MORE FROM HOLLYWOOD!

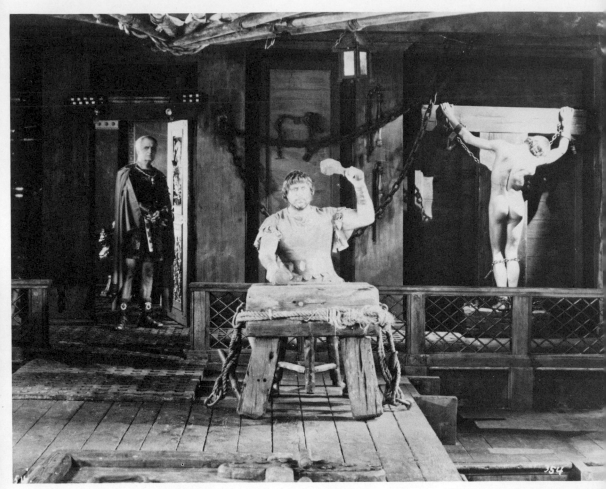

A rare still from M-G-M's silent version of *Ben-Hur*, directed by Fred Niblo; Frank Currier is entering the room of the galley slaves.

MORE FROM HOLLYWOOD
The Careers of 15 Great
American Stars

DeWitt Bodeen

SOUTH BRUNSWICK AND NEW YORK: A. S. BARNES AND COMPANY
LONDON: THE TANTIVY PRESS

© 1977 by A. S. Barnes and Co. Inc.

A. S. Barnes and Co., Inc.
Cranbury, New Jersey 08512

The Tantivy Press
Magdalen House
136-148 Tooley Street
London SE1 2TT, England

Library of Congress Cataloging in Publication Data

Bodeen, DeWitt.
    More from Hollywood!

    CONTENTS: Elsie Ferguson. — Pauline Frederick. — Greta Garbo. (etc.)
    Includes index.
    1. Moving-picture actors and actresses — United States — Biography. I. Title.
PN1998.A2B623   1977   791.43'028'0922 (B)   77-3213
ISBN 0-498-01533-5

ALSO BY DEWITT BODEEN:

Ladies of the Footlights
Romances by Emma
Who Wrote the Movie? (Associate Editor)
"A Glass of Water" (Translation from the French in the book *Camille
    and Other Well-Made Plays*)
The Films of Cecil B. DeMille (In collaboration with Gene Ringgold)
The Films of Maurice Chevalier (In collaboration with Gene Ringgold)
13 Castle Walk, a novel about Hollywood, then and now
From Hollywood

SBN 0-904208-20-6 (U.K.)
Printed in the United States of America

CONTENTS

ACKNOWLEDGEMENTS

These screen career stories first appeared in shorter and somewhat different forms in the American film magazine, "Films in Review" and in the English quarterly, "Focus on Film." They are herewith printed in revised, corrected, and, in some cases, up-dated versions.

I am grateful to Henry Hart and Charles Phillips Reilly, the former and present editors for "Films in Review"; and to Allen Eyles, editor of "Focus on Film," for permission to use those pieces as a basis for revising them into their new form and thus to issue them, through the services of Julien Yoseloff, in two volumes.

I am also grateful to librarian Mrs. Mildred Simpson and the entire staff of the Margaret Herrick Library at the Academy of Motion Picture Arts and Sciences in Hollywood for their assistance in my first researching of these pieces; and likewise I wish to acknowledge the help of Miss Brenda Davies and the staff at the library of the British Film Institute in London, who so kindly lent me their resources for double-checking and bringing up-to-date these articles. I also acknowledge gratefully the help of Jacobo Brender, of Caracas.

And, finally, I am most appreciative of the help of Peter Cowie, who, as editor for this book, has been of invaluable aid and encouragement to me.

PHOTO ACKNOWLEDGEMENTS

The author acknowledges his gratitude to the following organisations and individuals for the stills which illustrate this text:
The Academy of Motion Picture Arts and Sciences
(Robert Cushman, still dept.)
The British Film Institute
William C. Brooks (Pebble Beach, CA)
The Cinema Bookshop (London)
The Movie Memorabilia Shop of Hollywood
(Kenneth G. Lawrence)
Barrie Pattison (London)
Gene Ringgold (Hollywood, CA)
Anthony Slide (London)
Edna May Sobey (London)
Movie Star News

PART
ONE

SILENTS AND SOUND

1
ELSIE FERGUSON

The sobriquet "aristocrat of the screen" was bestowed on Elsie Ferguson by film critics and public alike, and deservedly.

In each of the twenty-two silent pictures she starred in for Paramount, as well as the one for Vitagraph, and in the one talkie she made for First National, Miss Ferguson was a well-bred heroine — beautiful, intelligent, exquisitely mannered and clothed — with a problem.

Dramatically, a *lady* is most interesting when she is opposed by a villain. In Miss Ferguson's films the villains were rarely double-dyed deceivers or that man you love to hate. Her antagonists were much subtler. In fact, they were psychological — a basic weakness, dormant in her personality, which she either conquered or was conquered by. The plots of almost all her pictures could be subtitled: The Lady and the Fatal Flaw.

Today, seemingly, it is impossible to see an Elsie Ferguson film. It is said that no prints are in existence, and that the negatives were destroyed in studio laboratory fires. Personally, I can't believe this, but it's the excuse offered. Her screen career, therefore, can only be examined by memory — at this time.

Time can be kind, as well as cruel, to remembered images. Sarah Bernhardt hoped her screen performances would be "my immortality." But because she never adapted to acting for the camera, her film appearances are now embarrassing to watch, and interesting only historically.

It was different with Elsie Ferguson.

When she came to the moving picture, Miss Ferguson was an established star of the theatre, but she realised that stage and screen are different media, and require entirely different techniques. After Adolph Zukor offered her a contract so attractive monetarily that it could not be resisted, she determined to be as effective on the screen as she had been on the stage.

She was a skilful actress, as well as one of the great beauties of her day, and was the precursor of such later ladies of the screen as Norma Shearer, Billie Dove, Ruth Chatterton, Ann Harding, Irene Dunne, and Deborah Kerr. I saw her on the stage twice, and saw almost all her screen performances, and my memories testify to the accuracy of the sobriquet "aristocrat of the screen."

She was born Elsie Louise Ferguson in New York City on August 19 — the year most probably 1883. Her father, Hiram Benson Ferguson, was a New York attorney, with a highly respectable annual income. Her mother, accord-

Elsie Ferguson

ing to an interview Miss Ferguson gave Gladys Hall for "Filmplay Journal," was a prosaic woman who wanted her only child to be the same. "Whenever I went to her bursting with some exuberant dream or thought," Miss Ferguson told Miss Hall, "Mother would say: 'Oh Elsie, how can you be so silly!'"

All the biographical material on Miss Ferguson states that she was educated in Manhattan's "Normal School." If she attended any such school, it couldn't have been for more than a few months, because she wasn't quite seventeen when she made her stage *début* as a member of the chorus of "The Belle of New York". "Through a friend's efforts," she said later, "I went into the chorus more through child-like curiousity than anything else...But musical comedy didn't satisfy me. It didn't seem serious enough."

She was five feet six, blue-eyed, golden-haired, and carried herself in a way that set her apart from the other chorines. But the following year — 1901 — she was still in the chorus, this time in "The Liberty Belles." She had, however, one line to speak. She toured with this show and learned, from forty-one one-night stands, some of the realities of stage life. "I knew then," she said later, "that my fight had begun, and I determined to climb to the top."

Every role she subsequently played on the stage was a step up, and she soon graduated from musical comedy. In only a few years she was playing leads in such stage dramas and melodramas as "The Bondman," "Pierre of the Plains," "The Battle," and "The Travelling Salesman." On August 31, 1909, she was starred at the Hackett Theatre in "Such a Little Queen," and from then until 1917 no Broadway season was complete until the new Elsie Ferguson play had opened. Several screen companies wooed her during those years, but she wouldn't let herself be won.

Early in 1916 she played Portia to Sir Herbert Tree's Shylock in "The Merchant of Venice," and later that year, while starring on Broadway in the title-role of "Shirley Kaye," Adolph Zukor offered her $5,000 a week for eighteen pictures to be made for Paramount-Artcraft over a three-year period. She found such a contract irresistible — and signed.

She was in her thirties by then, but she could, and did, look like a young girl if the role demanded it. She could also, and did, impersonate a sophisticated woman of the world. "One can only love once in a big way," she was fond of saying, and of repeating, "and I loved the stage first!"

Early in her career she had married Fred Hoey, the son of an express company executive. But the marriage hadn't lasted, and after it was dissolved, she always referred to it as unhappy.

When she was in the chorus, she had been much feted, and Evelyn Nesbitt, in her autobiography, "Prodigal Days — The Untold Story," tells of an intimate luncheon given by Stanford White. The other girl present was Elsie Ferguson. "Her companion, white-haired, slightly lame Thomas B. Clarke, a dealer in priceless Chinese porcelains and antiques, looked to me to be as old as Methuselah, and walked with the aid of a cane. He seemed devoted to Elsie."

In the 1907 newspaper accounts of the trial of Harry K. Thaw for the murder of Stanford White, Miss Ferguson's was one of the theatrical names mentioned, along with those of John Barrymore and Edna Goodrich (who had introduced Miss Nesbitt to Stanford White), as persons who knew of the Nesbitt-White liaison in the days when Miss Nesbitt swung high in a red

15

velvet swing. To avoid testifying at the trial, Miss Ferguson quietly sailed for London, and employed her stay there in a leading role on a West End stage in "The Earl of Pawtucket."

Some years before Zukor won her to the screen, Miss Ferguson had gone into the Harriman National Bank to withdraw money to pay for a try-out tour of a play in which she didn't have much faith. A young bank executive smiled cordially and introduced himself as Thomas B. Clarke Jr. He was the son of the man Evelyn Nesbitt described as being "devoted to Elsie." Miss Ferguson confided her concern about the new play. Clarke confided that he had seen her in her first starring vehicle nineteen times and that if she would revive it, he would commute between New York and wherever it was playing.

When Miss Ferguson returned from the tour — the play was a success in spite of her misgivings — Clarke became her second husband. She was Mrs. Clarke at the time of her film *début* and lived in an elegant apartment at 350 Park Avenue, just above 50th Street. More than once, she remarked: "I'm glad I did not marry an actor."

An exotic vehicle was chosen for her screen *début:* Robert Hichens's popular novel, *Barbary Sheep,* in which she played a titled lady come with her English lord to romantic Algiers. She was fortunate in having so sensitive and understanding a director as Maurice Tourneur. They hit it off so well that they made three more pictures together. Some critics called these films "picture poems," because Tourneur's sense of *mise-en-scène* and photography made them as beautiful to look upon as the star who graced them.

In the beginning, Miss Ferguson was not happy as a film actress. "At first I was frightfully confused," she told Frederick James Smith in an interview for "Classic." And to another interviewer, she said: "I shall never forget my state of mind during the making of *Barbary Sheep*. My experience before the camera was the most painful thing I have ever known in life. It seemed to me that the little black box became a monster that was leering and scoffing at my feeble efforts to register an emotion before it. I went home in tears. But the next morning I returned."

She was determined to conquer the camera, and later came to revere it, even though she missed "the spontaneous magnetism of an audience, which every actress knows and loves, and the inspiration which comes from that audience out front when the curtain rolls up upon the first act."

Tourneur was a gentle and persuasive man who quietly nurtured her self-confidence, and Miss Ferguson was appreciative. "I soon found my audience in my director," she said later. "But, if he cannot feel with me, react to my emotions, then I am lost. That is why, it seems to me, a great director must be a man of infinite, delicately-strung feelings."

Tourneur remained her favourite director, but she also worked well with, and praised, George Fitzmaurice, Emile Chautard, Hugh Ford, and John S. Robertson.

Barbary Sheep was received glowingly, and made money. So did her second picture, *The Rise of Jennie Cushing,* which almost every New York critic thought resembled the play "Outcast," in which she had distinguished herself on Broadway in 1914. Her third picture with Tourneur, *Rose of the World,* was Miss Ferguson's personal favourite of her first eighteen films.

By the time it was finished, she had come to grips with the problems of screen acting. "I return from the studio infinitely tired," she once said. "I

16

used to laugh at the idea of the tired business man and his love of light entertainment of the chorus-girl type. But after my months in the studios, I can understand his mood. My eyes are too tired to permit night reading, and, when I do feel able to go out in the evening, I want to go to something frothy, something that will rest my numbed nerves. Yes, I am a tired business woman these days.''

Because she was admired as a woman of taste, her advice on clothes was sought and appreciated. ''The average woman,'' she said, ''is more interested in the fashions displayed in motion picture productions than in the plots!...With the advent of the War, however, and the curtailed transportation facilities, many Manhattan designers were forced to create special models of their own, which soon became as popular, in their original appeal and far greater suitability to American women, as the modified Paris fashions.''

Miss Ferguson was one of the first American actresses to advocate *American* designers. ''A clever actress can carry her clothes with a nonchalance which often proves half the charm of the garment,'' she told American women, and added: ''It is not what you wear so much as how you wear it.''

I have never forgotten the remarkable taste with which she did a drunk scene that could so easily have been offensive in her fourth film, *The Song of Songs*. Of this picture ''Motion Picture Magazine'' said: ''Because of the Ferguson art, it is a masterpiece of screen literature — without her it would have been just another young girl's life shot to pieces.'' The same magazine later also praised her performance in *The Lie:* ''Elsie Ferguson's acting is the feat of a virtuoso ringing true in every tone;'' and Peter Milne in the ''Motion Picture News'' said of the same performance: ''...Miss Ferguson is her own best artist. Aside from playing with incomparable skill, she has an air of refinement that distinguishes her.''

Neither she nor Tourneur was entirely happy about *A Doll's House*. Both thought it too static. Nor did it do well at the box-office, as all her previous pictures had. Nevertheless, I find that I still remember vividly her scenes with her children, and the final scene in which she walks out on her husband, and closes the door on her life as a doll wife — ''the door slam that was heard around the world.''

Miss Ferguson was never self-deceived in her evaluations of her screen roles. She wanted to make a movie of ''Pierre of the Plains,'' which she had played on the stage, and it was re-written for her to do on the screen and re-named *Heart of the Wilds*. When it was finished, she forthrightly declared: ''I was young, undeveloped, and fired with extreme youth when I played Jen behind the footlights. When I came to do her on the screen, I found I had developed. I could no longer feel her ingenuous view of life.''

Paramount spared no expense on any of her productions, which were shot in its Eastern studio, then an ex-riding academy on 56th Street. One whole floor of it was turned into an elaborate replica of a Venetian scene, replete with balconies and gondolas gliding on a canal, for one of Miss Ferguson's most successful pictures, *A Society Exile*, which George Fitzmaurice directed.

My own favourite Ferguson pictures of this period are, first, *The Danger Mark*, a Robert W. Chambers story, in which she was never more beautiful, and in which she played a society girl with a taste for alcohol. The scene in which she feels her lover has turned against her and is bitterly tempted to

MORE FROM HOLLYWOOD

resume her secret drinking, especially remains in my memory. So, also, does the triple role she essayed in *The Avalanche,* another Fitzmaurice-directed film from a Gertrude Atherton novel. In it, she played 1) a young mother tormented by a fever for gambling; 2) the embittered woman that mother becomes years later as queen of an elegant gambling casino; and 3) the lovely daughter who turns up, as an extravagant gambler, in her own mother's salon.

Miss Ferguson took only one vacation during this three-year period of movie-making — a cruise to the Orient. When she finished her eighteenth picture and Paramount pressed a new and more rewarding contract upon her, she declined. She had found a play she wanted to do on Broadway — ''Sacred and Profane Love,'' dramatised from Arnold Bennett's novel, ''The Book of Carlotta.''

Elsie Ferguson in *The Avalanche.*

CHICHITA DANCES FOR HER FATHER'S COMPANIONS

ELSIE FERGUSON

Despite her enormous success as a screen actress, she credited her entire development as an actress to the stage. "One does not develop in the studio," she said. "The necessary method of doing disjointed scenes here and there from the photoplay prevents a genuine living of the character. On the stage you play a character straight through for many nights. It grows, expands, mellows — and you develop with it."

But she also acknowledged that her years in motion pictures had been a fruitful experience and that "I feel I am better equipped for the spoken drama because of it." When asked how she had liked working in pictures, she replied: "One moment I am wildly enthusiastic over them. Then, again — while not exactly bearish — I do get impatient. There is nothing mentally tiring about pictures, and...they are a branch of my art. I think it essential for an actress to know the mechanics of them, just as I think an actress should know how to play the piano and sing."

And she missed the spoken line. "In pictures," she explained, "I use the real lines, using the same vocal expressions I would on the stage — even the little nuances, which of course can't register on the silent screen."

"Sacred and Profane Love" opened in February, 1920, in New York's Morosco Theatre, and was an immediate success. She followed it the next year with Zoë Akins's "The Varying Shore," and when Zukor offered her a second Paramount contract, to begin with a movie version of her play-hit, *Sacred and Profane Love,* she signed to do four pictures over a two-year period.

Her second picture, on this contract, was *Footlights,* and it revealed a new facet to her screen personality. She played a lady, of course, but a phoney one who had a sparkling awareness of the comic, for she played a New England stage aspirant who attains success on the stage as a glamorous Russian actress, accent definitely hinted at in the sub-titles.

It was her third picture on the new contract which was, without any doubt, her greatest screen portrayal. With George Fitzmaurice again directing, she played the Duchess of Towers in the film version of Du Maurier's "Peter Ibbetson," which was re-titled for the American screen *Forever.* Wallace Reid was her co-star, and he also gave his best screen characterisation in it. Her re-creation of the unhappy Duchess was a thing of beauty, and she and Mr. Reid made their romance a deathless love. Were I to make a list of my ten favourite pictures, *Forever* would be high on it.

Fitzmaurice himself, when asked who was his favourite actress, said: "Miss Elsie Ferguson has the greatest personal charm of any actress I have directed, and I consider her one of the finest artists the screen has ever known...The charm of Elsie Ferguson lies in her womanliness. She is most feminine. Therefore she is at her best in romantic drama, where her femininity has full sway, and the exquisite delicacy of portrayal, and the brilliant nuances she achieves, can best be appreciated.

"Miss Ferguson is a woman of culture and has an active mind which is constantly stimulated by a diversity of interests. One is never bored in her company.

"Surely no one has forgotten Miss Ferguson's most moving portrayal as the Duchess of Towers in 'Peter Ibbetson,' a photoplay (retitled *Forever*) in which she and the late Wallace Reid worked under my direction. I always remember with pleasure the weeks in which we worked together on this picture.''

Forever, incidentally, is supposed to be another of those film masterpieces marked down as ''lost.'' Dorothy Reid, however, once had a print of it, given her after her husband's tragic death by Jesse L. Lasky. She gave that print, along with another of Reid's successes, *The Roaring Road,* to the ill-fated Hollywood Museum, from where, since its demise, both have reportedly disappeared or been stolen. I hope whoever has *Forever* realises its unique value and has made safety dupes of it for posterity's sake.

For her fourth and final film for Paramount Miss Ferguson chose to make a screen version of *Outcast,* in which she had been such a success on the stage. Next to *Forever,* it is probably her best screen performance. She had so mastered screen acting that her interpretation of the subtleties of hidden thought was as skilful in the dramatic as in the comic moments. Laurence Reid, reviewing this picture for ''Motion Pictures News,'' wrote: ''Miss Ferguson's performance is truly wonderful. She achieves the effect of seeming the perfect creature she pretends to be. This is sincerity of the highest order. It is positively one of the greatest contributions to the silver sheet. Her mute suffering when she thinks her lover has discarded her is rich with pathos.''

When Paramount proposed another contract, she demurred. ''The mere smell of the theatre stirs me,'' she said. So she played ''*The Wheel of Life*'' on Broadway in 1923, and toured it.

This was the first time I saw her on stage. I had seen almost every film she made, and the performance of ''The Wheel of Life'' I saw at the old White Theatre in Fresno, California, was superb. Admittedly, the play was hocus-pocus and full of English colonial bits in a Tibetan lamasery Kipling would have scorned to use. But every minute Miss Ferguson was onstage was real theatre magic.

When she got back to New York, she did a drama Zoë Akins had adapted from the Hungarian, ''The Moon-Flower.'' Then she portrayed Kate Hardcastle in a production at the Empire of ''She Stoops to Conquer,'' and starred in a melodrama called ''Carnival.''

Concurrently, Paramount was pressing her to resume her screen career. It had bought *The Wheel of Life* for her, and wanted her for a film version of Molnar's *The Swan.* She was tempted, and almost signed, when the script of the Alfred Savoir stage comedy, ''The Grand Duchess and the Waiter,'' fell into her hands, and she signed to do that instead. Paramount bought the screen rights at once and urged her to agree to make the screen version. But ''The Grand Duchess and the Waiter'' was one of Miss Ferguson's most dazzling stage successes, and she preferred to stick with it for two years on Broadway and the road. Paramount made *The Swan* with a newcomer, Frances Howard, as the princess, who shortly thereafter terminated her brief and successful screen career to become Mrs. Samuel Goldwyn. And the studio finally filmed *The Grand Duchess and the Waiter* with Florence Vidor and Adolphe Menjou, and hung onto *The Wheel of Life* until the talkie turnover, when it was used as an unimportant feature with Esther Ralston and Richard Dix. In 1927, Miss Ralston also re-made one of Miss Ferguson's most memorable films, *Footlights,* under a new title, *The Spotlight.*

Meanwhile, Miss Ferguson had divorced her second husband, and, al-

Elsie Ferguson as The Duchess of Towers with Wallace Reid as Peter Ibbetson in *Forever*.

aid she would never marry an actor, she changed her mind.
nd was Frederic Worlock, a British actor who had been in her
both "The Wheel of Life" and "The Grand Duchess and the

ne of the reasons for Miss Ferguson's reluctance to resume her
hat in 1925 the reactivated Vitagraph Company had induced her to
ne screen in a marital drama, *The Unknown Lover.* It was the only
insig   ant movie she ever made, and fortunately almost nobody saw it. She
did, and hated it so much that she never mentioned it.

The advent of sound prompted almost every studio to woo Miss Ferguson
with starring offers. She had preferred to open on Broadway in "The House of
Women," from Louis Bromfield's novel "The Green Bay Tree," and was
playing it when an SOS was sent out for her services. On the Pacific Coast,
Pauline Frederick had created the starring role in a new Samuel Shipman-
John B. Hymer melodrama, "The Crimson Hour," which, re-titled "Scarlet
Pages," was to go to Broadway. But Miss Frederick who suffered from
chronic asthma, which later killed her, decided for reasons of health against a
New York season, and Miss Ferguson was asked to star. She consented to do
it upon the closing of "The House of Women." The play was only the most
hackneyed of "Madame X" plots, with Miss Ferguson playing a renowned
lawyer defending a girl on trial for murder and then discovering that the
defendant is really her own daughter; but it was sound theatre, and Miss
Ferguson scored a big hit in it.

The screen rights were bought by First National, and Miss Ferguson agreed
to make her talkie *début* in *Scarlet Pages.* The picture was a success — in 1930
anything with a soundtrack was. Said "Variety:" Miss Ferguson's perfect
playing of the emotional makes it genuinely affecting." When Warner
Bros.-First National offered her a contract for more talking pictures, she
refused. She who had lamented the fact that an actress couldn't talk in silent
films said she hated talking pictures. They were going to talk themselves out
of existence, she warned, and the truth is, they almost did.

But the whole truth was simpler: she was nearly fifty years old. What had
appalled her about the way she was photographed in *The Unknown Lover,* she
could not deny, especially to herself, in *Scarlet Pages:* if she returned to the
screen, she could only play mature character roles. At the moment, her vanity
would not permit that.

Stage lighting is kinder than the camera, however, and so, in Hollywood
and San Francisco, she played the role Emily Stevens had created for the
Theatre Guild in its stage production of Ernest Vajda's comic-tragedy, "Fata
Morgana." I saw this production, and was again pleasantly pleased by Miss
Ferguson's admirable stage presence. I've since learned she didn't like the
role, and fought with the producers, her author, and her director every
moment, even making an unscheduled curtain speech one night, explaining
why she had done it and why she hated playing it, and bawling the audience
out for having bothered to come there to sit on their hands (Los Angeles
theatre audiences are noted for the paucity of their applause). I can only say,
however, that on the two occasions I saw "Fata Morgana" in Hollywood, I,
knowing nothing then of the drama going on backstage, relished every moment of what I saw onstage. Actresses do not always know what parts they're
right for, and I do not think Miss Ferguson could have been bettered as the

fickle, sophisticated older first love of Tom Douglas as the youth. I was also impressed, I remember, by a pretty young girl in that cast named Karen Morley.

Miss Ferguson, for all her ladylike image, was not without temperament. At the dress rehearsal on Broadway of "Such a Little Queen," her very first starring vehicle, when, as usual, everything went wrong, she gave vent to her emotions in language anything but ladylike. There was shocked silence, and then Lowell Sherman, a member of the cast, remarked casually: "Such a little queen!" It broke the tension. Miss Ferguson went into gales of laughter, and after that everything went right.

In the latter part of 1930, Miss Ferguson travelled in Europe, and there divorced her third husband. Soon afterwards, she married a British Navy officer, Victor Augustus Seymour Egan. At the time, she was quoted as saying: "A woman doesn't want to be a queen. She wants to be mastered. Every woman wants a caveman."

When Lowell Sherman was signed by RKO to direct *Becky Sharp,* he induced Miss Ferguson to agree to play the Duchess of Richmond. But when Sherman suddenly died, she asked to be released from the commitment, and Billie Burke replaced her. Most of the footage, unfortunately, was cut.

Miss Ferguson spent the next decade with her fourth husband at the farm they had purchased in East Lyme, Connecticut, and at Cap d'Antibes. She was adamant about not making another movie, and even for a time didn't want to return to the theatre. But Rose Franken, who had an adjoining farm, one day in 1943 gave Miss Ferguson the script of her new play, "Outrageous Fortune," and Miss Ferguson, liking the play, agreed to star in it. In November of that year she opened at the 48th Street Theatre in the role of Crystal Grainger. "Outrageous Fortune," although praised by Broadway's best critics, became the most distinguished failure of that early war year.

Ten years later, she made her summer stock *début* by opening the season at the Berkshire Playhouse in Stockbridge, Massachusetts, with Courtney Abbot's two-character drama, "And Two Make Four." Anthony Kemble Cooper played with her in it — but the play did not go beyond its summer engagement.

Miss Ferguson's husband died in France in 1956, and for some years thereafter she lived almost exclusively at Cap d'Antibes. Then, in July of 1961, she entered Lawrence Memorial Hospital in New London, Connecticut, and was there until November 15, when she died at the age of seventy-eight.

ELSIE FERGUSON FILMOGRAPHY

BARBARY SHEEP (1917). Romantic drama, set in Algiers; as Katherine, Lady Wyverne. *Dir:* Maurice Tourneur. *Sc:* Charles Maigne (from a novel by Robert Hichens). *With* Pedro de Cordoba, Lumsden Hare, Macy Harlan, Alex Shannon, Maude Ford. *Prod:* Paramount/Artcraft. 6 reels.

THE RISE OF JENNIE CUSHING (1917). Romantic drama of a girl who overcomes a sordid past; as Jennie Cushing. *Dir:* Maurice Tourneur. *Sc:* Charles Maigne (from a novel

by Mary S. Watts). *With* Elliott Dexter, Fania Marinoff, Frank Goldsmith, Sallie Delatore, Mae Bates, Edith McAlpin, Isabel Vernon. *Prod:* Paramount/Artcraft. 6 reels.

ROSE OF THE WORLD (1918). Romantic drama amongst the Colonials in British India; as Rosamond English. *Dir:* Maurice Tourneur. *Sc:* Charles Maigne (from a story by Agnes and Egerton Castle). *With* Wyndham Standing, Percy Marmont, Ethel Martin, June Sloane, Clarence Handysides, Maria Benedetta. *Prod:* Paramount/Artcraft. 5 reels.

THE SONG OF SONGS (1918). Romance of a woman's downfall; as Lily Kardos. *Dir:* Joseph Kaufman. *Sc:* Charles Maigne (from the Edward Sheldon play version of the Hermann Suderman novel). *With* Crauford Kent, Robert Cummings, Frank Losee, Gertrude Berkeley, Henry Leone, Corinne Uzell, Cyril Fletcher, (Re-made with Pola Negri [*Lily of the Dust*] and as a talkie with Marlene Dietrich). *Prod:* Paramount/Artcraft. 5 reels.

THE LIE (1918). Romantic drama of a lady who lives down her sister's vicious lie; as Eleanor. *Dir:* J. Searle Dawley. *Sc:* Charles Maigne (from the play by Henry Arthur Jones). *With* David Powell, Percy Marmont, Betty Howe, John L. Shine, Charles Sutton, Maude Turner Gordon, Bertha Kent. *Prod:* Paramount/Artcraft. 5 reels.

A DOLL'S HOUSE (1918). Sociological drama of a wife's revolt; as Nora. *Dir:* Maurice Tourneur. *Sc:* Charles Maigne (from the play by Henrik Ibsen). *With* Holmes E. Herbert, Alex Shannon, Ethel Grey Terry. (Universal released its production of *A Doll's House* with Dorothy Phillips, 1917; Nazimova released her version through United Artists in 1922; both Clare Bloom and Jane Fonda starred in separate versions, released in 1973.) *Prod:* Paramount/Artcraft. 5 reels.

THE DANGER MARK (1918). Drama of a woman who conquers her secret craving for alcohol; as Geraldine. *Dir/Sc:* Hugh Ford, (from the novel by Robert W. Chambers). *With* Mahlon Hamilton, Crauford Kent, Gertrude McCoy, Edmund Burns, Maude Turner Gordon, W.T. Carlton. *Prod:* Paramount/Artcraft. 5 reels.

HEART OF THE WILDS (1918). Romantic drama of the Canadian Northwest; as Jen Galbraith. *Dir:* Marshall Neilan. *Sc:* Charles Maigne (from the play, "Pierre of the Plains," by Edgar Selwyn, adapted from two Sir Gilbert Parker stories; using the heroine from "Jen of the Triple Chevron" and the plot from, mostly, "Pierre and His People".) *With* Thomas Meighan, Matt Moore, Joseph Smiley, Escamillo Fernandez, Sidney D'Albrook. (Re-made as *Over the Border,* 1922, starring Betty Compson as Jen; again as a talkie, *Pierre of the Plains,* M-G-M, 1942, with Ruth Hussey as Jen.) *Prod:* Paramount/Artcraft. 5 reels.

UNDER THE GREENWOOD TREE (1918). Romantic drama of a well-born Englishwoman who masquerades as a gypsy; as Mary Hamilton. *Dir:* Emile Chautard. *Sc:* Adrian Gil-Spear (from the play by Henry V. Esmond that had served as a vehicle onstage for Maxine Elliott). *With* Eugene O'Brien, Edmund Burns, Mildred Havens, John Ardizoni, Robert Milach, Robert Vivian, Charles Craig, Henry Warwick, James Fury. *Prod:* Paramount/Artcraft. 5 reels.

HIS PARISIAN WIFE (1918). Domestic drama; as the Parisienne, Fauvette, who becomes the writer, Marie Trieste. *Dir:* Emile Chautard. *Sc:* Eve Unsell. *With* David Powell, Courtenay Foote, Frank Losee, Cora Williams, Captain Charles Charles, Louis Grizel. *Prod:* Paramount/Artcraft. 5 reels.

THE MARRIAGE PRICE (1919). Romantic drama; as Helen Tremaine, who marries for money and finds love. *Dir:* Emile Chautard. *Sc:* Eve Unsell. *With* Wyndham Standing, Lionel Atwill, Robert Schable, Maud Hosford, Marie Temper, Clariette Anthony. *Prod:* Paramount/Artcraft. 5 reels.

EYES OF THE SOUL (1919). Romantic drama of a chorus girl who falls in love with a blind soldier; as Gloria Swan. *Dir:* Emile Chautard. *Sc:* Eve Unsell (from a story, "Salt of the Earth," by George Weston). *With:* Wyndham Standing, J. Flanigan, G. Backus, F. Dupree, Cora Williams, Captain Charles Charles. *Prod:* Paramount/Artcraft. 5 reels.

THE AVALANCHE (1919). Romantic melodrama of the gambling curse; in a triple role: as Chichita, who becomes the hardened gambler, a mystery woman known as Mme. Delano; and her daughter, Helen, caught up in the gambling fever. *Dir:* George Fitzmaurice. *Sc:* Ouida Bergere (from a novel by Gertrude Atherton). *With:* Lumsden Hare, Zeffie Tilbury, Fred Esmelton, William Roselle, Grace Field, Warner Oland. *Prod:* Paramount/Artcraft. 6 reels.

A SOCIETY EXILE (1919). Romantic drama of England and Venice; as Nora Shard. *Dir:* George Fitzmaurice. *Sc:* Ouida Bergere (from a play "We Can't Be as Bad as All That," by Henry Arthur Jones). *With* William P. Carleton, Warburton Gamble, Julia Dean, Henry Stephenson, Zeffie Tilbury, Bijou Fernandez, Alexander Kyle. *Prod:* Paramount/Artcraft. 6 reels.

WITNESS FOR THE DEFENSE (1919). Romantic melodrama of love and death in India; as Stella Derrick, on trial for the murder of her husband. *Dir:* George Fitzmaurice. *Sc:* Ouida Bergere (from the novel by A. E. Mason). *With* Vernon Steele, Warner Oland, Wyndham Standing, George Fitzgerald, J. G. Gilmore, Amelia Summerville, Cora Williams, Blanche Standing, Leslie King, Captain Charles Charles, Etienne Girardot. *Prod:* Paramount/Artcraft. 5 reels.

THE COUNTERFEIT (1919). Romantic melodrama of counterfeiters in high society; as a well-born heroine who becomes a Secret Service agent. *Dir:* George Fitzmaurice. *Sc:* Ouida Bergere (from a story by Robert Baker). *With* David Powell, Charles Kent, Charles Gerard, Ida Waterman, Robert Lee Keeling. *Prod:* Paramount/Artcraft. 5 reels.

ELSIE FERGUSON

HIS HOUSE IN ORDER (1920). Romantic drama; as Nina Graham. *Dir/Sc:* Hugh Ford. (from a play by Sir Arthur Wing Pinero). *With* Holmes E, Herbert, Vernon Steele, Margaret Linden, Marie Burke. (Filmed in 1929 in England with Tallulah Bankhead as Nina Graham). *Prod:* Paramount/Artcraft. 5 reels.

LADY ROSE'S DAUGHTER (1920). Romantic drama of three ladies whose names bear the curse of illegitimacy; in a triple role: as Lady Maude of 1860; Lady Rose of the nineties; and Julie Le Breton of the post first World War period. *Dir:* Hugh Ford. *Sc:* Burns Mantle (from the novel by Mrs. Humphrey Ward). *With* David Powell, Frank Losee, Holmes E. Herbert, Ida Waterman, Warren Cook. *Prod:* Paramount/Artcraft. 5 reels.

SACRED AND PROFANE LOVE (1921). Romantic drama; as Carlotta Peel. *Dir:* William Desmond Taylor. *Sc:* Julia Crawford Ivers (from the play by Arnold Bennett, in which Miss Ferguson had starred on Broadway, dramatised from his novel, "The Book of Carlotta".) *With* Conrad Nagel, Thomas Holding, Helen Dunbar, Winifred Greenwood, Raymond Brathwayt, Clarissa Selwynne, Howard Gaye, Forrest Stanley, Jane Keckley. *Prod:* Paramount. 6 reels.

FOOTLIGHTS (1921). Romantic comedy about a New England girl who becomes a great "Russian" star in the theatre; as Lizzy Parsons, who becomes known as Mme. Peffisima. *Dir:* John S. Robertson. *Sc:* Josephine Lovett (from the "Sat.Eve.Post" story by Rita Weiman). *With* Reginald Denny, Marc MacDermott, Octavia Handworth. (re-made in 1927, as *The Spotlight,* with Esther Ralston in the Ferguson role.) *Prod:* Paramount. 7 reels.

FOREVER (AKA, GB, *Peter Ibbetson*) *(1921).* Romance and fantasy; as The Duchess of Towers. *Dir:* George Fitzmaurice. *Sc:* Ouida Bergere (from the novel, "Peter Ibbetson," by George Du Maurier, as adapted to the stage by John Nathan Raphael and Constance Collier). *With* Wallace Reid, Montagu Love, George Fawcett, Dolores Cassinelli, Paul McAllister, Elliott Dexter, Barbara Dean, Nell Roy Buck, Charles Eaton, Jerome Patrick. (Re-made as a talkie, 1936, with Gary Cooper and Ann Harding.) *Prod:* Paramount. 7 reels. (Compare listing in Wallace Reid filmography).

OUTCAST (1922). Romantic drama; as Miriam Moore. *Dir:* Chet Withey. *Sc:* Josephine Lovett (from the play by Hubert Henry Davies in which Miss Ferguson had starred on Broadway). With David Powell, William David, Mary MacLaren, Charles Wellesley, Teddy Sampson, William Powell. (Filmed previously by Charles Frohman, 1918, with Ann Murdoch; re-made as a late silent starring Corinne Griffith; also story basis for *The Girl from Tenth Avenue,* 1935.) *Prod:* Paramount. 7 reels.

THE UNKNOWN LOVER (1925). Marital drama; as Elaine Kent, research chemist. *Dir/Sc:* Victor Hugo Halperin. *With* Frank Mayo, Mildred Harris, Peggy Kelly, Leslie Austen. *Prod:* Vitagraph. 7 reels.

SCARLET PAGES. (1930). Courtroom melodrama; as the attorney for the defence, Mary Bancroft. Miss Ferguson's first and only talking film. *Dir:* Ray Enright. *Sc:* Walter Anthony, with dialogue by Maude Fulton (from the Samuel Shipman and John B. Hymer play, in which Miss Ferguson had starred on Broadway). *With* Grant Withers, Marian Nixon, John Halliday, DeWitt Jennings, Charlotte Walker, Wilbur Mack, Daisy Belmore, William Davidson, Helen Ferguson. *Prod:* First National. 7 reels.

(Miss Ferguson appeared as herself in 1922 *A Trip to Paramountown;* she also appeared as herself arriving at a theatre premiere in Monta Bell's *Broadway after Dark,* Warner Bros., 1924.)

2
PAULINE FREDERICK

In recent years I've become more than a little impressed by how *different* are the things for which Pauline Frederick is remembered.

One man has never forgotten the brilliant blue of her eyes; another, the beautiful formation of her shoulders; a third, the style with which she wore clothes and carried herself. A shrewd woman of the world still speaks of her "unique ability to exude charm without seeming to." And those who remember how believably Miss Frederick projected the tragedy of "the fallen woman" in *Madame X,* both on stage and screen, are still innumerable.

She was born Pauline Beatrice Libbey on August 12, 1883 at 82 Berkeley Street in Boston, Massachusetts. She was a seven months baby, weighing only four pounds at birth, and spent her first month of life in an incubator.

Her mother's family was Scottish, of the MacDonald clan, and her father was the son of a Yankee farmer in Aroostook County, Maine. Neither had ever had any connection with the theatre.

At an amateur church bazaar one evening, Pauline sang with such style that somebody dared her to go down to the Boston Music Hall and sing in one of its vaudeville acts. Any kind of a dare she was always to find irresistible. Her mother, who was preparing to leave her husband, encouraged her. She auditioned, and was signed to a contract as a singer at $50 a week. In doing so, she assumed the surname of Frederick, which was the given name of her first piano accompanist.

Her mother was elated, but her father disapproved. So much so that Mrs. Libbey packed up and left him. Her accomplished daughter and she departed at once for New York City.

The father, Richard O. Libbey, was a railroad conductor, and after his first wife secured a divorce, he married a woman of some means. She financed an invention of his, which brought in a modest profit, and when he died, he left a respectable estate of around $30,000.

His will contained the following: "I leave to my daughter, Pauline Beatrice Libbey, nothing. Lest leaving her out of my will be construed as unintentional, I repeat that I leave her nothing." Commented Miss Frederick: "I'm surprised he left anything. He was always a spendthrift. He hated me because, when he separated from my mother, I went with her."

Her mother foolishly prevailed on Pauline to contest the will. She did so — unsuccessfully. The resultant publicity was not pleasant.

MORE FROM HOLLYWOOD

In New York, Miss Frederick landed a job in the chorus of a Klaw and Erlanger musical farce, "The Rogers Brothers in Harvard," co-starring Max and Gus Rogers. It opened in New York on September 1, 1902, at the Knickerbocker Theatre, and was a great success. Miss Frederick's presence in the chorus did not go unnoticed. Her salary was then only $15 a week.

"People who think the path of a chorus girl is strewn with roses," Miss Frederick said some years later, "have a lot to learn. I knew going on the stage would entail hardships, but I now venture to say a man with a pick and shovel has an easier time."

Was it Miss Frederick's beauty, or her mother's driving ambition, which hastened her escape from the chorus? Certainly it was the former that won her commissions to pose for Harrison Fisher, the magazine artist, who called her "the purest type of American beauty." In one of his portraits of her, Fisher made her eyes amber-coloured, which led to the sobriquet, "Girl with the Topaze Eyes." It couldn't have been more inexact, since her eyes were so startlingly blue that their blueness was the first thing one noticed about her magnetic presence.

After Victor Herbert's "It Happened in Nordland," in which Miss Frederick had obtained a supporting role, went on tour, Blanche Ring quarrelled with her co-star, Lew Fields, and walked out. Pauline Frederick stepped in, and the next morning the drama page headlines read: PAULINE FREDERICK BECOMES PRIMA DONNA IN A NIGHT. Her regal beauty was praised, but so was her voice. "She possesses a powerful soprano voice with the range of three octaves," said one critic. "Her high tones are full and clear and wonderfully sustained."

She soon graduated from musicals to straight drama, however, and played opposite such male stars as Richard Bennett, John Barrymore, Francis Wilson, William Gillette, and Charles Waldron.

"I went on the stage because it offered me a chance to escape being a nobody," she said. "It means work, lots of it, and hardships and disappointments, and perhaps failure in the end, but I am trying to succeed with all the energy I possess."

She was on the threshold of achieving stardom when she fell in love and married a man sixteen years older than she herself. Frank Mills Andrews was a noted architect who objected to being known as "Pauline Frederick's husband." So she willingly retired from the stage and spent most of the next three years travelling abroad with him.

When she returned to New York, she was apparently trying to ignore with some show of dignity her husband's growing interest in another woman, and when producer George Tyler offered her the role of the Marchioness of Joyeuse in "The Paper Chase," she accepted. Two years later, in 1914, Andrews and she were divorced.

It was the lead as Potiphar's Wife in Louis N. Parker's mammoth Biblical extravaganza, "Joseph and His Brethren," that brought her to the attention of Adolph Zukor, who was about to begin production on his most expensive film to date, *The Eternal City,* which was based on Hall Caine's novel and budgeted at $100,000. Zukor signed her for the lead, Donna Roma.

It was filmed in Rome, during the Pope's Jubilee Year, in order to catch on film the massive processions that emanated from the Vatican. Permission had even been gained to shoot certain intimate scenes in the Pope's own Vatican

Pauline Frederick

gardens. There was also a great deal of political disturbance in Rome that year, with mass meetings in the Coliseum and strikers marching between walls of armed soldiers down Roman avenues. Director Hugh Ford got his co-director and cameraman, Edwin S. Porter, to use all of this on film, and the mob scenes figured importantly on screen. Castle St. Angelo, the Villa d'Este gardens, and the Appian Way, also provided background for the story.

Although production wasn't completed when the First World War broke out, the company was ordered to leave. But one scene, in which the heroine had to be shown ascending and then descending the steps of the Vatican, was vital. So Hugh Ford dared Pauline Frederick to make the shot, knowing full well that daring her would be the only way she'd do it. She walked up the steps with high bravado, and was chased down, while Porter, at the camera, managed to keep the guards out of the shot. The resulting Roman "pasta" made excellent publicity.

The Eternal City premiered at the Astor Theatre in New York in April 1915, and was an instant hit. Miss Frederick was called the most glamorous star Famous Players had yet presented, and Zukor offered her a three year contract at a thousand a week. She was still under contract for only a few hundred a week to stage producer Al Woods and when she asked him to release her, he consented, but said: "Tell Zukor you want $2,000 a week the first year, $3,000 a week the second year, and $4,000 a week the third year." Zukor agreed without even going through the motions of protest.

In the three years that followed, Miss Frederick starred in twenty-eight features for Famous Players and enjoyed top popularity with Zukor's other stars, Mary Pickford and Marguerite Clark. All of these pictures were shot in the East, at the New York studio or on location in Florida or New Jersey, so she could live in a Park Avenue apartment with her mother, who was known as "Mumsy" and "queened it" more outrageously than her daughter ever did.

Studio workers, to whom Miss Frederick was just "Polly," liked her, for she was friendly and loyal to a fault. Friendliness and loyalty always breed a kind of blind, wilful gullibility, and Pauline Frederick was probably taken in by more bad advice from friends and admirers than any other actress. Had she not been the actress she was, her career might have gone down the drain any number of times.

When she loved, she adored without reason, and the men she married wanted either to destroy or rule her career, with equally disastrous results.

"I think I should have been willing to give up my career for the right man," she said later, "but he never came along."

With the man who was to be her second husband she took an impulsive step that all but wrecked her as actress and woman. He was Charles W. McLaughlin, the playwright-actor known professionally as Willard Mack. When she first met him, he had just separated from his second wife, the velvet-eyed, velvet-voiced Marjorie Rambeau. He wrote, and played opposite Miss Frederick in, the worst film she made for Zukor, *Nanette of the Wilds,* and she was so ecstatically happy she was blind to the mediocrity of the film itself.

The United States had entered the First World War, and Miss Frederick was constantly campaigning for Liberty Loan Bonds. She had also begun knitting furiously, a hobby that was to keep her occupied on set between takes and backstage for the rest of her life. Mack had just finished writing "Tiger

PAULINE FREDERICK

Rose," which was to be one of Lenore Ulric's greatest triumphs as a Belasco star. During its trial run in Washington, D.C., in September 1917, Pauline Frederick and he were married.

Mack was also in charge of the scenario department of the new Goldwyn Studios at Fort Lee, New Jersey, and he advised his wife that when her Zukor contract expired she should form her own production company. They would head it jointly, call it the Frederick Feature Film Company, and release through Goldwyn.

Zukor was abject when informed of her new plans, and accused Samuel Goldwyn of robbing his stable. "Pauline Frederick was a different type, tall and dark," Zukor later wrote in his memoirs. "Her neck and shoulders were regarded by artists as the most beautiful in the world. She was a few years older than the others and a player of more sophisticated roles. But there was nothing aloof about her at the studio. Her former husband was an architect and from him she had learned to draw. She used to sit with Dick Murphy (Zukor's production-designer) in his tiny office, helping design sets."

Zukor tried to persuade her to continue with him; but Willard Mack had chosen, and she willingly followed the path her husband set for her. And this despite the fact that all her Famous Players films had the benefit of carefully selected stories and full production values, and that many were notable films, and some distinguished.

With one notable exception, every picture she made for Goldwyn release was below the calibre of her Famous Players pictures. The exception, paradoxically, had her greatest screen performance. The title role of "Madame X" became synonymous with her own name, and she later played it on the stage time and again with overwhelming success. But "Madame X," be it noted, was post-Willard Mack.

"Madame X" was a Parisian courtroom melodrama written by Alexandre Bisson, and is what the French are pleased to call a "well-made play." A gifted and intelligent American actress, Dorothy Donnelly, discovered it, translated it, appeared in it to wide acclaim on the stage, and made an effective movie appearance in it for Pathé in 1916. Sarah Bernhardt's attention was called to it after Miss Donnelly's success, and she played it in French on several of her American tours, and included it later in her international repertory, with Lou Tellegen playing the role of her son.

When Pauline Frederick played it first in films in 1920, critics were already complaining that it was out-dated. But none of them denied the impact of Miss Frederick's performance. As the mother defended in a murder trial by the son she had abandoned as a baby, she was sensational. It was a tear-jerker, a four-handkerchief picture; nobody was unmoved by the way Miss Frederick played it. The part has as carefully a calculated range of emotions as *Camille*.

I do not think anybody who saw the twenty-four sheets of Pauline Frederick pictured as both the once-elegant Jacqueline Floriot and the absinthe-drinking Madame X, above the caption, "On the road to God knows where," will ever forget them. "She's on the road to God knows where" went into the popular vocabulary of the day.

Miss Frederick's personal life was also not without drama.

After she married Willard Mack, they took an elegant apartment in New York at 50 Central Park South, and had a country home at Darien in Connecticut. Both of them were making fabulous amounts of money, and spending

33

road to God knows where."

Pauline Frederick as *Madame X*.

every cent. They were great friends with Geraldine Farrar and Lou Tellegen, who lived in the same apartment house.

But Miss Frederick's life with Willard Mack soon became a nightmare. He was a heavy drinker, and sadistic when drunk. Several times he tried to kill her. When she found out that he was also taking drugs, she had to admit the situation was hopeless. She left him in 1919, and they divorced. Several years later they almost re-married. She still loved him, but he rolled up his sleeve and showed her the hypodermic marks on his arm. "I can't ruin your life again," he muttered, and walked out of her life. He always said, "Pauline, my third wife, was the best one I ever had."

In 1920, when the Goldwyn Company opened its studios at Culver City, the site of the later M-G-M lot, Miss Frederick moved to California with her mother, the ever-present "Mumsy." She fell in love with Hollywood as it was then, and bought a mansion on Sunset Boulevard and a beach-house at Malibu.

She always loved the out-of-doors, and was delighted when she had to do a lot of horseback riding in one of her first Hollywood movies. Cowboys, wranglers, and cow-queens were among her most intimate friends, and to go to Polly Frederick's on a Sunday afternoon at the then-numbered 503 Sunset Boulevard, was often like going to the circus. Will Rogers, Lew Cody, an old cowgirl known as "Prairie Annie," and Julian Eltinge, mingled with the most glamorous stars of the day and directors like Henry King, Frank Lloyd, and Robert G. Vignola. "Polly" shot craps or discussed literature with equal facility, and prepared dinner for all those who lingered on (she was an excellent cook). When everybody had gone, she enticed sleep by knitting or working a crossword puzzle. Her experiences with Mack had frightened her of alcohol, and she rarely drank anything except a little champagne at dinner.

She even liked riding in rodeos. The greatest compliment she ever received, she always said, came from "Prairie Annie," who, after clobbering a cowboy who had stood her up on a date, came up to Miss Frederick at a Bakersfield rodeo and asked, "What outfit do you ride for?" I myself remember her vividly when she was Queen of Raisin Day one year in Fresno, California, and rode on top of a float, with a red sunbonnet framing her beautiful face, and threw kisses with both hands to the cowboys and farmers who lined the streets.

Because of her reputation for complete amenability, Samuel Goldwyn was surprised whenever she did not like a story which he'd bought for her. He soon learned, however, that he had only to tell her that Geraldine Farrar was dying to do it for Miss Frederick to be completely amenable again, and leave his office with a happy smile, clutching the scenario to her breast.

Then, suddenly, an astonishing item appeared in the newspapers: "One of the best known Goldwyn stars, Pauline Frederick, has severed her connection with that corporation, and has signed up with another."

It soon became known that she had agreed to star for a new company, Robertson-Cole, which was listing as its other acquistions Sessue Hayakawa, Betty Blythe, Georges Carpentier, Bessie Barriscale, ZaSu Pitts, and her own predecessor as Mrs. Willard Mack, Marjorie Rambeau.

Goldwyn was sorry to lose Miss Frederick. When she showed him the contract, however, which Robertson-Cole had offered — a salary surpassed only by Mary Pickford's, the right to select not only her stories but also her directors, cameramen and supporting casts, a portable dressing-unit that would follow her even on location — Goldwyn shook her hand and said with admiration: "Goodbye, Pauline."

As things turned out, he might better have said, "Poor Pauline."

Her first picture under the new banner was based upon a Sir Arthur Wing Pinero play, "Iris," and was titled *A Slave of Vanity*. But for all its story prestige, it was certainly no *Madame X*.

Her subsequent Robertson-Cole pictures were worse, and as the realisation that leaving Goldwyn had been a mistake of the first magnitude slowly dawned on her, she decided to marry.

It was a typical gesture on her part. Whenever her career became too confusing, she simply took a new husband, as if that would change her luck or solve everything. The new husband, Dr. C. A. Rutherford, was a second cousin who had known her since their Boston childhood and who, encouraged by "Mumsy," had several times asked her to marry him.

They were married in Santa Ana, and the doctor immediately gave up his practice in Seattle to become her manager. "You're such a safe person," she told him in the beginning. Less than four months later, she had changed her mind about him and realised that he wasn't a "safe person" at all. He returned to Seattle to resume his practice, and two years afterward they were divorced. Rutherford, a nice man, knew nothing about managing an actress's career, and Miss Frederick, who was regretting her move to Robertson-Cole, needed professional help, not the bungling advice of a well-meaning husband. "There was never a misunderstanding beteween us," she told a reporter. "It was a total lack of understanding. I don't know where Dr. Rutherford is. I do not care."

When FBO (Film Booking Office) took over Robertson-Cole, Miss Frederick did not renew her contract. She was miserably unhappy about her career and said that if she couldn't make pictures like *Madame X,* she didn't want to make any. In March 1923, she returned to Al Woods's management and appeared for him, with Charles Waldron, in a play called "The Guilty One." It was a popular success and gave her the courage to try the movies again.

She returned to Hollywood and made *Let No Man Put Asunder* for the briefly revitalised Vitagraph studios. Her leading man was a friend, Lou Tellegen. He was by then divorced from Geraldine Farrar and was trying to make it on his own. Dutch born, he had lived most of his life in France and had been a favourite model for Rodin before becoming Sarah Bernhardt's leading man. English was always a puzzlement to him and when he appeared for work on *Let No Man Put Asunder,* he asked Miss Frederick: "What is this thing no man puts? What is a sunder?"

That film, in the opinion of "Photoplay," and of many others, was "one of the worst ever made," and Miss Frederick confessed that she was about ready to throw in the towel as far as her film career was concerned.

But when Ernst Lubitsch, who had always admired her, offered to cast her in *Three Women,* she accepted. In it she played the stylish mother of May McAvoy. Mother and daughter battled Marie Prevost, the other woman, for Lew Cody's affections, and the mother is eventually driven to kill him in order to protect her daughter. Miss Frederick carried off the acting honours in fine style, and her career in films was spurred forward again.

PAULINE FREDERICK

Clarence Brown then gave her the part of Laura La Plante's older sister in *Smouldering Fires,* which he was directing for Universal. I saw it again a few years ago at the National Film Theatre in London and thought Miss Frederick's performance as the business tycoon who marries a young man in her employ, and then finds he has fallen in love with her younger sister, still full of dramatic poignancy.

At Metro-Goldwyn, Robert G. Vignola, who had guided her through eight films and was one of her favourite directors, co-starred her with Conrad Nagel in an amusing comedy called *Married Flirts,* which had a sequence wherein she was hostess at a mahjong luncheon for movie stars and Norma Shearer, John Gilbert, Mae Murray, May McAvoy, and Aileen Pringle were among the guests, in cameo bits as themselves.

But for the most part Hollywood producers were not clamouring for Miss Frederick's services, and she went back to the theatre. Some of her thinking at that time is in the interiew with her which Adela Rogers St. Johns published in the September 1926 issue of "Photoplay:"

"There are too many angles to the motion picture business for a lone woman to combat. If I'd been a better picker, had a husband who was a big producer or a fine director, or even a good sound business man who could look after my stories, my casts, my releases, I should feel safe. When I left Goldwyn some years ago, I ran into bad luck. I was influenced to do the wrong thing. I didn't see what it would lead to, didn't understand. And I found myself with no one to advise me, no one to give me the surrounding support I needed. I am an actress, not a director, a story writer, a salesman. And — well, I just didn't do the right thing. And since then I've never found the right stories in the companies where they wanted me to work, and I haven't found any companies that wanted to make the stories I wanted to do."

Miss Frederick may have been discouraged, but she had not lost the personal magnetism that had made her a star. Wrote Mrs. St. Johns: "Oh, the charm of that woman off-screen! I forget about it, not seeing her for months and maybe years, and it captures me all over again. She is so *real.* She is so *natural.* No posing, no affectation, no languid boredom about her. She sparkles with life. She glows with enthusiasm. Her voice is rich, vibrant, entrancing. And she has the nicest handshake of any woman I have ever known — strong, firm, cordial, sweet."

Miss Frederick was playing in Frederick Lonsdale's "Spring Cleaning" on a Los Angeles stage when an Australian impresario, E. J. Carroll, persuaded her to go to the Antipodes with two plays — the Lonsdale piece and "The Lady" — which she had already acted in California. When she arrived in Sydney, *Smouldering Fires* had just opened to capacity business and a big banner, "Australia Welcomes Pauline Frederick" stretched across Oceanic Wharf. The Sydney stores were advertising "Pauline Frederick hats" and "Madame X perfume." She played to packed houses in both Sydney and Melbourne.

On her return to Hollywood, she revived, and toured, a stage production of "Madame X" for Louis O. Macloon, then the West Coast's foremost producer of stage plays and musicals.

Interestingly enough, the small role of the public prosecutor in this revival was played by Clark Gable. He had just been separated from his first wife (Josephine Dillon). Miss Frederick first saw him, ill-at-ease in a badly tailored, yellowing-gray suit, but obviously ambitious. She befriended him and

37

encouraged him to persist as an actor. Her dominating spirit and well-intended advice, however, secretly antagonised Gable. Fresh from having been squire to Jane Cowl during her tour with "Romeo and Juliet" — in which he had been a spear-carrier — Gable grumbled that "Miss Frederick is forever complaining she has a sore back. She likes me to rub it for her."

Miss Frederick also persuaded him to go to a good dentist, and paid for the work herself, so he could open his mouth without the gold in his upper teeth gleaming. Grateful, he always gallantly fell to one knee and kissed her hand, as he had done before with Miss Cowl. Years later, after he had achieved screen stardom, he visited Miss Frederick at her New York City hotel. He called her "Polly," and she asked with a wry smile: "Remember that lil ole yellow suit, Clark?"

After the American tour of "Madame X," she took it to London, under E. J. Carroll's auspices. It opened at the Lyceum on the night of March 2, 1927, and she took twenty-eight curtain calls. Said the critic of the London "Observer:"

"It looked as though neighbouring Covent Garden had been raided and completely divested of every flower in the market. Never have I seen such an exhibition of hysteria as greeted the American actress at the Lyceum Theatre on Wednesday night."

On the run's final night, there were more flowers and the audience wouldn't let her go. Even after she had removed her make-up, she had to go back, in her *negligée,* for one last call. It's a pity no film producer ever thought of including a cameo shot of her taking a bow after the final fade-out of one of her pictures. No actress ever took a curtain call better. She bent low from the waist, her hair sweeping down over the top of her head, then the quick flash of her head back, with the hair flying into place, and a wide, friendly smile that included everybody from top gallery to first row orchestra.

While appearing in "Madame X" in London, she made a movie for Herbert Wilcox. Appropriately named *Mumsie,* it was all about "smother love," and was not a memorable picture. But it did mark Herbert Marshall's film *début* and he later paid tribute to Miss Frederick's kindness to a newcomer, as did many other performers throughout her career.

On her return to Hollywood, she made three talkies for Warner Bros. — *On Trial, Evidence,* and *The Sacred Flame.* Early Vitaphone was kind to no one, but the reviewer for the "Los Angeles Times" said: "A star who was gone but never forgotten left Hollywood more in sorrow than anger and toured the world. Thanks to the talkies, this beautiful woman — Pauline Frederick — is back on the screen. She has a triumphant return in *On Trial."*

Evidence was a marital-problem tear-jerker, in which Miss Frederick also sang two songs, one of which, "Little Cavalier," enjoyed a brief popularity. The film version of Maugham's *The Sacred Flame* enabled her to be arresting as a devoted mother forced to become a mercy-killer.

The physical resemblance between Miss Frederick and Joan Crawford had often been remarked, and when Marjorie Rambeau, then under contract at M-G-M and playing Miss Crawford's mother in *This Modern Age,* fell ill and couldn't complete the film, it was re-shot with Pauline Frederick as Crawford's mother. In 1917, when Miss Crawford was still Billie Cassin and lived in Kansas City, she had written Miss Frederick requesting an autographed picture, and when she was married to Douglas Fairbanks Jr., she had

Pauline Frederick with Joan Crawford in *This Modern Age*.

met Miss Frederick backstage. Said Miss Frederick of the Crawford of that time: "If they will give the child a chance, she'll do big things. That girl's a fighter."

It is commonly believed that "Mumsy" — Miss Frederick's mother — once more persuaded her, "for security," to marry a hotel man named Hugh C. Leighton, in New York City on April 19, 1930. Miss Frederick left him a few months later, and the marriage was annulled the following December.

She resumed playing mothers in films — mothers who were good or bad, and mothers-in-law who were all bad. Even when she was young, Miss Frederick had never balked at mother roles. Injuries sustained in an early automobile accident had made it impossible for her to have a child of her own, and she was especially good in scenes involving a child. She especially loved "letting it rip with the old rips," as she called silver-cord mothers. She never acknowledged that she had one of them herself.

The best of her films in that phase of her career was *Ramona*, in which she played the aristocratic Señora Moreno. On the stage, she played Queen

MORE FROM HOLLYWOOD

Elizabeth in West Coast productions of Maxwell Anderson's "Elizabeth the Queen" and "Mary of Scotland," and the Empress Elizabeth of Austria in the Theatre Guild's New York production of Anderson's "The Masque of Kings."

Miss Frederick married her fifth husband, Colonel Joseph A. Marmon, in Scarsdale, N.Y., on January 21, 1934. He was commanding the 16th Infantry at Governor's Island and when he brought his lady there, the regiment, in formation on the dock, sang: "She's in the Army now."

Miss Frederick was devoted to Marmon, but her happiness was short-lived. He was dying of cancer, which had first been diagnosed as arthritis. He thought she didn't know the truth; she thought he didn't — and all the time they both knew. He died in December of the year in which they were married.

During that same time, Willard Mack, ravaged by alcohol and drugs, also died.

"The fuller we live, the more we experience; and the more we experience, the less vulnerable we are," Miss Frederick had once said.

She too was enduring poor health, and hated to admit it. For a decade she had been tormented by attacks of asthma.

She opened a new play, "Suspect," in San Francisco, which had always been a "Frederick city." Wrote one of the San Francisco critics of "Suspect": "No Fontanne, Cornell or Claire has ever received the welcome she got, for this is Polly Frederick's bailiwick. Finally, she capitulated and rose to give that unique Frederick bow, that deep bend at the waist that is her trademark."

She had hoped to take "Suspect" on to Broadway, but collapsed after the final night in San Francisco and had to go to a hospital.

She made one more movie — *Thank You, Mr. Moto,* with Peter Lorre. It was another mother role, an oriental one, and required her to die on the screen.

Simultaneously, "Mumsy" was dying in their Beverly Hills home, and didn't recognise her daughter when Miss Frederick was allowed to see her. After the mother's death in February 1938, Miss Frederick continued to live in the big house on Sunset Boulevard with a widowed aunt (Mrs. George Pettengill).

One night, some months after her mother died, she was dressing to go out to dine with some friends and suddenly changed her mind about wearing a white dinner dress embellished with red. "I'll leave it for another time," she told her aunt.

Two days later, on Septermber 19, 1938, an asthmatic attack again had her fighting for breath — in vain. She was buried in the dress she was saving "for another time."

An autopsy revealed that an intestinal obstruction, for which she had been operated on after her tour of "Mary of Scotland," had not been entirely cleared and was probably the basic cause of the recurrent and fatal asthma.

PAULINE FREDERICK FILMOGRAPHY

THE ETERNAL CITY (1915). Romantic drama of Rome; as Donna Roma. *Dir:* Edwin S. Porter and Hugh Ford. *Sc:* Hugh Ford (from the novel by Hall Caine). *With* Thomas Holding, Frank Losee, Fuller Mellish, George Majeroni, Macey Harlan, Exteriors filmed in Rome immediately prior to the First World War. (Re-made by Goldwyn/First National, 1923, with Barbara La Marr and Bert Lytell.) *Prod:* Famous Players (Paramount). 5 reels.

SOLD (1915). Romantic drama; as Helen Bryant, wife, who had been Helen Raymond, model. *Dir:* Edwin S. Porter and Hugh Ford. *Sc:* Hugh Ford (from a play by Henri Bernstein). *With* Thomas Holding, Julian L'Estrange, Lowell Sherman, Russell Bassett. *Prod:* Famous Players (Paramount). 4 reels.

ZAZA (1915). Romantic drama of the French music halls; as Zaza, favourite chanteuse. *Dir:* Edwin S. Porter and Hugh Ford. *Sc:* Hugh Ford (from the David Belasco play that was based on the Parisian success by Pierre Berton and Charles Simon). *With* Julian L'Estrange, Maude Grainger, Charles Butler, Mark Smith, Madge Evans, Ruth Sinclair, Walter Craven, Blanche Fisher, Helen Sinnot. (Re-filmed, 1923, with Gloria Swanson as Zaza; as a talkie, 1939, with Claudette Colbert.) *Prod:* Famous Players (Paramount). 4 reels.

BELLA DONNA (1915). Exotic romantic drama; as Ruby Chepstow, adventuress. *Dir:* Edwin S. Porter and Hugh Ford. *Sc:* Hugh Ford (from the play by Robert Hichens and James B. Fagan, as dramatised from the novel by Hichens). *With* Thomas Holding, Julian L'Estrange, Eugene Ormonde, George Majeroni, Edward Shalet, Helen Sinnot. *Prod:* Famous Players (Paramount). 5 reels.
(Re-filmed as Pola Negri's first Hollywood-made vehicle; as a talkie in England starring Mary Ellis; and in 1946 as *Temptation*, starring Merle Oberon).

LYDIA GILMORE (1916). Courtroom melodrama; as Lydia Gilmore, doctor's wife who lies on the witness stand to protect her husband, on trial for the murder of the husband of his mistress. *Dir:* Edwin S. Porter and Hugh Ford. *Sc:* Hugh Ford (from the play by Henry Arthur Jones). *With* Vincent Serrano, Thomas Holding, Robert Cain, Helen Luttrell, Jack Curtis, Michael Hale. *Prod:* Famous Players (Paramount). 5 reels.

THE SPIDER (1916). Mother love melodrama; in a dual role: as Valerie St. Cyr, mother, and Joan Marche, the grown daughter she deserted as a baby. *Dir:* Robert G. Vignola. *Sc:* William H. Clifford. *With* Thomas Holding, Frank Losee. *Prod:* Famous Players (Paramount). 5 reels.

AUDREY (1916). Romance of early America; as Audrey, an orphan who is rescued from her half-wild drudgery by a man who loves her. *Dir:* Robert G. Vignola. *Sc:* Hugh Ford (from the novel by Mary Johnson). *With* Charles Waldron, Henry Hallam, Helen Lindroth , Jack Clark. *Prod:* Famous Players (Paramount). 5 reels.

THE MOMENT BEFORE (1916). Romantic drama; as Madge, a gypsy, who fights her way up to become the Duchess of Maldon. *Dir:* Robert G. Vignola. *Sc:* Hugh Ford (from the play by Israel Zangwill). *With* Thomas Holding, J. W. Johnston, Frank Losee, Henry Hallam. *Prod:* Famous Players (Paramount). 5 reels.

THE WORLD'S GREAT SNARE (1916). Romantic drama of the West; as Myra, dance-hall girl. *Dir:* Joseph Kaufman. *Sc.* Hugh Ford (from a novel by E. Phillips Oppenheim). *With* Irving Cummings, William Riley Hatch, Ferdinand Tidmarsh, Frank Evans. *Prod:* Famous Players (Paramount). 5 reels.

THE WOMAN IN THE CASE (1916). Romantic melodrama; as Margaret Hughes, who poses as an adventuress to gain the evidence that will free her husband of a false murder charge. *Dir/Sc:* Hugh Ford (from the play by Clyde Fitch). *With* Alan Hale, Paul Gordon, Clarence Handysides, Marie Chambers, George Larkin. (Re-made, 1922, as *The Law and the Woman*, with Betty Compson.) *Prod:* Famous Players (Paramount). 5 reels.

ASHES OF EMBERS (1916). Romantic melodrama; in a dual role: as Agnes Ward, the good twin and as Laura Ward, the bad one. *Dir:* Joseph Kaufman. *Sc:* Forrest Halsey. *With* Earle Foxe, Frank Losee, Maggie Halloway Fisher. *Prod:* Famous Players (Paramount). 5 reels.

NANETTE OF THE WILDS (1916). Romantic melodrama of the Canadian Northwest; as Nanette Gautier. *Dir:* Joseph Kaufman. *Sc:* Willard Mack. *With* Willard Mack, Wallace MacDonald, Frank Joyner, Charles Brand, Daniel Pennell, Jean Stewart. *Prod:* Famous Players. (Paramount). 5 reels.

THE SLAVE MARKET (1917). Romantic melodrama of the West Indies; as Romana. *Dir/Sc:* Hugh Ford (from a story by Frederick Arnold Kummer). *With* Thomas Meighan, Albert Hart, Wellington Playter, Ruby Hoffman. *Prod:* Famous Players (Paramount). 5 reels.

SAPHO (1917). Romantic drama of Paris; as Fanny Le Grand, who becomes known as the notorious model, Sapho. *Dir/Sc:* Hugh Ford (from the novel and play by Alphonse Daudet). *With* Thomas Meighan, Pedro de Cordoba, Frank Losee, John Sainpolis, (*Sapho* formed the story basis for Garbo's third talkie, *Inspiration*.) *Prod:* Famous Players (Paramount). 5 reels.

SLEEPING FIRES (1917). Courtroom drama; as Zelma Bryce, on trial for having killed her philandering husband. *Dir/Sc:* Hugh Ford (from a story by George Middleton). *With* Thomas Meighan, John Sainpolis, Helen Dahl, Joseph Smiley. *Prod:* Famous Players (Paramount). 5 reels.

HER BETTER SELF (1917). Romantic drama; as Vivian, a daughter of the rich who loves a charity doctor. *Dir:* Robert G. Vignola. *Sc:* Margaret Turnbull. *With* Thomas Meighan, Alice Hollister, Charles Wellesley, Maud Turner Gordon. *Prod:* Famous Players. (Paramount). 5 reels.

THE LOVE THAT LIVES (1917). Realistic mother-love drama; as Molly McGill who becomes a scrubwoman in order to raise her two children. *Dir:* Robert G. Vignola. *Sc:* (from a story by Scudder Middleton). *With* Pat O'Malley, Violet Palmer, John Sainpolis. *Prod:* Famous Players (Paramount). 5 reels.

DOUBLE-CROSSED (1917). Melodrama; as Eleanor Stratton, a wife forced into thievery. *Dir:* Robert G. Vignola. *Sc:* Hector Turnbull. *With* (William) Riley Hatch, Crauford Kent, Clarence Handysides, Joseph Smiley. *Prod:* Famous Players (Paramount). 5 reels.

THE HUNGRY HEART (1917). Romantic drama; as Courtney, a neglected wife. *Dir:* Robert G. Vignola. *Sc:* Charles Maigne (from the novel by David Graham Phillips). *With* Howard Hall, Robert Cain, Helen Lindroth. *Prod:* Famous Players (Paramount). 5 reels.

MRS. DANE'S DEFENSE (1918). Drama of a woman trying to live down her past; as the respectable Mrs. Dane, trying to forget that she was once the indiscreet Felicia Hindemarsh. *Dir:* Hugh Ford. *Sc:* Margaret Turnbull (from the play by Henry Arthur Jones). *With* Leslie Austen, Frank Losee, Maud Turner Gordon, Ormi Hawley, Howard Hall, John L. Shine, Ida Darling, Cyril Chadwick, Amelia Summerville. (Re-made as a talkie, 1934, by Paramount-British, starring Joan Barry.) *Prod:* Famous Players (Paramount). 5 reels.

MADAME JEALOUSY (1918). Modern morality play; as Madame Jealousy ruling her "House of Heavy Hours." *Dir:* Robert G. Vignola. *Sc:* Eve Unsell (from a story by George V. Hobart). *With* Thomas Meighan, Frank Losee, Elsie McCloud, Charles Wellesley, Isabel O'Madigan, Frances Cappelano. *Prod:* Famous Players (Paramount). 5 reels.

LA TOSCA (1918). Period romantic melodrama; as Floria Tosca, Rome's greatest diva. *Dir:* Edward Jose. *Sc:* Charles E. Whittaker (from the French tragedy by Victorien Sardou in which Sarah Bernhardt had once starred). *With* Jules Raucourt, Frank Losee, W. H. Forestelle, Henry Herbert. Puccini turned the story into one of his best operas; and it has been filmed as a talkie and opera in Europe on several occasions. *Prod:* Famous Players (Paramount). 5 reels.

RESURRECTION (1918). Romantic drama of Tsarist Russia; as Katusha Maslova. *Dir:* Edward Jose. *Sc:* Charles E. Whittaker (from the novel by Count Leo Tolstoi). *With* Robert Elliott, John Sainpolis, Jere Austin. (See Dolores Del Rio for listing of other productions of *Resurrection*.) *Prod:* Famous Players (Paramount). 5 reels.

HER FINAL RECKONING (1918). Romantic melodrama; as Marsa Tcheretoff, a gypsy, who becomes a princess. *Dir:* Emile Chautard. *Sc:* Charles E. Whittaker (from a play, "Prince Zilah," by Jules Claretie). *With* John Miltern, Robert Cain, Warren Cooke, Joseph Smiley, James Laffey, Karl Dane. *Prod:* Famous Players (Paramount). 5 reels.

FEDORA (1918). Romantic Russian melodrama; as the Princess Fedora. *Dir:* Edward José. *Sc:* Charles E, Whittaker (from the play by Victorien Sardou, a favourite of Sarah Bernhardt's). *With* Alfred Hickman, Jere Austin, W. L. Abingdon, Wilmuth Merkyll. (Filmed by Fox, 1915, as *Princess Romanoff;* re-filmed by Paramount, 1928, as *The Woman from Moscow,* starring Pola Negri.) *Prod:* Famous Players (Paramount). 5 reels.

A DAUGHTER OF THE OLD SOUTH (1918). Romantic drama of the Old South; as Dolores Jardine, a Spanish girl. *Dir:* Emile Chautard. *Sc:* Margaret Turnbull (from a story by Alicia Ramsay and Rudolph De Cordova). *With* Pedro de Cordoba, Vera Beresford, James Laffey, Mrs. T. Randolph. *Prod:* Famous Players (Paramount). 5 reels.

OUT OF THE SHADOWS (1919). Romantic melodrama; as Ruth Minchin. *Dir:* Emile Chautard. *Sc:* Eve Unsell (from a story, "The Shadow of the Rope." by Ernest William Hornung). *With* Wyndham Standing, Ronald Byram, William Gross. *Prod:* Famous Players (Paramount). 5 reels.

PAID IN FULL (1919). Romantic drama; as Emma Brooks. *Dir:* Emile Chautard. *Sc:* Charles E. Whittaker (from the play by Eugene Walter). *With* Wyndham Standing, Robert Cain, Frank Losee, Jane Farrell, Vera Beresford. *Prod:* Famous Players (Paramount). 5 reels.

THE WOMAN ON THE INDEX (1919). Melodrama of murder and blackmail; as Sylvia

Martin. *Dir:* Hobart Henley. *Sc:* Willard Mack (from the play by Lillian Trimble Bradley and George Broadhurst). *With* Wyndham Standing, Willard Mack, Ben Hendricks, Jere Austin, *Prod:* Samuel Goldwyn. 5 reels.

ONE WEEK OF LIFE (1919). Romantic melodrama; in a dual role: as Helen Sherwood and Marion Roche. *Dir:* Hobart Henley. *Sc:* Willard Mack (from a novel by Cosmo Hamilton). *With* Thomas Holding, Sydney Ainsworth, Corinne Barker. *Prod:* Samuel Goldwyn. 5 reels.

THE FEAR WOMAN (1919). Drama of a woman who fears she has inherited the family taint of alcoholism; as Helen Winthrop. *Dir:* John A. Barry. *Sc:* (from a story by Izola Forester). *With* Milton Sills, Emmett King, Harry S. Northrup, Beverly Travers, Walter Hiers, Lydia Yeamans Titus. *Prod:* 'Samuel Goldwyn. 5 reels.

THE PEACE OF ROARING RIVER (1919). Western romance; as Madge Nelson. *Dir:* Victor Schertzinger. *Sc:* (from a story by George Van Schaick). *With* Thomas Holding, Hardee Kirkland, Corinne Barker, Lydia Yeamans Titus. *Prod:* Samuel Goldwyn. 5 reels.

BONDS OF LOVE (1919). Romantic drama; as Una Sayre, governess, who becomes Una Cabot. *Dir:* Reginald Barker. *Sc:* (from a story by Louis Sherwin). *With* Percy Standing, Betty Schade, Leslie Stuart, Charles Clary, Kate Lester, Frankie Lee. *Prod:* Samuel Goldwyn. 5 reels.

THE LOVES OF LETTY (1920). Romantic drama; as Letty Shell. *Dir:* Frank Lloyd. *Sc:* (from the play "Letty Shell," by Sir Arthur Wing Pinero). *With* John Bowers, W. Lawson Butt, Willard Louis, Florence Deshon, Leila Bliss, Leota Lorraine, Sydney Ainsworth, Harland Tucker, Joan Standing. *Prod:* Samuel Goldwyn. 5 reels.

THE PALISER CASE (1920). Courtroom melodrama; as Cassy Cora, a Portuguese woman accused on circumstantial evidence of murder. *Dir:* William Parke. *Sc:* Edfrid A. Bingham (from a story by Edgar Saltus). *With* Albert Roscoe, James Neill, Kate Lester, Warburton Gamble, Alec B. Francis. *Prod:* Samuel Goldwyn. 5 reels.

THE WOMAN IN ROOM 13 (1920). Murder mystery; as Laura Bruce. *Dir:* Frank Lloyd. *Sc:* Percival Wilde (from a play by Samuel Shipman and Max Marcin). *With* John Bowers, Charles Clary, Robert McKim, Sydney Ainsworth, Marguerite Snow, Kate Lester, Golda Madden, Richard Tucker. *Prod:* Samuel Goldwyn. 6 reels.

MADAME X (1920). Romantic melodrama; as Jacqueline Floriot. *Dir:* Frank Lloyd. *Sc:* J. E. Nash and Frank Lloyd (from the French play by Alexandre Bisson, which Miss Frederick played many times in the theatre). *With* Casson Ferguson, William Courtleigh, Hardee Kirkland, Albert Roscoe, Sydney Ainsworth, Lionel Belmore, Willard Louis, Cesare Gravina, Maude George. (A previous version was filmed by Pathé, 1916, starring Dorothy Donnelly. Subsequently re-filmed in 1929 with Ruth Chatterton; in 1937 with Gladys George; in 1965 with Lana Turner.) *Prod:* Samuel Goldwyn. 7 reels.

A SLAVE OF VANITY (AKA, GB, Iris) (1920). Romantic drama; as Iris, daughter of luxury, fallen upon poverty-stricken times. *Dir/Sc:* Henry Otto (from the play by Sir Arthur Wing Pinero). *With* Nigel Barrie, Willard Louis, Daisy Robinson, Arthur Hoyt. (Hepworth, in London, filmed *Iris*, 1915, with Alma Taylor.) *Prod:* Robertson-Cole. 6 reels.

ROADS OF DESTINY (1921). Romantic drama; as Rose Merritt, who cannot escape her fate, no matter which turn of the road she takes. *Dir:* Frank Lloyd. *Sc:* J. E. Nash (from the play by Channing Pollock, dramatised from an O. Henry story). *With* John Bowers, Jane Novak, Richard Tucker, Hardee Kirkland, Willard Louis, Maude George, Maurice B. "Lefty" Flynn). *Prod:* Samuel Goldwyn. 6 reels.

THE MISTRESS OF SHENSTONE (1921). Romantic drama; as Myra, Lady Ingleby. *Dir:* Henry King. *Sc:* (from a novel by Florence L. Barclay). *With* Roy Stewart, Emmett King, Arthur Clayton. *Prod:* Robertson-Cole. 6 reels.

SALVAGE (1921). Mother love drama; in a dual role: as two young mothers, one rich, Bernice Ridgeway; and the other poor, Kate Martin. *Sc:* (from a story by Daniel F. Whitcomb). *Dir:* Henry King. *With* Milton Sills, Ralph Lewis, Helen Stone, Raymond Hatton. *Prod:* Robertson-Cole. 6 reels.

THE STING OF THE LASH (1921). Western romantic drama; as Dorothy Keith, an Easterner, who marries a miner out West. *Dir:* Henry King. *Sc:* H. Tipton Steck (from a story by Harvey W. Gates). *With* Clyde Fillmore, W. Lawson Butt, Lionel Belmore, Jack Richardson, Edwin Stevens. *Prod:* Robertson-Cole. 6 reels.

THE LURE OF JADE (AKA, GB, *Houses of Glass*). (1921). Melodrama; in a dual role: as Sara Vincent, the mistress of "The Sea Gull," who tries to revenge herself upon a rival who looks like her. *Dir:* Colin Campbell. *Sc:* Marion Orth (from a play, "*The House of Glass*," by Max Marcin and George M. Cohan). *With* Thomas Holding, Arthur Rankin, Leon Barry, Hardee Kirkland, Clarissa Selwynne. (In 1918, Select released a Clara Kimball Young vehicle, *The House of Glass*, based on the same play; but Miss Young did not play the two roles, and the story varied.) *Prod:* Robertson-Cole. 6 reels.

TWO KINDS OF WOMEN (1922). Romantic Western , with California ranch setting; as Judith Sanford. *Dir:* Colin Campbell. *Sc:* Winifred Dunn (from a novel, "Judith of Blue Lake Ranch," by Jackson Gregory). *With* Tom Santschi, Charles Clary, Eugene Pallette, Clarissa Selwynne, Otis Harlan, Lydia Yeamans Titus, Stanhope Wheatcroft. *Prod:* Robertson-Cole. 6 reels.

THE GLORY OF CLEMENTINA (1922). Romantic drama; as Clementina Wing, a painter. *Dir:* Emile Chautard. *Sc:* E. Richard Schayer and Winifred Dunn (from a novel by William J. Locke). *With* Edward Martindel, Louise Dresser, Truly Shattuck, George Cowl, Lydia Yeamans Titus. (Previously filmed by Edison, 1915, with Miriam Nesbitt and Marc McDermott). *Prod:* Robertson-Cole. 6 reels.

LET NO MAN PUT ASUNDER (AKA, *Let Not Man Put Asunder)* (1924). Marital melodrama; as Petrina Farneuil. *Dir:* J. Stuart Blackton. *Sc:* Charles L. Gaskell (from a novel by Basil King). *With* Lou Tellegen, Leslie Austen, Helena D'Algy, Maurice Costello, Clifton Webb. *Prod:* Vitagraph. 9 reels.

THREE WOMEN (1924). Romantic drama; as Mabel Wilton. *Dir:* Ernst Lubitsch. *Sc:* Hans Kraly (from a story by Kraly and Lubitsch). *With* May McAvoy, Lew Cody, Marie Prevost, Willard Louis, Pierre Gendron, Mary Carr, Raymond McKee. *Prod:* Warner Bros. 8 reels. (Compare listing in May McAvoy filmography.)

SMOULDERING FIRES (1924). Romantic drama; as Jane Vale. *Dir:* Clarence Brown. *Sc:* Sada Cowan, Howard Higgin and Melville Brown. *With* Laura LaPlante, Malcolm MacGregor, Wanda Hawley, Tully Marshall, Helen Lynch, George Cooper. Some beautiful exteriors filmed at Yosemite Valley, California. *Prod:* Universal. 8 reels.

MARRIED FLIRTS (1924). Romantic comedy drama; as Nellie Wayne, a writer who spends too much time at her typewriter and then goes to Paris, where she becomes the glamorous "Mrs. Paramour." *Dir:* Robert G. Vignola. *Sc:* Julia Crawford Ivers (from the novel by Louis Joseph Vance). *With* Conrad Nagel, Mae Busch, Huntley Gordon, Paul Nicholson, Patterson Dial, Alice Hollister; and with cameo bits by famous stars at a studio commissary scene. *Prod:* Metro-Goldwyn. 7 reels.

HER HONOR THE GOVERNOR (AKA, GB, *The Second Mrs. Fenway)* (1926). Political drama; as Adele Fenway, governor of her state, fighting political corruption, scandal and impeachment. *Dir:* Chet Withey. *Sc:* Doris

Anderson (from a story by Hyatt Daab and Weed Dickinson). *With* Carroll Nye, Tom Santschi, Boris Karloff, Greta Von Rue, Stanton Heck, Jack Richardson, Kathleen Kirkham, Charles McHugh, William Worthington. *Prod:* FBO. 6300 ft.

DEVIL'S ISLAND (1926). Melodrama; as Jeannette Picot, who elects to accompany her husband when he is sent for life to Devil's Island. *Dir:* Frank O'Connor. *Sc:* Anthony Coldeway and Raymond L. Schrock. *With* Richard Tucker, Marian Nixon, Leo White, John Miljan, George Lewis, Harry Northrup. (Re-made by Warner Bros., 1940.) *Prod:* Chadwick. 6 reels.

JOSSELYN'S WIFE (1926). Marital drama; as Lillian Josselyn. *Dir:* Richard Thorpe. *Sc:* Agnes Parsons (from a novel by Kathleen Norris). *With* Holmes Herbert, Armand Kaliz, Josephine Hill, Carmelita Geraghty. *Prod:* Tiffany. 6 reels. (Previously filmed, 1919, starring Bessie Barriscale).

THE NEST (1927). Domestic drama; as Polly Hamilton, a widow with jazz-mad children. *Dir:* William Nigh. *Sc:* Charles E. Whittaker (from a French play, "Les Noces d'argent," by Paul Geraldy). *With* Holmes Herbert, Thomas Holding, Ruth Dwyer, Reginald Sheffield, Jean Acker, Wilfred Lucas. *Prod:* Excellent Pictures. 8 reels.

MUMSIE (1927). Mother love tear-jerker; as Mrs. Symonds, who loses the son she adores in the First World War. *Dir:* Herbert Wilcox. *Sc:* (from the play, "Mumsee," by Edward Knoblock). *With* Herbert Marshall, Nelson Keys, Frank Stanmore, Rolf Leslie. *Prod:* Herbert Wilcox Productions 7 reels.

ON TRIAL (1928). Courtroom murder trial drama; as Joan Trask. *Dir:* Archie Mayo. *Sc:* Robert Lord and Max Pollack (from the play by Elmer Rice). *With* Bert Lytell, Lois Wilson, Holmes Herbert, Richard Tucker, Jason Robards, Johnny Arthur, Franklin Pangborn, Vondell Darr, Edmund Breese, Edward Martindel. Miss Frederick's first talking film. (A silent version filmed by Essanay, 1917; remade by Warner Bros., 1939.) *Prod:* Warner Bros. 9290 ft.

EVIDENCE (1929). Mother love drama; as Myra Stanhope. *Dir:* John Adolfi. *Sc:* (from a play by J. Du Rocher MacPherson). *With* Conway Tearle, Lowell Sherman, William Courtenay, Alec B. Francis, Myrna Loy, Ivan Simpson, Lionel Belmore. *Prod:* Warner Bros. 8 reels.

THE SACRED FLAME (1929). Domestic drama about mercy killing; as Mrs. Taylor. *Dir:* Archie Mayo. *Sc:* Harvey Thew (from a play by W. Somerset Maugham). *With* Conrad Nagel, Lila Lee, William Courtenay, Walter

Byron, Dale Fuller, Alec B. Francis. (Re-filmed in 1935 as *The Right to Live*). *Prod:* Warner Bros. 7 reels.

THIS MODERN AGE (1931). Mother-daughter romantic drama; as Diane. *Dir:* Nicholas Grindé. *Sc:* Dialogue continuity by Sylvia Thalberg and Frank Butler, with added dialogue by John Meehan (from a story by Mildred Cram). *With* Joan Crawford, Neil Hamilton, Monroe Owsley, Hobart Bosworth, Emma Dunn, Albert Conti. *Prod:* M-G-M. 8 reels.

WAYWARD (1932). Mother-son drama; as Mrs. Frost, whose possessiveness almost ruins her son's marriage. *Dir:* Edward Sloman *Sc:* Gladys Unger and Lillian Day (from a novel, "Wild Beauty," by Mateel Howe Farnham). *With* Nancy Carroll, Richard Arlen, John Litel, Margalo Gillmore, Dorothy Stickney, Gertrude Michael. *Prod:* Paramount. 8 reels.

THE PHANTOM OF CRESTWOOD (1932). Murder mystery; as Faith Andes. *Dir:* J. Walter Ruben. *Sc:* Bartlett Cormack (from a story by Cormack and Ruben). *With* Karen Morley, Ricardo Cortez, H. B. Warner, Robert McWade, Aileen Pringle, Skeets Gallagher, Mary Duncan, Gavin Gordon, Anita Louise, Robert Elliott, Ivan Simpson, Hilda Vaughn, George E. Stone, Sam Hardy, Matty Kemp, Tom Doluglas, Eric Linden. *Prod:* RKO-Radio. 8 reels.

SELF-DEFENSE (1933). (Re-issued as *My Mother*). Mother-daughter murder mystery; as Katy DeVoux, who runs a gambling salon disguised as a resort hotel. *Dir:* Phil E. Rosen. *Sc:* (from a Peter B. Kyne story, "The Just Judge"). *With* Claire Windsor, Theodore von Eltz, Barbara Kent, Robert Elliott, Henry B. Walthall, Jameson Thomas, George Hackathorne. *Prod:* Monogram. 69m.

SOCIAL REGISTER (1934). Dramatic comedy; as Mrs. Breene, who tries to show up the chorus girl her son wants to marry. *Dir:* Marshall Neilan. *Sc:* William Ashmore Creelman (from a Clara Beranger adaptation of a play by Anita Loos and John Emerson). *With* Colleen Moore, Charles Winninger, Alexander Kirkland, Margaret Livingston, Robert Benchley, Ross Alexander, John Miltern, Frey and Braggiotti. *Prod:* Columbia. 8 reels.

MY MARRIAGE (1936). Society drama; as Mrs. DeWitt Tyler II, who opposes her son's marriage to the daughter of a racketeer. *Dir:* George Archainbaud. *Sc:* Frances Hyland. *With* Claire Trevor, Kent Taylor, Thomas Beck, Helen Wood, Colin Tapley, Paul Kelly, Henry Kolker, Frank Dawson, Lynn Bari, Paul McVey. *Prod:* 20th Century-Fox. 6,213 ft.

RAMONA (1936). Early California romantic drama; as Señora Moreno. *Dir:* Henry King. *Sc:* Lamar Trotti (from the novel by Helen Hunt Jackson). *With* Loretta Young, Don Ameche, Charles Waldron, Pedro de Cordoba, Kent Taylor, Jane Darwell, Katherine De-Mille, Victor Kilian, John Carradine, J. Carrol Naish, Claire Du Brey, Russell Simpson. (*Ramona* had been filmed in three silent versions: D. W. Griffith's for Biograph, with Mary Pickford; one by W. H. Clune, 1916, with Adda Gleason; and one by UA with Dolores Del Rio, 1928; it was re-made as a Mexican film in 1946, starring Esther Fernández.) *Prod:* 20th Century-Fox. Technicolor. 7,536 ft.

THANK YOU, MR. MOTO (1937). Murder mystery melodrama, about a lost treasure scroll of Genghis Khan; as Madame Chung. *Dir:* Norman Foster. *Sc:* Foster and Willis Cooper (from a story by John P. Marquand). *With* Peter Lorre, Thomas Beck, Jayne Regan, Sidney Blackmer, Sig Rumann, John Carradine, Nedda Harrigan, Philip Ahn. *Prod:* 20th Century-Fox. 6,100 ft.

3
GRETA GARBO

At the most, there are no more than a half-dozen movie stars who have become legends in their own time. The Queen of them all — "La Divina," as she is known in Europe — remains the one and only Garbo.

Over thirty-five years have gone by since she made a film, yet she is still the best press copy of all screen celebrities, and the re-releases of her M-G-M films, both for theatrical and television viewing, have made her the only movie actress whose name by itself spells instant box-office.

In the last decade, the top ten moneymakers picked every year by exhibitors include names that are almost exclusively male; in some years, one actress — Elizabeth Taylor, Joanne Woodward, Doris Day, Julie Andrews, Ali MacGraw, or Barbra Streisand — is numbered among the chosen ten; but almost every exhibitor will admit that if stars of revivals were eligible for the list, Garbo's name, above all other actresses, would be there regularly. An ironic admission, because during the years when she was acting, while she was always among the favoured international few, she rarely made the exclusively American top-ten lists. She makes them now, by proxy as it were, even though American audiences are no longer responsive to the star image of the actress. Thus for today's worldwide audience, Garbo is up there with the men of the hour — John Wayne, Clint Eastwood, Paul Newman, Marlon Brando, Steve McQueen.

Whenever the current release product lags or does not attract, an exhibitor books a season of Garbo films, and her lovely face saves his. It started one spring not so long ago in Chelsea when a theatre manager booked a Garbo season. Crowds queued in lines around the block. Subsequently, a West End revival of her films in a larger house brought out longer lines. Movie managers in the bigger American cities tried the same experiment starting in the late Fifties, and I well remember standing then in line to see *Camille* at the Beverly Canon in Beverly Hills with a friend who had never seen a Garbo film. I had already stopped counting the number of times I'd seen Garbo as the Lady of the Camelias because after the fiftieth occasion, those who knew were looking at me as if I were some kind of religious fanatic. I still am, I suppose, about Garbo, because I think I've now seen *Camille* a good twenty-five times more.

When the Museum of Modern Art, several years ago in Manhattan, scheduled a festival of all her films, both foreign and American (except for *The Divine Woman,* of which M-G-M says the negative has disintegrated and all prints are lost), tickets were sold out two days after they went on sale, and the programme was immediately scheduled for repetition.

She is a great favourite among the younger set, who know her from seeing revivals of her films both in theatres and television. The common query of today's teen-ager of an adult is "I knew Garbo was beautiful, but why didn't you tell me what a marvellous actress she is?"

In the autumn of 1972, when I was living in Spain, Spanish television showed all the M-G-M films of Garbo, silent and sound (except, of course, for *The Divine Woman*), and television viewing soared on the twice-weekly nights when her pictures were shown. All the top Spanish weeklies — "Hola!," "Lecturas," "Gaceta Ilustrada," and the very magazine that owes its name, "Garbo," to her — were quick sell-outs at the news stands. "Gaceta Ilustrada" indicated that this, the tenth time they had featured a Garbo article since 1957, was like the other nine, a collector's item before it came out.

In the Spanish language, incidentally, "garbo" means "elegance" or "graceful air," so the Spaniards, in honouring her, also pay homage to her for being the leading exponent of "garbo." It is not unusual to hear a Spaniard comment, "Garbo tiene garbo." (Garbo has elegance.)

Twelve years ago, when I was in Vienna, I remember seeing *Camille* and then on another afternoon, *Conquest* (known as *Marie Walewska* in both Europe and England). It was something of a shock at first, because both pictures had been dubbed into German, and a voice other than Garbo's was speaking the lines in German of Marguerite Gautier and Marie Walewska. The packed house, two-thirds of whom were young, was enthralled, and when the houselights came up, viewers remained in their seats for a few moments to wipe the tears from their eyes. One young girl was weeping uncontrollably, and her companions clung to her, weeping with her. I myself was moved, even though the voice I'd heard was not Garbo's.

And then I remembered how it was when I first saw Garbo on the screen. The appeal then was purely visual, because the movies had not found their voice, and missing then were the low, thrilling, bemused tones of the actress. But there was the face, which has been called "the face of the century," a face which, like Helen's, could have launched a thousand ships and topped many a topless tower. It was 1926, and although I was a senior at Fresno High School in Fresno, California, I had cut classes to catch the first matinee of a new M-G-M film, *The Torrent,* from the novel by Ibáñez. I don't know why I was attracted to that particular picture, but for the next three days, while *The Torrent* was playing the Kinema Theatre, nobody saw me. I spent afternoons and nights at the Kinema, because up there on the screen was an actress named Greta Garbo who was the most wonderful image I'd ever seen. I was glad when I learned she had come from Sweden, because I'm half Swedish, and felt a closer affinity.

I always read Robert E. Sherwood in those days, when he was reviewing films for the old weekly "Life," and when he called Garbo a "goddess" and the "dream princess of his department," I entirely concurred. It was after seeing Garbo in her second M-G-M feature, *The Temptress,* and Mr. Sherwood wrote: "I want to go on record as saying that Greta Garbo in *The Temptress* knocked me for a loop...(She) qualifies herewith as the official Dream Princess of the Silent Drama Department of 'Life.'" Two years later, Mr. Sherwood was reviewing *The Mysterious Lady,* and Garbo had become his "dream princess of eternity — the knockout of the ages." I was precisely of the same persuasion.

I was at Fresno State College when I saw her third film, *Flesh and the Devil*. I was reviewing for the paper, and was given *Ben-Hur* to review, an assignment which ordinarily would have delighted me, as it was the biggest prize of the season. But then I found that *Flesh and the Devil,* opening the same time at another theatre, had been handed to somebody I'd thought was a good friend. To my horror, he didn't like the picture and said so, and, what's worse, he liked the *ingénue* Barbara Kent better than Garbo. *Barbara Kent*? After that, I didn't like him. From that point on, there was nothing but a cool indifference between both of us, and ever since then, the very few I've known who are not Garbo worshippers I've dismissed as either trying to attract attention by being different, or as just having no taste whatsoever.

Soon thereafter I was in Los Angeles, a student at UCLA. Whatever I did, wherever I was then and in all the years to come, Garbo remained the serene goddess, and whenever a new picture of hers opened, I abandoned whatever I was doing or studying to pay homage to the faraway princess.

Actually, she wasn't so far away. She was filming at M-G-M studios in Culver City, living at numerous resident addresses in Santa Monica on San Vicente or Chevy Chase, or on Linden Drive in Beverly Hills (although that, I think, was actually her brother Sven's residence — her sister Alva died in Stockholm while Garbo was filming *The Temptress*). I began to see her, always alone, being driven to work early in the morning, and once when I was staying in Santa Monica for a weekend and took a midnight walk along the beach (one could walk alone there in those days at any hour with no fear of being hit over the head), coming toward me, walking barefooted in the wet sand, was Garbo, alone and perfectly content. She didn't look my way, and I looked the other way as we passed for fear she'd think I was staring — which I was.

I saw her again one night shortly afterward at the Shrine Auditorium during the annual opera season. It was for a performance, as I remember, of Strauss's "Salome," and Jeritza was singing. Suddenly, as I lingered in the foyer, there came Garbo, head lowered, walking quickly, one hand on the arm of her manager, Harry Edington (the only manager she ever had). Years later, when I was working on a script at RKO for Edington * (*Walk Away from 'Em,* which never got produced), I recalled that evening to Edington, and he smiled.

"Yes," he said, "I remember that night when I took her to the opera. She had actually expressed a desire to go, and then at the last minute almost bowed out because she didn't have anything in her own wardrobe elegant enough to wear. I phoned the studio and M-G-M wardrobe lent her an evening dress and a wrap for the occasion. Even then, she was so self-effacing and there were so many other stars present that night who wanted to be photographed that I think few recognised her and no photographer, to my knowledge, tried to steal a shot of her."

Meanwhile, I'd caught her appearances in the two major European films, which were shown to enthusiastic foreign film audiences in Hollywood — as the lovely Italian bride in love with the dissolute man of God in the Swedish,

*Ironically, Harry Edington by this time had become the husband of that ingenue I had once termed the least likely to succeed, Barbara Kent.

Stiller-directed *Gösta Berlings Saga;* and in Pabst's German-made film, *The Joyless Street,* as the Viennese girl from a good family who is forced through circumstances to enter what was once called "a house of assignation," and her first client is the young man she loves.

During those last few years of the silent film, which I sometimes cherish as the best in motion picture making, the films Garbo made are all filled with unforgettable moments: the youthful, laughing love scene on the floor between her and Lars Hanson in *The Divine Woman;* the tender scenes between her and the young Phillipe De Lacy, playing her son, in *Love,* as well as the impassioned ones between her as Anna and John Gilbert as Vronsky in the same picture; the suspenseful moment in *The Mysterious Lady,* when she, a spy, kills her enemy, Gustav von Seyffertitz, and then when a servant enters the room, sits on the dead man's knee and pretends to be his favourite for the evening as she signals to the servant to leave them alone; the scene of dismay when she learns in *The Single Standard* that Nils Asther, her lover with whom she is enjoying a yachting cruise, has dismissed her from his life and she distractedly but thoughtfully begins to wash her hair; the impassioned love scene in *A Woman of Affairs* when she gives herself to Gilbert and lets the loose ring slip from her finger, and again in the final reel when the bitter truth of her gallant lie is exposed and she turns up the death card in a solitaire pack and says via subtitle, "You've taken from me the only decent thing I ever did," before going out to her death; the strange attraction she feels in *Wild Orchids* drawing her to the handsome but half-barbaric oriental prince, Nils Asther, when she has become resignedly happy with her elderly husband, Lewis Stone, and finally, in her last silent, *The Kiss,* when she is on trial for murdering her insanely jealous husband and the defiant dignity she evinces when being defended by the attorney, Conrad Nagel, who loves her.

The talkies came, and gradually even the last three big hold-outs — Chaney, Garbo, and Chaplin — spoke. GARBO TALKS, all the choice twenty-four sheets in town announced, and it was an electric moment in *Anna Christie* when she makes her entrance after the first reel of preparation and finally, with deliberate calculation, speaks her first lines in that wonderful husky voice: "Whiskey — ginger ale on the side — and don't be stingy with the whiskey, baby."

Thereafter in most of her other talking features only her very presence illuminated her films. It's especially true of *Romance,* in which she is stunningly photographed and gowned, but even in 1930 it was a creaky vehicle. Recently, on re-visiting her third talking picture *Inspiration,* which I had not remembered as being as good as it is, I was pleased to note that the screenplay, suggested as it is by that old warhorse of the French theatre, Daudet's "Sapho," is well constructed and the dialogue has real charm and sophistication. Gene Markey did his homework well on this one; but on the other hand, *As You Desire Me,* which I had remembered fondly (and it also has a Markey script), seems poorly directed, with hackneyed dialogue and unbelievable scenes, with some very bad performances by some very good actors. And, again, it's only Garbo as the Pirandello heroine who lights up the screen with her own special incandescence.

Four other features from the talking era are most unworthy of her: *Susan Lenox: Her Fall and Rise, Mata Hari, The Painted Veil,* and her last — the clumsy, embarrassing *Two-Faced Woman.*

GRETA GARBO

To the role of the fading ballerina, Grusinskaya, in *Grand Hotel,* for which she was actually more than a little miscast, Garbo brought a nervous, restless quality that somehow made Grusinskaya's dilemma very real, and her love scenes with John Barrymore are some of the best she ever played, they had great admiration for one another as fellow artists, and the sincerity came through abundantly.

The three near-perfect and two perfect Garbo talking features are *Queen Christina, Anna Karenina,* and *Conquest* on the one hand; and *Camille* and *Ninotchka* at the peak.

She herself is wonderfully moving and believable as Sweden's unhappy Queen Christina; Rouben Mamoulian's direction of the somewhat artificial story often transcends the manufactured plot; and the two big silent moments with Garbo are unforgettable: when she memorises the room wherein she has loved for a night; and the end, when her lover is slain and the sails of the ship are unfurled while she goes to the prow and remains staring out like a beautiful ship's figurehead, not moving a muscle of her exquisite face while the camera slowly moves in for what is without doubt her most glorious closeup. Every viewer of those final moments has his own translation of what she is feeling, what she is thinking — it is perfect abstraction on film — and that is precisely the way Mamoulian wanted it.

Several years ago, when I was one of a chosen few who picked scenes from

Greta Garbo and John Gilbert in Mamoulian's *Queen Christina.*

MORE FROM HOLLYWOOD

films of the past for a three-hour programme called *The Movies* shown at a midnight viewing for those attending the live and film benefit show for the Motion Picture Relief Fund, (it had three subsequent showings for Academy members at the Academy Award Theatre, which came off magnificently as well as special television broadcasts), these scenes from *Queen Christina* were chosen to represent Garbo. Mamoulian one Sunday afternoon brought two cans of film containing the only filmed tests Garbo is ever known to have made. One of them, Mr. Mamoulian knew, had decomposed and could not be shown; it turned out to be the test Garbo had made with Laurence Olivier, who almost got the part until it was decided he photographed too young for her — and at her insistence John Gilbert was then engaged to play the Spanish lover. It would have been interesting to see Olivier with her, because Gilbert's performance is still regrettably the only weak one in *Christina*. The other reel, however, was in good condition, and was a silent wardrobe test, mostly of Garbo in the costume she wore when she masqueraded as the young man, since these Adrian-designed clothes had to be exactly right. Garbo turned obligingly, putting on and taking off hats with just the right swagger or tying on capes, while that bemused smile lighted her eyes, framed as they were, and still are, with those incredible, naturally long lashes that curl down upon her cheeks like miniature ski-runs.

Greta Garbo and John Gilbert in *Queen Christina*.

GRETA GARBO

The talking version of *Anna Karenina* is especially interesting when seen as a companion piece to *Love,* its silent counterpart. There are moments in the modern-styled silent version which top those same episodes in the talking version. Garbo was always tremendously moving when she played scenes with children, and her scenes with young Freddie Bartholomew as her son are just as memorable as they had been previously in the silent version when she played them with Philippe De Lacy. As the silent Vronsky, Gilbert is more in the picture as a dashing lover than is the talking Fredric March, who seems to be busy acting in this one. Better in the talking version, however, is the final moment at the train. David O. Selznick wanted in this scene that same mystic imperturbability which Mamoulian got from her. He had his then-assistant Val Lewton select a single frame of Garbo's best close-up as she stands watching the train. Over this close-up projected continuously on a screen, the lights of the passing train flashed and the sounds of the engine and the wheels of the cars on the track were all that was heard. And then the sad, forsaken, enigmatic face is obscured, and the passing lights, the steam, the sound rise, while the train itself disappears.

Camille remains the only movie I've ever seen where the audiences, no matter how many times they've seen it, always react as if they were at a live performance. When a sequence finishes and the fade-out begins, there is spontaneous applause just as there would be in a theatre when the curtain falls on a scene. *Camille* is a film which represents a meeting of talents that were perfect for its interpretation, and although it is beautifully cinematic, it is also soundly theatrical. It plays with effortless ease, like the well-made vehicle it is.

One of my favourite scenes is where Garbo, having made a rendezvous with Robert Taylor for late supper in her apartment, is suddenly surprised by the unexpected return of Henry Daniell, her baronial lover. It was an added scene, and Daniell told me once how on the morning he was to shoot it, he crossed the lot to his dressing-room and enountered Garbo on the way to hers.

She smiled wanly. "How do you like the new scene, Mr. Daniell?" she asked.

"I think it's a good scene," he said cautiously, "but I'm honestly worried about it. You see, I don't laugh very well."

"I don't either," she confessed plaintively.

That, of course, was the whole point of the scene, and Cukor staged it with an electric brilliance.

Ninotchka was billboarded everywhere with two words — GARBO LAUGHS. M-G-M had tried a campaign on *Camille* with a catchphrase, GARBO LOVES ROBERT TAYLOR, which was too much like school kids writing on a board fence. It didn't catch on as GARBO TALKS had and GARBO LAUGHS did. *Ninotchka* is a jewel of a comedy, and Garbo worked superbly with that master of subtle comedy, Ernst Lubitsch. *Ninotchka* brought her her last Academy Award nomination. She never won an Oscar, although she was first nominated in the 1929-30 season for both *Anna Christie* and *Romance;* in 1937, for *Camille;* and in 1939, for *Ninotchka.* In 1954, the Academy awarded her a special honorary Oscar for having brought magic to the screen with her unforgettable performances.

But these are, and will always be, the two flawless gems in her crown — the perfect romance, *Camille* and the perfect comedy, *Ninotchka.*

I don't think she meant to withdraw permanently from the screen after the unfortunate *Two-Faced Woman,* which she liked as little as her director Cukor. They and the picture were victims of the new and fleeting morality code which ruined the lightweight comedy, making a heavy pudding out of what should have been a *soufflé.*

Eventually, M-G-M released her from any commitment owed them, because they could find no suitable vehicles for her. Actually, by the time the Second World War was on, the international market, where she reigned as a top favourite, was lost to Hollywood. She might have made Daphne du Maurier's *My Cousin Rachel,* with Cukor directing, but she backed out, and so then did he. In the late Forties, she almost did another film with Cukor directing, playing George Sand, with Laurence Olivier as her leading man — but nothing came of that project. When the War was over, Selznick tried to interest her in starring as the lovely but deadly heroine of *The Paradine Case,* and at much the same time RKO commissioned Cukor to interest her in playing the Norwegian mother in *I Remember Mama.* She sent back the message: "No murderesses; no mamas."

The pictures she nearly did are almost legion. Zanuck did everything to interest her in *Anastasia;* she remained uninterested. Visconti wanted her recently for the film he has never made of Proust's "Remembrance of Things Past;" some time ago, according to a Spanish magazine, Cukor found an original called *Sacrifice* which would have starred her with Alain Delon; but she turned it down, and it has never been made. Before that, Selznick had tried to interest her, and then Ingrid Bergman, in a picture about Sarah Bernhardt; she would not commit herself.

Only once did she actually sign to make a picture, which Walter Wanger would produce abroad in Technicolor, an adaptation of Balzac's "La Duchesse de Langeais," in which James Mason was to have been her leading man and Max Ophuls would have directed. She accepted a cheque and journeyed to Italy, where costume tests were shot of her in colour by William Daniels, James Wong Howe, and an unnamed Italian cinematographer, probably a Technicolor adviser. And then, suddenly, due to reasons never satisfactorily explained, Wanger's financial backing faded out, and he could not get new backers. James Mason has said that Garbo herself was not cooperative about wooing the men with the money interests. Wanger disavowed that. I do know that Garbo was mortified when she learned that her name would no longer guarantee financial backing for a film starring her, for she told a close mutual friend, "It's over. Never again." It has come to the place where when she agrees to read a screenplay, she has confessed that almost simultaneously she begins to think of good reasons why she should *not* do the script in question.

And so it has been.*

Although she made frequent trips to Hollywood after her final picture, they were only business and social journeys. She once owned considerable real estate in Southern California, but has now reportedly sold most of it and

---

*The one big mystery remains: Whatever happened to those colour tests she made in Italy? They would be the only colour film ever shot on Garbo. About fourteen years ago in London, I asked Wanger about that film, and he merely shook his head sadly. "I don't know what happened to it," he said. "Your guess is as good as mine."

Greta Garbo and Robert Taylor in *Camille*.

Greta Garbo and Melvyn Douglas in Lubitsch's *Ninotchka*.

invested the money in other securities in other parts of the world. She remains frugal, and is a rich woman in her own right. Once she had a coterie of friends in and around the film colony, but most of them have died or moved from the Pacific Coast. Only George Cukor, Rouben Mamoulian, and Gaylord Hauser are still on hand to receive her when she comes West.

Shortly after the *débâcle* of *Two-Faced Woman,* she took up residence in New York City, and it was during the War years and subsequently right up to 1960, when I was frequently in Manhattan that I would again catch glimpses of her around town.

I once went to an exclusive candy store, Altman & Kuhne, on Fifth Avenue, to buy a gift box. A woman wearing a fur coat and fur hat was ahead of me at the counter, her back thus to me. And then I heard her voice as she gave George Cukor's address as the place where the candy should be sent. It was the one and only voice. She turned, stared at me a brief second, the lids with those incredible lashes fluttering down over the high cheekbones, and then she went out alone into the brisk air.

In New York nobody bothers her; they respect her desire for privacy. As a matter of fact, only once in Southern California, when she was lunching at the Beverly Hills Hotel with a good friend, the late Virginia Burrowes, did I ever see somebody try to get her autograph. He was a promising young actor, and should have known better. Garbo only ignored him, while Miss Burrowes coolly but firmly turned him off. I've seen Garbo walk casually alone down Fifth Avenue or Madison, be recognised, and allowed to go her serene way. Admirers look, but don't speak — and, of course, never touch.

In Hollywood, as I say, she was not always so lucky. Quite by accident, I learned that her dentist, a big and very competent Swede (he's now dead, a suicide, alas!), was also mine. I learned only because early one morning I left his office and went towards the elevator, just as the elevator doors opened and Garbo came out and went to his office. Sometime later on a subsequent visit, I said to the dentist, "I didn't know Garbo was a patient of yours." He looked at me over the tops of his glasses with big sad eyes. "She used to be," he said. "It was that damned stupid girl who used to operate the elevator who ruined everything. She stopped the elevator between floors when Miss Garbo was her only passenger and told her how she idolised her and was crazy about her. Miss Garbo was terrified, persuaded her to bring the elevator down to street level, and then fled. She phoned me when she got home to say she was sorry but she could never come back to me. God damn that stupid elevator girl!"

On the other hand, a great-aunt of mine returning by ship to her native Sweden, used to pass Garbo, who was also a passenger, as they walked the promenade deck. To her pleasure and surprise, she was stopped one day by Garbo, who engaged her in conversation in Swedish. I've always thought that perhaps much of her withdrawal from strangers, especially in the beginning, stemmed not only from her natural distrust of them, but also a reluctance to speak in a language in which she did not spontaneously think; it's not easy to think in Swedish and simultaneously translate to speak in English, a difficult language at best for foreigners. She was, and still is, like many of her countrywomen, a very shy and extremely sensitive person, and few have ever got to know what a charming sense of humour and droll wit she often evinces when she's comfortable with those she knows.

She made a friend of Allen Porter, when he was in the Cinema Department

GRETA GARBO

of the Museum of Modern Art, and often sat alone or with him or some other close friend, viewing one of her films, especially run off for her. The Garbo up on the screen she never thought of in the first person; it was always "she" or "that girl." Sometimes she even got her sexes confused, and the image became "that fellow." She would say, "Watch that girl; she's about to do something rather interesting;" or "Oh, she wasn't very good in that scene, was she?" or "That fellow sure does have a lot to learn."

Once, walking down Madison Avenue, I saw her ahead of me, and I remained discreetly behind, stopping to look into store windows when she stopped, and moving on when she walked on, always lingering some yards behind whenever she paused at a street corner. Finally, the inevitable happened. She caught a green light, but by the time I got to the curb, the light had changed to red and I had to wait. I saw her across the street as she paused. She half-turned with an amused little smile, lifted one gloved hand in farewell, as if to let me know that she had known all along that I was following her — and then went on her way, lost quickly in the milling crowds.

I made my first trip to Sweden early in that fabulous summer of 1959 — fabulous because that long summer went on and on until there was no time for autumn and full winter was suddenly at hand early one December morning. Stockholm was not only redolent with its own dramatic history, but it became memorable to me because I found the places where Garbo had lived and worked when she was young before she became famous. Even when I left Stockholm, in the university town of Uppsala, there on a hill is the big castle where Queen Christina formally abdicated, renouncing the crown of Sweden as Garbo had so movingly done in her picture about Christina. But in old Stockholm, across the river, on the South Side (the Söder), now as it was then a tenement area with ancient cobblestoned streets, is Blekingegatan, 32. There on the third floor of this cold-water flat, in a four-room apartment, is the house where she was born on September 18, 1905, Greta Lovisa Gustafsson, the youngest daughter of an unskilled labourer, Karl Gustafsson, and his wife, *née* Anna Karlsson. She had an older sister named Alva, with whom she was never as close as she was to the handsome brother, Sven, the middle child.

I don't know whether Blekingegatan, 32 still stands, as it did in 1959, nor do I know if there are still local barbershops in the neighborhood, as there still were then, very much like Einer Wideback's, where she went to work as a soap-lather girl after her father died. I haunted the places where she once lived and worked, looking as one might look on Delos for some sign of Apollo or on the shores of the Cyprian isle for some hint of Aphrodite rising from the sea foam.

At that time, in 1959, the department store known as PUB offered for sale at a modest price a photocopy of her application for a job there. For years I had such a copy — God knows where it is now — and noted on the form was that revealing statement: "Reason for leaving: To enter the films" (naturally, in Swedish). Thanks to PUB, she did some modelling of millinery there, and the door was opened to her for commercial films.

She was persuaded to try for acceptance as a student in the Royal Dramatic Academy of Sweden's own state theatre, the Royal Dramatic Theatre. She was accepted, and began her studies. More than anything else, she wanted to be a stage actress, and once anybody has seen a performance of a play at Sweden's Royal Dramatic Theatre, he can understand why: Sweden's na-

Greta Garbo, a portrait by Clarence Bull, taken shortly after the completion of *Two-Faced Woman*.

tional playhouse, like London's, is the home of some of the best acting in the world. Garbo, however, made only a few stage appearances in small support-ing roles while she was learning her craft at the Academy: in a German comedy, "The Tortoise Shell"; as a lady's maid in J. M. Barrie's "The Admirable Crichton"; in a Russian drama, "Violins of Autumn"; as a prosti-tute in a Swedish drama, "The Invisible"; and in Jules Romain's French farce, "Knock," or "The Triumph of Medicine."

Outside Stockholm in a suburb known as Råsunda were the studios of Svensk Filmindustri. From there one day in the summer of 1923, a disting-uished Russian-Jewish director, Mauritz Stiller, sent word to the Academy's director, Gustaf Molander, asking if two promising young female students could be sent over for a film he was going to make of the Nobel Prize novelist, Selma Lagerlöf's *Gösta Berlings Saga*. Molander sent a dark-haired girl, Mona Mårtenson, and the fair-haired Greta Gustafsson. Miss Mårtenson was signed almost at once for one of the principal roles. Stiller deliberated about the younger Greta Gustafsson, and when he sent for her to come to his home, he had already decided to use her and had almost decided to re-name her "Mona Gabór." By the time Miss Gustafsson arrived, however, he had the name for her — Greta Garbo! She signed a contract to work for him as the Countess Elisabeth Dohna in *Gösta Berlings Saga* on July 23, 1923. Stiller warned her, "You'll have to reduce ten kilos." She did. She did everything Stiller told her to do. Only once did she flare up in protest to cry with tears of rage, "Damn you, Stiller, I hate you!" When Louis B. Mayer signed Stiller to a director's contract at M-G-M, Stiller signed only if the studio also signed his protegee, Greta Garbo, with whom he wanted to work. She was signed at a starting weekly salary of $350, and she arrived with Stiller in New York Harbour on board the "Drottningholm" on July 6, 1925, not quite two years after she had first signed a contract to work for him in films. Fate was not kind to Stiller at M-G-M; he was taken off every project he began there. Garbo, on the other hand, became the idol and the legend.

There is no doubt that Stiller taught her almost everything she knew about acting. He may have been Svengali to her Trilby, but when he could not adapt himself to the Hollywood ways of M-G-M, she, unlike Trilby, was able to go on alone, displaying for the camera all that he had taught her. Because of him, the camera became her friend and allowed her to be its most beloved mistress. From her first American film in 1926, she of course had a remarkable cinematographer, the late William Daniels, who photographed twenty of her M-G-M films. She was the perfect model for the instrument; he, its perfect master.

She has never forgotten Mauritz Stiller, however. How could she? Death has claimed others who were close to her, but death robbed her of him who had made it all possible. In 1929, when she was making one of her last silent films, *Wild Orchids,* she was in her dressing-room when the cablegram was delivered, bringing her word of Stiller's death in Sweden. For a moment she nearly collapsed, but when concern was expressed, she quickly regained her composure and steeled herself to say, "Tell them I'll be made up and ready to go on in twenty minutes."

She is almost never lonely, although there are times when she prefers to be left alone, which is quite a different thing. There have been many friends and companions in her life — both male and female. Even in the summer of 1972, aged sixty-seven, she was squired all over Italy by a handsome, well-to-do, thirty-two-year-old Neapolitan, Massimo Gargia, a conquest many a forty-year-old American woman would have coveted. She is not alone, unless she wants to be. But Mauritz Stiller was her great love and her first great loss. "Damn you, Stiller, I hate you!" she may have said when he reduced her to tears while directing the only picture they ever made together, but she always openly worshipped him.

In the spring of 1973, the front page of "The Daily Telegraph" in London headlined a story that Greta Garbo was a patient in a Barcelona hospital, where she had undergone a successful operation twelve days previously for cataracts on both eyes, which had threatened her with blindness. Shortly thereafter, Miss Garbo issued a denial to the story, and since it's the first and only time she has ever bothered to deny anything printed about her, I'm inclined to think there may be little or no truth in the Barcelona story.

I like best to think of her as she was on one of the last days I caught a glimpse of her. I was in New York, on a spring day with showers. I was waiting as before, but better than before, for a signal light to change at Fifth Avenue at 57th Street, and suddenly I saw her on the other side of the street. She was with another woman. She was wearing a shiny blue belted raincoat, and her companion, a green one. The signal changed, and I stepped aside to wait, as the two women crossed the street, laughing and talking gaily like very young schoolgirls. I watched them go west on 57th towards a favourite ice cream parlour — and then I realised that beside me was a middle-aged woman, from the Bronx or perhaps Brooklyn, who was also looking after them. She turned to inquire of me, "That was Greta Garbo, wasn't it?"

I nodded. "Yes, it was."

She looked down at the solemn-faced young boy she held by the hand. "You see now," she said, "I been telling you not to stay indoors all the time. You go out, and who knows? You might see Greta Garbo!"

GRETA GARBO FILMOGRAPHY

Greta Garbo is reputed to have made her film *début* in 1920, when she and her older sister Alva both appeared as extras in a Swedish film *En lyckoriddare,* by John Brunius.

In 1921, while she was employed as a model by a leading department store in Stockholm, PUB (named for its founder, Paul U. Bergström), she appeared in two commercial films, advertising Swedish products. They were (in translation):

HOW NOT TO DRESS (1921). *Prod:* Harse W. Tullborgs. *Dir:* Captain Ragnar Ring.

OUR DAILY BREAD (1922). *Prod:* Fribergs Filbyrå, for the Consumers' Co-operative Association of Stockholm. *Dir:* Captain Ragnar Ring.

The Feature Films

LUFFAR—PETTER (*Peter, the Tramp*) (1922). Comedy; as Greta, a bathing beauty. *Dir/Sc:* Erik A. Petschler. *With* Erik A. Petschler, Helmer Larsson, Fredrik Olsson, Tyra Ryman, Gucken Cederborg. *Prod:* Erik A. Petschler Production. 5 reels.

GÖSTA BERLINGS SAGA (AKA, *The Saga of Gösta Berling, The Legend of Gösta Berling,* or *The Atonement of Gösta Berling*) (*1924*). Nineteenth century drama; as the Countess Elisabeth Dohna. *Dir:* Mauritz Stiller. *Sc:* Stiller and Ragnar Hyltén-Cavallius (from the novel by Nobel Prize author, Selma Lagerlöf). *With* Lars Hanson, Ellen Cederström, Mona Mårtensson, Jenny Hasselqvist, Karin Swanström, Gerda Lundeqvist, Torsten Hammarén, Svend Kornbauk, Otto Elg Lundberg, Sixten Malmerfelt, Hilda Forslund, Sven Scholander. *Prod:* Svensk Filmindustri by Svenská Biograf. Released in Sweden in two parts: Part 1 — 2,345 mtrs; Part 2 — 2,189 mtrs. Released in England and USA, 12 reels.

DIE FREUDLÖSE GASSE (AKA *La rue sans joie* (France); *The Joyless Street* (GB and USA), or *The Street of Sorrow* (USA 1925). Drama of post First World War in Vienna; as Greta Rumfort. *Dir:* Georg Wilhelm Pabst. *Sc:* Willi Hass (from the novel by Hugo Bettauer). *With* Werner Kraus, Asta Nielsen, Jaro Fürth, Agnes Esterhazy, Grigori Chmara, Valeska Gert, Einar Hanson, Loni Nest, Marlene Dietrich, Ilka Grüning, Robert Garrison, Tamara Tolstoi, Maria Forescu, Karl Etlinger. *Prod:* A Sofar-Film, by Hirschel-Sofar, (Germany) 3,000 mtrs.

THE TORRENT (AKA, *Ibáñez Torrent*). (1926). Romantic drama; as Leonora Moreno. *Dir:* Monta Bell. *Sc:* Dorothy Farnum (from the novel, "Entre Naranjos." by Vicente Blasco-Ibáñez). *With* Ricardo Cortez, Gertrude Olmstead, Edward Connelly, Lucien Littlefield, Martha Mattox, Lucy Beaumont, Tully Marshall, Mack Swain, Arthur Edmund Carewe, Lillian Leighton, Mario Carillo. *Prod:* M-G-M (Cosmopolitan Pictures). 7 reels.

THE TEMPTRESS (1926). Romantic tragedy; as Elena Torrebianca. *Dir:* Fred Niblo (Mauritz Stiller, uncredited). *Sc:* Dorothy Farnum (from the novel, "La tierra de Todos," by Vicente Blasco-Ibáñez). *With* Antonio Moreno, Roy D'Arcy, Marc MacDermott, Lionel Barrymore, Virginia Brown Faire, Armand Kaliz, Alys Murrell, Robert Anderson, Francis McDonald, Hector V. Sarno, Inez Gomez, Steve Clemento, Ray Coulson. *Prod:* M-G-M (Cosmopolitan Pictures). 9 reels. (Compare listing in Antonio Moreno filmography.)

FLESH AND THE DEVIL (1926). Romantic drama; as Felicitas von Klaetzingk. *Dir:* Clarence Brown. *Sc:* Benjamin F. Glazer (from the novel, "Es War." by Hermann Sudermann, known in translation as "The Undying Past"). *With* John Gilbert, Lars Hanson, Barbara Kent, William Orlamond, George

Fawcett, Eugenie Besserer, Marc MacDermott, Marcelle Corday. *Prod:* M-G-M. 9 reels.

LOVE (1927). Romantic tragedy: as Anna Karenina. *Dir:* Edmund Goulding. *Sc:* Frances Marion (adapted by Lorna Moon from the novel, "Anna Karenina," by Count Leo Tolstoy). *With* John Gilbert, George Fawcett, Emily Fitzroy, Brandon Hurst, Philippe De Lacy. (It was shot with an alternative ending, wherein Anna does not kill herself at the train station, but is reunited with Vronsky three years after the death of her husband.) (*Anna Karenina* was made by France-Pathé (1911): by Russia-Pathé (1914); by Fox, dir. by J. Gordon Edwards, 1915, re-made as a talking film by M-G-M, again with Garbo starring and Clarence Brown directing (1935); by Alexander Korda for London Film Co., dir. by Julien Duvivier with Vivien Leigh (1948); and by the U.S.S.R, as *Anna Karénine*, dir. by Alexandre Zarkhi with Tatiana Samoflova (1967). *Prod:* M-G-M. 8 reels.

THE DIVINE WOMAN (1928). Romantic drama; as the unwanted French girl called Marianne, who becomes a great Parisian actress. *Dir:* Victor Seastrom. *Sc:* Dorothy Farnum (adapted by Gladys Unger from her own play, "Starlight," based on an incident in the life of Sarah Bernhardt; with story treatment (uncredited) by Victor Seastrom and Frances Marion). *With* Lars Hanson, Lowell Sherman, Polly Moran, Dorothy Cumming, John Mack Brown, Cesare Gravina, Paulette Du Val, Jean De Briac. (As of 1973, M-G-M maintains that the negative has decomposed and, so far, no prints have been found; it is the only Garbo feature of which there is now no film record.) *Prod:* M-G-M. 8 reels.

THE MYSTERIOUS LADY (1928). Romantic espionage drama; as Tania, a Russian spy. *Dir:* Fred Niblo. *Sc:* Bess Meredyth (from a German novel by Ludwig Wolff, "War in the Dark"). *With* Conrad Nagel, Gustav von Seyffertitz, Albert Pollet, Edward Connelly, Richard Alexander. *Prod:* M-G-M. 9 reels.

A WOMAN OF AFFAIRS (1928). Romantic drama; as Diana Merrick (Iris March, in the novel). *Dir:* Clarence Brown. *Sc:* Bess Meredyth (from the novel, "The Green Hat," by Michael Arlen). *With* John Gilbert, Lewis Stone, John Mack Brown, Douglas Fairbanks Jr., Hobart Bosworth, Dorothy Sebastian. (Re-made as a talkie, *Outcast Lady,* 1934, starring Constance Bennett.) *Prod:* M-G-M. (Movietone: sound effects and music score). 9 reels.

WILD ORCHIDS (1929). Romantic drama; as Lili Sterling. *Dir:* Sidney Franklin. *Sc:* Hans Kraly and Richard Schayer (adapted by Willis Goldbeck from a story, "Heat," by John Colton). *With* Nils Asther, Lewis Stone. *Prod:* M-G-M. (Movietone: sound effects and music score). 11 reels.

A MAN'S MAN (1929). Romantic comedy drama; as Greta Garbo herself, idol of the heroine, Peggy, played by Josephine Dunn. *Dir:* James Cruze. *Sc:* Forrest Halsey (from the play by Patrick Kearney). *With* William Haines, Josephine Dunn, Sam Hardy, Mae Busch, John Gilbert, Gloria Davenport. *Prod:* M-G-M. (Movietone: sound effects and music score). 8 reels.
(While this is little more than a cameo appearance, the entire personality of the heroine, her Achilles' heel, in fact, is her adoration of Garbo; in the play, the heroine's goddess was Mary Pickford.)

THE SINGLE STANDARD (1929). Romantic drama; as Arden Stuart. *Dir:* John S. Robertson. *Sc:* Josephine Lovett (from a novel by Adela Rogers St. Johns). *With* Nils Asther, John Mack Brown, Dorothy Sebastian, Lane Chandler, Robert Castle, Mahlon Hamilton, Kathlyn Williams, Zeffie Tilbury, Joel McCrea (uncredited). *Prod:* M-G-M. (Movietone: sound effects and music score). 8 reels.

THE KISS (1929). Romantic drama; as Irene Guarry. *Dir:* Jacques Feyder. *Sc:* Hans Kraly (from a story by George M. Saville). *With* Conrad Nagel, Anders Randolph, Holmes Herbert, Lew Ayres, George Davis. *Prod:* M-G-M (Movietone: sound effects and music score). 7 reels. (This was Garbo's last silent film.)

ANNA CHRISTIE (1930). Drama; as Anna Christie. *Dir:* Clarence Brown. *Sc:* Frances Marion (from the play by Eugene O'Neill). *With* Charles Bickford, George F. Marion, Marie Dressler, James T. Mack, Lee Phelps. (Previously filmed as a silent, 1923, prod. by Thomas H. Ince for First National release, with Blanche Sweet as Anna.) *Prod:* M-G-M (Movietone: All-talking, with sound effects). 10 reels. A silent version was also issued, with titles by Madeleine Ruthven and sound effects. (In spite of the fact that *Anna Christie* was well-received and Garbo's *début* in talking films was highly acclaimed, she herself neither liked the picture nor her performance in it. "Isn't it terrible?" she said of it. "Who ever saw Swedes act like that?" She *did* like, however, the German version of her film, which was made shortly after the English version.)

ANNA CHRISTIE (1930) (GERMAN VERSION) Drama; as Anna Christie (but played with no concession to Hollywood glamour). *Dir:* Jacques Feyder. *Sc:* Frances Marion (translated and adapted into German by Walter Hasenclever, from the play by Eugene O'Neill). (Feyder, the Belgian director, and Garbo, Swedish star, also worked together, uncredited, on the script, making the German more idiomatic.) *With* Theo Shall, Hans Junkermann, Salka Steuermann (Viertel), Herman Bing. *Prod:* PARUFAMET (Paramount-Ufa-Metro — Verleihbetriebe). (Filmed in Culver City at the M-G-M studios for release in

Germany.) 82m. (There was much talk of filming a third version in the Swedish language, but it was this version in German, with Swedish super-imposed titles, that played in Sweden.)

ROMANCE (1930). Romantic drama; as Rita Cavallini, opera star. *Dir:* Clarence Brown. *Sc:* Bess Meredyth (from the play by Edward Sheldon). *With* Lewis Stone, Gavin Gordon, Elliott Nugent, Florence Rice, Clara Blandick, Henry Armetta, Mathilde Comont, Countess De Liguoro. (A silent version was released, 1920, by United Artists, starring Doris Keane, who had created Rita Cavallini onstage.) *Prod:* M-G-M. (Movietone: All-talking, with sound effects and music.) 10 reels.

INSPIRATION (1931). Romantic drama; as Yvonne, a Parisienne. *Dir:* Clarence Brown. *Sc:* Gene Markey (story by Markey, suggested by Daudet's "Sapho," uncredited). *With* Robert Montgomery, Lewis Stone, Marjorie Rambeau, Judith Vosselli, Beryl Mercer, John Miljan, Edwin Maxwell, Oscar Apfel, Joan Marsh, Zelda Sears, Karen Morley, Gwen Lee, Paul McAllister, Arthur Hoyt, Richard Tucker. *Prod:* M-G-M. 74m.

SUSAN LENOX: HER FALL AND RISE (AKA *The Rise of Helga*) (1931). Romantic drama; as Susan Lenox. *Dir:* Robert Z. Leonard. *Sc:* Wanda Tuchock (with dialogue by Zelda Sears and Edith Fitzgerald; from the novel by David Graham Phillips). *With* Clark Gable, Jean Hersholt, John Miljan, Alan Hale, Hale Hamilton, Hilda Vaughn, Russell Simpson, Cecil Cunningham, Theodore von Eltz, Marjorie King, Helene Millard, Ian Keith. *Prod:* M-G-M. 73m.

MATA HARI (1932). Romantic espionage drama; as the spy, Mata Hari, *Dir:* George Fitzmaurice. *Sc:* Benjamin Glazer and Leo Birinski (from their story, with dialogue by Doris Anderson and Gilbert Emery). *With* Ramon Novarro, Lionel Barrymore, Lewis Stone, C. Henry Gordon, Karen Morley, Alec B. Francis, Blanche Friderici, Edmund Breese, Helen Jerome Eddy, Frank Reicher. (In 1965, a Paris-Roma production distributed by Gala Films, *Mata Hari Agent H-21*, starred Jeanne Moreau.) *Prod:* M-G-M. 90m. (Compare listing in Ramon Novarro filmography.)

GRAND HOTEL (1932). Romantic drama; as Grusinskaya, ballerina. *Dir:* Edmund Goulding. *Sc:* William A. Drake (from the German novel and play by Vicki Baum). (Edmund Goulding always maintained that Drake had only translated the play, that the real screenplay which he shot was written by Frances Marion, uncredited.) *With* John Barrymore, Joan Crawford, Wallace Beery, Lionel Barrymore, Lewis Stone, Jean Hersholt, Robert McWade, Purnell B. Pratt, Ferdinand Gottschalk, Rafaela Ottiano, Morgan Wallace, Tully Marshall, Frank Conroy, Murray Kinnell, Edwin Maxwell. (In 1945, M-G-M made an "up-dated" version, *Weekend at the Waldorf*, with Ginger Rogers playing a weary actress, supposedly a parallel of Grusinskaya; released in Europe in 1961, was a German version *Menschen im Hotel*, with Michèle Morgan playing the Garbo role.) *Prod:* M-G-M. 112m. (Compare listing in John Barrymore filmography.)

AS YOU DESIRE ME (1932). Psychological romantic drama; as Zara, once possibly Maria, wife of Count Bruno Varelli. *Dir:* George Fitzmaurice. *Sc:* Gene Markey (from the play by Luigi Pirandello). *With* Melvyn Douglas, Erich von Stroheim, Owen Moore, Hedda Hopper, Rafaela Ottiano, Warburton Gamble, Albert Conti, William Ricciardi, Roland Varno. *Prod:* M-G-M. 71m.

QUEEN CHRISTINA (1933). Romantic historical drama; as Christina, Queen of Sweden. *Dir:* Rouben Mamoulian. *Sc:* H.M. Harwood and Salka Viertel; with dialogue by S.N. Behrman (from a story by Salka Viertel and Margaret F. Levin). *With* John Gilbert, Ian Keith, Lewis Stone, Elizabeth Young, C. Aubrey Smith, Reginald Owen, Lawrence Grant, David Torrence, Gustav von Seyffertitz, Ferdinand Munier, George Renevant, Cora Sue Collins. *Prod:* M-G-M. 9000 ft.

THE PAINTED VEIL (1934). Romantic drama; as Katrin Fane. *Dir:* Richard Boleslawski. *Sc:* John Meehan, Salka Viertel, Edith Fitzgerald (from a novel by W. Somerset Maugham). *With* Herbert Marshall, George Brent, Warner Oland, Jean Hersholt, Bodil Rosing, Katherine Alexander, Cecelia Parker, Soo Young, Forrester Harvey. M-G-M. 83m. (Re-made M-G-M, 1957, as *The Seventh Sin*, starring Eleanor Parker.)

ANNA KARENINA (1935). Romantic tragedy; as Anna Karenina. *Dir:* Clarence Brown. *Sc:* Clemence Dane, Salka Viertel, S. N. Behrman (from the novel by Count Leo Tolstoy). *With* Fredric March, Freddie Bartholomew, Maureen O'Sullivan, May Robson, Basil Rathbone, Reginald Owen, Reginald Denny, Phoebe Foster, Gyles Isham, Buster Phelps, Ella Ethridge, Joan Marsh, Sidney Bracey, Cora Sue Collins, Olaf Hytten, Joe E. Tozer, Guy D'Ennery, Harry Allen, Mary Forbes, Constance Collier, Ethel Griffies, Harry Beresford, Sarah Padden. *Prod:* M-G-M. 95m.

CAMILLE (1937). Romantic tragedy; as Marguerite Gautier, known as Camille. *Dir:* George Cukor. *Sc:* Zoë Akins, Frances Marion, James Hilton (from the novel and play by Alexandre Dumas, *fils*). *With* Robert Taylor, Lionel Barrymore, Elizabeth Allan, Jessie Ralph, Henry Daniell, Lenore Ulric, Laura Hope Crews, Rex O'Malley, Russell Hardie, E. E. Clive, Douglas Walton, Marion Ballou, Joan Brodel, (Leslie) June Wilkins, Fritz

GRETA GARBO

Leiber Jr., Elsie Esmonds, Eily Malyon. (In 1915 World released *Camille* with Clara Kimball Young; in 1917 it was a Fox feature with Theda Bara; and there was also in 1917 a foreign version released by Foreign-Hanover-General, starring Mme. Hesperia; in 1920 there was Metro's with Nazimova and Valentino; in 1927, Norma Talmadge and Gilbert Roland did it for First National; in 1912 Sarah Bernhardt filmed her version in France for Film d'Art released as *La dame aux camelias;* it was also produced by Abel Gance in 1935 in France, starring Yvonne Printemps, and titled *La dame aux camelias;* in Mexico, 1943, as *La dama de las camelias* with Lina Montés; a very ''mod'' version was released in 1969, made in Europe by Audubon, starring Danièle Gaubert, *Camille 2000.* In 1952, Micheline Presle played *Camille* under Raymond Bernard's direction, with Roland Alexandre as her Armand; and in 1953 in Argentina Zully Moreno played it for director Ernesto Arancibia, with Carlos Thompson as Armand. *Prod:* M-G-M. 109m.

CONQUEST (AKA, GB and Europe, *Marie Walewska).* (1937). Romantic historical drama; as the Countess Marie Walewska, Polish mistress of Napoleon Bonaparte. *Dir:* Clarence Brown. *Sc:* Samuel Hoffenstein, Salka Viertel, S.N.Behrman (from a Polish novel, ''Pani Walewska,'' by Waclaw Gasiorowski; and also a dramatisation by Helen Jerome). *With* Charles Boyer, Reginald Owen, Alan Marshal, Henry Stephenson, Leif Erickson, Dame May Whitty, Maria Ouspenskaya, C. Henry Gordon, Vladimir Sokoloff, Claude Gillingwater, George Houston, George Zucco, Scotty Beckett. *Prod:* M-G-M. 115m.

NINOTCHKA (1939). Romantic comedy; as Ninotchka. *Dir.* and *Prod:* Ernst Lubitsch. *Sc:* Charles Brackett, Billy Wilder, Walter Reisch (from a story by Melchior Lengyel). *With* Melvyn Douglas, Ina Claire, Bela Lugosi, Sig Rumann, Felix Bressart, Alexander Granach, Gregory Gaye, Rolfe Sedan, Edwin Maxwell, Richard Carle. (It was made into a successful Broadway musical with a Cole Porter score, starring Hildegarde Neff, which was then filmed in 1957 by M-G-M under its stage title, *Silk Stockings*, starring Cyd Charisse.) *Prod:* M-G-M. 110m.

TWO-FACED WOMAN (1941). Romantic comedy; as Karin Blake, who impersonates her ''twin.'' *Dir:* George Cukor. *Sc:* S. N. Behrman, Salka Viertel, George Oppenheimer (from a play by Ludwig Fulda). *With* Melvyn Douglas, Constance Bennett, Roland Young, Robert Sterling, Ruth Gordon, Frances Carson, Bob Alton. (Filmed as a silent and released by First National, 1925, as *Her Sister from Paris* starring Constance Talmadge; filmed as a musical romance and released by United Artists, 1933, as *Moulin Rouge*, starring Constance Bennett.) *Prod:* M-G-M. 94m

4
DOROTHY GISH

Dorothy Gish had china-blue eyes, light brown hair, a retroussé nose, and a rosebud mouth out of which came a voice tone so deep it was a surprise, if not a shock.

She never liked the way she looked. "I have a crooked face," she once told an interviewer. "You can't imagine how tired I get seeing it on the screen. I always think of myself as a squirrel, with two nuts stored in one cheek and only one in the other." She thought television made her "look like a basset hound."

She was also tongue-in-cheek about her career, and was, or affected to seem, uninterested in the fact that the Gish sisters are so important a part of the all-important period in which movies evolved from their sideshow beginnings. Throughout her life, Dorothy almost always turned conversation away from herself and toward Lillian.

It is impossible to imagine what Dorothy Gish's life would have been like without Lillian. Not primarily because of Lillian's greater fame, but fundamentally because of Lillian's incomparably greater sense of responsibility. Lillian was as intelligent in her protection of Dorothy as she was about business, and exhibited lifelong ingenuity in putting Dorothy forward, rescuing her in crises, and otherwise sustaining her. "When Dorothy arrives, the party begins," Lillian never tired of saying, nor of adding: "When I arrive, it usually ends."

Dorothy was born March 11,1898, in Dayton, Ohio, the younger daughter of James Lee and Mary Robinson McConnell Gish. Her father was a travelling salesman from the Pennsylvania "Dutch" country who had stopped off in Urbana, Ohio, and there met and wooed a harness-maker's daughter, whose respectable parents claimed President Zachary Taylor and poetess Emily Ward as ancestors.

The Gish sisters spent much of their earliest years with their mother in Masillon, Ohio, where Mrs. Gish's sister lived on a farm. Shortly after the turn of the century, however, their mother brought them to New York City "partly to look for our father, who had left us,"* Dorothy once told an interviewer, "and partly to earn a living for all three of us. We were practically

*Mrs. Gish located her husband, and for a time he lived with them again in their Manhattan apartment on West 39th Street. When she was working as a demonstrator in a Brooklyn department store, she gave him the money to pay on furniture she had bought and came home one day to find debt collectors had picked up the furniture and James Lee Gish was gone. When, with Dorothy and Lillian, she toured in plays, Mr. Gish sometimes showed up at the theatres. Mrs. Gish always feared he might take her daughters away from her, even though she had secured a legal separation from him and the care of the girls was lawfully hers. Eventually, Gish disappeared from their lives. No one knows what became of him.

destitute. She rented one of the old-fashioned railroad apartments, and advertised for 'genteel lady roomers.' One of the genteel ladies who rented a room was an actress (Dolores Lorne), and after she had been with us a few weeks, she had an offer for a part in a road company production of "East Lynne," provided she could find a small child — sex didn't matter — to play the part of Little Willie. She asked mother if she could borrow me for the role, and mother was willing, and so, at four, I became Little Willie. Then Lillian got parts too, and so did mother, and there we were, all three of us, actresses."

Dorothy made her stage *début* in 1902, and the following year the three Gishes toured together for a season in a popular melodrama called "Her First False Step." Dorothy then appeared, for four seasons, with Fiske O'Hara's company. As a little Irish girl in "Dion O'Dare," she made her New York *début* at the Lincoln Square Theatre in 1907. She toured in such well-liked dramas of the day as "Mr. Blarney from Ireland," "Editha's Burglar," "At Duty's Call," and "The Volunteer Organist."

Dorothy hated having to play little boy parts and whenever she balked at having to go onstage in knickerbockers, her mother had one effective threat: to make her walk home in them. "There wasn't all this talk of children hating their parents then," said Dorothy some years ago. In fact, when "The Ladies Home Journal," asked Dorothy to write her memories, she replied: "What I'd be interested in trying to write is the story of my mother. There's a real story, and I have the proper perspective for it."

Unfortunately, unlike Lillian, she never got around to doing it.

One summer Mrs. Gish ran a taffy concession at Brooklyn's Fort George Amusement Park, and her daughters helped. So did three child-actors named Gladys, Lottie and Jack Smith. Gladys Smith was soon to take a stage name: Mary Pickford. And Lottie and Jack would also adopt her surname. The Pickfords and Gishes always remained intimate.

Occasionally, the Gish girls ran afoul of the Gerry Society, which had been organised to protect the welfare of stage children. Dorothy once appeared before a well-meaning judge who took her on his lap and asked her how many Commandments there were. She answered correctly and the judge conceded she was getting a proper education. As her mother led her out of the courtroom, Dorothy remarked: 'What kind of judge is he? He doesn't even know there are Ten Commandments."

The Gishes toured in melodramas every winter, and their chief "treat" on the road was to go to "the pictures." One afternoon in Baltimore, while they were looking at Biograph's *Lena and the Geese,* they suddenly recognised their friend Gladys Smith on the screen.

When the Gishes finished their tour and got back to New York, Mrs. Gish took her daughters to visit their good friend Gladys Smith at Biograph's studio at 111 East 14th Street. Little Miss Smith was delighted to renew their acquaintance and introduced them to her director, D. W. Griffith.

"I want you to meet three of my dearest friends, Mr. Griffith — Mrs. Gish and her daughters, Lillian and Dorothy," she said, "and I think they would be perfectly lovely on the screen."

Said Griffith: "You have courage to introduce me to two such pretty girls. Aren't you afraid of losing your job? You'll be sorry."

DOROTHY GISH

Mary Pickford never was.

Griffith offered the Gish girls work as extras at five dollars a day. Since they usually hadn't earned more than ten dollars a week as stage actresses, they were glad to accept.

One day, so that oft-told story goes, Griffith started chasing them around a table, waving a pistol and firing blanks. They thought he'd gone mad and registered fear so eloquently that he stopped as suddenly as he had begun and congratulated them, explaining he had wanted to see their behaviour before hiring them to play two sisters at the mercy of safe robbers in *An Unseen Enemy*.

That was the first picture in which the Gish sisters had real parts and after it they were Biograph "regulars." One day, when a passerby on the street recognised them, Dorothy excitedly told her mother they had become famous. "Yes," said Mrs. Gish cynically, "but remember — people would notice you if you had a ring in your nose too."

Griffith always refused to take credit for his actors' development, and never took it for developing the Gish sisters. "I did not 'teach' the players with whom my name has been linked," he told "The Dramatic Mirror" (January 14, 1914). "We developed together; we found ourselves in a new art, and, as we discovered the possibilities of that art, we learned together."

Lillian progressed faster at Biograph than Dorothy and played more important parts sooner. Actress Linda Arvidson, who was Griffith's first wife, says of the Gish girls in her book, "When the Movies Were Young:" "For quite a long time they merely extra-ed in and out of the pictures. Especially Dorothy — Mr. Griffith paid her no attention whatever, and she cried because he wouldn't, but he wouldn't so she just kept on crying and trailed along." Linda Arvidson, however, preferred, or said she preferred, Dorothy as an actress because "she was that rare thing, a comedienne, and comediennes in the movies have been scarcer than hen's teeth." Lillian also admired Dorothy's talent to create laughter. "It was a rare gift for a woman," Lillian wrote me shortly after Dorothy's death. "She had it as a child, and as a girl. She was born with it."

When Griffith took his company to California in the winter of 1913, Lillian was one of the regular members of the troupe. Dorothy naturally accompanied her sister and their mother, but she had to pay her own train fare. Griffith had not invited her to come as a member of his company.

Fifteen years old and something of a madcap, Dorothy had become friendly with Blanche Sweet, the company's real star, and remained so throughout their lives. Says Miss Sweet: "When Dorothy and Lillian first came to Biograph, I recall Griffith asking me which I liked better. I replied that both were lovely, but the younger had sparkle and lilt. Dorothy and I shared a long and dear friendship, and an interest in our profession of acting. No rivalry, only the desire to help the other."

Constance Talmadge and Dorothy also became close friends. The youngest of the Talmadges was gawky and eager, and, like Dorothy, was never anything but herself. Both were over-shadowed by an older sister, but they feared nobody, not even the great Mr. Griffith. Constance's open friendliness with Griffith delighted him, but Dorothy's flippant ways didn't always please him.

Sincerely Dorothy Gish.

DOROTHY GISH

Linda Arvidson says Griffith considered Dorothy too forward. Nonetheless, because of him, Dorothy became a star at Mutual, as did Lillian, although Griffith did not use Dorothy in either *The Birth of a Nation* or *Intolerance,* and had given her only small roles in the two specials which preceded his masterpieces: *Judith of Bethulia* and *Home Sweet Home.*

Dorothy's career was also affected adversely by an accident. In December, 1914, while crossing the intersections of Virgil, Sunset and Hollywood, near the Mutual studio, she was hit by an automobile and dragged nearly forty feet. She was in the hospital for four weeks.

Griffith paid her a call, and even brought a projector so she could see the film she had been working on when the accident occurred (*How Hazel Got Even*).

Griffith supervised the production of *Old Heidelberg,* which John Emerson directed for Triangle in 1915, and was instrumental in casting Dorothy in the all-important role of Kathy, the tavern waitress who loves "the student prince" (Wallace Reid). It was Dorothy's sixty-second picture, and the one that got her a contract as a Triangle-Fine Arts star.

She was in eleven features under this contract, and they made her name known sufficiently for there to be general agreement that one really outstanding feature would put her in the big league. Lillian skilfully paved the way for the opportunity.

Griffith had cast Lillian as the heroine of *Hearts of the World,* which he intended filming in England and as near the front-line trenches of the First World War as he could safely get. After reading the story Griffith had written for it, Lillian recognised at once that the role of The Little Disturber was exactly right for Dorothy. Griffith said Constance Talmadge was to play it. Lillian insisted, and, since Griffith wanted Lillian for the feminine lead, he gave the part to Dorothy (he even gave a small part to Mrs. Gish). Lillian and her mother sailed for England in April 1917, on the first camouflaged ship to leave the United States, and two weeks later Dorothy sailed on the "Baltic," which also had General Pershing as a passenger.

As soon as Dorothy reached London, she learned that Griffith wanted her to play The Little Disturber in a bobbed black wig. She loathed it, but did it because he demanded it. Little did she realise that she would be stuck with a black wig throughout much of her subsequent film career.

Julian Johnson, in the August 1918 issue of "Photoplay," wrote: "Want to know where The Little Disturber character really came from? Well, she was a little Cockney girl — she's English, not French at all. Mr. Griffith saw her on the Strand one day, freshness, wig-wag walk, and all. He followed her for hours — or, rather, we did. I thought he was dreadful to make me play her. I didn't like her; I thought she was crazy. But Mr. Griffith insisted, and I cried. He insisted some more — and I did. I'm glad, now."

Dorothy, as The Little Disturber, walked off with *Hearts of the World's* acting honours, and Paramount-Artcraft offered her a million dollar starring contract (fifteen pictures over a two-year period).

She declined it, in order to stay with Griffith at her regular salary. Such loyalty was unprecedented, and had, additionally, a very ironic twist: Griffith supervised a series of comedies starring her, which were released by Paramount-Artcraft, and for doing these she got from Griffith about $1,000 a week!

The arithmetic of all this never failed to perplex her. She had turned down a million dollars for 104 weeks of work, and then turned right around to accept the same deal at less than a thousand dollars a week, because Mr. Griffith would be supervising. To be a Griffith Star was more important to her than a lot of money.

The series she made consisted of some charming but inconsequential programmers, in which she exploited the hoyden image she had created as The Little Disturber. Dorothy always had a good eye for new talent and was instrumental in giving the second lead in one of her comedies, *Out of Luck,* to a struggling, young, Italian-born actor who was calling himself Rudolph Valentino. She later suggested him for the Mexican romantic lead in *Scarlet Days,* which Griffith was then about to direct. Griffith thought he was too foreign-looking to become popular on the American screen, and so gave the *Scarlet Days* role to Richard Barthelmess, who had already been leading man to Dorothy in four of her feature comedies. Later, Griffith did employ Valentino to dance with his new *protégée,* Carol Dempster, in stage prologues when two Griffith films — *The Greatest Thing in Life* and *Scarlet Days* — premiered at a downtown Los Angeles movie palace.

Dorothy herself did not fall under the Valentino spell. "To me he was just the real domestic type," she later confessed, "a gardener by trade, who designed our riding habits for $35 apiece."

Reports Romano Tozzi in a "Films in Review" career-article on Lillian Gish: "In 1919, Griffith built a studio of his own on a water-side estate in Mamaroneck NY, and later that year, before going to Florida to make a picture, he encouraged Lillian in her desire to direct Dorothy in a movie. Lillian felt no director had ever brought out all of her sister's potentiality.

"*Remodeling Her Husband,* a romantic comedy about a young married couple was shot in Griffith's Mamaroneck studio and in the Thanhouser studio in New Rochelle, at a cost of $28,000. Its five reels were finished in December 1919, and made a profit of $150,000. Dorothy Parker wrote its titles. And James Rennie, who later married Dorothy, was the leading man. Lillian utilised all she had learned from Griffith, including what he had taught her about advertising and promotion."

James Rennie was one of Broadway's better leading men. Born in Toronto in 1890, he made a name for himself as an actor in American stock companies. He first appeared on Broadway in 1916 in *His Bridal Night,* a farce, and immediately thereafter joined Britain's Royal Air Force. He returned to Broadway in 1919 as leading man to Ruth Chatterton in *Moonlight and Honeysuckle.* His film *début* was in *Remodeling Her Husband,* and not long after it was released, he and Dorothy married (December 20, 1920).

Dorothy was fond of saying things were always being decided for her and she even claimed that marrying Rennie "wasn't my idea. It was Connie Talmadge's. She was busting to marry a fellow named John Pialoglou, and they talked Jim Rennie and me into eloping to Greenwich, Connecticut, with them. It was Sunday and I thought we probably couldn't get a licence anyway. But Connie had everything fixed, even the rings and the flowers."

After the two ceremonies, the newly-wed Rennies hastened back to Manhattan, where he gave a Sunday night stage performance in "Spanish Love," after which Dorothy took him home to the suite which the Gishes occupied

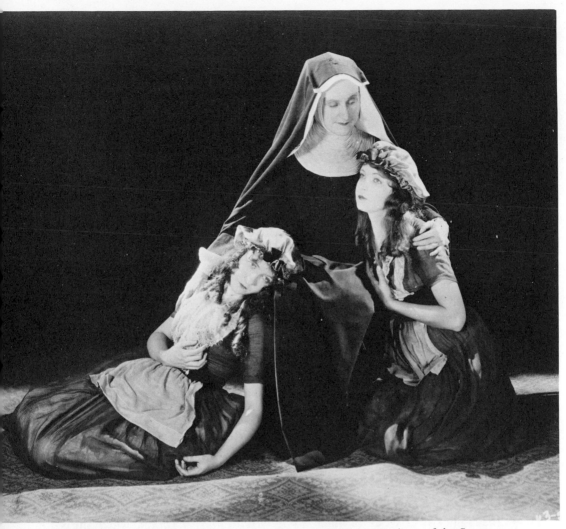

Dorothy Gish with Lillian Gish and Kate Bruce in Griffith's *Orphans of the Storm*.

then in the Savoy Hotel. A few weeks later, Mrs. Gish discreetly moved Dorothy's things to Rennie's apartment, which he still maintained, and told her younger daughter that the least the nice Mr. Rennie deserved was not to have to live with his in-laws.

After the fifteen "black wig" comedies that Dorothy did for Griffith, and for Paramount-Artcraft release, were completed, Griffith co-starred Dorothy and Lillian in *Orphans of the Storm*, a big spectacle based on the popular stage melodrama called *The Two Orphans*. Griffith set it in the time of the French Revolution and the Gish girls played two provincial sisters who come to Paris seeking a doctor who can cure Dorothy's blindness. Lillian is kidnapped by a venal aristocrat, and Dorothy is forced to sing and beg on the streets by one of the wickedest hags ever conceived (inimitably played by Lucille La Verne).

Orphans of the Storm was one of the most widely appreciated of Griffith's

75

major films and proved to be, to everybody's surprise, the Gish sisters' final appearance in any Griffith-directed feature. They left him for Inspiration Pictures, a new company formed by Richard Barthelmess and Charles H. Duell.

"We never called our first director, the man who discovered us and made us," said Dorothy much later, "anything but Mr. Griffith, and even today I can't get informal with a director on the set. Offstage yes, but while we are working — well, I just couldn't. I wasn't brought up that way."

She also reminisced to Herb Sterne for a "New York Times" interview: "Mr. Griffith spent months in rehearsing his players and plots before a camera turned. By the time a photoplay went into actual production, an actor was thoroughly familiar with his own part as well as the tempo, approach and reactions of the other members of the cast. Most of Mr. Griffith's films were shot without scripts and were improvised in the manner of the Commedia dell' Arte. Individual scenes were staged and re-staged until a maximum effect was realised, and footage was closely clocked with a stop-watch so the running time of the finished photoplay was known before production started. This saved large sums in raw film and time."

In 1923, Dorothy Gish appeared with Richard Barthelmess in two features for Inspiration Pictures. In *Fury* she is a Limehouse street girl who falls in love with a sailor who is determined to avenge a wrong done his parents. In *The Bright Shawl* she is La Clavel, a fiery, tragic, Cuban dancer. Barthelmess had wanted a newcomer, Jetta Goudal, for that part, and Goudal sailed for Havana believing she was to play La Clavel; she was partially compensated by being given the role of the exotic La Pilar, an informer. Dorothy could not have been more miscast, though her scenes with Barthelmess do have romantic allure; Barthelmess was always at his best opposite either of the Gishes.

Dorothy was then used by Inspiration in the cinematic version of George Eliot's *Romola,* which Henry King directed in Italy. She was well cast as Tessa, the plucky Florentine peasant who has an illegitimate child and is drowned in the River Arno; in fact, Dorothy took acting honours in *Romola,* and her sister was the first to say as much.

After her return to the United States, she played in several movies filmed on the East Coast, the best of which was *Night Life of New York,* in which she is a vivacious telephone operator wooed by a wealthy Westerner (Rod La Rocque). But the hoydenish child-woman sub-structure of her acting "image" had gone out of fashion, and her movie stardom, like Lillian's (and Mary Pickford's, too), was in peril. Dorothy's, in fact, might well have been over had British producer Herbert Wilcox not given it an unexpected boost.

He was just getting started as a producer and had the wit to offer Dorothy a contract as soon as he heard contracts were hard for her to get in Hollywood. She made four pictures for him in England, of which the best was the first, *Nell Gwyn*. She had the title role, of course, and was prefectly cast. Many think her performance in it the best of her career. Said "Variety": "She is Gish, Pickford, Negri and Swanson in one."

Wilcox in his autobiography, "25,000 Sunsets," says of Dorothy: "The wittiest woman I have met is undoubtedly Dorothy Gish. Usually without malice — but sometimes — for instance, whilst in New York I took her to Pavillon, the smartest and darkest restaurant in the city. About that time a columnist who called herself 'Hortense' was dishing out her daily column of

Dorothy Gish as *Nell Gwyn*.

poison. 'Hortense' was universally loathed, particularly by her pet target — film stars.

Whilst eating, I thought I saw her at a far table, but in the low-key lighting was not certain. 'Isn't that Hor*tense* over there?' I asked. Dorothy looked and without a flicker of a smile answered: 'She looks perfectly relaxed to me.'"

While Dorothy was filming for Wilcox, her mother, who was in London with her, became ill. Lillian, in Hollywood, worked all one night — her co-workers co-operating — to complete her scenes in *The Scarlet Letter* so she could hurry by train and boat to London. Mrs. Gish had suffered a serious stroke, and never walked or spoke again. Lillian took her back to California.

In October 1928, Dorothy returned to Broadway in Samson Raphaelson's play, "Young Love," which also starred her husband, James Rennie. In the summer of 1929 she played the same role in London, and shortly thereafter made her talking-picture *début* in Wilcox's *Wolves,* in which Charles Laughton made one of his first film appearances. It is not a good picture and wasn't shown in the States until years later, and then only in a bowdlerised version called *Wanted Men.*

That unsuccessful venture into talking films put Dorothy off them for nearly fifteen years. Throughout the Thirties she played on Broadway — in such revivals as Gogol's "The Inspector General," Shaw's "Getting Married," Boucicault's "The Streets of New York," and Ibsen's "The Pillars of Society," and in such new plays as "The Bride the Sun Shines On" and "Brittle Heaven," in which she played Emily Dickinson. She toured in Dodie Smith's "Autumn Crocus"; was directed by Guthrie McClintic in Elizabeth Gintie's "Missouri Legend," a drama about Jesse James; and, in 1939, she appeared in one of her very favourite plays, Paul Osborne's "Mornings at Seven."

She had definitely re-established herself as an important actress on Broadway, as had Lillian, who, in 1930, had begun a new chapter of her acting career by appearing on the stage for Jed Harris as Helena in Chekhov's "Uncle Vanya."

In the beginning of this Broadway period, each sister had her own suite at the Hotel Elysée, which Dorothy always referred to as "the rich actor's Royalton." Then Lillian bought an apartment on East 57th Street large enough for her mother and a nurse-companion, and later moved in with her mother. Lillian still lives there.

Also early in this Broadway period, Dorothy and James Rennie separated, and in 1935 Dorothy filed for divorce. When her suit came to court, she was hard put to particularise why a divorce should be granted — Rennie and she had remained on the best of terms — and the judge finally said: "Do you want this divorce, or don't you?" Dorothy thereupon alleged that Rennie had once worried her into a six-day case of hiccoughs, and a divorce was forthcoming.

Not long afterward, a stomach ulcer, and complicating ailments, began to plague her. She was in and out of hospitals for years, and in the latter part of her stage career she would lie on a couch backstage during a performance, but always got up to enter a scene on cue as if nothing were wrong with her. Finally, she had half her stomach removed. Afterward, for a while, she seemed to have her erstwhile bounce, and she was quick to suggest to anybody suffering even the mildest indigestion that he ought to have half his stomach taken out.

She did quite a bit of radio work in the Thirties and liked it, I think, better than any other form of performing. Her deep voice was unusually effective over the air. I especially remember three of her Lux Radio Theatre broadcasts of 1935: with Claude Rains in "The Green Goddess;" with Lillian, Helen Chandler, and Sylvia Field in "Little Women;" and with Lillian and Richard Barthelmess in "Way Down East."

In 1940, Dorothy took over from Dorothy Stickney the role of Vinnie in "Life with Father," and went out on its national tour with Louis Calhern playing Mr. Day. Lillian, incidentally, was playing the same role in Chicago with Percy Waram, and subsequently toured in it with him. Thus, the Gish sisters were playing the same role at the same time in theatres all over the United States. When, in the middle of Dorothy's San Francisco engagement, she was stricken ill and could not perform, Lillian, who had finished her tour, completed Dorothy's San Francisco engagement for her.

In 1944 Dorothy returned to Hollywood for what she called "my talkie *début,"* for she always hoped people would forget *Wolves*. In *Our Hearts Were Young and Gay,* she played with great natural charm the role of Mrs. Otis Skinner. Her performance was much admired, but she didn't try talkies again for two years, when she played the mother of Jeanne Crain and Linda Darnell in 20th Century Fox's *Centennial Summer,* a light-hearted musical in which, along with Constance Bennett and Esther Dale, she sang one of the Hammerstein-Kern songs: "I Was Up with the Lark This Morning."

She was frequently asked during the production of those two talkies what she thought of the new Hollywood. "Today it's more like an assembly line," she averred. "Whatever you play — a windshield or a mudguard — you are somehow detached. You miss the old feeling...making movies used to be fun. A medium is always more fun to work in when it is new. When Lillian and I were in silent films, we did everything for ourselves — mother made our costumes, we did our own hair, put on our own make-up. Nowadays, you have a couple of people getting you into costume, another couple fussing around on your hair, others with your face. You feel, somehow, like Marie Antoinette, rather aloof and removed, even with the best will in the world."

Dorothy liked practical jokes and her own were skilfully manoeuvered. During her last period in Hollywood, she happened to see *Salome, Where She Danced* (1945). She couldn't believe one film could contain so many *clichés* and so much flowery language. So, with a perfectly straight face, she went about saying *Salome, Where She Danced* was the greatest film ever made and insisting that her friends accompany her to a showing. As the picture progressed from one unbelievable situation to another, and her friends began stealing glances at her, she kept a straight face until the final fade-out. Whenever she was spotted with a fresh, unsuspecting group hurrying to the movies, those in the know would say: "There goes Dorothy, off to *Salome, Where She Danced* again!"

During this period when both Lillian and she were in Hollywood, D. W. Griffith included me on the list for some of the Sunday night showings of his films in a University of Southern California projection room. At the showing of *The White Rose,* Dorothy and Lillian were present (so was Mae Marsh). Dorothy's elderly Pekinese ("Rover"), a gift from Mary Pickford, was also there, and napped peacefully under Dorothy's chair. By coincidence he woke up just as Carol Dempster, who plays a second lead role in *The White Rose,* appeared, whereupon "Rover" went up to the screen and barked furiously at

Dempster. Dorothy led the laughter, and even Mr. Griffith chortled a few times.

I remember Dorothy breezing into tea at Lillian's apartment on East 57th Street one afternoon with an armful of new books she had just purchased. As she put them on a table, she explained that she had just received her first residual, and so was splurging. "I used to be perplexed when television actors would ask me if I'd had my residuals yet," she said. "I thought it had something to do with a physical check-up of some kind. But now I've had a residual — and I like 'em!"

In 1946, she and Louis Calhern co-starred on Broadway as Chief Justice Holmes and his wife in "The Magnificent Yankee." They seemed so perfect a couple and people had grown so used to them as a team after "Life with Father," that now everybody was wondering if they would marry in real life. They never did.

In 1950, she opened on Broadway in psychological suspense thriller by Mel Dinelli called "The Man," playing a housewife terrorised by a psychopathic young killer she has befriended. During the out-of-town try-out, she came down with a severe case of influenza, and Lillian, who was travelling with the company and knew the role by heart, went on for her several times. On such occasions, Lillian always said: "It doesn't matter who plays it — Dorothy or Lillian — so long as it's a Gish."

I think Dorothy was grateful for, not resentful of, Lillian's protection. During Lillian's stage run in "Crime and Punishment," I went for Thanksgiving dinner at her apartment and Dorothy met me at the door with: "Isn't Lil simply wonderful in 'Crime and Punishment'! I'm going every night I can! I think it's the best thing she's ever done on the stage."

Dorothy's last two films were made in 1951 and 1963. In the earlier, *The Whistle at Eaton Falls,* she played the widow-owner of a factory in that Louis de Rochemont semi-documentary which was actually filmed in a New England factory town; and in her last picture, *The Cardinal,* she is the mother of the Boston priest who becomes a cardinal, a role played by Tom Tryon, now a best-selling novelist.

Between her last two films and other professional engagements, Dorothy made several trips abroad. "I've discovered the joys of ocean voyages by freighter," she declared. "Now that I've found out about freighters, I feel I've wasted the best part of my leisure life. Last time I boarded a freighter at the Fulton Fish Market and ten days later was on the North African coast. There were only eight passengers — all women — and we had the most heavenly time. The captain and crew hated it — I think there's some superstition about women on board a ship being bad luck — but we landed without mishap, and, once ashore, we gave the captain a grand party."

In the summer of 1956, Lillian and Dorothy played in thirteen summer-stock engagements of Enid Bagnold's "The Chalk Garden." It was the first time they had played together in a theatre since their childhood. George Cukor says their performance opened to him facets of the play he had not noticed when he started directing the initial pre-Broadway production (he withdrew after only a few weeks). Dorothy played Mrs. St. Maugham, which had been Gladys Cooper's role on Broadway, and Lillian had the part Siobhan McKenna originated.

DOROTHY GISH

Not long after "The Chalk Garden" tour, there was a gradual, but perceptible, change in Dorothy. The simplest thing became an effort, and the fun seemed to have gone out of everything. Finally, she refused to go out, and to see people, and no longer seemed to care even about herself.

Lillian, deeply concerned, took her to their childhood home in Masillon, and for a time something of the old spark seemed to be rekindled. Dorothy accepted a role in Howard Teichmann's play, "The Girls in 509," but as soon as rehearsals began, she complained about not being able to remember lines, and asked to be replaced. Peggy Wood took over the part.

Sometime in the early Sixties, she started rehearsals for a television show. Although it was not a live production, but was to be filmed, she became distraught and again could not remember her lines. Lillian stepped in for her. Contrite and humiliated, Dorothy declared: "This is the end — no more acting."

Occasionally thereafter, she would go out with an old friend. Says Blanche Sweet: "I like to remember her as she was one of the last times we were together. We went to see *The Knack*, a fast-paced and quick-witted hilarious comedy film directed by Richard Lester. We never stopped laughing. Dorothy never missed a point or line; her perception was swift and keen."

But her physical and mental condition grew worse.

Lillian closed Dorothy's apartment in the Hotel Elysée and took her, with their life-long friend, Laura McCullaugh, to a sanatorium in Rapallo, Italy. Not long after her arrival there, Dorothy suffered a stroke, and from then on, she was in seclusion.

In the spring of 1968, when Lillian was playing on Broadway in "I Never Sang for My Father," she received a cable that Dorothy had contracted pneumonia, and the worst was feared. After a Saturday evening performance — the theatre would be dark Sunday and Monday — Lillian flew to Italy, and Lois Wilson, her standby, was notified to be ready to play the Tuesday night performance. But Tuesday afternoon Lillian flew in, and said Dorothy seemed to be recovering.

After "I Never Sang for My Father" closed, Lillian and Helen Hayes taped a television production of "Arsenic and Old Lace," and it was while Lillian was putting the final polish on her autobiography. "The Movies, Mr. Griffith and Me," that she received word Dorothy was again gravely ill with bronchial pneumonia. She flew to Rapallo and was at her sister's bedside when Dorothy succumbed on Tuesday, June 4, 1968.

Lillian arranged for Dorothy's cremation, and as soon as she got back to New York City, she placed her sister's ashes beside those of their mother in the family crypt at St. Batholomew's Protestant Episcopal Church on Park Avenue.

Except for a few minor bequests, Dorothy left her estate, valued at over $500,000 to Lillian in trust. After Lillian's death, it will go to the Actor's Fund, in memory of their mother.

DOROTHY GISH FILMOGRAPHY

AN UNSEEN ENEMY (The Terrible Experience of Two Young Girls in a Lonesome Villa) (1912). Melodrama; as one of two young sisters terrorised by a safe-cracker and a drunken maidservant. *Dir:* D. W. Griffith. *Sc:* Edwin Acker. *With* Lillian Gish, Robert Harron, Harry Carey, Lionel Barrymore, Elmer Booth, Grace Henderson. *Prod:* Biograph. 1143 ft.

THE MUSKETEERS OF PIG ALLEY (1912). Realistic gang-war drama; as one of the girls of Pig Alley. *Dir/Sc:* D. W. Griffith. *With* Lillian Gish, Harry Carey, Robert Harron, Elmer Booth, W. Chrystie Miller, Antonio Moreno, Marie Newton, Jack Pickford. *Prod:* Biograph. 1314 ft.

GOLD AND GLITTER (1912). Romantic drama; as one of the girls in the hero's odyssey. *Dir:* D. W. Griffith. *Sc:* George Henessy. *With* Lillian Gish, Lionel Barrymore, Elmer Booth. *Prod:* Biograph. 999 ft.

THE INFORMER (1912). Civil War romance; as a Southern girl. *Dir:* D. W. Griffith. *Sc:* George Henessy. *With* Mary Pickford, Lillian Gish, Walter C. Miller, (W. Chrystie Miller). Henry B. Walthall, Kate Bruce, Robert Harron, W. Christy Cabanné, Joseph Graybill, Harry Carey. *Prod:* Biograph. 1080 ft.

THE NEW YORK HAT (1912). Romance; as one of the girls in the town. *Dir:* D. W. Griffith. *Sc:* Anita Loos. *With* Mary Pickford, Lionel Barrymore, Lillian Gish, Mae Marsh, Robert Harron, Charles H. Mailes, Jack Pickford, Mack Sennett. *Prod:* Biograph. 999 ft.

MY HERO (1912). Drama; as a very young girl. *Dir/Sc:* D. W. Griffith. *With* Robert Harron, Henry B. Walthall, Charles H. Mailes, Harry Carey, Kate Bruce, Lionel Barrymore. *Prod:* Biograph. 1458 ft.

A CRY FOR HELP (1912). Drama; as a passerby with Harron. *Dir:* D. W. Griffith. *Sc:* Edwin Acker. *With* Lillian Gish, Lionel Barrymore, Harry Carey, Walter C. Miller, (W. Chrystie Miller), Kate Bruce, Robert Harron, Claire McDowell. *Prod:* Biograph. 1458 ft.

OIL AND WATER (1913). Society vs. theatre drama; as a girl in one scene. *Dir:* D. W. Griffith. *Sc:* E. J. Montagne. *With* Blanche Sweet, Henry B. Walthall, W. Chrystie Miller, Lionel Barrymore, Charles H, Mailes, Alfred Paget, Robert Harron, Lillian Gish. *Prod:* Biograph. 1546 ft. (Compare listing in Blanche Sweet filmography.)

THE PERFIDY OF MARY (1913). Small town romance; as one of two cousins who trips up a small-time Lothario. *Dir:* D. W. Griffith. *Sc:* George Henessy. *With* Mae Marsh, Lionel Barrymore, Henry B. Walthall, Harry Hyde, Walter C. Miller. *Prod:* Biograph. 1012 ft.

THE LADY AND THE MOUSE (1913). Small-town drama; as one of the daughters of the grocer. *Dir:* D. W. Griffith. *With* Lillian Gish, Lionel Barrymore, Henry B. Walthall, Robert Harron, Mae Marsh, Kate Toncray, Harry Hyde. *Prod:* Biograph. 2060 ft.

JUST GOLD (1913). Drama of a search for gold; in a small role. *Dir/Sc:* D. W. Griffith. *With* Lionel Barrymore, Lillian Gish, Charles West, Alfred Paget, Charles H. Mailes, Joseph McDermott, Kate Bruce. *Prod:* Biograph. 1007 ft.

ALMOST A WILD MAN (1913). Comedy; as a girl captivated by an out-of-work actor's performance as a wild man. *Dir:* Del Henderson. *Sc:* William Beaudine. *With* Gus Pixley, Charlie Murray, Edward Dillon. *Prod:* Biograph. 584 ft.

HER MOTHER'S OATH (1913). Drama; as a girl in love whose mother opposes the romance. *Dir/Sc:* D. W. Griffith. *With* Jennie Lee, Henry B. Walthall, Robert Harron, Charles H. Mailes, Jack Dillon, Mae Marsh. *Prod:* Biograph. 1386 ft.

PA SAYS (1913). Comedy; as a girl whose father opposes her romance. *Dir:* Del Henderson *Sc:* Anita Loos. *With* Edward Dillon. *Prod:* Biograph. 490 ft.

THE VENGEANCE OF GALORA (1913). Gypsy drama; as the unwitting rival of the gypsy girl. *Dir:* W. Christy Cabanné. *Sc:* Lionel Barrymore. *With* Blanche Sweet, Henry B. Walthall, Lionel Barrymore. *Prod:* Biograph. 1040 ft. (Compare listing in Blanche Sweet filmography.)

THOSE LITTLE FLOWERS (1913). Farce; as the young Mrs. Saunders. *Sc:* Marion Leonard. *With* Gertrude Bambrick, Gus Pixley, Kate Toncray. *Prod:* Biograph. 570 ft.

THE WIDOW'S KIDS (1913). *Sc:* Anita Loos. *Prod:* Biograph. 455 ft.

THE ADOPTED BROTHER (1913). Western drama; as a heroine who has a virtuous adopted brother and an evil blood one. *Dir/Sc:* W. Christy Cabanné. *With* Robert Harron, Elmer Booth, W. Chrystie Miller, Charles Gorman. *Prod:* Biograph. 1015 ft.

THE LADY IN BLACK (1913). Western melodrama; as a heroine who is rescued from being forced into an unwanted marriage. *Sc:* Anita Loos. *With* Edward Dillon, Gertrude Bambrick. *Prod:* Biograph. 607 ft.

82

DOROTHY GISH

THE HOUSE OF DISCORD (1913). Mother-daughter drama; as May, the daughter. *Dir:* James Kirkwood. *Sc:* A. Clayton Harris. *With* Blanche Sweet, Jack Mulhall, Antonio Moreno, Lionel Barrymore, Marshall Neilan. *Prod:* Klaw and Erlanger/Biograph. 2020 ft. (Compare listings in Antonio Moreno and Blanche Sweet filmographies.)

HER OLD TEACHER (1914). Character drama; as a onetime student of a now-destitute teacher. *Sc:* Elizabeth Lonergan. *With* Glen White. *Prod:* Biograph.

JUDITH OF BETHULIA (1914). The story of how Judith saved her people; as a crippled beggar. *Dir:* D. W. Griffith. *Sc:* Frank E. Woods (from the Apocryphal Book of Judith and a play by Thomas Bailey Aldrich). *With* Blanche Sweet, Henry B. Walthall, Kate Bruce, Lillian Gish, Mae Marsh, Robert Harron, Charles H. Mailes, Harry Carey, Antonio Moreno, Gertrude Bambrick, Alfred Paget. *Prod:* Biograph. 4 reels. (Re-issued, with additional footage, as 6 reels, 1917, as *Her Condoned Sin.*) (Compare listings in Blanche Sweet and Antonio Moreno filmographies.)

HER FATHER'S SILENT PARTNER (1914). Crook melodrama; in a small role. *Dir:* Donald Crisp. *Sc:* Belle Taylor. *With* Harry Carey, Claire McDowell. *Prod:* Biograph.

THE MYSTERIOUS SHOT (1914). Western drama; as Mary Lee Price, forced into a loveless marriage, who falls in love with a Mexican rancher. *Dir:* James Kirkwood. *Sc:* (from a story "The Higher Law," by George Patullo). *With* Henry B. Walthall, Jack Pickford, Donald Crisp. *Prod:* Mutual/Reliance. 1902 ft.

THE FLOOR ABOVE (1914). Mystery drama; as a chorus girl who helps unravel the mystery. *Dir:* James Kirkwood. *Sc:* (from a novel, "The Mystery of Charlecot Mansions," by E. Phillips Oppenheim). *With* Henry B. Walthall, Earle Foxe, Ralph Lewis, Estelle Coffin. *Prod:* Mutual/Reliance.

THE OLD MAN (1914). Character drama; as a maid of all work. *With* Henry B. Walthall. *Prod:* Mutual/Reliance. 988 ft.

LIBERTY BELLES (1914). Romantic farce; as Dorothy Ketchum. *Dir:* James Kirkwood. *Sup:* D. W. Griffith. *With* Gertrude Bambrick, Marion Sunshine, Jack Pickford, Reggie Morris, Spottiswoode Aitken, Charles H. Mailes, Kate Toncray, David Morris. *Prod:* Klaw and Erlanger/Biograph. 2615 ft.

THE MOUNTAIN RAT (1914). Dorothy Gish's first starring role. Western drama; as a dance hall girl, known as "Nell, the Mountain Rat." *Dir:* James Kirkwood. *Sc:* (from a story by Mary Rider Mechtold). *With* Henry B. Walthall, Donald Crisp, Irene Hunt. *Prod:* Mutual/Reliance.

SILENT SANDY (1914). Romantic drama; as a romance-starved slavey who puts an ad in a matrimonial column. *Sup:* D. W. Griffith. *Sc:* H. R. Durant and Russell E. Smith. *With* Fred Kelsey. *Prod:* Mutual/Reliance.

THE NEWER WOMAN (1914). Comedy about the emancipation of women; as one of "the newer women." *Dir:* Donald Crisp. *Sc:* Russell E. Smith. *With* Robert Harron, Donald Crisp. *Prod:* Mutual/Majestic.

THEIR FIRST ACQUAINTANCE (1914). Romantic drama; as a housemaid who gets involved in a burglary. *Dir:* John G. O'Brien. *Sc:* George Henessy. *With* Robert Harron, F. A. Turner, Miriam Cooper. *Prod:* Mutual/Majestic.

ARMS AND THE GRINGO (AKA, GB, *The Rifle Smugglers*) (1914). Romantic drama of the Mexican border; as a Mexican señorita involved in contraband and romance. *Dir:* W. Christy Cabanné. *Sc:* Anna Tupper Wilkes. *With* Wallace Reid, F. A. Lowery, Fred Kelsey, Howard Gaye. *Prod:* Mutual/Majestic. 2034 ft. (Compare listing in Wallace Reid filmography.)

THE SUFFRAGETTE'S BATTLE IN NUT-TYVILLE (1914). A travesty about the battle of the sexes; as the leader of the females. *Dir:* W. Christy Cabanné. *Prod:* Mutual/Majestic. 1 reel.

THE CITY BEAUTIFUL (1914). Romance of early film-making in Los Angeles; as a girl who falls in love with a country boy. *Dir:* W. Christy Cabanné. *With* Wallace Reid. *Prod:* Mutual/Majestic. 1 reel. (Compare listing in Wallace Reid filmography.)

THE PAINTED LADY (1914). Drama of two country girls, sisters, who go to the big city; as the younger sister. *Sup:* D. W. Griffith. *Sc:* (from a story, "The Cavalier," by Charles S. Thompson). *With* Blanche Sweet, W. E. Lawrence, Josephine Crowell. *Prod:* Mutual/Majestic. 2 reels. (Compare listing in Blanche Sweet filmography.)

HOME SWEET HOME (1914). Romantic drama of the effect the song, "Home Sweet Home" has on a number of people; as the younger sister of the character played by Lillian Gish, who is in love with John Howard Payne, writer of the song. *Dir:* D. W. Griffith. *Sc:* Griffith and H. E. Aitken. *With* Henry B. Walthall, Josephine Crowell, Lillian Gish, Fay Tincher, Mae Marsh, Spottiswoode Aitken, Robert Harron, Miriam Cooper, Mary Alden, Donald Crisp, James Kirkwood, Jack Pickford, Courtenay Foote, Blanche Sweet, Owen Moore, Edward Dillon, Earle Foxe, Karl Brown, George Seigmann, Ralph Lewis, John Dillon, Irene Hunt. This film is often cited as the first all-star feature. *Prod:* Mutual. 6 reels. (Compare listing in Blanche Sweet filmography.)

THE TAVERN OF TRAGEDY (1914). Civil War melodramatic tragedy; as the daughter of Corto, a Confederate tavern-keeper. *Dir:* Donald Crisp. *Sc:* Russell E. Smith. *With* F. A. Turner, Donald Crisp. *Prod:* Mutual/Majestic. 1252 ft.

HER MOTHER'S NECKLACE (1914). Domestic drama; as a resentful daughter of a father who plans to marry again. *Dir:* Donald Crisp. *With* Irene Hunt, Howard Gaye. *Prod:* Mutual/Majestic. 1974 ft.

A LESSON IN MECHANICS (1914). Romance; as a rich girl who loves to tinker with motor engines. *Dir:* W. Christy Cabanné. *With* Robert Harron. *Prod:* Mutual/Majestic. 2 reels.

GRANNY (1914). Romantic drama; as Nell who prevents a boarder from committing a burglary. *Dir:* W. Christy Cabanné. *With* W. A. Lawrence, A. T. Sears, Ida Wilkinson. *Prod:* Mutual/Majestic. 984 ft.

A FAIR REBEL (1914). Civil War romantic drama; as Joan Fitzhugh, a Confederate young lady in love. *Dir:* James Kirkwood. *Sup:* D. W. Griffith. *With* Linda Arvidson, Charles West, Lillian Gish, Clara T. Bracey, Charles Perley, J. H. Elsky, Walter T. Lewis, J. Martin, G. Pierce, Robert Drouet, Jack Brammall, Florence Ashbrooke. *Prod:* Klaw and Erlanger/Biograph. 2569 ft.

DOWN THE ROAD TO CREDITVILLE (1914). Comedy; as an extravagant bride. *Dir:* Donald Crisp. *With* Wallace Reid. *Prod:* Mutual/Majestic. 992 ft.

THE WIFE (1914). Marital drama; as the ingenue. *Dir:* James Kirkwood. *Sup:* D. W. Griffith. *With* Linda Arvidson, Charles West. *Prod:* Klaw and Erlanger/Biograph. 2575 ft.

THE REBELLION OF KITTY BELLE (1914). Romantic drama; as Kitty Belle. *Dir/Sc:* W. Christy Cabanné (from a story by George Patullo). *With* Robert Harron, Lillian Gish, Raoul Walsh. *Prod:* Mutual/Majestic. 2 reels.

SANDS OF FATE (1914). Drama of the desert; as a girl who learns which of the two men she loves is the better. *Dir:* Donald Crisp. *With* Robert Harron, Raoul Walsh, Cora Drew. *Prod:* Mutual/Majestic.

THE WARNING (1914). Moral drama; as Dorothy, who goes to sleep in her hammock and dreams of what may happen to her in the city. *Dir:* Donald Crisp. *Sc:* Russell E. Smith. *Prod:* Mutual/Majestic. 1003 ft.

BACK TO THE KITCHEN (1914). Romantic drama of the West; as the rancher's daughter. *Dir:* John G. O'Brien. *Prod:* Mutual/Majestic.

CLASSMATES (1914). Drama of West Point rivalry and redemption; in a secondary role. *Dir:* James Kirkwood. *Sup:* D. W. Griffith. *Sc:* (from the play by William C. de Mille and Margaret Turnbull). *With* Henry B. Walthall, Marshall Neilan, Blanche Sweet, Lionel Barrymore, Jack Mulhall, Antonio Moreno, Gertrude Robinson, Thomas Jefferson. (Re-made, 1924, with Richard Barthelmess and Madge Evans.) *Prod:* Klaw and Erlanger/Biograph. 3449 ft. (Compare listing in Blanche Sweet and Antonio Moreno filmographies.)

THE AVAILING PRAYER (1914). Drama; as an ailing daughter whose father almost steals for her. *Dir:* Donald Crisp. *Sc:* Richard Barker Shelton. *With* Raoul Walsh, Spottiswoode Aitken. *Prod:* Mutual/Majestic. 980 ft.

THE SAVING GRACE (1914). Drama of revenge; as an illiterate daughter of the town drunk, who becomes educated by a minister. *Dir:* W. Christy Cabanné. *With* Fred Burns, George Seigmann. *Prod:* Mutual/Majestic.

THE SISTERS (AKA, GB, *A Duel for Love*) (1914). Drama of sister love; as the sister who makes a tremendous sacrifice to insure her sister's happiness. *Dir/Sc:* W. Christy Cabanné. *With* Lillian Gish, Elmer Clifton, W. E. Lawrence. *Prod:* Mutual/Majestic. 1871 ft.

THE BETTER WAY (1914). Father-daughter drama; as a young servant girl in a wealthy home who prevents her ex-convict father from burgling the house where she works. *Dir/Sc:* W. Christy Cabanné. *With* F. A. Turner. *Prod:* Mutual/Majestic. 1000 ft.

AN OLD-FASHIONED GIRL (1915). A romantic pastorale; as a country girl, Abigail, whose lover becomes infatuated with a city girl. *Dir:* Donald Crisp. *Sc:* Russell E. Smith. *With* Seena Owen, William Hinckley, Eleanor Washington. *Prod:* Mutual/Majestic. 973 ft.

HOW HAZEL GOT EVEN (1915). Romantic comedy; as Hazel, a restaurant cashier who loves a bus-driver. *Dir:* George Seigmann. *With:* Eugene Pallette, W. E. Lawrence, Fred Burns. This became known as a jinx production: Donald Crisp started it as director, but became ill and George Seigmann took over; then Dorothy Gish was struck by an automobile, and was four weeks in the hospital. *Prod:* Mutual/Majestic. 1940 ft.

THE LOST LORD LOVELL (1915). Romantic comedy; as an ill-treated maid-of-all-work. *Dir:* Paul Powell. *Sc:* W. Carey Wonderly. *With* Frank Bennett, Catherine Henry, Chet Withey. *Prod:* Mutual/Majestic. 1958 ft.

MINERVA'S MISSION (1915). Satiric comedy on the fads of modern reformers; as Minerva, whose mission is reforming everybody. *Dir;* Paul Powell. *With* W. E. Lawrence,

Cora Drew, James Gorman. *Prod:* Mutual/Majestic. 1992 ft.

HER GRANDPARENTS (1915). Old age vs. youth drama; as a shop-girl. *Dir:* Frank Powell. *Prod:* Mutual/Majestic. 963 ft.

OUT OF BONDAGE (1915). Underworld drama; as the daughter of a notorious crook. *Sc:* Chester B. Clapp. *With* William Hinckley, Walter Long, F. A. Turner, Richard Cummings. *Prod:* Mutual/Majestic.

HER MOTHER'S DAUGHTER (AKA, *The Nun*). (1915). Spiritual drama; as a repentant mother's daughter who chooses to become a nun. *Dir:* Paul Powell. *Sc:* Russell E. Smith. *With* W. E. Lawrence, Mary Alden, F. A. Turner, Jennie Lee. Filmed at the Santa Barbara Mission and surrounding country. *Prod:* Mutual/Majestic.

THE MOUNTAIN GIRL (1915). Mountaineer drama; as a mountain girl who falls in love with a stranger whose life she has saved. *Dir:* James Kirkwood. *Sc:* (from a story by Mary Rider Mechtold). *With* Frank Bennett, Ralph Lewis, W. E. Lawrence. *Prod:* Mutual/Majestic.

THE LITTLE CATAMOUNT (1915). Romantic drama; as a moonshiner's shrewish daughter who is tamed by a young fisherman. *Dir:* Paul Powell. *With* Ralph Lewis, W. E. Lawrence, Frank Bennett, William Brown. *Prod:* Mutual/Majestic. 929 ft.

VICTORINE (1915). Carnival romance; as a carnival girl who has knives thrown at her. *Dir:* Paul Powell. *Sc:* (from a story, "The Going Ons of Victorine", by Julian Street). *With* Ralph Lewis, William Hinckley, Walter Long, Mae Gaston. *Prod:* Mutual/Majestic.

BRED IN THE BONE (1915). Backstage drama; as a Quaker girl who becomes a great actress. *Dir:* Paul Powell. *Sc:* Russell E. Smith (from a story by Frank Kinsella). *With* Mary Alden, W. E. Lawrence, William Hinckley, George (André) Beranger, Margery Wilson, Alberta Lee, Richard Cummings, Seena Owen, Al Filson, Eleanor Washington. *Prod:* Mutual/Majestic. 4 reels.

OLD HEIDELBERG (1915). Romance; as Kathy, the tavern waitress who loves a prince. *Dir/Sc:* John Emerson (an updated dramatisation of the novel, "Karl Heinrich," by W. Meyer-Forster and a play by Richard Mansfield). *Sup:* D. W. Griffith. *With* Wallace Reid, Erich von Stroheim, Karl Forman, Raymond Wells, Madge Hunt, Erik von Ritzau, Kate Toncray, Harold Goodwin, Francis Carpenter. (See Reid filmography for other versions of the story on film.) *Prod:* Triangle/Fine Arts. 5 reels.

JORDAN IS A HARD ROAD (1915). Father-daughter drama; as Cora Minden, daughter of a reformed bandit. *Dir/Sc:* Allan Dwan (from the novel by Gilbert Parker). *Prod:* D. W. Griffith. *With* Owen Moore, Frank Campeau, Sarah Truax, Ralph Lewis, Mabel Wiles, Fred Burns, Lester Perry, Jim Ked, Walter Long, Joseph Singleton. *Prod:* Triangle/Fine Arts. 5 reels.

BETTY OF GREYSTONE (1916). Romantic drama; as Betty, daughter of the caretaker of Greystone Gables, who marries the young heir to Greystone. *Dir:* Allan Dwan. *Sc:* F. M. Pierson. *With* Owen Moore, George Fawcett, Kate Bruce, Albert Tavernier, Kid McCoy, John Beck, Warner Richmond, Grace Rankin, Macey Harlan, Eugene Ormond, Leonore Harris. *Prod:* Triangle/Fine Arts. 5 reels.

LITTLE MEENA'S ROMANCE. (1916). Romantic comedy drama; as Meena Bauer, a Pennsylvania Dutch girl. *Dir:* Paul Powell. *Sc:* F. M. Pierson (from his own story, "Katie Bauer)". *With* Owen Moore, Marguerite Marsh, Fred J. Butler, Robert Lawler, Alberta Lee, Mazie Redford, George Pierce, Fred A. Turner, Kate Toncray, James O'Shea, William Brown. *Prod:* Triangle/Fine Arts. 5 reels.

SUSAN ROCKS THE BOAT (AKA, GB, *Sweet Seventeen*) (1916). Romantic drama; as a rich girl, whose idol is Joan of Arc. *Dir:* Paul Powell. *Sc:* Bernard McConville. *With* Owen Moore, Kate Bruce, Fred J. Butler, Fred A. Turner, Edwin Harley, Clyde E. Hopkins, James O'Shea. *Prod:* Triangle/Fine Arts. 5 reels.

THE LITTLE SCHOOL MA'AM (1916). Romantic comedy; as Nan, a Southern girl who goes West to teach school. *Dir:* Chester M. and Sidney A. Franklin. *With* Elmer Clifton, George Pierce, Jack Brammall, Howard Gaye, Josephine Crowell, Luray Huntley, Millard Webb, Hal Wilson, Georgie Stone. *Prod:* Triangle/Fine Arts. 5 reels.

GRETCHEN, THE GREENHORN (1916). Comedy drama; as Gretchen, a Dutch immigrant who gets innocently involved as a counterfeiter's dupe. *Dir:* Chester M. and Sidney A. Franklin. *Sc:* Bernard McConville (from his story, "Gretchen Blunders In"). *With* Ralph Lewis, Frank Bennett, Eugene Pallette, Kate Bruce, Georgie Stone, Violet Radcliffe, Carmen DeRue, Beulah Burns, Francis Carpenter, Tom Spencer. *Prod:* Triangle/Fine Arts. 5 reels.

ATTA BOY'S LAST RACE (AKA, *The Best Bet*). (1916). Horse-racing comedy drama; as Sue Kean, who loves horses, but hates racetrack intrigue. *Dir:* George Seigmann. *Sc:* Tod Browning. *With* Keith Armour, Adele Clifton, Carl Stockdale, Loyola O'Connor, Fred A. Turner, Joe Neery, Tom Wilson. *Prod:* Triangle/Fine Arts. 5 reels.

CHILDREN OF THE FEUD (1916). Southern mountaineer drama, based on an occurrence which actually happened during a Virginia feud; as "Sairy" Ann Clayton, moonshiner's daughter, who gets involved in the feud between the Claytons and the Allens. *Dir:* Joseph Henabery. *Sc:* Bernard McConville (from his own story, "The Feud-Breakers"). *With* A. D. Sears, Fred A. Turner, Sam de Grasse, Alberta Lee, Elmo Lincoln, Charles Gorman, Violet Radcliffe, Beulah Burns, Tina Rossi, Georgie Stone. *Prod:* Triangle/Fine Arts. 5 reels.

THE LITTLE YANK (1917). Civil War romance; as Sally, a Yankee, who loves a Confederate soldier. *Dir:* George Seigmann. *Sc:* Roy Somerville. *With* Frank Bennett, A. D. Sears, Hal Wilson, Robert Burns, Fred A. Turner, Kate Toncray, Alberta Lee. *Prod:* Triangle/Fine Arts. 5 reels.

STAGE STRUCK (1917). Comedy romance; as Ruth Colby, who wants to be an actress. *Dir:* Edward Morrissey. *Sc:* Roy Somerville (from his own story, "The Failures"). *With* Frank Bennett, Spottiswoode Aitken, Kate Toncray, Jennie Lee, Fred A. Warren, Mazie Radford. *Prod:* Triangle/Fine Arts. 5 reels.

HER OFFICIAL FATHERS (1917). Romantic comedy; as Janice Webster, who holds the controlling interest on a bank's board of directors. *Dir:* Elmer Clifton and Joseph Henabery. *Sc:* Roy Somerville (from a story, "That Colby Girl," by Hugh S. Miller). *With* Frank Bennett, Fred A. Turner, Sam de Grasse, Charles Lee, Jennie Lee, Milton Schumann, Hal Wilson, Bessie Buskirk, Fred Warren. *Prod:* Triangle/Fine Arts. 5 reels.

HEARTS OF THE WORLD ("The Story of a Village. An Old-Fashioned Play with a New-Fashioned Theme") (1918). First World War story; as "The Little Disturber." *Dir:* D. W. Griffith. *Sc:* Gaston de Tolignac (D. W. Griffith). *With* Lillian Gish, Robert Harron, Josephine Crowell, Kate Bruce, Erich von Stroheim, George Seigmann, Jack Cosgrove, Robert Anderson, George Fawcett, Ben Alexander, Mary Gish, George Nichols, Adolphe Lestina, Mlle. Yvette Duvoisin, Mrs. Harron, Mary Harron, Jessie Harron, Johnny Harron, Mary Hay, Anna Mae Walthall, Nöel Coward. Exteriors filmed behind the fighting lines at Compiègne and St. Liège in France, in English studios, and back in Hollywood on the Griffith lot. *Prod:* Comstock-World. 10 reels.

THE HUN WITHIN (AKA, GB, *The Peril Within*) (1918). Romantic melodrama; as Beth. *Dir:* Chet Withey and W. Christy Cabanné. *Sc:* Granville Warwick (D. W. Griffith) and S. E. V. Taylor. *With* Douglas MacLean, Charles Gerrard, George Fawcett, Kate Bruce, Erich von Stroheim, Bert Sutch, Max Davidson, Lillian Clarke, Robert Anderson, Adolphe Lestina. *Prod:* Paramount/Artcraft. 5 reels.

BATTLING JANE (1918). Comedy drama in a small Maine town; as "Battling" Jane. *Dir:* Elmer Clifton. *Sc:* (from a story by Arnold Bernot). *With* George Nichols, May Hall, Katherine MacDonald, Ernest Marion, Bertram Grassby, Adolphe Lestina, Kate Toncray. *Prod:* Paramount/Artcraft. 5 reels.

THE HOPE CHEST (1919). Romantic comedy; as Sheila, daughter of a vaudevillian, who works in a candy store. *Dir:* Elmer Clifton. *Sc:* M. M. Stearns (from a novel by Mark Lee Luther). *With* Richard Barthelmess, George Fawcett, Sam de Grasse, Kate Toncray, Carol Dempster, Bertram Grassby. *Prod:* Paramount/Artcraft. 5 reels.

BOOTS (1919). Romance in wartime London: as a slavey who loves an American Secret Service agent. *Dir:* Elmer Clifton. *Sc:* M. M. Stearns (from a story by Martha Pittman). *With* Richard Barthelmess, Fontaine LaRue, Edward Peil. *Prod:* Paramount/Artcraft. 5 reels.

PEPPY POLLY (1919). Romantic comedy; as Polly Shannon, a hoyden in trouble with the law, who falls in love with a young physician. *Dir:* Elmer Clifton. *Sc:* (from a story by Marjorie Raynale). *With* Richard Barthelmess, Edward Peil, Emily Chichester. *Prod:* Paramount/Artcraft. 5 reels.

I'LL GET HIM YET (1919). Romantic comedy; as a rich girl in love with a young reporter. *Dir:* Elmer Clifton. *Sc:* (from a story by Harry Carr). *With* Richard Barthelmess, George Fawcett, Ralph Graves, Edward Peil, Porter Strong. *Prod:* Paramount/Artcraft. 5 reels.

NUGGET NELL (1919). Burlesque on Western melodrama; as a two-gun bandit known as "Nugget Nell." *Dir:* Elmer Clifton. *Sc:* Hugh R. Osborne (from a story by John R. Cornish). *With* Raymond Cannon, David Butler, Regina Sarle, James Farley, Bob Fleming, Wilbur Higeby, Emily Chichester. *Prod:* Paramount/Artcraft. 5 reels.

OUT OF LUCK (1919). Romantic comedy about superstition; as Frances Wadsworth. *Dir:* Elmer Clifton. *Sc:* George Morgan (from a story, "Nobody's Home," by Lois Zellner). *With* Ralph Graves, Rudolph Valentino, Raymond Cannon, Vera McGinnis, George Fawcett, Emily Chichester, Norman McNeill, Porter Strong, Kate Toncray, Vivian Montrose. *Prod:* Paramount/Artcraft. 5 reels.

TURNING THE TABLES (1919). Romantic comedy in a sanitarium; as an eccentric who is committed by a stern aunt. *Dir:* Elmer Clifton. *Sc:* Lois Zellner (from a story by Wells Hastings). *With* Raymond Cannon, George Fawcett, Eugenie Besserer, Kate Toncray, Fred Warren, Rhea Haines, Porter Strong, Norman McNeill. *Prod:* Paramount/Artcraft. 5 reels.

MARY ELLEN COMES TO TOWN (1920). Romantic comedy; as Mary Ellen from the country, who comes to the city. *Dir:* Elmer Clifton. *Sc:* Wells Hastings (from a story by Helen G. Smith). *With* Ralph Graves, Kate Bruce, Adolphe Lestina, Charles Gerrard, Raymond Cannon, Bert Apling, Rhea Haines. *Prod:* Paramount/Artcraft. 5 reels.

REMODELING HER HUSBAND (1920). Romantic comedy; as a young wife who makes over her husband to suit her own taste. *Dir:* Lillian Gish (the only time Miss Gish ever directed a full feature). *Sc:* Dorothy E. Carter. *With* James Rennie, Marie Burke, Downing Clark, Frank Kingdon. *Prod:* Paramount/Artcraft. 5 reels.

LITTLE MISS REBELLION (1920). Mythical kingdom-Manhattan romantic comedy; as the Grand Duchess Marie Louise, who escapes a Bolshevik rebellion and comes to New York, where she works in a restaurant. *Dir:* George Fawcett. *Sc:* Wells Hastings (from a story by Harry Carr). *With* Ralph Graves, George Seigmann, (William) Riley Hatch, Marie Burke. *Prod:* Paramount/Artcraft. 5 reels.

FLYING PAT (1920). Romantic comedy of aviation; as the young wife of a plane manufacturer. *Dir:* F. Richard Jones. *Sc:* Harry Carr and F. R. Jones (from a story by Virginia P. Withy). *With* James Rennie, Morgan Wallace, Harold Vizard, William Black, Porter Strong, Tom Blake, Kate Bruce. *Prod:* Paramount/Artcraft. 5 reels.

THE GHOST IN THE GARRET (1921). Romantic comedy; as Daisy (Delsie) O'Dell, who finds thieves in a "haunted" house. *Dir:* F. Richard Jones. *Sc:* Fred Chaston (F. Richard Jones) (from a story by Wells Hastings). *With* William E. Park, Downey Clark, Mrs. David Landau, Ray Gray, Tom Blake, Porter Strong. *Prod:* Paramount/Artcraft. 5 reels..

ORPHANS OF THE STORM (1922). Historical drama of the French Revolution; as Louise Girard, blind sister. *Dir/Sc:* D. W. Griffith (from the play "The Two Orphans," by Adolphe D'Ennery). *With* Lillian Gish, Joseph Schildkraut, Monte Blue, Frank Losee, Catherine Emmett, Morgan Wallace, Lucille La Verne, Sheldon Lewis, Frank Puglia, Creighton Hale, Leslie King, Sidney Herbert, Leo Kolmer, Adolphe Lestina, Kate Bruce, Flora Finch, Louis Wolheim, Kenny Delmar. *Prod:* United Artists. 12 reels. (Previously filmed by Selig and then by Fox as *The Two Orphans.*)

THE COUNTRY FLAPPER (1922). Slapstick comedy; as Jolanda, a bucolic tease. *Dir:* F. Richard Jones. *Sc:* Harry Carr and Joseph W. Farnham (from a story, "Cynic Effect," by Nalbro Bartley). *With* Glenn Hunter, Mildred

Marsh. Harlan Knight, Tom Douglas, Raymond Hackett, Albert Hackett, Catherine Collins. *Prod:* Producers Security. 5 reels. (Once announced as *Oh, Jo!* in 1921 as an Artcraft film.)

FURY (1923). Drama of vengeance; as Minnie, a Limehouse waif. *Dir:* Henry King. *Sc:* Edmund Goulding. *With* Richard Barthelmess, Tyrone Power Sr., Pat Hartigan, Barry Macollum, Jessie Arnold. *Prod:* Inspiration-First National. 8860 ft.

THE BRIGHT SHAWL (1923). Romantic drama of the Cuban rebellion from Spain; as La Clavel, a Cuban dancer. *Dir:* John S. Robertson. *Sc:* Edmund Goulding (from the novelette by Joseph Hergesheimer). *With* Richard Barthelmess, Edward G. Robinson, Andre de Beranger, Mary Astor, Margaret Seddon, William Powell, Jetta Goudal, Luis Alberni, Anders Randolph, George Humbert. *Prod:* Inspiration-First National. 8 reels.

ROMOLA (1924). Romantic drama of Florentine Renaissance; as Tessa, the peasant girl. *Dir:* Henry King. *Sc:* Will M. Ritchey (from the novel by George Eliot). *With* Lillian Gish, Ronald Colman, William Powell, Charles Lane, Herbert Grimwood, Frank Puglia, Bonaventura Ibañez. Filmed in Florence, Italy. *Prod:* Inspiration/Metro-Goldwyn. 12 reels.

NIGHT LIFE OF NEW YORK (1925). Romantic comedy drama; as Meg (Madge), a Manhattan switchboard operator who yearns for the wide open spaces of the West. *Dir:* Allan Dwan. *Sc:* Paul Schofield (from a story by Edgar Selwyn). *With* Rod La Rocque, Ernest Torrence, Helen Lee Worthing, George Hackathorne, Arthur Housman, (William) Riley Hatch. *Prod:* Paramount. 8 reels.

THE BEAUTIFUL CITY (1925). Romantic melodrama of New York's East Side; as Mollie. *Dir:* Kenneth Webb. *Sc:* Don Bartlett and C. Graham Baker (from a story by Edmund Goulding). *With* Richard Barthelmess, William Powell, Frank Puglia, Florence Auer. *Prod:* Inspiration-First National. 7 reels.

CLOTHES MAKE THE PIRATE (1925). Costume comedy; as Betsy Tidd, shrewish wife of a hen-pecked tailor. *Dir:* Maurice Tourneur. *Sc:* Marion Fairfax (from a novel by Holman Day). *With* Leon Errol, Nita Naldi, George Marion, James Rennie, Tully Marshall, Edna Murphy, Frank Lawler, Walter Law, Reginald Barlow. *Prod:* First National. 8 reels.

NELL GWYN (1926). Romantic comedy of the court of Charles II; as Nell Gwyn. *Dir/Sc:* Herbert Wilcox (from the novel, "Mistress Nell Gwyn," by Marjorie Bowen). *With* Randle Ayrton, Juliette Compton, Sidney Fairbrother, Judd Green, Edward Sorley.

Filmed in England.(Said George Jean Nathan: "It took a British director and an English-made film to reveal how sexy Dorothy Gish can be.") (Mary Pickford played Nell Gwyn for Famous Players; Anna Neagle was Nell Gwyn in Wilcox's talking version.) *Prod:* Paramount/British National. 7760 ft.

LONDON (AKA, GB, *Limehouse*) (1927). Romantic drama; as Mavis Hogan, a Limehouse ragamuffin who becomes a lady. *Dir/Sc:* Herbert Wilcox (from a story by Thomas Burke). *With* John Manners, Elissa Landi, Adelqui Millar, Jeff McLaughlin. *Prod:* Paramount/British National. 6 reels.

TIP TOES (1927). Romantic comedy about three American vaudevillians stranded in London; as "Tip Toes," a cabaret dancer. *Dir/Sc:* Herbert Wilcox (from a play by Fred Thompson and Guy Bolton). *With* Will Rogers, Nelson Keys, John Manners, Ivy Ellison, Annie Esmond, Miles Mander, Dennis Hoey, Ray Raymond. *Prod:* Paramount/British National. 7 reels.

MME. POMPADOUR (1927). Romantic drama of the court of Louis XV; as the King's mistress, Mme. Pompadour. *Dir:* Herbert Wilcox. *Sc:* Frances Marion (from a play by Rudolph Schanzer and Ernst Wellisch). *With* Antonio Moreno, Henry Bosc, Jeff McLaughlin, Nelson Keys, Cyril McLaglen, Marcel Beauplan, Marie Ault, Tom Reynolds. *Prod:* Paramount. 7 reels. (Compare listing in Antonio Moreno filmography.)

WANTED MEN (AKA, GB, *Wolves*) (1936, USA: 1930, England). Melodrama; as Leila McDonald, a girl held prisoner in a whaling camp. *Dir:* Herbert Wilcox. *Sc:* Reginald Berkeley (from a play by Georges Toudouze). *With* Charles Laughton, Malcolm Keen, Jack Ostermann, Arthur Margetson, Franklyn Bellamy, Griffith Humphreys, Andrews Engelmann, Betty Boulton. *Prod:* British Dominion. 5140 ft. First English all-talkie (not a silent converted into a talkie); Dorothy Gish's debut in talking films.

OUR HEARTS WERE YOUNG AND GAY (1944). Romantic comedy; as Mrs. Otis Skinner. *Dir:* Lewis Allen. *Sc:* Sheridan Gibney (from the book by Cornelia Otis Skinner and Emily Kimbrough). *With* Gail Russell, Diana Lynn, Charles Ruggles, Beulah Bondi, James Brown, Bill Edwards, Jean Heather, Alma Kruger, Helen Freeman, George Renevant, Roland Varno, Holmes Herbert, Reginald Sheffield. *Prod:* Paramount. 81m.

CENTENNIAL SUMMER (1946). Romantic film musical about Philadelphia's 1876 Centennial Exposition; as Harriet Rogers. *Dir:* Otto Preminger. *Sc:* Michael Kanin (from the novel by Albert E. Idell). *With* Jeanne Crain, Linda Darnell, Constance Bennett, Cornel Wilde, William Eythe, Walter Brennan, Barbara Whiting, Larry Stevens, Kathleen Howard, Gavin Gordon, Reginald Sheffield. *Prod:* 20th Century-Fox. 10 reels.

THE WHISTLE AT EATON FALLS (AKA, GB, *Richer than the Earth*) (1951). Social drama; as Mrs. Doubleday, widow-owner of a New Hampshire plastics company. *Dir:* Robert Siodmak. *Sc:* Lemist Esler and Virginia Shaler (from an idea by J. Sterlin Livingston). *With* Lloyd Bridges, Carleton Carpenter, Murray Hamilton, James Westerfield, Russell Hardie, Lenore Lonergan, Doro Merande, Ernest Borgnine, Parker Fennelly, Diana Douglas, Arlene Francis, Anne Seymour, Joe Foley. *Prod:* Columbia. 96m.

THE CARDINAL (1964). Drama of the rise of a young Bostonian priest to Cardinal; as Celia Fermoyle, his devoted mother. *Dir:* Otto Preminger. *Sc:* Robert Dozier (from the novel by Henry Morton Robinson). *With* Tom Tryon, Carol Lynley, Maggie McNamara, John Saxon, John Huston, Robert Morse, Cecil Kellaway, Burgess Meredith, Jill Haworth, Raf Vallone, Tullio Carminati, Ossie Davis, Romy Schneider. (Sequences filmed in Rome and Vienna). *Prod:* Columbia. 175m.

5
FRANCES MARION

Of all the arts and crafts that contribute to the creation of a movie, screenwriting has been the least appreciated, and, except for occasional oratorical pats on the back, almost all of which include the phrase, "In the beginning was the Word," screenwriters have been unmentioned men — and women. Their contributions to particular films are usually underestimated, and their importance in film history has been almost totally suppressed.

One screenwriter whose place in motion picture history *is* beginning to be recognised is Frances Marion, who wrote the scenarios of some of Mary Pickford's major pictures and of such other important silents as Lillian Gish's *The Scarlet Letter* and *The Wind;* Valentino's *The Son of the Sheik;* "Photoplay's Best Pictures of the Year." *Humoresque* (1920) and *Abraham Lincoln* (1924); and the screenplays of such important sound films as Garbo's *Anna Christie* and *Camille;* Pickford's last picture, *Secrets;* Cukor's *Dinner at Eight;* and the Oscar-winning *The Big House* and *The Champ*.

In addition, she was the wife of one of the great Western stars — Fred Thomson — and theirs is one of the real love stories of Hollywood.

Frances Marion Owens was born in San Francisco on November 18, 1888, and was named after a — collaterally — paternal ancestor, the Revolutionary War general, Francis Marion, known as "The Swamp Fox." Her father, Len Douglas Owens, was a partner in an advertising firm which prospered by specialising in railroad, street railway, and other forms of outdoor advertising. At one time, he owned seven thousand acres of Napa Valley vineyards and farmland, exported wine, and owned several San Francisco warehouses. He had been born in Council Bluffs, Iowa, to which his father had emigrated from South Carolina when Iowa Territory was opened to settlers.

His wife, *née* Minnie Hall, was the daughter of a concert violinist (Charles R. Hall) and a coloratura soprano (Aimee Griswold Hall), and was herself an accomplished pianist who had been taught by one of Liszt's pupils. After her marriage, she entertained the foremost artists of the time, including Melba and Tetrazzini, whom she accompanied when they sang in her home. In addition to Frances, she had two other children — an older boy and a younger girl.

Frances Marion evinced an early talent for drawing, and when she was expelled from San Francisco's Hamilton Grammar School for caricaturing the teachers, her parents put her in St. Margaret's Hall, a fashionable private school in Burlingame, which prepared students for Bryn Mawr. In summertime she studied at the Mark Hopkins Art School. The San Francisco fire and earthquake of 1906 so crippled her father financially that instead of going East to Bryn Mawr, she entered the University of California at Berkeley.

Miss Marion's clearest memories of the earthquake and fire which destroyed a good part of San Francisco fix upon her concern for a new Easter bonnet she had worn for the first time the preceding Sunday. Says the Frances Marion of today:

"For a long time I'd had my eye on a very handsome art student and teacher named Wesley DeLappé. He hadn't known I was alive until that Easter bonnet caught his eye. I hung on to that hat through quake and fire because I needed it to further my conquest of young Mr. DeLappé. It worked. He soon suggested that we elope, and we did! I wasn't yet seventeen, and he was only nineteen.

"His parents and mine objected, but we paid no attention to their protests. I dropped out of the University at Berkeley, and we lived in a ramshackle studio on Russian Hill. Our romance was youthfully ardent and very *La Bohème*. When our paths first crossed, he was the youngest instructor the Mark Hopkins Art School had ever had. He had far greater talent as an artist than I, but wasn't half so ambitious. We were both temperamental and high-spirited. Our marriage lasted less than two years."

Although she wasn't yet nineteen at the time she divorced, she thought it too late to return to college and took a cub reporter job on the "San Francisco Examiner." "I was not a good reporter," Miss Marion says. "Adela Rogers St. Johns, a close friend since our teens, said I was too soft, too chicken-hearted, and she was right. When I was assigned hot leads, I blew them because I felt sorry for the culprits. The rival papers got the scoops, and I got the gate."

She thereupon turned to commerical art and illustrated advertisements for the Western Pacific Railway Company and Baker's Chocolate. For the latter, she also posed for some of its advertising. She also illustrated verses of her own composition which she sold to "Sunset Magazine," which led to writing stories for the Pacific Coast publication. She had been introduced there by Ella Wheeler Wilcox, whose early encouragement was of great importance in the Frances Marion career.

And posing for advertisements for Baker's Chocolate led to her becoming a model for Arnold Genthe, one of America's great photographers.

"When I began posing for Genthe," Miss Marion says, "my first marriage was just coming to an end. In exchange for my modelling, Mr. Genthe instructed me in psychology and philosophy. The two models he used for the photographs which won him international prizes were myself and a girl named Hazel Tharsing. Hazel was just out of a convent and as pure as a lily, but Genthe saw her as a gypsy with flashing eyes and a rose between her teeth. He posed me, then known as "The Wild Rose of Telegraph Hill," in the robes of one of the saints. Both Hazel and I changed our names shortly thereafter. Marion DeLappé became Frances Marion again, and Hazel Tharsing took the name of Carlotta Monterey. Years later she became Mrs. Eugene O'Neill."

Genthe says in his autobiography ("As I Remember"): "And there was little Marion Owens with her extraordinary blue eyes and chestnut-colored hair. She had come to me with a letter from Dr. Millicent Cosgrove, asking me

to try to find some work for her, since her family had lost everything in the fire. I was looking for someone to help me in the studio and she fitted very nicely. Today, under the pen name of Frances Marion, she is one of Hollywood's most successful scenario writers, and a novelist and short story writer besides.''

Frances Marion was only twenty when she married Robert Pike, a man of good family name years older than she. ''The failure of my second marriage was entirely my fault,'' she admits. ''Robert was a fine man, but conservative. He felt uneasy with my artist and writer friends, and wanted us to live a formal mid-Victorian existence. I didn't give a hoot about Nob Hill, but was immensely concerned with what Frank Norris, Jack London, and the poet George Sterling, and our California painters were achieving.* Such differences in our social instincts did not promise contentment, and we parted.''

She again resumed the name of Frances Marion, and returned to commercial art. Luckily, Oliver Morosco was visiting San Francisco, saw her posters, and offered her a job painting portraits, for reproduction on posters, of the players and visiting stars who appeared weekly with his stock company in Los Angeles.

Her first assignment — in Los Angeles — was Laurette Taylor in ''Peg o' My Heart.'' ''I loved Laurette Taylor,'' Miss Marion says. ''I hated Peg o' My Heart.' but nobody could say a word against 'Peg,' because Miss Taylor's husband, J. Hartley Manners, whom she adored, had written it for her. It was all an ordeal, but I gritted my teeth, and drew a portrait about which everybody was enthusiastic, and so I survived.''

Subsequently, Miss Marion drew portraits of Hazel Dawn, Charlotte Greenwood, Elsie Janis, Kitty Gordon, Bert Lytell, as well as all the fine actors who then made up Morosco's regular stock list, e.g., Lewis Stone, Warner Baxter, Jimmy Gleason, Bob Leonard, Richard Dix, Edmund Lowe.

She later came to know all these players intimately. She wrote special screen stories for Elsie Janis, Kitty Gordon, and Lewis Stone, and at least four important scripts for Bob Leonard, who became director Robert Z. Leonard. She and Leonard were the best of friends, and Miss Marion was sympathetic when Leonard married the temperamental Mae Murray, delighted when he later divorced and married actress Gertrude Olmstead. The three remained close friends until Leonard's death in August 1968. His widow and Miss Marion are still friends.

''I drew many posters of Bert Lytell,'' Miss Marion says, ''both up in San Francisco when he was playing at the Alcazar and then when he was starring in Los Angeles for Morosco. When he married Claire Windsor, I thought they made a handsome couple. Claire may not know this, but I gave her that name when she first came to Hollywood, a beautiful young girl from Kansas named Olga Kronk. Lois Weber asked me to think of a name to fit her. I suggested ''Claire'' because she was a natural blonde with delicate features and light complexion, and ''Windsor'' because she suggested aristocracy.''

Miss Marion had arrived in Los Angeles in 1913, and soon became one of a group which dined, as often as its finances permitted, in Levy's Restaurant, to discuss the future of motion pictures — and themselves.

*The canvasses Miss Marion painted during her second marriage were signed ''Marion Pike,'' and she takes special pride in the art work of another Marion Pike, a niece by marriage and now one of California's foremost painters.

FRANCES MARION

"Among us were Adela Rogers, soon to marry Ivan St. Johns, who saw nothing but the greatest future for the movies; Vienna-born Erich von Stroheim, who worked as a rower of boats on Lake Tahoe the summer before he came down to Hollywood and got a bit in D. W. Griffith's *The Birth of a Nation;* handsome Frank Borzage, who was already playing supporting roles for Thomas Ince; and those two beautiful Japanese, Sessue Hayakawa and his *fiancée,* Tsuru Aoki.

"When Ince produced a story called *The Geisha,* Borzage was given the romantic lead and he was instrumental in getting the role of the Japanese heroine for Tsuru. All of us went out to Inceville one day to see the film being shot. I was thrilled and began to wonder how I could fit into movie-making."

When Oliver Morosco could no longer ignore the fact that money was being made in movies and set up his own film company, Miss Marion became convinced "the camera was my passport to a modern Xanadu."

Through Adela Rogers St. Johns, she wangled a personal introduction to Lois Weber,* who was then directing a film for Bosworth. Of Lois Weber, Miss Marion says: "She was a gifted and very generous woman. Buxom and well-corseted, she sailed into her office, where I was waiting that afternoon, and favored me with a gracious smile. She looked at my drawings as I told her how much I wanted to design costumes and sets in a movie studio. Then we talked, and to my joy she said she'd take me on as a *protégée.*

"Working at the Bosworth studios was Sidney Franklin, who had come down from San Francisco, a restless soul like myself, in search of new adventures. He had tremendous faith in the future of movies, a faith that was justified when he became one of the foremost directors and producers in the industry, with such credits to his name as *The Guardsman* and *The Barretts of Wimpole Street,* and many other great films. When Lois Weber gave me the green light, I did exactly what Sidney was doing: started to learn every phase of the picture business. We played extra bits, worked in the cutting-room, read scripts and dared suggest changes, and even hauled furniture around to make the sets more attractive. No one would have been surprised to see us sweeping the floor."

In her autobiography, "So Far, So Good," Elsie Janis, then filming several features for Bosworth, recalls her first meeting with Frances Marion: "There was a pretty blue-eyed girl very much in evidence around the studio. It was difficult to find what her job was, for she did a little of everything. She played in the picture one week, helped 'cut' the next, wrote a story the next, and in her spare moments handled the publicity. I told Mr. Garbutt (Frank Garbutt, production head of Bosworth, Inc.) that she would be heard from some day.

---

*Pittsburgh-born Lois Weber had trained to be a concert pianist, but an uncle persuaded her to become a musical-comedy leading lady at his Chicago Theatre, and it was there she met and married actor Phillips Smalley. They entered films in New York City as a team — co-producing, directing, writing, acting — for Kessel and Bauman's New York Motion Picture Co., and later for Rex. After they went to California, Miss Weber continued, on a constantly expanding scale, to win recognition, both with her husband and alone, in those four branches of film-making.

She was the first American woman to win really top acclaim as a film director, did much to further the careers of actresses Mary MacLaren, Mildred Harris, Claire Windsor and Billie Dove, and was an important director throughout most of the silent period. Her best and most representative films were two Billie Dove vehicles released by Universal — *The Marriage Clause* (1926) and *The Sensation Seekers* (1927). Although she had no directorial success in talking pictures, her husband enjoyed a run as a successful actor into the Thirties. Sometime after his death, she remarried, and, continuing to live on a scale no longer within her means, died destitute. Frances Marion paid the funeral expenses.

MORE FROM HOLLYWOOD

The last time I heard from her she had just signed a new contract for $3,500 a week and had written scenario, continuity and dialogue for three of the biggest pictures of 1931. Her name was, and (though she has had several others, due to a weakness for 'marrying the man') still is, Frances Marion!''

It was at Bosworth that Miss Marion met Owen Moore and through him that she met his wife, Mary Pickford. He was leading man to Elsie Janis, and he suggested that his wife might be interested in Miss Marion's painting her portrait, although, he confessed, she was not what he thought of as a real actress. ''That,'' says Miss Marion, ''I put down to professional jealousy. Right from the beginning, Mary and I became the best of friends. We still are.''

When Lois Weber signed a new contract and went to Universal, Miss Pickford got in touch with Frances Marion about playing the second lead in her new picture, which she had also written, *A Girl of Yesterday*. ''It was a modern vampish role,'' explains Miss Marion, ''and I accepted, first because I had a story for Mary in mind and wanted to stay close to her so I could present it when the moment was right, and second because the idea of my playing a vamp struck my sense of humour. Allan Dwan directed, and, besides Mary, her brother Jack was in the cast, along with Gertrude Norman, Donald Crisp, Marshall Neilan, and a young aviator who became one of America's foremost plane builders, Glenn L. Martin.''

Miss Marion wrote her first original scenario for Mary Pickford. It was titled *The Foundling* and as soon as its filming was finished, Miss Pickford entrained for New York to attend its *première*.

''Mary wanted me to come East too, because she thought it might be good for me to be on the spot with a hit to my credit,'' Miss Marion says. ''But I didn't have the money for such a gamble, much as I wanted to go. I saw Mary off at the depot, and that very day I got a break: I was asked if I would be interested in playing leading lady to Monte Blue in a Western that was ready to go into production. Much as I disliked acting, I seized the chance, for it guaranteed me enough money to make the trip East. Two weeks later, the shooting finished, I wired Mary I was coming and was on a train headed for New York. I didn't have a lot of money, and was counting on making a deal with the boys in the New York office. I went directly from Grand Central to the Algonquin, and then took a cab over to the Riverside Drive apartment where Mary was staying. She received me with a tearful embrace.

.'''Oh, Frances, you don't know!' she exclaimed. 'A terrible thing has happened! The negative and all the prints of *The Foundling* have been destroyed in a studio fire!'

''My high hopes went crashing, but I was not going back to Hollywood. Not right away. Nor was I going to be stranded and starving in New York. I checked out of the Algonquin and into a less expensive hotel. Then I sat down and wrote an identical letter to the heads of all major studios in the city. I cited the name of Lois Weber, and played up — *big* – Mary Pickford and *The Foundling*. For two weeks, I said, I would write scenarios for absolutely nothing. If at the end of that time, my services were acceptable, I wanted $200 a week.

''William Fox was the first to reply. He had had a great success that year with Theda Bara's *A Fool There Was,* the film which made his studio possible. He admitted he was searching desperately for properties to fit Miss Bara's

96

vamp personality. But he didn't think any writer was worth $200 a week and he offered me $150. I thanked him politely, said I'd think it over and let him know, and left. I'm glad I did, because there was another reply awaiting me at my hotel. William A. Brady, head of the World Company, wanted to see me.

Brady and I got along fine. He parried at first, but when he found out that I had been born in San Francisco, which was also his home-town, I could see I was in. Brady never could resist a gamble, thank heaven, and he had a weakness for sponsoring other San Franciscans.

"He said I could start right away. I asked if I could have an office, any little cubby-hole, but he said there were no rooms for writers in the studio. I asked for a story to adapt, and he said all the stories World had bought were already assigned and told me to write something original.

"I tried, but after several days, panic set in. I went to the studio and, for want of anything else to do, watched the film editor at work. Cutting a film had always fascinated me, and I was already aware that a good editor can make even a mediocre film seem important. There were some tins of films on a shelf which, I was told, were all bad. I asked to see some of them, hoping I'd get an idea and be able to salvage the film.

"That's exactly what happened. One picture, the worst of the lot, starr3d Brady's talented daughter Alice, and I suggested shooting a prologue and epilogue which would give an entirely new meaning to the body of the story itself.

"Mr. Brady was delighted, and put me on salary. I was so relieved that I wrote a story, "The Fisher-Girl," and sold it to a magazine. World bought it for their new star, Muriel Ostriche, re-titling it *A Daughter of the Sea.*"

Meantime, Famous Players had salvaged some of *The Foundling,* but re-shot most of the picture in the East, even changing some of the cast members. It opened in New York City in January 1916.

Fox also bought one of Miss Marion's published stories, "The Iron Man," and filmed it as *The Battle of Hearts,* starring William Farnum. His leading lady, then known as Elda Furry, was to have a career of her own as Hedda Hopper, and became one of Miss Marion's closest friends.

The amount of work Frances Marion did at World during the next twenty-four months is staggering. There is scarely a Brady release of that time in which she was not involved, and the scenarios she wrote are some of the best of 1916-17. Some were adaptations of such well-known literary properties as "Camille" and "La vie de Bohème"; some were adaptations of currently popular plays — e.g., the French "Frou-Frou" (which became *The Hungry Heart);* George Broadhurst's "Bought and Paid For"; and Leo Ditrichstein's "Mlle. Fifi" (which became *The Divorce Game).*

The number of *original* scenarios she wrote compels admiration, not only for their quantity, but also for the quality of their cinematic dramatisation. Her scenarios *moved* when they were acted for the camera, and required a minimum of sub-titles (Miss Marion usually wrote her own). At least nine original scenarios are credited to her in the two years she spent at World, and all nine were successful programme fare.

Clara Kimball Young was the first star for whom Miss Marion wrote at World, and the version of *Camille* that she prepared helped make Miss Young a bigger box-office attraction. Other Marion scenarios were for Ethel Clayton, Kitty Gordon, Gail Kane, June Elvidge, Robert Warwick, Carlyle

Blackwell, and the actress she cherished most, who remained a good friend until her death, Alice Brady.

"There are few actresses comparable to Alice," says Miss Marion. "She could play anything, tears or laughter, modern or period, young or old, and make it believable. And she was so much fun to be with! A very real woman with a very big heart. She was terribly near-sighted and in those days when she was young — we were all young then — I'd go with her to parties, and as we entered, she'd look around with those beautiful dark eyes and say,'Frances, is there anybody here I already know?'"

It was at World that Miss Marion first met Doris Kenyon, just beginning her film career, and Milton Sills, and there that she renewed her friendship with Marie Dressler. She had first met Miss Dressler in San Francisco when her own spirits were at a low ebb, and the comedienne had mothered her until she emerged from a dark time. Miss Dressler had contracted to make a programmer for World which was eventually released as *Tillie Wakes Up*. Frances Marion developed what amounted to an original scenario for her.

William Brady keenly appreciated Miss Marion's work and called her his story editor. He had a penchant for buying screen rights to big stage successes, and believed a sound piece of theatre could *always* be adapted to the screen. When rival producers complained of the prices he paid for movie rights, he replied that "no price is too high when it comes to a story." He was proud of his production of *La vie de Bohème* and arranged a private showing of it for members of the Metropolitan Opera Company.

When Mary Pickford had had two flops in a row at Famous Players — *Less Than the Dust* and *Pride of the Clan* — she came East and talked Frances Marion into leaving her comfortable berth at World and writing the scenario for the next Pickford film, which was to be an adaptation of Eleanor Gates's successful play, "Poor Little Rich Girl." Maurice Tourneur directed, and Miss Pickford acknowledges in her autobiography, "Sunshine and Shadow," that she and Miss Marion gave him a bad time by inventing on set impromptu scenes. Tourneur kept protesting: "My dear young ladies, it has nothing to do with the picture. It is not in the play. I do not find it in the script. *Mais non! C'est un horreur!*"

When *A Poor Little Rich Girl* opened, it was called a classic. Mary Pickford's work was praised without reservation, and so were Tourneur's direction and Miss Marion's scenario.

Miss Pickford then made two films directed by Cecil B. DeMille: *Romance of the Redwoods* and *The Little American*. The first restored to the screen the Mary her fans loved; the second, a patriotic melodrama played with all stops out, added sex to the Pickford image (she is nearly raped in one scene).

While Miss Pickford was so engaged, Miss Marion was assigned to write a scenario, from the Pinero play called "The Amazons," in which Adolph Zukor starred Marguerite Clark, the only rival Mary Pickford ever acknowledged. It's one of Miss Clark's most charming portrayals, and she often spoke of her pleasure in filming it.

Jesse L. Lasky, who realised how important the next Pickford films would be both for the studio and Miss Pickford, announced on May 10, 1917, that Frances Marion had been signed to write exclusively for Paramount and that

FRANCES MARION

her first assignment would be the Artcraft production of Mary Pickford's *Rebecca of Sunnybrook Farm*.

Frances Marion had become a woman of undeniable importance in Hollywood, and it is interesting to read an interview she gave a few months later.

The October 20, 1917 issue of "Dramatic Mirror" reports her saying: "The scenario of today is vastly different from the scenario of five, three, or even a

Mary Pickford and Josephine Crowell in *Rebecca of Sunnybrook Farm,* scenario by Frances Marion.

year ago. In fact, it has changed considerably within the last six months, and we no longer have to do our pictures in words of one syllable. The movie audience has developed so fast we can write more and more intricate stories.''

Rebecca of Sunnybrook Farm is one of the most beloved of all Pickford films, and for many the most beloved. Miss Marion also wrote Miss Pickford's next four pictures, which were beautifully directed by Marshall Neilan. I find it difficult to choose a favourite from such a quintet as *Rebecca of Sunnybrook Farm, A Little Princess, Stella Maris, Amarilly of Clothes-line Alley,* and *M'liss*.

Between her Pickford assignments, Miss Marion also turned out other scripts — an adaptation for Douglas Fairbanks *(He Comes Up Smiling);* two originals for Sessue Hayakawa *(City of Dim Faces* and *Temple of Dusk);* and an original comedy about movie-studio life for Fred Stone *(The Goat)*.

Then, as the First World War came to an end. Mary Roberts Rinehart suggested to the U.S. Army that Miss Marion be hired to observe and report on the plight of women and children in the countries the Allies were occupying.

It was in France that she re-met Fred Thomson, an ordnance officer and chaplain of the 143rd Field Artillery. Their first meeting occurred in Southern California when Thomson, who had broken a leg playing football with his outfit, was hospitalised at Camp Kearney, and Mary Pickford, an honorary colonel of the 143rd, had taken Miss Marion with her on a visit there. Both were especially gracious to Thomson.

He had been born in Pasadena, California, and was the son of a Presbyterian minister. He had distinguished himself at Occidental College both as a student and athlete, and after graduating there went to Princeton to study for the ministry. At Princeton he won the national all-around athlete championship in 1910, 1911, and 1913. After Miss Marion's visit to Camp Kearney, they saw one another as often as possilble until he was shipped overseas with his regiment.

When Miss Marion turned up in France, he was one of the first to welcome her. Tall and handsome, with wavy, chestnut-coloured hair, and very blue eyes, he had always been attractive to women. But he had eyes only for Frances Marion.

''Fred and I were very much in love,'' says Miss Marion. ''But he was the son of a Presbyterian minister, was himself ordained, and planned to follow in his father's footsteps. If he married me, a twice-divorced woman, as he wanted to, it would mean the end of his very promising career in his church.

''I belong to no established faith — I never have — and the members of my family are not church-goers, but they are strict adherents to the Golden Rule. I felt I could not selfishly ruin a career the man I loved cherished. For the first time I bitterly regretted my two marital indiscretions. Only, they really hadn't been that; they were both more like youthful experimentations.

''I returned to the United States and after officially filing my Special Service report in Washington, threw myself into film-writing in the East — *The Misleading Widow* for Billie Burke and *Anne of Green Gables,* Mary Miles Minter's first at Realart on her new million dollar contract. I think I had the most fun with a scenario I wrote for Elsie Janis. She, too, had just returned from overseas, and Lewis J. Selznick had asked her to make a movie for him, for $5,000 a week plus the privilege of choosing her own story.''

FRANCES MARION

Says Miss Janis in her autobiography: "I not only chose the story, I wrote it, and Frances Marion (you remember the little girl I said would be heard from at the Bosworth studio?) adapted it for the screen, adding the invaluable touches which make her the highest paid scenario writer of the present day! It was called *The Regular Girl*, and the story was about a society girl who had been a nurse in France and, unable upon her return to take up her old life, went down and worked as a maid-of-all-work (Well! Almost all work!) in a boarding-house where a crowd of ex-service men lived.

"Frances, who had been overseas, felt as I did about the War, and so between us we put everything in the picture but a de-lousing station. We had great fun. Practically every man in the cast was ex-service, and for the hospital scenes we had the real thing, mostly fellows who had seen me in France. What a party! The director, James Young, had to grab me out of 'sing songs' and crap games when he wanted me for a scene!"

By 1920, the year she adapted *Pollyanna* for Miss Pickford, Miss Marion was considered Hollywood's most versatile screenwriter. She herself hates *Pollyanna*, and so does Miss Pickford. It was the first Pickford release for the newly incorporated United Artists, and its grosses put UA on a sound financial basis.

It has frequently been said — especially after W. A. Swanberg's biography, "Citizen Hearst" — that Frances Marion's rise to fame was accelerated because she was the *secret* story editor for Hearst's Cosmopolitan Pictures. She denies it, and says, "I did write scenarios for Cosmopolitan, including some of Marion Davies's early films — *The Cinema Murder* and *The Restless Sex*. I was proudest of having done the scenario for Fannie Hurst's *Humoresque*, and I liked doing *The World and His Wife* for my good friend, Bob Vignola. For *Humoresque*, I urged that Frank Borzage be given the director's job. It was Frank's first truly important directorial assignment, and he went on to be one of the tops, as I always knew he would. He had that unique and enviable combination in a director: good taste and the ability to play on the heartstrings.

"I think the rumour that I was the story power behind Mr. Hearst's company started because I once told him to be sure and see the play, "Little Old New York." I had gone to its opening and thought he should buy it for Marion [Davies]. After seeing it, he thought so too, and purchased it. That picture established her as a comedienne. Afterwards, I was told I could have my pick of any Cosmopolitan property, and did. That's all! Secret story editor I was not!"

Meanwhile, Fred Thomson had been taking part in the Inter-Allied Games held in Paris shortly after the Armistice, and once again had proved himself a top athlete by winning the decathlon event and France's gold medal for grenade-throwing. On his return to the United States, he resumed pleading his cause with Miss Marion. Finally, very quietly, they were married in New York City — Mary Pickford was matron of honour — and sailed for a European honeymoon. Seeing them off at the boat, Hedda Hopper asked Miss Marion why she had relented and married Thomson. Replied Miss Marion with a wry smile: "I couldn't get him any other way."

About a month later, the Thomsons were joined in Europe by Mary Pickford and Douglas Fairbanks, who had just married.

Not long after the Thomsons' return to America, they heard that a magnificent grey outlaw stallion was for sale in New England, and went to see it. The minute Fred Thomson laid eyes upon the animal, Miss Marion says, he decided to buy it and even gave it the name ''Silver King.'' As they came away, he talked of nothing but producing outdoor action movies starring ''Silver King.''

Says Miss Marion: ''At this time I had adapted another Fannie Hurst story, 'Just Around the Corner,' and Mr. Hearst gave me the chance to direct it. I cast it, and we went up-State, where it was snowing, on location. An actor who was supposed to have reported for an important supporting role, sent word that he was ill and would have to be replaced. The rest of the cast goaded Fred into stepping into the part, and, rather than hold up production, he consented.

''If I had any qualms, they were instantly dispelled as soon as I saw the rushes. I knew then I'd married an actor. Was there ever a confirmed preacher who wasn't also a confirmed actor? Mr. Hearst also praised Fred, but as for continuing his acting career, Fred couldn't have been less interested. He was still trying to set up a production company to make films starring 'Silver King.'

''Meanwhile, I had written a story for Mary Pickford called 'The Love Light.' She liked it so much she not only bought it but asked me to direct her in it. This was a challenge in more ways than one. Mary had never been directed by a woman, and my story offered her a highly dramatic role where she, a simple Italian peasant girl, learns that the man she has saved from the sea, fallen in love with, and married, is a German spy. Torn between love for him and loyalty to her country, she exposes him and he is shot.

''The picture was ready to go into production, but we hadn't yet been able to find the right actor for the German. An actor named Raymond Bloomer, who had been selected to play the real heroic lead, one day turned to Fred and said, 'Why don't you play the German?' Fred treated it as a big joke, but Bloomer persisted, and when Mary and I took up the idea, Fred gave up and played the part. He still wasn't considering himself as an actor, however, although there were those in Hollywood who were.

''Especially Maurice B. Flynn, known to all of us as 'Lefty.' He was a New Yorker who had played football for Yale when Fred was at Princeton, and they had become close friends. After graduating from Yale, 'Lefty' was a rancher in Colorado, but after a stint in the First World War, he decided to try acting in Hollywood. He was lean and tall, about six feet four, and had a most engaging smile. In the Twenties, he was in about fifty features, and played leads opposite Pauline Frederick, Jacqueline Logan, Alice Brady, Dorothy Dalton, Mary Miles Minter, and the star he married in 1925, Viola Dana. Until they divorced in the Thirties, they were one of Hollywood's most popular couples. 'Lefty' died in 1959.

''When 'Lefty' urged Fred to play a villainous rumrunner in a picture Dustin Farnum was about to start called *Oath-Bound,* and Farnum enthusiastically seconded the idea, Fred capitulated.

''Then Universal offered to star him as the hero of a 15-episode serial, *The Eagle's Talons.* It was Joe Kennedy who pointed out to Fred that unwittingly, *by acting,* he had already learned a great deal about the camera and could do good on a bigger scale as an actor than he ever could do as a minister. Joe said the serial was good exposure and that Universal's salary offer was excellent. Meanwhile, Joe and I planned a series of Westerns starring Fred with 'Silver King' that would be released through Joe's company (FBO). When Fred protested that wasn't the way he wanted it, Joe pointed out that a horse can't be starred by itself — a man's got to ride it and guide its tricks and stunts.

"'And you're the only man who can ride 'Silver King,'' Joe added. 'You're stuck, Fred, if you want to make 'Silver King' a big star!'

"And that, so help me, is the true story of how my husband became a movie hero."

Starting with *The Mask of Lopez* (1923), the Fred Thomson pictures were better-than-average Westerns, and very profitable. They were family films, rich in folk humour, and expensive in production detail. Nothing in a Fred Thomson movie ever glorified villainy or violence, and their outdoor action and first-class stunt work* were always on the side of life. More than one critic noted that nobody would know from Thomson's Jesse James that James had been a notorious killer and outlaw (he was shown holding up a stagecoach only once, and did that for a Robin Hood motive). "Silver King" and Fred Thomson were idolised as much as Tom Mix and "Tony," and in no time at all Thomson was making $10,000 a week.

Frances Marion contributed more than a little to her husband's scenarios, although most of them were credited to Marion Jackson, a charming little lady from Walla-Walla who had established herself as a dependable screenwriter. "I didn't want to go on record as the writer of my husband's scripts," Miss Marion says. "Neither Fred nor I thought it wise professionally. Besides, there were times when I couldn't legally write Fred's stories — when I was under exclusive contract elsewhere. Our friends around the lot, however, would look at me knowingly, and say, 'Aw, come on, Mrs. T! Fred's pictures are just too darn well-written. We know you're moonlighting.' I would affect a nice show of surprise, grin, and say: 'Well boys, you can't stop pillow conferences, can you? If a man and his wife want to talk story all night long, who's to stop them?'

"I wanted no story credit for Fred's pictures, however, and I took none. We had a deal with Marion Jackson: she got the credit and the cash. There were times, I will admit, when she was so busy with the current script she had no time for the subsequent scenario, and I'd stay up half the night writing it under a nom de plume. You'll find all sorts of men's names listed as Fred's writers. 'Frank M. Clifton' was one I remember, and he's nobody else but me. Some other pen-names Fred and I thought up were dillies. The main point is — the only credit I really want is for my work as Frances Marion."

And she was very busy, in those days, as Frances Marion. After writing two charming comedies for Constance Talmadge, she worked for Norma Talmadge's unit and wrote seven of her biggest hits. And when director Chester M. Franklin started *Song of Love,* which Miss Marion had adapted, and became ill, it was Miss Marion who replaced him as director, and brought the picture in on schedule and budget.

She then wrote an original scenario for *The Toll of the Sea,* the second

---

*Before he himself played film roles, Thomson had often doubled for well-established he-man stars, and performed even difficult stunts with ease.

all-Technicolor feature-length film. It's a Madame Butterfly story, with Anna May Wong as the unhappy heroine.

Miss Marion is sincerely proud of *Abraham Lincoln,* which "Photoplay's" readers picked as 1924's best film. "Financially," she admits, "it did almost nothing. I believed in it so much that I accepted a percentage of the profits in lieu of salary — and there were no profits."

Three years before the birth of their sons — Fred Clifton Thomson Jr. (1926) and Richard Gordon Thomson (1927) — the Thomsons bought a hilltop site overlooking Beverly Hills and on its twenty-four acres constructed a twenty-room home they named "The Enchanted Hill." In addition to the main house there were separate servants' quarters, swimming-pool, tennis courts, and a stable for "Silver King" that had mahogany floors. Furthermore, Thomson was buying a line of beautiful gray horses and to house them he purchased ten thousand acres in that part of San Fernando Valley now known as Chatsworth.

By that time Miss Marion had become Samuel Goldwyn's favourite screenwriter. *Cytherea, Tarnish, A Thief in Paradise, The Dark Angel, His Supreme Moment,* all directed by George Fitzmaurice, and *Stella Dallas,* directed by Henry King, are merely some of the Goldwyn achievements she wrote.

She considers Goldwyn her all time favourite producer, and says: "Sam has taste and integrity. There is never any pretence about him. He has always worked harder than any one he ever hired, and his appreciation for a job well done is always immense and completely genuine."

Said Goldwyn of Miss Marion when (January 1926) he signed her to an exclusive contract with Samuel Goldwyn Productions: "The work accomplished from Miss Marion's scenarios is so directly to the point, whether of comedy, dramatic or novelty values, that I feel we have solved one of the great problems of film production by securing her uninterrupted association."

In her autobiography, "From Under My Hat," Hedda Hopper tells how Miss Marion, who always had an eye for potential stars, especially of the male gender, was responsible for bringing Gary Cooper to the attention of Goldwyn and Henry King. Cooper was given the second most important male role in *The Winning of Barbara Worth,* instead of a mere bit, because of the awareness of Miss Marion, who had written the scenario. After seeing the daily rushes, she advised Goldwyn not only to promote Cooper but to put him under personal contract. Goldwyn admits this, but, for reasons which are still obscure, he didn't make an immediate contract offer, and when he did, the salary he offered wasn't particularly enticing.

"It's the only time I ever knew Sam to hesitate too long and then offer too little," says Miss Marion. "When Paramount countered with a better contract and more money, Cooper naturally signed with them. Sam was chagrined and still doesn't like to talk about it. He used Cooper often in later years, borrowing him when he had to or signing him for a single film. And never once did he begrudge Cooper the enormous salary he had to pay him.

"When my contract was running out, Sam quickly raised my weekly salary to $3,000. He knew, he said, that M-G-M was angling to sign me as soon as I was free, and, if I signed with them they'd now be required to start me at least at $3,000. They started me at $3,500. Sam and I regretted parting, but Sam knew a long-term contract at M-G-M was to my advantage."

Lillian Gish and Lars Hanson in *The Wind,* screenplay by Frances Marion.

Before signing with M-G-M, Miss Marion adapted *Son of the Sheik* for Valentino and in doing so virtually discarded the original novel. When Valentino died, United Artists was left with a film that had played in only a few major cities in the United States. Joseph Schenck decided to issue it immediately on a saturation booking which included *all foreign outlets*. It was an unprecedented move, and it produced a financial bonanza. Always before, when death claimed the star of an unreleased film, distribution was sloughed off in the belief that the public found the films of recently deceased stars distasteful. Everybody wanted to see *Son of the Sheik.*

As soon as Miss Marion was installed at M-G-M, she decided to do something for her old friend and benefactress, Marie Dressler, whose career had hit rock bottom. Allan Dwan had given Miss Dressler a character part in an Olive Borden film shot in Florida, *The Joy Girl,* but no jobs had been offered her after that, and she was thinking of opening a *trattoria* in Rome that specialised

105

in American hamburgers. She also had a legitimate offer to go to work as housekeeper-cook for a wealthy Long Island family.

In the course of adapting Kathleen Norris's *The Callahans and the Murphys,* Miss Marion persuaded Irving Thalberg to have Marie Dressler and Polly Moran. It also so aroused the ire of Hibernian societies that M-G-M withdrew it shortly after its release, and for a while Miss Dressler's spirits sank again. But Miss Marion persuaded her to linger on in Hollywood and accept supporting roles.

Miss Marion was then at the peak of her career. Every scenario she devised for M-G-M became a money-maker, whether an adaptation of a comic strip (*Bringing Up Father*) the Garbo-Gilbert *Love* (adapted from Tolstoi's "Anna Karenina"), or Lillian Gish's version of Hawthorne's "The Scarlet Letter."

Her reputation in Hollywood was then so great that when it became known she was going to Europe for her vacation (summer of 1928), Joseph Schenck asked her to drop by Salzburg and give him an objective opinion of the story Max Reinhardt was planning to film with Lillian Gish. Fred Thomson was getting ready to shoot *Jesse James* and couldn't go with her, and she sailed for Europe accompanied by her favourite niece and Hedda Hopper.

Reinhardt's story had been outlined by Hugo von Hoffmanstal and was based on the history of a contemporary peasant girl, Theresa Neumann, who had suffered the stigmata of the Holy Cross on her hands.

"I was appalled," Miss Marion confesses. "Reinhardt, von Hoffmanstal, and all their *confrères* had sold Lillian an idea that could never be filmed. Lillian looked enchantingly lovely and spiritual, with her hair down to her waist and pearls intertwined throughout its length. I hated doing it, but I had to send back a very negative report on the venture to Joe Schenck."

It was in the summer of 1928 that Warners released their first all-talkie, *Lights of New York,* but when Miss Marion returned to Hollywood, and to "The Enchanted Hill," the talkies were not yet the ominous cloud they soon became. Even Louella O. Parsons had predicted they were a fad and would never last.

The cup of the Thomsons seemed filled to the brim: two fine sons, good health, fabulous incomes, successful careers, and love. A week before Christmas of 1928, however, Fred Thomson, who had never been ill a day in his life, realised something was the matter internally, and entered the Queen of Angels Hospital. Doctors thought at first he was suffering from gallstones, and operated, but he did not rally. When, the day before Christmas, it was discovered that ten days before entering the hospital he had stepped on a rusty nail and never done anything about it, blood transfusions were ordered.

Christmas Day was a nightmare. Len Douglas Owens Jr., Miss Marion's brother, was with her at the Queen of Angels, and so were Marie Dressler, Hedda Hopper, Thomson's brother and his wife.

Shortly before midnight, Fred Thomson died — of tetanus.

His death altered not only the pattern of Frances Marion's life but the heart of her self-confidence. Transformed, in a few weeks, from a happily married career woman into a widow with two small sons to raise, she sometimes wondered if she had any career as a writer left.

She asked Hedda Hopper to find a buyer for "The Enchanted Hill," which had been placed solely in her name and was not part of Thomson's estate, and accepted Marion Davies's invitation to rest at San Simeon. To everybody's

surprise, including Miss Marion's own, Hedda Hopper found William Barnes, who paid $450,000 in cash for the hilltop property and home (Hopper's commission: $10,000).

The entire Thomson estate, which consisted chiefly of the Chatsworth ranch and Thomson's production company, had, in the economically desperate winter of 1929-30, more liabilities than assets. "Silver King" was taken and cared for by Fred Thomson's brother, professor of ancient history Harrison Thomson, and Thomson's other horses were sold. After everything was settled, Miss Marion put into annuities what remained from "The Enchanted Hill." "If I hadn't," she says, "I'd probably be living in the Motion Picture Country Home — if I could get in there."

She then rented the Beverly Hills home Florence Vidor and Jascha Heifetz had lived in right after their marriage, and let it be known she was ready to go back to work.

The talkies' advent had obliged the studios to re-negotiate, or liquidate, the contracts of writers as well as the contracts of players, directors, *et al,* but Miss Marion had a friend at court: Irving Thalberg. He respected not only her screenwriting ability but her advice on production problems, and in time he came to depend on her judgement of every script he produced. Miss Marion thought Thalberg second only to Samuel Goldwyn in what a film producer should be.

Her opinion of Louis B. Mayer was quite different. She had first worked for Mayer early in 1922, when he had his own company, and engaged her to adapt a popular post-war play, "The Famous Mrs. Fair." According to Bosley Crowther's "Hollywood Rajah," Mayer, at his first meeting with Miss Marion, indicated the silver-framed photographs of his wife and two daughters, Edith and Irene, and said: "I'm determined that my little Edie and my little Irene will never be embarrassed. All my pictures are moral and clean." This won Miss Marion's respect at the time, but by 1929, when she resumed her career at M-G-M she knew him much better. He had not only encouraged her to buy stocks on margin in the disastrous year of 1929, but she had several personally unpleasant experiences with him. Once in the studio commissary, as she passed his table, where he was eating his favourite matzo ball soup, he looked up and grinned, and then pinched her well-groomed *derrière.* She paused to look at him. "Mr. Mayer," she said, "Be careful, or you may find your face in that matzo ball soup."

When she returned to work after Thomson's death, it was Thalberg who claimed her services and assigned her to the screenplay of *Their Own Desire,* which was an adaptation of a Sarita Fuller novel, and starred Thalberg's wife, Norma Shearer.

In the early years of the talking film, a well-established scenarist would construct the "screenplay" that served as a blueprint for the filming. The term "screenplay," although infrequently used in the late silent era, came into general usage after sound came in, and embraced not only continuity, with full camera sets-ups, but also the spoken dialogue. However, in sound's early days, it was considered "the thing" to have dialogue re-phrased and polished by a "dialoguer," who almost always would be some "name" playwright who was willing to pick up a fat cheque for doing a job that had already been set up for him, or even already done perfectly, by the scenarist. James Forbes — ironically, the playwright of "The Famous Mrs. Fair" — is

credited for the dialogue of *Their Own Desire,* but the entire screenplay was Frances Marion's.

Norma Shearer was nominated for an Academy Best Actress Award for her performance in *Their Own Desire.*

For at least two things Miss Marion was then better than anybody else in her business: her characters were always original and their conflicts were not only dramatic but genuinely human; and her stories were eye-mindedly conceived, written with the camera always in mind. Even in the early days of sound, before the techniques of it were understood, and everything was too often slowed down for the sake of constant yackety-yak on the soundtrack, and consequently every scene was static, Frances Marion's screenplays *moved,* and could be *acted.* She often deliberately wrote sequences without a single line of dialogue, well aware that action and re-action expressed pantomimically are more effective than the most scintillating of dialogue.

Miss Marion's second talkie assignment was the screenplay from Eugene O'Neill's *Anna Christie,* which was Garbo's talking-film *début.* One sequence in this film version was not in O'Neill's play: the scene on the amusement pier, which adds to and builds the relationship between Anna and Matt Burke. It also takes the action off the coal barge, and provides a real threat with the re-entry of old drunken Marthy into the scene. It is so good an acting sequence I've heard student actors, seeing a stage production of O'Neill's play, remember this scene and ask why it had been cut.

Miss Marion induced Thalberg and director Clarence Brown to test Marie Dressler for the role of Marthy Owen and was delighted when they agreed that no other actress should play it. It turned out that Miss Dressler's performance was the only one that impressed Garbo, who disliked herself in the English film version of *Anna Christie* as much as she approved of her performance in the German version directed by Jacques Feyder. She contended that Swedes didn't act the way the characters in the English version did; and she hated the glamourised Anna she had to play. The morning after she had seen the completed English version, however, she took a large bouquet of chrysanthemums to Miss Dressler's home. Garbo's first nomination for an Oscar was for *Anna Christie* (in tandem with her performance in *Romance*). Director Clarence Brown and cameraman William Daniels were also nominated for their work on it.

Miss Marion herself won an Oscar for the original story and screenplay of another 1930 film: *The Big House.* And that same year, *The Rogue Song,* for which Miss Marion wrote the screenplay (with John Colton), brought Lawrence Tibbett an Academy Award nomination. Although Miss Marion usually shied away from the film musical, she did write the screenplays of three at M-G-M — *The Rogue Song, Good News,* and *Going Hollywood.*

She wrote the screenplays of three other M-G-M releases in 1930: Norma Shearer's *Let Us Be Gay,* the musical *Good News,* and *Min and Bill,* which co-starred Marie Dressler and Wallace Beery, and won a Best Actress Award for Miss Dressler. Said Miss Dressler on accepting her Oscar: "You can be the best actress in the world, have the best producer, director and cameraman, but it won't matter a bit if you don't have the story."

Min and Bill was made from an original story by Frances Marion, although its source material is credited as being a novel by Lorna Moon called "Dark Star," which was dedicated to Miss Marion. Goldwyn publicist Sam Marx

revealed the true story about a decade later in a release to a syndicated column: "Frances Marion had worked out an original untitled story for Marie Dressler, which she told to Kate Corbelay, then one of the bright lights of M-G-M's story department and a good friend of Miss Marion's. Both women were saddened by the plight of Lorna Moon, who had written many scenarios for silents, including Lon Chaney's *Mr. Wu* and Norma Shearer's *Upstage*. Lorna had asked them to help push the picture sale of "Dark Star," a very downbeat novel of the Scottish moors.

"Lorna Moon was dying of tuberculosis in an Arizona sanitarium. Miss Marion had paid her expenses there, and Lorna was obsessive about paying the debt and having enough left over to stay in the sanitarium until she died.

"So Kate Corbelay and Frances Marion cooked up this scheme: At the next executive council meeting, when it came time for Kate to recommend the purchase of story properties, she would start to tell the story of "Dark Star" and at that point Miss Marion would enter the room and say, 'Oh, Kate, it's about "Dark Star!" I know the story so well, let me tell it.' Then she would relate the plot of her own untitled original for Dressler.

"All went as they planned. When Miss Marion finished telling the story, she could see by the executives' and producers' faces that she had won them.

" 'What do you think the author wants for her story?' she was asked. When Kate said $10,000, Louis B. Mayer ordered: 'Offer her seventy-five hundred.' Miss Marion volunteered to persuade Miss Moon to take it 'if you'll guarantee that I get to write the screenplay.'

"There was no argument on that point. Miss Marion looked at Mrs. Corbelay — Miss Moon had asked that they get her at least $3,000. Miss Marion was scared some smart boy might read the novel, so she said: 'I'm going to write Lorna later today, and if you'll have the cheque made out, I'll send it to her and tell her the contracts for the story purchase are on the way.'

"In another five minutes a cheque for $7,500 to the order of Lorna Moon for the movie rights of "Dark Star" was on its way special delivery. Lorna paid her few debts — and died before *Min and Bill* was released."

Adds Miss Marion: "That same day I asked for Marion Jackson to be put on the assignment with me — and we were off! We had to get the script done in a rush. Very few — in fact, I sometimes wonder if anybody except Kate and I — ever read "Dark Star." We kept our secret until years later, when it no longer mattered."

In 1931, Miss Marion wrote the original stories and screenplays of two more M-G-M winners: *The Secret Six* and *The Champ*. In the former, she is credited with giving Clark Gable his first important part. He did not have top billing, but his performance made M-G-M decide he warranted "the build-up."

The Champ was a four-handkerchief picture if there ever was one, and earned Miss Marion her second Oscar. And Wallace Beery won a Best Actor Award for his performance in that picture, tying with Fredric March, who got his for *Dr. Jekyll and Mr. Hyde*.

Frances Marion wrote two other original screenplays on her M-G-M contract: *Emma*, a moving character study co-starring Jean Hersholt with Marie Dressler, which gained an Academy Award nomination for Miss Dressler; and *Blondie of the Follies*, an amusing Marion Davies comedy, which had wonderful backstage atmosphere and beguiling performances by ex-Follies beauties Davies and Billie Dove.

MORE FROM HOLLYWOOD

Early in 1930, in a Phoenix, Arizona, judge's chambers, Miss Marion became the bride of film director George William Hill, whom she had known since the First World War and who had escorted her to Hollywood *premières* and parties after Fred Thomson's death. He had been born in Douglas, Kansas, and had begun his film career at Fine Arts-Triangle, first as a stagehand and then as a cameraman for D. W. Griffith. During the First World War, he was attached to the photographic division of the Signal Corps, served in Italy and around Gallipoli, and attained the rank of captain. At the war's end, he became a contract director at Fox and was very skilled in handling male stars in both comedies and dramas. He was one of Fred Thomson's closest friends and would have directed Thomson's features with "Silver King," had Fox not put him under contract. When he married Frances Marion, he had already directed three scripts she had written, and, after their marriage, he directed three more: *The Big House, Min and Bill,* and *The Secret Six.*

The marriage was short-lived. They separated, reconciled, separated again, and on October 26, 1931, Hill obtained a divorce in Reno. His estranged wife, he said, was travelling in Europe.

"We should not have married," says Miss Marion. "We got along well as director and writer, and I hoped it would be good if my sons had a father whom they liked, one who had known their own father well. But it turned out that George Hill had a weakness I discovered only after I'd married him, one which I'm certain even Fred knew nothing about, good friends as they were: George Hill was a compulsive and secret drinker.

"Time and again, when he was drinking, his crews and I would cover up for him, but things got so bad the studio threatened to fire him. Our home life became harrowing; he belittled and threatened to kill me; and many a time the weeping, loyal servants in the house locked themselves behind doors in an attempt to shut out the abuse from my sons. When, finally, we discussed divorce in one of his sober moments, I did not want to state the real reason since that would make his getting directorial assignments impossible.

"So we agreed that I would send him a letter saying I was going to Europe and that I did not wish to resume our marital relationship when I returned. But when he got to Reno, he found he could not obtain a divorce on so cooked-up a desertion and he was forced to charge me with extreme cruelty, which was about as far from the truth as you can get.

"I always felt sorry for him, for he was finding it hard to get any work to do since everybody at M-G-M was aware of his drinking problem and knew he couldn't be trusted."

Meanwhile, Miss Marion bought an attractive home for herself and her sons on Selma Avenue between Hollywood and Sunset Boulevards, only a short walk from where Hedda Hopper lived on Fairfax Avenue; and she went to work for Samuel Goldwyn again, this time on the screenplay for *Cynara,* adapted from a hit play about a successful and happily married man who happens to fall in love, in his fashion, with a lonely young woman. When he returns to his wife, the deserted girl kills herself, which almost destroys him. Ronald Colman, Kay Francis, and Phyllis Barry played husband, wife, and other love.

By that time, Goldwyn was filming on the United Artists lot exclusively, and Miss Marion stayed on there to work for Mary Pickford on what turned out to be Miss Pickford's last film. Although her first talkie, *Coquette,* had been successful and won Miss Pickford an Academy Award, her few subsequent features were ill-chosen. She hoped to recoup her prestige by re-doing one of Norma Talmadge's most popular silents, *Secrets,* and hired Marshall Neilan to direct her in it, with Kenneth MacKenna as her leading man. When about six reels were completed and roughly cut, Miss Pickford was so unhappy with both the film and her own performance that she decided to scrap what had been done and start all over again. For the new screenplay, she chose Frances Marion, who had written not only the best of the earlier Pickford scripts but also the scenario of the silent Talmadge version of *Secrets.*

The new screenplay gave Miss Pickford the scope of characterisation she visualised. Frank Borzage was engaged as director (she had been very unhappy with Neilan, who hadn't the flare for directing talkies which he had shown in his silents), and Leslie Howard was the leading man. Miss Pickford and Howard began as youthful lovers and went through the years until they were the elderly parents of Ethel Clayton, Huntley Gordon, Bessie Barriscale, and Theodore von Eltz. The result had audience appeal, and if Miss Pickford had planned to end her career with *Secrets,* she could not have chosen a more becoming vehicle.

When Irving Thalberg induced Frances Marion to return to M-G-M, she was sorry to learn that her first assignment was to adapt *Peg o' My Heart* for Marion Davies. Both Miss Davies and she felt the sentimentality of the memorable Laurette Taylor vehicle had become even shabbier with the years.

"*Peg o' My Heart* seems to have haunted me," Miss Marion says. "My first poster for Morosco years before had been of Laurette Taylor in the role. I had to struggle now to make a story in which I had never believed suitable for Marion. Everybody concerned with the production managed to pull it off, however, and it became one of Marion's best-liked pictures. I still don't like *Peg o' My Heart,* and Marion always clowned about it in private."

Miss Marion's next at M-G-M was the screenplay of the all-star production, *Dinner at Eight*, which David O. Selznick produced and George Cukor directed. Although one of the most successful films she ever adapted, it ironically didn't win an Oscar nomination in any category.

Miss Marion wrote original stories for two other 1933 pictures: *The Prizefighter and the Lady* for Max Baer, Myrna Loy, and Walter Huston, which at the time was considered Hollywood's best film about prizefighting; and the Marion Davies-Bing Crosby comedy with music, *Going Hollywood*. The former brought Frances Marion her third Academy Award nomination.

In 1934, Thalberg assigned her to do a screenplay from Pearl Buck's *The Good Earth*. Although worried about George Hill's alcoholism, Thalberg agreed to take the chance of letting him direct it, since the story was so much up Hill's alley. And because Hill hadn't worked for almost two years, Miss Marion agreed to work with her ex-husband and help him make the picture one of the great ones, and thereby to re-establish himself. Hill went to China with a crew and filmed some exteriors, and seemed to be in control of himself. When he came back, the front office praised the film he had taken.

On the evening of August 10, 1934, Thalberg summoned him to a production

Marie Dressler in *Dinner at Eight*.

and story conference. His ex-wife naturally was present, and everybody was in unusually fine humour and enthusiastic about the picture's prospects.

All present were shocked when Hill, very late, arrived in so drunken a condition that he could hardly stand. The excited talk became stunned silence, Miss Marion says, and adds: "He looked from one face to another and I felt sad for him, because he must have known he was through, that this was the end of his career."

Hill was driven by his chauffeur to Miss Marion's oceanside home in South Venice, where he was then living by himself. Sometime during the night he shot himself in the head with his Army revolver.

Miss Marion was so stunned that she could no longer work on the screenplay of *The Good Earth,* and asked Thalberg to replace her. She spent her days in the artist's studio behind her house, working with sculptor's clay. She also took courses at USC's summer school — in philosphy, art history, sculpture, and ceramics.

Finally, she felt able to write again and returned to M-G-M to do one of Jean Harlow's most popular pictures: *Riffraff,* in which Spencer Tracy was leading man.

But Miss Marion was no longer willing to accept what the writer's position in Hollywood had become.

"Bess Meredyth, Anita Loos, and I were asked our advice on virtually every script M-G-M produced during the Thirties," says Miss Marion. "It would have been embarrassing had other writers discovered that the executives asked our opinions about their work and that we were, without credit, making revisions. When we carried the scripts on which we were doing re-writes, we made sure they were in unmarked, plain covers. But we knew also that some male writers were complaining about 'the tyranny of the woman writer' supposedly prevalent at all studios then, and particularly at M-G-M.

"It was a ridiculous accusation — they were lucky to have us on their side. And the three of us were not exempt, on our own scripts, from writers being assigned to revise and then demanding credit, no matter how small their contribution to the final shooting script. The Credit Arbitration Board of the Writers' Guild was not set up as strongly then as it is now, and it was appalling how some over-ambitious writers horned in on credits to which they were not always entitled. I was beginning to feel that film writers are like Penelope — knitting their stories all day just to have somebody else unravel their work by night.

"I'd always worked closely with directors and producers on my own scripts, and, at their request, often worked as writer on the set, making script changes during actual production. Clarence Brown, Frank Borzage, Frank Lloyd, and many other directors personally requested me to be on hand during production, and all thanked me, publicly as well as privately, for any aid I gave during shooting, for which I never requested or received credit when the screenplay was originally not my own.

"But it was apparent that if a writer wanted to maintain any control over what he wrote, he would have to become a writer-director, or a writer-producer. Writing a screenplay had become like writing on sand, with the wind blowing."

Marlene Dietrich and Robert Donat in *Knight without Armour,* screenplay by Frances Marion.

FRANCES MARION

One of M-G-M's most curious writing credits is that for *Grand Hotel,* where the sole credits go to Vicki Baum for the play and novel and to William Drake for the screenplay, when actually Drake was Miss Baum's translator. But this was apparently the way Irving Thalberg wanted the credits to read, or the way he was forced by purchase to state them. Director Edmund Goulding, however, always claimed that the screenplay he filmed had been written by Frances Marion, and it is known that Miss Marion did work at length on the shooting script — but without credit.

Miss Marion's final M-G-M contractual assignment was adapting *Camille* for Garbo to play and George Cukor to direct. She relished doing it. It was the third screenplay she wrote for Garbo to play, and more than twenty years previously, one of her first great hits had been the scenario for Clara Kimball Young's *Camille*. But by the time the Cukor-Garbo *Camille* reached the screen, two other writers shared the credit on the screenplay.

"Full credit for that picture," Miss Marion says, "should go to George Cukor and Greta Garbo. They made it what it is, a classic love story done for the films in exquisite taste, believable because of the artistry they brought to it.

"Today it is fashionable to discredit both sentiment and sentimentality in a story. I can only remember back to my brief newspaper days when sentiment did me in as a reporter, and how well it served me later when I began to write stories for the screen. Although tear-jerkers have always been made fun of by the critics, there's a streak of sentimentality in most of us, and audiences will always respond to lachrymose yarns, and will often even applaud them."

After Miss Marion finished *Camille,* she wrote two films in England: *Love from a Stranger,* starring Ann Harding, from a play fashioned from an Agatha Christie story, and the Marlene Dietrich-Robert Donat *Knight without Armour,* which was adapted from a James Hilton novel.

"Even in England it was the same story as far as writers went, especially, as I found, on *Knight without Armour,*" she says. "I returned to Hollywood, determined that I would have some control over my writing efforts and that any writing I did for films would involve either production or direction, or both.

"Whereupon a jinx seemed to hound me. I finally went to Columbia, where I obtained a contract to produce a big-scale Western on the order of *The Covered Wagon.* We bought a Courtney Riley Cooper story and I got Frank R. Adams to write the screenplay, for I had decided to concentrate on producing. Unfortunately, Columbia had had a big setback with *Lost Horizon,* which was not a money-maker when it was first released. I sat down with Harry Cohn and systematically, although reluctantly, tried to cut the costs because Columbia couldn't afford a big-budget picture that year. But no matter where we trimmed, the story lost its impact, so I finally said, 'Harry, I think we'd better call the whole thing off. It isn't going to work. I ask only that you pay my writers, Cooper and Adams, in full. You don't have to pay me.'

"Harry Cohn agreed with me about shelving the picture and paying the writers, but insisted on paying me in full as well. I refused to take the cheque, but when I got home, there was a bouquet of flowers from Harry and the cheque was in the envelope with the card. This went on, back and forth, several times, and as soon as I would return the money, it would come back to me with more flowers. Finally, I accepted the cheque and turned it over to charity.

115

MORE FROM HOLLYWOOD

"I tell this because today it's fashionable to denigrate Harry Cohn. He may have had his faults, but I always found him a fair shooter and, as far as I'm concerned, he discharged his every obligation."

Another Marion attempt to produce at Columbia — *The Second Mrs. Draper* for Gloria Swanson — was also shelved.

"I had always wanted to do a story for Gloria," Miss Marion says, "but it never worked out. I'm sad, too, that I've never written anything for two of my favourite actresses: Katharine Hepburn and Joan Blondell. Nobody ever asked me to."

Miss Marion says she was so determined not to write screenplays that would be re-written by some other writer that she forgot about movie writing temporarily and began doing magazine stories and serials. "Valley People," generally regarded as her best piece of published fiction, is still a remarkable book. A study of some of the people of Napa Valley, it has an unforgettable, haunting beauty. She also spent much time on a textbook on the technique of screenwriting: "How to Write and Sell Film Stories."

In the summer of 1937, she took her two sons to the Scandinavian countries and had, she thinks, "the most perfect summer I've ever spent."

When she got back to Hollywood, she tried for several months to set up a production-writing deal for herself, and finally she resumed screenwriting. She did an original screenplay for Universal, *Green Hell,* but was not pleased with the way it turned out. She agreed then to return to M-G-M, but only in an advisory and editorial capacity; her main concern for many years was the supervision of the work of younger and inexperienced contract writers at M-G-M.

When Bess Meredyth and her husband, Michael Curtiz, set up an independent company to release through Warners, Miss Marion left M-G-M to work with them. But their company never got off the ground, and was eventually dissolved.

In the past two decades, Miss Marion has been painting and sculpting. The walls of the terrace apartment she leased for many years were covered with her colourful canvasses, which included an extraordinary portrait of her oldtime friend, ZaSu Pitts. Miss Marion has been offered sizeable sums for the Pitts portrait as well as another she did of Marie Dressler, but she always said decisively, "Not for sale." They hang today in the homes of her sons.

In the early Fifties, she sold her attractive home on Selma Avenue and went to Connecticut to live. "It meant easy access to Manhattan," she says, "and I've always loved New York. I wrote a lot of magazine stories; I painted; and I wrote a play with Anita Loos, which, alas, never got to Broadway. I wanted to try writing for television, too. But illness prevented."

A clot of blood moved into one eye, and totally destroyed its sight.

When she returned to Hollywood, she lived in The Colonial House, one of the oldest deluxe apartment houses bordering the Sunset Strip and Beverly Hills. She gave it up and went East once more to live near her sons, but then returned to Beverly Hills, where she lived in a small exclusive residential hotel.

"I hope my story shows one thing," she says. "While it's perfectly true many important men like Oliver Morosco, William A. Brady, William Randolph Hearst, Samuel Goldwyn, and Irving Thalberg helped and encouraged me,

116

it's consoling to know how many women gave me real aid when I stood at the crossroads. Too many women go around these days saying women in important positions don't help their own sex, but that was never my experience. In my case there were Marie Dressler, Lois Weber, Mary Pickford, Elsie Janis, Mary Roberts Rinehart, Adela Rogers St. Johns, Hedda Hopper, Bess Meredyth, Anita Loos, Ella Wheeler Wilcox, who encouraged me when I was young to write poetry and helped me sell my poems and short stories, and Genevieve Parkhurst, the editor of 'Pictorial Review,' who encouraged me to write magazine serials. The list is endless, believe me!"

Not having had the advantage of a formal education, and regretting it, Miss Marion has been a student all her life. "I've always believed no one can have a well-rounded writing career without at least a modicum of knowledge of all the arts," she told me recently. Over the years, she taught herself to speak French and Spanish; took piano lessons from Fanchon Armitage, and singing lessons from Dr. Marifiotti, Grace Moore's mentor; took college courses in English, philosophy, and psychology. In the Fifties, she studied anatomy and sculpture with Merrill Gage, ceramics with Glen Lukens, and painting with Francis de Erdely. She calls herself "the oldest co-ed at USC." On January 30, 1966, that university made her the first recipient of its Pioneer Film Award "for distinguished contributions and long-standing devotion toward advancing the art of the motion picture."

Her elder son, Fred Thomson Jr., received his PhD from Yale in English literature, taught there six years, and is now professor of English literature at Chapel Hill, North Carolina. Her younger son, Richard Thomson, is a Naval Air captain, was flying jets in Vietnam, but is now stationed in the East, near Annapolis. Both are happily married. Fred has one son, and Richard two sons and a daughter.

For years Fred encouraged his mother to write a book about Hollywood and the people she knew and still knows, and in the spring of 1968 she settled down to do it, following a line she had set forth in a series of diaries. She was determined, however, not to write an autobiography. Nor did she want to have any truck with another scandal *exposé*. When she was writing the manuscript, she frequently said, "My book will start when I come down to Hollywood, aged twenty-three, to paint posters for Morosco. I'm not going to talk about any of my husbands or lovers except Fred Thomson, the father of my sons, because he was the best of them all. Mostly, the book's going to be about all the wonderful, and sometimes slightly nutty, people I knew and worked with."

In the summer of 1972 that book, "Off With Their Heads!," subtitled "A Serio-Comic Tale of Hollywood," was published by Doubleday, and drew wholehearted praise from many a critic as well as top figures in the industry, like Gloria Swanson (who wrote a glowing foreword), Lillian Gish, Jean Renoir, Frank Capra, Joan Blondell, and Mary Pickford.

Her mind was still very quick and if there be any who think it overlaid with sentiment, I can testify that her words were often more than faintly etched in acid. For instance, we were speaking of a prominent Hollywood writer and she said casually: "I hear she doesn't like me. I can't understand why. I never did her a favour."

And she says: "Of course Hollywood isn't the same. The fun went out of

117

everything when we got so damned rich. Money never meant anything to me. I spent it faster than I made it. I'm proudest of all of the way my two sons have turned out, because I raised them myself.

"As for the stories, scenarios, and screenplays I wrote, they were a business, a job, a hard buck to earn. I was glad when they were acclaimed, and ready on all occasions to accept the blame when they flopped. Writers, happily, are blessed with a kind of anonymity, and I've always welcomed that. I've always regarded publicity as a time-taker, and I've avoided giving out stories about myself.

"It's pretty evident, I think, that a new and better film world may be emerging. The war and postwar years, that utter and terrible wasteland, have passed. We've gone through the valley of indecision, and now each year there are always a few American, and a few foreign-made, films that are indicative of the cinema that's going to be. The industry is all the better for becoming international.

"I don't think Hollywood will ever again be as glamorous, or as funny, or as tragic, as it was during the Teens, the Twenties, and the Thirties. But that's what everybody says about the past as he grows older and looks back on the days of his youth, when everything was new and exciting and beautiful. Was it really that way? Frankly, too often, all I can remember are the heartbreak and the hard work."

In September 1972, I dined for the last time with Frances Marion. I was flying to Europe to live in Spain, and I knew I'd probably never see her again. I kissed her cheek in farewell, and turned at the door to look back at her. She stood in the centre of the room and smiled as she raised one hand in farewell.

"Goodbye, DeWitt," she said.

I knew it was goodbye.

I received a few scribbled notes from her during the fall. She was in wretched health, and was in and out of hospitals. Then in May in London, where I'd gone to complete this manuscript, I received word that she had endured a 7½ hour surgery for cancer, and was also suffering an aneurism of the aorta for which, obviously, nothing could be done. She died in Los Angeles at the Good Samaritan Hospital on May 12, 1973.

FRANCES MARION FILMOGRAPHY

(The following pictures comprise, in order of release, the films to which Frances Marion was an accredited contributor, either as actress, producer, director, or, and most often, writer.

As a writer, Miss Marion wrote original stories; adapted other writers' novels and plays to scenario form; wrote many original scenarios; wrote sub-titles. When the movies found their voice, she was equally proficient as screenplay writer, adapter, continuity writer, constructionist, dialoguer. Some of these latter terms are now obsolete, even though they connoted branches of the screenplay that still exist today.

The following filmography attempts to list only the acknowledged screen credits of Frances Marion. It must be emphasised, however, as stated in my article about her, that she made other writing contributions under many *noms de plume*, and she is known to have written some produced screenplays which for some reason, are not accredited to her.)

A GIRL OF YESTERDAY (1915). Described as "A Novel Romance of the Past and the Present"; as an actress: in the role of Rosanna Danford, city vamp. *Dir:* Allan Dwan. *Sc:* Mary Pickford. *With* Mary Pickford, Gertrude Norman, Jack Pickford, Donald Crisp, Marshall Neilan, Glenn L. Martin. *Prod:* Famous Players (Paramount). 4 reels.

THE WILD GIRL FROM THE HILLS (1915). Romance of a girl from the hills and a young man from the city; as an actress: leading lady, in the title role to Monte Blue, the only other actor known by name to be in the cast. Director and writer are also unknown, and so is the releasing company; it is likely that it is a two-reeler made for Mutual or Bosworth release.

A DAUGHTER OF THE SEA (1915). Romantic drama of the sea; as writer of the original story, "The Fisher Girl." *Dir:* Charles Seay. *Sc:* Russell Smith. *Cast:* Muriel Ostriche, W. H. Tooker, Catherine Calhoun, Clara Whipple, Clifford Gray, Roy Applegate. *Prod:* Equitable-World. 5 reels.

CAMILLE (1915). Romantic tragedy; as scenarist. *Dir:* Albert Capellani. Adapted from the novel and play by Alexandre Dumas, *fils*. *Cast;* Clara Kimball Young, Paul Capellani, Frederick C. Truesdell, William Jefferson, Louie Ducey, Lillian Cook, Robert Cummings, Edward M. Kimball, Stanhope Wheatcroft. *Prod:* World. 5 reels.

THE FOUNDLING (1916). Sentimental drama of an orphan's problems; as writer of an original scenario. *Dir:* John B. O'Brien. *Cast:* Mary Pickford, Mildred Morris, Gertrude Norman, Maggie Weston, Edward Martindel, Marcia Harris. Originally filmed in Hollywood early in 1915, the negative and all prints were partially destroyed in the fire on Sept. 11, 1915, which burned Famous Players Manhattan studio on West 26th Street. The film was almost entirely re-shot, however, using different actors in several roles, and the new re-edited film belatedly premiered in Manhattan during January, 1916. *Prod:* Famous Players (Paramount). 5 reels.

THE YELLOW PASSPORT (1916). Dramatic version of "The Yellow Ticket" play; as cowriter, with Edwin August, of the scenario. *Dir:* Edwin August. adapted from the story and play by Abraham Schomer. *Cast:* Clara Kimball Young, John Sainpolis, Alec B. Francis, Edwin August. *Prod:* Shubert-World. 5 reels.

THEN I'LL COME BACK TO YOU (1916). Romantic drama; as scenarist. *Dir:* George Irving. Adapted from a novel by Larry Evans. *Cast:* Alice Brady, Jack Sherrill, Eric Blind, Leo Gordon, George Kline, Marie Edith Wells, Ted Dean. *Prod:* World-Frohman. 5 reels.

THE SOCIAL HIGHWAYMAN (1916). Drama; as scenarist. *Dir:* Edwin August. Adapted from a play by Mary Stone. *Cast:* Ormi Hawley, Edwin August, John Sainpolis, Alice Clair Elliott, Noah Berry. *Prod:* Peerless-World. 5 reels.

THE FEAST OF LIFE (1916). Romantic drama; as writer of an original scenario. *Dir:* Albert Capellani. The picture was filmed on location in Cuba. *Cast:* Clara Kimball Young, Paul Capellani, Robert Frazer, Doris Kenyon, Mr. and Mrs. Edward M. Kimball. *Prod:* Paragon-World. 5 reels.

TANGLED FATES (1916). Romantic drama; as scenarist. *Dir:* Travers Vale. Adapted from a story by William Anthony McGuire, known as both "Grub Stake" and "Grubstakers." *Cast:* Alice Brady, Arthur Ashley, George Morgan, Edward M. Kimball. *Prod:* Peerless-World. 5 reels.

THE BATTLE OF HEARTS (1916). Sea drama; as writer of the original story, "The Iron Man." *Dir./Sc:* Oscar C. Apfel. *Cast:* William Farnum, Elda Furry (Hedda Hopper), Wheeler Oakman, Willard Louis. *Prod:* Fox. 5 reels.

LA VIE DE BOHEME (AKA, GB, *La Boheme*) (1916). Romantic drama; as scenarist. *Dir:* Albert Capellani. Adapted from "Scènes de la vie de Bohème" by Henri Murger. *Cast:* Alice Brady, Paul Capellani, June Elvidge, Leslie Stowe, Chester Barnett, Zena Keefe. *Prod:* Paragon-World. 5 reels.

THE CRUCIAL TEST (1916). Drama; as writer of an original scenario. *Dir:* John Ince and Robert Thornby. *Cast:* Kitty Gordon, Niles Welch, J. Herbert Frank, W. Cahill, Winifred Harris. Working title; *The Eternal Sacrifice*. *Prod:* Paragon-World. 5 reels.

A WOMAN'S WAY (1916). Romantic drama; as scenarist. *Dir:* Barry O'Neill. Adapted from a play by Thompson Buchanan. *Cast:* Ethel Clayton, Carlyle Blackwell, Montagu Love, Alec B. Francis, Edith Campbell Walker. *Prod:* Peerless—World. 5 reels.

THE SUMMER GIRL (1916). Romantic drama; as scenarist. *Dir:* Edwin August. Adapted from a story, "Contrary Mary," by Louis V. Jefferson. *Cast:* Mollie King, Arthur Ashley, Dave Ferguson, Ruby Hoffman, Harold Entwhistle, Dora Mills Anderson. *Prod:* Peerless—World. 5 reels.

FRIDAY, THE 13TH (1916). Drama; as scenarist. *Dir:* Emile Chautard. Adapted from a novel by Thomas W. Lawson. *Cast:* Robert Warwick, Gerda Holmes, Charles Brandt, Charles Harvey, Lenore Harris. *Prod:* Peerless—World. 6 reels.

THE REVOLT (1916). Drama; as scenarist. *Dir:* Barry O'Neill. Adapted from the play by Edward A. Locke. *Cast:* Frances Nelson, Arthur Ashley, Clara Whipple, Frank Beamish, ggeorge MacQuarrie, Madge Evans, Ada Price. *Prod:* Peerless—World. 6 reels.

THE HIDDEN SCAR (1916). Drama; as scenarist. *Dir:* Barry O'Neill. Adapted from a story, "The Scorching Way," by Mrs. Owen Bronson. *Cast:* Holbrook Blinn, Ethel Clayton, Irving Cummings, Montagu Love, Madge Evans, Edward M. Kimball, Mrs. Woodward. *Prod:* Peerless-World. 6 reels.

THE GILDED CAGE (AKA, GB, *The Heart*

of a Princess) (1916). Romantic mythical kingdom drama; as scenarist. *Dir:* Harley Knoles. Adapted from a story, "Her Majesty," by J. I. C. Clarke. *Cast:* Alice Brady, Irving Cummings, Arthur Ashley, Montagu Love, Gerda Holmes, Clara Whipple, Alec B. Francis, Sidney D'Albrook. *Prod:* Peerless-World. 5 reels.

BOUGHT AND PAID FOR (1916). Marital drama; as scenarist. *Dir:* Harley Knoles. Adapted from the play by George Broadhurst. *Cast:* Alice Brady, Montagu Love, Frank Conlan, Josephine Drake. *Prod:* Peerless-World. 5 reels.

ALL MAN (1916). Drama; as scenarist. *Dir:* Emile Chautard. Adapted from a story by Willard Mack. *Cast:* Robert Warwick, Mollie King, Johnny Hines, Henry West, Louis Grisel, Alec B. Francis, Gerda Holmes, George MacQuarrie. *Prod:* Peerless World. 5 reels.

THE RISE OF SUSAN (1916). Romantic drama; as writer of an original scenario. *Dir:* S. E. V. Taylor. *Cast:* Clara Kimball Young, Eugene O'Brien, Warner Oland, Jenny Dickerson, Marguerite Skirwin. Working title: *Cosette.* Prod: Peerless-World. 5 reels.

ON DANGEROUS GROUND (1916). Drama; as scenarist. *Dir:* Robert Thornby. Adapted from a novel, "Little Comrade," by Burton E. Stevenson. *Cast:* Gail Kane, Carlyle Blackwell, William Bailey, Stanhope Wheatcroft, Frank Leigh, John Burkell, Florence Ashbrooke. *Prod:* Peerless-World 5 reels.

A WOMAN ALONE (1917). Romantic drama; as scenarist. *Dir:* Harry Davenport. Adapted from a story, "Loneliness," by Willard Mack. *Cast:* Alice Brady, Edwin T. Langford, Arthur Ashley, J. Clarence Harvey, Edward M. Kimball, Justine Cutting, Walter D. Greene. *Prod:* Peerless-World. 5 reels.

TILLIE WAKES UP (1917). Farce-comedy; as scenarist. *Dir:* Harry Davenport. Adapted from an idea by Mark Swan. *Cast:* Marie Dressler, Johnny Hines, Frank Beamish, Rubye de Remer, Ruth Barrett, Jack Brown, Working title: *Tillie's Night Out. Prod:* Peerless-World. 5 reels.

THE HUNGRY HEART (AKA, GB, *Frou-Frou)* (1917). Romantic drama; as scenarist. *Dir:* Emile Chautard. Adapted from a play, "Frou-Frou," by Henri Meilhac and Ludovic Halévy. *Cast:* Alice Brady, Gerda Holmes, Edward Langford, George MacQuarrie, Alec B. Francis, John Dudley, Edna Whistler, Mrs. H. J. Brundage, Josephine Earle. *Prod:* Peerless-World. 5 reels.

A SQUARE DEAL (1917). Romantic drama; as scenarist. *Dir:* Harley Knoles. Adapted from a story, "The Parasites," by Louis V. Jefferson. Cast: Carlyle Blackwell, June Elvidge, Henry Hull, Charlotte Granville, Muriel Ostriche. *Prod:* Peerless-World. 5 reels.

A GIRL'S FOLLY (1917). Romantic drama of early film-making; as co-writer of the original scenario with Maurice Tourneur. *Dir:* Maurice Tourneur. *Cast:* Robert Warwick, Doris Kenyon, June Elvidge, Jane Adair, Johnny Hines, Chester Barnett. Working title: *A Movie Romance. Prod:* Paragon-World. 5 reels.

THE WEB OF DESIRE (1917). Romantic drama; as scenarist. *Dir:* Emile Chautard. Adapted from a story by E. Lloyd Sheldon. *Cast:* Ethel Clayton, Rockcliffe Fellowes, Doris Kenyon, Madge Evans, Doris Field, Edward M. Kimball, Richard Turner, William Williams. *Prod:* Peerless-World. 5 reels.

A POOR LITTLE RICH GIRL (1917). Drama; as scenarist. *Dir:* Maurice Tourneur. Adapted from the play by Eleanor Gates. Cast: Mary Pickford, Charles Wellesley, Frank McGlynn, Emile La Croix, Charles Craig, Frank Andrews, Madlaine Traverse, Marcia Henderson, Maxine Elliott Hicks, Gladys Fairbanks, Herbert Prior. *Prod:* Paramount/Artcraft. 7 reels.

AS MAN MADE HER (1917). Drama; as scenarist. *Dir:* George Archainbaud. Adapted from a story, "Her Higher Destiny," by Helen Beare. *Cast:* Gail Kane, Frank Mills, Edward Langford, Gerda Holmes. *Prod:* Peerless-World. 5 reels.

THE SOCIAL LEPER (1917). Drama; as scenarist. *Dir:* Harley Knoles. Adapted from a story by Flordece C. Bolles. *Cast:* Carlyle Blackwell, June Elvidge, Arthur Ashley, Evelyn Greeley, Mrs. Eugene Woodward, Edna Whistler, Isabel Berwin, George MacQuarrie. *Prod:* Peerless-World. 5 reels.

FORGET-ME-NOT (1917). Drama; as writer of an original scenario. *Dir:* Emile Chautard. *Cast:* Kitty Gordon, Montagu Love, Alec B. Francis, Norma Phillips, George MacQuarrie, Lillian Herbert. Entire production shot on location in Cuba. *Prod:* Peerless-World. 5 reels.

DARKEST RUSSIA (1917) Melodrama of Jewish persecution in imperial Russia; as scenarist. *Dir:* Travers Vale. Adapted from the play by H. Gratten Donnelly and Sidney R. Ellis. *Cast:* Alice Brady, John Bowers, Lillian Cook, Norbert Wicki, J. Herbert Frank, Jack Drumier, Kate Lester, Frank De Vernon, Herbert Barrington, Boris Korlin (Karloff?). *Prod:* World. 5 reels.

THE CRIMSON DOVE (1917). Romantic drama; as writer of an original scenario. *Dir:* Romaine Fielding. *Cast:* Carlyle Blackwell, June Elvidge, Marie LaVerre, Henry West, Edward N. Hoyt, Louis Grisel, Dion Titheradge, Maxine Elliott Hicks. *Prod:* World. 5 reels.

THE STOLEN PARADISE (1917) Romantic drama; as writer of an original scenario. *Dir:* Harley Knoles. *Cast:* Ethel Clayton, Edward

Langford, Pina Nesbit, George MacQuarrie, Robert Forsyth, George Cowl, Lew Hart, Edward Reed, Edwin Roe, Ivan Dobble. *Prod:* World. 5 reels.

THE DIVORCE GAME (1917). Marital drama; as scenarist. *Dir:* Travers Vale. Adapted from a play, "Mlle. Fifi," by Leo Ditrichstein. *Cast:* Alice Brady, John Bowers, Arthur Ashley, Kate Lester, Joseph Herbert, Jack Drumier. *Prod:* Peerless-World. 5 reels.

THE BELOVED ADVENTURESS (1917). Romantic melodrama; as writer of an original scenario. *Dir:* William A. Brady and George Cowl. *Cast:* Kitty Gordon, Madge Evans, Lillian Cook, Frederick C. Truesdell, Pina Nesbit, William Sherwood, Jack Drumier, Inez Shannon, Robert Forsyth, Edward Elkas, R. Payton Gibbs, Katherine Johnston. *Prod:* World. 5 reels.

THE AMAZONS (1917). Romantic comedy; as scenarist. *Dir:* Joseph Kaufman. Adapted from the play by Sir Arthur Wing Pinero. *Cast:* Marguerite Clark, Elsie Lawson, Helen Greene, William Hinckley, Edgar Norton, Andre Bellon, Adolphe Menjou, Jack Standing. *Prod;* famous Players (Paramount). 5 reels.

REBECCA OF SUNNYBROOK FARM (1917). Comedy drama; as scenarist. *Dir:* Marshall Neilan. Adapted from the book by Kate Douglas Wiggin & Charlotte Thompson. *Cast:* Mary Pickford, Eugene O'Brien, Josephine Crowell, Maym Kelso, Marjorie Daw, Jane Wolff, Helen Jerome Eddy, Charles Ogle, Jack MacDonald, Violet Wilkey, Frank Turner, Kate Toncray, Emma Gerdes. *Prod:* Paramount-Artcraft. 6 reels.

A LITTLE PRINCESS (1917). Romantic comedy-fantasy; as scenarist. *Dir:*Marshall Neilan. Adapted from the novel by Mrs. Frances Hodgson Burnett. *Cast:* Mary Pickford, Norman Kerry, ZaSu Pitts, Katherine Griffith, Anne Schaeffer, Theodore Roberts, Gertrude Short, Gustav von Seyffertitz. *Prod:* Paramount/Artcraft. 5 reels.

STELLA MARIS (1918). Romantic drama; as scenarist. *Dir:* Marshall Neilan. Adapted from a novel by William J. Locke. *Cast:* Mary Pickford, Conway Tearle, Camille Ankewich (Marcia Manon), Ida Waterman, Herbert Standing, Josephine Crowell. *Prod:* Paramount-Artcraft. 6 reels.

AMARILLY OF CLOTHES-LINE ALLEY (1918). Romantic comedy; as scenarist. *Dir:* Marshall Neilanm Adapted from a story by Belle K. Maniates. *Cast:* Mary Pickford, Norman Kerry, William Scott, Kate Price, Ida Waterman, Margaret Landis, Thomas H. Wilson, Fred Goodwins, Herbert Standing, Wesley Barry, Frank Butterworth, Antrim Short, George Hackathorne, Gertrude Short. *Prod:* Paramount/Artcraft. 5 reels.

M'LISS (1918). Western romance; as scenarist. *Dir:* Marshall Neilan. Adapted from the story by Bret Harte and the stage play therefrom by Clay M. Greene. *Cast:* Mary Pickford, Theodore Roberts, Thomas Meighan, Charles Ogle, Tully Marshall, Monte Blue, Helen Kelly, Winifred Greenwood, Val Paul, W. H. Brown, John Burton, Bud Post, Guy Oliver. *Prod:* Para- mount/Artcraft. 5 reels.

HOW COULD YOU, JEAN? (1918). Romantic comedy; as scenarist. *Dir:* William D. Taylor. Adapted from a novel by Eleanor Hoyt Brainerd. *Cast:* Mary Pickford, Casson Ferguson, Herbert Standing, Spottiswoode Aitken, Fanny Midgely, Larry Peyton, ZaSu Pitts, Mabelle Harvey, Lucille Ward. *Prod:* Paramount/Artcraft. 5 reels.

THE CITY OF DIM FACES (1918). Romantic melodrama of San Francisco; as writer of an original scenario. *Dir:* George Melford. *Cast:* Sessue Hayakawa, Doris Pawn, Marin Sais, James Cruze, Winter Hall. *Prod:* Famous Players-Lasky/Paramount. 5 reels.

JOHANNA ENLISTS (1918). Romantic wartime comedy; as scenarist. *Dir:* William D. Taylor. Adapted from a story, "The Mobilising of Joanna," by Rupert Hughes. *Cast:* Mary Pickford, Emory Johnson, Monte Blue, Douglas MacLean, Jon Steppling, Anne Schaeffer. *Prod:* Paramount/Artcraft. 5 reels.

HE COMES UP SMILING (1918). Romantic comedy; as scenarist. *Dir:* Allan Dwan. Adapted from a play by Byron Quigley and Emil Mytray, which was based on a novel by Charles Sherman. *Cast:* Douglas Fairbanks, Marjorie Daw, Herbert Standing, Bull Montana, Albert McQuarrie, Frank Campeau, Jay Dwiggins, Kathleen Kirkham. *Prod:* Paramount-Artcraft. 5 reels.

THE TEMPLE OF DUSK (1918). Romantic drama; as writer of an original scenario. *Dir:* James Young. *Cast:* Sessue Hayakawa, Jane Novak, Sylvia Breamer, Lewis Willoughby, Henry Barrows, Mary Jane Irving. *Prod:* Exhibitors-Mutual (Haworth). 5 reels.

THE GOAT (1918) Comedy drama with a Hollywood studio background; as writer of an original scenario. *Dir:* Donald Crisp. *Cast:* Fred Stone, Fanny Midgely, Charles McHugh, Rhea Mitchell, Sylvia Ashton, Philo McCullough, Winifred Greenwood; Noah Beery, Raymond Hatton, Charles Ogle, Ernest Joy, Clarence Geldart, Ramon Samaniegos (Novarro). *Prod:* Paramount/Artcraft. 5 reels.

CAPTAIN KIDD, JR. (1919). Romantic comedy; as scenarist. *Dir:* William D. Taylor. Adapted from the play by Rida Johnson Young. *Cast:* Mary Pickford, Douglas MacLean, Spottiswoode Aitken, Robert Gordon, Winter Hall, Marcia Manon, Victor Potel, Clarence Geldart. *Prod:* Paramount/Artcraft. 5 reels.

121

THE MISLEADING WIDOW (1919). Romantic comedy; as scenarist. *Dir:* John S. Robertson. Adapted from a play, "Billeted," by F. Tennyson Jesse and H. M. Harwood. *Cast:* Billie Burke, Jame L. Crane, Frank Mills, Madeline Clare, Fred Hearn, Mrs. Priestly Morrison, Frederick Esmelton, Dorothy Waters. *Prod:* Paramount/Artcraft. 5 reels.

ANNE OF GREEN GABLES (1919). Romantic comedy; as scenarist. *Dir:* William D. Taylor. Adapted from the four "Anne" novels by L. M. Montgomery. *Cast:* Mary Miles Minter, Paul Kelly, Marcia Harris, Frederick Burton, Laurie Lovelle, Lila Romer, Lincoln Stedman, Albert Hackett, George Stewart. *Prod:* Realart (Paramount). 6 reels.

A REGULAR GIRL (1919). Romantic comedy; as co-writer, with Edmund Goulding, of an original scenario. *Dir:* James Young. *Cast:* Elsie Janis, Robert Lytton, Matt Moore, Robert Ayerton, Tammany Young. *Prod:* Selznick/Select. 6 reels.

THE CINEMA MURDER (1920). Murder mystery; as scenarist. *Dir:* George D. Baker. Adapted from a novel by E. Phillips Oppenheim. *Cast:* Marion Davies, Nigel Barrie, Eulalie Jensen, Anders Randolph, Reginald Barlow, Peggy Parry, W. Scott Moore. *Prod:* Paramount/Cosmopolitan. 6 reels.

POLLYANNA (1920). Romantic comedy; as scenarist. *Dir:* Paul Powell. Adapted from the novel by Eleanor H. Porter and the play dramatised therefrom by Catherine Chisholm Cushing. *Cast:* Mary Pickford, William Courtleigh, Katherine Griffith, J. Wharton James, Herbert Prior, Helen Jerome Eddy, George Berrell, Howard Ralston. *Prod:* United Artists. 6 reels.

HUMORESQUE (1920). Romantic mother-son drama; as scenarist. *Dir:* Frank Borzage. Adapted from the novel by Fannie Hurst. *Cast:* Vera Gordon, Gaston Glass, Alma Rubens, Dore Davidson, Louis Sterns, Maurice Levigne, Miriam Battista, Bobby Connelly. Winner of "Photoplay Magazine's" first Gold Medal Award for the year's "Best Picture." *Prod:* Paramount/Cosmopolitan. 6 reels.

THE FLAPPER (1920). Romantic comedy; as writer of an original scenario. *Dir:* Alan Crosland. *Cast:* Olive Thomas, Theodore Westman, Warren Cook, Katherine Johnston, Arthur Housman (Norma Shearer had an uncredited bit). *Prod:* Lewis J. Selznick. 6 reels.

THE RESTLESS SEX (1920). Drama; as scenarist. *Dir:* Robert Z. Leonard and Leo D'Usseau. Adapted from the novel by Robert W. Chambers. *Cast:* Marion Davies, Ralph Kellard, Carlyle Blackwell, Charles Lane, Robert Vivian, Vivienne Osborne. *Prod:* Paramount/Cosmopolitan. 7 reels.

THE WORLD AND HIS WIFE (1920). Marital triangle drama; as scenarist. *Dir:* Robert G. Vignola. Adapted from Charles F. Nirdlinger's translation of "El Gran Galeoto," a play by José Echegaray. *Cast:* Alma Rubens, Montagu Love, Gaston Glass, Charles Gerrard, Pedro de Cordoba, Byron Russell, Margaret Dale. Paramount/Cosmopolitan. 6 reels.

THE LOVE LIGHT (1921). Romantic drama of Italy during the First World War; as writer of an original story and as director. *Cast:* Mary Pickford, Fred Thomson, Raymond Bloomer, Evelyn Duma, Jean De Briac, Edward Phillips. *Prod:* United Artists. 8 reels.

STRAIGHT IS THE WAY (1921). Romantic comedy drama; as scenarist. *Dir:* Robert G. Vignola. Adapted from a story, "The Manifestations of Henry Ort," by Ethel Watts Mumford. *Cast:* Matt Moore, Gladys Leslie, Mabel Bert, Emily Fitzroy, Van Dyke Brooks, George Parsons. *Prod:* Paramount / Cosmopolitan. 6 reels.

JUST AROUND THE CORNER (1922). Romantic drama; as scenarist and as director. Adapted from a novel by Fannie Hurst. *Cast:* Fred Thomson, Sigrid Holmquist, Margaret Seddon, Lewis Sargent, Edward Phillips, Peggy Parry, Mme. Rosa Rosanova, William Nally. *Prod:* Paramount/Cosmopolitan. 7 reels.

BACK PAY (1922). Drama; as scenarist. *Dir:* Frank Borzage. Adapted from the novel by Fannie Hurst. *Cast* Seena Owen, Matt Moore, J. Barney Sherry, Ethel Duray, Charles Craig, Jerry Sinclair. *Prod:* Paramount / Cosmopolitan. 7 reels.

THE PRIMITIVE LOVER (1922). Romantic comedy; as scenarist. *Dir:* Sidney A. Franklin. Adapted from a play, "The Divorcee," by Edgar Selwyn. *Cast:* Constance Talmadge, Harrison Ford, Kenneth Harlan, Joe Roberts, Charles Pina, Chief Big Tree, Matilda Brundage *Prod:* First National. 7 reels.

SONNY (1922). Mother-son drama; as scenarist. *Dir:* Henry King. Adapted from a play by George V. Hobart. *Cast:* Richard Barthelmess, Pauline Garon, Margaret Seddon, Patterson Dial. *Prod:* Inspiration-First National. 7 reels.

EAST IS WEST (1922). Romantic comedy; as scenarist. *Dir:* Sidney A. Franklin. Adapted from the play by Samuel Shipman and John B. Hymer. *Cast:* Constance Talmadge, Nigel Barrie, Warner Oland, Edmund Burns, Frank Lanning, Winter Hall, Lillian Lawrence. *Prod:* First National. 8 reels.

THE ETERNAL FLAME (1922). Romantic costume drama; as scenarist. *Dir:* Frank Lloyd. Adapted from the novel, "La Duchesse de Langeais," by Honoré de Balzac. *Cast:*

Norma Talmadge, Conway Tearle, Adolphe Menjou, Kate Lester, Irving Cummings, Juanita Hansen, Rosemary Theby, Wedgwood Nowell, Thomas Ricketts. *Prod:* First National. 8 reels.

MINNIE (1922). Ugly duckling romantic comedy; as writer of the sub-titles. (Miss Marion usually wrote the sub-titles for the scenarios she wrote; this is once when she stepped in at Neilan's request to write sub-titles for him.) *Dir:* Marshall Neilan and Frank Urson. *Sc:* Marshall Neilan (from a story by George Patullo). *Cast:* Leatrice Joy, Matt Moore, George Barnum, Josephine Crowell, Helen Lynch, Raymond Griffith, Richard Wayne, Tom Wilson. George Dromgold. *Prod:* First National. 7 reels.

THE TOLL OF THE SEA (1922). Oriental tragic romance; as writer of an original scenario. *Dir:* Chester M. Franklin. *Cast:* Anna May Wong, Kenneth Harlan, Beatrice Bentley. This was the second all-Technicolor feature-length film; the first had been *The Gulf Between,* released Sept., 1917. *Prod:* Metro / Technicolor. 5 reels.

THE VOICE FROM THE MINARET (1923). Romantic drama; as scenarist. *Dir:* Frank Lloyd. Adapted from the novel and play by Robert Hichens. *Cast:* Norma Talmadge, Eugene O'Brien, Edwin Stevens, Winter Hall, Carl Gerrard, Claire Du Brey. *Prod:* First National. 7 reels.

THE FAMOUS MRS. FAIR (1923). Domestic drama; as scenarist. *Dir:* Fred Niblo. Adapted from the play by James Forbes. *Cast:* Myrtle Stedman, Huntley Gordon, Marguerite de la Motte, Cullen Landis, Ward Crane, Carmel Myers, Helen Ferguson. *Prod:* Mayer/Metro. 8 reels.

THE NTH COMMANDMENT (1923). Drama; as scenarist. *Dir:* Frank Borzage. Adapted from a novel by Fannie Hurst. *Cast:* Colleen Moore, James Morrison, Edward Phillips, Charlotte Merriam. *Prod:* Paramount / Cosmopolitan. 8 reels.

WITHIN THE LAW (1923). Romantic crook melodrama; as scenarist. *Dir:* Frank Lloyd. Adapted from the play by Bayard Veiller. *Cast:* Norma Talmadge, Jack Mulhall, Eileen Percy, Lew Cody, Joseph Kilgour, Helen Ferguson, Lincoln Plummer, Ward Crane. *Prod:* First National. 8 reels.

THE LOVE PIKER (1923). Romantic comedy; as scenarist. *Dir:* E. Mason Hopper. Based on a story by Frank R. Adams. *Cast:* Anita Stewart, Robert Frazer, William Norris, Carl Gerrard, Arthur Hoyt, Betty Francisco, Maym Kelso. *Prod:* Goldwyn/Cosmpolitan. 7 reels.

POTASH AND PERLMUTTER (1923).

Comedy; as scenarist. *Dir:* Clarence G. Badger. Adapted from the play by Montague Glass and Charles Klein. *Cast:* Alexander Carr, Barney Bernard, Vera Gordon, Martha Mansfield, Ben Lyon, Edward Durand, Hope Sutherland. *Prod:* Goldwyn/First National. 8 reels.

THE FRENCH DOLL (1923). Romantic comedy; as scenarist. *Dir:* Robert Z. Leonard. Adapted from a play by A. E. Thomas which derived from a French farce by Paul Armont and Marcel Gerbidon. *Cast:* Mae Murray, Orville Caldwell, Rod La Rocque, Rose Dione, Willard Louis, Lucien Littlefield. *Prod:* Tiffany/Metro. 7 reels.

THE SONG OF LOVE (1924). Romantic drama; as scenarist and co-director, with Chester M. Franklin, the latter of whom started as director, but became ill, and Miss Marion took over. Adapted from a novel, "Dust of Desire," by Margaret Peterson. *Cast:* Norma Talmadge, Joseph Schildkraut, Arthur Edmund Carewe, Lawrence Wheat, Maude Wayne, Earl Schenck, Hector V. Sarno. *Prod:* First National. 8 reels.

THROUGH THE DARK (1924). Melodrama; as scenarist. *Dir:* George W. Hill. Adapted from a story, "The Daughter of Mother McGinn," by Jack Boyle. *Cast:* Colleen Moore, Forrest Stanley, Carmelita Geraghty, Edward Phillips. *Prod:* Goldwyn / Cosmopolitan. 8 reels.

ABRAHAM LINCOLN (1924). Historical drama; as writer of an original scenario. *Dir:* Philip E. Rosen. *Cast:* George A. Billings, Ruth Clifford, Irene Hunt, Otis Harlan, Louise Fazenda, William Humphrey, Fred Kohler, Nell Craig, Genevieve Blinn, Eddie Sutherland. Winner of "Photoplay Magazine's" fifth Gold Medal Award as "Best Picture of 1924." *Prod:* Rockett-Lincoln Film Co. 12 reels.

SECRETS (1924). Romantic costume drama; as scenarist. *Dir:* Frank Borzage. Adapted from the play by Rudolf Besier and May Edington. *Cast:* Norma Talmadge, Eugene O'Brien, Claire McDowell, Gertrude Astor, Alice Day, Emily Fitzroy, Donald Keith, Doris Lloyd, Dick Sutherland, Winter Hall. *Prod:* First National. 8 reels.

CYTHEREA (1924). Marital drama; as scenarist. *Dir:* George Fitzmaurice. Adapted from the novel by Joseph Hergesheimer. *Cast:* Lewis Stone, Alma Rubens, Irene Rich, Constance Bennett, Norman Kerry, Charles Wellesley, Betty Bouton, Mickey Moore, Peaches Jackson, Brandon Hurst. Two dream sequences were in Technicolor. *Prod:* Goldwyn/First National. 8 reels.

TARNISH (1924). Romantic drama; as scenarist. *Dir:* George Fitzmaurice. Adapted from the play by Gilbert Emery. *Cast:* Ronald

Colman, May McAvoy, Marie Prevost, Albert Gran, Norman Kerry, Harry Myers. *Prod:* Goldwyn/First National. 7 reels.

IN HOLLYWOOD WITH POTASH AND PERLMUTTER (1924) Comedy with a studio film-making background; as scenarist. *Dir:* Alfred E. Green. Adapted from a play, "Business before Pleasure," by Montague Glass and Jules Eckert Goodman. *Cast:* Alexander Carr, George Sidney, Vera Gordon, Betty Blythe, Belle Bennett, Anders Randolph, Peggy Shaw, Charles Meredith, Lillian Hackett, Joseph W. Girard, Louis Payne, Cyril Ring. Sidney Franklin also appears in this directing Norma Talmadge as herself, and David Butler appears directing Constance Talmadge. *Prod:* Goldwyn/First National. 7 reels.

SUNDOWN (1924). Western romantic drama; as co-writer, with Kenneth B. Clarke, of the scenario. *Dir:* Laurence Trimble and Harry O. Hoyt. Adapted from a story by E. J. Hudson. *Cast:* Bessie Love, Roy Stewart, Hobart Bosworth, Arthur Hoyt, Charlie Murray, Jere Austin, Charles B. Crockett, E. J. Radcliffe, Margaret McWade. *Prod:* First National. 8 reels.

A THIEF IN PARADISE (1925). Romantic melodrama; as scenarist. *Dir:* George Fitzmaurice. Adapted from a novel, "The Worldlings," by Leonard Merrick. *Cast:* Ronald Colman, Aileen Pringle, Doris Kenyon, Alec B. Francis, Claude Gillingwater. *Prod:* Goldwyn/First National. 8 reels.

A TIGHT CORNER (1925). Western mystery romance; as writer of an original scenario. *Dir:* Al Rogell. *Cast:* Fred Thomson, "Silver King," Ann May, Fred Huntley, William Lowery, Carrie Ward. (Although Miss Marion had something to do with the writing of every one of Fred Thomson's Westerns, this is the only one on which she took any credit under her own name as a writer. She was between writing contracts at the time, and the credit reads: "Specially written by Frances Marion.") *Prod:* Ideal/Pathé. 5 reels.

THE LADY (1925). Mother-son drama; as scenarist. *Dir:* Frank Borzage. Adapted from the play by Martin Brown. *Cast:* Norma Talmadge, Wallace MacDonald, Brandon Hurst, Doris Lloyd, Walter Long, George Hackathorne, Marc McDermott, Paulette Du Val, Emily Fitzroy, Margaret Seddon. *Prod:* First National. 8 reels.

THE FLAMING FORTIES (1925). Western romance; as co-scenarist, with Harvey Gates. *Dir:* Tom Forman. Adapted from a story, "Tennessee's Pardner," by Bret Harte; with screen story by Elliott S. Clawson. *Cast:* Harry Carey, James Mason, William Bailey, Jacqueline Gadsden. *Prod:* Producers Distributing Co. 6 reels.

HIS SUPREME MOMENT (1925). Romantic drama; as scenarist. *Dir:* George Fitzmaurice. Adapted from a novel, "World without End," by May Edington. *Cast:* Blanche Sweet, Ronald Colman, Jane Winton, Belle Bennett, Cyril Chadwick, Ned Sparks, Kathlyn Myers. A play within the play, featuring Miss Sweet, Anna May Wong and Kalla Pasha, was in Technicolor. *Prod:* First National. 8 reels.

ZANDER THE GREAT (1925). Romantic comedy; as co-scenarist, with Lillie Hayward. *Dir:* George W. Hill. Adapted from the play by Salisbury Field. *Cast:* Marion Davies, Holbrook Blinn, Harrison Ford, Harry Watson, Harry Myers, George Seigmann, Emily Fitzroy, Hobart Bosworth, Richard Carle, Hedda Hopper, Olin Howland. *Prod:* Metro-Goldwyn/Cosmopolitan. 8 reels.

LIGHTNIN'. (1925). Comedy drama; as scenarist. *Dir:* John Ford. Adapted from the play by Frank Bacon and the story by Bacon & Winchell Smith. *Cast:* Jay Hunt, Madge Bellamy, J. Farrell MacDonald, Wallace MacDonald, Ethel Clayton, Richard Travers, James Marcus, Otis Harlan, Edythe Chapman, Brandon Hurst. *Prod:* Fox. 8 reels.

GRAUSTARK (1925). Mythical kingdom romance; as scenarist. *Dir:* Dimitri Buchowetzki. Adapted from the novel by George Barr McCutcheon. *Cast:* Norma Talmadge, Eugene O'Brien, Wanda Hawley, Roy D'Arcy, Frank Currier, Winter Hall, Albert Gran. *Prod:* First National. 7 reels.

THE DARK ANGEL (1925). Romantic drama; as scenarist. *Dir:* George Fitzmaurice. Adapted from a play by H. B. Trevelyan. *Cast:* Ronald Colman, Vilma Banky, Helen Jerome Eddy, Florence Turner, Wyndham Standing, Frank Elliott, Charles Lane. *Prod:* Goldwyn-First National. 8 reels.

LAZYBONES (1925). Bucolic romance; as scenarist. *Dir:* Frank Borzage. Adapted from the play by Owen Davis. *Cast:* Buck Jones, Madge Bellamy, ZaSu Pitts, Edythe Chapman, Leslie Fenton, Emily Fitzroy. *Prod:* Fox. 8 reels.

THANK YOU (1925). Comedy drama; as scenarist. *Dir:* John Ford. Adapted from the play by Winchell Smith and Tom Cushing. *Cast:* Alec B. Francis, Jacqueline Logan, George O'Brien, J. Farrell MacDonald, George Fawcett, Cyril Chadwick, Edith Chadwick, Marion Harlow. *Prod:* Fox. 7 reels.

SIMON, THE JESTER (1925). Romantic comedy drama; as producer and scenarist. *Dir:* George H. Melford. Adapted from the novel by William J. Locke. *Cast:* Eugene O'Brien, Lillian Rich, Edmund Burns, Henry B. Walthall. *Prod:* Producers Distributing Co. 7 reels.

STELLA DALLAS (1925). Mother-daughter drama; as scenarist. *Dir:* Henry King. Adapted from the novel by Olive Higginsprouty. *Cast:* Belle Bennett, Lois Moran, Ronald Colman, Jean Hersholt, Douglas Fairbanks Jr., Alice Joyce, Vera Lewis. *Prod:* Goldwyn/United Artists. 11 reels.

THE FIRST YEAR (1926). Marital comedy; as scenarist. *Dir:* Frank Borzage. Adapted from the play by Frank Craven. *Cast:* Matt Moore, Kathryn Perry, John Patrick, Frank Currier, Frank Cooley, Virginia Madison, Margaret Livingston, Carolynne Snowden, J. Farrell MacDonald. *Prod:* Fox. 6 reels.

PARTNERS AGAIN — POTASH AND PERLMUTTER (1926). Comedy; as scenarist. *Dir:* Henry King. Adapted from the play by Montague Glass and Jules Eckert Goodman. *Cast:* George Sidney, Alexander Carr, Betty Jewel, Allan Forrest, Lillian Elliott, Lew Brice, Robert Schable, Earl Metcalf. *Prod:* Goldwyn/United Artists. 6 reels.

PARIS AT MIDNIGHT (1926). Parisian drama; as producer and scenarist. *Dir:* E. Mason Hopper. Adapted from the novel, "Père Goriot", by Honoré de Balazc. *Cast:* Lionel Barrymore, Jetta Goudal, Mary Brian, Edmund Burns, Emile Chautard, Brandon Hurst, Jocelyn Lee, Carrie Daumery. *Prod:* Producers Distributing Co. 7 reels.

THE SON OF THE SHEIK (1926) Romantic drama; as scenarist. *Dir:* George Fitzmaurice. Adapted from the novel, "The Sons of the Sheik," by E. M. Hull. *Cast:* Rudolph Valentino, Vilma Banky, Montagu Love, Agnes Ayres, George Fawcett, Karl Dane, Bull Montana. *Prod:* United Artists. 7 reels.

THE SCARLET LETTER (1926). American classic drama of the Puritans; as scenarist. *Dir:* Victor Seastrom. Adapted from the novel by Nathaniel Hawthorne. *Cast:* Lillian Gish, Lars Hanson, Henry B. Walthall, William H. Tooker, Karl Dane, Joyce Coad. *Prod:* M-G-M. 9 reels.

THE WINNING OF BARBARA WORTH (1926). Romantic drama; as scenarist. *Dir:* Henry King. Adapted from the novel by Harold Bell Wright. *Cast:* Ronald Colman, Vilma Banky, Gary Cooper, Charles Lane, Clyde Cook, Paul McAllister. *Prod:* Goldwyn/United Artists. 9 reels.

THE RED MILL (1927). Romantic comedy of Holland; as scenarist. *Dir:* William Goodrich (Roscoe Arbuckle). Adapted from the musical comedy by Victor Herbert and Henry Blossom. *Cast:* Marion Davies, Owen Moore, Louise Fazenda, Karl Dane, Snitz Edwards, George Seigmann. *Prod:* M-G-M / Cosmopolitan. 7 reels.

THE CALLAHANS AND THE MURPHYS (1927). Comedy; as scenarist. *Dir:* George W. Hill. Adapted from the novel by Kathleen Norris. *Cast:* Marie Dressler, Polly Moran, Sally O'Neil, Lawrence Gray, Frank Currier, Gertrude Olmstead, Eddie Gribbon, Dawn O'Day (Anne Shirley). *Prod:* M-G-M. 7 reels.

MADAME POMPADOUR (1927). Romantic drama of the French court; as scenarist. *Dir:* Herbert Wilcox. Adapted from the play by Rudoph Schanzer and Ernst Wellisch. *Cast:* Dorothy Gish, Antonio Moreno, Henry Bosco, Jeff McLaughlin, Nelson Keys, Cyril McLaglen, Marcel Beauplan, Marie Ault, Tom Reynolds. *Prod:* Paramount. 7 reels.

LOVE (1927). Romantic tragedy; as scenarist. *Dir:* Edmund Goulding. Adapted by Lorna Moon from the novel, "Anna Karenina," by Count Leo Tolstoy. *Cast:* Greta Garbo, John Gilbert, George Fawcett, Emily Fitzroy, Brandon Hurst, Philippe De Lacy. *Prod:* M-G-M. 8 reels.

BRINGING UP FATHER (1928). Slapstick comedy; as scenarist. *Dir:* Jack Conway. Adapted from a George McManus story written by him from his newspaper comic strip. *Cast:* J. Farrell MacDonald, Jules Cowles, Polly Moran, Marie Dressler, Gerorude Olmstead, Grant Withers, David Mir, Tenen Holtz. *Prod:* M-G-M. 7 reels.

THE COSSACKS (1928). Romantic drama of Old Russia; as scenarist. *Dir:* George W. Hill. Adapted from the novel by Count Leo Tolstoy. *Cast:* John Gilbert, Renée Adorée, Ernest Torrence, Dale Fuller, Mary Alden, Paul Hurst. *Prod:* M-G-M. 10 reels.

EXCESS BAGGAGE (1928). Backstage romantic drama; as scenarist. *Dir:* James Cruze. Adapted from the play by John McGowan. *Cast:* William Haines, Josephine Dunn, Neely Edwards, Kathleen Clifford, Greta Granstedt, Ricardo Cortez, Cyril Chadwick. *Prod:* M-G-M. 8 reels.

THE WIND (1928). Psychological drama; as scenarist. *Dir:* Victor Seastrom. Adapted from the novel by Dorothy Scarborough. *Cast:* Lillian Gish, Lars Hanson, Dorothy Cumming, Montagu Love, Edward Earle, William Orlamond. *Prod:* M-G-M. 8 reels.

THE AWAKENING (1928). Romantic drama; as writer of the original story. *Dir:* Victor Fleming. *Sc:* Carey Wilson. *Cast:* Vilma Banky, Walter Byron, Louis Wolheim, George Davis, William Orlamond, Carl von Hartmann. (The soundtrack featured Irving Berlin's theme song, "Marie.") *Prod:* Goldwyn-United Artists. 9 reels.

THE MASKS OF THE DEVIL (1928). Psychological drama; as scenarist. *Dir:* Victor Seastrom. Adapted from the novel, "Die Masken Erwin Reiners." *Cast:* John Gilbert, Alma

Rubens, Theodore Roberts, Frank Reicher, Eva Von Berne, Ralph Forbes, Ethel Wales, Polly Ann Young. *Prod:* M-G-M. 8 reels.

THEIR OWN DESIRE (1929). Sophisticated romantic drama; as writer of the screenplay (with dialogue by James Forbes). *Dir:* E. Mason Hopper and James Forbes. Adapted from a novel by Sarita Fuller. *Cast:* Norma Shearer, Belle Bennett, Lewis Stone, Robert Montgomery, Helene Millard, Cecil Cunningham, Henry Herbert, Mary Doran, June Nash. (Miss Marion's first screenplay for the talking film.) (Norma Shearer was nominated for an Oscar.) *Prod:* M-G-M. 7 reels.

ANNA CHRISTIE (1930). Drama; as screenplay writer. *Dir:* Clarence Brown. Adapted from the play by Eugene O'Neill. *Cast:* Greta Garbo, Charles Bickford, George Marion, Marie Dressler, Lee Phelps, James R. Mack. (Garbo, director Brown and cameraman William Daniels were nominated for Oscars.) (Miss. Marion's screenplay was also translated into German for the German talking version.) *Prod:* M-G-M. 10 reels.

THE ROGUE SONG (1930). Romantic operetta; as co-writer, with John Colton, of the screenplay. *Dir:* Lionel Barrymore. Adapted from an operetta, "Gypsy Love", by Franz Lehar, a. m. Wilner and Robert Bodansky. Technicolor. *Cast:* Lawrence Tibbett, Catherine Dale Owen, Nance O'Neil, Judith Vosselli, Ulrich Haupt, Elsa Alsen, Florence Lake, Lionel Belmore, Wallace MacDonald, Kate Price, H. A. Morgan, Burr MacIntosh, James Bradbury, Stan Laurel, Oliver Hardy. (Tibbett was nominated for an Oscar.) *Prod:* M-G-M. 12 reels.

THE BIG HOUSE (1930). Prison drama; as writer of the original story, screenplay, and dialogue (with additional dialogue by Joe Farnham and Martin Flavin). *Dir:* George W. Hill. *Cast:* Chester Morris, Wallace Beery, Robert Montgomery, Lewis Stone, Leila Hyams, George Marion, J. C. Nugent, Karl Dane, DeWitt Jennings, Matthew Betz, Claire McDowell, Robert Emmett O'Connor, Tom Kennedy, Tom Wilson, Eddie Foyer, Roscoe Ates, Fletcher Norton. (Miss Marion won her first Oscar; Beery was nominated for his performance; so was Douglas Shearer, who won for Sound Recording; and the picture was one of the five nominees for best of the year.) (Miss Marion's screenplay was also the basis for the translations for the German, French and Spanish-speaking versions.) *Prod:* M-G-M. 10 reels.

LET US BE GAY (1930). Drawing-room comedy; as writer of the screenplay (with additional dialogue by Lucille Newmark). *Dir:* Robert Z. Leonard. Adapted from the play by Rachel Crothers. *Cast:* Norma Shearer, Rod La Rocque, Marie Dressler, Gilbert Emery, Hedda Hopper, Raymond Hackett, Sally Eil-

ers. (Miss Marion's screenplay was also translated into French for the French talking version.) *Prod:* M-G-M. 8 reels.

GOOD NEWS (1930). Musical comedy; as screenplay writer (with dialogue by Joe Farnham). *Dir:* Nick Grinde and Edward J. MacGregor. Adapted from the musical comedy by Lawrence Schwab, Frank Mandel, B. G. DeSylva, Lew Brown and Ray Henderson. *Cast:* Bessie Love, Mary Lawlor, Cliff Edwards, Stanley Smith, Lola Lane, Gus Shy, Thomas Smith, Delmer Daves, Frank McGlyn, Dorothy McNulty, Abe Lyman and his band. *Prod:* M-G-M. 11 reels.

MIN AND BILL (1930). Character comedy drama; as co-writer, with Marion Jackson, of the screenplay. *Dir:* George W. Hill. Supposedly based on a novel, "Dark Star," by Lorna Moon; actually adapted from a story written by Frances Marion. *Cast:* Marie Dressler, Wallace Beery, Dorothy Jordan, Marjorie Rambeau, Donald Dillaway, DeWitt Jennings, Russell Hopton, Frank McGlynn, Greta Gould. (Dressler won a Best Actress Oscar.) (Miss Marion's screenplay was also translated into Spanish for the Spanish talking version.) *Prod:* M-G-M. 7 reels.

THE SECRET SIX (1931). Underworld vs. police melodrama; as sole writer of the original story and screenplay. *Dir:* George W. Hill. *Cast:* Wallace Beery, Lewis Stone, John Mack Brown, Jean Harlow, Marjorie Rambeau, Paul Hurst, Clark Gable, Ralph Bellamy, John Miljan, DeWitt Jennings, Murray Kinnell, Fletcher Norton, Louis Natheaux, Frank McGlynn, Theodore von eltz. *Prod:* M-G-M. 9 reels.

THE CHAMP (1931). Father-son drama; as writer of the original story (with dialogue continuity by Leonard Praskins and additional dialogue by Wanda Tuchock). *Dir:* King Vidor. *Cast:* Wallace Beery, Jackie Cooper, Irene Rich, Roscoe Ates, Edward Brophy, Hale Hamilton, Jesse Scott, Marcia Mae Jones. (Miss Marion won her second Oscar; Wallace Beery won a Best Actor Oscar, tying with Frederic March for *Dr. Jekyll and Mr. Hyde;* King Vidor was nominated for Best Director; the picture was one of eight nominees for best of the year.) *Prod:* M-G-M 10 reels.

EMMA (1932). Drama; as writer of the original story (with adaptation and dialogue by Leonard Praskins; additional dialogue by Zelda Sears). *Dir:* Clarence Brown. *Cast:* Marie Dressler, Richard Cromwell, Jean Hersholt, Myrna Loy, John Miljan, Purnell Pratt, Leila Bennett, Barbara Kent, Kathryn Crawford, George Meeker, Dale Fuller. (Dressler was nominated for a Best Actress award.) *Prod:* M-G-M. 8 reels.

BLONDIE OF THE FOLLIES (1932). Backstage romantic comedy; as writer of the original story (with dialogue by Anita Loos). *Dir:* Edmund Goulding. *Cast:* Marion Davies, Billie Dove, Robert Montgomery, Jimmy Durante, James Gleason, ZaSu Pitts, Sidney Toler, Douglas Dumbrille, Sarah Padden, Clyde Cook. *Prod:* M-G-M/Cosmopolitan. 9 reels.

CYNARA (1932). Romantic drama; co-author, with Lynn Starling, of the screenplay. *Dir:* King Vidor. Adapted from the play by H. M. Harwood and Robert Gore-Brown, which was based on Gore-Brown's novel, "An Imperfect Lover." *Cast:* Ronald Colman, Kay Francis, Phyllis Barry, Henry Stephenson, Viva Tattersall, Florine McKinney, Clarissa Selwynne, Paul Porcasi. *Prod:* Samuel Goldwyn. 9 reels.

SECRETS (1933). Romantic drama; as writer of the screenplay. *Dir:* Frank Borzage. Adapted from the play by Rudolf Besier and May Edington. *Cast:* Mary Pickford, Leslie Howard, C. Aubrey Smith, Blanche Friderici, Doris Lloyd, Herbert Evans, Ned Sparks, Allan Sears, Mona Maris, Huntley Gordon, Virginia Grey, Ethel Clayton, Bessie Barriscale, Theodore von Eltz. *Prod:* United Artists. 9 reels.

PEG O' MY HEART (1933). Romantic comedy drama; as adapter of the J. Hartley Manners play. *Dir:* Robert Z. Leonard. *Sc:* Frank R. Adams. *Cast:* Marion Davies, Onslow Stevens, J. Farrell MacDonald, Juliette Compton, Irene Browne, Tyrell Davis, Alan Mowbray, Doris Lloyd, Billy Bevan, Robert Greig. *Prod:* M-G-M. 9 reels.

DINNER AT EIGHT (1933). Comedy drama; as co-writer, with Herman J. Mankiewicz, of the screenplay (with additional dialogue by Donald Ogden Stewart). *Dir:* George Cukor. Adapted from the play by George S. Kaufman and Edna Ferber. *Cast:* John Barrymore, Lionel Barrymore, Billie Burke, Marie Dressler, Jean Harlow, Wallace Beery, Lee Tracy, Edmund Lowe, Madge Evans, Jean Hersholt, Karen Morley, Louise Closser Hale, Phillips Holmes, May Robson, Grant Mitchell, Phoebe Foster, Elizabeth Patterson, Hilda Vaughn, Harry Beresford, Edwin Maxwell, John Davidson, Edward Woods, George Baxter, Herman Bing, Anna Duncan. *Prod:* M-G-M. 11 reels.

THE PRIZEFIGHTER AND THE LADY (1933). Romantic drama of the prizefighting ring; as writer of the orginal story, "The Sailor and the Lady." *Dir:* W. S. Van Dyke. *Sc:* John Lee Mahin and John Meehan. *Cast:* Max Baer, Myrna Loy, Walter Huston, Primo Carnera, Jack Dempsey, Otto Kruger, Vince Barnett, Robert McWade, Muriel Evans, Jean Howard. (Miss Marion was nominated for a Best Original Story award.) *Prod:* M-G-M. 11 reels.

GOING HOLLYWOOD (1933). Hollywood comedy, with music; as writer of the original story. *Dir:* Raoul Walsh. *Sc:* Donald Ogden Stewart. *Cast:* Marion Davies, Bing Crosby, Fifi D'Orsay, Stuart Erwin, Ned Sparks, Patsy Kelly, Bobby Watson. *Prod:* M-G-M / Cosmopolitan. 9 reels.

RIFFRAFF (1935). Romantic comedy drama; as writer of the original story, and as co-writer, with H. W. Hanemann and Anita Loos, of the screenplay. *Dir:* J. Walter Ruben. *Cast:* Jean Harlow, Spencer Tracy, Una Merkel, Joseph Calleia, Victor Kilian, Mickey Rooney, J. Farrell MacDonald, Paul Hurst, Juanita Quigley, Roger Imhof, Vince Barnett, Dorothy Appleby, Judith Wood, Arthur Housman, Wade Boteler, Joe Phillips, William Newell, Al Hill, Helen Flint, Lillian Harmer, Bob Perry, George Givot, Helene Costello, Rafaela Ottiano. *Prod:* M-G-M. 10 reels.

CAMILLE (1937). Romantic tragedy; as co-writer, with Zoë Akins and James Hilton, of the screenplay. *Dir:* George Cukor. Adapted from the play and novel, "La Dame aux Camellias," by Alexandre Dumas, *fils.* *Cast:* Greta Garbo, Robert Taylor, Lionel Barrymore, Elizabeth Allen, Jessie Ralph, Henry Daniell, Lenore Ulric, Laura Hope Crews, Rex O'Malley, Russell Hardie, E. E. Clive, Douglas Walton, Marion Ballou, Joan Brodel (Leslie), June Wilkins, Fritz Leiber Jr., Elsie Esmonds, Eily Malyon. (Garbo was nominated for a Best Actress Academy Award.) *Prod:* M-G-M. 109m.

LOVE FROM A STRANGER (1937). Suspense murder mystery; as writer of the screenplay and dialogue. *Dir:* Rowland V. Lee. Adapted from the play by Frank Vosper, which had been based on a short story by Agatha Christie. *Cast:* Ann Harding, Basil Rathbone, Binnie Hale, Bruce Seton, Jean Cadell. *Prod:* Trafalgar/United Artists. 9 reels.

KNIGHT WITHOUT ARMOUR (1937). Romantic drama; as adapter of the novel, "Without Armour," by James Hilton. *Dir:* Jacques Feyder. *Sc:* Lajos Biros, with scenario and dialogue by Arthur Wimperis. *Cast:* Marlene Dietrich, Robert Donat, Irene Vanbrugh, Herbert Lomas, John Clements, Austin Trevor, Basil Gill, Davie Tree, Frederick Culley, Miles Malleson, Lyn Harding, Raymond Huntley. *Prod:* London Films (Korda)/United Artists. 11 reels.

GREEN HELL (1940). Melodrama in South America; as writer of an original screenplay. *Dir:* James Whale. *Cast:* Douglas Fairbanks Jr., Joan Bennett, Vincent Price, George Bancroft, Alan Hale, John Howard, George Sanders, Gene Garrick, Francis McDonald, Ray Mala, Peter Bronte. *Prod:* Universal. 10 reels.

MOLLY AND ME (1945). Character comedy drama; as writer of the novel, "Molly Bless Her," which formed the basis of the story. *Dir:*

Lewis Seiler. *Sc:* Leonard Praskins (from Roger Burford's adaptation). *Cast:* Gracie Fields, Monty Woolley, Roddy McDowall, Reginald Gardiner, Natalie Schafer, Edith Barrett, Queenie Leonard, Doris Lloyd, Ethel Griffies. *Prod:* 20th Century-Fox. 6400 ft.

THE CLOWN (1953). Father-son drama; as writer of the original story, "The Champ," of which this was a re-make. *Dir:* Robert Z. Leonard. *Sc:* Martin Rackin. *Cast:* Red Skelton, Tim Considine, Jane Greer, Loring Smith, Fay Roope, Philip Ober, Walter Reed, Edward Marr, Jonathan Cott, Don Beddoe, Steve Forrest.

Addenda

The films Lois Weber made for Bosworth Productions during 1914-15, on which Frances Marion worked as Miss Weber's *protégée*, include *False Colours, Hypocrites, It's No Laughing Matter, Like Most Wives, Traitor* (all produced in 1914), and *Sunshine Molly* (1915). The features Elsie Janis made for Bosworth when Miss Marion and she first knew each other include *Caprices of Kitty, Betty in Search of a Thrill, Nearly a Lady,* and *'Twas Ever Thus* (all released in 1915). Dustin Farnum starred in *Captain Courtesy* for Bosworth in 1915, and Miss Marion, an excellent horsewoman, doubled for his leading lady, Winifred Kingston (who later became Mrs. Farnum) in all her riding scenes.

The professional compatibility between Frances Marion and Mary Pickford cannot be over-emphasised. Theirs was a remarkably happy professional union, one which benefited both careers. Several joint-ventures which were publicised but never realised are sometimes listed as actual films, but the ones listed in the preceding filmography are the only ones that actually got before the camera.

In the late Twenties and into the mid-Thirties most major Hollywood studios made foreign-language versions of their films, and some of Miss Marion's screenplays were translated into French, Spanish, and German. Although identical sets were used in shooting these foreign-language versions, the directors often chose different set-ups, abd the actors frequently gave different characterisations from those in the English-speaking originals. Garbo, for example, who played the title role in both the American and the German versions of *Anna Christie,* gave an entirely different characterisation in the German version, in which Anna, from her first entrance, looks like a dejected prostitute who has suffered a breakdown and has only just been released from a hospital.

In the foreign versions of other Frances Marion screenplays, Lili Damita played the Norma Shearer role in *Soyons Gai,* the French version of *Let Us Be Gay* directed by Arthur Robison, in which Adolphe Menjou and Françoise Rosay also played; Charles Boyer played the Chester Morris role in the French version of *The Big House* directed by Paul Fejos, who also directed the German version, *Menschen hinter Gittern,* while Ward Wing directed the Spanish version; and Virginia Fabregas played the Marie Dressler role in the Spanish version of *Min and Bill* directed by Arthur Gregor and called *La fruta amarga.*

Frances Marion is the author of innumerable short stories, poems, and non-fiction articles in "Sunset Magazine," "Pictorial Review," "Photoplay," and other magazines; and she is the writer of the following books:

"Minnie Flynn" (1925), a novel dedicated "To My Father and Mother." It has a background of early movie-making at Biograph and Famous Players in New York City.

"The Secret Six" (1931), a novel adapted from her original screenplay and illustrated with scenes from the film.

"Valley People" (1935), a series of vignettes of California's Napa Valley, which, viewed as a whole, forms a *genre* novel that critics have compared favourably to Sherwood Anderson's "Winesburg, Ohio," and to Edgar Lee Masters's "Spoon River Anthology."

"Molly, Bless Her" (1937), a novel based on incidents in the life of Marie Dressler.

"How to Write and Sell Film Stories" (1937), a manual and textbook on the technique of screenwriting in which Samuel Goldwyn allowed Miss Marion to use the complete screenplay of Robert E. Sherwood's "Adventures of Marco Polo" as an analytical example of a well-constructed talking picture script.

"Westward the Dream" (1948), historical novel of early California.

"The Powder Keg" (1953), a novel set in a California woman's prison.

Miss Marion's work forms part of the following books: her scenario for *The Scarlet Letter* is in Frances Taylor Patterson's "Motion Picture Continuities" (1929); her one-act play, "The Cup of Life," is in Kenyon Nicholson's "Hollywood Plays" (1930); and her essay, "Scenario Writing," is in Stephen Watts's "Behind the Screen" (1938).

"Off With Their Heads!," (1972), described as "A Serio-Comic Tale of Hollywood," provides some fascinating recollections by her of a town and a time that are no more, and is in no sense to be construed as an autobiography, but only reminiscences of some of the talented and amusing and, sometimes, tragic people she has known in the film business.

6
MAY McAVOY

The persistence of the child-woman as a favourite focus for the male imagination is a human fact worth serious study. So are the changes in the child-woman depicted by American movies in the course of their evolution.

Until the advent of sound — or, perhaps appropriately, the advent of the Depression — the child-woman in American films was virginal mentally as well as physically. It has been only the image of the actress herself that has saved the type from banality, actresses like Mary Pickford and Marguerite Clark. And May McAvoy, who could light up the screen like a dazzling star coming into orbit. She also enjoyed two other distinctions: she was a full-fledged movie star *before* she went to Hollywood, having served her apprenticeship in Eastern-made films; and she was leading lady to Al Jolson in *The Jazz Singer,* the film that spelled the end of the silent era.

During the last quarter of the Nineteenth century, her paternal grandfather owned and operated a big livery stable in Manhattan, which filled the block between Park and Lexington Avenues now occupied by the Waldorf-Astoria Hotel. Her father became a partner in that thriving enterprise, and with his wife, and their first-born (a son), resided in a brownstone house at 41st and Park, in which, on September 8, 1901, the daughter christened May was born.

While May was still in grammar school — St. Patrick's Parochial School — her father suddenly died at the age of thirty-six, and Grandfather McAvoy thereupon sold the livery stable at a substantial profit. "I scarcely remember my father at all," May says.

Her widowed mother was not hard pressed, but she did move her small family uptown to 106th Street and Amsterdam Avenue, and May to Public School 54. Subsequently, the McAvoys moved further west on 106th Street almost to Riverside Drive. May's brother Frank became an electrical engineer and today is head of the McAvoy Target Engineering Co. in New York.

"I wanted to be somebody," May says, "and was utterly miserable at high school. I had absolutely nothing in common with the other girls. All they thought about were good times, pretty clothes, and boys. I was there to work. I left high school in my third year, and decided I was going to succeed in pictures."

There was more to it than that.

She had made a friend of a dancer in a variety act named Ruth Wells* and one afternoon visited her backstage. While she watched her performance from the wings, a man nearby observed her closely. She was then in her mid-teens, and a very diminutive person — she never attained a height greater than 4 feet 11 inches, never weighed more than one hundred pounds — and in the eager innocence of her face there were large Irish blue eyes fringed with dark lashes. The man asked if she were "in the profession." She didn't know what he was talking about. He explained he was an agent for modelling and acting talent, and gave her his card.

When she got home, she showed her mother the card and said she had decided to become a model and actress. Mrs. McAvoy regarded her daughter sceptically, and tore up the card.

"That could have been the end of it all," says Miss McAvoy, "except that I soon realised I was not cut out to be a schoolteacher, which is what it was then assumed I would be. Every time I saw Ruth Wells I longed to be, like her, 'in the profession.' Finally, Mother saw that I was making myself and everybody else miserable, so she told me I could try my luck and at least get it out of my system."

Miss McAvoy immediately had good professional photographs taken, wrote her name and address and information about herself on their backs, and left them in as many casting offices as she could.

"Almost at once I had a call from Cliff Robertson, the casting director at Metro," Miss McAvoy says. "He'd been very reassuring when I left my photograph and had said, 'You'll hear from us.' A couple of days later he phoned to ask me to come down to Metro that evening at 7:30 and film a short for Domino Sugar. I was so naive I said, 'Couldn't we please do it tomorrow night? I'm invited to a birthday party tonight.' There was a pause at Robertson's end of the line. Then he said curtly that if I wanted the job I'd have to be there that night promptly at 7:30. I promised I'd be on hand without fail.

"Mother went with me, and it wasn't at all a glamorous evening. A wardrobe woman handed me a gingham dress and an apron, and the director told me to put on make-up. I didn't even know what that meant. The wardrobe woman did the best she could with powder, rouge and lipstick from her handbag."

Other movie commercials followed, and Miss McAvoy got modelling jobs for hats, gloves, shoes. But never full figure, since she was not considered tall enough to model a dress. However, through modelling, she met and became friendly with some of the top models of the time, including Helene Chadwick, Justine Johnstone, and Edna Murphy. Beautiful Martha Mansfield advised her to concentrate on movie casting directors. "You're born for movies," Miss Mansfield insisted. "You're young and you're small. They prefer small actresses, not show girls like me, because few actors are really tall."

Miss McAvoy took her advice, and broke into feature films at Fox in New York, as an extra in a George Walsh picture called *I'll Say So*. Other extra jobs

---

*Ruth Wells and May McAvoy met in Public School 54. Even then, Miss Wells was a talented dancer and she quit school to join a vaudeville dance-act. But her early promise was not fulfilled, and years later Miss McAvoy was able to get small parts for her in films. Ultimately, she committed suicide.

133

followed, and she became aware that some directors would place her in the foreground so she could be seen. Audiences responded to her, and in 1917 she was given an *ingénue* lead in an independent movie called *Hate,* the exteriors of which were filmed in Savannah, Georgia. The picture was sold on the State-rights basis, and Miss McAvoy received critical attention for the first time.

Her notices were so good that they helped get her next break: a flashy dramatic part as a wounded girl forced to serve Prussian officers who had taken over a Belgian convent, in some First World War propaganda called *To Hell with the Kaiser!* Her next two roles — as "Australy" with Marguerite Clark in *Mrs. Wiggs of the Cabbage Patch* and as Madge Kennedy's younger sister in *A Perfect Lady* — established her as one of the screen's most promising *ingénues.*

"Madge Kennedy was absolutely marvellous to me," says Miss McAvoy. "It was the first and only time a star deliberately turned her back to the camera and gave me the scene. Miss Kennedy did it not once but several times, until the director reminded her that *she* was the star audiences paid money to see."

After two more years as a supporting *ingénue* — young sister to Norma Talmadge in *The Way of a Woman;* youthful nurse to Alice Joyce in *The Sporting Duchess;* a tragic young sister to Florence Reed in *The Woman Under Oath,* where she again proved she could handle a dramatic scene — Miss McAvoy became leading lady in a series of features J. Stuart Blackton directed for Pathé.

While so employed, she heard that director John S. Robertson was preparing to film James M. Barrie's *Sentimental Tommy* at Paramount-Artcraft's new studio on Long Island. Barrie's heroine, Grizel, was one of Miss McAvoy's favourite fictional characters, and she at once decided the role was for her. She tried to get an interview with Robertson, only to learn he had already cast Faire Binney as Grizel.

She was disappointed, but an important role with Lionel Barrymore in *The Devil's Garden* made her forget about losing the part of Grizel in *Sentimental Tommy.*

"The luck of the Irish then played into my hands," Miss McAvoy says. "Kenneth Webb, the director of *The Devil's Garden,* was shooting a sequence up-State and John Robertson came up to our location to see Webb about something. He arrived on a morning when Mr. Webb had arranged to see the previous day's rushes in a local theatre before it opened for its matinee, so Webb asked Mr. Robertson to accompany him. By sheer chance, the rushes contained rough footage of one of my best scenes, Mr. Robertson was impressed, and stored the memory of me in a corner of his mind.

"Anyway, when I finished on *The Devil's Garden,* Mr. Webb told me to go at once to see John Robertson, who had started shooting *Sentimental Tommy,* but was shooting around Faire Binney, who wasn't working out and Robertson was going to replace her. I tore over to Robertson's office. He remembered me! And gave me the part of Grizel."

Today, *Sentimental Tommy* is considered one of the "lost films." The negative has presumably disintegrated, and no prints are known to exist. I hope a print will one day show up (probably in Russia or behind the Iron Curtain, where so many have come to light), for *Sentimental Tommy* remains

May McAvoy with Mabel Taliaferro in *Sentimental Tommy*.

in my memory as a beautiful picture, and as the best adaptation to the screen of any Barrie work. Exquisite stills corroborate my memory. Robertson was a sensitive director and had both a feeling for mood and an artist's eye for pictorial composition. In the village of Scottish weavers (Thrums) that Robertson constructed on Long Island, May McAvoy and Gareth Hughes, as Grizel and Tommy, gave performances that lifted them to stardom.

Her success as Grizel was so outstanding that Paramount signed her to a starring contract before *Sentimental Tommy* was finished. As soon as it was, Miss McAvoy set out, accompanied by her mother, for Hollywood, to star for Realart (a Paramount subsidiary).

She was only twenty when she arrived in Hollywood and she quickly discovered that contract stars were studio work-horses: they dressed up the programmers that made the high-budgeted pictures possible. But she was fortunate in having Kathlyn Williams with her in most of her Realart vehicles. Miss Williams was the wife of Charles Eyton, Paramount's production manager, and anything she played in was treated a little more considerately.

Most of Miss McAvoy's films were shot at the Lasky Studios, then at Vine between Selma and Sunset. Hector Turnbull, one of filmdom's most expensive writers (he had written Fannie Ward's *The Cheat* for DeMille), provided three stories for Miss McAvoy, and her pictures were relatively well-mounted. At least one of those Realart programmers, *Morals,* an adaptation of William J. Locke's "The Morals of Marcus Ordeyne," was liked by many critics. Oddly enough, Miss McAvoy dislikes this film. When I reminded her that Marie Doro had previously done it, that Lupe Velez re-made it, and that Mabel Normand had lamented to William Desmond Taylor, its director, that she hadn't been allowed to do it, Miss McAvoy replied: "I wish to heaven they had let Mabel do it! I hated it. I don't care how good the critics said it was — I thought it much ado about nothing."

135

MORE FROM HOLLYWOOD

When the anti-trust division of the United States Department of Justice forced Paramount to divest itself of Realart, and Paramount elected to dissolve the company, Paramount also took over Miss McAvoy's contract. Although it had provided for solo star billing, Miss McAvoy says she was relieved when Paramount co-starred her.

"How could I object?" she now asks. "The stories were better; the budgets were bigger; and I could really do something with the parts in which I was cast. It was much easier if you had something to work with and time to develop a characterisation; and the directors were more compatible, especially William C. de Mille, who became, next to John Robertson, my favourite. Like Robertson, he had great taste, intelligence, and sensitiveness. And George Fitzmaurice was also very simpatico. I loved working for him in *Kick In,* and I was very pleased when the critics and public singled out my portrayal of that tragic girl."

Paramount had high hopes for her, and Jesse L. Lasky soon announced that she had been chosen for Lady Babbie in *The Little Minister,* and that John Robertson, then "conferring" in London with James M. Barrie, had specified McAvoy for the title role in *Peter Pan* if Paramount should decide he would be the director.

Barrie himself declared, in an interview, his admiration for her depiction of Grizel, and Carl Sandburg called her a "star-eyed goddess." Robert E. Sherwood, then reviewing movies for "Life" (when it was the American "Punch"), was unreserved in his praise of her performance. Those were the days Miss McAvoy walked on air.

While filming *Only 38,* which was directed by William C. de Mille, Miss McAvoy kept catching glimpses of that director's celebrated brother Cecil on the set, and soon realised he was watching *her.*

"He made me very nervous," she says. "Then one day, just after I finished a scene, he was introduced to me, and he said, smiling, 'I've been watching you, Miss McAvoy.' I told him I knew he had, and he rejoined: 'I've made up my mind. I'd like you to play the lead in my next picture.'

"I was naturally very flattered. Then, without taking his eyes off me, he said, 'You may not be so pleased, Miss McAvoy, when you hear the two conditions. First, you'll have to cut your hair very short.'

"That didn't bother me, really. I'd been thinking about having my hair fashionably shingled anyway. I told him I had no objections to cutting my hair for him. He still hadn't taken his eyes off me. 'In this picture,' he said, 'there are flashbacks to the Stone Age. You'll be wearing practically no clothes.'

"My Scottish-Irish backbone went very stiff. I've always behaved with great propriety, and I guess it's given people the impression I'm prudish, which I'm not. I was offended only by the manner in which the subject had been broached.

"'I'm afraid, Mr. DeMille, you've got the wrong girl,' I said as coldly as I could.

"The smile faded from his face and he walked from the set. He never spoke to me again. I had said 'no' to him.

"At first, I didn't realise there would be consequences. The studio didn't have anything ready for me after *Only 38,* and I was grateful for a respite. I was amused when Mr. DeMille gave the girl's role in *Adam's Rib* to one of my good friends, Pauline Garon, and she wasn't half as nude in her tiger skins as

136

most of us were when we went bathing at Santa Monica. But *Adam's Rib* was one of the worst pictures DeMille ever made, and I was glad I had no part of it.

"Then I read in Louella Parson's column that Betty Compson was going to play Babbie in *The Little Minister** — this only a few months after Lasky had announced me for it. On top of that, *Peter Pan* was given not to John Robertson to direct but to Herbert Brenon, who chose an unknown, Betty Bronson, for the lead.

"I was heartsick, and beginning to get the message. For eight months I sat at home, assigned to no role because I had dared say 'no' to Mr. DeMille. I was still on salary and went to Mr. Lasky, who was every actor's friend, and pleaded my case. I asked him, if Paramount didn't have anything for me, to lend me to another studio. So he did, to Thomas Ince for a thriller called *Her Reputation*. Ince paid Paramount twice what Paramount was paying me.

"When I was through shooting *Her Reputation*, I went home and sat some more. Finally, I couldn't stand it any longer and asked my lawyer, Neil McCarthy, if he could arrange for me to buy up the remainder of my Paramount contract. He got them to let me do so for ten thousand dollars cash, which I paid. Then Mother and I packed up and took a train to New York."

Which changed her luck. John Robertson, who had contracted to direct Richard Barthelmess in a movie version of the Pinero play called *The Enchanted Cottage*, offered her the role of the lonely, ugly spinster who falls in love with a young man who has been crippled, and their love enables the two of them to see each other as beautiful and desirable.

"We didn't have union make-up artists then — it was before the days of the Westmores," says Miss McAvoy, "and Mr. Robertson let me work out my own make-up. I built up an unattractive fake nose and wore an awkward dental bridge that altered the whole appearance of my jaw and made my front teeth protrude. I pulled my hair back until it was lifelessly straight. I built up my eyebrows and brushed them the wrong way. I raised one heel so that I limped. And I wore a kind of humped brace on my back so that I stooped and all my clothing hung gracelessly. I was about as unfeminine and pathetic as a girl can get, but I was delighted. I'd come a long way from that ambitious teenager who hadn't known what make-up was."

The Enchanted Cottage did as much to revive interest in May McAvoy as *Sentimental Tommy* had done to establish her. The picture and everybody who worked on it were praised. It is a property that has always opened doors, as I myself was to discover years later when I was hired to write the screenplay for the talking version of it.

As soon as Miss McAvoy completed *The Enchanted Cottage*, Jesse Lasky asked if she would be interested in a film Paramount was about to make with Glenn Hunter — a screen version of Homer Croy's bestselling novel, *West of the Water Tower*. Miss McAvoy replied that she was interested, but the price for her services had gone up. She had been getting $500 a week when she

---

*Today, Miss Compson says: "Oh, how I wish May McAvoy had played Babbie. It was nothing but a headache to me. First of all, the director, Penrhyn Stanlaws, and I were no longer compatible at all; and then halfway through shooting, when we were on location up in the Hollywood hills, I was told to hide in some shrubbery. Shrubbery? I said. That's poison ivy if I ever saw it. I was persuaded that I was wrong, so I hid in the shrubbery. Unfortunately, I was right; it was poison ivy. So *The Little Minister* was really more than a headache to me."

137

bought out her Paramount contract. Now, she told Lasky, her weekly salary was $1,500.

"There was a momentary silence," Miss McAvoy says, "followed by: 'Very well, the studio will accept that salary.' I realised then that Lasky was on my side all along."

West of the Water Tower led to another Paramount picture, *The Bedroom Window*, directed by William C. de Mille. Her salary was increased for that picture, and for subsequent ones, until she was receiving $3,000 a week, the highest salary then paid to a free-lance actress. And her roles improved. Fitzmaurice used her again very effectively in *Tarnish*, with Ronald Colman and Marie Prevost, and Lubitsch used her in *Three Women* in a highly dramatic role, one in which she played a young girl who unknowingly weds her mother's lover.

May McAvoy with Richard Barthlemess in *The Enchanted Cottage*.

MAY McAVOY

"Later, I signed to do Lady Windermere for Lubitsch in *Lady's Windermere's Fan*," Miss McAvoy says, "but I got to thinking about it and decided Lady Windermere is a terrible prig. I began to hate her, and everything about the picture, especially my clothes, which I didn't like at all. Just before we were scheduled to start shooting, I'm sorry to say I did a very unprofessional thing: I took off for Catalina Island and hid out there. Mr. Lubitsch located me, and got me on the phone. He was a charmer and had had plenty of experience handling temperament. He persuaded me to return quietly and make the picture. Ironically, it turned out to be one of my very best. Nevertheless, I'm sorry it's one of the very few silent pictures of mine available to today's cinemaddicts.*

Miss McAvoy spent part of 1924, and virtually all of 1925, playing Esther in M-G-M's 1926 production of *Ben-Hur*. Like Grizel, Esther was a part she got on the rebound. Gertrude Olmstead had been playing Esther for months in Rome, with George Walsh as Ben-Hur and Charles J. Brabin directing, when M-G-M decided to start all over, with McAvoy and Ramon Novarro as Esther and Ben-Hur, and with Fred Niblo directing.

"Mother, of course, accompanied me abroad," Miss McAvoy says. "*Ben-Hur* was a tremendous undertaking, and shooting on it seemed interminable. I don't know why Esther had to be a blonde doll, but I had to wear a golden wig which I didn't like. The Italian-made wig, which had been fashioned at great expense for Miss Olmstead was too big for me, and I could never get the new one the way I wanted it.

"On those rare days when we weren't required to be on the set, Ramon, mother and I went sight-seeing. We asked Carmel Myers to come along too, but Carmel, smart girl, had brought her own publicist to Europe and on the days she didn't work, she was posing against the ruins of Pompeii, or some other antiquity. I think magazines featured candid shots of Carmel photographed against the ruins of the Roman Empire for the next two years."

Miss McAvoy is very frank about her role of Esther. "I'm glad I did it," she says, "although any young actress could have played it. It demanded almost nothing, except for the sequence in which Esther, on her own, goes to the Valley of the Lepers to find Ben-Hur's mother and sister. That did require some decisive action on Esthers's part. She also shows she's capable of thinking on the night before the big chariot race when she drives her own chariot to Ben-Hur's tent to warn him of his enemies (a sequence unfortunately omitted in the re-edited version). Otherwise, she's just decorative romance.

"Incidentally, I drove that chariot myself — my father and grandfather hadn't run a livery stable in Manhattan for nothing. It was one of the last scenes I shot in Rome, and when I boarded the 'Berengaria' to return to America, I still sported a right hand and arm in bandages. In being my own charioteer, I had pulled tendons, bruised flesh, and strained muscles."

In 1927, Warners put Miss McAvoy under contract, and her first three features there were routine programmers. But Warners was then experimenting with sound and Miss McAvoy was used in a series of experimental

* A cut-down version of *Ben-Hur* is in existence, and the silent version of *The Enchanted Cottage* is now in the American Film Institute vaults, donated by RKO.

Vitaphone shorts and called "The Vitaphone Girl." She was also selected to be Al Jolson's leading lady in *The Jazz Singer*.

"When Jolson came to Hollywood that time," Miss McAvoy says, "he was a very lonely man. He wasn't married, and he knew very few people. He was at our house for dinner nearly every night. I don't mean to insinuate there was a romance between him and me, despite the fact that I, too, was lonely then. He adored my mother. That was the amusing thing. Actors might call on me, but they'd come back because they'd fallen for mother. When I worked with Ronald Colman and with Richard Barthelmess, they'd come for dinner, but it wasn't I who made them come back. My mother was a hearty Irishwoman with a lovely sense of humour. She managed to be both tolerant and very proper. Nothing ever really shocked her except bad taste. She was truly proud of me. I've never got over the feeling of loss her death produced in me.

"During my stardom, I went to dances and parties and *premières*," Miss McAvoy says, "but I suppose I didn't really mingle and lived a rather withdrawn life. I have to admit this, but I suppose it's true that those who stay in the public consciousness do so because their names have been involved in scandals or in some kind of notoriety. Sometimes I wish my Irish impulsiveness had smothered my stronger, Scottish, conservative strain."

Miss McAvoy says nobody concerned with the making of *The Jazz Singer*, except possibly Jolson, realised the revolutionary importance of its talking and singing sequences. Like almost everybody else in Hollywood, she thought the Vitaphone a toy which would attract and then bore the public. She was sure the international pantomimic art of the movies would survive the novelty, and that everybody would go back to making pictures "that moved."

"Our stumbling block was really the Vitaphone device itself," she now explains. "Once they got sound off an accompanying record and onto a filmed sound track, the whole conception changed. Nobody sounded like himself on those early Vitaphone records, and they were always getting out of sync. I don't mind saying I hated the Vitaphone."

And she didn't like her own early Vitaphone efforts. Later, she was both angry and disgusted when critics said she hadn't registered effectively in talking films because her voice was hampered by a lisp.

"I never lisped in my life," she says in perfectly enunciated speech. "I wasn't an established stage star like Lionel Barrymore or Pauline Frederick, but they didn't sound like themselves on the Vitaphone either.

"The stories Warners gave me after *The Jazz Singer* were awful. Moreover, the fun of making films disappeared — they were ground out under the most exasperating working conditions. So, when I really fell in love in 1929 and Maurice Garrett Cleary and I married, I decided to retire. To save face, the studio — and I don't mean Jack Warner, whom I personally like — gave out a story that my voice was not right for talkies and that they were dropping me. It was I who dropped them. They were still billing me as their 'Vitaphone Girl.'

"Subsequent film historians accepted the stories the studio put out as gospel. Not long ago, when a Wolper television documentary revived the falsehood again, I filed a lawsuit. I was angry, and determined to have the truth established. But then I thought, 'Oh, what the hell! You're really retired now.' And I let the whole thing drop. Maybe I should have gone on with it, and proved my point."

She had met the man she married, Maurice Cleary, at a party at "Pickfair."

140

MAY McAVOY

He had been secretary-treasurer of United Artists and had resigned when Joseph Schenck came into the company. Cleary then became assistant to the president of Lockheed Aircraft, a position from which he retired in the late Sixties. A few months later, Cleary suffered a stroke, and is now confined to his home, a semi-invalid.

In 1932, Miss McAvoy had given birth to their only child, a son, Patrick Garrett Cleary. When eighteen, he enlisted in the Navy Air Corps, and in his last months of service, while stationed in San Diego, he married Marilyn Bennett. They have three children, and he is now with the A. B. Dick office equipment company. His wife is one of Miss McAvoy's closest friends, and she is a devoted grandmother.

In the early Forties, when war work kept Lockheed busy, and hence her husband, and her son was at boarding school, Miss McAvoy made a contract arrangement with M-G-M whereby she was on call for bit parts and appearances as an extra. She says she did this in the hope that it would lead to a juicy character part, and that such a part would enable her to lay the rumour that she spoke with a lisp. But such a part never came. Only once was she put on the payroll of a picture's entire shooting schedule (as distinct from the payroll of the studio for day work). That one time was when John Ford was making a picture for M-G-M. In looking over the list of "stock players," he noticed the names of May McAvoy and Mae Marsh, and he exclaimed: "My God! Put both those girls on my picture!"

"There was a group of us to whom M-G-M gave stock contracts," Miss McAvoy says. "They told us we were dependable old guard. I hadn't thought of myself that way, but I guess that's how we were. The studio wanted reliable players at hand and so kept us on. One after another quit or died, and finally there were just three of us left — Naomi Childers, Mahlon Hamilton, and I. Then Naomi and Mahlon died, and there was I going on and on, alone, the last of the old guard. Most of the time my scenes were shot over my shoulder — and I was eternally some middle-aged secretary with her back to the camera. You could blink your eyes and miss me altogether in some of those parts. Or I was an off-scene voice — without a lisp, may I add."

Today Miss McAvoy is genuinely appreciative because young filmgoers admire her silent movies. "Most of them are so young they could have seen me only in revivals of *Lady Windermere's Fan, The Jazz Singer,* or a rare showing of the silent *Ben-Hur,*" she says fondly. "Nevertheless, they somehow find out where I live in Beverly Hills — we're not listed in the phonebook. About once a week an individual, or a group, from all parts of the world, is on my doorstep, wanting to meet me, with a photograph or book they've bought on their own for me to sign.

"Usually, if I can, I ask them in and give them a cup of tea and talk to them while I autograph the photographs or books. I do this because I can't help feeling it's the young who sense there was something in the silent movies that's not in today's films, and, if they ever get in authority, might some day, somehow, restore to movies the magic that's been lost."

MAY McAVOY FILMOGRAPHY

HATE (1917). Melodrama of pre-natal influence, with propaganda directed against illegitimate hospitals and doctors; in the feminine lead. *Dir:* Walter Richard Stahl. *Sc:* J. Walter Meade. *With* T. Henderson Murray, Adelaide Holland, Jack McLean, Morgan Jones, Norman Acker. Exteriors filmed in Savannah, Georgia. *Prod:* Fairmont Film Co.

TO HELL WITH THE KAISER! (1918). Propaganda melodrama; as The Wounded Girl. *Dir:* George Irving. *Sc:* June Mathis. *With* Olive Tell, Lawrence Grant, Betty Howe, Earl Schenck, John Sunderland, Frank Currier, Karl Dane. *Prod:* Metro. 7 reels.

A PERFECT LADY (1918). Romantic comedy, with a backstage setting; as Claire Higgins, sister to the heroine. *Dir:* Clarence G. Badger. *Sc:* (from the play by Channing Pollock and Rennold Wolf, which has starred Rose Stahl on Broadway). *With* Madge Kennedy, Jere Austin, Walter Law, Rod La Rocque, Ben Hendricks Sr., Harry Spingler, Agnes Marc. *Prod:* Goldwyn. 5 reels.

MRS. WIGGS OF THE CABBAGE PATCH (1919). American comedy; as Australy, one of Mrs. Wiggs's brood. *Dir:* Hugh Ford. *Sc:* Eve Unsell (from the play by Alice Hegan Rice and Anne Crawford Flexner). *With* Marguerite Clark, Mary Carr, Vivia Ogden, Gareth Hughes, Gladys Valerie, Jack MacLean, Lawrence Johnson, (See Marguerite Clark filmography for other film versions of *Mrs. Wiggs.*) *Prod:* Famous Players (Paramount). 5 reels.

THE WOMAN UNDER OATH (1919). Revenge drama; as the wronged sister. *Dir:* John M. Stahl. *With* Florence Reed, Gareth Hughes, David Powell, Florida Kingsley, Mildred Cheshire, Hugh Thompson, Harold Entwhistle, Thomas McGurie, Edward Brennan, Edward Elkas. *Prod:* United Picture-Tribune Prod. 5 reels.

THE WAY OF A WOMAN (1919). Society drama; as the heroine's young sister. *Dir:* Robert Z. Leonard. *Sc:* (from a play, "Nancy Lee," by Eugene Walter). *With* Norma Talmadge, Conway Tearle, Gertrude Berkeley, Colonel Vernon, Jobyna Howland, Hassard Short, George Le Guerre, William Humphreys, Stuart Holmes. *Prod:* Select. 5 reels.

MY HUSBAND'S OTHER WIFE (1919). Marital drama; as the second wife of a divorced doctor. *Dir:* J. Stuart Blackton. *Sc:* Stanley Olmsted. *With* Sylvia Breamer, Robert Gordon, Warren Chandler, Fanny Rice. *Prod:* Pathé. 5 reels.

THE SPORTING DUCHESS (1920). Melodrama of the race track; as the heroine's nurse.

Dir: George Terwilliger. *Sc:* Lucien Hubbard (from the play by August Harris, Cecil Raleigh and Henry Hamilton, which had been a popular hit at Drury Lane). *With* Alice Joyce, Percy Pape, John Goldworthy, Dan Comfort, William Turner. *Prod:* Vitagraph. 5 reels.

MAN AND HIS WOMAN (1920). Romantic drama; as Eve Cartier, a nurse, who falls in love with her patient, a once-important doctor now on the skids. *Dir:* J. Stuart Blackton. *Sc:* Stanley Olmsted (from a story by Shannon Fife). *With* Herbert Rawlinson, Eulalie Jensen, Warren Chandler, Louis Dean, Charles Kent. *Prod:* Pathé. 5 reels.

THE HOUSE OF THE TOLLING BELL (1920). Romantic mystery; as Lucy Atherton. *Dir:* J. Stuart Blackton. *Sc:* (story by Edith Sessions Tupper). *With* Bruce Gordon, Morgan Thorpe, Edward Elkas, Eulalie Jensen, William R. Dunn, Edna Young, William Jenkins. *Prod:* Pathé 5 reels.

FORBIDDEN VALLEY (1920). Feudal drama in the Southern hills; as Morning Glory, who learns that the man she loves is her blood enemy. *Dir:* J. Stuart Blackton. *Sc:* Stanley Olmsted (from a story by Randolph Lewis). *With* Bruce Gordon, William R. Dunn, Warren Chandler, Charles Kent, Emil Link. *Prod:* Pathé. 5 reels.

THE DEVIL'S GARDEN (1920). Drama; as Mavis Petherick. *Dir:* Kenneth Webb. *Sc:* Violet Clark (from a story by W. B. Maxwell). *With* Lionel Barrymore, Doris Rankin, H. Cooper Cliffe. *Prod:* First National. 5 reels.

LOVE WINS (1920). Romantic drama; as a secretary to the hero. *With* Violet Mersereau. *Prod:* H. & H. Productions. 5 reels.

THE TRUTH ABOUT HUSBANDS (1921). Drama; as a wife who learns the truth about her own husband. *Dir:* Kenneth Webb. *Sc:* Violet Clark (from a play, "The Profligate," by Sir Arthur Wing Pinero). *With* Anna Lehr, Holmes E. Herbert, Richard Gordon, Ivo Dawson, Lorraine Frost, Arthur Rankin. *Prod:* First National. 5 reels.

SENTIMENTAL TOMMY (1921). Romantic drama of a Scottish village; as Grizel. *Dir:* John S. Robertson. *Sc:* Josephine Lovett (from two stories by Sir James M. Barrie: "Sentimental Tommy" and "Tommy and Grizel"). *With* Gareth Hughes, George Fawcett, Mabel Taliafero, Harry L. Coleman, Leila Frost, Kempton Greene, Virginia Valli, Alfred Kappeler, Malcolm Bradley. *Prod:* Paramount/Artcraft. 6 reels.

A PRIVATE SCANDAL (1921). Drama of loyalty when scandal strikes; as Jeanne Millet,

142

an adopted Belgian orphan. *Dir:* Chester M. Franklin. *Sc:* Eve Unsell (from a story by Hector Turnbull). *With* Bruce Gordon, Ralph Lewis, Kathlyn Williams, Lloyd Whitlock, Gladys Fox. *Prod:* Realart (Paramount). 5 reels.

EVERYTHING FOR SALE (1921). Romance almost thwarted by smother love; as Helen Wainwright. *Dir:* Frank O'Connor. *Sc:* Hector Turnbull. *With* Eddie Sutherland, Kathlyn Williams, Edwin Stevens, Richard Tucker, Betty Schade, Dana Todd, Jane Keckley. *Prod:* Realart (Paramount). 5 reels.

A VIRGINIA COURTSHIP (1922). Romantic comedy drama; as Prudence Fairfax. *Dir:* Frank O'Connor. *Sc:* Edfrid A. Bingham (from a play by Eugene Presbrey). *With* Alec B. Francis, Casson Ferguson, Jane Keckley, L. M. Wells, Kathlyn Williams, Richard Tucker. Guy Oliver, George Reed, Washington Blue, Vern Winters. *Prod:* Realart (Paramount). 5 reels.

A HOMESPUN VAMP (1922). Romantic comedy drama; as Meg Mackenzie, a drudge who gets a city fellow for a husband. *Dir:* Frank O'Connor. *Sc:* Harvey Thew (from a story, "The Happy Ending," by Hector Turnbull). *With* Darrell Foss, Lincoln Stedman, Josephine Crowell, Charles Ogle, Guy Oliver, Helen Dunbar, Kathleen Kirkham. *Prod:* Realart (Paramount). 5 reels.

MORALS (1922). Romantic comedy drama; as Carlotta. *Dir:* William Desmond Taylor. *Sc:* Julia Crawford Ivers (from the novel and play, "The Morals of Marcus Ordeyne," by William J. Locke). *With* William P. Carleton, William E. Lawrence, Kathlyn Williams, Bridgeta Clark, Sydney Bracey, Starke Patterson, Nicholas de Ruiz, Marian Skinner. *Prod:* Realart (Paramount). 5 reels. (Previously filmed for Paramount by Marie Doro, who had created the role on Broadway; subsequently filmed as a talking feature starring Lupe Velez.)

THROUGH A GLASS WINDOW (1922). Romantic comedy drama; as Jenny Martin, a doughnut maker. *Dir:* Major Maurice Campbell. *Sc:* Olga Printzlau. *With* Raymond McKee, Fanny Midgely, Burwell Hamrick, Fred Turner, Carrie Clark Ward, Frank Butterworth, Wade Boteler, Russ Powell. *Prod:* Realart (Paramount). 5 reels.

THE TOP OF NEW YORK (1922). Romance of the tenements; as Hilda O'Shaughnessy. *Dir:* William Desmond Taylor. *Sc:* George Hopkins (from a story by Sonya Levien). *With* Walter McGrail, Pat Moore, Edward Cecil, Charles Bennett, Mary Jane Irving, Carrie Clark Ward, Arthur Hoyt. *Prod:* Paramount. 5 reels.

CLARENCE (1922). Comedy drama; as Cora Wheeler, pampered daughter of the rich. *Dir:* William C. de Mille. *Sc:* Clara Beranger (from a play by Booth Tarkington). *With* Wallace Reid, Agnes Ayres, Kathlyn Williams, Edward Martindel, Robert Agnew, Adolphe Menjou, Bertram Johns, Dorothy Gordon, Maym Kelso, *Prod:* Paramount. 7 reels. (Remade as a talkie, 1937, by Paramount.) (Compare listing in Wallace Reid filmography.)

KICK IN (1922). Crook melodrama; as Myrtle, a tragic young gangster's moll. *Dir:* George Fitzmaurice. *Sc:* Ouida Bergere (from the play by Willard Mack). *With* Bert Lytell, Betty Compson, Robert Agnew, Gareth Hughes, John Miltern, Charles Stevenson, Jed Prouty, Charles Ogle, Kathleen Clifford, Maym Kelso, Walter Long. (Prevously filmed by Fitzmaurice for Astra-Pathé, 1917; re-made as a talkie by Paramount, starring Clara Bow.) *Prod:* Paramount. 7 reels. (Compare listing in Betty Compson filmography.)

GRUMPY (1923). Mystery comedy; as Virginia Bullivant. *Dir:* William C. de Mille. *Sc:* Clara Beranger (from the play by Horace Hodges and T. Wigney Percyval). *With* Theodore Roberts, Conrad Nagel, Casson Ferguson, Bertram Johns, Robert Bolder, Charles French, Bernice Frank. *Prod:* Paramount. 6 reels. (Re-made as talkie, 1930.)

ONLY 38 (1923). Romantic comedy; as Lucy Stanley. *Dir:* William C. de Mille. *Sc:* Clara Beranger (from the play by A. E. Thomas, which had been dramatised from a story by Walter Prichard Eaton). *With* Lois Wilson, Elliott Dexter, George Fawcett, Robert Agnew, Jane Keckley, Lillian Leighton, Taylor Graves, Ann Cornwall. *Prod:* Paramount. 7 reels.

HER REPUTATION (1923). Newspaper melodrama; as Jacqueline Lanier, scandal-sheet victim. *Dir:* John Griffith Way. *Sc:* Bradley Page (from a novel by Talbot Mundy). *With* Lloyd Hughes, Brinsley Shaw, George Larkin, James Corrigan, Louise Lester, Winter Hall, Eric Mayne, Casson Ferguson. *Prod:* Ince/First National. 7 reels.

WEST OF THE WATER TOWER (1924). Small town romance; as Bee Chew, daughter of the town's richest man. *Dir:* Rollin S. Sturgeon. *Sc:* Doris Schroeder (adapted by Lucien Hubbard from the novel by Homer Croy). *With* Glenn Hunter, Ernest Torrence, George Fawcett, ZaSu Pitts, Anne Schaeffer, Riley Hatch. *Prod:* Paramount. 8 reels.

THE ENCHANTED COTTAGE (1924). Romantic drama; as Laura Pennington. *Dir:* John S. Robertson. *Sc:* Josephine Lovett (from the play by Sir Arthur Wing Pinero). *With* Richard Barthelmess, Ida Waterman, Alfred Hickman, Holmes E. Herbert, Florence Short, Marion Coakley, Ethel Wright. (Re-made as a talking picture by RKO, 1945,

143

with Dorothy McGuire and Robert Young.) *Prod:* First National. 7 reels.

THE BEDROOM WINDOW (1924). Mystery romance; as Ruth Martin. *Dir:* William C. de Mille. *Sc:* Clara Beranger. *With* Malcolm MacGregor, Ethel Wales, Robert Edeson, George Fawcett, Ricardo Cortez, Charles Ogle, Medea Radzina, Guy Oliver, Lillian Leighton, George Callega. *Prod:* Paramount. 7 reels.

TARNISH (1924). Romantic drama; as Letitia Tevis. *Dir:* George Fitzmaurice. *Sc:* Frances Marion (from the play by Gilbert Emery). *With* Ronald Colman, Marie Prevost, Albert Gran, Mrs. Russ Whytall, Priscilla Bonner, Kay Deslys, Lydia Yeamans Titus, Norman Kerry, Harry Myers, *Prod:* Goldwyn/First National. 7 reels.

THREE WOMEN (1924). Romantic drama; as Jeanne Wilton, who weds her mother's lover. *Dir:* Ernst Lubitsch. *Sc:* Hans Kraly (from a story by Kraly and Lubitsch). *With* Pauline Frederick, Marie Prevost, Lew Cody, Willard Louis, Pierre Gendron, Mary Carr, Raymond McKee. *Prod:* Warner Bros. 8 reels. (Compare listing in Pauline Frederick filmography.)

THE MAD WHIRL (1924). Jazz drama and alcoholic reformation; as Cathleen Gillis. *Dir:* William A. Seiter. *Sc:* Edward T. Lowe Jr. (from a story, "Here's How," by Richard Washburn Child). *With* Jack Mulhall, Myrtle Stedman, Barbara Bedford, Alec B. Francis, Ward Crane, George Fawcett, Marie Astaire, Joseph Singleton. *Prod:* Universal. 7 reels.

TESSIE (1925). Romantic comedy; as Tessie, a gum-chewing candy clerk. *Dir-Sc:* Dallas M. Fitzgerald (from a "SatEvePost" story, "Tessie and the Little Sap," by Sewell Ford). *With* Robert Agnew, Myrtle Stedman, Gertrude Short, Lee Moran, Walter Perry, Mary Gordon. *Prod:* Arrow. 7 reels.

LADY WINDERMERE'S FAN (1925). Sophisticated drawing-room comedy; as Lady Windermere. *Dir:* Ernst Lubitsch. *Sc:* Julien Josephson (from a play by Oscar Wilde). *With* Irene Rich, Ronald Colman, Bert Lytell, Edward Martindel, Helen Dunbar, Carrie D'Aumery, Billie Bennett. (Re-made as a talkie, *The Fan,* by Otto Preminger.) *Prod:* Warner Bros. 8 reels.

BEN-HUR (1926). A tale of the Christus; as Esther. *Dir:* Fred Niblo. *Sc:* Carey Wilson (from the adaptation by June Mathis of the novel by General Lew Wallace). *With* Ramon Novarro, Francis X. Bushman, Carmel Myers, Claire McDowell, Kathleen Key, Nigel de Brulier, Mitchell Lewis, Leo White, Frank Currier, Charles Belcher, Betty Bronson, Dale Fuller, Winter Hall. (Re-made as a talkie, with Haya Harareet as Esther.) *Prod:*

M-G-M. 12 reels. (Compare listing in Ramon Novarro filmography.)

THE ROAD TO GLORY (1926). Drama of regeneration through blindness; as Judith Allen. *Dir:* Howard Hawks. *Sc:* L. G. Rigby (from a story by Hawks, "The Chariot of the Gods"). *With* Leslie Fenton, Ford Sterling, Rockcliffe Fellowes, Milla Davenport, John MacSweeney. *Prod:* Fox. 6 reels.

THE SAVAGE (1926). Romantic comedy; as Ysabel Atwater. *Dir:* Fred Newmeyer. *Sc:* Jane Murfin and Charles Whittaker (from a story by Ernest Pascal). *With* Ben Lyon, Tom Maguire, Philo McCullough, Sam Hardy, Charlotte Walker. *Prod:* Fist National. 6 reels.

THE PASSIONATE QUEST (1926). Romantic drama of London; as Rosina Vanet. *Dir:* J. Stuart Blackton. *Sc:* Marion Constance Blackton (from the novel by E. Phillips Oppenheim). *With* Willard Louis, Louise Fazenda, Gardner James, Holmes E. Herbert, DeWitt Jennings, Vera Lewis, Nora Cecil, Charles Stevenson, William Herford, Mathilde Comont, Jane Winton, Frank Butler. *Prod:* Warner Bros. 7 reels.

MY OLD DUTCH (1926). Romantic drama of London costermongers; as Sal Gratton. *Dir:-Sc:* Laurence Trimble (from the play by Arthur Shirley and Albert Chevalier). *With* Pat O'Malley, Cullen Landis, Jean Hersholt, Patsy O'Bryne, Edgar Kennedy, Frank Crane, Rolfe Sedan, Newton Hall, George Seigmann. (Re-made as a talking film, 1934, by British Gaumont, starring Betty Balfour.) *Prod:* Universal. 8 reels.

THE FIRE BRIGADE (1927). Melodrama and homage to the fire fighters; as Helen Corwin. *Dir:* William Nigh. *Sc:* Robert Lee (from a story by Kate Corbelay). *With* Charles Ray, Holmes E. Herbert, Tom O'Brien, Eugenie Besserer, Warner P. Richmond, Bert Woodruff, Vivia Ogden, DeWitt Jennings, Dan Mason, Erwin Connelly, James Bradbury. *Prod:* M-G-M. 9 reels. (Compare listing in Charles Ray filmography.)

MATINEE LADIES (1927). Jazz melodrama; as Sally Smith, cigarette girl. *Dir:* Byron Haskins. *Sc:* Graham Baker (from a story by Albert S. Howson). *With* Malcolm MacGregor, Hedda Hopper, Richard Tucker, Cissy Fitzgerald, William Demarest, Margaret Seddon. *Prod:* Warner Bros. 7 reels.

IRISH HEARTS (1927). Romantic comedy drama; as Patsy Shannon, a hash-slinger. *Dir:* Byron Haskins. *Sc:* Bess Meredyth and Graham Baker (from a story by Melville Crosman). *With* Jason Robards, Warner Richmond, Kathleen Key, Walter Perry, Walter Rodgers, Les Bates. *Prod:* Warner Bros. 6 reels.

SLIGHTLY USED (1927). Romantic comedy;

as Cynthia Martin. *Dir:* Archie K. Mayo. *Sc:* Graham Baker (from a story by Melville Crosman). *With* Conrad Nagel, Robert Agnew, Audrey Ferris, Anders Randolph, Eugenie Besserer, Arthur Rankin, Sally Eilers, David Mir. *Prod:* Warner Bros. 7 reels.

THE JAZZ SINGER (1927). Backstage drama; as Mary Dale. *Dir:* Alan Crosland. *Sc:* Alfred A. Cohn (from the play by Samson Raphaelson). *With* Al Jolson, Warner Oland, Eugenie Besserer, Otto Lederer, Cantor Josef Rosenblatt, Bobbie Gordon, Richard Tucker, William Demarest, Myrna Loy, Anders Randolph, Will Walling. The first part-talkie, with songs; the feature film that made talking features inevitable. *Prod:* Warner Bros. 9 reels.

A RENO DIVORCE (1927). Romantic comedy; as Carla. *Dir:* Ralph Graves. *Sc:* Robert Lord (from a story by Ralph Graves). *With* Ralph Graves, Hedda Hopper, Robert Ober, Anders Randolph. *Prod:* Warner Bros. 6 reels.

IF I WERE SINGLE (1928). Romantic comedy; as May Howard. *Dir:* Roy Del Ruth. *Sc:* Robert Lord. *With* Conrad Nagel, Myrna Loy, Andre Beranger. *Prod:* Warner Bros. 7 reels.

THE LITTLE SNOB (1928). Romantic comedy; as May Banks. *Dir:* John G. Adolfi. *Sc:* Robert Lord (from a story by Edward T. Lowe, Jr). *With* Robert Frazer, Alec B. Francis, John Miljan, Virginia Lee Corbin, Frances Lee. *Prod:* Warner Bros. 6 reels.

MAY McAVOY IN SUNNY CALIFORNIA (1928). One of several experiments in sound and outdoor photography, with Miss McAvoy driving around to a number of tourist spots in Southern California. *Dir:* Bryan Foy. *Sc:* Murray Roth and Hugh Herbrt. *Prod:* Warner Bros. 1 reel (Vitaphone No. 2239). Warner Bros. started billing May McAvoy as "The Vitaphone Girl."

THE LION AND THE MOUSE (1928). Drama; as Shirley Ross, whose father is ruined by the father of the man she marries. *Dir:* Lloyd Bacon. *Sc:* Robert Lord (from a play by Charles Klein). *With* Lionel Barrymore, Alec B. Francis, William Collier Jr., Emmett Corrigan, Jack Ackroyd, Audrey Ferris. Part-Talkie. (Previously filmed by Vitagraph, with Alice Joyce.) *Prod:* Warner Bros. 7 reels.

THE TERROR (1928). Murder suspense drama; as Olga Redmayne. *Dir:* Roy Del Ruth. *Sc:* Harvey Gates (with dialogue by Joseph Jackson, from the play by Edgar Wallace). *With* Louise Fazenda, Edward Everett Horton, Alec B. Francis, Matthew Betz, Holmes E. Herbert, John Miljan, Otto Hoffman, Joseph Gerard, Frank Austin. The second all-talking Vitaphone feature. *Prod:* Warner Bros. 9 reels.

CAUGHT IN THE FOG (1928). Crook melodrama; as "The Girl," who is on her first job as a jewel thief. *Dir:* Howard Bretherton. *Sc:* Charles R. Condon (from a story by Jerome Kingston). *With* Conrad Nagel, Charles Gerard, Emile Chautard, Ruth Cherrington, Mack Swain, Hugh Herbert. Part-Talkie. *Prod:* Warner Bros. 7 reels.

STOLEN KISSES (1929). Romantic comedy; as May Lambert. *Dir:* Ray Enright. *Sc:* Edward T. Lowe Jr., with dialogue by James A. Starr (from a story by Franz Suppé). *With* Reed Howes, Claude Gillingwater, Hallam Cooley, Edna Murphy. Part-Talkie. *Prod:* Warner Bros. 7 reels.

NO DEFENSE (1929). Romantic Western; as Ruth Harper. *Dir:* Lloyd Bacon. *Sc:* Robert Lord (from a story by J. Raleigh Davis). *With* Monte Blue, William Tooker, William Desmond, Kathryn Carver, Lee Moran. Part-Talkie. *Prod:* Warner Bros. 6 reels.

Addenda

Miss McAvoy is to be seen in a cameo as herself in a two-reel exploitation film put out by Paramount in 1922. *A Trip to Paramountown.* It was directed by Jerome Beatty, and photographed by the eminent cinematographer, Karl Brown. Jack Cunningham wrote the continuity, and Rob Wagner composed the sub-titles.

Again, Miss McAvoy is to be seen in a cameo appearance as herself in Paramount's *Hollywood,* 1923, directed by James Cruze. In *Married Flirts,* a Pauline Frederick vehicle Metro-Goldwyn released in 1924, there is a scene of stars and players lunching in the studio commissary, and Miss McAvoy is one of them.

In 1940 Miss McAvoy returned to films as a contract player at M-G-M. Although she remained under contract there until the mid Fifties, she played only unbilled bits, dress extras, and voice-overs. She is now retired.

7
ANTONIO MORENO

Antonio Moreno's film career was one of the long ones. He made his cinematic *début* in the spring of 1912 for Rex-Universal in *The Voice of the Million,* and his last important appearance before the cameras was for John Ford in *The Searchers,* released in 1956.

Within those forty-four years of film activity, nearly all the female stars of the silent screen's golden period appeared opposite him, including Mary Pickford, Lillian and Dorothy Gish, Blanche Sweet, Pearl White, Norma and Constance Talmadge, Irene Castle, Gloria Swanson, Alice Terry, Bebe Daniels, Pola Negri, Colleen Moore, Clara Bow, Marion Davies, Billie Dove, Greta Garbo — to name only some.

He played comedy and tragedy equally well, and was successful in every kind of melodrama — romantic, suspense, the Far West. For a while, because of his work in action-filled serials, he was called "King of the Cliff-hangers." But his greatest fame came as a pre-Valentino "Latin Lover."

Antonio Garrido Monteaguado y Moreno was born in Madrid, Spain, on September 26, 1886.* His father, Juan Moreno, was a non-commissioned officer in the Spanish Army. Not long after Antonio's birth, his father was transferred to Seville, and shortly afterward died there.

The impoverished widow was determined her only child should attend school, even if it meant he worked evenings in a bakery for one peseta a night, which he did. In a few years, she moved to Algeciras, and then to Gibraltar, where young Antonio became a sort of mascot to the English soldiers stationed there.

"Although I was only a little boy," he said many years later, "I tried to learn English, but didn't make much progress."

In his very early teens, he worked as a common labourer on the buildings for Gibraltar's annual fair, and had made so much progress with English that he attracted the attention of Enrique de Cruzat Zanetti, a Spaniard and Harvard graduate, who was a wealthy Cuban attorney, and his American friend, Benjamin Curtis, a nephew of Seth Lowe (president of Columbia University and New York's Mayor between 1901-02). Curtis was in ill health, and young Moreno was hired as interpreter and companion-nurse for the duration of the two friends' travels in Spain. From this, young Moreno earned

*Moreno's birth-year was always given, during his career, as 1888, but in 1965 a court proceeding established his age: seventy-nine. Thus, 1886 becomes the correct year.

enough to move his mother to the small coastal town of Campamento, in which she lived the rest of her life.

When Zanetti and Curtis returned to New York, they did not forget the alert, proud Spanish youth who had expressed such keen interest in everything American and so determinedly had striven to learn English, and they cabled him the fare to New York. He arrived in 1902, and was enrolled in a school conducted by Catholic nuns. After a year there, he knew enough English to attend a New York high school.

Then, through a wealthy Manhattan social worker, Adeline Moffet, who often staged entertainments at downtown schools, he was introduced to Mrs. Charlotte Morgan, a widow of considerable means who had just lost a son of the same age as he. She took Antonio to her home in Northampton, Massachusetts, and enrolled him in the nearby Williston Seminary. His mother in Spain, who had re-married, was under the impression he was studying for the priesthood.

Independent by nature, he insisted on working, and for a time was employed in a Northampton silk hosiery factory, then by a New England telephone company as a sweeper and tester, and eventually as a meter-reader for the gas company. The Calvin Coolidges resided there then, and in later years, Mrs. Coolidge, with a twinkle in her eyes, said, "Of course I remember Tony Moreno. He used to read my meter."

It was in Northampton that Moreno got his first taste of the theatre by playing small roles one summer with the resident stock company. The engagement whetted his appetite for acting and when, at the summer's end, the other members of the company went on to other theatrical engagements, he went to New York City to start work as an electrician and be near Broadway.

As luck would have it, he was sent one day to fix the switchboard in the Empire Theatre, where Maude Adams was beginning rehearsals for Barrie's "The Little Minister." After he completed the repairs, Moreno asked the stage manager if he could work as a super in Miss Adams's company. He was signed on as an actor, and in time was given a few lines to speak.

In the subsequent five years, he played with Mrs. Leslie Carter in "DuBarry"; was a Spanish count with her in "Two Women," a Rupert Hughes play; was with Constance Collier and Tyrone Power Sr. in "Thais"; with Wilton Lackaye's company in "The Right to Happiness"; toured a sketch with Beatrice Ingraham in vaudeville; played in two productions with William Hawtrey; was a member of the musical comedy company for "The Man from Cook's"; and played a season of stock with the Manhattan Players at the Lyceum Theatre in Rochester.

When, in 1910, he returned to Spain to visit his mother, she, disappointed that he wasn't becoming a priest, urged him to ponder the wisdom of continuing his acting career; but on board ship coming home, he met Helen Ware, a prominent American actress, who encouraged him to stick to it. She said he had a devil-may-care dash few American-born actors possessed, as well as Castilian grace and a natural air of Latin romance. He could become, she thought, a unique star.

Considerably heartened, he went with Sothern and Marlowe for a season of Shakespearean repertory, and then, in 1912, while he was acting in a stage farce called C.O.D., an elderly English actor, Walter Edwin, suggested he try his luck in motion pictures.

ANTONIO MORENO

Moreno went to Rex-Universal Studios on Eleventh Avenue at 43rd Street, and was given a role in a film starring Marion Leonard called *The Voice of the Million*. It was a sociological drama about a mill-town strike, and Moreno played one of the dedicated young strikers. He photographed so well that he was soon so busy acting for the camera he had no time for the stage.

D. W. Griffith induced him to switch to Biograph, which he later left for Mutual Reliance, enjoying there a long association in the *Our Mutual Girl* series, which starred Norma Phillips. By 1914 he was so established as an ingratiating and photogenic personality that Albert E. Smith, president of Vitagraph, signed him as a contract player. Moreno continued as an actor for Vitagraph until the summer of 1917, when he went to Pathé. But a year later, he returned to Vitagraph to star in features and four fifteen-episode serials.

During his first stretch at Vitagraph, Moreno co-starred with almost all the Vitagraph queens, but was usually paired with Edith Storey. Moreno said of her: "I think we should have married if we had stayed together any longer." And he added: "I don't think I'll get married until some lady makes up her mind otherwise. Then I'll be lost, of course." When asked what qualities in a wife he preferred, Moreno said: "Brains, a fine intellect, because I have so little. I don't know a thing. I'm just a mutt."

In his year at Pathé, Moreno co-starred with Irene Castle, who had personally asked for him, and with the exotic dancer Doraldina, in one of the most popular movies he ever made: *The Naulahka*.

More importantly, however, Pathé had assigned him to Pearl White in her serial, *The House of Hate* (1918). It was one of the best of the serials in which fearless, peerless Pearl queened it as a Dauntless Damsel in Distress, for Moreno's Latin allure lent an exotic touch to the romantic phases of her exploits and perils. She was usually so athletic and competent that the identities of her leading men rarely registered. But the twenty-chapter *The House of Hate* put black-haired Tony, as well as blonde Pearl, on the crest of the serial wave.

So much so that Albert E. Smith offered Moreno an attractive contract to return to Vitagraph as a serial star. But Moreno wanted to get out of serial work and into feature pictures exclusively, and asked Vitagraph's former top actor, William Desmond Taylor, who had become an ace director at Paramount, to intercede for him.* Taylor was unable to convince Smith that Moreno could win audiences in non-serial pictures, and, after much temporising on both sides, Moreno made two pictures for Samuel Goldwyn: *Lost and Found* (1923) paired him on location in the South Seas with Pauline Starke; *Look Your Best* merely required him to be handsome and admired by Colleen Moore (playing a heroine whose greatest enemy was too much rich food).

Moreno had contracted to play the lead in Selznick's *Rupert of Hentzau* opposite Elaine Hammerstein, when Paramount offered him a term contract as its top leading man. Selznick released him, and Paramount cast him first as lead to Mary Miles Minter in the last film she ever made, which was, ironi-

*Moreno and Taylor had been friends since Moreno's early days at Vitagraph. The both lived for quite a time at the Los Angeles Athletic Club, and after Taylor became a director, Moreno sought, and valued Taylor's opinions of his acting roles. Moreno may even have been the last person to talk by phone to Taylor before Taylor's murder on the night of February 1, 1922. Moreno told the Los Angeles Police he had called Taylor to confirm an appointment they had for the following day. Officially, the Taylor murder is still unsolved.

cally, one of her best and most successful, *The Trail of the Lonesome Pine*, and then opposite Gloria Swanson in *My American Wife*. As soon as he finished that picture, Paramount sent him East to join Bebe Daniels for a romantic thriller called *The Exciters*.

Serials were now behind Moreno, and this improvement in his acting career was matched by one in his private life. When *The Exciters* was finished, he married, on January 27, 1923, an extremely wealthy socialite divorcee, Daisy Canfield Danziger. Her father, Charles A. Canfield, had been a partner of oilman Edward L. Doheny, and she had achieved further status via her first husband, J. M. Danziger, by whom she had two daughters and a son. She was the kind of woman Moreno had always said he would marry: intelligent, witty, socially accomplished.

The Morenos spent their honeymoon in Europe and when they visited his mother in Spain, practically the entire village turned out to welcome him and his bride. "I wanted to run away, my heart was beating so," Moreno said later. "I felt so damned unworthy of it all."

On their return, they bought a six-acre estate on the crest of a wide hill overlooking Los Angeles and built one of the show-homes of the Twenties — a magnificent Mediterranean villa they named "Crestmount." It still affords one of the best scenic views of Los Angeles. Now, however, the whole Micheltorena Street hillside is a real estate sub-division called Moreno Highlands.

In the Twenties, Mary Pickford and Douglas Fairbanks ruled Hollywood social life from "Pickfair"; but Mrs. Antonio Moreno was also one of Hollywood's social arbiters, and invitations to "Crestmount" were prized. Her "Sundays" were often the event of the social week, for John McCormack, Jascha Heifetz, Raquel Meller, and similar artists performing in Los Angeles were often present to entertain. Moreno guests were not confined to the movie colony. Society, and California's old Spanish families, who rarely accepted invitations outside their own group, also liked to go to "Crestmount."

Paramount continued using Moreno as a leading man — opposite Estelle Taylor, Agnes Ayres, Jacqueline Logan, and Helene Chadwick, until the end of 1924. They also gave him one of his best film assignments, which was in support of Pola Negri in *The Spanish Dancer*. She played a tempestuous gypsy, and Moreno was her Robin Hood lover. *The Spanish Dancer* far outshone *Rosita*, which Mary Pickford made at the same time, and which derived from the same source — an old Continental play, "Don Cesar de Bazan." *The Spanish Dancer's* script had originally been titled *A Spanish Cavalier*, and had been prepared as a Valentino vehicle to follow *The Young Rajah*. When Valentino broke his Paramount contract, the script was revised so as to be a starring vehicle for Miss Negri. It provided Moreno with one of his most dazzling roles.

Nevertheless, he was far from satisfied with the roles Paramount had given him and asked to be released from his contract. Whereupon he went to First National, but his only film of any importance there was *Learning to Love*, a bright comedy starring Constance Talmadge, with whom he had played in his Vitagraph days.

Like Richard Dix and Thomas Meighan, the latter his best friend, Moreno

152

Antonio Moreno while filming Rex Ingram's *Mare Nostrum*.

was always going out of his way to help fellow actors. Once at Vitagraph, he had hidden Ramon Novarro in his car in order to get him inside the studio, where Novarro then obtained extra work in a serial. When Henry King wanted Moreno to play opposite Lillian Gish in *The White Sister,* and Moreno, who had just married, couldn't accept, he suggested that King consider a rising young Englishman then on the Broadway stage, Ronald Colman.

In 1925, director Rex Ingram, a friend since Vitagraph days, offered Moreno the male lead in his adaptation of Ibáñez's *Mare Nostrum,* and Moreno accepted eagerly, for it was to be shot in Europe and the Ingram company would be based in the studios in Nice. Mrs. Moreno, of course, accompanied him.

Mare Nostrum was Rex Ingram's personal favourite of all the films he directed, and it became the personal favourite of its two stars, Alice Terry and Moreno. They made a handsome pair of ill-fated lovers, and I don't think either ever appeared to better advantage. Its story gave Miss Terry an opportunity to play the *femme fatale* kind of role she had always wanted, and Moreno, as a romantic Spanish sea captain who loves, and is claimed by, the sea, had a chance for facets of rich characterisation none of his other romantic roles had so plenteously afforded. And all against lovely Mediterranean backgrounds. It is a beautiful picture, and after its release M-G-M offered Moreno a contract. It enabled him to be co-starred with, or be leading man to, some of the most popular actresses on the M-G-M roster.

The best known of Moreno's M-G-M movies is a screen version of another Ibáñez novel, *The Temptress,* which was Garbo's second American-made film. Garbo's sponsor, Mauritz Stiller, was assigned to direct it, but his Russian-Jewish temperament soon clashed with Moreno's Spanish one. When he wanted Moreno to shave off his mustache and to wear larger shoes so Garbo's slippered feet would not seem so big, Moreno walked off the set. Louis B. Mayer supported Moreno, for Stiller had not only alienated other players (Lionel Barrymore had to be brought in to replace H. B. Warner, who can be seen in some of the still photographs shot for this picture), but had dropped far behind schedule. Stiller was replaced by Fred Niblo. Despite this, Garbo has said several times that *The Temptress* is her favourite of all her M-G-M silents. It certainly contains one of her better performances, and one of Moreno's most colourful.

Moreno has had very little to say about working with Garbo. But then he was never one to speak of the ladies he has loved on the screen. "Marion Davies was the most fun," he once said. "When I worked with her in *Beverly of Graustark,* she was the cutest thing on the screen. Always the same — gay, unassuming, loyal, and considerate."

Moreno was a pet of the redoutable Elinor Glyn, one of whose stories was the basis of *Love's Blindness,* in which he had played with Pauline Starke at M-G-M. Mme. Glyn had asseverated that in her opinion only four Hollywood personalities had the quality she called "It": Clara Bow, Antonio Moreno, the doorman at the Ambassador Hotel, and Rex, King of the Wild Horses. Paramount couldn't do much about the Ambassador Hotel doorman or the stallion known as "Rex," but they did cast Moreno opposite Clara Bow in *It,* Bow's first starring vehicle.

154

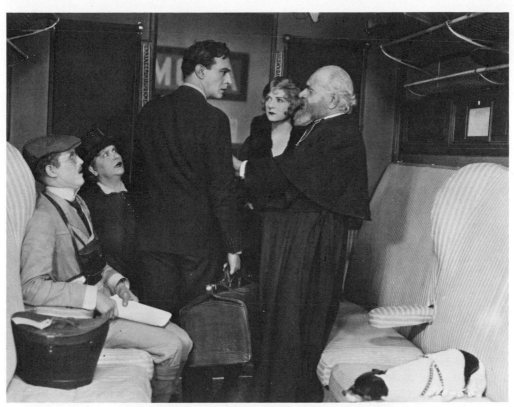

Antonio Moreno with Alice Terry in *Mare Nostrum*.

Antonio Moreno with Greta Garbo in *The Temptress*.

MORE FROM HOLLYWOOD

After suppporting Constance Talmadge again in one of the most charming of her romantic comedies, *Venus of Venice,* Moreno went to London to appear opposite Dorothy Gish in *Madame Pompadour*. While abroad, he also appeared in a Spanish film, *En la tierra del sol*.

When he returned to America, the talkies had taken over; he knew that the roles he assumed would have to change. His years betrayed him more than his voice; his age made it impossible for him to continue as a romantic lead. In 1929 he was forty-three years old, and although he did not look it, youth was the treasured commodity of the time — and it still is. He had a definite asset, however, as a talking actor: he was bilingual, and United States studios were shooting many of their productions simultaneously in several languages. As soon as an English-speaking company finished a day's work on a set, another company, usually with another director, moved in to shoot the same sequences in Spanish, French or German. Moreno's career was thus diverted into playing leads in the Spanish versions of Hollywood films.

In 1931, he went to Mexico to help establish the Mexican sound film. He directed Mexico's first talking feature of importance, *Santa,* and another Mexican feature, *Aguilas frente al sol*.

One of the reasons for his going to Mexico was his separation from his wife. After he moved out of "Crestmount," she gave the property to the Roman Catholic Church, and for some years it was a school for exceptionally talented girls who were orphans or near-orphans; it was called the Chloe P. Canfield Memorial Home. Later, it was acquired by the Franciscan nuns and is now Our Lady of the Sacred Heart Home for Girls, a semi-charity residence for homeless or orphaned girls aged nine through sixteen.

In 1933, Mrs. Moreno was killed when, in a fog, her chauffeur-driven limousine plunged three hundred feet from Mulholland Drive. The chauffeur's back was broken, but he survived, crawling up the mountainside in great pain to summon help. Mrs. Moreno's three children by her first husband had all adopted Moreno's name. Today the son is known as Robert C. Moreno, and the two older daughters as Beth Moreno Tappan and Daisy Fickeisen.

In 1936 Moreno went to Spain to appear, with a young Carmen Amaya, in a film called *Maria de la O*. Moreno might have stayed on in his native Spain had civil war not ended film production there for several years.

On his return to Hollywood, he was not exactly forgotten, but he was fifty years old. Ben Piazza, RKO-Radio's casting director, got him several jobs, and I remember seeing him on the lot when he played Cochise in *The Valley of the Sun,* and a conquistador in *The Spanish Main*. In the latter role, he looked as if he had stepped from a Velasquez canvas. His was a noble face, to which the years had given dignity, and throughout the Forties and Fifties his presence graced a number of films, even though his roles were not leads.

He was absent from the screen all of 1943 and most of 1944, for it was during this time that his mother died in Spain after a long illness, as did the friend who had brought Moreno to this country — Enrique Zanetti. In the Second World War, Moreno was an air-raid warden for his residential district in Hollywood. When the war was over, he bought the home on South Peck Drive in Beverly Hills, in which he lived the rest of his life.

He returned to the screen to play Tyrone Power's father in *Captain from Castille,* and subsequently did a few other roles. He had practically written "finis" to his career when John Ford asked him to play a part in *The Searchers,* the last important film in which he appeared. He later went to Havana for a picture, and decided to stay on and direct (which he liked). This was rendered impossible when the Castroites overthrew Batista. "Rebellions, seldom my own, have put an end to more than one movie dream of mine," Moreno said resignedly.

In May 1965, he suffered a stroke, but recovered; he remained, however, too ill to manage his own affairs properly, and petitioned the courts to appoint his friend, Mrs. Mary G. Westbrook, conservator of his estate, which for the first time was acknowledged to be of substantial size. His three step-children objected to Mrs. Westbrook on the grounds that she was not "a long and dear friend," as was claimed, but "a comparatively new acquaintance." Although Moreno proved he had first met her in 1942 when he was air-raid warden and she had been his assistant, Mrs. Westbrook withdrew, and Moreno's longtime friend and accountant, Leon P. Scammon, was appointed.

During the 1966 Christmas holidays, Moreno's precarious health took a serious turn. Early in February 1967 he suffered two strokes, the second of which, on February 15, killed the "Latin Lover" who had preceded Rudolph Valentino on the world's silent screens.

ANTONIO MORENO FILMOGRAPHY

THE VOICE OF THE MILLION (1912). Social drama about a milltown strike; as one of the strike leaders. *Dir-Sc:* Stanner E. V. Taylor. *With* Marion Leonard. *Prod:* Rex-Universal. 988 ft.

TWO DAUGHTERS OF EVE (1912). Backstage drama; as an actor. *Dir:* D. W. Griffith. *Sc:* George Henessy. *With* Henry B. Walthall, Claire McDowell, Lillian Gish, Elmer Booth, W. Chrystie Miller, Gertrude Bambrick, Marion Kerby, George Nicholls. *Prod:* Biograph. 1057 ft.

SO NEAR, YET SO FAR (1912). Romantic comedy drama; in the background. *Dir:* D. W. Griffith. *Sc:* George Henessy. *With* Mary Pickford, Elmer Booth, Robert Harron, W. Chrystie Miller, Lionel Barrymore, Charles H. Mailes. *(Subtitled:* "The Reward of Persistence May Be Delayed, But It Is Inevitable.") *Prod:* Biograph. 999 ft.

THE MUSKETEERS OF PIG ALLEY (1912). Realistic gang-war drama; as one of the boys of Pig Alley. *Dir.-Sc:* D. W. Griffith. *With* Lillian Gish, Harry Carey, Robert Harron, Elmer Booth, W. Chrystie Miller, Dorothy Gish, Marie Newton, Jack Pickford. *Prod:* Biograph. 1314 ft. (Compare listing in Dorothy Gish filmography.)

NO PLACE FOR FATHER (1913). Father-son drama; as the son. *With* Hector Dion, Julia Brunns. *Prod:* Biograph.

BY MAN'S LAW (1913). A social document; as "Slaver," to whom a capitalist brings every woe. *Dir:* D. W. Griffith. *Sc:* William E. Wing.

With Mae Marsh, Robert Harron, Mildred Manning, Donald Crisp, Alan Hale, Charles H. Mailes. *Prod:* Biograph. 1116 ft.

THE HOUSE OF DISCORD (1913). Mother-daughter drama; as one of the young men in the drama. *Dir:* James Kirkwood. *Sup:* D. W. Griffith. *Sc:* A. Clayton Harris. *With* Blanche Sweet, Jack Mulhall, Dorothy Gish, Lionel Barrymore, Marshall Neilan. *Prod:* Klaw & Erlanger/Biograph. 2020 ft. (Compare listings in Blanche Sweet and Dorothy Gish filmographies.)

JUDITH OF BETHULIA (1914). The story of how Judith saved her people; in the background. *Dir:* D. W. Griffith. *Sc:* Frank E. Woods (from the Apocryphal Book of Judith and a play by Thomas Bailey Aldrich). *With* Blanche Sweet, Henry B. Walthall, Kate Bruce, Lillian Gish, Mae Marsh, Dorothy Gish, Robert Harron, Charles H. Mailes, Harry Carey, Gertrude Bambrick, Alfred Paget. *Prod:* Biograph. 4 reels. (Re-issued, with additional footage, as 6 reels, 1917, as *Her Condoned Sin*). (Compare listings in Blanche Sweet and Dorothy Gish filmographies.)

HIS FATHER'S HOUSE (1914). Romantic drama; as a jealous husband whose dance-hall girl wife takes refuge in his father's house. *Prod:* Biograph. 1001 ft.

CLASSMATES (1914). Drama of West Point rivalry and redemption; in a small role. *Dir:* James Kirkwood. *Sup:* D. W. Griffith. *Sc:* (from the play by William C. de Mille and Margaret Turnbull). *With* Henry B. Walthall, Marshall Neilan, Blanche Sweet, Lionel Barrymore, Jack Mulhall, Dorothy Gish, Gertrude Robinson, Thomas Jefferson. (Re-made, 1924, with Richard Barthelmess and Madge Evans.) *Prod:* Klaw and Erlanger/Biograph. 3449 ft. (Compare listings in Blanche Sweet and Dorothy Gish filmographies.)

OUR MUTUAL GIRL (1914). Programme series of twenty-six episodes, each featuring a visit to some celebrity, or some historic or popular site in Manhattan; as "The Country Lover," whose romance with the Mutual Girl (Norma Phillips) is progressed with each episode. Episodes were released fortnightly in two-reels each. *Prod:* Mutual/Reliance. Total of fifty-two reels.

STRONGHEART (1914). Drama of an Indian brave, who goes to a white man's college, and falls in love with a white girl; as Frank Nelson, the heroine's brother, who is saved from drowning by Strongheart. *Dir:* James Kirkwood. *Sup:* D. W. Griffith. *Sc:* (from the play by William C. de Mille). *With* Henry B. Walthall, Lionel Barrymore, Blanche Sweet, Alan Hale, Gertrude Robinson. (Re-made as *Braveheart*, 1925, with Rod La Rocque.) *Prod:* Klaw and Erlanger/Biograph. 2471 ft. (Compare listing in Blanche Sweet filmography.)

TOO MANY HUSBANDS (1914). Farce comedy; as Harry Brown. *Dir:* Sidney Drew. *Sc:* (from a story by Anthony E. Wills). *With* Harry Davenport, Sidney Drew, Jane Morrow, Etienne Girardot, Lillian Burns, Hughie Mack, Miss Gray, Ethel Lloyd. *Prod:* Vitagraph. 2122 ft.

THE ACCOMPLISHED MRS. THOMPSON (1914). Domestic comedy; as Dick Osborne, a newlywed husband whose housekeeper is the estranged wife of his best friend. *Dir:* Wilfrid North. *Sc:* (from a story by Norval Richardson). *With* Lillian Walker, Cissy Fitzgerald, Harry Davenport. *Prod:* Vitagraph. 1004 ft.

THE LADIES' WAR. (1914). Comedy; as Mr. Blenkinsop. *Dir:* Wilfrid North. *Sc:* Roy L. McCardell. *With* Cissy Fitzgerald, Jane Fearnley, Albert Roccardi, Mandy Wilson, Karin Norman. *Prod:* Vitagraph. 1 reel.

THE PERSISTENT MR. PRINCE (1914). Farce comedy; as Prunella's brother. *Dir:* Wilfrid North. *Sc:* Gelett Burgess. *With* Lillian Walker, Wallie Van, Edwina Robbins. *Prod:* Vitagraph. 1027 ft.

THE SONG OF THE GHETTO (1914). Romantic drama; as Mario Amata, who sails to America, where his sweetheart joins him. *Dir:* William Humphrey. *Sc:* (from a story by Louise Braganza). *With* Carolyn Birch, William Humphrey, Eulalie Jensen. *Prod:* Vitagraph. 2106 ft.

JOHN RANCE, GENTLEMAN (1914).

Romantic drama; as John Rance, tempted by the love of his best friend's wife. *Dir:* Van Dyke Brooke. *Sc:* (from a story by Elizabeth R. Carpenter). *With* Norma Talmadge, Harry Kendall. *Prod:* Vitagraph. 1710 ft.

THE MEMORIES IN MEN'S SOULS (1914). Marital drama; as Graham's son, a husband who is tempted. *Dir:* Van Dyke Brooke. *Sc:* (from a story by James Hopper). *With* Norma Talmadge, Van Dyke Brooke. *Prod:* Vitagraph. 1010 ft.

THE HIDDEN LETTERS (1914). Marital drama; as John Reynolds, the husband. *Dir:* Van Dyke Brooke. *Sc:* Edward Montagne (from a story by Isabelle W. Sterne). *With* Norma Talmadge, Julia Swayne Gordon, Frank Currier. *Prod:* Vitagraph. 1954 ft.

POLITICS AND THE PRESS (1914). Newspaper exposure of a ruthless political gang; as John Marsden, the newspaper editor. *Dir:* Van Dyke Brooke. *Sc:* (from a story by W. A. Tremayne). *With* Norma Talmadge, Van Dyke Brooke. *Prod:* Vitagraph. 968 ft.

THE LOAN SHARK KING (1914). Drama; as Harry Graham, an artist. *Dir:* Van Dyke Brooke. *Sc:* (from a story by Laura Colfax). *With* Norma Talmadge, Van Dyke Brooke. *Prod:* Vitagraph. 1073 ft.

THE PEACEMAKER (1914). Romantic comedy; as Jack Strong, a man in love. *Dir:* Van Dyke Brooke. *Sc:* William A. Tremayne. *With* Norma Talmadge, Constance Talmadge, Van Dyke Brooke, Garry McGarry. *Prod:* Vitagraph. 1018 ft. (Compare listing in Constance Talmadge filmography.)

UNDER FALSE COLORS (1914). Romantic comedy; as Private Warring, a fortune hunter. *Dir:* Van Dyke Brooke. *Sc:* (from a story by Jane Lennox). *With* Norma Talmadge, Van Dyke Brooke, Edwina Robbins, *Prod:* Vitagraph. 1068 ft.

GOODBYE SUMMER (1914). Romantic drama; as Hugo St. Clair, sculptor. *Dir:* Van Dyke Brooke. *Sc:* (from a story by Mrs. Owen Bronson). *With* Norma Talmadge, Van Dyke Brooke, Paul Scardon, Bobby Connelly. *Prod:* Vitagraph. 2040 ft.

THE OLD FLUTE PLAYER (1914). Romantic drama; as John Vanderlyn, rich socialite. *Dir:* Lionel Belmore. *Sc:* Eugene Mullin (from a story by C. T. Dazey and Edward Marshall). *With* Edith Storey, Charles Kent, Maud Milton, Ethel Lloyd. *Prod:* Vitagraph. 2640 ft.

IN THE LATIN QUARTER (1915). Romantic drama; as Andrew Lenique, artist. *Dir:* Lionel Belmore. *Sc:* Florence Bolles. *With* Edith Storey, Constance Talmadge, S. Rankin Drew, William Dunn. *Prod:* Vitagraph. 2 reels. (Compare listing in Constance Talmadge filmography.)

ANTONIO MORENO

THE ISLAND OF REGENERATION (1915). Romance on a desert island; as John Charnock, castaway. *Dir:* Harry Davenport. *Sc:* (from a novel by the Rev. Cyrus Townsend Brady). *With* Edith Storey, S. Rankin Drew, Bobby Connelly, Leo Delaney, Naomi Childers, Jack Brawn, Lillian Herbert, Logan Paul. *Prod:* Vitagraph. 6 reels.

THE QUALITY OF MERCY (1915). Romantic drama; as personal secretary to the father of the girl he loves. *Dir:* Lionel Belmore. *Sc:* (from a story by George Bronson Howard). *With* Edith Storey, Frank Currier, S. Rankin Drew. *Prod:* Vitagraph. 1064 ft.

THE PARK HONEYMOONERS (1915). Romantic comedy; as Billy, a newly-wed husband. *Dir:* Tefft Johnson. *Sc:* J. Stuart Blackton. *With* Betty Gray, George Stevens. *Prod:* Vitagraph. 932 ft.

LOVE'S WAY (1915). Romantic drama; as Rand Cornwall, idler, goaded by the girl he fancies into making something of himself. *Dir:* S. Rankin Drew. *Sc:* (from a story by Arthur H. Miller). *With* Edith Storey, Charles Kent. *Prod:* Vitagraph. 1034 ft.

ON HER WEDDING NIGHT (1915). Romantic drama; as a man who weds his murdered friend's *fiancé*. *Dir:* William Humphrey. *Sc:* (from a story by Eugene Mullin). *With* Edith Storey, Carolyn Birch, Denton Vane, William Dunn, Louise Beaudet, Charles Kent. *Prod:* Vitagraph. 4 reels.

DUST OF EGYPT (1915). Romantic comedy fantasy; as a man who on his betrothal night dreams a wild romantic dream about an Egyptian princess come to life. *Dir:* George Baker. *Sc:* (from a story by Alan Campbell, son of Mrs. Patrick Campbell). *With* Edith Storey, Naomi Childers, Hughie Mack, Cissy Fitzgerald, Charles Brown, Jay Dwiggins. *Prod:* Vitagraph. 6 reels.

YOUTH (1915). Marital drama; as a sculptor who falls in love with his model. *Dir:* Harry Handworth. *Sc:* (from a story by Lanier Bartlett). *With* Mlle. Valkyrien, Donald Hall, Frankie Mann. *Prod:* Vitagraph. 3 reels.

ANSELO LEE (1915). Romantic drama; as Anselo Lee, gypsy. *Dir:* Harry Handworth. *Sc:* (from a story by Paul Kester). *With* Naomi Childers, Mrs. Nellie Anderson, Donald Hall, Frankie Mann. *Prod:* Vitagraph. 3 reels.

THE GYPSY TRAIL (1915). Romantic drama; as a gypsy who becomes infatuated with a trollop. *Dir:* Harry Handworth. *Sc:* (from a story by Paul Kester). *With* Frankie Mann, Donald Hall, Josephine Earle, Mrs. Nellie Anderson. *Prod:* Vitagraph. 2 reels.

A "MODEL" WIFE (1915). Romantic drama; as the son of the owner of a large dressmaking establishment. *Dir:* Wilfrid North. *Sc:* (from a story by E. Lawrence Gibson). *With* Lillian Walker, Louise Beaudet, L. Rogers Lytton, Lillian Burns, Helen Pillsbury. *Prod:* Vitagraph. 2 reels.

A PRICE FOR FOLLY (1915). Romantic comedy fantasy; as a young man fascinated by a temptress. *Dir:* George Baker. *Sc:* (from a story by George P. Dillenbeck). *With* Edith Storey, Arthur Conzie, Louise Beaudet, Charles Kent, Ethel Corcoran, Harry T. Morey. *Prod:* Vitagraph. 5 reels.

KENNEDY SQUARE (1916). Romantic drama; as Harry Rutter, a gallant Southerner. *Dir:* S. Rankin Drew. *Sc:* (from a novel by F. Hopkinson Smith). *With* Muriel Ostriche, Charles Kent, Thomy Brooke, Raymond Bloomer, Dan Jarrett, Harold Foshay, Logan Paul. *Prod:* Vitagraph. 5 reels.

THE SUPREME TEMPTATION (1916). Romantic drama; as a medical student who becomes a surgeon. *Dir:* Harry Davenport. *Sc:* (from a story by Arthur J. Westermayr). *With* Dorothy Kelly, Evart Overton, Charles Kent, Mary Maurice, Kate Davenport, Templar Saxe, Jack Brawn, Marguerite Blake. *Prod:* Vitagraph. 5 reels.

SUSIE, THE SLEUTH (1916). Romantic comedy; as Hank, the sweetheart of a girl who wants to become a detective. *Dir:* George Baker. *Sc:* Kenneth S. Webb. *With* Edith Storey, John Costello, Rose E. Tapley, George Stevens, Arthur Robinson. *Prod:* Vitagraph. 1044 ft.

SHE WON THE PRIZE (1916). Romance; as a young business man who doesn't recognise his own secretary on holiday, and falls in love with her. *Dir/Sc:* George D. Baker (writing in collaboration with Elizabeth R. Carpenter). *With* Edith Storey, Josephine Earle, Donald McBride. *Prod:* Vitagraph. 1 reel.

(WINIFRED) THE SHOP GIRL (1916). Romantic drama; as a rich New Yorker who falls in love with a fashion model. *Dir:* George D. Baker. *Sc:* George Plympton (from a story by C. N. and A. M. Williamson). *With* Edith Storey, Lillian Burns, John Costello, Mrs. Soule, Harold Foshay, Marion Henry, Josephine Earle, Clara McCormack, Eddie Dunn, Templar Saxe. *Prod:* Vitagraph. 5 reels.

THE TARANTULA (1916). Drama of revenge; as Pedro Mendoza, lover of the Cuban girl who has sworn a terrible revenge on the American *roué* who has wronged her. *Dir-Sc:* George D. Baker. *With* Edith Storey, Eulalie Jensen, L. Rogers Lytton, Charles Kent, Harry Hollingsworth, Emmanuel A. Turner, Raymond Walburn, Harold Foshay, Gordon Gray, Templar Saxe. *Prod:* Vitagraph. 6 reels.

THE DEVIL'S PRIZE (1916). Drama; as Hugh Roland, newspaper owner. *Dir/Sc:* Marguerite Bertsch. *With* Naomi Childers, Albert S. Howson, Templar Saxe, Lark Taylor, Clio Ayres, Mildred Platz. *Prod:* Vitagraph. 5 reels.

ROSE OF THE SOUTH (1916). Romantic tragedy; as Randolph, a dashing young Confederate cavalry leader known as "The Flying Colonel." *Dir:* Paul Scardon. *Sc:* Joseph F. Poland (from a novel, "Randolph," by Arthur Train). *With* Peggy Hyland, Gordon Gray, Rose E. Tapley, Mary Maurice, Charles Kent. *Prod:* Vitagraph. 5 reels.

HER RIGHT TO LIVE (1917). Murder and innocence of guilt story; as a man falsely accused of murdering a political boss. *Dir:* Paul Scardon. *Sc:* Paul West. *With* Peggy Hyland, Mrs. Costello, Helen Connelly, Julia Swayne Gordon, Mildred Platz, John Robertson, Jack Ellis, Bobby Connelly. *Prod:* Vitagraph. 5 reels.

MONEY MAGIC (1917). Western romance, with two lovers stalemated; as Ben Fordyce, bound to an invalid sweetheart. *Dir:* William Wolbert. *Sc:* A. Van Buren Powell (from a story by Hamlin Garland). *With* Edith Storey, William Duncan, Lawrence Winston, Florence Dyer. *Prod:* Vitagraph. 5 reels.

ALADDIN FROM BROADWAY (1917). Romantic adventure in Mecca; as Jack Stanton. *Dir:* William Wolbert. *Sc:* Helmer Walton Bergaman (from a story by Frank Isham). *With* William Duncan, Laura Winston, George Holt, Otto Lederer. *Prod:* Vitagraph. 5 reels.

THE CAPTAIN OF THE GRAY HORSE TROOP (1917). Western romance; as Army Captain George Curtiss, who protects the Indians against the cattlemen. *Dir:* William Wolbert. *Sc:* A. Van Buren Powell (from a story by Hamlin Garland). *With* Edith Storey, Otto Lederer, Mrs. Bradbury, Al Jennings, Robert Burns, Neola May, H. A. Barrows. *Prod:* Vitagraph. 5 reels.

THE MAGNIFICENT MEDDLER (1917). Western drama; as Montague Emerson, newspaper reformer from the East who tangles with political bosses in the West. *Dir:* William Wolbert. *Sc:* Garfield Thompson (from a story by Lawrence McCloskey). *With* Mary Anderson, Leon D. Kent, Otto Lederer. *Prod:* Vitagraph. 5 reels.

A SON OF THE HILLS (1917). Almost autobiographical in that it is about a poor boy who, befriended by a wealthy old man, rises in the world; as Sandy Morley. *Dir:* Harry Davenport. *Sc:* Joseph F. Poland (from a novel by Harriet T. Comstock). *With* Belle Bruce, Robert Gaillord, Julia Swayne Gordon, Florence Radinoff, William Balfour. *Prod:* Vitagraph. 5 reels.

BY RIGHT OF POSSESSION (1917). Western comedy, with lovers running against one another in an election for sheriff; as Rom Beraer, sheriff. *Dir:* William Wolbert. *Sc:* Garfield Thompson (from a story by Alvah Milton Kerr). *With* Mary Anderson, Otto Lederer, Leon D. Kent. Working title: *The Lady Sheriff. Prod:* Vitagraph. 5 reels.

THE ANGEL FACTORY (1917). Social drama on the education of slum children; as a wealthy young philanthropist. *Dir:* Lawrence McGill. *Sc:* Will M. Ritchey (from a story by Lucien Hubbard). *With* Helene Chadwick, Armand Cortez, Margaret Greene, Suzanna Wills, Francis X. Conlay. *Prod:* Pathé. 5 reels.

THE MARK OF CAIN (AKA, *Thou Shalt Not*) (1917). Murder mystery; as Kane Langton, suspected of the murder of his rich uncle. *Dir:* George Fitzmaurice. *Sc:* Philip Bartholomae (from a novel by Carolyn Wells). *With* Irene Castle, J. H. Gilmour, Elinor Black, John Sainpolis. *Prod:* Pathé. 5 reels.

THE NAULAHKA (1918). Adventure drama in India; as Nicholas Tarvin, in quest of a "naulahka" (a famed jewelled girdle). *Dir:* George Fitzmaurice. *Sc:* George B. Seitz (from the novel by Rudyard Kipling and Walcott Balestier). *With* Doraldina, Warner Oland, Helene Chadwick, Mary Alden, J. H. Gilmour. *Prod:* Pathé. 6 reels.

THE HOUSE OF HATE (1918). Adventure serial in twenty chapters; as Harvey Gresham, young scientist. *Dir:* George B. Seitz. *Sc:* Arthur B. Reeve and Charles A. Logue. *With* Pearl White, Floyd Buckley, Peggy Shanor, John Webb Dilleon, J. H. Gilmour. *Prod:* Pathé. 41 reels (1st chapter, 3 reels; 19 subsequent chapters, 2 reels each).

THE FIRST LAW (1918). Mystery, murder, blackmail adventure; as Herbert Goodwin, a wealthy young man blackmailed by a detective. *Dir:* Lawrence McGill. *Sc:* Ray Somerville (from the novel by Gilson Willets). *With* Irene Castle, J. H. Gilmour, Marguerite Snow, Edward J. Connelly. *Prod:* Pathé. 5 reels.

THE IRON TEST (1918). Adventure serial in fifteen episodes; as Albert Beresford, circus acrobat. *Dir:* R. N. Bradbury and Paul C. Hurst. *Sc:* Graham Baker (from a story by Albert E. Smith and Cyrus Townsend Brady). *With* Carol Holloway. *Prod:* Vitagraph. 31 reels (1st chapter, 3 reels; 14 susbsequent chapters, 2 reels. each).

THE PERILS OF THUNDER MOUNTAIN (1919). Adventure serial in fifteen episodes; as John Davies, who conquers every mountain hazard, including snow, forest fire, flood, storm, and a set of villains intent upon his destruction. *Dir:* R. N. Bradbury and W. J. Bowman. *Sc:* Graham Baker (from a story by Albert E. Smith and Cyrus Townsend Brady).

160

ANTONIO MORENO

With Carol Holloway, Kate Price. *Prod:* Vitagraph. 31 reels (1st chapter, 3 reels; 14 subsequent chapters, 2 reels. each).

THE INVISIBLE HAND (1920). Adventure serial in fifteen episodes; as John Sharpe, known as "The Needle." *Dir:* William J. Bowman. *Sc:* Graham Baker (from a story by Albert E. Smith and Cyrus Townsend Brady). *With* Pauline Curley, Brinsley Shaw, Jay Morley, Sam Polo, George Mellcrest. *Prod:* Vitagraph. 31 reels (1st chapter, 3 reels; 14 susbsequent chapters, 2 reels each).

THE VEILED MYSTERY (1920). Adventure serial in fifteen episodes; as Ralph Moore, hounded by a mysterious menace. *Dir:* Antonio Moreno, Webster Cullison, William J. Bowan and F. J. Grandon. *Sc:* Graham Baker (from a story by Albert E. Smith and Cleveland Moffett). *With* Pauline Curley, H. A. Barrows, Nenette de Courcy, W. L. Rogers, George H. Reed. *Prod:* Vitagraph. 31 reels (1st chapter, 3 reels: 14 subsequent chapters, 2 reels each).

THREE SEVENS (777) (1921). Prison break thriller; as Daniel Craig, Convict No. 777. *Dir:* Chester Bennett. *Sc:* E. Magnus Ingleton (from a novel by Perley Poore Sheehan). *With* Jean Calhoun, Emmett King, Jefferson Webb, DeWitt Jennings. *Prod:* Vitagraph. 5 reels.

THE SECRET OF THE HILLS (1921). Romantic adventure; as Guy Fenton, whose life is changed when he is given the wrong hat by a hat-check girl. *Dir:* Chester Bennett. *Sc:* E. Magnus Ingleton (from a novel by William Garrett). *With* Lillian Hall, Kingsley Benedict, George Claire, Walter Rodgers, Oleta Otis, J. Gunnis Davis, Frank Thorne, Arthur Sharpe. *Prod:* Vitagraph. 5 reels.

A GUILTY CONSCIENCE (1922). Romantic drama in India; as Gilbert Thurston, British civil service employee. *Dir:* David Smith. *Sc:* Jay Pilcher. *With* Betty Francisco, Harry Van Meter, Lillie Leslie, J. MacFarlane. *Prod:* Vitagraph. 5 reels.

MY AMERICAN WIFE (1923). Romantic drama; as Manuel Tassa (Santos), a South American cavalier. *Dir:* Sam Wood. *Sc:* Monte M. Katterjohn (from a story by Hector Turnbull). *With* Gloria Swanson, Josef Swickard, Gino Corrado, Eric Mayne, Edythe Chapman, Aileen Pringle, Walter Long, F. R. Butler, Loyal Underwood. *Prod:* Paramount. 6 reels.

LOST AND FOUND ON A SOUTH SEA ISLAND (AKA, GB *Lost and Found*) (AKA, GB, *Passions of the Sea*) 1923. Adventure in the South Seas; as Lloyd Warren. *Dir:* Raoul Walsh. *Sc:* Paul Bern (from a story, "Captain Blackbird," by Carey Wilson). *With* House Peters, Pauline Starke, Mary Jane Irving, Rosemary Theby, George Seigmann, William V. Mong, Carl Harbaugh, David Wing. Exteriors filmed in the South Seas. *Prod:* Goldwyn. 7 reels.

LOOK YOUR BEST (1923). Romantic comedy; as Carlo Bruni. *Dir:* Rupert Hughes (from his story, "The Bitterness of Sweets"). *With* Colleen Moore, Earl Metcalfe, Martha Mattox, William Orlamond, Francis McDonald. *Prod:* Goldwyn. 6 reels.

THE TRAIL OF THE LONESOME PINE (1923). Mountaineer feud drama; as John Hale, civil engineer. *Dir:* Charles Maigne. *Sc:* Will M. Ritchey (from the novel by John Fox Jr. and the play therefrom by Eugene Walter). *With* Mary Miles Minter, Ernest Torrence, Edward Brady, Beulah Bains, J. S. Stembridge, Cullen Tate. (Previously filmed, 1916, by Cecil B. DeMille, with Thomas Meighan in the male lead; re-made as a talkie, 1936, by Henry Hathaway.) *Prod:* Paramount. 6 reels.

THE EXCITERS (1923). Rum-running melodrama; as Pierre Martel, secret service man posing as a burglar. *Dir:* Major Maurice Campbell. *Sc:* John Colton and Sonya Levien (from a play by Martin Brown). *With* Bebe Daniels, Burr McIntosh, Diana Allen, Cyril Ring, Jane Thomas, Ida Darling. *Prod:* Paramount. 6 reels. (Compare listing in Bebe Daniels filmography.)

THE SPANISH DANCER (1923). Romantic drama of Old Spain; as Don César de Bazan, scapegrace hero. *Dir:* Herbert Brenon. *Sc:* June Mathis and Beulah Marie Dix (from the play, "Don César de Bazan," by Adolphe D'Ennery and Phillippe François Pinel Dumanoir). *With* Pola Negri, Adolphe Menjou, Wallace Beery, Kathlyn Williams, Gareth Hughes, Robert Agnew, Dawn O'Day (Anne Shirley), Edward Kipling, Charles A. Stevenson. (*Rosita*, simultaneously produced by Mary Pickford with Ernst Lubitsch directing, had its story basis in the same play.) *Prod:* Paramount. 9 reels.

FLAMING BARRIERS (1924). Forest fire-fighting melodrama; as Sam Barton. *Dir:* George Melford. *Sc:* Harvey Thew (from a story by Byron Morgan). *With* Jacqueline Logan, Walter Hiers, Charles Ogle, Luke Cosgrove, Robert McKim. *Prod:* Paramount. 6 reels.

BLUFF (1924). Comedy drama about the power of bluff; as Robert Fitzmaurice, attorney. *Dir:* Sam Wood. *Sc:* Willis Goldbeck (from a story by Rita Weiman and Josephine Quirk). *With* Agnes Ayres, Fred Butler, Roscoe Karns, Clarence Burton, Pauline Pasquette, Jack Garden. *Prod:* Paramount. 6 reels.

TIGER LOVE (1924). Romantic drama; as the bandit called "The Wildcat." *Dir:* George Melford. *Sc:* Howard Hawks (from a Spanish operetta, "El Gato Montes," by Manuel Penella). *With* Estelle Taylor, G. Raymond Nye, Manuel Camere, Edgar Norton, David Torrence, Snitz Edwards, Monte Collins. *Prod:* Paramount. 6 reels.

THE STORY WITHOUT A NAME (AKA, GB *Without Warning*) (1924). Adventurous melodrama about a U.S. Army death machine; as Alan Holt, radio expert. *Dir:* Irvin V. Willat. *Sc:* Victor Irvin (from a story by Arthur Stringer). *With* Agnes Ayres, Tyrone Power Sr., Louis Wolheim, Dagmar Godowsky, Jack Lionel Bohn, Maurice Costello, Frank Currier, Ivan Linow. *Prod:* Paramount. 6 reels.

THE BORDER LEGION (1924). Western melodrama; as Jim Cleve, who joins an outlaw band. *Dir:* William K. Howard. *Sc:* George Hull (from a novel by Zane Grey). *With* Helene Chadwick, Rockcliffe Fellowes, Gibson Gowland, Charles Olge, James Corey, Edward Gribbon, Luke Cosgrove. (Previously filmed by Goldwyn, 1919; first re-made as a talkie by Paramount starring Richard Arlen, 1930; re-made as *The Last Round-Up,* with Randolph Scott.). *Prod:* Paramount. 7 reels.

LEARNING TO LOVE (1925). Romantic comedy; as Scott Warner, legal guardian to the flirtatious heroine. *Dir:* Sidney Franklin. *Sc:* John Emerson and Anita Loos. *With* Constance Talmadge, Edythe Chapman, Emily Fitzroy, Wallace MacDonald, Ray Hallor, John Harron, Byron Munson, Alf Goulding, Edgar Norton. *Prod:* First National. 7 reels. (Compare listing in Constance Talmadge filmography.)

ONE YEAR TO LIVE (1925). Romantic melodrama; as Captain Tom Kendrick. *Dir:* Irving Cummings. *Sc:* J. G. Hawks (from a newspaper series by John Hunter). *With* Aileen Pringle, Dorothy Mackaill, Rosemary Theby, Sam de Grasse, Joseph Kilgour, Rose Dione, Leo White, Chester Conklin. *Prod:* First National. 5889 ft.

HER HUSBAND'S SECRET (1925). Romantic drama of rehabilitation; as Eliot Owen. *Dir:* Frank Lloyd. *Sc:* J. G. Hawks (from a novel, "Judgement," by May Edington). *With* Patsy Ruth Miller, Ruth Clifford, David Torrence, Frankie Darro, Walter McGrail, Phyllis Haver, Pauline Neff, Frances Teague, Margaret Fielding, James Girard. *Prod:* First National. 7 reels.

MARE NOSTRUM (*Our Sea*) (1926). Romantic drama of the Mediterranean; as Ulysses Ferragut, Spanish sea captain. *Dir:* Rex Ingram. *Sc:* Willis Goldbeck (from the novel by Vicente Blasco Ibáñez). *With* Alice Terry, Hughie Mack, Mlle. Kithnou, Mme. Paquerette, Fernand Mailly, Andre von Engelman, Michael Brantford, Uni Apollon, Alex-Nova, Kada-Abd-el-Kader, Rosita Ramirez, Frederick Marlotti. Filmed in Madrid, Naples, Pompeii, Paestum, Marseilles, Monte Carlo, and the Metro studio at Nice. (Moreno's favourite role.) *Prod:* M-G-M. 10 reels.

BEVERLY OF GRAUSTARK (1926). Mythical kingdom romance; as Danton, bodyguard of the heroine, who is masquerading as her boy cousin, heir to Graustark's throne, *Dir:* Sidney Franklin. *Sc:* Agnes Christine Johnston (from the novel by George Barr McCutcheon). *With* Marion Davies, Creighton Hale, Roy D'Arcy, Albert Gran, Paulette Duval, Max Barwyn, Charles Clary. *Prod:* M-G-M (Cosmopolitan Pictures). 7 reels.

THE TEMPTRESS (1926). Romantic tragedy; as Ribledo, South American engineer. *Dir:* Fred Niblo (Mauritz Stiller, uncredited). *Sc:* Dorothy Farnum (from the novel, "La tierra de todos," by Vicente Blasco Ibáñez). *With* Greta Garbo, Roy D'Arcy, Marc MacDermott, Lionel Barrymore, Virginia Brown Faire, Armand Kaliz, Alys Murrell, Robert Anderson, Francis McDonald, Hector V. Sarno, Inez Gomez, Steve Clemento, Ray Coulson. *Prod:* M-G-M (Cosmopolitan Pictures). 9 reels. (Compare listing in Greta Garbo filmography.)

LOVE'S BLINDNESS (1926). Romantic drama of an impoverished nobleman who agrees to wed a money-lender's daughter; as Hubert Culverdale, Eighth Earl of St. Austel. *Dir:* John Francis Dillon. *Sc:* Elinor Glyn. *With* Pauline Starke, Lilyan Tashman, Sam de Grasse, Douglas Gilmore, Earl Metcalfe. *Prod:* M-G-M. 7 reels.

THE FLAMING FOREST (1926). Melodrama of the Northwest; as Sergeant David Carrigan, of the North West Mounted Police. *Dir:* Reginald Barker. *Sc:* Waldemar Young (from the novel by James Oliver Curwood). *With* Renée Adorée, Gardner James, William Austin, Tom O'Brien, Emile Chautard, Clarence Geldart, Charles Ogle, Claire McDowell, Bert Roach. Filmed in Natural Color. *Prod:* M-G-M/Cosmopolitan. 7 reels.

IT (1927). Romantic comedy; as Cyrus Waltham, son of a big department store owner. *Dir:* Clarence Badger. *Sc:* Louis D. Lighton and Hope Loring (from a novel by Elinor Glyn). *With* Clara Bow, William Austin, Jacqueline Gadsden, Julia Swayne Gordon, Priscilla Bonner, Eleanor Lawson, Rose E. Tapley, Gary Cooper, Elinor Glyn. *Prod:* Paramount. 7 reels.

VENUS OF VENICE (1927). Romantic comedy; as Kenneth Wilson, whose heart is stolen by a Venetian thief. *Dir:* Marshall Neilan. *Sc:* Wallace Smith. *With* Constance Talmadge, Julanne Johnston, Edward Martindel, Hedda Hopper, Michael Vavitch. *Prod:* First National. 7 reels. (Compare listing in Constance Talmadge filmography.)

MADAME POMPADOUR (1927). Romantic drama of the court of Louis XV; as a romantic innkeeper who loves the king's mistress. *Dir:* Herbert Wilcox. *Sc:* Frances Marion (from a play by Rudolph Schanzer and Ernst Wellisch). *With* Dorothy Gish, Henry Bosc, Jeff MacLaughlin, Nelson Keys, Cyril McLaglen, Marcel Beauplan, Marie Ault, Tom Reynolds. *Prod:* Paramount. 7 reels. (Compare listing in Dorothy Gish filmography.)

EN LA TIERRA DEL SOL. Filmed in Spain, 1927. Not released in U.S.A. or Great Britain. *Dir:* Ramon Martinez de la Riva. *With* Elisa Ruiz Romero, Alfredo Hurtado.

COME TO MY HOUSE (1928). Metropolitan melodrama; as Floyd Bennings. *Dir:* Alfred E. Green. *Sc:* Marion Orth (from a story by Arthur Somers Roche). *With* Olive Borden, Ben Bard, Cornelius Keefe, Doris Lloyd, Richard Maitland. *Prod:* Fox. 6 reels.

THE WHIP WOMAN (1928). Romantic melodrama; as Count Michael Ferenzi. *Dir:* Joseph C. Boyle. *Sc: Earle Roebuck (from a story by Forrest Halsey and Leland Hayward).* *With* Estelle Taylor, Lowell Sherman, Hedda Hopper, Julanne Johnston, Loretta Young, Jack Ackroyd. *Prod:* First National. 6 reels.

NAMELESS MEN (1912). Prison melodrama; as Robert Strong, secret service man who gets himself into Sing Sing in order to gain confidence of bank robbers. *Dir:* W. Christy Cabanné. *Sc:* John F. Natteford (from a story by E. Morton Hough). *With* Claire Windsor, Ray Hallor, Sally Rand, Charles Clary. *Prod:* Tiffany. 6 reels.

THE MIDNIGHT TAXI (1928). Melodrama; as Tony Driscoll, reformed crook who wants to go straight. *Dir:* John Adolfi. *Sc:* Freddie Fay (from a story by Gregory Rogers). *With* Helene Costello, William Russell, Tommie Dugan, Myrna Loy, Pat Hartigan, Robert Agnew. *Prod:* Warner Bros. 65 reels.

THE AIR LEGION (1928). Romantic aviation drama; as Steve Rogers, mail pilot. *Dir:* Bert Glennon. *Sc:* Fred Myton (from a story by James Ashmore Creelman). *With* Ben Lyon, Martha Sleeper, Colin Chase. *Prod:* FBO. 7 reels.

ADORATION (1928). Romantic drama; as the Russian Prince Serge Orloff. *Dir:* Frank Lloyd. *Sc:* Winifred Dunn (from a story by Lajos Biro). *With* Billie Dove, Lucy Dorraine, Nicholas Soussanin, Winifred Bryson, Nicholas Bela, Lucien Prival, Emile Chautard. *Prod:* First National. 7 reels.

SYNTHETIC SIN (1928). Romantic comedy; as Donald Anthony. *Dir:* William A. Seiter. *Sc:* Tom J. Geraghty (from a play by Frederic and Fanny Hatton).*With* Colleen Moore, Kathryn McGuire, Montagu Love, Edythe Chapman, Gertrude Astor, Ben Hendricks Jr., Julanne Johnston, Gertrude Howard, Raymond Turner. *Prod:* First National. 7 reels.

CAREERS (1929). Romantic drama of the Orient; as Victor Gromaire, French magistrate in a small town in Cochin-China. *Dir:* John Francis Dillon. *Sc:* Forrest Halsey (from a play, "Karriere", by Alfred Schirokauer and Paul Rosenhayn). *With* Billie Dove, Carmel Myers, Thelma Todd, Noah Beery, Holmes E. Herbert, Robert Frazer, Sojin. (Moreno's talking feature *début.*) *Prod:* First National. 8455 ft.

EL CUERPO DEL DELITO (1929). Spanish-speaking version of *The Benson Murder Case;* in the role enacted in the English-speaking version by William (Stage) Boyd. *Dir:* Cyril Gardner and A. Washington Pezet. *With* Ramon Pereda, Maria Alba, Barry Norton. *Prod:* Paramount. 5,794 ft.

ROMANCE OF THE RIO GRANDE (1929). Romantic melodrama, with music, of the Rio Grande; as Juan, a villainous nephew seeking to discredit the real heir. *Dir:* Alfred Santell. *Sc:* Marion Orth (from a novel, "Conquistador," by Katherine Fullerton Gerould. *With* Warner Baxter, Mary Duncan, Mona Maris, Robert Edeson. (Moreno also played in the Spanish-speaking version, *Vieja Hildalguia.*) *Prod:* Fox. 8400 ft.

ONE MAD KISS (1930). Romantic drama, with music; as Don Estrada, a corrupt governor. *Dir:* James Tinling and Marcel Silver. *Sc:* Dudley Nichols (from a play by Adolph Paul). *With* Jose Mojica, Mona Maris, Tom Patricola. (Moreno played the same role in the Spanish-speaking version, *El precio de un beso,* directed by Marcel Silver.) *Prod:* Fox. 7 reels.

EL HOMBRE MALO (1930). Spanish-speaking version of *The Bad Man;* as Pancho Lopez, the title role, which Walter Huston had played in the English-speaking version. *Dir:* William McGann. *With* Rosita Ballesteros, Juan Torena. *Prod:* First National. 9 reels.

ROUGH ROMANCE (1930). Lumberjack melodrama of the Northwest; as Loup Latour, a French-Canadian villain. *Dir:* A. F. Erickson. *Sc:* Elliott Lester (from a story by Kenneth B. Clarke). *With* George O'Brien, Helen Chandler, Roy Stewart, Harry Cording, John Wayne, Noel Francis, Frank Lanning, Eddie Borden. Working title: *The Girl Who Wasn't Wanted. Prod:* Fox. 6 reels.

LA VOLUNTAD DEL MUERTO (*The Will of the Deceased*) (AKA, *El Gato*) (1930). Spanish-speaking version of *The Cat Creeps,* adapted from "The Cat and the Canary," a play by John Willard; Spanish version translated from the screenplay by Gladys Lehman and William Hurlbut. *Dir:* George Melford. *With* Lupita Tovar, Soledad Jimenez, Andre de Segurola, Maria Calvo, Conchita Ballesteros. Manuel Grando, Paul Ellis (Moreno played the role which Neil Hamilton had enacted in the English-speaking version, directed by Rupert Julian.) *Prod:* Universal. 8 reels.

LOS QUE DANZAN (1931). Spanish-speaking version of *Those Who Dance* (See Betty Compson and Blanche Sweet filmographies); as Dan Hogan (played by Monte Blue in the English-speaking talkie; by Warner Baxter in the silent). *Dir:* William McGann. *With* Maria Alba, Pablo Alvarez Rubio. *Prod:* First National. 7 reels.

THE WIDE OPEN SPACES (1931). Western satire; as a Westerner. *Dir:* Arthur Rosson. *Sc:* Walter Weems and Edward Earle. *With* William Farnum, Earle Foxe, Dorothy Sebastian, Charles Wilder. *Prod:* RKO (Masquers Club Comedy). 2 reels.

FIN DE FIESTA (1931). Political adventure; in the male lead. *With* Maria Alba, Pablo Alvarez Rubio, Martin Garralaga, Tito Davison. *Prod:* First National.

SANTA (1931). Romantic tragedy; Moreno did not act in this. *Dir:* Antonio Moreno (assistant director was Ramón Peón, who became a director in Mexican films). *Sc:* Carlos Noriega Hope (from the novel by Federico Gamboa). *With* Lupita Tovar, Carlos Orellana, Juan José Martinez Casado, Donald Reed, Antonio R. Frausto, Mimi Derba, Rosita Arriaga, Raul de Anda, Joaquin Busquets, Feliciano Rueda, Jorge Peón, Jorge Marrón. (*Santa* is often referred to as the film that marked the birth of the Mexican talking feature film.) (Re-made in Mexico, 1943, with Esther Fernández and Ricardo Montalban; directed by Norman Foster.) *Prod:* Compañia Nacional Productora de Películas. 81m.

AGUILAS FRENTE AL SOL *(Eagles Across the Sun)* (1932). International adventure; Moreno did not act in this. *Dir:* Antonio Moreno. *Sc:* Gustavo Sáenz de Sicilia. *With* Jorge Lewis, Hilda Moreno, Joaquin Busquets, Conchita Ballesteros, José Soriano Biosca, Manuel Tamés, Joaquin Pardavé, Julio Villarreal, Ramón Péon, Alberto Marti, Joaquin Coss, Ina del Mar, Paco Martinez, Armando Arriola, jorge Péon, Raúl de Anda, Ballet de la Compañia "Roberto Soto." *Prod:* Comañia Nacional Productora de Películas. 80m.

PRIMAVERA EN OTONO (*Springtime in Autumn*) (1932). Romantic comedy; as the male lead. *Dir:* Eugene S. Forde. *Sc:* Gregorio Martinez Sierra (from his play). *With* Catalina Barcena, Raoul Roulien. *Prod:* Fox.

LA CIUDAD DE CARTON (*The Cardboard City*) (1932). Romantic comedy with a Hollywood setting; in the male lead. *Dir:* Louis King. *Sc:* Gregorio Martinez Sierra (original). *With* Catalina Barcena, José Crespo. *Prod:* Fox.

ROSA DE FRANCIA (1933). Romantic comedy of a crown princess who marries an Asturian prince; as the prince. *Dir:* Gordon Wiles. *With* Rosita Diaz, Julio Peña, Consuelito Frank, Enrique de Posas, Don Alvarado, Maria Calvo. Prod: Fox.

SENORA CASADA NECESITA MARIDO (1933). Romantic comedy; in the male lead. *Dir:* Eugene S. Forde. *With* Catalina Barcena, Valentin Parera. *Prod:* Fox. 6 reels. (English-speaking version starred George Sanders, Michael Whalen and Gloria Stuart; it was released as *My Second Wife,* but during production it was also known as *The Lady Escapes, Escape from Love,* and *Married Woman Needs a Husband,* the last becoming the Spanish version's title.)

STORM OVER THE ANDES (1935). Romantic triangle; as Major Tovar, the flying squadron major who battles it out with Holt, who is on the make for the major's wife. *Dir:* W. Christy Cabanné. *Sc:* Albert De Mond, Frank Wead, Eve Greene (from a story by Eliot Gibbons and La Clade Christy). *With* Jack Holt, Mona Barrie, Gene Lockhart, Grant Withers, Juanita Garfias, Barry Norton, George Lewis. Moreno played the same role in the Spanish-speaking version, ALAS SOBRE EL CHACO, with Jose Crespo and Lupita Tovar in the Holt and Barrie roles. *Prod:* Universal. 83m.

MARIA DE LA O (1936). Romantic drama; as an American painter in Spain. *Dir:* Francisco Elias. *With* Carmen Amaya, Pastora Imperio, Julio Peña. Filmed in Spain.

THE BOHEMIAN GIRL (1936). Farce comedy; as Devilshoof, a philandering gypsy. *Dir:* James Horne and Charles Rogers. *Sc:* Alfred Bunn (from the operetta by William Balfe). *With* Stan Laurel, Oliver Hardy, Jacqueline Wells, Darla Hood, Mae Busch, William P. Carleton, James Finlayson, Thelma Todd. *Prod:* M-G-M. 8 reels.

ROSE OF THE RIO GRANDE (1938). Romantic Western, with music; as the villainous rebel captain. *Dir:* William Nigh. *Sc:* Dorothy Reid and Ralph Bettinson (from a story by Johnston McCulley). *With* Movita, John Carroll, Lina Basquette, George Cleveland, Duncan Renaldo, Don Alvarado. *Prod:* Monogram. 7 reels.

AMBUSH (1939). Bank robbery melodrama; as the Detective-Captain. *Dir:* Kurt Neumann. *Sc:* Laura and S. J. Perelman (from a story by Robert Ray). *With* Gladys Swarthout, Lloyd Nolan, William Henry, William Frawley, Ernest Truex, Broderick Crawford, Richard Denning, Polly Moran, Wade Boteler, Raymond Hatton, Ethel Clayton, Bryant Washburn, George Melford. (The only non-singing role in Gladys Swarthout's film career). *Prod:* Paramount. 6 reels.

ANTONIO MORENO

SEVEN SINNERS (1940). Romantic melodrama; as Rubio, one of the admirers of Dietrich. *Dir:* Tay Garnett. *Sc:* John Meehan and Harry Tugend (from a story by Ladislaus Fodor and Laslo Vadnay). *With* Marlene Dietrich, John Wayne, Broderick Crawford, Mischa Auer, Albert Dekker, Billy Gilbert, Oscar Homolka, Anna Lee, Samuel S. Hinds, Reginald Denny, Vince Barnett, Herbert Rawlinson, James Craig, William Bakewell, Russell Hicks, William Davidson. *Prod:* Universal. 87m. (Re-made, 1950, as *South Sea Sinner.)*

THEY MET IN ARGENTINA (1941). Musical romance, with Rodgers and Hart score; as Don Carlos. *Dir:* Leslie Goodwins and Jack Hively. *Sc:* Jerry Cady (from a story by Lou Brock & Harold Daniels). *With* Maureen O'Hara, James Ellison, Alberto Vila, Buddy Ebsen, Robert Barrat, Joseph Buloff, Diosa Costello, Luis Alberni, Fortunio Bonanova. *Prod:* RKO. 64m.

TWO LATINS FROM MANHATTAN (1941). Comedy; as an authentic Latin who complicates matters for those pretending to be. *Dir:* Charles Barton. *Sc:* Albert Duffy. *With* Joan Davis, Joan Woodbury, Jinx Falkenburg, Fortunio Bonanova, Lloyd Bridges, Sig Arno. *Prod:* Columbia. 65m.

THE KID FROM KANSAS (1941). (AKA, *The Americanos*). Comedy drama; as a Police Chief. *Dir:* William Nigh. *Sc:* Griffin Jay and David Silverstein (from a story by Griffin Jay). *With* Leo Carrillo, Andy Devine, Dick Foran, Ann Doran, Marcia Ralston, James Seay, Francis McDonald, Nestor Paiva, Wade Boteler. *Prod:* Universal. 61m.

FIESTA (1942). Romantic comedy; as Don Hernandez. *Dir* LeRoy Prinz. *Sc:* Cortland Fitzsimmons (from an adaptation of his own story by Kenneth Higgins). *With* Anne Ayars, George Negrete, Armida, George Givot, Nick Moro. *Prod:* United Artists-Hal Roach. Technicolor. 5 reels.

THE VALLEY OF THE SUN (1942). Western; as Cochise. *Dir:* George Marshall. *Sc:* Horace McCoy (from a novel by Clarence Buddington Kelland). *With* James Craig, Dean Jagger, Lucille Ball, Sir Cedric Hardwicke, Peter Whitney, Billy Gilbert, Tom Tyler (Geronimo), George Cleveland. *Prod:* RKO. 79m.

UNDERCOVER MAN (1942). A Hopalong Cassidy Western; as Tomas Gonzalez. *Dir:* Lesley Selander. *Sc:* J. Benton Cheney. *With* William Boyd, Andy Clyde, Jay Kirby, Nora Lane, Chris-Pan Martin. *Prod:* Paramount. 68m.

TAMPICO (1944). Below-the-border Nazi espionage melodrama; as a Mexican Justice of the Peace. *Dir:* Lothar Mendes. *Sc:* Kenneth Gamet, Fred Niblo Jr. Richard Macaulay (from a story and adaptation by Ladislaus Fodor). *With* Edward G. Robinson, Lynn Bari, Victor McLaglen, Robert Bailey, Marc Lawrence, Mona Maris, Tonio Selwart, Ralph Byrd, Nestor Paiva. *Prod:* Fox. 76m.

THE SPANISH MAIN (1945). Romantic drama of piracy on the high seas; as a Spanish Commandanto. *Dir:* Frank Borzage. *Sc:* George Worthing Yates, Herman J. Mankiewicz (from a story by Aeneas MacKenzie). *With* Paul Henreid, Maureen O'Hara, Walter Slezak, Binnie Barnes, John Emery, Barton MacLane, J. M. Kerrigan, Fritz Leiber, Nancy Gates, Jack LaRue, Ian Keith, Mike Mazurki. Technicolor. *Prod:* RKO. 100m.

SOL Y SOMBRA (*Sunlight and Shadow*) (1945). Father-son drama; as Manuel Campos, once a great Spanish torero, who retires to Mexico. *Dir:* Rafael E. Portas. *Sc:* Enrique Bahórquez and Rafael Solana (from a play by Antonio Quintero and Pascual Guillén). *With* Luis Procuna, Josefina Romagnoli, Rubén Rojo, Florencio Castelló, Luana Alcañiz, Emma Roldán, Eliva Salcedo. *Prod:* Films Mundiales. 85m.

NOTORIOUS (1946). Espionage suspense melodrama in South America; as Señor Ortiza, one of the villainous Nazi agents. *Dir:* Alfred Hitchcock. *Sc:* Ben Hecht (from an idea by Hitchcock). *With* Cary Grant, Ingrid Bergman, Claude Rains, Louis Calhern, Leopoldine Konstantin, Reinhold Schunzel, Lenore Ulric, Moroni Olsen, Ivan Triesault, Alexis Minotis, Wally Brown, Sir Charles Mendl, Fay Baker. (Footage of the Moreno role, as well as that of Lenore Ulric, landed almost entirely on the cutting-room floor.) *Prod:* RKO. 101m.

CAPTAIN FROM CASTILLE (1947). Drama of Cortez and his *conquistadores* in Mexico; as Don Francisco, *hidalgo* father of Power. *Dir:* Henry King. *Sc:* Lamar Trotti (from the novel by Samuel Shellabarger). *With* Tyrone Power, Jean Peters, Cesar Romero, Lee J. Cobb, John Sutton, Thomas Gomez, Alan Mowbray, Barbara Lawrence, George Zucco, Ray Roberts, Marc Lawrence, Virginia Brissac. *Prod:* 20th Century-Fox. Technicolor. 140m.

LUST FOR GOLD (1949). Western drama; as Ramon Peralta, who discovers a fabulous but accursed gold mine in Arizona's Superstition Mountains, and is the first to meet his death. *Dir:* S. Sylvan Simon. *Sc:* Ted Sherdeman and Richard English (from a novel, "Thunder God's Gold," by Barry Storm). *With* Ida Lupino, Glenn Ford, Gig Young, William Prince, Edgar Buchanan, Will Geer, Paul Ford. Working title: *For Those Who Dare*. *Prod:* Columbia. Technicolor. 91m.

CRISIS (1950). Melodrama in Latin America; as Dr. Nierra, a South American surgeon. *Dir/Sc:* Richard Brooks (from a story, "The

Doubters," by George Tabori). *With* Cary Grant, Jose Ferrer, Paula Raymond, Signe Hasso, Ramon Novarro, Gilbert Roland, Leon Ames, Pedro de Cordoba. *Prod:* M-G-M. 95m. (Compare listing in Ramon Novarro filmography.)

SADDLE TRAMP (1950). Western; as Martinez, a rival rancher. *Dir:* Hugo Fregonese. *Sc:* Harold Shumate (from a story by Shumate). *With* Joel McCrea, Wanda Hendrix, John McIntire, John Russell, Jeanette Nolan Ed Begley, John Ridgely, Michael Steele, Russell Simpson. *Prod:* Universal. Technicolor. 76m.

DALLAS (1950). Western about Texas and the days of Will Bill Hickok; as Don Felipe, harassed father of the heroine. *Dir:* Stuart Heisler. *Sc:* John Twist. *With* Gary Cooper, Ruth Roman, Steve Cochran, Raymond Massey, Barbara Payton, Leif Erickson, Jerome Cowan, Monte Blue, *Prod:* Warner Bros. Technicolor. 91m.

MARK OF THE RENEGADE (1951). Romantic drama of early California; as Jose de Vasquez, leader of the California Republic and father of the heroine. *Dir:* Hugo Fregonese. *Sc:* Robert Hardy Andrews and Louis Solomon (from a story by Johnston McCulley). *With* Ricardo Montalban, Cyd Charisse, J. Carrol Naish, Gilbert Roland, Andrea King, George Tobias, Georgia Backus, Robert Warwick, Robert Cornthwaite. *Prod:* Universal-International. Technicolor. 81m.

THUNDER BAY (1953). Thriller of an offshore oil well in the Gulf of Mexico opposed by bayou fisherman; as Dominique Rigaud, fisherman father of the heroine. *Dir:* Anthony Mann. *Sc:* John Michael Hayes (from a story by George W. George and George F. Slavin). *With* James Stewart, Joanne Dru, Gilbert Roland, Dan Duryea, Marcia Henderson, Robert Monet, Jay C. Flippen, Henry Morgan, Fortunio Bonanova. *Prod:* Universal-International. Technicolor. 103m.

WINGS OF THE HAWK (1953). Period melodrama of the Mexican insurrection; as Father Perez, a priest. *Dir:* Budd Boetticher. *Sc:* James E. Moser (from an adaptation by Kay Lenard of a novel by Gerald Drayson Adams). *With* Van Heflin, Julie Adams, Abbe Lane, George Dolenz, Noah Beery, Rodolfo Acosta. *Prod:* Universal-International. Technicolor. 3-dimension. 81m.

UNTAMED FRONTIER (1953). Western of cattle barons vs. settlers who cross their land; as Bandera. *Dir:* Hugo Fregonese. *Sc:* Gerald Drayson Adams, John and Gwen Bagni (adapted by Polly James from a story by Houston Branch and Eugenia Nigh). *With* Joseph Cotten, Shelley Winters, Scott Brady, Suzan Ball. *Prod:* Universal-International. Technicolor. 75m.

THE CREATURE FROM THE BLACK LAGOON (1954). Science fiction horror story; as Carl Maia, the scientist who discovers the huge web-fingered skeleton in the Amazon River. *Dir:* Jack Arnold. *Sc:* Harry Essex and Arthur Ross (from a story by Maurice Zim). *With* Richard Carlson, Julie Adams, Richard Denning, Nestor Paiva, Whit Bissell. *Prod:* Universal. Three-dimension. 79m.

SASKATCHEWAN (AKA, GB, *O'Rourke of the Royal Mounted*) (1954). Western melodrama in the Canadian Rockies; as Chief Dark Cloud. *Dir:* Raoul Walsh. *Sc:* Gil Doud. *With* Alan Ladd, Shelley Winters, Robert Douglas, J. Carrol Naish, Hugh O'Brien, Richard Long, Jay Silverheels. *Prod:* Universal. Technicolor. 87m.

THE SEARCHERS (1956). Western drama of the five-year search for a girl who has been carried off by the Comanches; as an early Spanish-American trader. *Dir:* John Ford. *Sc:* Frank S. Nugent (from a novel by Alan LeMay). *With* John Wayne, Jeffrey Hunter, Vera Miles, Ward Bond, Natalie Wood, John Qualen, Olive Carey, Henry Brandon, Ken Curtis, Harry Carey Jr., Walter Coy, Dorothy Jordan, Pat Wayne. *Prod:* Warner Bros./C. V. Whitney. VistaVision/Technicolor. 116m.

EL SENOR FARON Y LA CLEOPATRA (*Mr. Pharaoh and Cleopatra*) (1958). Romantic comedy. *Dir:* Don Weiss. *With* Dina Merrill, Gilbert Roland, Jonathan Harris, Gina Roman. Filmed in Cuba and never released in the U.S.A.

8
NAZIMOVA

There has never been any doubt about the greatness of Alla Nazimova as an actress. I would not hesitate to name her the foremost actress of the Twentieth century American theatre. Certainly, for what she brought to this country as a disciple of the realistic school of acting, she is a towering figure. She reformed and revitalised acting in America just as Eleonora Duse did throughout Europe.

But I'd be forced to withhold such accolades in estimating Nazimova's place in film annals. There is about her screen appearances a feeling of waste. She had a unique and superlative talent; she was a star of the first order — and yet the pictures in which she starred were, for the most part, beneath her. Her directors were always capable, sometimes remarkably gifted; her writers were more than competent; the entire production value of all her pictures was high; but the stories she chose to film were so bizarre as to be weird and unbelievable, or they were juvenile enough to be more suitable for a Mary Pickford. Only her illuminating presence gave her films any real value.

In time, she herself admitted the banality of her scenarios. When she finished her Metro contract in 1921 after *Camille* and did not sign again, Hollywood was startled by her announcement that she would put all the money she had saved — and it was more than a modest fortune — into financing and starring in two cinematic ventures that she hoped might expiate her Metro sins.

"I must purge myself," she said.

The two features — *A Doll's House* and *Salome* — were box-office failures. Though she did win a divided critical acclaim, her public, already contemptuous of her arty *Camille,* was bored by the Ibsen production and both bored and outraged by the Oscar Wilde play. She never gained a financial profit from either film, and forced herself to appear in three features that were little better than the gaudy tripe she had done at Metro. These did bring her some money, and she thereupon embarked upon a four-year tour on the vaudeville stage in vehicles every bit as meretricious as the worst of those she had starred in at Metro. In October 1928, however, she joined Eva Le Gallienne's company at the Civic Repertory Theatre in New York and played a Madame Ranevsky in Chekhov's "The Cherry Orchard" that re-established her at once as a truly unforgettable actress. All could be forgiven, and was. Like all great players, she was always only at her incomparable best when challenged by a great play. The mistakes she made when she herself chose to play showy roles in shoddy plays were of her own making. Yet when she did not try to manoeuvre her career, but submitted to wise management and so appeared under the best auspices in the best plays, she always shone like a privileged angel.

Alla Nazimova had an enviable and perfect background for an acting career. She was, indeed, the first student of Constantin Stanislavsky to star on the American stage and screen. She was also one of the first to be star-billed by her surname alone — NAZIMOVA. Only her family and very close friends ever called her Alla. To her co-workers she was always known affectionately and proudly as Madame. Actually, her real name was Adelaide Leventon, but by the time she decided to become an actress, that name was abandoned. Few ever knew about it.

She was born at Yalta on the Black Sea in the Crimea, Russia, on June 4, 1879.* Her parents, the Yacov Leventons, were wellborn and of the Jewish faith. Reputedly, the family had come originally from Spain, and their proper name was Lavendera; so, at least, Madame told Mercedes de Acosta — but "lavendera" in Spanish means "laundress," and one wonders if Nazimova were not in one of her frequent playful, *Madame Sans-Gêne* moods, when she permitted herself the indulgence of this confidence. When she was six years old, her father, a chemist, arranged for her to be sent to a private Catholic school at Montreux, Switzerland. Six years later, she returned to the Crimea to take up her study of music at the Philharmonic Music Academy, playing the violin in the school orchestra under such conductors as Tchaikovsky and Rimsky-Korsakov. Born a Jewess, raised a Catholic, she renounced both religions. First and foremost, she was an artiste, and if she believed at all, she believed in herself.

Shortly after her father's death, she gave up her career as a musician to enter the Academy of Acting in Moscow. She had fallen in love with the theatre, and was now determined to be an actress. Three years later she graduated with the Academy's highest honour — won for her performance in Ibsen's "Little Eyolf" — a gold medal awarded to only one student in every five thousand. It granted her an apprenticeship in Stanislavsky's Moscow Art Theatre, where she spent a year acting what she called "thinking" roles. Truthfully, the parts she played were atmospheric bits and it was only by "thinking" that she could make anything of them. This she really managed to do and was singled out by Moscow critics for what she contributed to certain plays' interpretations. She was barely out of her teens when she was faced with an inevitable decision: she could stay at the Moscow Art, graduating to the performance of minor roles which would prepare her eventually for the leads: or she could become leading lady at once in any number of provincial companies. She settled for the latter choice, and reigned as the star of Kostroma, Kerson, and then Vilna, performing over two hundred leading roles in theatres of those three provincial towns. In 1903, when she was not yet twenty-four, she was in Russia's capital, St. Petersburg, where she was the leading actress in the Nemetti Theatre, which she has described as being "across the river from the best part of the city; a theatre for working people . . . a place where we gave serious plays with a message."

The male star of the company was Paul Orleneff, an extraordinary actor who was also known as a wild kind of revolutionary. Nazimova and he fell

*Some sources claim May 22, 1879 — but June 4 is in most references and was in all obituaries.

170

Nazimova

madly in love, and were married. He was then thirty-six; she, twenty-five. As a pair, the two were more than doubly temperamental and stormy. Physically, they were not unalike — thin, small in stature, wiry but graceful, blessed with huge, expressive, long-lashed eyes that were a chameleon blue. Both were veritable human dynamos. To work fifteen hours daily in the theatre — rehearsing and studying by day, playing a performance every night — was routine with them. They were dedicated, driven actors, not as tall as most American adolescents, but on stage they could tower like giants. It was always a shock to realise how petite Nazimova was, because on stage and screen there was never anything diminutive about her, unless she wanted you to think her small. Nazimova was blessed with one gift that was almost completely denied Orleneff: she had a divine sense of humour. Her wit was quick, intellectually adult, yet she sometimes went out of her way to enact a humorous and often malicious prank that was only funny to her.

By 1904, Imperial Russia was reeling under the blows for freedom struck by the nihilist rebels, and Tsarist censorship tightened in all the arts. Orleneff was officially forbidden to produce a play about the early Zionist movement, Chirikov's "The Chosen People." As usual, when in a fury, he got insanely drunk. Then, sober, he decided that he would present "The Chosen People" outside Russia with such success that the government would beg him to present it in St. Petersburg. Nazimova was in accord, and so their company travelled to Berlin late in 1904 and then on to London. The play was performed, of course, in the Russian language; none of the actors spoke German or English. Audiences in both cities were sparse, and the reviewers, although impressed by the acting, were apathetic about the vehicle. Undismayed, Orleneff and Nazimova sailed for America with their players to present "The Chosen People" to New York audiences, opening at the Herald Square Theatre on March 23, 1905. Every Russian then in Manhattan must have been in attendance sometime during that engagement, but the audience that really understood and applauded the actors were the Jews. The Orleneff company itself gained its most favourable notices from the critic of the "New York Times," who praised the "naturalistic acting of the players from St. Petersburg." Nazimova herself, then billed as Mme. Nasimoff, was singled out for her "inspired performance."

Heartened by their first good reception away from their native country, the Orleneff company moved to a lecture hall on East Third Street, near Third Avenue, which became known as Orleneff's Russian Lyceum, and it was advertised as being modelled on the famous Stanislavsky's Art Theatre in Moscow. There they presented in Russian a repertory season of some of the best modern classics of the European theatre — Gorki, Chekhov, Dostoievsky, Ibsen, Strindberg, and Hauptman. In all of these, Orleneff and his wife were especially hailed. In an article in "Theatre Magazine" for December 1905, Kellog Durland wrote: "Mme. Nasimoff, who is the leading actress in the Orleneff company, is a handsome woman of pronounced Slavonic type. She is a thorough artist and has interpreted all the great roles with mental grasp and power. Her method reminds one forcibly of Duse's." The comparison of Nazimova with Duse became frequent. Said Nazimova: "When they speak of me as Duse, I smile. It is ridiculous. Duse is a Goddess!"

For two seasons Russian repertory was popular in Manhattan, and it became the fashion to sponsor Orleneff and his players. Charles Frohman, Edith Wharton, Mrs. W. K. Vanderbilt, and Ethel Barrymore sponsored a benefit for them at the Criterion, where "Ghosts" was staged. Nazimova elected to play the small role of Regina, because she wanted Orleneff to show himself to best advantage, which she felt he did as Oswald. Orleneff wrote in his own memoirs that "Dollars flowed in a river. I remember we often departed from the show with suitcases crammed with dollars — gold, silver, and paper." Daniel Frohman arranged for the company to perform in Chicago and Boston, and even Andrew Carnegie and J. P. Morgan contributed to their welfare. But in their travels about America, poverty nonetheless tracked the Russian actors constantly like wolves pursuing them across the Siberian steppes. At one point Nazimova not only quarrelled with her husband, but left him temporarily to return to Europe. He enticed her back with promises of building a new theatre for her, but that was only a dream, and the kindest thing that the company's benefactors could do was to finance their return to their native land. Nazimova, however, refused to go. She feared the revolutionary tide rising in Russia, and implored her husband to remain in America, where they would learn to speak English and start anew. But Orleneff was disgusted with America and wanted to go home; he told his wife he expected her to accompany him.

"*I* am staying here!" said Nazimova.

She went down to the pier to see him and the rest of the company off. She waved the ship goodbye and then, an alien, turned back into the Manhattan jungle alone.

She was not alone long. She was introduced to producer and theatre owner Lee Shubert, who had seen her perform in Russian and was not only impressed, but begged to have the honour of presenting her to New York audiences in her first English-speaking role in any play of her own choice. It was a challenge, and there was nothing she loved better. She asked him to engage an English teacher for her, and he sent her an actress known as Caroline Harris, who had been leading lady to Robert Mantell, but was to be better known as the mother of one of filmdom's brightest stars, Richard Barthelmess. For nearly five months Mrs. Barthelmess met with Nazimova regularly, and taught her how to speak English. Like all educated Europeans, Nazimova was multi-lingual; she conquered almost at once the intricacies of a language whose grammar has defeated many an Englishman and American. In later years, Nazimova was to describe these months for a magazine interviewer: "Yes, Mrs. Barthelmess is lovely — a splendid woman. And Dickey — ah, Dickey! I have Dickey's first love letter. Yes, he wrote it to me! "I lived in Washington Square. You know Washington Square? Well, there is where I lived in a little room in the Judson Hotel, way up in the tower. Mrs. Barthelmess would come there to give me lessons. She, too, lived in a little room, somewhere uptown. She had no place to leave Dickey. He was nine then. I said, 'Why don't you bring your little boy with you?' So she brought Dickey, and Dickey brought his cage of white rats. He would turn them loose to scamper around my room. Dickey would play with his rats, and I would play with Dickey. Then he went to the seaside. He wrote me on a postal card. He said — 'Dear Madame: The white rats are fine. I hope you are, too. Love, Dickey.'"

The method by which she learned English was unique. "Every day she

173

came to me," Nazimova related of Mrs. Barthelmess, "and stayed with me three or four hours. We talked and read. There was no grammar. It was all conversation or reading books and newspapers and magazines. It was not hard. I have a remarkable memory for form, and once I see a word I never forget it...I avoided all Russians, for I did not want to hear the hard accent of northern Russia. I wanted my ear to forget it."

It was on June 23, 1906 that Nazimova took her first English lesson from Mrs. Barthelmess. Not five months later, she made her *début* as an English-speaking actress, appearing at the Princess Theatre in November in the title role of Ibsen's "Hedda Gabler." Lee Shubert presented her in this, the first of a series of special matinees, directed by Henry Miller. It also marked the first time she dropped her previous billing as "Mme. Nasimoff," and was starred simply as NAZIMOVA. As one critic announced: "Since 'a' is the normal feminine ending in Russian, it is difficult to understand why the masculine version was ever used." NAZIMOVA she became, and NAZIMOVA she remained.

Overnight she was the talk of the town. Her first matinee audience had been largely professional and social; everybody who could buy or wheedle a ticket made up the subsequent capacity audiences. Critics reckoned her Hedda as being greater than that of the current favourite, Mrs. Fiske. Nazimova was called "a new and superbly different force in the theatre." The critic for the "New York Times" ended his panegyric with "She is, in short, one of the most remarkable actresses of the times."

On January 14, 1907, Shubert next presented her as Nora in an English translation of Ibsen's "A Doll's House." Audiences and critics were stunned by her versatility. When she made her initial entrance, she was so physically unlike Hedda Gabler that first-night audiences did not immediately recognise her. When they did, a gasp of genuine surprise rippled throughout the house. Alan Dale, in the "New York American," wrote: "Was this the stately creature who had charmed us in Hedda? Was this the silent feline atrocity that had made the most impossible of Ibsen's plays possible? This Nora seemed smaller, slighter, cast in another mould." And he summed up: "You saw the actress in the part, not the part in the actress."

Similarly, the critic for the "New York Times" noted of Nazimova: "Her Nora is astonishing in its revelation of what might be termed a new personality — one as distinct and far removed from Hedda as possible...The Russian woman is a genius."

In an excellent career piece for "Century" magazine in June 1907, Owen Johnson summarised what Nazimova was doing for the art of acting in America: "The advent to the American stage of the Russian actress, Mme. Alla Nazimova, is more than the opening of a great career. It is significant both of the evolution of the drama and the development of the art of dramatic interpretation. For nothing is more significant of the last half-century than the evolution of the art of acting in direct response to the evolution of the drama. The classic and romantic schools (which differed in methods rather than ideas) had produced a school of acting often brilliant and grandiose, but operatic, statuesque and artificial, just as the drama itself was an idealisation or a sentimentalisation of life. When the realistic school arose, it became imperative that new methods should prevail in the dramatic interpretation.

174

NAZIMOVA

The new drama sought the ruthless facts of life. Eleonora Duse headed the revolt that humanised the art and brought the actress from the pedestal on which she had stood, to suffer and rejoice as a woman of the mold of her own audience.''

Like a delighted child stringing a necklace of genuine pearls, Nazimova then proceeded to display her protean talents in two other Ibsen dramas — ''The Master Builder'' and ''Little Eyolf,'' the latter of which premiered a playhouse named for her — The Nazimova Theatre (later to become the 39th Street Playhouse). She interspersed her repertory with plays from other European writers — Schnitzler's ''The Fairy Tale'' and Benavente's ''The Passion Flower'' — and some gaudy paste pearls were strung into the necklace as well — baubles like ''The Comet'' amd ''The Comtesse Coquette.''

At the Empire Theatre in November 1912, she played Ruby Chepstow in Robert Hichens's ''Bella Donna,'' a femme fatale who so fascinated theatregoers that after the long Broadway run, Nazimova spent another year touring the play. ''Bella Donna'' brought her a fortune, even if the same reviewers who had praised her as an interpreter of Ibsen heroines made fun of the play and her in it. Was she mermaid or leopard? Reptile or animal? Woman of stone? Or Empress of hate? She later told actor Alexander Kirkland that whereas three days was more than enough time to prepare Zaza, Ruby Chepstow, and all the other rhinestone ladies of the theatre, three years were insufficient to the understanding of Hilda Wangel in ''The Master Builder.'' She only did ''The Comtesse Coquette,'' she asserted, because she wanted a rest between her Ibsen plays. '' 'The Comtesse Coquette' is a snap,'' she said. ''It is only child's play.''

Her leading man in ''Bella Donna'' was a tall handsome Englishman named Charles Bryant born in the same year as she. Nazimova fell in love with him; others hinted that it was hardly love, but she thought him right as her mate. Sometime during the endless run of ''Bella Donna'' they were supposed to have become man and wife, and for over a decade Nazimova in private life was known as Mrs. Charles Bryant. Actually, Paul Orleneff refused to give her a divorce, and she could not legally marry Bryant. Living as his common law wife finally became for her a kind of secret shame, and for years none but one or two very close friends knew the tormenting truth — tormenting only because she knew the pitfalls looming ahead of her.

She followed ''Bella Donna'' with another play unworthy of her remarkable talents — ''That Sort.'' It did not last long, but it led to her triumphant entry into vaudeville, where she premiered as the headliner at the Palace in a vehement anti-war one-acter, ''War Brides.'' It came at exactly the right psychological time. The year was 1915. A war that threatened to embrace the entire world had ignited in Europe, and the pacifist cause was never more popular than it was then in America. ''War Brides'' dramatically presented the folly of war, though the play itself was little better than melodramatic propaganda. However, Nazimova's performance as the beleaguered heroine, Joan, was another matter — dramatically persuasive and instantly empathic. She travelled on the Orpheum circuit from the Atlantic to the Pacific playing ''War Brides,'' and no one who saw her blazing performance ever forgot it or her in it.

''War Brides'' also opened the door to a screen career for her. Film producers had previously offered her tantalising projects, but she had always resisted them. She reported her feelings honestly: "I have been interested in moving pictures for five years, ever since a certain producer (D. W. Griffith) showed me through his plant, and I saw the process in operation. But whenever I was asked to appear in pictures, my answer was always the same — 'Let me see some of your work, so that I may know in what way my art will be presented to the public.' And always when I would see what they considered their best productions, I would say 'Not yet.' I was interested, you understand, and would have been glad to engage in the picture art, but could not find a man who possessed the imaginative faculty that I wanted.

"A mutual friend wanted to introduce Mr. Herbert Brenon, and I said I would be glad to know him, but he sent word, oh quite politely, that he would much prefer that I should see first his latest creation, *A Daughter of the Gods*. I saw it, at a private view, and was enchanted. It is a work of pure creative imagination. By his work I did know him and was satisfied that this was a director with whom I could work. After that, it was a very simple matter for us to come to terms."

Herbert Brenon acquired the film rights to her big hit, *War Brides,* and he himself adapted the play to scenario form, expanding its single act to eight reels. It was shot in the East under his direction, and it was an instantaneous hit when released by Lewis J. Selznick late in 1916. "There is nothing on Broadway that can begin to compare with *War Brides!*" exclaimed critic Alan Dale. "It is the finest movie I have ever seen."

The critic for "The Moving Picture World" wrote that *War Brides* "reaches a tragic height never before attained by a moving picture...To Nazimova and her associates belongs the credit of a fine artistic achievement in the acting of the play — a masterly control of the emotions and their expression by means of the silent drama."

Likewise the critic of the "New York Times" wrote of Nazimova's screen *début:* "In the language of the studios she screens well, which, translated, means that she is a good subject for motion photography, always a consummation devoutly to be wished for; and what is more to her credit, since it is the result of her intelligence and not her good fortune, she knows how to express herself in terms of the film. Her marvellously mobile face, capable of indicating varying shades of emotion, especially those of sorrow, is a priceless asset for the dumb show of the screen. So there was some reason for the word 'Success' on the floral offerings in the lobby."

It was after the *première* of *War Brides* that Mercedes de Acosta first met with Nazimova, a meeting which she relates in her memoirs, "Here Lies the Heart": "A friend of mine named Jane Wallach asked me to help with a large benefit to be given in Madison Square Garden. Nazimova was going to be in it. My excitement was such that of the entire performance, which was an elaborate and lengthy one, I remember not a single thing or person except Nazimova. Representing Russia (which was then still Imperial Russia), she made a sudden entrance through the door of the vast arena, then at Twenty-seventh Street, dressed as a cossack and resembling the photographs we had all seen of the Czarevitch. As the band struck up the Imperial Anthem, she waved the Russian flag as a great spotlight played over her. Then the music changed to a wild cossack strain and, still carrying the flag high, she ran the entire distance around the arena, leaping into the air every few steps. To run and leap around this enormous arena with such grace was a feat few dancers, or athletes, could have accomplished. She brought the house down.''

Nazimova had told Selznick that she would film *War Brides* for $1,000 a day. Selznick said he'd go her one better: he'd give her $1,000 in cash after every day's shooting. It took thirty days to shoot *War Brides,* and Nazimova was mightily impressed when she realised that in just one month she had a cash total of $30,000. That sum was a trifle compared to what she was to gain in the subsequent feature films she made, but it proved to her the fortune she could amass as a screen actress.

She was also pleased that in *War Brides* she could introduce her oldtime youthful friend, ''Dickey'' — Richard Barthelmess — to a movie career. He made his *début* as the youngest of four sons called up to battle. He had been attending Trinity College, and in the interval between his junior and senior years, he was playing bits in pictures to defray educational expenses. But after *War Brides,* Herbert Brenon wanted him for his next feature about the Borgias, *The Eternal Sin,* and from then on Barthelmess was kept so consistently busy that he never returned to finish his studies at Trinity. Barthelmess and Nazimova remained lifelong friends. Men were always fascinated by and adored her; women were awed by and worshipped her.

It was inevitable, after the great success of *War Brides,* that the major film companies and producers of the day would approach Nazimova with contracts for other screen appearances. She held off all offers, however, and returned to the Broadway stage, where she opened at the Princess Theatre in January 1917, in *'Ception Shoals,* and on being hailed for her acting skill (she played a very naïve teen-aged girl in it, and she was then thirty-eight), she made arrangements to be presented by Arthur Hopkins at the Plymouth during the spring of 1918 in a repertory of three Ibsen plays — ''A Doll's House,'' ''Hedda Gabler,'' and ''The Wild Duck.''

Those details affirmed, she finally signed with the Metro Company. It was an extraordinary contract which allowed her her own production unit as well as approval of all stories, directors, and casts. She was to be more than the mistress of her productions: she was acknowledged empress, with the power for any ultimate ukase, although the studio allowed itself loopholes which would curtail her doing Ibsen and Chekhov on the screen. For this contract she was guaranteed a splendid income starting at $13,000 a week, with raises; and she was granted the right to fulfill her stage appearances in the forthcoming 1918 Ibsen repertory season in Manhattan.

She chose as her first Metro film a property adapted from a somewhat synthetic novel, ''The Rosebush of a Thousand Years,'' that had delighted the starved hearts of many a lonely bachelor and spinster with its clouded romantic mysticism. Re-named *Revelation,* it provided a *tour de force* role for its star. Herb Sterne, in an article for ''Rob Wagner's Script'' in Beverly Hills in 1941, has reminisced most effectively about this film: ''A rococo little number, it concerned itself with an artist's model, of dubious morality, who masquerades as a boy, invades the sanctity of a monastery, and poses (surreptitiously) for a portrait of the Madonna. Under her touch a sacred rosebush blooms. Then regeneration...revelation...from the picture of the same name. The starring role was one of violent contrasts, permitted the actress to run the gamut between Vice and Virtue with dazzling effect. The movie public, bored with pretty faces and no talent, acclaimed Nazimova as an actress par excellence. Which, strangely enough, was an actual fact.''

Reviewing *Revelation,* the film critic for the "New York Times" reported the following incident at the *première:* "Some one among those who went to the Lyric Theatre last night to see the first evening showing of *Revelation,* Mme. Nazimova's latest motion picture, recognised the actress herself in one of the boxes during the intermission and shouted:

'' 'There she is!'

"The spectators turned and began to applaud. Nazimova seemed not to realise at first that she had been discovered, but as the applause became louder and louder she knew that it was for her, and rose to acknowledge it. The whole house greeted her with shouts and handclapping that did not cease until she had retreated from the box.

"When the performance was over, Mme. Nazimova hurriedly left the box which she had re-entered after the lights had been turned out for the showing of the second half of the picture, but the people wanted to see her again, and applauded so insistently that she came back into the box and smiled her appreciation. Not until she had left the theatre did the people stop their applause.''

With *Revelation* and *War Brides* both to her credit, Nazimova's name soared at once into the top lists of screen favourites. On every screen popularity contest of the time, she placed high among the ladies — in the top category with Mary Pickford, Norma Talmadge, Pearl White, and Marguerite Clark.

To be fair, her Metro career must be adjudged in the light of its day. After the First World War, American films had gained a supremacy which they didn't entirely deserve. Battle and invasion had called a halt to film production in England, France, Italy and other European countries, and when film-making could be resumed abroad, it took time to create, re-create, make up for time lost. The best film product was to come almost at once from the conquered nation, Germany, whose postwar films were to have a lasting effect on worldwide film production. But American films, during and after the war, had been ground out like assembly items on a factory line. Most of them were masterpieces of mediocrity.

I have already stated what Nazimova herself acknowledged — the stories she chose to make were unworthy of her. But her pictures were products of the time, and *she* was responsible for giving them far better production values than those accorded the movies of her contemporary exotics — Theda Bara, Valeska Suratt, Olga Petrova, Louise Glaum, Dorothy Dalton, and the whole sisterhood. Her pictures were beautifully photographed, handsomely designed, skilfully directed, well cast, and most of her own roles, while often bizarre, were sympathetic. They were certainly varied; she was not just a vamp. In fact, she was not a vamp at all. She loved the *tour de force* challenge the camera permitted her, and in four of her eleven Metro films she played dual roles — sisters, or mother and daughter. Six of the Metro films had the advantage of being written or co-written by June Mathis, whose flair for drama was always sure and everything she wrote bore the mark of innate good taste. The three best of the Metro releases were directed by Albert Capellani, a sensitive and talented man whose motto, ''Be natural,'' was in accord with Nazimova's own, ''Be real.''

178

NAZIMOVA

It's also interesting to note that Nazimova's lover, Charles Bryant, who had played an important role in her *début* film, *War Brides,* was her leading man in eight of her Metro pictures; he also wrote scenarios for three; and he directed or co-directed Nazimova three times.

The money she made at Metro (and for Metro, too) was, of course, what kept her in Hollywood. It was phenomenal, and she was paid in cash in a day before income tax took everything. She leased a mansion on the periphery of Hollywood, on Sunset Boulevard, and she made it into a showplace villa. In those days the boundaries of Hollywood ended where the Pacific-Electric red car terminated at Hollywood Boulevard and La Brea. Hollywood Boulevard itself stretched westward before rising into the heights of Laurel Canyon, a small dirt road, through avocado orchards and lemon and orange groves, in the midst of which one could spot an occasional farm dwelling and a very few sumptuous residences. Two blocks south of Hollywood Boulevard, however, and running parallel to it was Sunset Boulevard, another two-lane, tar-covered dirt road which stretched on through the county into the new real estate development known as Beverly Hills, and then continued winding westward through the foothill curves of the Santa Monica Mountains right down into Inceville, ending where the Pacific Ocean broke upon the California shore.

For $50,000, Nazimova took a ninety-nine year lease on her California villa at 8150 Sunset Boulevard, near the curve where it is crossed by Crescent Heights and east of where it turns rather abruptly into what is now known as The Strip. Here, in her home attractively landscaped in three and a half acres of cedars, roses, palms, semi-tropical flowers, and fruit trees bordering a lily pond and a swimming-pool in the shape of the Black Sea, Nazimova lived out her silent screen career with the man she called her husband, Charles Bryant. She named it appropriately "The Garden of Alla," and she always winced when some newspaper or magazine writer ended "Alla" with an "h."

In the Twenties, when her Hollywood career had crashed, she was forced to turn her lease over to a corporation which tore out most of the lovely gardens and built twenty-five guest bungalows around the main house and pool. It became then for several decades that fabulous hostelry known as "The Garden of Allah," home for many a literary light and rendezvous for all the beautiful people of the time. Nazimova was allowed to live there in a small upstairs apartment whenever she was in Hollywood, and it always made her melancholy to realise that she who had been the mistress of a great private home was now only an occasional non-paying courtesy guest.

In 1959, "The Garden of Allah," very much run-down, was sold, demolished by bulldozers, and on its grounds rose a new edifice — Bart Lytton's Loan & Savings Company. That, too, eventually went the way of most such companies, and now on the site, re-decorated in Sunset Strip moderne, is another savings company.

But Nazimova's "Garden of Alla," at the time she was its mistress, was a veritable oasis in the midst of that innocent desert called Hollywood. Her home was beautifully managed, restful, and she and Charles Bryant regularly entertained not only the biggest names of the industry, but all the visiting artists of the theatre, dance, music, art, and literary worlds. It was not just a contemporary salon. Indeed, "The Garden of Alla," was a crossroads of the world where Nazimova, an incomparable hostess, conversed intelligently on

179

almost any subject that could be discussed in English, French or Russian. She always gave generously of herself: when Mabel Normand wanted to be coached before she went East to try out a play for Al Woods, Nazimova did everything she could to teach Miss Normand how to project her voice to the last row in the auditorium, a feat pitifully beyond the Normand vocal range. She adored young people, especially those starting in the profession, and gave them encouragement and assistance: Patsy Ruth Miller, who became an important leading lady in the Twenties and Thirties, owes her *début* in films to Nazimova, who thought she had a future and gave her the role of Nichette in her *Camille*.

Nazimova's fans were enormously loyal during these beginning years, B.N.R. (before Natacha Rambova). After *Toys of Fate,* her second Metro feature released in the late spring of 1918, her public demanded more, yet the film critic for the "New York Times" expressed the general critical attitude in the East of her Hollywood success: "Many persons will wonder why Nazimova, who chose to play Ibsen's masterpieces at the Plymouth Theatre this season, selected such a play as *Toys of Fate* for the screen. Can it be that she doesn't have much respect for the movies?"

In 1918, the theatre critic for "Theatre Magazine" awarded Nazimova the year's palm for her stage performances of three Ibsen heroines, but qualified his selection thusly: "I shall breathe the name of Nazimova — thereby risking much critical opprobrium. I am thankful for her Ibsen. Great is Alla! But I feel that the movies are her principal profit."

It was an award that revealed a fact which could no longer be ignored: as an interpreter of Ibsen and the modern classics, Nazimova had no peer in the theatre world, but that audience was intellectual and therefore limited; when she played her sequin heroines like Ruby Chepstow, her audience was unlimited. Realising that and knowing the candystick tastes of the average film audience, she gave them the ultimate in sweet exoticism — the heroines of *Toys of Fate* and *Eye for an Eye.*

Her two best films for Metro were the first two released in 1919 — *Out of the Fog,* directed by Capellani, and adapted from her Broadway play success, "Ception Shoals;" followed by a very beautifully produced and exciting drama of the Boxer Rebellion in China, *The Red Lantern,* also directed by Capellani. Nazimova proved her immense versatility by playing dual roles in both, and all four women she created were immensely sympathetic. The most exotic of them, the Eurasian Mahlee of *The Red Lantern,* brought tears that audiences usually reserved for the sad plights of Mary Pickford and Norma Talmadge. "I still see Nazimova curled in a peacock chair in *The Red Lantern,*" Alexander Kirkland reminisced in his article on Nazimova in "Theatre Arts," and similarly Herb Sterne, in "Rob Wagner's Script," wrote: "The tragedy of the Chinese child, a suicide, huddled in the depths of a peacock chair murmuring 'East is East and West is West...' as she is dying, remains one of the poignant moments in the history of the cinema."

Reviewing the picture in the May 10, 1919 issue of "Motion Picture News," Laurence Reid wrote: "In *The Red Lantern,* Metro has turned out a photoplay which will challenge attention with any special production ever presented. The ability to reproduce a picture of China, to catch a breath of its exotic atmosphere, to invest its barbaric splendour, and to translate its mystic

Nazimova and Warner Oland in *The Red Lantern*.

soul, so faithfutly, spells a triumph of film art. To Nazimova, the star, and Capellani, the director, belong the credit for the success of the picture. The former, undertaking a dual role in which the characters are entirely different, displays the highest form of histrionism. Her performance is superb in its vividness, poignancy, and sympathy.''

In her last six Metro films, and especially after she had met and collaborated with Natacha Rambova, she began to be tainted by affectation. For an actress who had pioneered in realism, she was becoming a disciple of the art for art's sake school. She was going against the very creed that had established her —

181

"Be real!" She played *outré* characterisations in both *Stronger than Death* and *Madame Peacock* that were too curiously mannered to be real; and she elected to play *gamines* in *The Brat, The Heart of a Child,* and *Billions* who were far too young for her to play before the camera. In 1920, she was forty-one years old. On the stage, flatteringly lighted in a rose-amber spot, she could have still played the *ingénue* effectively, because her body was, as always, slight and remarkably graceful; on the screen she looked what she was — a middle-aged woman miscast in youthful roles she should never have attempted. She was not only mannered in them; she was kittenish, full of tricks that betrayed unattractive fits of the "cutes."

Only gradually, however, did her faithful public begin to admit that this was not the Nazimova who had won them; then, little by little, her fans fell away until she had no following at all. They did not understand a posturing that had grown as deliberately artificial as that afflicting Mae Murray. By the time Nazimova did her version of *Camille,* she had reached the point of eccentricity. She had been attracted to Natacha Rambova, and allowed that lady to design the settings and costumes for *Camille.* Nazimova gave Rudolph Valentino, then rising to the top after playing Julio in *The Four Horsemen of the Apocalypse,* the role of Armand, but their love story was a series of *tableaux.* They were cardboard figures. Fans booed the film.

Dagmar Godowsky, in her autobiography, "First Person Plural," has related an anecdote that shows the more unflattering side of Nazimova's Gemini character: "We were at the Ship's Café at Santa Monica, where the executives at Metro were giving Nazimova a dinner party. We must have been twenty at table — the studio bigwigs; Milton Sills, the ex-professor; Nazimova and her husband; Jean Acker, her best friend, who was an actress at Metro; Viola Dana; May Allison, Bert Lytell, and so on.

"It was all very gay, and Maxwell Karger, the general manager of Metro, was toasting Nazimova when I saw a boy gliding across the dance floor toward me. He was handsome and dark, and as he came closer I recognised him. His name was Guglielmi and I had met him through Caruso at the Moulin Rouge in New York.

"He arrived at the table beaming with pleasure and I started to introduce him, but Nazimova lowered her head and froze. Her little frame was rigid and she looked as if she were having a divine fit. The whole table took its cue from her and one by one they too lowered their heads in this shocking form of grace. My voice trailed off and so did Guglielmi.

"Nazimova broke the tableau and thundered, 'How dare you bring that gigolo to my table? How dare you introduce that pimp to *Nazimova?'*

"I didn't understand. I soon found out. Signor Guglielmi had come to California to avoid a nasty scandal in New York. Biance de Saules, a wealthy Chilean, had murdered her husband all for love of this young man. Though he was innocent of any complicity, his name was anathema.

"When he started working as an extra in pictures, however, he changed it — to Valentino."

Later, Valentino married Jean Acker, but the marriage, never consummated, only lasted one night. Nazimova took Jean Acker back as her best friend, and forgave Valentino all his past errors. They became very good friends and when, during the making of *Camille,* she saw that he had become

182

infatuated by Natacha Rambova, she advised against their marriage. I think eventually she realised how Rambova had influenced her for the worst, and that the blame for the affectations of *Camille* and *Salome* could be laid to Rambova, and no one else.

After *Camille,* Nazimova not only wouldn't sign again with Metro, but the studio didn't really want her any more. The features she had filmed in 1920 were an apt illustration of the law of diminishing returns, and *Camille,* even with the added allure of the Valentino name, rising in power, was proving a disappointment, at the box-office.

A Doll's House, the first feature Nazimova made with her own money for United Artists release, is in my opinion one of her two best motion pictures; the other, *The Red Lantern. A Doll's House* was at least a valiant and honest effort to bring Ibsen to the screen, and in it are very few of the bad mannerisms Nazimova had allowed herself to acquire. "Photoplay" named it one of the six best of the month, and after calling it "a mental masterpiece," said of its star: "The Russian star, usually eccentric, curbs her Camille tendencies, and as Nora, one of the drama's most absorbing women, really acts. Or rather, thinks...Madame Bryant is regaining her artistic balance and her next celluloid should restore her to her first high histrionic standard."

Her next, however, was the *coup de grâce* for a career that was in trouble. When she announced that she would not only star in *Salome,* but would write the scenario (under her *nom de plume,* Peter M. Winters), and bring Oscar Wilde's play to the screen after the style of the Aubrey Beardsley illustrations as realised by Natacha Rambova, there was little doubt among those who knew the facts that Nazimova was committing professional suicide. The meagre audiences who saw *Salome* hated it and were openly derisive. It was said by the kindest that it might be ahead of its time, but its time has at least now come and gone. During the last decade it has been unreeled often at artsy-fartsy retrospectives, where modern audiences roll in the aisle with mirth, for it has become one of the great examples of both *kitsch* and high camp.

Salome ruined Nazimova financially. She had let Charles Bryant direct the production and gave him full credit, but it was soon evident that Bryant was only standing in for his wife as director, and his wife did as Natacha Rambova advised. Domestic relations between Bryant and Nazimova were already not the best, and he did not stay around long after the *Salome* fiasco. A couple of years later he did present Nazimova on the New York stage again; they did need and cherish one another for a very little while.

Edwin Carewe thought the Nazimova name still of value, and he engaged her to do *Madonna of the Streets,* in which she was a wicked, selfish, mature woman who is redeemed by the goodness and strength of Milton Sills; there was no chance in this one for any idle ingenuish posturing. First National paid her well for this film, and J. Stuart Blackton also paid her a tidy sum to do *The Redeeming Sin* at the briefly resurrected Vitagraph Studios. They were only adequate programme pictures.

Nazimova was very good in a second feature Edwin Carewe hired her to do, *My Son,* in which she played a Portuguese mother in a New England fishing village who saves her son, Jack Pickford, from the destructive wiles of a baby vamp, Constance Bennett. She was real and very moving.

MORE FROM HOLLYWOOD

It was obvious that the close personal relationship between her and Bryant was over, and there was no reason at all to stay in Hollywood. She signed over her lease of "The Garden of Alla," and let the hotel syndicate take over, while she took the train for Broadway.

The four-year interval that ensued brought her no artistic fame, but she began to replenish her waning fortune. In the latter part of 1923, she played in some colourful nonsense called "Dagmar" at the Frolic Theatre, which Bryant produced; after its closing, they never again worked together. She made a guest appearance with the French Grand Guignol Players, and she then returned to the Orpheum circuit, appearing in George Middleton's one-act, "Collusion," which met with audience approval but also incurred censorship trouble both here and in London, even when it was rechristened "The Unknown Lady." In a sophomoric one-act version of "Mother India," Nazimova also enjoyed a tremendous vogue in vaudeville, even though she played a mere child bride of twelve. Actually, the spots were so low-key on her that her performance was more than a little effective.

In 1927, she became an American citizen, and that same year she journeyed to London, where she played at the Coliseum in a trifling playlet, "A Woman of the Earth." At this time, Beverley Nichols wrote about her in "The Sketch" when she defended the art of screen acting: "Everything registers on the screen, especially insincerity. If you are not feeling acutely what you meant to be feeling, it is as though *'Insincerity'* were stamped across your face in letters of fire. The screen reads your thoughts, delves deep in your mind, and brings up secrets which perhaps even you yourself had hardly realised. So how can anybody talk about the film as though it had a coarsening effect on one's art? The exact opposite is the case."

Charles Bryant married a Marjorie Gilhooley, and when newspapermen admitted they didn't know that he and Nazimova were divorced, he came out bluntly with the truth.

"We were never married," he said.

Nazimova was in New York at the time, residing in a hotel, when she read the damning headline in a morning paper — CHARLES BRYANT, SUPPOSED HUSBAND OF NAZIMOVA, MARRIES. The truth was out, and humiliated, she felt she could not face the world. She later confided to Alexander Kirkland her instinctive reaction — to throw herself from her twelfth-story hotel window. As she moved to the window, there was a knock at her door, and, distraught, she turned back to open it, only to be confronted by a stranger offering her a great box of flowers. He presented himself as Paul Bern. She agreed to have dinner with him that night. He sent her orchids that afternoon, with a card: "We will dress." They dined at the Waldorf, and later attended several night-clubs. Everybody greeted her with warmth and genuine friendliness. No one mentioned Bryant's name. The shame and embarrassment vanished, and she confessed that the adventure of that night made her feel reborn. A friend, hearing the anecdote re-told later, said, "Thank God, Madame, you didn't jump!" That old mischievous twinkle lighted her eyes. "Ah yes," she agreed. "Think what the world would have lost!!" And she burst into hilarious laughter.

Ironically, the fact that she had never really been Mrs. Charles Bryant was forgotten, almost as if by common consent, by every newspaperman. When

NAZIMOVA

Nazimova died in 1945, every one of her obituaries listed her as having been married once — to Charles Bryant. The real legal marriage to Paul Orleneff was not even mentioned. Louella O. Parsons, who knew the truth, deliberately falsified it — and others followed her lead.

Nazimova was kidding when she said that the world would have been the loser, but actually ahead of Nazimova lay more than a decade that would contain some of her most memorable acting accomplishments. In 1928, she accepted an invitation from Eva Le Gallienne to become a guest of the Civic Repertory Company on 14th Street, and she starred there in Chekhov's "The Cherry Orchard" and Andreyev's "Katerina." As it had been when she first played in the English language, all of Gotham was again genuflecting to Alla, the Great, for with her return to the theatre, greatness came back. A most extraordinary tribute was paid her after her death by Kappa Phelan, writing in "The Commonweal" about her performance in "The Cherry Orchard." It's one of those tributes you wish the deceased could have lived to read: "It is true, certainly the part will never be as inevitably done; it was played as written; a woman as the wind turns, the air shapes. And its infinitesimal variations were effected immediately the curtain rose, when the humour of the house was taken and judged. These variations — solely of tempo and weight, never of reading — directly established that 'area of communication' where the player plays as much *from* as *to* the house, where the play is wholly experienced, gathered, rather than attended."

She was drawn back to the film world when talkies came in, and managed to get a personal appointment with Irving Thalberg to discuss a longterm contract with M-G-M. She had forgotten that she had already met Thalberg once years previously when she was the queen of Metro; the occasion then had been a small dinner party given by Dagmar Godowsky and her husband, Frank Mayo, and one of the guests had been a very young Thalberg, receptionist at the time for the general manager at Universal Studios. When Nazimova learned that he was only a mere office boy, she turned snobbish, cold, and cruel. She had been bored, and by the following day had forgotten the entire incident. Thalberg never got over her treatment of him, however, and was waiting for his moment of revenge. To quote Miss Godowsky: "When she entered his office, a little late, of course, Irving greeted her. 'You don't remember me, Madame?'

"Nazimova drew back and looked at him carefully. 'Why, no, Mr. Thalberg. Certainly I would remember had we met before.' And then she sat down with an expectant smile.

"'I doubt it, Madame, I was only the office boy then!'

"Nazimova's curious expression implored him to go on.

"'Yes. I was only an office boy and Dagmar Godowsky invited me to her house to dine with you. I was dying to meet the great Nazimova — and you snubbed me. I wasn't good enough to dine with you, Madame!'

"And then, Nazimova told me, he relived the whole evening and she sat, and she listened, and she died. She did not get the contract, but she left the office with the imperial dignity that was hers to the end."

It was fortunate she did not enter talking pictures on any kind of a contract at that time, for late in 1929 the Theatre Guild made a contract with her, and she appeared as Natalia Petrovna in Turgenev's "A Month in the Country," and won a glowing reception. Then, in October 1931, she gave one of her most vivid performances as Christine, the Clytemnestra-like mother, in Eugene O'Neill's "Mourning Becomes Electra."

As the Thirties rolled on, there were at least two more memorable performances from Nazimova for the Guild — Olan in Pearl Buck's "The Good Earth" and the Priestess Prola in Shaw's "The Simpleton of the Unexpected Isles." And then in 1935 came the first national tour, climaxed with the engagement at the Empire Theatre in New York, with Nazimova starring as Mrs. Alving in Ibsen's "Ghosts." Brooks Atkinson, writing of the production in the "New York Times," said: "'Great' is a word for sparing use; it paralyzes linotype machines toward midnight. But there is no other way to characterise a transcendent performance of a tragic role in a drama that is not especially pertinent now."

Nazimova as Mrs. Alving I consider not only the greatest single performance I've ever seen an actress give in the theatre, but also the most enthralling evening I've ever spent watching a play unfold. Nazimova invested the tragic mother with classic dignity, and the drama between her and Harry Ellerbe as her hapless son, the tainted Oswald, crackled with an electricity that was almost unbearable. As if to prove that this was no fluke, Nazimova in 1936 revived her first triumph in this country and again played the title role of Ibsen's "Hedda Gabler," touring it with "Ghosts."

It was George Cukor who in 1938 brought Nazimova back to Hollywood, not as an actress but as a consultant and research adviser on his Paramount production of *Zaza,* that old warhorse of the French romantic theatre that had served as a vehicle for both Pauline Frederick and Gloria Swanson in the silent days. It had been prepared this time as a feature for Isa Miranda, but Claudette Colbert stepped in at the last minute as a replacement star.

A little more than a year later, Nazimova came back to films as an actress, thanks to Mervyn LeRoy, and played Robert Taylor's mother in M-G-M-'s *Escape,* which starred Norma Shearer. It was a key role, not long in footage, but unforgettable and very believable dramatically. In 1941, Rouben Mamoulian used her as Tyrone Power's mother in his beautiful production of *Blood and Sand.* During the first day of shooting, Nazimova industriously scrubbed floors. At a rehearsal, Mamoulian had suggested that she was playing the part too young. "Play it older, as a character," he advised, "as if you were forty-five." "Ah yes," she said, and then began to laugh, explaining, "You tell me to play it older, a character role, forty-five, and I say 'Yes,' and here I am really in my sixties!"

During the war years that ensued, Nazimova was consumed by restlessness. She had hoped for more screen roles after the successful notices she garnered in both *Escape* and *Blood and Sand,* but the films that issued from Hollywood during the early Forties were little better than those turned out during the First World War. Almost no picture lost money during the first half of the Forties; one could stick film together with spit, and it paid off at the box-office. There were certainly very few good character roles being written for an experienced film actress like Nazimova.

She brooded over her past, and began to write her memoirs. She was the aunt of Val Lewton, whose production unit at RKO was, according to James Agee, "carrying films a long way out of Hollywood." Val's mother, Nina

186

Nazimova in Mamoulian's *Blood and Sand*.

Lewton, was for a considerable time a literary adviser and editor in M-G-M's foreign language department; she was Nazimova's older sister, and both Nazimova and Val respected and honoured her for having dramatised "Lay Down Your Arms," a novel written by Bertha von Suttner, winner of the Nobel Peace Prize in 1905. I frequently saw Nazimova during this period, as a dinner guest at Val's home, since I was under contract at RKO and wrote three screenplays for Val. She would not talk much about her former silent film career, dismissing it all with one wave of her expressive arm. "Trash, my dear young man," she said. "I sold my soul for trash." And then she looked at me pensively and added, "Just as you yourself may be doing now."

She was always dramatic, and since there was then so little activity in her own life, she sometimes made up dramas, just to see how the real-life actors would react to the situations in which she placed them. I remember coming into a story conference with Val at the studio and finding him more than merely a little upset. When I asked him what was wrong, he said, "Oh, it's Alla again! I wish to God somebody in town would give her a job. Maybe then she'd stop acting these personal dramas she invents."

It developed then that when he had gone home the previous evening, it was to find his wife weeping and near hysteria. During the afternoon she had gone into the living-room and, looking out the window, had seen Nazimova seated

187

in her car in front of the house. Perplexed, she went out and asked her to come in for tea. Nazimova kept watching her as she sipped her tea, and finally said, "Poor Ruth — ah, poor Ruth!" And then, as Mrs. Lewton only looked at her in bewilderment, Nazimova gave a little cry and said, "Ah, you do not known then! Forgive me!" Pressed to explain, Nazimova confided that Val had told her he was seeing his doctor, who had told him he had only a short time to live.

Val assured his wife that there was no truth in the drama. He told me he had immediately gone to see Nazimova and had chided his aunt for having so needlessly perturbed his wife, whereupon Nazimova had only turned her cool, smiling eyes upon him and said, "But wasn't she happy when she found out that you weren't going to die?"

Not until 1944 did Nazimova get another acting job, and then it was as the Marquesa de Montmayor in a re-make of Thornton Wilder's *The Bridge of San Luis Rey*. Unfortunately, there was little to recommend this version, which could not touch Charles Brabin's previous dramatisation of it at M-G-M, released in 1929. Nazimova was the only player who seemed to know what it was all about, and was always in scene.

For Warners Nazimova then played a Polish countess in *In Our Time*, a moving drama of Poland as the enemy swept into the country. It was, like her work in *Escape* and *Blood and Sand*, moody and excitingly dramatic. Only one other movie appearance followed — a very brief role, but one she loved doing and did make something of, a Polish-American welder doing her bit in the war effort — for David O. Selznick's *Since You Went Away*.

In her one scene she quoted the Emma Lazarus sonnet on the Statue of Liberty, "The New Colossus," and brought to it a very special meaning because she herself had benefited from American freedom. It meant something true when she said:

"Keep, ancient lands, your storied pomp!" cries she
With silent lips. "Give me your tired, your poor,
Your huddled masses yearning to breathe free,
The wretched refuse of your teeming shore.
Send these, the homeless, tempest-tost, to me.
I lift my lamp beside the golden door!"

But after *Since You Went Away*, it was inactivity again, broken only by the additional work she managed to get in on her memoirs. She was not well, and on June 30, 1945, entered the Good Samaritan Hospital in Los Angeles, following a severe attack of coronary thrombosis. A fortnight later, on July 13, she died there, aged sixty-six, attended at the last, as Louella O. Parsons wrote in her obituary and tribute, by "her faithful friend and companion of many years, Glesca Marshall, and her nephew, Val Ivan Lewton, RKO producer and son of her sister, who survives her."

Nearly a score of years before she died, Beverley Nichols wrote a paragraph about her in life that stands admirably as a tribute to her in death: "I cannot imagine the divine unrest ever dying down in Nazimova. There are some people who were born to live, mentally and spiritually, in a caravan. They are restless, always searching. Sometimes, for a space — it may be even for a year or two — the caravan comes to rest. But it is off again, sooner or later, and if I dared to quote that exceedingly sentimental little song which one used to sing at school, I should say that there was nothing left but a few flowers fading on the grass, and a couple of rapidly vanishing wheel-tracks."

188

NAZIMOVA FILMOGRAPHY

WAR BRIDES (AKA, GB, *Motherhood*) (1916). Melodramatic, anti-war propaganda; as Joan, a widow. *Dir/Sc:* Herbert Brenon (from the one-act play by Marion Craig Wentworth which Nazimova had toured on the vaudeville circuit). *With* Gertrude Berkeley, Nila Mac, Charles Hutchison, Charles Bryant, William Bailey, Richard Barthelmess, Alex K. Shannon, Robert Whitworth, Ned Burton, Theodora Warfield, Charles Challies. *Prod:* *Lewis J. Selznick. 5 reels.

REVELATION (1918). Drama of the revelation that comes with pure faith; as Joline. *Dir/Sc:* George D. Baker (from the novel, "The Rosebush of a Thousand Years," by Mabel Wagnall). *With* Charles Bryant, Frank Currier, Syn De Conde, John Martin, Eugene Borden, Philip Sandford, Bigelow Cooper, True James, Dave Turner, Fred Radcliff, A. C. Hadley. (Re-made by Metro-Goldwyn, 1924, with Viola Dana.) *Prod:* Metro. 7 reels.

TOYS OF FATE (1918). Romantic drama; in a dual role: as Hagar, wife of a gypsy chieftain; and as Azah, Hagar's gypsy daughter. *Dir:* George D. Baker. *Sc:* June Mathis. *With* Charles Bryant, Frank Currier, Irving Cummings, Dodson Mitchell, Edward J. Connelly, Nila Mac. *Prod:* Metro. 7 reels.

EYE FOR AN EYE (1918). Romantic drama of love and vengeance; as Hassouna, daughter of a sheik. *Dir:* Albert Capellani. *Sc:* June Mathis and Capellani (from the play, "L'Occident," by Henry Kistemaechers). *With* Charles Bryant, Donald Gallaher, Sally Crute, E. L. Fernandez, John Reinhard, Louis Stern, Charles Eldridge, Hardee Kirkland, Miriam Battista. *Prod:* Metro. 7 reels.

OUT OF THE FOG (1919). Romantic drama; in a dual role: as Faith Coffin, a mother; and as Eve, her daughter. *Dir:* Albert Capellani. *Sc:* June Mathis and Capellani (from a play, "'Ception Shoals," by H. Austin Adams, which Nazimova had created on the Broadway stage). *With* Charles Bryant, Henry Harmon, Nancy Palmer, T. Morse Koupal, George W. Davis, Charles Smiley, Tom Blake, Hugh Jeffrey, Dorothy Smaller. *Prod:* Metro. 7 reels.

THE RED LANTERN (1919). Romantic drama of the Boxer Rebellion in China; in a dual role: as half-sisters — the Eurasian Mahlee, who becomes Goddess of the Red Lantern, Queen of the Boxers; and as the white Englishwoman, Blanche Sackville. *Dir:* Albert Capellani. *Sc:* June Mathis and Capellani (from a novel by Edith Wherry). *With* Darrell Foss, Mrs. McWade, Virginia Ross, Frank Currier, Winter Hall, Amy Van Ness, Noah Beery, Harry Mann, Yukio Ao Yamo, Edward J. Connelly. *Prods:* Metro. 7 reels.

THE BRAT (1919). Comedy of a chorus girl who reforms a snobbish family; as "The Brat." *Dir:* Herbert Blaché. *Sc:* June Mathis (from an adaptation by Charles Bryant of the play by Maude Fulton). *With* Charles Bryant, Amy Van Ness, Frank Currier, Darrell Foss, Bonnie Hill. (Re-made by Fox, 1931, as a talkie, directed by John Ford, with Sally O'Neil in the Nazimova role.) *Prod:* Metro. 7 reels.

STRONGER THAN DEATH (1920). Romantic drama of India; as Sigrid Fersen, a dancer. *Dir:* Herbert Blaché and Charles Bryant. *Sc:* Charles Bryant (from a novel, "The Hermit Doctor of Gaya," by I. A. R. Wylie). *With* Charles Bryant, Charles W. French, Margaret McWade, Herbert Prior, William H. Orlamond, Millie Davenport, Henry Harmon. *Prod:* Metro. 7 reels.

THE HEART OF A CHILD (1920). Romantic comedy drama; as Sally Snape, a Limehouse child who becomes the wife of an English lord. *Dir:* Ray C. Smallwood. *Sc:* Charles Bryant (from a story by Frank Danby — pseudonym for Julia Davis Frankau). *With* Charles Bryant, Ray Thompson, Nell Newman, Victor Potel, Eugene Klum, Claire Du Brey, Jane Sterling, John Steppling, William J. Irving, Myrtle Rishell. *Prod:* Metro. 6 reels.

MADAME PEACOCK (1920). Mother-daughter backstage drama; in a dual role: as the mother, Jane Goring, a star known as "Madame Peacock"; and as the daughter she had selfishly abandoned who becomes her rival in the theatre, Gloria Cromwell. *Dir:* Ray C. Smallwood. *Sc:* Nazimova (from a story by Rita Weiman). *With* George Probert, John Steppling, William H. Orlamond, Rex Cherryman, Albert Cody, Gertrude Claire, Mrs. Woodthorpe. *Prod:* Metro. 6 reels.

BILLIONS (1920). Comedy of relative values; as the Russian Princess Tirloff. *Dir:* Ray C. Smallwood. *Sc:* Charles Bryant (from a French farce by Jean-José Frappa and Henri Dupuy Mazuel). *With* Charles Bryant, William J. Irving, Victor Potel, John Steppling, Marian Skinner, Bonnie Hill, Emmett King. *Prod:* Metro. 6 reels.

CAMILLE (1921). Romantic tragedy; as Marguerite Gautier. *Dir:* Ray C. Smallwood. *Sc:* June Mathis (from the novel and play, "La Dame aux Camellias" by Alexandre Dumas, *fils*). *With* Rudolph Valentino, Arthur Hoyt, Zeffie Tilbury, Rex Cherryman, Edward J. Connelly, Patsy Ruth Miller, William H. Orlamond, Consuelo Flowerton, Mrs. Oliver. See Garbo filmography for other versions of *Camille. Prod:* Metro. 5600 ft.

A DOLL'S HOUSE (1922). Drama of a wife

189

and mother who becomes an independent woman; as Nora Helmer. *Dir:* Charles Bryant. *Sc:* Peter M. Winters (nom de plume for Nazimova) (from the play by Henrik Ibsen). *With* Alan Hale, Nigel de Brulier, Elinor Oliver, Wedgwood Nowell, Clara Lee, Florence Fisher, Philippe de Lacy, Barbara Maier. See Elsie Ferguson filmography for other versions of *A Doll's House. Prod:* United Artists. 6650 ft.

SALOME (1923). Stylized version of the Biblical drama; as the daughter of Herodias, Salome, who demands the head of John the Baptist. *Dir:* Charles Bryant. *Sc:* Peter M. Winters (Nazimova) (from the play by Oscar Wilde). *With* Mitchell Lewis, Rose Dione, Nigel de Brulier, Earl Schenck, Arthur Jasmine, Frederick Peters, Louis Dumar. (Fox released Salome, 1918 with Theda Bara; Rita Hayworth played it for Columbia, 1953.) *Prod:* Allied Producers and Distributors. 5,595 ft.

MADONNA OF THE STREETS (1924). Drama of a magdalen redeemed by love; as Mary Carlson. *Dir:* Edwin Carewe. *Sc:* Frank Griffin (from a novel, "The Ragged Messenger," by W. B. Maxwell). *With* Milton Sills, Claude Gillingwater, Courtenay Foote, Wallace Beery, Anders Randolph, Tom Kennedy, John T. Murray, Vivien Oakland, Harold Goodwin, Rosa Gore, Maybeth Carr, Herbert Prior, Fred Kelsey, George Irving. (Re-made as a talkie by Columbia, 1930, directed by John S. Robertson, with Evelyn Brent and Robert Ames.) *Prod:* First National. 8 reels.

THE REDEEMING SIN (1925). Redemption of a girl of the Paris underworld; as Joan Billaire. *Dir:* J. Stuart Blackton. *Sc:* Marion Constance (Blackton) (from the novel by L. V. Jefferson). *With* Lou Tellegen, Carl Miller, Otis Harlan, Rosita Manstini, William Dunn, Rose E. Tapley. (Re-made by Warner Bros. as a talkie, 1929, starring Dolores Costello.) *Prod:* Vitagraph. 7 reels.

MY SON (1925). New England seacoast mother-son drama; as Ana Silva, Portuguese fisherwoman. *Dir:* Edwin Carewe. *Sc:* Finis Fox (from the play by Martha Stanley). *With* Jack Pickford, Constance Bennett, Hobart Bosworth, Ian Keith, Charles A. Murray, Mary Akin, Dot Farley. *Prod:* First National. 7 reels.

ESCAPE (1940). Melodrama in Hitler's Germany; as Emmy Ritter, actress, wanted by the Nazis. (Nazimova's talking film *début*.) *Dir:* Mervyn LeRoy. *Sc:* Arch Oboler and Marguerite Roberts (from the novel by Ethel Vance). *With* Norma Shearer, Robert Taylor, Conrad Veidt, Albert Basserman, Felix Bressart, Philip Dorn, Bonita Granville, Blanche Yurka, Edgar Barrier, Lisa Golm, Marek Windheim, Elsa Basserman, Gretl Sherk, Florine McKinney, Helmut Dantine, Winter Hall. *Prod:* M-G-M. 104m.

BLOOD AND SAND (1941). Dramatic tragedy of the bullring; as Señora Gallardo, mother of Juan Gallardo, who becomes Spain's favourite matador. *Dir* Rouben Mamoulian. *Sc:* Jo Swerling (from the novel by Vicente Blasco Ibáñez). *With* Tyrone Power, Linda Darnell, Rita Hayworth, Anthony Quinn, J. Carrol Naish, John Carradine, Lynn Bari, Laird Cregar, William Montague, George Reeves, Vicente Gomez, Pedro de Cordoba, Fortunio Bonanova, Victor Kilian, Michael Morris, Ann Todd, Cora Sue Collins, Russell Hicks, Rex Downing, Richard Allen. *Prod:* 20th Century-Fox. Technicolor. (Winner of the Academy Colour Cinematography Award, 1941.) 125m. (Pregiously filmed by Paramount, 1922, with Rudolph Valentino.)

THE BRIDGE OF SAN LUIS REY (1944). Philosophical drama of why five were chosen to fall to their deaths when the bridge collapsed; as the Marquesa de Montmayor, one of the five. *Dir:* Rowland V. Lee. *Sc:* Howard Estabrook and Eugene Vale (from the novel by Thornton Wilder). *With* Lynn Bari, Akim Tamiroff, Francis Lederer, Louis Calhern, Blanche Yurka, Donald Woods, Barton Hepburn, Joan Loring, Emma Dunn, Abner Biberman, Minerva Urecal, Antonio Triana and his dancers. (Previously filmed by M-G-M, 1929, with Charles Brabin directing and Emily Fitzroy playing the Nazimova role.) *Prod:* United Artists. 106m.

IN OUR TIME (1944). Suspenseful drama of Poland on the eve of German conquest; as the Polish Countess Zofya Orvid. *Dir:* Vincent Sherman. *Sc:* Ellis St. Joseph and Howard Koch. *With* Ida Lupino, Paul Henreid, Nancy Coleman, Mary Boland, Victor Francen, Michael Chekhov, Ivan Triesault, Leonid Snegoff, Ivan Lebedeff, Faye Emerson, Frank Reicher. *Prod:* Warner Bros. 110m.

SINCE YOU WENT AWAY (1944). Drama of an American home during World War Two; as Koslowska, a Polish-American welder in the shipyards. *Dir:* John Cromwell. *Sc:* David O. Selznick (from the adaptation by Margaret Buell Wilder of her own novel). *With* Claudette Colbert, Jennifer Jones, Joseph Cotten, Shirley Temple, Monty Woolley, Lionel Barrymore, Robert Walker, Agnes Moorehead, Keenan Wynn, Albert Basserman, Gordon Oliver, Craig Stevens, Guy Madison, Hattie McDaniel, Lloyd Corrigan, Florence Bates. *Prod:* United Artists-Selznick. 134m.

ADDENDA

Nazimova also acted as Consultant and Research Adviser on the making of *Zaza,* Paramount, 1939, for which George Cukor was director, Zoë Akins screenplay writer, and Claudette Colbert star.

9
RAMON NOVARRO

It is usually thought that Rudolph Valentino's great fame overshadowed Ramon Novarro, but I doubt whether Novarro's career would have been much different had there been no Valentino. The "Latin Lover" illusions of women in the Twenties were sufficiently widespread for there to be a need for Novarro as well as Valentino — and Antonio Moreno.

Novarro was born on February 6, 1899, in Durango, Mexico, and was the eldest of thirteen children.* At his christening he was given fourteen names, but when grown he signed himself: José Ramon Gil Samaniegos. His mother's family, the Gavilans, claimed to be descended from an Aztec noble, and his father's family from a conquistador. His father, who was born in Juarez, Mexico, was a graduate of the University of Pennsylvania and spoke English as fluently as he did Spanish. Dolores Del Rio, also a native of Durango, was a distant cousin. She and Novarro did not meet until they had become stars in Hollywood.

Novarro's childhood was happy and he always remembered "wonderful summers, while we were growing up, on the family ranch, where we lived out of doors, swam, and rode horseback. I'm sorry for children who grow up in the cities today. They miss too much."

His father, a successful dentist, eventually moved the family to Mexico City, where Novarro attended Mascarones College and studied music, French and English — and became a movie fan, with his eyes on Hollywood.

"One year my brother Mariano and I were allowed to visit relatives in El Paso, Texas," says Novarro. "We stayed long enough to be polite, but left as soon as we could for Los Angeles, my secret mecca. We arrived on Thanksgiving Day, 1916, and between us had ten dollars. For the next four years, we virtually starved."

Following the Huerta Revolution, Novarro's father who had retired because of failing eyesight, moved the family to Los Angeles, and shortly thereafter died. Since Ramon, as the eldest, was then the chief support of the Samaniegos family, his mother begged him to give up his idea of becoming an actor. With equal fervour, he begged her to be patient. "I am determined," he told her, "to succeed in the theatre somehow — as actor, singer, musician or dancer."

*Four died in their youth. Two sisters are Roman Catholic nuns in a Mexico City convent. His other two sisters, Luz and Carmen, married and lived near Novarro in the San Fernando Valley. One brother (Mariano) was a Los Angeles dentist; Eduardo was an architect; José a chemist; and Antonio a sound-technician at 20th Century-Fox Studios.

He worked at anything that brought in money until Marion Morgan chose him as one of her dancers in a ballet, "Attila and the Huns," which she toured on the Orpheum Circuit. Thereafter he often danced professionally with Carmen, the sister closest in years to him. Both of them were also able to secure work as extras in Hollywood studios. They tangoed together, and had bit parts, in Rex Ingram's *The Four Horsemen of the Apocalypse*.

Most movie historians list Novarro's first camera appearance as an extra in an Artcraft-Fred Stone film, *The Goat,* which was written by Frances Marion. But that was made in 1918, and by then Ramon was an established extra. One may catch fleeting glimpses of him in several Vitagraph serials and Ince productions; in DeMille's *The Little American* with Mary Pickford (1917); in Sessue Hayakawa's *The Jaguar's Claws*; in Wallace Reid's *The Hostage* (1917); and as a starving peasant in DeMille's *Joan the Woman,* which starred Geraldine Farrar (1917). Established actors — notably Antonio Moreno and Richard Dix — tried to help him, but with no success.

He was industrious. He doubled as stage manager and bit player for Los Angeles' Majestic Theatre Stock Company, which starred Edward Everett Horton, Evelyn Varden, and Franklin Pangborn; often served as usher at the Los Angeles Philharmonic concerts; forced himself to seek auditions with the great (he sang for Farrar, danced for Pavlowa, acted for Mrs. Fiske). Aged eighteen, he approached Mary Garden as she sat in a box at the Philharmonic and exclaimed: "Miss Garden, I want to sing and play and act for you!"

"My, my!" said Miss Garden. "What an accomplished young man!" Which was as far as his garden grew with the celebrated Mary.

One day he heard that D. W. Griffith was seeking a new leading man, and he bribed a chambermaid at the Alexandria Hotel to learn the number of "The Master's" suite. He had secured a letter of introduction and compiled a neat list of his accomplishments.

Griffith himself opened the door and Novarro proffered his papers, bowed, and said: "My future is in your hands, Mr. Griffith."

Griffith read through the papers, carefully scrutinised him, and gruffly told him to report at the studio the following morning for a test.

"I was there long before 8 a.m.," Novarro told me. "I made myself up, and waited patiently. About four in the afternoon, Mr. Griffith arrived. He directed me in a brief camera test. I thanked him, left, and never heard another word from him; I sometimes wonder if there was really any film in that camera."

It's an apocryphal story that Novarro owed his lucky break to Rex Ingram telling Rudolph Valentino, after a temperamental outburst from that actor during the making of *The Conquering Power,* that he, Ingram, could pick any extra from the ranks and make him as big a star as Valentino — and so had chosen Novarro.

"That was studio publicity — the usual bunk," Novarro told me when I asked about this. "It didn't happen like that at all. I'd already been featured with Derelys Perdue in a flashy Oriental dance sequence for a full-length Mack Sennett comedy, *A Small Town Idol;* and I'd been the lead dancer with the Marion Morgan group in a bacchanal sequence in Allen Holubar's *Man, Woman, Marriage;* I'd had billing in a Tom Moore feature, *Mr. Barnes of New York;* and a gifted artist-director, Ferdinand Pinney Earle, had chosen me to

194

Ramon Novarro

play the lead in his art movie, *The Rubaiyat of Omar Khayyam* (released as *A Lover's Oath*). Also, Mr. Ingram had been in the audience one night at the Hollywood Community Theatre when I was performing in a dance pantomime, "The Royal Fandango," and Mr. Earle had shown him a sequence or two from *Omar Khayyam*. Furthermore, an actress friend of mine, Margaret Loomis, had just finished a role for Mr. Ingram in *Turn to the Right,* and she suggested that I go see him about a lead in his next picture, *The Prisoner of Zenda.*

"But when I went to the Metro casting-office and asked to see Mr. Ingram, I got exactly nowhere. Then Mary O'Hara, who had written the scenario for *Zenda,* and was then trying to help Mr. Earle edit *Omar Khayyam,* suggested to Mr. Earle that he give me a personal letter of introduction to Ingram. He sat down at once and wrote a charming one, which got me into Mr. Ingram's office.

"Mr. Ingram was courteous, but didn't think me the type for Rupert of Hentzau. He said he wanted an actor over six feet tall, blond, and older than I. I had my make-up kit with me and asked him to describe exactly what type he had in mind. On the back of Mr. Earle's letter Ingram quickly sketched four facial studies of what he wanted his Rupert of Hentzau to resemble. My heart sank when I saw moustaches and a short Prussian beard. I was very young then and my own beard took months to become even scraggly.

"But I was good at make-up and fashioned a false moustache and beard. Mr. Ingram studied me a long time, and finally took me out on a set and made a camera test of me. In the next few days he made four tests of me as Rupert. After the third he said, "No, you're still too young." But he then changed his mind. "Let's try a test with a monocle, too," he said. When Mr. Ingram ran that test off, he was pleased, and signed me to a personal contract at $125 a week, which was more money than I had ever hoped to get. He said I would be his new leading man and that he would groom me for stardom. I was deliriously happy, and didn't dare believe it. But that's exactly what he did."

Incidentally, at the time I last talked to him, Novarro still had that letter of introduction from Ferdinand Pinney Earle with Ingram's four pencil sketches on the back. He asked Edward Weber, his secretary, to get it out of his safe. Ingram's sketches are just as Novarro described them.

In *The Prisoner of Zenda,* Novarro received fourth billing — after Lewis Stone, Alice Terry and Robert Edeson — as "Ramon Samaniegos."

"With one flip of a monocle in *The Prisoner of Zenda,*" wrote astute publicist Herb Howe, "he won the American public."

For his subsequent film, *Trifling Women,* Ingram suggested that his new discovery use the surname "Novarro" — a name from the maternal side of his family.

Samuel Goldwyn chanced to see *Trifling Women* before it was released and offered Novarro a two-year contract at $2,000 a week. "I turned him down," says Novarro. "Mr. Ingram had given me my break, and the least I could do was stay with him. Anyway, I enjoyed every moment I worked for Rex Ingram, and there wasn't a day I didn't learn something new. An Ingram picture was carefully mounted, beautifully designed, and the actors were well rehearsed before a camera ever started being turned. Also, although I might earn $2,000 a week starring for Mr. Goldwyn, my career might be finished at the end of two years. If Goldwyn didn't have anything for me, he'd have to

Ramon Novarro with Alice Terry in Rex Ingram's *Where the Pavement Ends*.

lend me out, and loan-outs were then more often disastrous than helpful. In all my career as a contract actor, I've never once gone on loan-out.

"Of course I told Mr. Ingram of the Goldwyn offer. He looked very sad and said I probably should accept it since he couldn't afford to pay such a salary. But I didn't want to leave Mr. Ingram. Also, I was more than a little annoyed, because Mr. Goldwyn had gone to my family, trying to get them to persuade me to accept.

"When Mr. Ingram heard Goldwyn had done that, and that Goldwyn had once turned me down when Richard Dix had made a test of me and tried to sell me to Goldwyn, he said: "No, Goldwyn can't have you. He didn't take you when he could have, so he shouldn't be allowed to have you now at any price."

Ingram often said Novarro "is the only actor who can walk in front of a camera and hand me a kick." And his publicity department even had Ingram say, "Novarro has the physique of Michelangelo's David and the face of an El Greco Don." Novarro kidded Ingram about this, saying, "Well, that proves what Mary Pickford once said — my face and body do not match." When, shortly thereafter, Miss Pickford tried to borrow Novarro for her leading man in *Rosita,* Ingram turned her down. "If she thinks your face and body don't match, she can't have you either," he told Novarro.

In his third picture with Ingram, *Where the Pavement Ends,* Novarro played a young native who loves and is loved by a prim missionary's daughter — played by Alice Terry — and gave one of the best performances of his career. He was so idolised after the initial release of that film that exhibitors demanded he not be killed off at its end, and Ingram was forced to recall the prints and give exhibitors a choice of two endings. In the final fade-out of the happy version, the native boy discovers he's really of white parentage and so can marry the missionary's daughter.

After that came *Scaramouche,* which was road-shown, and lifted Novarro into the first magnitude of Hollywood screen stars. Even Pola Negri, who rarely praised *any* actor, called him "the greatest actor of the screen," and added this gallantry: "When I saw Mr. Novarro as Scaramouche, I took off my hat to him!"

Alice Terry, his co-star, who remained a close friend for life, said of Novarro at the time: "He acts by thought rather than by gesture. I'm always curious as to what he's going to do next, so I watch his eyes to know what he's thinking. And that's fatal!"

Novarro made one more picture for Ingram, who, by the time of *The Arab,* was paying him $500 a week. That film was shot in North Africa, whither Novarro journeyed in the company of Ingram and Alice Terry who was not only *The Arab's* leading lady but also Ingram's wife.

It was while making *The Arab* that Ingram decided he would not return to Hollywood (Louis B. Mayer and he were antagonistic, and Metro, Ingram's home studio, was now part of Metro-Goldwyn-Mayer), but would remain in Europe and North Africa and make pictures in the studios in Nice. He advised Novarro to return to Hollywood, and there work only for well-established directors in carefully-selected vehicles.*

*The pictures Ingram then did in Europe were often imaginative and beautiful to look at — *The Garden of Allah* and *The Magician* especially, and *Mare Nostrum* became his masterpiece — but

RAMON NOVARRO

On his return to Hollywood, Novarro followed Ingram's advice in part — the part of working for an established director, and made two films directed by Fred Niblo: *Thy Name Is Woman,* with Barbara LaMarr, and *The Red Lily,* with Enid Bennett.

Whereupon M-G-M offered him a solo starring contract that guaranteed $10,000 a week. Its negotiation consumed five months, and when it was finally signed, Marcus Loew complained that "Ramon will make a great Shylock," and Louis B. Mayer cracked, according to the publicity: "Ramon, if you ever decide to give up acting, I'll make you head of my legal department."

Novarro began spending at once. He built a mammoth residence on 22nd Street in the then-fashionable West Adams district; acquired a staff of nine; and brought his mother, three brothers, and two sisters to live with him. He built a private theatre on the grounds of his estate, called it "El Teatro Intimo," and opened it with a concert by Louis Graveure, a distinguished baritone of the day. He gave many more concerts and entertainments there, and his audiences were always star-studded. He himself occasionally sang a repertory of songs, for, after becoming a movie star, he began to hope he could sing in opera, and to that end diligently studied music and voice.

His first starring picture (i.e., the first picture on which his name appeared alone above the title) was *The Midshipman,* which endeared him to those of the young who liked their movie heroes to be collegiate. Incidentally, it was while *The Midshipman* was being filmed that Mabel Normand, in one of whose films he had once worked as extra, visited the set and declared after seeing Novarro work: "You don't have to worry about that boy being a star. He can look out for himself!"

Meanwhile, M-G-M had embarked on its costliest production: *Ben-Hur.* Charles J. Brabin, who had been selected as director, and a cast headed by George Walsh, Gertrude Olmstead and Francis X. Bushman, were in Italy filming the galley slave and shipwreck sequences on the Mediterranean. Mishaps occurred, costs mounted, and M-G-M was not happy with the film Brabin sent back. Production was halted; Brabin was removed as director, and Fred Niblo took his place. Walsh and Miss Olmstead, in the roles of Ben-Hur and Esther, were replaced by Novarro and May McAvoy. When production was resumed, very little of Brabin's footage was salvaged.

Novarro had hoped that Rex Ingram would be chosen as the new director. Ingram wanted the assignment and was willing to declare an armistice with Louis B. Mayer. But Mayer could neither forgive nor forget, and the assignment went to Fred Niblo, for whom Novarro had already worked.

"Efficient craftsman though Mr. Niblo was," said Novarro later, "I really always regretted that Rex Ingram was not given the directorship. I think, although *Ben-Hur* was very good for me, the picture itself would have been a greater artistic triumph had Mr. Ingram been at the helm.".

Filmed at an estimated final cost of $5,000,000, *Ben-Hur* had these advantages going for it: a pre-sold audience which had read the pseudo-literary

they were moody and slow-paced and his reputation as a top director declined. In his last picture, he acted the male lead and let his wife, Alice Terry, direct. Not until he was in ill health, and the clouds of the Second World War had gathered, did he return to California. There he lived as a recluse in a guest cottage in back of the San Fernando Valley home of Miss Terry, who had given up her acting career. Her only recent public appearance was her presence in court during her suit for damages for the way she was depicted in *Valentino* (she received an out-of-court settlement).

Ramon Novarro as *Ben-Hur*.

novel; great spectacle, including a battle at sea and an exciting chariot race; enough sex and temptation to make even DeMille envious; enough spirituality to please the religious-minded; and Ramon Novarro as sure-fire box-office insurance.*

Novarro was a guest at the New York *première* of M-G-M's 1959 *Ben-Hur,* and said this of it: "A curious thing happened: the audience was rooting out loud for Messala to win the chariot race. The anti-hero was already in then, and he is even more so as time has passed. I think, had I been Charlton Heston, I would have wanted to play Messala." And Carmel Myers, who accompanied Novarro to this *première,* said, smiling when they noted that the part she had played in the 1926 version (the temptress, Iras) had been eliminated: "It must be because they couldn't find anyone in Hollywood as sexy as I am."

Of the first seven pictures Novarro made after *Ben-Hur,* only one is worth remembering — Lubitsch's production of *The Student Prince,* in which Novarro loved and lost Norma Shearer.

*It was the second filming of *Ben-Hur*. The 1907 Kalem production was pirated and was responsible for not only the establishment in law of the rights authors have when their work is used in motion pictures (Kalem had to pay $25,000 to novelist Lew Wallace), but for an avalanche of historical film spectacles. "Bigger than *Ben-Hur*" became the advertising slogan for every special any studio tried to road-show (none of which *was* bigger).

Ramon Novarro with Kathleen Key in *Ben-Hur*.

MORE FROM HOLLYWOOD

Novarro himself was bored with such pictures and in 1927 announced that he was seriously considering abandoning movies for operetta and opera. By the following year he had withdrawn so completely from the Hollywood scene that it was rumoured he intended abandoning music too, and enter a monastery. For years he had sung in the choir of the Church of Our Lady of Guadalupe, and had stopped only because his stardom attracted too many disturbing autograph-seekers.

"The stars of my day enjoyed a certain privacy," Novarro said. "We lived two lives: our film life, and our own private one. It wasn't only Garbo who lived as a recluse — almost all of us did. I don't know if we actually had better taste, or it was forced upon us. But the intimate details of our personal lives were never publicised unless we deliberately allowed them to be. And it wasn't all a desire for privacy. Some of us realised it was necessary in order to sustain the public illusion that made us stars.

"As for myself, I know that not until late in my M-G-M career was I photographed with my mother or any of my brothers or sisters, and then only because my mother wanted it. The interior of my home was not photographed, and certainly not my bedroom or bathroom. I lived one life — my professional one — at M-G-M when I was busy making films. When I left the studio, I took up my life as Ramon Samaniegos.

"I spent my time on weekends and between pictures studying music or rehearsing the acts for the revues I staged at my own intimate theatre. We worked six days a week making pictures in those days and often on Saturday evenings I was driven directly from the studio to the railroad station and rode up to San Francisco on the overnight "Lark," studied there on Sunday with my favourite vocal coach, and took the overnight train back to Los Angeles, arriving just in time to be driven directly to the Culver City lot for Monday's shooting.

"During the first two years of my stardom, I never entered the studio wearing anything but a black suit and tie. Even when conventions were relaxed, it would never have occurred to me to arrive for work wearing levis or a T-shirt, as some of the male stars do today. Nor did I have any social life, really. On a few occasions I was a guest at a dinner party at "Pickfair" — that was about it as far as parties went. I socialised with my mother, my brothers, and sisters. We were always a closely knit family. Later on, it was Elsie Janis who brought me out of my shell. She kept after me until I was almost forced to go out escorting her. She introduced me to Ruth Chatterton, and when I did go to parties, it was usually to escort Miss Janis, Miss Chatterton, or Beth Fairbanks, the first wife of Doug Senior, whom I liked."

After Ingram, Novarro has said that his most helpful directors were Jacques Feyder and Ernst Lubitsch. And although he was never in an F. W. Murnau film, he has said that director coached him privately and "proved to me how an actor might take a role to a certain peak, but then let the audience finish the scene, so to speak. He told me how, in *The Last Laugh,* which had no sub-titles, he wanted Emil Jannings, as the old man, simply to sit, abjectly, beyond all thought or tears, after a completely shattering day during which he had been unable to secure any kind of employment. When Jannings wanted a big emotional scene, the release of a veritable Niagara, Murnau did not argue, but just said, 'Okay, we'll shoot it both ways.' He ran both versions in the

202

projection room for Jannings, who, when he saw how much more effective Murnau's interpretation was, got up and said, 'You win!'

"It was fortunate, I suppose, that Murnau did not long survive the birth of the talking picture. He frequently complained of talkies to the very studio heads who were hiring him and told them: 'You have destroyed the art of acting.'

"In a way, I feel that Murnau was right. We of the silent screen had created a pantomimic art that had no language barriers. We were universal — any nationality could understand the story we were telling. When I go to the movies nowadays, which isn't often, I get a feeling that the actors, as actors, are coasting. They're neither creating nor interpreting."

Novarro was not proud of the pictures he made after sound came in. "With the exception of *The Pagan,* in which I only sing," he said, "and some of *Son of India* and a good part of Feyder's *Daybreak* — certainly not the ending, however — I didn't like any of the talkies in which I starred. I, too, coasted. It was, however, the vehicles themselves which were really at fault. They weren't right for me, and we were given no time to try and make them right. I'd been spoiled by the years when I'd worked with Ingram. I remember he would spend six months to a year in pre-production. Every detail of setting, costume, and prop was carefully planned and chosen. Mr. Ingram's pictures were beautifully designed. He was an artist, and a good one. Every frame was a tasteful and exciting picture in itself. And we actors were rehearsed. We knew exactly what we had to do when it came time to appear before the camera, and we did it."

In those days, movie audiences were overwhelmingly female and it was freely acknowledged that the chief requisite for male stardom was an "ability to please women." Novarro's thought on this subject: "Women must be wooed long and ardently, preferably under balconies." Which sounded better in the Twenties than it does today. Said Herb Howe, perhaps Hollywood's most literate publicity man: "Between Novarro and such hot knavish lovers as Valentino and Moreno there is no more resemblance than between Little Eva and Topsy." Novarro's technique, in a way, was Topsy-esque: he might convey the impression that he was "real wicked," but would wink or otherwise let his audience know it was all a celluloid lark.

M-G-M was intelligent about introducing him in a talkie. In 1929 it released *The Pagan,* much of which had been filmed on location in the Tahitian Islands. It was a silent film with sound effects and a score, but in it Novarro sang "The Pagan Love Song," which instantly became, and has remained, a standard. It enhanced his popularity, as did the recordings he made of it and of his subsequent songs.

His first all-talking and singing film, *Devil May Care* (late 1929), re-enforced his position as one of M-G-M's top stars. "When talkies came in," Novarro said, "my contract had, of course, to be re-negotiated. In a way, I suffered because I was caught in the middle of the personal fight for power which Irving Thalberg and Louis B. Mayer were staging. I was flattered that both wanted me in their corner. But Mr. Thalberg's first interest was the career of his wife, Norma Shearer, and what happened to the rest of us at M-G-M was of secondary interest. On the other hand, when, after *The Pagan,* M-G-M wanted me to sign a new exclusive contract, the terms Mr. Mayer presented were so restricted they would have controlled me body and soul. I politely handed the contract back to him and said: 'Excuse me, Mr. Mayer, you haven't put down here when I am allowed to go to the bathroom.'

"I stayed at home studying my music and let my attorney argue out the new contract with a battery of M-G-M lawyers. Eventually, I got things my way on paper, but, alas, I did not get any more really good roles!"

For the next five years Novarro danced, sang, and utilised his linguistic talents by starring in the Spanish and French versions of such films as *Call of the Flesh,* some of which he also directed. He always disapproved, both pantomimically and verbally, of *Laughing Boy,* one of his last M-G-M films. He disliked it so much that he never went to see it.

When Novarro finished his last picture under his long-term M-G-M contract, he was not interested in continuing in films. He thought his last seven M-G-M pictures had not only been unworthy but actually dishonest. Furthermore, he had all the money he needed, and it was wisely invested.

Music really interested him and his financial independence enabled him to devote all his time, if he so desired, to a concert career. Nor was he without assets in pursuing such a goal. His lyric tenor voice was pleasant, albeit too light for opera, and he could transpose music at sight.

But the film medium still fascinated him, though no longer as an actor. He wrote, financed, produced, and directed a Spanish-speaking feature-length film for the European and Latin American markets, *Contra la Corriente.*

But his work as a director didn't satisfy him. "The experiment only proved," he says, "that directing was not my field. I liked it, yes — but acting was my true *métier.* I'd long been in the game, had enjoyed the help of at least four wonderful directors, and it was not unreasonable for me to try to direct. But I saw quickly enough that what I could achieve as an actor was more satisfying than what I could do as a director."

So he began a series of song recitals. Then he went to London to co-star with Doris Kenyon in an operetta, "A Royal Exchange." It was a complete fiasco, and he used to wince at the mention of it.

In 1935, however, he appeared at the London Palladium with an act in which he sang songs from his movies, accompanying himself on either the piano or guitar (for both of which he had composed) and dancing with a partner, his sister Carmen. It was a success, and he toured both England and the Continent with it.

He returned to Hollywood in 1937 and made two romantic comedies at Republic, but didn't like them and terminated his contract. He then bought a forty-nine acre ranch near San Diego, which caused a revival of the rumour of his wanting a monastic life. Actually, in spite of his enduring Catholicism, he at that time was intrigued by yoga. .

He returned to Europe in 1940 to star in a charming comedy filmed in Italy with a cast of superlative French actors — *La comédie de bonheur* (better known in Europe by the title of its Italian-dubbed version, *Ecco la felicita*). It got few bookings in America, despite some amusing Cocteau dialogue. I saw it in Europe later and thought it not only witty and elegant but full of charming performances by Novarro, Jacqueline Delubac, Micheline Presle, Sylvie, Michel Simon, and Louis Jourdan.

Once, during the making of *La comédie de bonheur,* Novarro didn't go to the studio because his salary hadn't been paid. The producer hurried to his hotel, and, handing him a cheque, said, "Now, Mr. Novarro, let's go to the studio." Responded Novarro: "Excuse me, signor, but we'll first stop at the bank."

Europe was on the brink of the Second World War, and when the French director suddenly had to return to Paris, Novarro finished directing the picture himself. Whereupon some Italian producers offered him work, but the war clouds were too ominous, and he returned to California.

Two years later, Novarro starred in a big Mexican production called *La virgen que forjo una patria,* which was a success in Latin American countries and was favourably reviewed in the United States when exhibited in Spanish-speaking communities. The President of Mexico thought it so conducive to religious patriotism that he gave Novarro a special decoration.

Both before and after this Mexican film, Novarro appeared in road tours and summer stock engagements of such plays as "Tovarich," "The Command to Love," and a French play produced in Montreal called "In the Shadows of the Harem." He bought an Owen Wister story with an 1885 California background, "Padre Ignacio," developed it into a screenplay, and hoped to direct and star in it, but he never got it before the camera. In 1962 he went to New York to rehearse an adaptation of Shakespeare's "Julius Caesar" called "Infidel Caesar." After a series of previews, it failed to open, and Novarro quietly returned to Hollywood.

When his mother had died in February 1949, he had sold his seventeen-room house, and ultimately he built an attractive rustic home in Laurel Canyon near Studio City. And he relinquished all screen, stage, and musical ambitions.

But in this he was not altogether successful. He sang character roles in at least two productions at Fort Worth's Casa Mañana: General Birabeau in "The Desert Song" and Wang-Chi-Yang in "The Flower Drum Song." In 1949, John Huston offered him a character part in *We Were Strangers,* and later that year he played a character role in RKO's *The Big Steal.* Said "Time" of this one: "As the gentle, humourous, sly Mexican Army colonel, he steals the show." The following year his part in an M-G-M Western called *The Outriders* caused "Hollywood Reporter" to say: "Ramon Novarro's emergence as a character actor continues to be one of the joys of present day filmgoing."

Not all such appearances were pleasant and when on M-G-M's *Crisis* he had the feeling that the director, Richard Brooks, didn't want him, he found it all so hectic that as soon as the picture was over, he checked into Scripp's Clinic for tests and a rest.

In 1959, however, he did return to films to play the villain in a Western which George Cukor directed for Paramount, *Heller in Pink Tights.* Said Novarro: "John Barrymore once told me that if I ever got a chance to appear in a film directed by George Cukor, it would be an experience I'd value — and I did greatly enjoy every moment working for Mr. Cukor."

He then began appearing in television — in Disney's *Nine Lives of Elfego Baca* and Alfred Hitchcock's *La strega,* and in segments of *Dr. Kildare, Bonanza,* and *Rawhide.* Novarro enjoyed it. "I have none of the worries of being a star," he said, "and all of the fun."

In 1962 he told an interviewer the old Hollywood "was more leisurely, and I guess there was more security. When you arrived, you *had* arrived, and

Paula Raymond, Cary Grant, Ramon Novarro, Antonio Moreno, and Jose Ferrer in *Crisis*.

weren't frantic if a picture turned out not quite so good as its predecessor. But those days are over. As for me, well, I don't reminisce unless people want me to. After all, my idea of hell is to be a star all your life." Nevertheless, when the Ramon Novarro Fan Club of London congregated on one of his last birthdays, he telephoned them and spoke personally to each member. "I visit those loyal ladies every time I go abroad," he admitted, and added, with a flash of the old Novarro smile: "When they swoon over me now, somebody has to help them get up."

Late in 1965 he appeared on television with Luise Rainer and Kurt Kreuger in a *Combat* segment. Plagued by painful attacks of pleurisy, he was in and out of hospitals for months at a time. When not so afflicted, he lived quietly in the beautifully landscaped, rambling home he built in Laurel Canyon (two of his sisters, and three of his brothers lived relatively near). He saw a few of his old movie friends, most frequently Alice Terry, who also lived nearby. And he sometimes returned to TV, as when he did to play a roguish Mexican villain in *The Wild Wild West*.

Novarro never married, and said: "That's one mistake I did not make."

He did make other mistakes, however, far more self-injurious, and one of them was a growing addiction to alcohol. He had been arrested several times for driving while intoxicated, and was forbidden to drive a car. Alcoholism brought with it all the attendant evils, the foremost for him association with the lowest and worst of drinking companions.

206

RAMON NOVARRO

On October 31, 1968, the world was shocked to learn that Ramon Novarro, aged sixty-nine, had been cruelly bludgeoned to death in a drunken brawl in his home by two ne'er-do-well hustlers from Chicago — brothers: Robert Ferguson, aged twenty-two and Thomas Scott Ferguson, aged seventeen. The young brothers, convicted of murdering Novarro, were formally sentenced to prison for life on October 27, 1969.

It was one of the most savage murders Hollywood has ever known, a brutal ending to what had been a brilliant film career.

"He was born with a gift for laughter and a sense that the world was mad," wrote Raphael Sabatini of his picaresque hero in *Scaramouche*, which Novarro had played as if it had been specially created for him.

And in the end, the world in which Novarro lived was without laughter and completely gone mad.

RAMON NOVARRO FILMOGRAPHY

A SMALL TOWN IDOL (1921). Slapstick comedy; as burlesque of a hick who wants to be a movie star; as the lead dancer with the Marion Morgan dancers in the big harem scene. *Dir:* Erle C. Kenton. *Sc:* Mack Sennett. *With* Ben Turpin, James Finlayson, Phyllis Haver, Bert Roach, Marie Prevost, Al Cooke, Charles Murray, Dot Farley, Eddie Gribbon, Kalla Pasha, Billy Bevan, George O'Hara, Derelys Perdue. *Prod:* Associated Producers. 7 reels.

MR. BARNES OF NEW YORK (1922). Romantic comedy about a Corsican vendetta; as a Sicilian, Antonio Paoli. Novarro received billing under his real name, Ramon Samaniegos. *Dir:* Victor Schertzinger. *Sc:* Gerald Duffey (from a story by Archibald C. Gunter). *With* Tom Moore, Naomi Childers, Anna Lehr, Sydney Ainsworth, Lewis Willoughby, Otto Hoffman. *Prod:* Goldwyn. 5 reels.

THE PRISONER OF ZENDA (1922). Mythical kingdom romance; as Rupert of Hentzau. *Dir:* Rex Ingram. *Sc:* Mary O'Hara (from the novel by Anthony Hope and the play dramatised therefrom by Edward Rose). *With* Lewis Stone, Alice Terry, Robert Edeson, Barbara La Marr, Malcolm MacGregor, Edward J. Connelly, Lois Lee. (Novarro still billed as Ramon Samaniegos.) Famous Players filmed this story in 1913 with James K. Hackett. It was filmed as a talkie by Selznick in 1937 and by M-G-M in 1952.) (Ingram shot both a happy and unhappy ending and let exhibitors take their choice.) *Prod:* Metro. 10 reels.

TRIFLING WOMEN (AKA, GB, *The Fatal Orchids*) (1922). Romantic tragedy; as Ivan de Maupin and also, in the story frame, as the modern descendant, Henri de Maupin. (For the first time Novarro was billed as Ramon Novarro.) *Dir/Sc:* Rex Ingram. *With* Barbara La Marr, Lewis Stone, Edward J. Connelly, Hughie Mack, Pomeroy Cannon. (Previously filmed by Ingram at Universal, 1917, as *Black Orchids*). Prod: Metro. 9 reels.

WHERE THE PAVEMENT ENDS (1923). Romantic drama of the South Seas; as a native youth, Matauri. *Dir/Sc:* Rex Ingram (from a short-story, "The Passion Vine," by John Russell). *With* Alice Terry, Edward J. Connelly, Harry T. Morey, John George. Filmed on location in Florida and Cuba. (Again, Ingram shot two endings: in the original unhappy one Novarro drowns himself in a waterfall; in the happy ending he learns he isn't a native but is a heavily tanned Caucasian and so can marry the missionary's daughter.) *Prod:* Metro. 8 reels.

SCARAMOUCHE (1923). Romantic drama of the French Revolution; as André-Louis Moreau, later known as "Scaramouche." *Dir:* Rex Ingram. *Sc:* Willis Goldbeck (from the novel by Rafael Sabatini). *With* Alice Terry, Lewis Stone, Julia Swayne Gordon, Lloyd Ingraham, William Humphrey, Otto Matiesen, George Seigmann. (Re-filmed as a talkie by M-G-M in 1952 with Stewart Granger in the Novarro role.) *Prod:* Metro. 10 reels.

THY NAME IS WOMAN (1924). Romantic tragedy of the Spanish Pyrénées; as Juan Ricardo, a Spanish officer sent to entrap the beautiful wife of a crafty mountaineer smuggler. *Dir:* Fred Niblo. *Sc:* Bess Meredyth (from the play by Benjamin Glazer and Karl Schoenherr). *With* Barbara La Marr, William V. Mong, Wallace MacDonald, Robert Edeson, Claire McDowell, Edith Roberts. *Prod:* Metro-Goldwyn. 9 reels.

THE ARAB (1924). Romantic drama; as Jamil Abdullah Azam, a roguish Arabian dragoman. *Dir/Sc:* Rex Ingram (from the play by Edgar Selwyn). *With* Alice Terry, Gerald Robertshaw, Alexandresc, Maxudian, Adelqui Miller, Count de Limur, Rheda, Paul Vermoyal. Filmed on location in Algiers, the Sahara, and the Oulad Nail mountains. (Previously filmed by Cecil B. DeMille, 1915, with Edgar Selwyn; re-filmed as a talkie, 1933, by M-G-M, again starring Novarro and this time called *The Barbarian*.) *Prod:* Metro-Goldwyn. 7 reels.

207

THE RED LILY (1924). Romantic drama of the Parisian Montmartre; as Jean Leonnec. *Dir:* Fred Niblo. *Sc:* Bess Meredyth (from a story by Niblo). *With* Enid Bennett, Wallace Beery, Frank Currier, Rosemary Theby, Mitchell Lewis, Emily Fitzroy, George Periolat, Milly Davenport, Dick Sutherland, Gibson Gowland, George Nichols. *Prod:* Metro-Goldwyn. 7 reels.

A LOVER'S OATH (1925). Oriental romance; as Ben Ali, nephew of Omar Khayyam. *Dir/Sc:* Ferdinand Pinney Earle (from "The Rubaiyat of Omar Khayyam"). Supervised and edited by Milton Sills. *With* Kathleen Key, Edwin Stevens, Frederick Warde, Hedwiga Reicher, Snitz Edwards, Charles A. Post, Arthur Edmund Carewe, Paul Weigel, Philippe de Lacy. Actually filmed in 1922 when it was copyrighted under its original title, it did not gain a release until 1925. *Prod:* Astor. 6 reels.

THE MIDSHIPMAN (1925). Drama of the U.S. Navy Academy at Annapolis; as James Randall, midshipman. *Dir:* W. Christy Cabanné. *Sc:* F. McGrew Willis (from a story by Carey Wilson). *With* Harriet Hammond, Wesley Barry, Margaret Seddon, Crauford Kent, Maurice Ryan, Harold Goodwin, William Boyd, Gilbert Roland. Novarro's first as a star in his own right, it was produced at Annapolis under supervision of the U.S. Navy. *Prod:* Metro-Goldwyn. 8 reels.

BEN-HUR (1926). A tale of the Christus; as Ben Hur, young Prince of Judah. *Dir:* Fred Niblo. *Sc:* Carey Wilson (from the adaptation by June Mathis of the novel by General Lew Wallace). *With* Francis X. Bushman, May McAvoy, Claire McDowell, Kathleen Key, Carmel Myers, Nigel de Brulier, Mitchell Lewis, Leo White, Frank Currier, Charles Belcher, Betty Bronson, Dale Fuller, Winter Hall. (Filmed in Italy, on the Mediterranean, in Hollywood, and below the border in Mexico.) (Previously filmed by Kalem in 1907, and re-filmed as a talkie in 1959 with Charlton Heston in the Novarro role.) *Prod:* M-G-M. 12 reels. (Compare listing in May McAvoy filmography.)

LOVERS? (1927). Romantic drama; as José (Ernesto). *Dir:* John M. Stahl. *Sc:* Douglas Furber and Sylvia Thalberg (from the play by Charles Frederick Nirdlinger, "The World and His Wife," which was adapted from the Spanish play, "El Gran Galeoto," by José Echegaray. *With* Alice Terry, Edward Martindel, Edward J. Connelly, George K. Arthur, Holmes E. Herbert, John Miljan, Roy D'Arcy. (A happy ending was submitted for exhibitor's choice over the original tragic one.) (Previously filmed in 1920 as *The World and His Wife*.) *Prod:* M-G-M. 6 reels.

THE ROAD TO ROMANCE (1927). Romantic drama of piracy; as José Armando, captain of Spanish dragoons. *Dir:* John S. Robertson. *Sc:* Josephine Lovett (from the novel, "Romance," by Joseph Conrad and Ford Maddox Ford). *With* Marceline Day, Marc McDermott, Roy D'Arcy, Cesare Gravina, Bobby Mack, Otto Matiesen, Jules Cowles. *Prod:* M-G-M. 7 reels.

THE STUDENT PRINCE IN OLD HEIDELBERG (AKA, *The Student Prince*) (1927). Romantic drama; as Karl Heinrich who falls in love with a commoner. *Dir:* Ernst Lubitsch. *Sc:* Hans Kraly (from the Romberg-Donnelly operetta, "The Student Prince," and the novel, "Karl Heinrich," by W. Meyer-Forster). *With* Norma Shearer, Jean Hersholt, Gustav von Seyffertitz, Philippe de Lacy, Edgar Norton, Bobby Mack, Edward J. Connelly, Otis Harlan, John S. Peters. (Previously filmed in 1915 as *Old Heidelberg* with Wallace Reid and Dorothy Gish; and re-filmed in 1954 as a musical with Mario Lanza singing and Edmund Purdom acting the role of Karl Heinrich). *Prod:* M-G-M. 10 reels.

ACROSS TO SINGAPORE (1928). Romantic drama of the sea; as Joel Shore, youngest of the Shore brothers. *Dir:* William Nigh. *Sc:* Ted Shane and Richard Schayer (from the novel, "All the Brothers Were Valiant," by Ben Ames Williams). *With* Joan Crawford, Ernest Torrence, Frank Currier, Dan Wolheim, Duke Martin, Edward J. Connelly, James Mason. Working title: *China Bound*. (Previously filmed, 1923; filmed as a talkie, 1953). *Prod:* M-G-M. 7 reels.

A CERTAIN YOUNG MAN (1928). Romantic comedy drama; as Lord Gerald Brinsley, a gay young blade with many loves. *Dir:* Hobart Henley. *Sc:* Doris Bureel. *With* Marceline Day, Renée Adorée, Carmel Myers, Bert Roach, Huntley Gordon, Ernest Wood, Willard Louis. (Originally filmed in 1916, with Novarro in a character role of a greying *roué*, but that was shelved, and then entirely re-shot with a younger characterisation.) *Prod:* M-G-M. 6 reels.

FORBIDDEN HOURS (1928). Mythical kingdom romance); as His Majesty, Michael IV of Balanca. *Dir:* Harry Beaumont. *Sc:* A. P. Younger. *With* Renée Adorée, Dorothy Cumming, Edward J. Connelly, Alberta Vaughn, Roy D'Arcy. *Prod:* M-G-M. 5 reels.

THE FLYING FLEET (1929). Drama of the Navy Air Corps; as Tommy, one of six buddies who train for the Navy Air Crops as fliers; only two make it. *Dir:* George W. Hill. *Sc:* Richard Schayer (from a story by Frank Wead and Byron Morgan). *With* Ralph Graves, Anita Page, Eddie Nugent, Carroll Nye, Sumner Getchell, Gardner James, Alfred Allen. *Prod:* M-G-M. 11 reels.

THE PAGAN (1929). Romantic drama of the

South Seas; as a native boy, Henry Shoesmith Jr. *Dir:* W. S. Van Dyke. *Sc:* Dorothy Farnum (from a story by John Russell). *With* Renée Adorée, Dorothy Janis, Donald Crisp. Exteriors filmed in Tahiti. With Sound and Musical Score. Novarro sang "The Pagan Love Song." *Prod:* M-G-M. 9 reels.

DEVIL MAY CARE (1929). Romantic drama in France during the time of Napoleon; as Armand. *Dir:* Sidney Franklin. *Sc:* Hans Kraly (with dialogue by Zelda Sears; adapted from the Richard Schayer version of a French play, "La bataille des dames," by Eugene Scribe and Ernest Legouvé). *With* Dorothy Jordan, Marion Harris, John Miljan, William Humphrey, George Davis, Clifford Bruce. Novarro's first all-talkie, with four musical numbers, and a sequence in Technicolor. *Prod:* M-G-M. 11 reels.

IN GAY MADRID (1930). Romantic drama of a light-hearted Madrileno with two loves; as Ricardo. *Dir:* Robert Z. Leonard. *Sc:* Bess Meredyth, Salisbury Field and Edwin Justus Mayer (from a Spanish novel, "La casa de la Troya," by Alejandro Perez Lugin). *With* Dorothy Jordan, Lettice Howell, Claude King, Eugenie Besserer, William V. Mong, Beryl Mercer, Nanci Price, Herbert Clark, David Scott, George Chandler, Bruce Coleman, Nicholas Caruso. *Prod:* M-G-M. 9 reels.

CALL OF THE FLESH (1930). Romantic drama of Seville; as Juan, a carefree singer who becomes an opera star. *Dir:* Charles J. Brabin. *Sc:* Dorothy Farnum (with dialogue by John Colton). *With* Dorothy Jordan, Renée Adorée, Ernest Torrence, Nance O'Neil, Mathilde Comont, Russell Hopton. Technicolor sequence. Working title: *Singer of Seville. Prod:* M-G-M. 11 reels.

LA SEVILLANA (AKA, *Sevilla de Mis Amores*) (1930). the Spanish-speaking version of *Call of the Flesh;* with Novarro playing Juan in Spanish. *Dir:* Ramon Novarro. *With* Conchita Montenegro, Rosita Ballesteros, José Soriano Biosca, Martin Garralaga, Maria Calvo, Michael Vavitch. *Prod:* M-G-M.

LE CHANTEUR DE SEVILLE (1931). The French-speaking version of *Call of the Flesh;* with Novarro playing Juan in French. *Dir:* Ramon Novarro and Ivan Noe. *With* Pierrette Caillot. *Prod:* M-G-M.

DAYBREAK (1931). Realistic romance in Vienna; as Willi Kasda, a young guardsman so far in debt that he attempts suicide. *Dir:* Jacques Feyder. *Sc:* Ruth Cummings and Zelda Sears (with dialogue by Cyril Hume, from a novel, "Daybreak," by Arthur Schnitzler). *With* Helen Chandler, Jean Hersholt, C. Aubrey Smith, William Bakewell, Karen Morley, Kent Douglass (Douglass Montgomery), Glenn Tryon, Clyde Cook, Sumner Getchell,

Clara Blandick, Edwin Maxwell, Jackie Searle. *Prod:* M-G-M. 6280 ft.

SON OF INDIA (1931). Romantic drama of India; as Karim, son of a wealthy Indian jewel merchant, who is impoverished. *Dir:* Jacques Feyder. *Sc:* Ernest Vajda (with additional dialogue by John Meehan and Claudine West, from a novel, "Mr. Isaacs," by F. Marion Crawford). *With* Madge Evans, Conrad Nagel, Marjorie Rambeau, C. Aubrey Smith, Mitchell Lewis, John Miljan, Nigel de Brulier. (After the initial release, Louis B. Mayer insisted that the film be recalled, and a happy ending put onto it.) *Prod:* M-G-M. 7 reels.

MATA HARI (1923). Romantic drama of espionage; as Lt. Alexis Rosanoff. *Dir:* George Fitzmaurice. *Sc:* Benjamin Glazer and Leo Birinski (with additional dialogue by Doris Anderson and Gilbert Emery). *With* Greta Garbo, Lionel Barrymore, Lewis Stone, C. Henry Gordon, Karen Morley, Alec B. Francis, Blanche Friderici, Edmund Breese, Helen Jerome Eddy, Frank Reicher. *Prod:* M-G-M. 88m. (Compare listing in Greta Garbo filmography.)

HUDDLE (AKA, GB, *The Impossible Lover*) (1932). Yale football drama; as Tony Amatto. *Dir:* Sam Wood. *Sc:* Francis Wallace. *With* Madge Evans, Una Merkel, Ralph Graves, John Arledge, Kane Richmond, Frank Albertson, Martha Sleeper, Henry Armetta, Ferike Boros, Rockcliffe Fellowes, Joe Sawyer. Working title: *For Glory and the Girl. Prod:* M-G-M. 98m.

THE SON-DAUGHTER (1932). Romantic drama; as Tom Lee, a Chinese prince in disguise. *Dir:* Clarence Brown. *Sc:* John Goodrich and Claudine West (with dialogue by Leon Gordon, from the play by David Belasco and George M. Scarborough). *With* Helen Hayes, Lewis Stone, Warner Oland, Ralph Morgan, Louise Closser Hale, H. B. Warner, Edward McWade, Ben Bard. *Prod:* M-G-M. 7 reels.

THE BARBARIAN (AKA, GB, *A Night in Cairo*) (1933). Talking picture version of the 1924 success, *The Arab;* again, as Jamil. *Dir:* Sam Wood. *Sc:* Anita Loos and Elmer Harris (from the play, "The Arab," by Edgar Selwyn). *With* Myrna Loy, Reginald Denny, Louise Closser Hale, C. Aubrey Smith, Edward Arnold, Blanche Friderici, Marcelle Corday, Hedda Hopper, Leni Stengel. (Naturally, Mayer wanted and got a happy ending.) Novarro sang, "Love Song of the Nile." *Prod:* M-G-M. 79m.

THE CAT AND THE FIDDLE (1934). Musical romance in Paris; as Victor, a composer in love. *Dir:* William K. Howard. *Sc:* Bella and Sam Spewack (from the Jerome Kern-Otto Harbach operetta). *With* Jeanette MacDonald, Frank Morgan, Charles Butterworth, Jean

Hersholt, Vivienne Segal, Frank Conroy, Henry Armetta, Adrienne d'Ambricourt, Joseph Cawthorn, Sterling Holloway, Herman Bing, Henry Kolker, Irene Franklin. Technicolor sequence. *Prod:* M-G-M. 88m. (Compare listing in Jeanette MacDonald filmography.)

LAUGHING BOY (1934). Indian romantic tragedy; as the young brave, Laughing Boy. *Dir:* W. S. Van Dyke. *Sc:* John Colton and John Lee Mahin (from the novel by Oliver LaFarge). *With* Lupe Velez, William Dickenson, Chief Thunderbird, Catalina Rambula, Ruth Channing. *Prod:* M-G-M. 79m.

THE NIGHT IS YOUNG (1934). Romance, with music; as Paul Gustave, a Viennese archduke. *Dir:* Dudley Murphy. *Sc:* Edgar Allan Woolf and Frank Schultz (from a story by Vicki Baum and the Hammerstein-Romberg operetta). *With* Evelyn Laye, Charles Butterworth, Una Merkel, Henry Stephenson, Edward Everett Horton, Rosalind Russell, Donald Cook, Charles Judels, Herman Bing, Christian Rub, Gustav von Seyffertitz, Albert Conti, Snub Pollard, Joseph Swickard. Technicolor sequence. *Prod:* M-G-M. 80m.

CONTRA LA CORRIENTE (1936) Romance between a poor boy and a rich girl; Novarro does not act in it, but he produced, wrote, and directed it. It was a Spanish-speaking film, and had a big release in Latin American countries. *With* Luana Alcaniz, José Caraballo.

THE SHEIK STEPS OUT (1937). Romantic comedy; as Ahmed Ben Nesib, a desert chieftain who poses as a tourist guide. *Dir:* Irving Pichel. *Sc:* Adele Buffington. *With* Lola Lane, Gene Lockhart, Kathleen Burke, Stanley Fields, Billy Bevan, Charlotte Treadway, Robert Coote, Leonid Kinskey, Georges Renevant, Jamiel Hasson, C. Montague Shaw, George Sorel. Working title: *She Didn't Want a Sheik*. *Prod:* Republic. 66m.

A DESPERATE ADVENTURE (AKA, GB, *It Happended in Paris*) (1938). Romantic comedy; as André, a temperamental young Parisian painter. *Dir:* John H. Auer. *Sc:* Barry Trivers (from a story by Hans Kraly and M. Coates Webster). *With* Marian Marsh, Margaret Tallichet, Eric Blore, Andrew Tombes, Tom Rutherford, Maurice Cass, Erno Berebes, Cliff Nazarro. Working title: *As You Are*. *Prod:* Republic. 67m.

LA COMEDIE DE BONHEUR (1940). Romantic comedy; as Felix. *Dir:* Marcel l'Herbier. *Sc:* (from the play by Nicholas Evrelnoff, with dialogue by Jean Cocteau). Filmed in Rome in the French language. *With* Michel Simon, Jacqueline Delubac, Micheline Presle, Louis Jourdan, Sylvie, Marcel Vallé, Alermé, René Genin, M. Berubet. The version dubbed into the Italian language was called *Ecco la felicita*. Prod: Discina (Italo-Franco).

LA VIRGEN QUE FORJO UNA PATRIA (1942). Spanish-speaking feature made in Mexico; as Juan Diego, the Mexican peon who is the first to see a vision of Santa Guadalupe, Mexico's patron saint, the worship of whom played a big part in the forging of the Mexican nation. *Dir:* Julio Bracho. *Sc:* Bracho (from a story by René Capistián Garza). *With* Gloria Marin, Domingo Soler, Julio Villareal. Felipe Montoya, Fanny Schiller, Margarita Cortés. *Prod:* Films Mundiales. 110m. Working title: *Reina de reinas*.

WE WERE STRANGERS (1949). Suspense drama about a Cuban who returns to Havana with money for a revolution; as one of the revolutionaries, called "Chief." *Dir:* John Huston. *Sc:* Peter Viertel and Huston (from the "China Valdez" episode in "Rough Sketch," a book by Robert Sylvester). *With* Jennifer Jones, John Garfield, Pedro Armendáriz, Gilbert Roland, Wally Cassell, David Bond, Jose Perez, Morris Ankrum. *Prod:* Columbia. 105m.

THE BIG STEAL (1949). Romantic chase thriller for a thief who has stolen a big army payroll; as Colonel Ortega. *Dir:* Don Siegel. *Sc:* Geoffrey Homes and Gerald Drayson Adams (from a story, "The Road to Carmichael's," by Richard Wormser). *With* Robert Mitchum, Jane Greer, William Bendix, Patric Knowles, Don Alvarado, John Qualen, Pat O'Malley, Pascual Garcia Pena. *Prod:* RKO. 71m.

THE OUTRIDERS (1950). Civil War Western; as Don Antonio Chavez, leader of the U.S. train conducting gold bullion to safety. *Dir:* Roy Rowland. *Sc:* Irving Ravetch. *With* Joel McCrea, Arlene Dahl, Barry Sullivan, Claude Jarman Jr., James Whitmore, Jeff Corey, Ted de Corsia, Russell Simpson. *Prod:* M-G-M. 93m.

CRISIS (1950). Suspense drama in a Latin American country; as Colonel Adragon, who kidnaps an American surgeon and his wife. *Dir/Sc:* Richard Brooks (from a story, "The Doubters," by George Tabori). *With* Cary Grant, Jose Ferrer, Paula Raymond, Signe Hasso, Gilbert Roland, Leon Ames, Antonio Moreno, Teresa Celli, Pedro de Cordoba, Soledad Jimenez, George Lewis. *Prod:* M-G-M. 95m. (Compare listing in Antonio Moreno filmography.)

HELLER IN PINK TIGHTS (1960). Western action drama among a troupe of travelling players; as Señor De Leon. *Dir:* George Cukor. *Sc:* Dudley Nichols and Walter Bernstein (from a novel, "Heller with a Gun," by Louis L'Amour). *With* Sophia Loren, Steve Forrest, Anthony Quinn, Margaret O'Brien, Eileen Heckart, Edmund Lowe, George Mathews, Ken Clark, Frank Silvera, Frank Cordell. *Prod:* Paramount. 100m. Technicolor.

RAMON NOVARRO

For more than four years, between 1917 and 1921, Ramon Novarro (Samaniegos) worked as an extra and bit player in Hollywood, and appeared in nearly one hundred films in this capacity. Among these are such distinguished features as Cecil B. DeMille's *Joan the Woman*, Allen Holubar's *Man, Woman, Marriage*, Rex Ingram's *The Four Horsemen of the Apocalypse;* he worked with Mary Pickford in DeMille's *The Little American*, with Fred Stone in *The Goat*, with Sessue Hayakawa in *The Jaguar's Claws*, with Wallace Reid in *The Hostage*. These and many others are not cited in the preceeding filmography, because they were not large enough to warrant billing, and these filmographies contain only the titles of those films for which the actors received cast credit. Except, of course, in the case of pre-1915 release in which even leading players did not receive credit.

10
CHARLES RAY

Any star who believes the rug can never be pulled from under him will do well to consider the career of Charles Ray.

In Hollywood, Ray was know as "Ince's Wonder Boy," and throughout the United States the image he projected on the screen was deemed to be the very embodiment of the American ethos. Great Britain and all the other movie-going countries of the world subscribed to the same belief.

In 1920 Ray said to Katherine Anne Porter, who was then doing motion picture, and other kinds of, journalism: "I like country people. Maybe that is the reason I gravitated naturally toward this character. These country boys are the very spine of the nation...They come to town full of hopes and plans, and they grab at life like a pup grabbing at a thistle, and they don't let go when it stings. They just grab harder. At last, they get the job they want, and the girl they want, and they get a little polish without losing their clean country ideals. I like them, because they are Americans — just as the screen is distinctively an American art. You can't find their type anywhere else in the world."

A few years later, the country boy hero was *passé*, and when Ray tried to change his acting style, he did so without real comprehension of the post-First World War world. Then he sank everything he had, and more, into a big super-special intended to glorify the beginnings of America, *The Courtship of Myles Standish*. Costume pictures were momentarily in vogue, but it cost over $600,000 to produce and that much and more to promote. The public didn't care for it, and within a few years it no longer cared for Charles Ray.

Charles Edgar Ray was born on March 15, 1891, in Jacksonville, Illinois. His father was of Irish-Scottish descent, and his mother of French. He was an only son, but had an older sister, Beverly.

His father worked for railroads and was obliged to move his family around. Charles had attended schools in both Springfield and Peoria before the Rays moved to California — first to Needles, a railroad town in San Bernardino County near the Arizona border, and then to Los Angeles, where Charles attended Polytechnic High School.

His father urged him to take a business course at the Los Angeles Business College, and I believe Ray also studied commerce at Stanford University. But a business man he was not, and could never be. While he was living in Needles, he had haunted its one theatre — passing out handbills, ushering, scene-shifting, serving iced water at intermissions, cleaning the auditorium, helping in the box-office, and finally being allowed to do walk-ons and bits and then playing supporting juveniles. And while he was attending Los Angeles' Polytechnic High School, he had earned one dollar a performance for walk-ons and bits at the Burbank Theatre and the Mason Opera House, in plays which starred such actors as Lewis Stone and T. Daniel Frawley.

When it was clear the business courses weren't registering and that Ray's heart was in the theatre, his sister, who held a commercial job of some responsibility, gave him the money for a course at the Wallace Dramatic School. As soon as he graduated, he teamed up with two other stage-struck youths and put on, in local movie houses, playlets they concocted by plagiarising and cutting down to a single act, such favourites of the time as "Girl of the Golden West" and "The Lottery Man." The trio sometimes earned as much as eighty dollars a week, and toured the playlets from Santa Barbara to Phoenix.

In Phoenix one summer Ray landed a berth with a company that was giving a season of light musical comedy in an open-air theatre, featuring tenor Willis G. West. Ray, of course, was very green. At the first dress-rehearsal, an electrician asked him whether he wanted a spotlight or flood. The latter sounded like an awful lot of light, so he said, "Spotlight, please." He got it, and suddenly realised he had a star's light and was going to have to perform like a star on solo. He did, and was a hit.

Los Angeles was his home base, and he was naturally very much aware of motion pictures, although he knew nothing about them. When he heard, however, that Thomas Ince was hiring actors at his studio in Inceville, down by the sea near Santa Monica, he set his alarm clock for six a.m., and on the morning of December 12, 1912, journeyed to Inceville via Los Angeles' red inter-city Pacific Electric cars.

"I changed cars three times," he later remembered, "walked a lot, and suddenly landed on what I've ever since thought of as the most inspiring sight I've ever seen. About a hundred cowboys were riding around on ponies, and forty to fifty Indians, and there were sixty teepees. A most beautiful California morning brightened the scene, the shimmer of the Pacific Ocean, the liveliness, busy-ness of it all thrilled and charmed me. In all my life I never wanted to do anything so much as to get into the movies right then and there."

He did just that. He learned who was directing those cowboys and Indians and went up to him and asked for work. It was Charles Giblyn, who put him on the payroll as an extra, and told him to put on a beard. Ray had become expert at putting on his own make-up and later that day Thomas Ince noticed how professional his make-up was and praised him — not only for his beard but also for his characterisation.

Ray shyly remarked that cowboys-and-Indians were a little out of his line, and Ince asked what his line was. Ray said, "Juveniles." Ince looked him up-and-down, and told him to report back the following day. But only more bearded bits resulted. Ince was then making a series of Civil War stories and Ray made up as Lincoln or Grant one day and as Robert E. Lee the next.

"We used to wear Northern and Southern uniforms alternately," he later reminisced. "We'd charge upon ourselves, change uniforms, and charge back."

Ince finally cast Ray in a juvenile role in a Civil War drama called *The Favourite Son*. When that picture finished shooting, Ray was told Ince wanted to see him; he was then so modest and insecure that he thought Ince was going to give him the gate. Instead, Ince said: "I see good possibilities in you and hope you will stay with me." He asked how much a week Ray wanted. Ray knew the highest salary at Inceville was $50 a week and suggested $35, which Ince agreed to without further dickering. They were walking upstairs together at the time, and Ray was so overcome, he stumbled. Ince laughed, patted his shoulder, and said: "It's good luck, to fall upstairs."

Ray needed money coming in regularly since his father had died shortly before and he and his sister were the sole support of their mother. Until he could afford to buy a roadster, he rode to Inceville on the red electric-cars six days a week, studying his roles for the day each morning, and for the next day each night.

Throughout his first year with Ince, almost all of Ray's roles had either a Civil War or a Puritan background, and he played heroes and villains equally well. But in 1914 the background of Ince's stories became more varied, although Ince's producing practices remained the same: he would find a photogenic location and write, or have written, a series of variations on one plot capable of utilising that particular locale. In 1914, Ray played either the hero or principal villain in Westerns, Irish-English romances, or turgid melodramas about the wickedness of the city.

By 1915, Ince films had become, to exhibitors, more important than mere programmers and were considered features, for Ince insisted on good production values and carefully built a stock company of actors, which included such important players as Frank Borzage, J. Barney Sherry, Louise Glaum, Bessie Barriscale, Gertrude Claire, Enid Markey, Dorothy Dalton, and, of course, William S. Hart, who then was also billed as "Two-Gun" Hart. Ray first appeared with Hart early in 1915 in a Western called *The Grudge,* which Hart directed, but his best picture with Hart was *The Conversion of Frosty Blake,* in which Ray is a tubercular minister who reforms gunman Hart, gives up his life to save Hart's, and marries Hart to dancehall-girl Louise Glaum with his last dying breath.

Ray's first picture after Ince became part of Triangle is one that made him a star. This is *The Coward,* which was released in late October 1915. In it Ray played a young Confederate soldier so terrified of battle he deserts the Southern cause, but then vindicates himself by an act of outstanding heroism. Ray said later he never tried harder in any role, and his performance, even when judged in the abbreviated prints available today, stands up. He had learned so much about acting for the camera that, compared to his performance, those of veteran players Frank Keenan and Gertrude Claire are ham.

By 1917, Charles Ray had become one of the brightest stars in Hollywood and when it became obvious to Ince that Triangle was going to break up, Ince took Ray, and much of his unit, with him to Paramount, which guaranteed Ray $35,000 a picture. In 1918, Paramount released nine Ray features.

"When I skipped out with a dramatic and musical stock company years ago," Ray told Katherine Anne Porter, "I little thought my life role would be interpreting the country boy to the world. I did all sorts of parts, but chiefly was the dapper juvenile — the kind that wears incredible neckties and unheard of suits and makes romantic love to the soubrette. Well, I got out of that! Being fascinating was too much for me. Besides, that role was never real — never worthwhile. I wanted to interpret a live human being, one that people would recognise as true to life, like someone they knew, or someone they

217

Sincerely yours
Charles Ray

Sincerely yours,

Witzel
L.A.

Charles Ray

once were themselves. The screen gave me the chance to do this."

As a person, Ray was still a movie-struck, unspoiled young man. His was a household name long before he visited New York and during his starring years he never went abroad. But when he married Clara Grant, a quiet, petite, well-educated non-professional, he did buy a handsome Beverly Hills home and lived in the style he thought a movie star should — Persian rugs on highly polished floors; sixteenth century Italian marble fireplace; gold doorknobs and bathroom fixtures; Japanese butler; formal dress for dinner even when he and his wife were alone. And all this in a day when Hollywood and Beverly Hills had scarcely outgrown their orange-grove and avocado-orchard origins.

This living style was partly a reflex from the self-denial and poverty of Ray's early years, as was his admiration for director William Desmond Taylor, whose flair for elegance tinged even his mysterious murder in 1922. Ray once asked Taylor if he thought an actor should carry a cane before he was making $75 a week, and when Taylor heard that Ray's weekly salary had reached that figure, he sent him a gold-headed cane, which Ray flaunted at once (and was visibly hurt when his fellow-workers kidded him about it). Like most dedicated, hard-working people, Ray never had any humour about himself.

But there was loving humour in the way he portrayed American youth on the screen, and, often, real wit. Whereas Harold Lloyd made the bashful, backward American boy amusing, Ray made him real. It's true, perhaps, that Richard Barthelmess made the American youth a deeper character (*Tol'able David, Way Down East, The Bond Boy*). But Ray made him more simpatico.

Nevertheless, Ray tried to vary the country boy role. In *The Family Skeleton* he is a young millionaire who believes he has inherited the family curse of alcoholism. In *His Own Home Town* he is the black-sheep who disgraces himself and his family, but returns to town to manage the local newspaper and expose political chicanery.

He made other attempts, but the public wanted a Charles Ray picture to begin with him barefoot, straw-hatted, wearing tattered overalls and a faded gingham shirt. That same public wanted Mary Pickford in curls and child-woman roles; insisted on William S. Hart being a *good* bad-man; would accept Theda Bara only as Satan's sorceress.

Thirteen of the Ray films between 1917 and 1919 were directed by Victor Schertzinger, with whom Ray was remarkably compatible. Ray once said: "Just before doing a certain episode I may re-read it and talk it over with Vic...I can't explain how it is between Vic and me — we so thoroughly understand each other we don't have to talk when he directs. He looks at me; I look at him. It must be thought-transference or something, but I feel harmonious when he is around."*

*Schertzinger, probably Hollywood's best-liked director of all time, also had an infallible ear for melody and wrote many popular songs. Although Irving Berlin won the contest for the title-song of Mary Pickford's *Rosita*, no one today remembers his prize-winner, but the song Schertzinger unsuccessfully submitted, and later re-named "Marcheta," is now a standard. Even the silent films Schertzinger directed had a lyrical flow, and he directed not only some of Ince's best pictures but some of Goldwyn's. Mabel Normand felt about him as Ray did, and when Goldwyn tried to give her a different director, she balked and insisted on having "Vic." Even Grace Moore, who could be a prima donna on a Hollywood set as well as the Met, adored him. Her best picture, *One Night of Love,* was directed by Schertzinger.

CHARLES RAY

In the spring of 1920, Ray broke away from Thomas H. Ince, set up his own production company, and arranged to release his pictures through Associated First National. It was not, Ray explained, a precipitate action. "Mr. Ince and I talked the matter over many times," he said, "and naturally he tried to dissuade me, not because he would lose a box-office attraction — he could always promote someone else — but because he was really fond of me, and knew how hard it was for even an experienced swimmer to breast the fluctuating tides and hold his own against the occasional undertows, or panics, which sometimes beset the motion picture business. I replied that I must 'start my own grocery store,' which made him laugh. When he finally understood that I was determined to try my luck, he let me go and wished me success."

Adolph Zukor, in his book "The Public Is Never Wrong," explains Ray's departure from Ince-Paramount quite differently: "We tried Ray as other types, but the country boy was the only one he could play — it seemed to us he had only a few years to go before the public tired of him. It fell to my lot, as in the case with so many others, to endeavour to tell him the facts of movie life.

"He came to my office, and, as was the custom, I suggested that we look at the books.

"He was not interested.

"'But,' I argued, 'you are making four pictures a year and by taking the figures on a set of four we can get an average which will demonstrate your value to us.'

"'No, thank you,' he answered politely, 'I'm interested only in the salary you are prepared to offer.'

"'Mr. Ray,' I continued sympathetically, 'you aren't really a leading-man type. You can never be the romantic figure who commands a top salary. You play the farmer come to town, and you do it well. We want you to keep on playing that character and we will pay you the highest price we can.'

"He waited.

"'A quarter of a million dollars a year,' I said. 'Five thousand a week.'

"His brown eyes grew larger and I thought the deal was set. I was mistaken.

"'Mr. Zukor,' he said, 'that offer is an insult.'

"I quit right there, and I must say that I felt somewhat as a man who had intended to bet on a horse but failed to get his money down and it came in a loser. Here was an actor who had so far over-estimated himself as to lose touch with reality. I knew he was headed for trouble and did not care to be with him when he found it."

Ray wasn't as unrealistic as Zukor alleges. He was twenty-nine years old, however, and knew he could not play the country boy much longer. He also knew executives like Zukor would dump him at their convenience. A producing company of his own, he believed, was the answer. On the other hand, Zukor really knew all the answers — and even now, a centenarian, having celebrated his one hundredth birthday in January 1973, he still does. The public is not always right, in spite of the title of his book, but he himself has seldom been wrong in the entire century of his life.

Ray, on his own, got off to an uneasy start. He took on a property which had been adapted from George M. Cohan's play, *45 Minutes from Broadway*. The only thing he and Cohan had in common was that they were actors of Americana, but they didn't move in the same American circle. Burns Mantle, reviewing the film for "Photoplay," remarked: "Charles Ray was doing very nicely until he decided to go it alone. Since then he has lost ground. His stories have not been as carefully or wisely selected, and his own performances in them have been lacking in the ease and natural grace that a measure of irresponsibility begets. The old boyish charm is giving way to the mature and deliberative performances of an anxious actor." Much of this was true, even though Mantle was building a case from Ray's only release away from Ince.

But many others criticised Ray for wanting to do everything on his pictures, and for not delegating phases of production to those who specialised in them. He was particularly taken to task when, in 1921, he began directing his films.

He defended himself as follows: "I know I've been called stubborn, self-willed, bull-headed, presumptuous, 'a fool and his money,' a know-it-all, and all sorts of harsh and uncomplimentary things, simply because, after seven years of professional work under the guidance of one producer — good guidance, too — and sticking pretty closely to one type of portrayal, I felt an overwhelming urge to do something different.

"From the time I was a small boy the theatre has been my palace of dreams, and to be a mime my steadfast ambition. That, no doubt, is one reason I got somewhere in my chosen work at a comparatively early age. Starting my own productions has never meant I would give up acting, temporarily or ultimately. On the contrary, it was to enable me to do more acting, and a greater variety of acting, in characterisations I knew I should never be allowed to touch under producers. In other words, as my own employer I could take a chance on myself and do stories radically different from those I had become identified with. It would be unfair, and indeed useless, to ask a producer to allow me to do a story on which he might, if lucky, break even, when he had in hand a story for me on which he could roll up hundreds of thousands of dollars.

"I have not been motivated by a belief that 'if you want a thing well done, do it yourself.' My old stories had been admirably done, to the satisfaction of everybody. It was simply that if I was to work out certain ideas which have been hammering at my brain for years, I would have to find the capital to back them myself. Call it ambition, restlessness, anything you like, but I had this desire for new experience and new expression, and it had nothing to do with making money."

Ray's second picture on his own was better; he was happily in his own home town, treading ground he well knew. Entitled *Peaceful Valley,* it was adapted from a popular rustic play. Its author, Edward E. Kidder, after seeing the film, said glowingly: "Ray is more than a 'ray;' he is a dramatic X-ray. He illuminates everything and one misses the spoken word very little."

The last phrase may, in part, have inspired Ray to undertake a film that not only had no plot, but had no sub-titles whatsoever. First National, through which he released his pictures, begged him to insert quotations from James Whitcomb Riley's poem at appropriate places, but he refused. *The Old Swimmin' Hole* was widely praised, and made money. It still stands as a wholly successful example of the silent film at its very best — all pantomime, all charm, and Ray's country-boy image at its most appealing.

One of Ray's production associates was a genial, good-looking cousin, Albert Ray, a former publicist, who later assisted Ray in writing scripts and on at least one occasion assisted in the direction of a picture. It was at this

Charles Ray in *The Girl I Loved*.

cousin's suggestion that Ray and his wife, in 1921, journeyed for the first time to New York City to promote his First National successes. He made frequent stop-overs in crossing the continent and was everywhere received with all the fanfare accorded a true star. When he arrived in Manhattan, Mayor John F. Hylan officially greeted him on the steps of City Hall.

Late in 1922, United Artists offered to release Ray's pictures and the two films they released for him are among his very best: *A Tailor-Made Man* and *The Girl I Loved*. The latter is my own favourite Ray film. Also adapted from a James Whitcomb Riley poem, like *The Old Swimmin' Hole*, it embodies everything Ray had learned in projecting the country-boy hero, and does so in

223

a believable story about a youth who matures through heartbreak. I saw it again during the Second World War, when Charles Koerner was considering buying and re-making it. Unfortunately, Koerner died before RKO made a decision.

The Girl I Loved is the apogee of Ray's career as an independent producer. His next picture bankrupted him.

It was said that people stayed away in droves from *The Courtship of Myles Standish* because they had had to memorise Longfellow's poem in school. But there were more realistic reasons: its ponderous script (by cousin Albert); uninspired direction (Frederic Sullivan); and, except for leading lady Enid Bennett, mediocre cast, were far from compensated for by a Charles Ray, in Sixteenth century costume and wig, as John Alden. *The Courtship of Myles Standish* was so deadly dreary that United Artists didn't want to release it, and Ray had to distribute it through Associated Exhibitors.

Standish devoured every asset, every cent, Ray had, and every cent he had been able to borrow. He was flat broke.

Yet on the eve of bankruptcy, he invited all the Hollywood notables he thought would come, and all the people who had worked on the pictures he had produced, to a fantastic bash in his Beverly Hills home. He spared no expense — hiring a string orchestra, liveried servants, serving from jeroboams of champagne purchased from the best bootlegger.

When late-comers brought the first edition of the morning papers, Rob Wagner, who had written scripts for Ray, asked if the headlines about his bankruptcy were true.

"Yes," Ray said shyly, and added: "I'm broke. This is a farewell party."

"How are you going to pay for all this?"

"Credit."

He was not being smart-assed. He was a complete innocent who had been royally taken, like the characters he played best, and was now flat on his face.

The Rays moved out of their large house, which, with all it contained, was auctioned. They moved into an inexpensive apartment, and Clara Ray opened a dress shop on the Sunset Strip.

Thomas Ince then rescued his erstwhile "Wonder Boy." He was motivated not only by pity; he could use a star who could be salvaged on the cheap, and he was sure he knew better than Ray himself how Ray's stardom could be salvaged.

They both agreed the country-boy theme was *passé,* but the theme of innocence triumphant over evil is eternal. So Ince put Ray into *Dynamite Smith,* in which Ray, at the outset a timid reporter, overcomes cowardice and captures a murderer; and then he cast Ray in *Percy* in which Ray, as a mama's boy, is changed by what happens to him into a real man. The essential themes of both pictures are still innocence triumphing over evil, but the surface appearance was sufficiently different to adjust it to the changed mores of post First World War America.

Ray's hopes of salvation were suddenly blasted when Ince was fatally stricken, while weekending on William Randolph Hearst's yacht, and died in his Hollywood home on November 19, 1924. If *Dynamite Smith* and *Percy* are indicative of the new Ray image which Ince was building, Ince's death, even more than *The Courtship of Myles Standish,* doomed Ray to the misery most of the remainder of his life was.

Charles Ray with Joan Crawford in *Paris*.

First, Ray was reduced to working for a poverty-row studio (Chadwick), which put him into two bucolic comedies, *Some Pun'kins* and *Sweet Adeline*. They weren't altogether repulsive, but only because the director was Jerome Storm, who had guided Ray through many of his Paramount and First National releases.

Second, after M-G-M, late in 1925, signed him for four films, one of which, *The Fire Brigade,* had thrilling fire scenes and gave Ray a sympathetic role as the youngest of an Irish firefighting family, M-G-M didn't keep him.

Third, he did three programmers for Producers' Distributing Corporation, playing leads to Leatrice Joy in two and to Marie Prevost in one. His decline was a little less obvious when he did the very human prize-fight romance for Universal called *The Count of Ten,* and his last silent film, United Artists' *The Garden of Eden,* in which he was leading man to orchidaceous Corinne Griffith, and wore white tie and tails. Although directed by Lewis Milestone,

225

who was supposed to despise romantic comedy, *The Garden of Eden* had many Lubitsch-like touches and still has a certain light comedy charm.

But that was the last time Charles Ray had an important role in an important picture. Inability to adjust to sound was not the reason. He had had stage experience; his tenor voice recorded pleasantly; but no producer rushed to gain his services. Talkies were a whole new ball-game, and the companies preferred teams of new players. Ray tried to bring himself to the attention of Hollywood producers by going on tour with a vaudeville sketch. He starred in a stage version of "The Girl I Loved," and for Henry Duffy in a Pacific Coast tour of Channing Pollock's play, "The House Beautiful," which the late Dorothy Parker properly called "The Play Lousy."

His wife and he moved to New York City and lived for a while in one room in a West Side Hotel (the Plymouth, on West 49th Street, now demolished) while he sought stage employment, in the hope that a Broadway engagement would get him back to the top in Hollywood. Many other one-time Hollywood stars were trying to do the same thing — and learned that so far as Broadway was concerned, they were not only has-beens but never-weres.

Ray wrote a play, and "Of Youth and Rogues" was announced for production, but never got into rehearsal so far as I have been able to learn. He wrote a novel and a collection of short stories — "Seven Faces West" and "Writer's Cramp" — but they were amateurish and didn't sell.

In 1934, he and Clara Ray divorced,* and shortly thereafter he married Yvonne Guerin, a very pretty Parisienne. There are one or two vague allusions to her having acting ambitions, and to her having been considerably younger than Ray.

They took up residence in Los Angeles, and Ray made his talking film *début* in a Cary Grant comedy, *Ladies Should Listen*. In it he is a uniformed hotel doorman, and he barely had billing and only a few lines.

He was forty-three years old, and although his shoulders were slightly bowed, his face still shone with the scrubbed, apple-pie look of the perennial juvenile. Said he forthrightly to Louella O. Parsons: "I'm not staging a comeback. I'm a man looking for work."

He was offered bits in features, sometimes actual roles, but after *Hollywood Boulevard* (1936), which featured a lot of one-time stars and in which he had considerable footage, he gave up trying to get work as an actor.

Four years later, a casting director heard he was in dire need and gave him a bit in *A Little Bit of Heaven,* which led to other appearances. The best was as an American business executive in *A Yank in the RAF* (1941). Some critics went out of their way to notice him. Hope flickered for a last time, and he told an interviewer: "This role in *A Yank in the RAF* is a good start for a second career. I thought I had retired, but you can't retire once you've put on the greasepaint. I'm as happy as a kid with a new toy. I'm back in the world I enjoyed for so many years."

---

*For a time Mrs. Ray kept up with her successful dress shop on Sunset, which did not cater to the actress trade but to the more mature Los Angeles society strata. The last time I heard of her was during the Second World War when an agent tried unsuccessfully to negotiate a sale of the re-make rights to *The Girl I Loved*. It is my understanding that she became personal designer and dressmaker to Mrs. Henry Ford, and moved to Detroit.

His happiness was short-lived. In 1942 he was not only forced into bankruptcy a second time, but his second wife died.

He did not long survive her. An impacted tooth, which became infected, sent him to the Cedars of Lebanon Hospital, and there, on November 23, 1943, the infection wrought his death.

"That is the official diagnosis," wrote Louella O. Parsons. "But I think Charles Ray died of a heartbreak that began many years ago, when, broke and discouraged, he realised his bright, particular star had set, and that there was no comeback."

CHARLES RAY FILMOGRAPHY

THE FAVORITE SON (1913). Civil War drama; as Bill who, with his brother Jim, enlists in the Union cause. *Dir:* Francis Ford. *With* Grace Cunard, Francis Ford, Joseph King. *Prod:* Ince (Kay-Bee/Mutual). 2 reels.

THE SHARPSHOOTER (1913). Civil War drama; as a Union sharp-shooter. *With* Grace Cunard. *Prod:* Ince (Broncho/Mutual).

THE BARRIER (1913). One in the "Shorty" series of Westerns; as Sergeant Wade. *With* Shorty Hamilton. *Prod:* (Broncho/Mutual) 2 reels.

THE LOST DISPATCH (1913). Civil War drama; as a young man who enlists in the Confederate Army. *With* Hazel Buckham. *Prod:* Ince (Kay-Bee). 2100 ft.

THE SERGEANT'S SECRET (1913). As Lt. Jim Bryce. *With* Shorty Hamilton, Margaret Thompson, Richard Stanton, William Hadley, Ann Little. *Prod:* Ince (Broncho/Mutual) 2 reels.

THE SINEWS OF WAR (1913). Civil War drama; as a Northern officer. *With* Joe King, Miss Bracken. *Prod:* Ince (Broncho/Mutual) 2 reels.

THE GREY SENTINEL (1913). Civil War drama; as Hal Peters, Confederate soldier. *Dir:* Burton King. *With* J. Barney Sherry, John Emerson, Fred Mace, Mr. Weston, Mr. Cummings, Mr. Bailey, Mr. David. *Prod:* Ince (Broncho/Mutual). 2050 ft.

BREAD CAST UPON THE WATERS (1913). Civil War drama; as Captain Blake, a Union officer, whose company is saved from annihilation by a Southern boy whose pony Blake's men have rescued. *With* Hazel Buckham, Cyril Gottlieb. *Prod:* Ince (Broncho/Mutual). 2 reels.

A SLAVE'S DEVOTION (1913). Civil War drama; as Captain Craig, whose life is saved by his black slave. *Prod:* Ince (Broncho/Mutual). 2 reels.

THE BOOMERANG (1913). Civil War drama; as Lt. John Calhoun, a young Union soldier who had been deserted as a child by his father, and unwittingly becomes the cause of his father's death. *With* Louise Glaum, Gertrude Claire. *Prod:* Ince (Broncho/Mutual). 3000 ft.

THE TRANSGRESSOR (AKA *His Punishment* and *The Puritan*) (1913). As Philip Owen. *Sc:* (based on the novel, "The Scarlet Letter," by Nathaniel Hawthorne). *With* Louise Glaum. *Prod:* Ince (Broncho/Mutual). 2000 ft.

THE QUAKERESS (1913). Puritan drama; as John Hart, the new village schoolmaster, who loves a Quakeress. *With* Louise Glaum. *Prod:* Ince (Broncho/Mutual). 1800 ft.

THE BONDSMAN (1913). Puritan drama; as a Puritan who falls in love with the woman to whom he has been bonded. *With* Hazel Buckham. *Prod:* Ince (Domino/Mutual). 2 reels.

THE EXONERATION (1913). Puritan drama; as Richard, a Puritan falsely accused of embezzlement. *With* Hazel Buckham. *Prod:* Ince (Domino/Mutual). 2 reels.

THE BLACK SHEEP (1913). As Jim Foster. *Prod:* Ince (Broncho/Mutual). 2215 ft.

THE WITCH OF SALEM (1913). Puritan drama; as a young Puritan, Roger Hastings, who loves a girl accused of witchcraft. *With* Clara Williams. *Prod:* Ince (Domino/Mutual). 2 reels.

THE BURIED PAST (1913). In the male lead, Tom Winters. *With* Leona Hutton, Daniel Gilfether, Enid Markey. *Prod:* Ince (Broncho/Mutual.) 2 reels.

SOUL OF THE SOUTH (1913). Civil War drama; as Jim Page, who has enlisted in the Confederate Army, and falls asleep at his post. *With* J. Barney Sherry. *Prod:* Ince (Kay-Bee/Mutual). 2,234 ft.

THE OPEN DOOR (1913). Social drama; as young Blair who works with his sister for a deposed minister in the slums. *Sc:* William H. Clifford. *With* J. Barney Sherry, Hazel Buckham, Thomas Chatterton. *Prod:* Ince (NYMP-Bronco). 2054 ft.

EILEEN OF ERIN (1913). Drama of Irish emigration; as Dennis Morrissey, Irish rebel who escapes the gallows. *Dir:* Scott Sidney. *With* Bessie Barriscale, J. Barney Sherry. *Prod:* Ince (Domino/Mutual). 1949 ft.

A MILITARY JUDAS (1914). Civil War drama; as a Confederate lieutenant who sells military secrets. *Dir:* Jay Hunt and Thomas H. Ince. *Sc:* William H. Clifford. *With* Robyn Adair. *Prod:* Ince (Broncho/Mutual). 3 reels.

THE HOUSE OF BONDAGE (1914). Romantic Puritan drama; as a Puritan in love with a girl accused of witchcraft. *With* Ann Little. *Prod:* Ince (Kay-Bee/Mutual). 3 reels.

FOR HER BROTHER'S SAKE (1914) Drama about the curse of gambling; as John Frye, who is addicted to gambling. *Dir:* Jay Hunt. *With* J. Barney Sherry, Leona Hutton, C. K. French. *Prod:* Ince (Kay-Bee/Mutual). 1 reel.

IN THE TENNESSEE HILLS (1914). Drama of injustice; as a Southern boy who avenges himself at the risk of being hanged. *With* Enid Markey. *Prod:* Ince (Kay-Bee/Mutual).

REPAID (1914) Western about a railroad's fight to put its track through Indian territory; as the fighting hero. *Dir:* Walter Edwards. *With* Rhea Mitchell, William Enfe, Walter Edwards, Charles Edler, Mrs. Howard Swallow. *Prod:* Ince (Mutual).

DESERT GOLD (1914). (Re-issued as *After the Storm)*. Drama of jealousy and vengeance, very much inspired by Frank Norris's "McTeague" (*Greed*); as Hardy, a greedy prospector. *Dir:* Scott Sidney. *With* Clara Williams, Frank Borzage. *Prod:* Ince (Kay-Bee/Mutual). 1998 ft.

FOR THE WEARING OF THE GREEN (1914). Irish drama; as Dennis Grady, who nearly loses his life when he is accused of treachery to the Crown. *With* Ann Little, Fannie Midgley. *Prod:* Ince (Domino/Mutual).

THE PATHS OF GENIUS (1914). Romantic drama of Old England; as a painter who paints an inn sign to pay for a meal. *With* Ann Little, Fannie Midgley, Gordon Mullins, Louis Morrison, Gretchen Lederer. *Prod:* Ince (Kay-Bee/Mutual).

THE RIGHTFUL HEIR (1914). Drama; as one of two sons who fights to inherit his British father's title. *Sc:* Charles Brown (revised by R. V. Spencer and Thomas H. Ince). *With* John Kellar, George Osborne, Roy Laidlaw, Walter Belasco, Ramona Radcliffe. *Prod:* Ince (Kay-Bee/Mutual)

THE SQUIRE'S SON (1914). In the title role. *Dir:* Raymond B. West. *With* Ann Little, George Osborne, J. Barney Sherry, Jerome Storm. *Prod:* Ince (Kay-Bee/Mutual). 2 reels.

SHORTY'S SACRIFICE (1914). A tale of Old Arizona; in a secondary but important role. *With* Shorty Hamilton, Enid Markey, Scott Sidney, Herschel Mayall, Fanny Midgley. *Prod:* Ince (Broncho/Mutual). 2 reels.

THE CARD SHARPS (1914). Drama of two men released from prison; as one of the men. *With* Herschel Mayall, Enid Markey. *Prod:* Ince (NYMP/Domino).

IN THE COW COUNTRY (1914). Western drama; as the cowboy hero. *Sc:* Thomas H. Ince and R. V. Spencer. *With* Enid Markey, Roy Laidlaw. *Prod:* Ince (Kay-Bee/Mutual).

THE LATENT SPARK (1914). Drama of heroism; as a misunderstood youth who becomes a hero. *Sc:* Thomas H. Ince and W. H. Clifford. *With* Gertrude Claire, Fannie Midgley, J. Barney Sherry, Elizabeth Burbridge, William Enfe. *Prod:* Ince (Domino/Mutual).

DESERT THIEVES (1914). Western; in the lead role. *With* Gretchen Lederer, Mrs. Howard Swallow, Frank Keenan, Tsuru Aoki. *Prod:* Ince (Broncho/Mutual). 2 reels.

THE CURSE OF HUMANITY (1914). Drama of alcoholism; as an alcoholic who is able to reform. *Dir:* Scott Sidney. *Sc:* Thomas H. Ince and W. H. Clifford. *With* Elizabeth Burbridge, Fannie Midgley, Harry Keenan, Thelma Salter, Larry Smith, Gretchen Lederer. *Prod:* Ince (Domino/Mutual). 2 reels.

THE CITY (1914). Drama of big business; as a son who saves his father from financial ruin. *Dir:* Raymond B. West. *Sc:* Thomas H. Ince and W. H. Clifford. *Prod:* Ince (Kay-Bee/Mutual).

RED MASK (1914). Western drama; as an outlaw who daringly masquerades as the secret service man out to capture him. *With* Clara Simpson. *Prod:* Ince (Broncho/Mutual). 990 ft.

THE THUNDERBOLT (1914). Drama; in the lead. *With* Enid Markey, Margaret Thompson, Arthur Jarret, Fanny Midgley. *Prod:* Ince (Domino/Mutual).

THE GANGSTERS AND THE GIRL (1914). Underworld drama; in the lead as a detective posing as a crook. *With* Elizabeth Burbridge, Arthur Jarret, Thomas H. Ince, Margaret Thompson. *Prod:* Ince (Kay-Bee/Mutual).

THE SILVER BELL (1914). In the male lead role. *With* Enid Markey, Roy Laidlaw, Gertrude Claire, Joseph J. Dowling. *Prod:* Ince (Domino/Mutual).

228

JOE HIBBARD'S CLAIM (1914). Western of the mining country; as an ore thief, Joe Hibbard. *Prod:* Ince (Broncho/Mutual). 1017 ft.

ONE OF THE DISCARD (1914). Western drama; as an Easterner who falls in love with a dance-hall girl. *With* Gladys Brockwell, Jay Hunt, Elizabeth Burbridge. *Prod:* Ince (Kay-Bee/Mutual).

WORD OF HIS PEOPLE (1914). Romantic melodrama of the West; as the son of a Western fort's commander. *With* J. Barney Sherry, Webster Campbell, Elizabeth Burbridge. *Prod:* Ince (Kay-Bee/Mutual).

THE POWER OF THE ANGELUS (1914). In the male lead. *With* Enid Markey, Walter Edwards, J. Barney Sherry. *Prod:* Ince (Domino/Mutual).

THE FORTUNES OF WAR (1914). Romance of the Mexican War; as one of two suitors for the heroine's favour. *Dir:* Jay Hunt. *With* Enid Markey, Thomas Kurihara, Herschel Mayall, Jack Nelson, Louis Morrison. *Prod:* Ince.

THE CITY OF DARKNESS (1914). Murder and crime drama; as Donald, who barely escapes the electric chair for a crime he didn't commit. *With* Enid Markey, Gertrude Claire, Walter Edwards, Leona Hutton, Herschel Mayall. *Prod:* Ince.

THE FRIEND (1914). Romantic tragedy; as a young society artist who is responsible for his model's suicide. *With* Enid Markey, Webster Campbell. *Prod:* Ince (Domino/Mutual).

NOT OF THE FLOCK (1914). Romantic drama; as a young minister seeking a wife, who chooses the saloon keeper's daughter. *With* Enid Markey, Webster Thompson, Charles K. French, Webster Campbell. *Prod:* Ince (Domino/Mutual).

THE GRUDGE (1915). Western drama; as a young man who challenges a Westerner to a fight. *Dir:* William S. Hart. *With* William S. Hart, Margaret Thompson, Thomas Kurihara. *Prod:* Ince (Broncho/Mutual).

THE WELLS OF PARADISE (1915). Drama of the oil workers vs. the cattlemen; as a young man who strikes oil and is determined to keep his rights. *Dir:* Tom Chatterton. *With* Gertrude Claire, Thelma Salter, Roy Laidlaw, Ethel Ullman. *Prod:* Ince.

THE CUP OF LIFE (1915). Morality drama of two sisters who drink from the cup of life, one wisely, the other foolishly; as the young man who is spurned by the foolish sister. *Dir:* Raymond B. West. *Sc:* Thomas H. Ince. *With* Bessie Barriscale, Enid Markey, Gertrude Claire, Louise Glaum, Frank Borzage, Jerome Storm, J. Barney Sherry, Arthur Maude, Harry Keenan, Howard Hickman. *Prod:* Ince.

THE SPIRIT OF THE BELL (1915). (Re-issued as *The Mystery of the Mission*). Romantic drama of the Southwest; as the Mexican foreman of the ranch. *Dir:* Jay Hunt. *Sc:* Thomas H. Ince and W. H. Clifford. *With* Enid Markey, Jack Nelson, Herschel Mayall. *Prod:* Ince (NYMP).

THE RENEGADE (1915). (Re-issued as *African Love*). Romantic melodrama of Africa; as the young Englishman who is saved by a slave girl. *Dir:* Charles Swickard. *With* Louise Glaum, Ethel Ullman, Herschel Mayall. *Prod:* Ince (Broncho/Mutual).

THE SHOAL LIGHT (1915) (Re-issued as *After the Storm*). Romantic drama of the sea; as a young sea captain. *Dir:* Scott Sidney. *With* Estelle Allen, Joseph Dowling, Roy Laidlaw. *Prod:* Ince (Domino/Mutual).

THE CONVERSION OF FROSTY BLAKE (1915). Romantic Western drama; as a tubercular young minister. *With* Louise Glaum, William S. Hart. *Prod:* Ince (Broncho/Mutual).

THE ACE OF HEARTS (1915). (Re-issued as *The Clue*) (1915). Canadian Northwest murder melodrama; as a French-Canadian trapper falsely accused of murder. *With* Ethel Ullman, Walter Edwards, J. Frank Burke, Leo Willis. *Prod:* Ince (Domino/Mutual).

THE COWARD (1915). Drama of the Civil War; as Frank Winslow, a fear-obsessed youth who deserts, then vindicates himself. *Dir:* Reginald Barker. *Sc:* Thomas H. Ince. *With* Frank Keenan, Gertrude Claire, Margaret Gibson, Nick Cogley, Charles K. French. *Prod:* Ince-Triangle. 5500 ft.

CITY OF THE DEAD (AKA, *The Forbidden Adventure*). Romantic drama of Arabia; as an adventurer who claims a priestess of her tribe. *With* Louise Glaum, Herschel Mayall. *Prod:* Ince-Triangle. 5 reels.

THE PAINTED SOUL (1915). (Re-issued as *The Straight Road*). Romantic drama; as Edward Barnes, a painter who falls in love with his model, a streetwalker. *Dir:* Scott Sidney. *With* Bessie Barriscale, Milton Ross, Truly Shattuck. *Prod:* Ince-Triangle. 5 reels.

PEGGY (1916). Romantic comedy; as Colin the scapegoat son of the heroine's Scottish uncle. *Dir/Sc:* Thomas H. Ince. *With* Billie Burke, William Desmond, William H. Thompson, Gertrude Claire, Nona Thomas, Truly Shattuck, Claire Du Brey. *Prod:* Ince-Triangle. 5 reels.

THE DIVIDEND (1916) (Re-issued as *The Curse of the Poppy*). Social drama of the tragedy of a rich man's son; as the unfortunate son. *Sc:* C. Gardner Sullivan. *With* William H. Thompson, Ethel Ullman, Margaret Thompson. *Prod:* Ince-Triangle. 5 reels.

THE DESERTER (1916). Western drama; as Lt. Parker, who deserts his Army post, but proves himself a hero. *Dir:* Walter Edwards. *Sc:* R. V. Spencer (from a story by Thomas H. Ince). *With* Rita Stanwood, Wedgwood Nowell, Hazel Belford, Joseph Dowling. *Prod:* Ince-Triangle. 5 reels.

HONOR THY NAME (1916). Drama; as Castleton Jr., the only son of a proud Southern family, who marries a notorious Broadway gold-digger. *With* Frank Keenan, Louise Glaum, Blanche White, Gertrude Claire, George Fisher, Dorcas Matthews, Agnes Herring, Harvey Clarke. *Prod:* Ince-Triangle. 5 reels.

HOME (1916). Domestic comedy; as Bob Wheaton, who falls for a vulgar chorus girl. *With* Bessie Barriscale, George Fisher, Louise Glaum, Clara Williams, Agnes Herring, Thomas S. Guise, Joseph Dowling. *Prod:* Ince-Triangle. 5 reels.

A CORNER IN COLLEENS (AKA, GB, *Four Irish Girls*) (1916). Romantic comedy; as a young man who goes to Ireland to claim an inheritance, and marries an Irish colleen. *Dir:* Charles Miller. *Sc:* C. Gardner Sullivan. *With* Bessie Barriscale, Margery Wilson, Roy Neill, Agnes Herring, Walter Perry, Alice Taafe (Terry), Charles K. French, Alice Lawrence. *Prod:* Ince-Triangle. 5 reels.

THE WOLF WOMAN (AKA, *Dust*) (1916). drama of the destructive power of an evil woman; as a young man who becomes the victim of a vampire. (1916). *Sc:* C. Gardner Sullivan. *With* Louise Glaum, Howard Hickman, Marjory Temple, Gertrude Claire, Wyndham Standing. *Prod:* Ince-Triangle. 5 reels.

PLAIN JANE (1916). Romantic comedy; as Frank Sophomore Adams, working his way through college, who falls in love with an ugly-duckling housemaid. *Dir:* Charles Miller. *Sc:* C. Gardner Sullivan. *With* Bessie Barriscale, Mabel Johnson, Fannie Midgley. *Prod:* Ince-Triangle. 5 reels.

THE HONORABLE ALGY (1916). Romantic comedy; as the Honourable Algy, youngest of the Monteiths, sent to America to wed an heiress. *Dir:* Raymond B. West. *With* Margaret Thompson, Howard Hickman, Margery Wilson, Albert Cody, Jerome Storm, Charles K. French, Louise Brownell, Thomas V. Guise, Katherine Kirkwood, Walt Whitman. *Prod:* Ince-Triangle. 5 reels.

THE WEAKER SEX (1917). Courtroom murder mystery; as young Harding, son of the public prosecutor, defended on a murder charge by his father's lawyer-wife. *Dir:* Raymond B. West. *Sc:* Monte M. Katterjohn (from a story by Alice C. Brown). *With* Dorothy Dalton, Louise Glaum, Margaret Thompson, Robert McKim, Charles K.

French, J. Barney Sherry. *Prod:* Ince-Triangle. 5 reels.

BACK OF THE MAN (1917). Drama of the power of a woman; as a man who becomes somebody because of the woman he loves. *Dir:* Reginald Barker. *Sc:* Monte M. Katterjohn. *With* Dorothy Dalton, J. Barney Sherry, Margaret Thompson, Jack Livingston. *Prod:* Ince-Triangle. 5 reels.

THE PINCH HITTER (AKA, GB, *The Dud*) (1917). Baseball romantic comedy; as Parker, who, because of a woman, becomes a baseball hero. *Dir:* Victor Schertzinger. *Sc:* C. Gardner Sullivan. *With* Sylvia Breamer, Joseph Dowling, Jerome Storm, Darrell Foss, Louise Durham. *Prod:* Ince-Triangle. 5 reels.

THE MILLIONAIRE VAGRANT (1917). Comedy drama; as Steven du Peyster, millionaire, who bets he can live on six dollars a week. *Dir:* Victor Schertzinger. *Sc:* J. G. Hawks. *With* Sylvia Breamer, J. Barney Sherry, Dorcas Matthews, Agnes Herring, Walt Whitman, John Gilbert. *Prod:* Ince-Triangle. 5 reels.

THE CLODHOPPER (1917). Bucolic and backstage comedy drama; as Everett, a farm boy who goes to the city and becomes a hit in the theatre. *Dir:* Victor Schertzinger. *Sc:* Monte M. Katterjohn. *With* Margery Wilson, Charles K. French, Lydia Knott, Thomas B. Guise. *Prod:* Ince-Triangle. 5 reels.

THE SON OF HIS FATHER (1917). Comedy drama of big business; as Gordon Carbhoy. *Dir:* Victor Schertzinger. *Sc:* (from a story by Ridgewall Cullum). *With* Vola Vale, Charles K. French, Robert McKim, George Nichols, John P. Lockney, George Hoffman. *Prod:* Ince-Paramount. 5 reels.

HIS MOTHER'S BOY (1918). Romantic comedy; as Matthew Denton, New England youth who goes West to resolve a fraud. *Dir:* Victor Schertzinger. *Sc:* (from a story, "When Life Was Marked Down," by Rupert Hughes). *With* Doris Lee, William Elmer, Josef Swickard, Jerome Storm, Gertrude Claire, Lydia Knott. Ince-Paramount. 5 reels.

THE HIRED MAN (1918). Bucolic drama; as Ezry, the good-natured hired man on a farm. *Dir:* Victor Schertzinger. *Sc:* Julien Josephson (from his story, "Ezry"). *With* Doris Lee, Charles K. French, Carl Ullman, Gilbert Gordon, Lydia Knott. *Prod:* Ince-Paramount. 5 reels.

THE FAMILY SKELETON (1918). Romantic drama; as Billy Bates, who thinks he has inherited the family curse — drinking. *Dir:* Victor Schertzinger. *Sc:* Bert Lennon. *With* Sylvia Breamer, Andrew Arbuckle, William Elmer, Otto Hoffman, Jack Dyer. *Prod:* Ince-Paramount. 5 reels.

CHARLES RAY

PLAYING THE GAME (1918). Romantic drama; as a playboy who settles down into being a man of importance. *Dir:* Victor Schertzinger. *Sc:* Julien Josephson. *With* Doris Lee, Robert McKim, Harry Rattenberry, Charles Perley, Lillian Lorraine. *Prod:* Ince-Paramount. 5 reels.

HIS OWN HOME TOWN (1918). Smalltown drama; as the playboy son of a minister. *Dir:* Victor Schertzinger. *Sc:* (from a story by Larry Evans). *With* Katherine MacDonald, Andrew Arbuckle, Charles K. French, Otto Hoffman, John P. Lockney, Carl Forms, Milton Ross. *Prod:* Ince-Paramount. 5 reels.

THE CLAWS OF THE HUN (1918). Wartime propaganda drama; as John Stanton, unjustly accused of being a slacker, who uncovers a German espionage plot. *Dir:* Victor Schertzinger. *Sc:* R. Cecil Smith (from a story by Ella Stuart Carson). *With* Jane Novak, Robert McKim, Dorcas Matthews, Melbourne McDowell, Mollie McConnell. Working title: *The Hand of the Hun. Prod:* Ince-Paramount. 5 reels.

A NINE O'CLOCK TOWN (1918). Smalltown romantic comedy; as David Clary, saved from a city vamp by the town's clever little corset model. *Dir/Sc:* Victor Schertzinger. *With* Jane Novak, Otto Hoffman, Gertrude Claire, Catherine Young, Dorcas Matthews. *Prod:* Ince-Paramount. 5 reels.

THE LAW OF THE NORTH (1919). Northwest melodrama; as Alain de Montcalm, known as "L'aiglon," son of a French Canadian trading station commandant. *Dir:* Irvin V. Willat. *Sc:* (from a story by Ella Stuart Carson). *With* Doris Lee, Robert McKim, Gloria Hope, Charles K. French, Manuel Ojeda. *Prod:* Ince-Paramount. 5 reels.

STRING BEANS (1919). Smalltown romantic comedy; as Toby Watkins, who runs away from his father's farm to make it big as a newspaperman. *Dir:* Victor Schertzinger. *Sc:* Julien Josephson. *With* Jane Novak, Donald MacDonald, John P. Lockney, Al Filson, Otto Hoffman. *Prod:* Ince-Paramount. 5 reels.

THE GIRL DODGER (1919). Romantic comedy; as Cuthbert Trotman, who has literary aspirations. *Dir:* Jerome Storm. *Sc:* J. G. Hawks. *With* Doris Lee, Hallam Cooley, Jack Nelson, Leota Lorraine. *Prod:* Ince-Paramount. 5 reels.

THE SHERIFF'S SON (1919). Romantic melodrama; as Royal Beardry, who proves that he has the courage of his sheriff father. *Dir:* Victor Schertzinger. *Sc:* J. W. Hawks (from a story by William McLeod Raine). *With* Seena Owen, Charles K. French, John P. Lockney, Clyde Benson, Otto Hoffman, Lamar Johnstone. *Prod:* Ince-Paramount. 5 reels.

GREASED LIGHTING (1919). Romantic comedy; as Andy Fletcher, country blacksmith, who is mad about racing cars. *Dir:* Jerome Storm. *Sc:* Julien Josephson. *With* Wanda Hawley, Robert McKim, Willis Marks, Bert Woodruff, John P. Lockney, Otto Hoffman. *Prod:* Ince-Paramount. 5 reels.

THE BUSHER (1919). Romantic baseball comedy; as Ben, who becomes a Big Leaguer. *Dir:* Jerome Storm. *Sc:* Earl Snell. *With* Colleen Moore, John Gilbert, Jay Morley, Otto Hoffman, *Prod:* Ince-Paramount. 5 reels.

HAY FOOT, STRAW FOOT (1919). Romantic comedy about a small-town boy who becomes a soldier; as Ulysses S. Grant Briggs. *Dir:* Jerome Storm. *Sc:* Julien Josephson. *With* Doris Lee, Spottiswoode Aitken, William Conklin, John P. Lockney. *Prod:* Ince-Paramount. 5 reels.

BILL HENRY (1919). Romantic smalltown comedy; as Bill Henry. *Dir:* Jerome Storm. *Sc:* Julien Josephson. (from a story by Lois Zellner). *With* Edith Roberts, William Carroll, Bert Woodruff, Mrs. Jennie Lee Courtright, Walter Perkins, Walter Hiers. *Prod:* Ince-Paramount. 5 reels.

CROOKED STRAIGHT (1919). Drama of crime in a big city; as a poor boy in a city who becomes a professional safe cracksman's partner. *Dir:* Jerome Storm. *Sc:* Julien Josephson. *With* Margery Wilson, Wade Boteler, Gordon Mullins. *Prod:* Ince-Paramount. 5 reels.

THE EGG CRATE WALLOP (AKA, GB, *The Knock-Out Blow*) (1920). Prizefighting romantic comedy; as Jim Kelly, who goes from country express office worker to boxer. *Dir:* Jerome Storm. *Sc:* Julien Josephson. *With* Colleen Moore, Otto Hoffman, John P. Lockney, Jack Connolly. *Prod:* Ince-Paramount. 5 reels.

RED HOT DOLLARS (1920). Romantic comedy; as Tod Burke, adopted son of a big business man. *Dir:* Jerome Storm. *Sc:* Julien Josephson. *With* Gladys George, Charles H. Mailes, William Conklin, Mollie McConnell. *Prod:* Ince-Paramount. 5 reels.

ALARM CLOCK ANDY (1920). Romantic comedy; as Andy, bashful motor truck salesman. *Dir:* Jerome Storm. *Sc:* Agnes Christine Johnston. *With* Millicent Foster, George Webb, Thomas B. Guise, Andrew Robson. *Prod:* Ince-Paramount. 5 reels.

PARIS GREEN (1920). Romantic comedy; as Luther Green, who returns to his New Jersey hometown, followed soon by a French girl, who woos him. *Dir:* Jerome Storm. *Sc:* Julien Josephson. *With* Ann May, Bert Woodruff, Gertrude Claire, Donald MacDonald, Norris Johnson, William Courtwright, Ida Lewis, Otto Hoffman. *Prod:* Ince-Paramount. 5 reels.

45 MINUTES FROM BROADWAY (1920). Romantic comedy; as the pal of a playboy heir who falls in love with his friend's housemaid. *Dir:* Joseph De Grasse. *Sc:* Agnes Christine Johnston and Bernard McConville (from the play by George M. Cohan). *With* Dorothy Devore, Hazel Howell, Donald MacDonald, Eugenie Besserer, Harry Myers. *Prod:* First National. 6 reels.

THE VILLAGE SLEUTH (1920). Comedy; as William, a farmer's son who wants to be a detective. *Dir:* Jerome Storm. *Sc:* Agnes Christine Johnston. *With* Winifred Westover, Donald MacDonald, Dick Rush, George H. Hernandez, Betty Schade, Lew Morrison. Working title: *Watch Out, William! Prod:* Ince-Paramount. 5 reels.

PEACEFUL VALLEY (1920). Bucolic drama; as Hosiah Howe, a village boy who bests a city villain who has designs on both his sweetheart and sister. *Dir:* Jerome Storm. *Sc:* Agnes Christine Johnston (from a play by Edward E. Kidder). *With* Ann May, Harry Myers, Charlotte Pierce, Lydia Knott, Lincoln Stedman, Walter Perkins, William Courtwright, Vincent Hamilton, Jesse Herring, Melba Lorraine, Ida Lewis. *Prod:* First National. 6 reels.

HOMER COMES HOME (1920). Romantic drama of a country boy who comes home a success; as Homer Cavender. *Dir:* Jerome Storm. *Sc:* Agnes Christine Johnston (from a story by Alexander Hull). *With* Priscilla Bonner, Otto Hoffman, Ralph McCullough, Walter Higby, John H. Eliot, Harry Hyde, Gus Leonard, Joe Hazelton, Bert Woodruff, Lew Morrison. *Prod:* Ince-Paramount. 5 reels.

AN OLD-FASHIONED BOY (1920). Romantic comedy; as David Warrington, who finds he has to learn some new-fashioned tricks. *Dir:* Jerome Storm. *Sc:* Agnes Christine Johnston. *With* Ethel Shannon, Hallam Cooley, Wade Boteler, Grace Morse, Alfred Allen, Gloria Joy, Frankie Lee, Virginia Brown. *Prod:* Ince-Paramount. 5 reels.

NINETEEN AND PHYLLIS (1921). Romantic comedy; as Andrew Jackson Cavanaugh, who finds it hard to be a Beau Brummel on only $18 a week. *Dir:* Joseph De Grasse. *Sc:* Isabel Johnston and Bernard McConville (from a story by Frederick Stowers). *With* Clara Horton, Lincoln Stedman, George Nichols, Frank Norcross, Cora Drew. *Prod:* Ince-Paramount. 5 reels.

THE OLD SWIMMIN' HOLE (1921). A rustic idyll of Americana; as Ezra. *Dir:* Joseph De Grasse. *Sc:* Bernard McConville (from the narrative poem by James Whitcomb Riley). *With* Laura La Plante, Marjorie Prevost, James Gordon, Charlotte Pierce, Lincoln Stedman, Lon Poff, Blanche Rose. There were

no sub-titles in this film; it was pure pantomine. *Prod:* First National. 5 reels.

SCRAP IRON (1921). Prizefight drama; as John Steel, who becomes a top pugilist and learns that success brings loneliness. *Dir/Sc:* Charles Ray (from a story by Charles E. Van Loan). *With* Vera Stedman, Lydia Knott, Tom Wilson, Tom O'Brien, Stanton Heck, Charles Wheelock, Claude Berkeley. *Prod:* First National. 7 reels.

A MIDNIGHT BELL (1921). Romantic comedy; as Martin Tripp, who outwits a band of bogus ghosts. *Dir:* Charles Ray. *Sc:* Richard Andres (from the play by Charles H. Hoyt). *With* Doris Pawn, Donald MacDonald, Van Dyke Brooke, Clyde McCoy, Jess Herring, S. J. Bingham. *Prod:* First National. 6 reels.

TWO MINUTES TO GO (1921). College football romantic comedy; as Chester Burnett. *Dir:* Charles Ray. *Sc:* Richard Andres. *With* Mary Anderson, Lionel Barrymore, Tom Wilson, Lincoln Stedman, Trueman Vandyke, Burt Woodruff, Phil Dunham. *Prod:* First National. 6 reels.

R.S.V.P. (1921). Romantic comedy; as Richard Morgan, who becomes a successful artist. *Dir:* Charles Ray. *Sc:* Rob Wagner. *With* Jean Calhoun, Florence Oberle, Harry Myers, Tom McGuire, Robert Grey, William Courtwright, Ida Schumaker. *Prod:* First National. 6 reels.

THE BARNSTORMER (1922). Backstage romantic comedy; as Joel ("Utility"), who is stagestruck. *Dir:* Charles Ray. *Sc:* Richard Andres. *With* Charlotte Pierce, Wilfred Lucas, Florence Oberle, George Nichols, Blanche Rose, Lionel Belmore. *Prod:* First National. 6 reels.

GAS, OIL AND WATER (1922). Romantic espionage drama; as George Oliver Watson, U. S. secret service agent, posing as a gasoline station attendant. *Dir:* Charles Ray. *Sc:* Richard Andres. *With* Charlotte Pierce, Otto Hoffman, Robert Grey, William Carroll, Dick Sutherland. *Prod:* First National. 5 reels.

THE DEUCE OF SPADES (1922). Romantic comedy Western; as Amos, forced to become a two-gun man. *Dir:* Charles Ray. *Sc:* Richard Andres (from a story, "The Weight of the Last Straw," by Charles E. Van Loan). *With* Marjorie Maurice, Lincoln Plummer, Phil Dunham, Andrew Arbuckle, Dick Sutherland, Jack Richarson, John P. Lockney, Gus Leonard, William Courtwright. *Prod:* First National. 5 reels.

SMUDGE (1922). Romance of Southern California and the salvation of an orange crop from frost; as Stephen Stanton, who has invented a smokeless heater. *Dir:* Charles and

Albert Ray. *Sc:* Rob Wagner. *With* Ora Carewe, Charles K. French, Florence Oberle, John P. Lockney, Blanche Rose, Lloyd Bacon, Ralph McCullough. *Prod:* First National. 5 reels.

ALIAS JULIUS CAESAR (1922). A comedy of errors, as Billy Barnes. *Dir:* Charles Ray. *Sc:* Richard Andres. *With* Barbara Bedford, William Scott, Carl Miller, Wallace Beery, Robert Hernandez, Harvey Clark, Milton Ross, Phil Dunham, Eddie Gribbon, Gus Thomas, Tom Wilson, S. J. Bingham. *Prod:* First National. 5 reels.

A TAILOR-MADE MAN (1922). Romantic comedy; as John Paul Bart, clothes presser, who becomes an important business man. *Dir:* Joseph De Grasse. *Sc:* Albert Ray (from the play by Harry James Smith). *With* Jacqueline Logan, Thomas Ricketts, Ethel Grandin, Kate Lester, Douglas Gerrard, Stanton Heck, Victor Potel, Frank Butler, Nellie Saunders, Eddie Gribbon, Thomas Jefferson, Fred Thompson, Edythe Chapman, Charlotte Pierce, Irene Lentz. *Prod:* United Artists. 9 reels. (Re-made, 1931, talkie with William Haines.)

THE GIRL I LOVED (1923). A rural tale of Indiana; as John Middleton, who experiences his first disappointment in love. *Dir:* Joseph De Grasse. *Sc:* Harry L. Decker (from an adaptation by Albert Ray of the narrative poem by James Whitcomb Riley). *With* Patsy Ruth Miller, Ramsey Wallace, Edythe Chapman, William Courtwright, Charlotte Woods, Gus Leonard, Lon Poff, F. B. Phillips, George Marion. *Prod:* United Artists. 8 reels.

THE COURTSHIP OF MYLES STANDISH (1923). Classic Pilgrim romance; as John Alden, doing the courting for Standish. *Dir:* Frederic Sullivan. *Sc:* Albert Ray (from the narrative poem by Henry Wadsworth Longfellow). *With* Enid Bennett, Alyn Warren. *Prod:* Associated Exhibitors. 9 reels.

DYNAMITE SMITH (AKA, GB, *The Agony of Fear*). (1924). suspense drama of how a timid newspaper reporter overcame fear; as Gladstone Smith. *Dir:* Ralph Ince. *Sc:* C. Gardner Sullivan. *With* Jacqueline Logan, Wallace Beery, Bessie Love, Lydia Knott, S. D. Wilcox, Russell Powell, Adelbert Knott. *Prod:* Ince-Pathé. 7 reels.

PERCY (1925). Action drama of how a "mama's boy" became a man; as Percival Rogeen. *Dir:* R. William Neill. *Sc:* Eve Unsell and J. G. Hawks (from a novel, "The Desert Fiddler," by William H. Handy). *With* Barbara Bedford, Louise Dresser, Charles Murray, Betty Blythe, Joseph Kilgour, Victor McLaglen. *Prod:* Ince-Pathé. 6 reels.

SOME PUN'KINS (1925). Bucolic comedy ; as Lem Blossom, country boy. *Dir:* Jerome Storm. *Sc:* Bert Woodruff and Charles E. Banks. *With* Duane Thompson, George Fawcett, Fannie Midgley, Bert Woodruff, Hallam Cooley, William Courtwright, Ida Lewis. *Prod:* Chadwick. 6 reels.

BRIGHT LIGHTS (1925). Romantic comedy with backstage background; as Tom Corbin, New Jersey farm boy, who follows a chorus girl he loves to Manhattan. *Dir:* Robert Z. Leonard. *Sc:* Jessie Burns and Lew Liston (from a story by Richard Connell). *With* Pauline Starke, Lilyan Tashman, Lawford Davidson, Ned Sparks. *Prod:* Metro-Goldwyn. 7 reels.

SWEET ADELINE (1926). Backstage story; as Ben Wilson, country boy, who gets a job in a city cabaret and is a hit, singing the title song. *Dir:* Jerome Storm. *Sc;* Charles E. Banks. *With* Gertrude Olmstead, Jack Clifford, John P. Lockney, Ida Lewis, Sibyl Johnston, Gertrude Short. *Prod:* Chadwick. 7 reels.

THE AUCTION BLOCK (1926). Romantic comedy; as Bob Wharton, son of a millionaire, who makes his marriage to a beauty contest winner work. *Dir:* Hobart Henley. *Sc:* Frederic and Fanny Hatton (from the novel by Rex Beach). *With* Eleanor Boardman, Sally O'Neil, Ernest Gillen, Charles Clary, David Torrence, Forrest Seabury. *Prod:* M-G-M. 7 reels.

PARIS (1926). Romantic drama; as Jerry, a rich American in Paris, who falls in love with a dancing girl from Montmartre. *Dir/Sc:* Edmund Goulding. *With* Joan Crawford, Douglas Gilmore, Michael Visaroff, Rose Dione, Jean Galeron. *Prod:* M-G-M. 6 reels.

THE FIRE BRIGADE (1927). Epic drama of a big city's fire department; as Terry O'Neil, firefighter. *Dir:* William Nigh. *Sc:* Kate Corbelay. *With* May McAvoy, Holmes E. Herbert, Tom O'Brien, Eugenie Besserer, Warner P. Richmond, Bert Woodruff, Vivia Ogden, DeWitt Jennings, Dan Mason, Erwin Connelly, James Bradbury. *Prod:* M-G-M. 9 reels. Technicolor and tinted sequences. (Compare listing in May McAvoy filmography.)

THE FLAG MAKER (1927). Drama of a man who went to fight in the First World War; as the veteran who comes back to his smalltown home to find his girl and job pre-empted. This was the first of George K. Spoor's stereoscopic "Natural Vision Motion Pictures." It had a very limited showing and a disappointing reception, but it is important as one of the first experiments in 3-D on the screen. *Dir:* J. Stuart Blackton. *Sc:* Marion Constance Blackton (from a story, "The American," by Jewel Spencer, the theme of which had been suggested by Theodore Roosevelt). Exteriors filmed in San Diego, California. *With* Bessie Love, Ward Crane, Maurice Murphy, Evelyn

MORE FROM HOLLYWOOD

Selbie, Dickie Brandon, John P. Lockney, Banks Winter. *Prod:* Spoor-Blackton. 6 reels.

NOBODY'S WIDOW (1927). Romantic farce comedy; as the Honourable John Clayton. *Dir:* Donald Crisp. *Sc:* Clara Beranger and Douglas Z. Doty (from the play by Avery Hopwood). *With* Leatrice Joy, Phyllis Haver, David Butler, Dot Farley, Fritzi Ridgeway, Charles West. *Prod:* PDC. 7 reels.

GETTING GERTIE'S GARTER (1927). Romantic farce; as Ken Walrick, who finally retrieves the jewelled garter bearing a photo of himself which he had indiscretly bestowed once upon a girl friend. *Dir:* E. Mason Hopper. *Sc:* F. McGrew Willis (from the play by Avery Hopwood and Wilson Collison). *With* Marie Prevost, Harry Myers, Sally Rand, Fritzi Ridgeway, Lila Leslie, William Orlamond, Dell Henderson, Franklin Pangborn. *Prod:* PDC. 7 reels.

VANITY (1927). Romantic melodrama; as Lloyd Van Courtland, who loves a vain society girl. *Dir:* Donald Crisp. *Sc:* Douglas Z. Doty. *With* Leatrice Joy, Alan Hale, Noble Johnson, Maym Kelso, Helen Lee Worthing. *Prod:* PDC. 6 reels.

THE COUNT OF TEN (1928). Prizefight drama; as Johnny McKinney, champ fighter, who has a freeloading family. *Dir:* James Flood. *Sc:* Harry Hoyt (from a story by Gerald Beaumont). *With* Jobyna Ralston, James Gleason, Edythe Chapman, Arthur Lake, Charles Sellon. *Prod:* Universal. 6 reels.

THE GARDEN OF EDEN (1928). Sophisticated romantic comedy; as Richard Spanyi, a Riviera Prince Charming. *Dir:* Lewis Milestone. *Sc:* Hans Kraly (from a play by Rudolph Bernauer and Rudolph Osterreicher). *With* Corinne Griffith, Louise Dresser, Lowell Sherman, Maud George, Edward Martindel, Freeman Wood, Hank Mann. *Prod:* United Artists. 8 reels.

THE BRIDE'S BEREAVEMENT (1932). Farce; as the comedy lead. *Dir:* Robert F. Hill. *Sc:* Walter Weems and Edward Earle. *With* Aileen Pringle. *Prod:* RKO. 2 reels.

LADIES SHOULD LISTEN (1934). Romantic comedy; as Henri, a doorman. *Dir:* Frank Tuttle. *Sc:* Claude Binyon and Frank Butler (from a play by Alfred Savoir and Guy Bolton). *With* Cary Grant, Frances Drake, Edward Everett Horton, Nydia Westman, Rosita Moreno, George Barbier, Charles E. Arnt, Clara Lou (Ann) Sheridan. *Prod:* Paramount. 61m.

TICKET TO A CRIME (1934). Detective comedy drama; as Courtney Mallory. Dir: Lew Collins. *Sc:* Charles A. Logue (from a story by Carroll J. Daly). *With* Ralph Graves,

Lois Wilson, Lola Lane, James Burke, Edward Earle. *Prod:* Beacon. 67m.

SCHOOL FOR GIRLS (1935). Social drama of a reform school; in a key supporting role. *Dir:* William Nigh. *Sc:* Albert De Mond (from a story, "Our Undisciplined Daughters," by Reginald Wright Kauffman). *With* Sidney Fox, Paul Kelly, Lois Wilson, Lucille La Verne, Dorothy Lee, Toby Wing, Dorothy Appleby, Lona Andre, Russell Hopton, Barbara Weeks, Kathleen Burke, Anna Q. Nilsson, Purnell Pratt, Robert Warwick, William Farnum, Dawn O'Day (Anne Shirley), Myrtle Stedman, Helene Chadwick, Helen Foster, Fred Kelsey, Edward Le Saint. *Prod:* Liberty. 66m.

WELCOME HOME (1935). Comedy; in a supporting role. *Dir:* James Tinling. *Sc:* Marion Orth and Arthur Horman (from a story by Arthur Horman). *With* James Dunn, Arline Judge, Raymond Walburn, Rosina Lawrence, William Frawley, Charles Sellon, Frank Melton, George Meeker, James Burke, Arthur Hoyt. *Prod:* Fox. 73m.

JUST MY LUCK (1936). Comedy drama; as Homer Crowe, who invents a formula for making synthetic rubber. *Dir:* Russell Ray Heinz. *Sc:* Wallace Sullivan and Scott E. Cleethorpe (from a story by Sullivan). *With* Anne Grey, Eddie Nugent, John Roche, Snub Pollard, Matthew Betz. *Prod:* Corona-Guaranteed. 65m.

HOLLYWOOD BOULEVARD (1936). Romantic drama about Hollywood; as an assistant director. *Dir:* Robert Florey. *Sc:* Marguerite Roberts (from a story by Faith Thomas). *With* John Halliday, Marsha Hunt, Robert Cummings, C. Henry Gordon, Esther Ralston, Esther Dale, Frieda Inescort, Albert Conti, Rita La Roy, Francis X. Bushman, Maurice Costello, Betty Compson, Mae Marsh, Roy D'Arcy, Creighton Hale, Ruth Clifford, Edmund Burns, Mabel Forrest, Herbert Rawlinson, Jane Novak, Bryant Washburn, William Desmond, Jack Mulhall, Frank Mayo, Jack Mower, Richard Powell, Charles Morton, Harry Myers, Tom Kennedy, Pat O'Malley, Thomas Jackson, Oscar Apfel, Purnell Pratt, Irving Bacon, Hyman Fink. *Prod:* Paramount. 68m. (Compare listing in Betty Compson filmography.)

A LITTLE BIT OF HEAVEN. (1940). Rags-to-riches romance, with music, as Uncle Wes. *Dir:* Andrew Marton. *Sc:* Daniel Taradash, Gertrude Purcell, Harold Goldman (from a story by Grover Jones). *With* Gloria Jean, Robert Stack, Hugh Herbert, C. Aubrey Smith, Stuart Erwin, Nan Grey, Eugene Pallette, Nana Bryant, Billy Gilbert, Noah Beery Jr., Maurice Costello, Fred Kelsey, Monte Blue, William Desmond, Kenneth Harlan, Pat O'Malley. *Prod:* Universal. 87m.

THE LADY FROM CHEYENNE (1941). Romantic comedy about women's suffrage; in the supporting cast. *Dir:* Frank Lloyd. *Sc:* Catherine Scola and Warren Duff (from a story by Jonathan Finn and Theresa Oaks). *With* Loretta Young, Robert Preston, Edward Arnold, Gladys George, Frank Craven, Jessie Ralph, Samuel S. Hinds. *Prod:* Universal. 88m.

WILD GEESE CALLING (1941). Northwest romantic adventure; in the supporting cast. *Dir:* John Brahm. *Sc:* Horace McCoy (from a novel by Stewart Edward White). *With* Henry Fonda, Joan Bennett, Warren William, Ona Munson, Barton MacLane, Russell Simpson, Iris Adrian. *Prod:* 20th Century-Fox. 78m.

THE MAN WHO LOST HIMSELF (1941) Drama; in the supporting cast. *Dir:* Edward Ludwig. *Sc:* Eddie Moran (from a story by H. DeVere Stacpoole). *With* Brian Aherne, Kay Francis, Henry Stephenson, S. K. Sakall, Nils Asther, Sig Rumann, Dorothy Tree, Janet Beecher, Marc Lawrence, Henry Kolker, Sarah Padden, Eden Gray. *Prod:* Universal. 72m.

A YANK IN THE R.A.F. (1914). Second World War thriller of the Royal Air Force; in the supporting cast. *Dir:* Henry King. *Sc:* Darrell Ware and Karl Tunberg (from a story by Melville Crossman). *With* Tyrone Power, Betty Grable, John Sutton, Reginald Gardiner, Richard Fraser, Ralph Byrd, Ethel Griffies, Frederic Worlock, Lester Matthews. *Prod:* 20th Century-Fox. 97m.

THE MAGNIFICENT DOPE (1942). Country boy beats city slickers; in the supporting cast. *Dir:* Walter Lang. *Sc:* George Seaton (from a story by Joseph Schrank). *With* Henry Fonda, Lynn Bari, Don Ameche, Edward Everett Horton, George Barbier. *Prod:* 20th Century-Fox. 83m.

11
BLANCHE SWEET

It is an interesting fact, and one of some sociological importance, that the actresses who became the first great screen stars did so under the guidance of ambitious and indomitable female relatives.

Mary Pickford, the Gishes, Mae Marsh, and the Talmadge sisters had mothers who pushed their careers. Marguerite Clark had an older sister who directed hers. And Blanche Sweet had a grandmother whose *raison d'être* was Blanche.

Blanche Sweet appeared in her first movie in 1909, when she was only thirteen years old. But by that time she had been on the stage almost twelve years. Her movie stardom came from the early pictures of D. W. Griffith, from whom she parted in 1913 when Jesse Lasky, Cecil B. DeMille, and Samuel Goldfish (Goldwyn) formed the Lasky Feature Play Company. She continued to be a star until after the advent of sound.

She was born in Chicago on June 18, 1896, and christened Sarah Blanche. Her mother, *née* Pearl Alexander, was a professional dancer who died when she was only nineteen years old, after her husband, Charles Sweet, a wine salesman, deserted her for another woman.

Mrs. Sweet's mother, Cora Blanche (Ogden) Alexander, was then a divorcée of thirty-seven who had had five children, four of whom had died in infancy. When Pearl Alexander Sweet, her last child, died at the age of nineteen, the helpless baby she left seemed to Mrs. Alexander a gift to her loneliness from God.

Mrs. Alexander, a small woman of large faith, was descended from a Richard Ogden who had come in 1640 from Southampton in England to help settle Southampton on Long Island. She did not hesitate to solicit help from her daughter's stage friends and when Blanche was only eighteen months old, obtained work for her in a popular melodrama of the day, "Blue Jeans." She was carried on stage and one of the actors kissed her foot. Other stage work followed, and the infant was soon being billed as "Baby Blanche."

"It never occurred to me that I was different from other children," Blanche Sweet has said. "My wonderful grandmother was both mother and father to me. And she was always ready for anything. When I was very young, she got me a between-season job in a tent show in Ohio and had her hat on, I remember, and was saying, 'Let's go' before I even knew where we were going.''

By the time she was four, "Baby Blanche" was touring in "The Battle of the Strong," which starred Marie Burroughs, with Maurice Barrymore and Holbrook Blinn. In it she clung to Barrymore's neck as he fought a duel with Blinn, and years later Blinn told her he had often feared for both their safeties because Barrymore sometimes removed the button from his fencing foil.

While she and her grandmother were living in a rooming-house on 34th Street, Barrymore came there several times to rehearse "Baby Blanche" for "Editha's Burglar." But she never got to play it with him. One afternoon he disappeared, and shortly thereafter was confined to an asylum.

"I remember my grandmother sitting in a rocking chair, humming to me as she held me in her lap," Miss Sweet says. "She would drink coffee, dipping a Uneeda biscuit in it, and I never knew until later that she was listening fearfully for Barrymore's light step on the stairs. Our room had been the last place he'd been before being committed, and she was afraid he'd escape and come to us.''

When she had become "Little Blanche" and was six years old, her grandmother secured an engagement for her with Chauncey Olcott's company that lasted three seasons, first in New York and then in various parts of the country. The Olcotts liked Blanche so much they wanted to adopt her, but her grandmother refused, although, Miss Sweet recalls "She threatened whenever I was naughty to let the Olcotts adopt me."

While playing in Denver, and being billed as Blanche Alexander, her father, who had remarried, saw her. He went backstage afterward, and tried vainly to induce the grandmother to let him raise Blanche. But Mrs. Alexander did listen to his suggestion that she and his child should come to San Francisco, where he was living, and that Blanche should be sent to school there.

Says Miss Sweet: "My father was a tall, handsome man with a personality like Gaylord Ravenal's in 'Show Boat.' He was then selling champagne, and prospering, and lived with his new wife in the St. Francis Hotel." For Blanche and her grandmother he took a room in a small residential hotel on Geary Street not far away. Blanche was entered in a girls' public school nearby.

"I learned more from my grandmother and from being in the theatre than I did in school," Miss Sweet says. "And I was embarrassed most of the time because all the other girls had their hair in two neat pigtails with hair ribbons, which was the fashion, and my grandmother insisted on putting mine up in curls."

On the morning of the 1906 earthquake and fire that devastated San Francisco, her grandmother wakened and hastily dressed her. When they went out on the street and learned that the Embarcadero was in flames, her grandmother wanted to go back to the hotel for their possessions, but wasn't allowed to, and their hotel was dynamited in one of the early attempts to establish a fire-break. Mrs. Alexander and Blanche were herded with other civilians to the Presidio grounds.

"I was only nine," Miss Sweet says, "and thought the whole fire and earthquake a magnificent spectacle. I had no feeling of fear since my grandmother was with me."

Eventually, they found a room in Berkeley across the Bay, where Blanche was given some dancing lessons by Ruth St. Denis. Meanwhile, her father was

240

Blanche Sweet

suffering reverses; champagne was the least of the things stricken San Francisco needed at that time, and so he assented to "Little Blanche" resuming her stage career in New York. She did so in a popular melodrama of the day called "Charlotte Temple."

But she had fallen in love with the world of the dance, and began studying with Gertrude Hoffman. To pay for her lessons, she applied for work at the Edison studio.

Her screen *début* was in a featured role in a comedy. *A Man with Three Wives,* in which she played one of the young "wives," although she was only a little more than thirteen years old.

Then, through some friends of her grandmother — Will Nichols and his sister Helen — she contacted Biograph and made her first appearance there in D. W. Griffith's *A Corner in Wheat.* "I was placed very deep in the corner," she says. Griffith also used her as "The Spirit of the New Year" in another comedy, *The Day After.*

She was then very thin, very blonde, very pale — a Dresden china creature — and Griffith thought her too young for dramatic roles. So did William Λ. Brady, who told her grandmother, when she brought Blanche to his office for a stage role: "How can I use a leading woman who isn't old enough to have had all her teeth yet?"

But Griffith was impressed by how remarkably natural she was in front of the camera. "Frankly, I never knew then where the camera was," says Miss Sweet. "I just did what I was told to do."

She was so seriously interested in dancing, however, that when Griffith and his Biograph Players were about to go to California for a winter of filming, she grandly turned down an offer to accompany them because Miss Hoffman had hired her as a featured member of her ballet, "The Spring Song," at $18 a week.

"My grandmother was terribly disappointed, for I'd been earning considerably more than that with Biograph," Miss Sweet says. "But those who will dance soon learn that the piper must be paid. When the tour with Miss Hoffman was over, there were no other dancing engagements. So my grandmother wrote to Mr. Griffith in California. They all remembered their 'Biograph Blonde,' and Frank Powell, an actor-director for Griffith, wrote us to come on out. I think Mr. Griffith was really bowled over when he got another look at me. I'd been thin and scrawny when I was with him before. Now, little more than a year later, I was plumped out with adolescent fat."

Griffith gave her a real chance by putting her in a railroad melodrama of the Old West called *The Lonedale Operator,* in which the screen image that was Blanche Sweet emerged full-blown. As Griffith's wife, Linda Arvidson Griffith, says in her book, "When the Movies Were Young": "That was the picture in which he first recognised the potentiality of Blanche Sweet."

Miss Sweet adored Griffith. "Anything he told me to do I did," she says. "*Anything* to gain his praise! The competition for the leads among 'the Griffith girls' was keen. Heaven knows why I got so stubborn and refused to do the heroine of *Man's Genesis.* I'd danced around with Gertrude Hoffman in little more than a piece of gauze, but suddenly I was determined I wouldn't wear a grass skirt and expose my bare legs and feet. Mary Pickford and others also refused for the same reason. We were both snooty to Mae Marsh when Mr. Griffith gave the role to her, an unknown, and my grandmother and Mrs.

Pickford, who hadn't been too friendly because each was loyal to her own, drew together in their disapproval of Mae. My grandmother even accused Mae of not having enough hair on her head! We can laugh about it now, because Mae became one of our closest friends, but at the time we were filled with rage when, to punish us, Mr. Griffith gave the lovely heroine's role in *Sands of Dee* to Mae, knowing both Mary and I wanted it so desperately."

Linda Arvidson Griffith wrote of Blanche: "It was strange that the one woman in whom Mr. Griffith had seen the least promise came to play the most important roles in his Biograph pictures."

She was even chosen for the title role in his first major film, the four-reel milestone, *Judith of Bethulia,* which he began in 1913, mostly at Chatsworth outside Los Angeles in the San Fernando Valley, and completed in 1914 at Biograph's new studio in the Bronx. The budget was $32,000.

In her book on Griffith, Iris Barry says *Judith* "remains both in his own career, and in the memories of those who saw it at the time, a real landmark." Adds Lewis Jacobs in "The Rise of the American Film": "The unusual pattern of *Judith of Bethulia,* modelled on the four-part pattern of Griffith's earlier *Pippa Passes,* presaged the form of Griffith's future masterpiece, *Intolerance.* The four movements were in counterpoint not unlike a musical composition; they reacted to each other simultaneously, and the combination produced a cumulative, powerful effect. The individual episodes had a tight internal structure. The imagery was not only lavish in detail but fresh in camera treatment, and was enhanced by expert cutting."

In his "The Art of the Moving Picture," Vachel Lindsay, the first important American author to write seriously of the movies as an artistic medium, praised *Judith* as "one of the two most significant photoplays I have ever encountered," and he wrote of Blanche Sweet's performance as being "dignified and ensnaring, the more so because in her abandoned quarter of an hour the Jewish sanctity does not leave her."

All of which is indeed remarkable in view of the fact that Miss Sweet was then only seventeen years old. She assigns to the directorial genius of Griffith the credit for her performance.

After the exteriors, and some of the interiors, for *Judith* were filmed in California, "the Biograph westerners" entrained for New York, but paused in Albuquerque, New Mexico, so Griffith could direct a Mary Pickford vehicle, *A Pueblo Legend.* Since Miss Sweet wasn't to appear in it, she wanted to go on to New York with her grandmother and await the company there. But Griffith insisted on the company staying together.

"Mr. Griffith could be even more stubborn than I ever was," Miss Sweet says. "My revenge was, I'm afraid, a very feminine one. Every afternoon I had a cold bath, put on a cool fresh dress, and was sitting on the hotel veranda with an ice-clinking glass in one hand to welcome the company when they all returned, hot and tired, from a long day's shooting on the New Mexican desert. They must have hated me."

After they finished *Judith* in New York, Griffith supervised a series of programme pictures in which Miss Sweet starred under the direction of such Griffith *protégés* as William Christy Cabanné, James Kirkwood, and John O'Brien. She also starred in three specials that Griffith personally directed — *The Escape, Home Sweet Home,* and *The Avenging Conscience.*

The Escape was begun in New York and after shooting all of one bitterly cold Christmas Eve, Miss Sweet came, exhausted, to the hotel room she shared with her grandmother, who had ordered her a special treat — clams. When the waiter brought them, Miss Sweet was too ill to eat them.

She had scarlet fever, and work on *The Escape* had to be postponed. The Griffith company returned to California to do *The Battle of the Sexes* while waiting for Miss Sweet to get well and finish *The Escape*. When she rejoined the company, she learned that Griffith was going to form his own company and had bought *The Clansman* — eventually re-titled *The Birth of a Nation*. He told Miss Sweet there would be a part in it for her.

"But by the time we'd completed *The Avenging Conscience*," says Miss Sweet, "he wasn't ready to give me a definite commitment. I was proud, I suppose, upset, and hurt. All 'the Griffith girls' were begging him for roles in *The Clansman,* and I was fearful of being overlooked. Then Jeanie Macpherson, who had been an actress with Griffith, came to me and said that Jesse Lasky, Cecil B. DeMille, and Samuel Goldfish (later Goldwyn) had been impressed with my performance in *Judith of Bethulia* and that they needed stars for their company and had learned I had no contract with Mr. Griffith — none of us ever had. They came to my house in Hollywood and offered me a wonderful financial deal. They'd brought out stage stars to play for them, but they wanted to pioneer with me as their first fully-established screen star.

"I went to Mr. Griffith and told him of the offer, hoping he'd counter with an offer of his own, for I definitely would have preferred staying with him. Instead, he told me he thought I'd learned everything I could from him, and that it would probably be better if I tried my own wings somewhere else. So I signed with Lasky."

The 1914 issue of "Motion Picture News" which contains the story of Lasky's signing Miss Sweet as his new star, says: "Nobody is aiming to make Blanche Sweet just a pretty girl on the screen. On the contrary, she will have the widest range of opportunity in the Belasco dramas, and the ambition of Mr. DeMille is that she shall be not only great in appeal but supreme as an artist in her field of endeavour."

DeMille himself directed her first two Lasky films — *The Warrens of Virginia* and *The Captive*. "I'd been spoiled, however," says Miss Sweet. "I'd had the greatest director of them all, the real master, Mr. Griffith, and I was still angry and sulking in my humiliation, because Mr. Griffith had so indifferently advised me to leave him. Years later I confessed apologetically to poor Mr. DeMille that if I'd seemed sullen and uncooperative, it was really because I was afraid of him. He smiled and said chivalrously: "You know, Blanche, you're the only actress I was ever afraid of."

Goldwyn always said Griffith "had played Svengali to Miss Sweet's Trilby," and it is true that Miss Sweet was not content with any of her Lasky directors until her eighth Lasky film, *The Ragamuffin,* which was William C. de Mille's *début* as a director. In his autobiography, de Mille says of *The Ragamuffin:* "I considered myself lucky to have so good a star for my first directorial venture." He also directed her two subsequent films, *Blacklist* and *The Sowers.*

Nevertheless, her Lasky vehicles were ahead of their time. *The Clue* was a gripping suspense melodrama that anticipated Japanese spy pictures; *The Case of Becky,* from a Belasco stage play, was an absorbing psychological study of a girl with a dual personality; and such pictures as *Blacklist, Public*

244

BLANCHE SWEET

Opinion, Unprotected, and *The Evil Eye* were full of much more sociological import than most silent programme pictures.

Miss Sweet's favourite of the features she did at this time is *The Thousand Dollar Husband.* "I so rarely got a chance to play comedy," she says. "I started in films in comedy and they switched me to the most exhausting of dramas until I even had a guilty feeling about any picture I enjoyed making. You have to have a certain amount of joy in making a comedy, or it's going to come out as heavy drama, and I seldom had occasion to be joyous.

"I also loved making Westerns, and heaven knows I made plenty of them. I didn't even know how to ride in the beginning. They put me on a horse and said, 'Ride.' So I did. Mr. Griffith once asked me if I thought I could rear my horse back on its hind legs and shoot a gun. I said, 'Sure,' and I did that, too.

"On the other hand, I could be very stubborn, and still can be — ridiculously. They even sometimes said I was temperamental. The truth is that no screen role of mine ever completely satisfied me. I always come away from a performance feeling I could have done better, and resolving never to fall short again. I wonder if that's conceit?"

Her last three pictures for Lasky were directed by Marshall Neilan, who had played in several of the films Griffith supervised for the Klaw & Erlanger interest. Miss Sweet had persuaded Lasky to take on Neilan as a contract director. He was to direct her again in some special features later, and in 1922 they were married.

After making nineteen pictures for Lasky, Miss Sweet left the screen for two years. She was tired and ill; she had worked constantly for eight years and been in over seventy films. "I took everything too seriously," she said later. "I worked too hard, and I was very unhappy in other ways."

The unhappiness was personal and stemmed from a lover's quarrel which she and Neilan had, whereupon he married another Griffith girl, Gertrude Bambrick.

Adela Rogers St. Johns wrote in "Photoplay" for September 1924: "The sum total of Blanche Sweet to me is that I don't know anybody I'd rather have for a side-kick in a tight place than Blanche...There would probably be times when you wanted to smack her, but I have never met a personality so stimulating, so intriguing, so full of interesting vibration, as Blanche Sweet's — and she'd certainly never, never bore you."

Of Miss Sweet's prolonged absence from films at the height of her career, Mrs. St. Johns wrote: "Then came the years of absence from the screen — the long illness. Some day, perhaps, the story of those years can be told. Some day, when we are all old and gray and the sting of things, and the joy of things, no longer burns so brightly. But not now. Because much of that time Blanche walked in the valley of the shadow where — I think — we have no right to follow her. From it she emerged — the woman of today, wearing a new deep sweetness, a new charm, a new power...Do you remember Kipling's description of the woman who 'had known all the sorrow in the world and was laughing at it?' That is a perfect description of Blanche Sweet Neilan."

Actually, she returned to film production during the last year of the First World War in a dual role in *The Unpardonable Sin,* which was adapted from a Rupert Hughes novel and directed by Marshall Neilan. Its treatment of shocking German atrocities in Belgium anticipated by forty-some years the horrifying rape sequence of mother and daughter in Sophia Loren's *Two*

245

Women. Miss Sweet and Mary Alden played a daughter and mother who seek refuge from German soldiers in a Belgian convent, only to be savagely raped by the invading Germans and left pregnant. Wallace Beery, fresh from a series of comedy roles, played a villainous Prussian officer.

"I remember vividly two incidents about that production," says Miss Sweet. "We were the only picture shooting in Hollywood because of the Spanish influenza epidemic, and when the cameras weren't being ground, everybody had to don a flu mask. I was in nearly every shot, playing one sister or the other, and I finally said, 'To hell with it!' and wouldn't wear a mask at all.

"The other incident was that when we were almost through shooting, the State Department, which had fully authorised our frank treatment of German atrocities, suddenly requested that we soften the brutalities. We all knew that meant one thing — the war was in its last months. So we tried to get the picture out before the Armistice. We didn't, and it was tough sledding to sell in 1919 a picture about a war everybody was sick and tired of and glad was over."

In 1919, Miss Sweet signed a contract to star for Jesse Hampton Productions, and at last had a chance to make some comedies. The best of these was an adaptation of a Bret Harte story, *Fighting Cressy*. She also enjoyed making *The Deadlier Sex,* on which she first met Boris Karloff, who, she says, is one of the pleasantest and most gentlemanly actors she ever knew. "He never scared me in all those later horror pictures," she says, "because even in them I could think of him only as he actually was."

Sometime after she married Neilan, Miss Sweet gave what many, including myself, consider her finest screen performance — in the title role of Thomas H. Ince's production of Eugene O'Neill's *Anna Christie*.

"Ince was the first who dared to bring an O'Neill play to the screen, and he stepped out of character to make it, for he had achieved his reputation from financially successful melodramas, shockers, and Westerns," says Miss Sweet. "He pioneered with *Anna*, and I considered it a great honour and thrill to be chosen to pioneer with him."

Her peformance as Anna was liked both by critics and public, and Eugene O'Neill sent her a telegram to say how much he approved of it. When she visited New York soon afterward, he was ill, but sent Robert Edmond Jones to congratulate her on his behalf.

Garbo re-did *Anna Christie* as her first talkie, but wasn't happy with the English-speaking version. O'Neill never saw Garbo's version because friends told him he wouldn't like it.

Miss Sweet's Anna is certainly, nearer the O'Neill heroine than Garbo's and the Bradley King scenario expanded the play's background so that action was shown pictorially which is only talked about in the play. Thus, one sees Anna's early life in Sweden; her life with her brutal, woman-hungry cousins on the lonely American farm; and an exciting ship collision sequence, shot near San Francisco, which catapulted the stoker-hero Matt Burke, played by William Russell, into the foggy sea, to be rescued to the Christopherson's barge.

"Had I seen Pauline Lord's performance as Anna in the theatre, I'd never have had the courage to play it," Miss Sweet confesses. "I finally did see it in Los Angeles after the picture was released, and I remember sinking lower and lower in my seat, absolutely awed. I went backstage afterward to tell her so."

Blanche Sweet as *Anna Christie*.

MORE FROM HOLLYWOOD

In 1924, the Neilans contracted to make pictures for Goldwyn, and went abroad several times, first to shoot exteriors for *Tess of the D'Urbervilles,* especially the sequence in which Tess takes refuge amid the ruins of Stonehenge, and later to shoot exteriors for *The Sporting Venus,* in which Miss Sweet had as her leading man Ronald Colman. These were shot at the castle on the Cortachy estate in Kirriemuir, and Miss Sweet remembers viewing for the first time authentic Scottish dancing — "How the feet did fly!"

While they were abroad shooting *Tess,* Metro and Goldwyn merged, and Neilan was forced to shoot a "happy" ending, which everybody hated, and it completely negated Hardy's intention. Eventually the picture was released with both endings, and exhibitors were allowed to choose whichever finale they preferred.

While the Neilans were in Britain for *The Sporting Venus,* Miss Sweet bought the film rights to a story of Rebecca West's involving amnesia called

Blanche Sweet as Tess, with Stuart Holmes in *Tess of the D'Urbervilles.*

"Return of a Soldier." She filmed some exteriors for it, but the picture itself was never made, and Miss Sweet eventually sold the rights to Warner Bros., who thought it might make a vehicle for Bette Davis. But Warners never made it either. At one time Sidney Howard also wanted to dramatise it as a stage vehicle for his then-wife, Clare Eames.

"When I look back on my career," says Miss Sweet, "I seem to have always been fighting to make pictures I never got to do. After *Judith of Bethulia*, Mr. Griffith waxed enthusiastic about starring me in Flaubert's "Salammbo," but nothing came of that. When I was with Lasky, I was to have done *The Puppet Crown* and *The Cheat*. Ina Claire got the first; Fannie Ward, the second. Then, when we were planning "Return of the Soldier," Rebecca West and H. G. Wells had me to dinner to meet Michael Arlen. I told him I would adore playing Iris March in "The Green Hat," and Arlen told me to tell my husband, who'd gone back to New York, to contact Al Woods, who was to produce a play version with Katharine Cornell. I cabled Marshall, who replied that I was to contact Mr. Woods on my return to New York. When I got back, the play had opened to tremendous business, and M-G-M was already negotiating for it for Garbo, who got the part."

After the Goldwyn pictures, Miss Sweet made several for First National, of which she liked best one from a Frances Marion script that was directed by George Fitzmaurice, *His Supreme Moment*, in which she again had Colman as her leading man. "'Fitz's pictures," she says, "always had a lot of polish, and they were a joy to look at."

When Neilan directed a tongue-in-cheek version of Sardou's *Diplomacy* for Paramount, Miss Sweet wanted to play the adventuress Zita, but was talked into playing Dora. "I wasn't really right for the wife," she says. "I'd done enough of those pounding-on-the-door women, but the front office — and Marshall — convinced me at the time that playing an adventuress might hurt my screen image. I argued that I'd played a prostitute in *Anna Christie*, which certainly hadn't hurt my image. While we were making *Diplomacy*, I used to glare so effectively at Arlette Marchal playing the Countess because she had the part I wanted that I think I rather frightened Mlle. Marchal."

After *Diplomacy* Miss Sweet returned to London to do Wilkie Collins's *The Woman in White* for Herbert Wilcox. "We had the picture half-way shot when word came about Al Jolson's *The Jazz Singer*. Wilcox deliberated about re-shooting it as a talkie, but there were then no top sound technicians in London, and it was decided to finish it as a silent, which meant it got only a limited release."

At that time (1929), Miss Sweet had to cope not only with problems incident to the coming of sound but with those attending the end of her marriage to Neilan. She divorced him soon after her return from London.

Her first experiment with sound was a one-reel Vitaphone short, *Always Faithful*, but her real talkie *début* was at M-G-M in the Paul Bern-produced *The Woman Racket*, adapted from a Broadway play, "The Night Hostess." She sang in it, and also in *Show Girl in Hollywood*. "I've never been able to forgive myself for that," she says.

She appeared in only one more movie — in a minor role in Rex Beach's *The Silver Horde*, the stars of which were Evelyn Brent, Jean Arthur, and Joel McCrea.

With considerable valour, she then put together a vaudeville act called "Sweet and Lovely," and for two years toured it on the Fanchon & Marco and Orpheum circuits. It consisted of songs, a comedy sketch, and a dramatic scene from "Anna Christie" (for the last John Qualen coached her Swedish accent).

She was then offered a road tour of "The Party's Over," in which Raymond Hackett was to be the male lead. She had met him when he was a leading man for M-G-M, and says: "I don't think I knew it then, but the real reason I decided to tour in 'The Party's Over' was because Raymond was to be in it."

In 1935, the year before they married, they both were playing on Broadway, but not in the same play. Miss Sweet was portraying the society woman who, with others, is trapped in the service-station lunchroom in Robert E. Sherwood's "The Petrified Forest." Simultaneously, she had a five-day-a-week radio programme going in Manhattan.

After their marriage, they played together in a number of out-of-town engagements, notably "Storm over Patsy."

"Raymond was a great help to me," she says. "There was an awful lot I had to learn about the theatre and everything I ever did I always first worked out at home with him advising, rehearsing, cueing me in my lines.

"Raymond and I must have known each other as children, for when my grandmother and I were living on the north side of 34th Street, the Hackett family was living in the same block on the south side. I often wish Raymond and I could have come together when we were young, and could have had more than those twenty-two years which we did have, the happiest of my life."

Her grandmother died in 1939 and was buried in Long Island, to which her ancestors had come centuries before. Even now, when Miss Sweet speaks of her grandmother, affectionate tears rise to her blue eyes.

She continued to live in Los Angeles after the death of her husband, and for a time worked in a department store, where she was known simply as "Mrs. Hackett." Today she is retired, and has lived for a number of years in New York City.

In 1963, the British Broadcasting Corporation asked her to come to London and appear as a surprise guest on a "This Is Your Life" programme featuring Bessie Love's life-story. "I'm no devotee of that or any other television programme," Miss Sweet says, "but I'd go anywhere for Bessie. We still take up right where we left off as 'Frank' and 'Blunt,' which is what Bessie used to call the two of us. If you could hear what we have to say about 'the good old days,' I'm afraid you wouldn't print it.

"But the pictures we made then had more entertainment value than pictures do now. And we were *idolised!*"

BLANCHE SWEET FILMOGRAPHY

A MAN WITH THREE WIVES (1909). A comedy of marital mix-ups involving two young artists in Greenwich Village, one of whom passes off three different women as his wife; as one of the "wives." *Prod:* Edison. 440 ft.

A CORNER IN WHEAT (1909). Drama of the wheat market; in a bit role. *Dir/Sc:* D. W. Griffith (from the novel, "The Pit," by Frank Norris). *With* Henry B. Walthall, James Kirkwood, Frank Powell, Jeanie Macpherson, Mack Sennett, Kate Bruce, W. Chrystie Miller, Arthur Johnson, Billy Quirk. *Prod:* Biograph. 967 ft.

THE DAY AFTER (1909). A comedy about the day after New Year's Eve; as The Spirit of the New Year. *Dir:* D. W. Griffith. *With* Marion Leonard, Linda Arvidson, Henry B. Walthall, W. Chrystie Miller, Arthur Johnson, Mack Sennett. *Prod:* Biograph. 460 ft.

ALL ON ACCOUNT OF THE MILK (1910). Rural comedy; as the maidservant who changes places with the daughter of the house to confound the milkman. *Dir:* Frank Powell. *With* Mary Pickford, Arthur Johnson, Mack Sennett, Jack Pickford. *Prod:* Biograph. 989 ft.

CHOOSING A HUSBAND (1910). Comedy; in a supporting role. *Dir:* D. W. Griffith. *With* Florence Barker, Mack Sennett, Billy Quirk, Kate Bruce, Henry B. Walthall. *Prod:* Biograph. 531 ft.

A ROMANCE OF THE WESTERN HILLS (1910). Romantic Western; in a supporting role. *Dir:* D. W. Griffith. *With* Mary Pickford, Charles West, Arthur Johnson, Alfred Paget, Kate Bruce. *Prod:* Biograph. 980 ft.

THE ROCKY ROAD (1910). Drama; in a supporting role. *Dir:* D. W. Griffith. *With* Wilfred Lucas, Linda Arvidson, Tony O'Sullivan, Kate Bruce, Adele De Garde, Harry Saltzer, W. Chrystie Miller, James Kirkwood, Stephanie Longfellow, George Nicholls, Frank Powell. *Prod:* Biograph. 1020 ft.

COUNTRY LOVERS (1911). Comedy; as one of two country girls whose boy friends try to frighten them. *Dir:* Mack Sennett. *Prod:* Biograph.

WAS HE A COWARD? (1911). Romantic drama; as a Western heroine. *Dir:* D. W. Griffith. *Sc:* Emmett Campbell Hall and Wilfred Lucas. *Prod:* Biograph. 994 ft.

THE LONEDALE OPERATOR (1911). Railroad melodrama; as the girl who is the telegraph operator at Lonedale. *Dir:* D. W. Griffith. *With* Wilfred Lucas, Frank Grandin,

Charles West. (Re-made by Griffith as *The Girl and Her Trust*.) *Prod:* Biograph. 998 ft.

HOW SHE TRIUMPHED (1911). Subtitled as "An Argument in Favour of Physical Culture"; as an ugly duckling who goes in for exercises and becomes a beauty. *Dir:* D. W. Griffith. *With* Linda Arvidson, Joseph Graybill, Vivian Prescott, Florence La Badie, Kate Bruce, Charles West. *Prod:* Biograph. 1045 ft.

THE WHITE ROSE OF THE WILDS (1911). Western drama of innocence and its triumph over evil; as the older sister who gives the outlaw who had saved her and her sister a white rose. *Dir:* D. W. Griffith. *With* Mack Sennett, Robert Harron, W. Chrystie Miller, Wilfred Lucas, Joseph Graybill. Filmed in the Santa Monica hills and palisades. *Prod:* Biograph. 1055 ft.

A SMILE OF A CHILD (1911). Period drama; as a young girl whose smile wins the regard of an ill-tempered ruler. *Dir:* D. W. Griffith. *With* Edwin August, W. Chrystie Miller. *Prod:* Biograph. 1044 ft.

A COUNTRY CUPID (1911). Bucolic romance. *Prod:* Biograph. 1080 ft.

THE PRIMAL CALL (1911). Drama. *Dir:* D. W. Griffith. *Sc:* Emmett Campbell Hall. *With* Claire McDowell, Florence La Badie, Wilfred Lucas, Donald Crisp, Frank Grandin, Vivian Prescott. *Prod:* Biograph. 1028 ft.

THE LAST DROP OF WATER (1911). Western drama; as the girl at the apex of a romantic triangle. *Dir:* D. W. Griffith. *With* Joseph Graybill, Charles West, W. Chrystie Miller, William J. Butler, Jeanie Macpherson, Robert Harron, Del Henderson. Filmed in the "wastes of San Fernando Valley." *Prod:* Biograph. 1057 ft.

OUT FROM THE SHADOW (1911). Drama; as a woman who stops mourning and resumes life. *Dir:* D. W. Griffith. *With* Edwin August, Alfred Paget, Charles West, Jeanie Macpherson, Marion Sunshine. *Prod:* Biograph.

THE BLIND PRINCESS AND THE POET (1911). A morality fantasy; as the blind princess. *Dir:* D. W. Griffith. *With* Charles West, Florence La Badie, Francis Grandin, W. Chrystie Miller. Filmed in the rose gardens of the celebrated flower-painter, Paul De Longpre, in Hollywood. *Prod:* Biograph. 1000 ft.

THE STUFF HEROES ARE MADE OF (1911). Domestic melodrama; in the feminine lead. *With* Marion Sunshine. *Prod:* Biograph. 1031 ft.

251

THE MAKING OF A MAN (1911). Backstage romance; as a girl who falls in love with a *matinée* idol. *Dir:* D. W. Griffith. *With* Del Henderson, Joseph Graybill. *Prod:* Biograph. 1046 ft.

THE LONG ROAD (1911). Subtitled "Destiny's Roadway with Its Many Turns"; as Edith, a flirt, who becomes a sister of mercy. *Dir:* D. W. Griffith. *With* Charles West, Joseph Graybill. *Prod:* Biograph. 1038 ft.

LOVE IN THE HILLS (1911). Romantic drama; as a soldier's daughter with a choice of three suitors. *Dir:* D.W.Griffith. *Sc:* Del Henderson. *With* Charles West, Jacques Lenoir, Kate Toncray. *Prod:* Biograph. 1054 ft.

THE BATTLE (1911). Civil War drama; as a Rebel heroine who goads her lover into becoming a hero. *Dir:* D. W. Griffith. *With* Charles West, Robert Harron, Charles H. Mailes, W. Chrystie Miller, Donald Crisp, Spottiswoode Aitken, Lionel Barrymore. *Prod:* Biograph. 1135 ft.

THROUGH DARKENED VALES (1911). Romantic drama of blindness; as a girl who loses her eyesight in an accidental explosion. *Dir:* D. W. Griffith. *Sc:* Stanner E. V. Taylor. *With* Charles West, Joseph Graybill. *Prod:* Biograph. 1047 ft.

A WOMAN SCORNED (1911) (AKA, in a cut-down version, *Woman of Sin*). Drama of vengeance; as a sweetheart of a thief who schemes for justice. *Dir:* D. W. Griffith. *Sc:* George Henessy. *With* Claire McDowell, Vivian Prescott, Charles H. Mailes, Wilfred Lucas, Adolphe Lestina. *Prod:* Biograph. 1084 ft.

THE VOICE OF THE CHILD (1911). Drama; in the feminine lead. *Dir:* D. W. Griffith. *Sc:* George Henessy. *With* Joseph Graybill, Kate Bruce. *Prod:* Biograph. 1055 ft.

THE ETERNAL MOTHER (1912). Drama; as the divorced wife of a man, whose second wife, on dying, wants her to have their baby. *Dir:* D. W. Griffith. *With* Mabel Normand, Edwin August. *Prod:* Biograph. 1011 ft.

FOR HIS SON (1912). Social drama; as the nurse of a doctor, whose son becomes a drug addict. *Dir:* D. W. Griffith. *Sc:* Emmett Campbell Hall. *Prod:* Biograph. 1000 ft.

THE TRANSFORMATION OF MIKE (1912). Drama of a gang leader's reformation; as the girl he hopes to marry. *Dir:* D. W. Griffith. *Sc:* Wilfred Lucas. *Prod:* Biograph. 999 ft.

UNDER BURNING SKIES (1912). Subtitled "A Tale of the American Desert"; as a girl loved by two men. *Dir:* D. W. Griffith. *With* W. Christy Cabanné, Wilfred Lucas. *Prod:* Biograph. 1125 ft.

THE GODDESS OF SAGEBRUSH GULCH (1912). A romantic thriller of the West; as the prettiest girl of a mining camp, known as "The Goddess." *Dir:* D. W. Griffith. *Sc:* George Henessy. *With* Dorothy Bernard, Charles West, Wilfred Lucas, Alfred Paget, Charles H. Mailes, W. Christy Cabanné. *Prod:* Biograph. 972 ft.

THE PUNISHMENT (1912). Romantic tragedy of California; as a poor fruit-grower's daughter wed to a landowner, and coveted by his son. *Dir:* D. W. Griffith. *Sc:* Bernadine R. Leist. *With* Harry Hyde, Verner Clarges, Wilfred Lucas, Kate Bruce, W. Christy Cabanné. *Prod:* Biograph. 957 ft.

ONE IS BUSINESS, THE OTHER CRIME (1912). Social drama of parallel thieveries among the rich and the poor; as the rich man's bride. *Dir:* D. W. Griffith. *Sc:* George Henessy. *With* Charles West, Dorothy Bernard, Edwin August, Kate Bruce, Alfred Paget, Mae Marsh. *Prod:* Biograph. 1007 ft.

THE LESSER EVIL (1912). Melodrama; as a girl trapped on a smuggler's boat. *Dir:* D. W. Griffith. *Sc:* George Henessy. *With* Edwin August, Alfred Paget, Mae Marsh, Charles West, Herbert Prior, Owen Moore, Charles H. Mailes. *Prod:* Biograph. 1009 ft.

AN OUTCAST AMONG OUTCASTS (1912). Melodrama; as the postmaster's daughter. *Dir:* D. W. Griffith. *With* W. Chrystie Miller, David Miles, Dorothy Bernard, Charles West. *Prod:* Biograph. 985 ft.

A TEMPORARY TRUCE (1912). A story of the early West; as Jack's wife. *Dir:* D. W. Griffith. *Sc:* George Henessy. *With* Charles H. Mailes, W. Chrystie Miller, Claire McDowell, Robert Harron, W. Christy Cabanné, Charles West. *Prod:* Biograph. 1507 ft.

THE SPIRIT AWAKENED (1912). Bucolic melodrama; as The Girl. *Dir:* D. W. Griffith. *With* Edward Dillon. Mae Marsh, Kate Bruce, W. Chrystie Miller, Charles West, Jacques Lenoir. *Prod:* Biograph. 999 ft.

MAN'S LUST FOR GOLD (1912). Western; as The Girl. *Dir:* D. W. Griffith. *Sc:* George Henessy. *With* Robert Harron, William J. Butler, David Mills. *Prod:* Biograph. 1000 ft.

THE INNER CIRCLE (1912). Social melodrama; as the Second Lead. *Dir:* D. W. Griffith. *Sc:* George Henessy. *With* Mary Pickford, Henry B. Walthall, Charles West, Alfred Paget, Jack Pickford, Adolphe Lestina, Gladys Egan. *Prod:* Biograph. 911 ft.

WITH THE ENEMY'S HELP (1912). Western gold mining drama; as the Prospector's Wife. *Dir:* D. W. Griffith. *With* Mary Pickford (Faro Kate), Charles West. *Prod:* Biograph. 973 ft.

A CHANGE OF SPIRIT (1912) Reformation drama; as The Girl, whose love reforms a happy-go-lucky crook. *Dir:* D. W. Griffith. *With* Henry B. Walthall, W. Chrystie Miller, Charles H. Mailes, William J. Butler, Kate Toncray. *Prod:* Biograph. 998 ft.

BLIND LOVE (1912). Romantic drama; as The Girl. *Dir:* D. W. Griffith. *Sc:* M. B. Harvey. *With* Edward Dillon, Charles West. *Prod:* Biograph. 1027 ft.

THE CHIEF'S BLANKET (1912). A sacred Indian blanket is stolen and finally returned, but it has its effect on all those through whose hands it passes; as The Girl. *Dir:* D. W. Griffith. *Sc:* Wilfred Lucas. *With* Lionel Barrymore, Wilfred Lucas. *Prod:* Biograph. 1692 ft.

THE PAINTED LADY (1912). Romantic tragedy; as a fallen girl, who shoots her lover and goes mad. *Dir:* D. W. Griffith. *Sc:* George Henessy. *With* Madge Kirby, Charles H. Mailes, Kate Bruce, William J. Butler, Joseph Graybill. *Prod:* Biograph. 1152 ft9

A SAILOR'S HEART (1912). Comedy drama about the undoing of an over-romantic sailor; as The Sailor's Second Sweetheart. *Dir:* Wilfred Lucas. *With* Wilfred Lucas, Bess Meredyth, Claire McDowell, Charles H. Mailes, W. Chrystie Miller. *Prod:* Biograph. 1007 ft.

THE GOD WITHIN (1912). Mother love drama; as a young mother bereft of her child who finds happiness in an adopted baby. *Dir:* D. W. Griffith. *Sc:* T. P. Bayer. *With* Lionel Barrymore, Henry B. Walthall, Claire McDowell, Charles H. Mailes. *Prod:* Biograph. 1000 ft.

THREE FRIENDS (1913). Romantic comedy drama; as a girl who weds a man who had claimed to be a misogynist. *Dir:* D. W. Griffith. *With* Henry B. Walthall, Lionel Barrymore, Jack Dillon, Harry Carey. *Prod:* Biograph. 936 ft.

PIRATE GOLD (1913). Piracy, mutiny, stolen gold melodrama; as The Captain's Daughter. *Sc:* George Henessy. *Prod:* Biograph. 1008 ft.

OIL AND WATER (1913). Society vs. theatre drama; as Genova, a dancer. *Dir:* D. W. Griffith. *Sc:* E. J. Montagne. *With* Henry B. Walthall, W. Chrystie Miller, Lionel Barrymore, Charles H. Mailes, Alfred Paget, Robert Harron, Lillian Gish, Dorothy Gish. *Prod:* Biograph. 1546 ft. (Compare listing in Dorothy Gish filmography.)

A CHANCE DECEPTION (1913). Romantic mistaken identity drama; as a young wife suspected of an indiscretion by her husband. *Dir:* W. Christy Cabanné. *With* Harry Carey, W. Christy Cabanné. *Prod:* Biograph. 1004 ft.

BROKEN WAYS (1913). Western romantic drama; as a telegraph operator, married to a bandit, but loving the sheriff. *Dir:* D. W. Griffith. *With* Henry B. Walthall, Robert Harron, Harry Carey, Mae Marsh. *Prod:* Biograph. 1074 ft.

THE HERO OF LITTLE ITALY (1913). Romantic drama among American Italians; as Maria, a flirt, who nearly precipitates a tragedy. *Dir:* D. W. Griffith. *Sc:* Grace C. de Sellon. *With* Charles West, Kate Toncray, Harry Carey, Charles H. Mailes, William J. Butler. *Prod:* Biograph. 1006 ft.

THE STOLEN BRIDE (1913). Drama of the California orange groves; as a kidnapped bride. *Dir:* D. W. Griffith. *Sc:* Grace Barton. *Prod:* Biograph. 531 ft.

LOVE IN AN APARTMENT HOTEL (1913). Comedy of misplaced loves; as the *fiancée* of a wealthy bachelor, who is loved by the maid. *Dir:* D. W. Griffith. *Sc:* William M. Marston. *With* Edward Dillon, Mae Marsh, Henry B. Walthall, W. Chrystie Miller, Robert Harron, Jack Dillon, Harry Carey, Lionel Barrymore, Kate Toncray. *Prod:* Biograph. 1008 ft.

IF WE ONLY KNEW (1913). Melodrama; as the mother of a child nearly lost at sea. *Dir:* D. W. Griffith. *Sc:* George Henessy. *With* Henry B. Walthall. *Prod:* Biograph. 976 ft.

DEATH'S MARATHON (1913). Melodrama of a suicide; as the estranged wife of a gambler. *Dir:* D. W. Griffith. *Sc:* William E. Wing. *With* Henry B. Walthall, Lionel Barrymore, W. Chrystie Miller, Kate Bruce, Robert Harron. *Prod:* Biograph. 1008 ft.

THE COMING OF ANGELO (1913). Romantic tragedy; as Theresa, who is responsible for the death of her first lover. *Dir:* D. W. Griffith. *With* Charles H. Mailes, W. Chrystie Miller, Jennie Lee, Robert Harron, W. Christy Cabanné. *Prod:* Biograph. 1030 ft.

THE MISTAKE (1913). Western tragedy; as The Girl. *Dir/Sc:* D. W. Griffith. *With* Henry B. Walthall, Charles H. Mailes. *Prod:* Biograph. 1074 ft.

TWO MEN ON THE DESERT (1913). Dramatic tragedy of Death Valley; as The Girl. *Dir/Sc:* D. W. Griffith (story basis attributed to Jack London, but the finale is right out of Frank Norris's "McTeague"). *With* Harry Carey, Donald Crisp, Henry B. Walthall, Mae Marsh, W. Chrystie Miller, Marshall Neilan. *Prod:* Biograph. 1060 ft.

THE VENGEANCE OF GALORA (1913). Gypsy drama; as Galora, the vengeful gypsy. *Dir:* W. Christy Cabanné. *Sc:* Lionel Barrymore. *With* Henry B. Walthall, Lionel Barrymore, Dorothy Gish. *Prod:* Biograph. 1040 ft. (Compare listing in Dorothy Gish filmography.)

THE HOUSE OF DISCORD (1913). Mother-daughter drama; as Mildred, the mother. *Dir:* James Kirkwood. *Sc:* A. Clayton Harris. *With* Dorothy Gish, Jack Mulhall, Antonio Moreno, Lionel Barrymore, Marshall Neilan. *Prod:* Klaw and Erlanger-Biograph. 2020 ft. (Compare listings in Antonio Moreno and Dorothy Gish filmographies.)

HER WEDDING BELL (1913). Romantic drama; as the lady of the house whose life is saved by the immigrant gardener. *Dir:* James Kirkwood. *Sc:* Edward Acker. *Prod:* Biograph. 1065 ft.

THE SENTIMENTAL SISTER (1914). Romantic drama; as a girl who runs away to find love in the city. *Dir:* James Kirkwood. *Sc:* Harry Hyde. *With* Marshall Neilan, Gertrude Robinson. *Prod:* Biograph. 915 ft.

THE MASSACRE (1914). Drama of the West and a disgraceful massacre; as The Girl, saved from the massacre. *Dir/Sc:* D. W. Griffith. *With* Robert Harron, Charles West, Claire McDowell, Wilfred Lucas, Edward Dillon, Charles H. Mailes, Alfred Paget, Del Henderson, W. Chrystie Miller, Charles Craig. (Although filmed late in 1912 and registered then, this was not released until early in 1914.) *Prod:* Biograph. 1834 ft.

JUDITH OF BETHULIA (1914). Romantic tragedy; as Judith, the beautiful widow, who saves her people from Holofernes. *Dir:* D. W. Griffith. *Sc:* Frank E. Woods (from the Apocryphal Book of Judith and a play by Thomas Bailey Aldrich). *With* Henry B. Walthall, Kate Bruce, Lillian Gish, Mae Marsh, Dorothy Gish, Robert Harron, Antonio Moreno, Charles H. Mailes, Harry Carey, Gertrude Bambrick, Alfred Paget. *Prod:* Biograph. 4 reels. (Re-issued, with additional footage, in 6 reels, 1917, as *Her Condoned Sin.*) (Compare listings in Dorothy Gish and Antonio Moreno filmographies.)

CLASSMATES (1914). Drama of West Point rivalry and redemption; as Sylvia Randolph. *Dir:* James Kirkwood. *Sup:* D. W. Griffith. *Sc:* (from the play by William C. de Mille and Margaret Turnbull). *With* Henry B. Walthall, Marshall Neilan, Lionel Barrymore, Antonio Moreno, Jack Mulhall, Dorothy Gish, Getrude Robinson, Thomas Jefferson. (Re-made, 1924, with Richard Barthelmess and Madge Evans.) *Prod:* Klaw and Erlanger/Biograph. 3449 ft. (Compare listings in Dorothy Gish and Antonio Moreno filmographies.)

STRONGHEART (1914). Romantic drama; as Dorothy Nelson, a white girl, who is loved by an Indian. *Dir:* James Kirkwood. *Sup:* D. W. Griffith. *Sc:* (from the play by William C. De-Mille). *With* Henry B. Walthall, Lionel Barrymore, Antonio Moreno, Alan Hale, Gertrude Robinson. *Prod:* Klaw and Erlanger-Biograph. 2471 ft. (Re-made as *Braveheart*,

1925, with Rod LaRocque.) (Compare listing in Antonio Moreno filmography.)

MEN AND WOMEN (1914). Drama; as the daughter of a man who had been an emblezzler and is now Arizona's governor. *Dir:* James Kirkwood. *Sup:* D. W. Griffith. *Sc:* (from the play by David Belasco and Henry C. DeMille). *With* Lionel Barrymore, Marshall Neilan, Lillian Gish, Claire McDowell, Vivian Prescott, Alan Hale, Frank Crane, Gertrude Robinson. (Re-made in 1925 by William C. de Mille.) *Prod:* Klaw and Erlanger-Biograph. 2815 ft.

ASHES OF THE PAST (1914). Drama of reformation; as the wife of an alcoholic. *Dir:* James Kirkwood. *With* James Kirkwood. *Prod:* Mutual-Majestic. 2 reels.

THE SOUL OF HONOUR (1914). Civil War tragedy; as a young wife. *Dir:* James Kirkwood. *Sup:* D. W. Griffith. *With* Henry B. Walthall, Ralph Lewis. *Prod:* Mutual-Majestic. 1943 ft.

THE PAINTED LADY (1914). Drama of two country girls, sisters, who go to the big city; as the older sister. *Sup:* D. W. Griffith. *Sc:* (from a story, "The Cavalier," by Charles S. Thompson). *With* Dorothy Gish, W. E. Lawrence, Josephine Crowell. *Prod:* Mutual-Majestic. 2 reels. (No relation to *The Painted Lady* Miss Sweet filmed in 1912.) (Compare listing in Dorothy Gish filmography.)

THE SECOND MRS. ROEBUCK (1914). Domestic drama; as Mabel Mack, who marries the widower Roebuck, and comes into conflict with his elder sister, the mistress of his house. *Dir:* W. Christy Cabanné and John O'Brien. *Sup:* D. W. Griffith. *Sc:* (from a "Smart Set" story by W. Carey Wonderly). *With* Wallace Reid, Mary Alden, Raoul Walsh. *Prod:* Mutual-Majestic. 1979 ft. (Compare listing in Wallace Reid filmography.)

FOR THE UNBORN (1914). Romantic drama; as an Eastern girl who renounces her lover and comes West because she thinks she has tuberculosis. *Dir/Sc:* W. Christy Cabanné. *Sup:* D. W. Griffith. *With* Robert Harron, Wallace Reid, Irene Hunt. *Prod:* Mutual-Majestic. 2 reels. (Compare listing in Wallace Reid filmography.)

HER AWAKENING (1914). Romantic drama; as an heiress who is almost done out of her inheritance and her life. *Dir:* W. Christy Cabanné. *Sup:* D. W. Griffith *With* Wallace Reid, Ralph Lewis, *Prod:* Mutual-Majestic. 2 reels. (Compare listing in Wallace Reid filmography.)

FOR HER FATHER'S SINS (1914). Social problem drama; as a daughter out to reform her father of his sweat-shop practices. *Dir:* John O'Brien. *Sup:* D. W. Griffith. *Sc:* Anita Loos.

With Wallace Reid, Billie West, Al Fillson. *Prod:* Mutual-Majestic. 1710 ft. (Compare listing in Wallace Reid filmography.)

THE TEAR THAT BURNED (1914). Melodrama; as a girl who dies and the crook who had been her lover gets another girl to impersonate her. *Dir:* John O'Brien. *Sup:* D.W . Griffith. *With* Lillian Gish, Josephine Crowell, John Dillon. W. E. Lowery. (A cut-down version was re-issued, which utilised only the second half of the film.) *Prod:* Mutual-Majestic. 1862 ft.

THE ODALISQUE (1914). Drama; as a model who almost gets into trouble because of her love for fine clothes. *Sup:* D. W. Griffith. *Sc:* (from a Leroy Scott story). *With* Henry B. Walthall, Wallace Reid, Miriam Cooper, Robert Harron. *Prod:* Mutual-Majestic. 2 reels. (Compare listing in Wallace Reid filmography.)

THE LITTLE COUNTRY HOUSE (1914). Romantic drama; as Dorothy, a clergyman's daughter. *Sup:* D. W. Griffith. *With* Wallace Reid, Mary Alden, Raoul Walsh. *Prod:* Mutual-Majestic. 989 ft. (Compare listing in Wallace Reid filmography.)

THE OLD MAID (1914). Romantic drama; as Dorothy, a spinster secure in her memories. *Dir:* John O'Brien. *Sup:* D. W. Griffith. *Sc:* (from a poem, "Dorothy in the Garret," by John Townsend Trowbridge). *With* Mary Alden, Spottiswoode Aitken, Jack Conway, Billie West. *Prod:* Mutual-Majestic. 1927 ft.

THE ESCAPE (1914). Sociological drama, beginning in documentary style, dealing with eugenics, crime and sex problems in the slums; as May Joyce. *Dir:* D. W. Griffith. *Sc:* (from the play by Paul Armstrong). *With* Mae Marsh, Donald Crisp, Robert Harron, Owen Moore, Ralph Lewis, F. A. Turner. *Prod:* Mutual. 7 reels. (Re-filmed, 1928, with William Russell and Virginia Valli.)

HOME SWEET HOME (1914). Anthology drama, showing the effect of the song, "Home Sweet Home," on a number of people, as well as dramatising the life of John Howard Payne, who wrote it; as the heroine of the third story, "The Marriage of Roses and Lilies." *Dir:* D. W. Griffith. *Sc:* Griffith and H. E. Aitken. *With* Henry B. Walthall, Josephine Crowell, Lillian Gish, Dorothy Gish, Fay Tincher, Mae Marsh, Spottiswoode Aitken, Robert Harron, Miriam Cooper, Mary Alden, Donald Crisp, James Kirkwood, Jack Pickford, Courtenay Foote, Owen Moore, Edward Dillon, Earle Foxe, Karl Brown, George Seigmann, Ralph Lewis, John Dillon, Irene Hunt. This film is often cited as the first all-star feature; it was billed as featuring "18 World Famous Stars." *Prod:* Mutual. 6 reels. (Compare with listing in Dorothy Gish filmography.)

THE AVENGING CONSCIENCE (AKA, GB, *Thou Shalt Not Kill*) (1914). Anthology drama, featuring two short-stories and one poem by Edgar Allan Poe; as Annabel Lee, in the dramatised poem of that name. *Dir/Sc:* D. W. Griffith (from the stories, "The Tell-Tale Heart" and "The Pit and the Pendulum," and the poem, "Annabel Lee" by Edgar Allan Poe). *With* Henry B. Walthall, Spottiswoode Aitken, George Seigmann, Ralph Lewis, Wallace Reid. *Prod:* Mutual. 6 reels. (Compare listing in Wallace Reid filmography.)

THE WARRENS OF VIRGINIA (1915). Civil War romantic drama; as Agatha Warren, daughter of a Confederate general in love with a Union lieutenant. *Dir:* Cecil B. DeMille. *Sc:* William C. de Mille (from his own play, produced by David Belasco on Broadway). *With* House Peters, James Neill, Page Peters, Mabel Van Buren, Marguerite House (Marjorie Daw), Dick La Reno, Mrs. Lewis McCord, Sydney Deane, Raymond Hatton, Milton Brown, Lucien Littlefield, Gerald Ward, Mildred Harris. *Prod:* Lasky-Paramount. 5 reels. (Re-made, Fox, 1924, with Martha Mansfield, who was accidentally burned to death filming the last scene.)

THE CAPTIVE (1915). Romantic drama in Montenegro; as Sonya, a widowed peasant girl. *Dir:* Cecil B. DeMille. *Sc:* DeMille, with Jeanie Macpherson. *With* House Peters, Theodore Roberts, Page Peters, Gerald Ward, Jeanie Macpherson, Marjorie Daw, William Elmer. *Prod:* Lasky-Paramount. 5 reels.

STOLEN GOODS (1915). First World War romantic drama; as Margery Huntley, Red Cross nurse, who impersonates a rich woman, Helen North. *Dir:* George Melford. *Sc:* Margaret Turnbull. *With* House Peters, Theodore Roberts, Cleo Ridgely, Horace B. Carpenter, Sydney Deane. *Prod:* Lasky-Paramount. 5 reels.

THE CLUE (1915). Romantic courtroom melodrama; as a girl who stands by her lover when he is tried for a murder he did not commit. *Dir:* James Neill. *Sc:* Margaret Turnbull. *With* Edward MacKay, Sessue Hayakawa, Gertrude Keller, Page Peters, Ernest Joy, William Elmer. *Prod:* Lasky-Paramount. 5 reels.

THE SECRET ORCHARD (1915). Romantic drama; as Diane, convent raised, her mother a Parisian demi-mondaine. *Dir:* Frank Reicher. *Sc:* William C. DeMille (from the play by Channing Pollock, dramatised from the novel by Alice and Egerton Castle). *With* Edward MacKay, Cleo Ridgely, Carlyle Blackwell, Theodore Roberts, Marjorie Daw, Gertrude Keller. *Prod:* Lasky-Paramount. 5 reels.

THE CASE OF BECKY (1915). Drama of a split personality; in a dual role: as Dorothy, the good girl, and as Becky, her bad self. *Dir:*

Frank Reicher. *Sc:* (from the play by Edward Locke, which Belasco had produced on Broadway, starring Frances Starr). *With* Carlyle Blackwell, Theodore Roberts, James Neill. *Prod:* Lasky-Paramount. 5 reels. (Remade by Realart, 1921, with Constance Binney and Glenn Hunter.)

THE SECRET SIN (1915). Drama of drug addiction in San Francisco's Chinatown; in a dual role: as twin sisters, Edith and Grace Martin, the latter being a drug addict. *Dir:* Frank Reicher. *Sc:* Margaret Turnbull. *With* Thomas Meighan, Sessue Hayakawa, Hal Clements, Alice Knowland. *Prod:* Lasky-Paramount. 5 reels.

THE RAGAMUFFIN (1916). Romantic comedy drama about a crook who reforms and tries to become a dressmaker; as Jenny. *Dir/Sc:* William C. de Mille (his first directorial effort). *With* Tom Forman, Minnette Burnette, Mrs. Lewis McCord, Park Jones, James Neill, William Elmer. (Re-Made by de Mille as *The Splendid Crime*, in 1925, starring Bebe Daniels.) *Prod:* Lasky/Paramount. 5 reels.

BLACKLIST (1916). Melodrama of strike leaders in a mine being blacklisted; as a schoolteacher, who throws in her lot with them. *Dir:* William C. de Mille. *Sc:* De Mille and Marion Fairfax. *With* Charles Clary, Ernest Joy, Horace B. Carpenter, Lucien Littlefield, Jane Wolff, William Elmer. *Prod:* Lasky / Paramount. 5 reels.

THE SOWERS (1916). Romantic drama of the Russian revolution; as Karina, a rebel in love with a prince. *Dir/Sc:* William C. de Mille (from a novel by Henry Seton Merriman). *With* Thomas Meighan, Ernest Joy, Mabel Van Buren, Horace B. Carpenter, Raymond Hatton, Theodore Roberts. *Prod:* Lasky / Paramount. 5 reels.

THE THOUSAND DOLLAR HUSBAND (1916). Romantic comedy; as Olga Nelson, a Swedish maid-of-all-work in a college boarding house. *Dir:* James Young. *Sc:* Margaret Turnbull. *With* Tom Forman, Theodore Roberts, Jane Wolff, Horace B. Carpenter, James Neill. *Prod:* Lasky/Paramount. 5 reels.

THE DUPE (1916). Drama; as Ethel Hale, secretary to and dupe for a society woman. *Dir:* Frank Reicher. *Sc:* Hector Turnbull. *With* Thomas Meighan, Ernest Joy, Veda McEvers. *Prod:* Lasky-Paramount. 5 reels.

PUBLIC OPINION (1916). Drama of a nurse accused of murdering a doctor; as Hazel Grey, found not guilty, but public opinion is against her. *Dir:* Frank Reicher. *Sc:* Margaret Turnbull. *With* Elliott Dexter, Earle Foxe, Tom Forman, Edythe Chapman, Raymond Hatton. *Prod:* Lasky-Paramount. 5 reels.

THE STORM (1916). Romantic drama; as

Natalie Raydon, compromised when she is marooned overnight on an island with a minister. *Dir:* Frank Reicher. *Sc:* Beatrice C. DeMille and Leighton Osmun. *With* Thomas Meighan, Theodore Roberts, Richard Sterling. *Prod:* Lasky-Paramount. 5 reels.

UNPROTECTED (1916). Melodrama about the mistreatment of female prisoners in a Southern convict camp; as a female prisoner brutalised by a guard who desires her. *Dir:* James Young. *Sc:* James Hatton. *With* Tom Forman, Theodore Roberts, Walter Long, Ernest Joy, Mrs. Lewis McCord, Jane Wolff, Robert Gray. *Prod:* Lasky-Paramount. 5 reels.

THE EVIL EYE (1917). Drama of social work among Mexican labourers; as a young doctor regarded as a witch with an evil eye because of the lamp she wears around her forehead. *Dir:* George Melford. *Sc:* Hector Turnbull. *With* Tom Forman, Webster Campbell, J. Parks Jones, Ruth King, William Dale, Walter Long. *Prod:* Lasky-Paramount. 5 reels.

THOSE WITHOUT SIN (1917). Drama of the Civil War; as Melanie, daughter of a government clerk of the Old South. *Dir:* Marshall Neilan. *Sc:* George DuBois Proctor and Tom J. Geraghty (from a story by Harvey F. Thew) *With* Tom Forman, James Neill, Charles Ogle, Mabel Van Buren, Dorothy Abril, Billy Jacobs. *Prod:* Lasky-Paramount. 5 reels.

THE TIDES OF BARNEGAT (1917). Drama of sacrifice; as Jane Cogden, schoolteacher, who sacrifices her own reputation to save her younger sister's. *Dir:* Marshall Neilan. *Sc:* Eve Unsell (from the novel by F. Hopkinson Smith). *With* Elliott Dexter, Norma Nichols, Tom Forman, Harrison Ford, Lillian Leighton, Billy Jacobs. *Prod:* Lasky-Paramount. 5 reels.

THE SILENT PARTNER (1917). Drama of sacrifice; as Jane Golby, a secretary who sacrifices her savings and good name to save her boss. *Dir:* Marshall Neilan. *Sc:* Edmund Goulding. *With* Thomas Meighan, Maym Kelso, Ernest Joy, George Herbert, Florence Smythe, Mabel Van Buren. (A film with the same title, 1923, starring Leatrice Joy does not have the same story) *Prod:* Lasky-Paramount. 5 reels.

THE UNPARDONABLE SIN (1919). First World War propaganda drama of the brutal treatment of women by invading Germans; in a dual role: as Alice and Dimny Parcot. *Dir:* Marshall Neilan. *Sc:* Rupert Hughes. *With* Mary Alden, Matt Moore, Wallace Beery, Wesley Barry. *Prod:* Garson. 7 reels.

THE HUSHED HOUR (1919). Separate dramas told in flashback as four children of a famous judge spend a hushed hour at his bier; as Virginia, the society-loving daughter. *Dir:* Edmund Mortimer. *With* Milton Sills, Rosemary Theby, Gloria Hope, Wyndham Standing, Ben Alexander, Wilfred Lucas, Winter Hall, Lydia Knott, Mary Anderson, Harry Northrup, Norman Selby. *Prod:* Garson. 5 reels.

A WOMAN OF PLEASURE (1919). Romantic melodrama; as Alice Dane, compelled to marry a nobleman whom she has seen commit a murder, *Dir:* Wallace Worsley. *Sc:* James Willard. *With* Wheeler Oakman, Wilfred Lucas, Wesley Barry, Josef Swickard, Spottiswoode Aitken. *Prod:* Pathé. 7 reels.

FIGHTING CRESSY (1919). Gun feud drama of the Sierras; as Cressy, who has decided that the McKinstry-Harrison feud must come to an end. *Dir:* Robert Thornby. *Sc:* Fred Myton (from the story by Bret Harte). *With* Pell Trenton, Edward Peil, Russell Simpson, Antrim Short, Frank Lanning, Billie Bennett, Georgie Stone. *Prod:* Pathé.

THE DEADLIER SEX (1920). Romantic duel of a railroad owner and a Wall Street broker; as Mary Willard. *Dir:* Robert Thornby. *Sc:* Fred Myton. *With* Mahlon Hamilton, Winter Hall, Roy Laidlaw, Boris Karloff, Russell Simpson. *Prod:* Pathé. 5187 ft.

SIMPLE SOULS (1920). Comedy drama; as a girl who marries a duke. *Dir:* Robert Thornby. *Sc:* John Hastings Turner (from a story by Fred Myton). *With* Charles Meredith, Kate Lester, Maym Kelso, Herbert Standing. *Prod:* Pathé. 5 reels.

THE GIRL IN THE WEB (1920). Melodrama; as Esther Maitland, secretary. *Dir:* Robert Thornby. *Sc:* (from a story by Geraldine Bonner). *With* Nigel Barrie, Haywood Mack, Christine Mayo, Thomas Jefferson, Adele Farrington. *Prod:* Pathé. 5 reels.

HELP WANTED - MALE (1920). (AKA *Object Matrimony*). Romantic comedy; as Leona, a telephone operator who gains an inheritance and goes looking for a husband. *Dir:* Henry King. *Sc:* George Plympton (from a story, "Leona Goes a-Hunting," by Edwina Levin). *With* Henry King, Frank Leigh, Maym Kelso, Thomas Jefferson, Jay Belasco, Jean Acker. *Prod:* Pathé.

HER UNWILLING HUSBAND (1920). Comedy of mistaken identity; as Mavis, a stage star. *Dir:* Paul Scardon. *Sc:* (from a story by Kenneth B. Clarke). *With* Albert Roscoe, Edwin Stevens. Working title: *Port o' Caprice*. *Prod:* Pathé. 5 reels.

THAT GIRL MONTANA (1921). Western of the gold rush days; as Montana Rivers. *Dir:* Robert Thornby. *Sc:* George H. Plympton. *With* Mahlon Hamilton, Frank Lanning, Edward Peil, Claire Du Brey, Kate Price. *Prod:* Pathé. 5 reels.

QUINCY ADAMS SAWYER (1922). Roman-

tic melodrama; as the blind heroine, Alice Pettengill. *Dir:* Clarence Badger. *Sc:* Bernand McConville (from the novel by Charles Felton Pidgin). *With* John Bowers, Lon Chaney, Barbara LaMarr, Elmo Lincoln, Louise Fazenda, Joseph S. Dowling, Claire McDowell, Edward J. Connelly, June Elvidge, Vic Potel, Gale Henry, Hank Mann, Kate Lester. *Prod:* Metro. 8 reels.

THE MEANEST MAN IN THE WORLD (1923). Romantic comedy; as Jane Hudson. *Dir:* Eddie Cline. *Sc:* Austin McHugh (from a play by George M. Cohan and Everett S. Ruskay). *With* Bert Lytell, Bryant Washburn, Ward Crane, Victor Potel, Carl Stockdale, Lincoln Stedman, Bill Conklin. (Re-filmed, 1943, as a Jack Benny-Priscilla Lane comedy.) *Prod:* First National. 6 reels.

ANNA CHRISTIE (1923). Drama of the sea; as Anna Christie. *Dir:* John Griffith Wray. *Sc:* Bradley King (from the play by Eugene O'Neill). *With* William Russell, George Marion, Chester Conklin, Eugenie Besserer, George Seigmann. (Re-made, 1930, as Garbo's first talkie.) *Prod:* Ince/First National. 8 reels.

IN THE PALACE OF THE KING (1923). Romantic costume drama of Spain in the days of Philip II; as Dolores de Mendoza, *Dir:* Emmett Flynn. *Sc:* June Mathis (from the novel by F. Marion Crawford). *With* Edmund Lowe, Hobart Bosworth, Pauline Starke, Sam de Grasse, William V. Mong, Aileen Pringle, Lucien Littlefield, Charles Clary. (Previously filmed by Essanay, 1916, with Nell Craig and Richard Travers.) *Prod:* Goldwyn. 9 reels.

THOSE WHO DANCE (1924). Bootlegging and murder melodrama; as Ruth Jordan, gangster's moll, also known as Rose Carney. *Dir:* Lambert Hillyer. *Sc:* Hillyer and Arthur Statter (from a story by George Kibbe Turner). *With* Warner Baxter, Bessie Love, Matthew Betz, Robert Agnew, Frank Campeau. (Re-made as a talkie by Warner Bros., with Betty Compson in Miss Sweet's role; also a Spanish-speaking version, *Los que danzan.*) *Prod:* Ince/First National. 8 reels.

TESS OF THE D'URBERVILLES (1924). Drama of Tess, trapped by fate; as Tess. *Dir:* Marshall Neilan. *Sc:* Dorothy Farnum (from the novel by Thomas Hardy). *With* Conrad Nagel, Stuart Holmes, George Fawcett, Victory Bateman, Courtney Foote, Joseph J. Dowling. Exteriors filmed abroad in England. Exhibitors had their choice of two endings: one, the original tragic ending; and the other, an absurdly happy one. *Prod:* Metro-Goldwyn. 8 reels. (Previously filmed by Famous Players, 1913, starring Mrs. Fiske.)

THE SPORTING VENUS (1925). Romantic drama; as Lady Gwendolyn Grayle, a Scottish heiress. *Dir:* Marshall Neilan. *Sc:* Thomas J. Geraghty (from the "Red Book" story by Gerald Beaumont). *With* Ronald Colman, Lew

Cody, Josephine Crowell, George Fawcett, Edward Martindel, Kate Price, Hank Mann, Arthur Hoyt. Exteriors shot in Scotland. *Prod:* Metro-Goldwyn. 7 reels.

HIS SUPREME MOMENT (1925). Romantic drama; as Carla King, an actress who falls in love with a mining engineer. *Dir:* George Fitzmaurice. *Sc:* Frances Marion (from the novel, "World without End," by May Edington). *With* Ronald Colman, Jane Winton, Belle Bennett, Cyril Chadwick, Ned Sparks. In the Technicolor sequence opening the film, Anna May Wong and Kalla Pasha may be glimpsed as the harem favourite and the sultan. *Prod:* First National. 8 reels.

WHY WOMEN LOVE (1925). Sea drama; as Molla Hansen, daughter of a Norwegian sea captain. *Dir:* Edwin Carewe. *Sc:* Lois Leeson (from a play, "The Sea Woman," by Willard Robertson). *With* Edward Earle, Robert Frazer, Dorothy Sebastian, Charles Murray, Russell Simpson. *Prod:* First National. 7 reels.

THE NEW COMMANDMENT (1925). Drama of expatriates before, during, and after the First World War; as René Darcourt, dancing daughter of a wealthy American family. *Dir:* Howard Higgin. *Sc:* Sada Cowan and Howard Higgin (from a novel, "Invisible Wounds," by Frederick Palmer). *With* Ben Lyon, Holbrook Blinn, Clare Eames, Effie Shannon, Dorothy Cumming, Pedro de Cordoba, George Cooper, Diana Kane. *Prod:* First National. 7 reels.

BLUEBEARD'S SEVEN WIVES (1926). Satire on the ways of Hollywood; as a movie queen impersonating Juliet in a sequence with Ben Lyon as Romeo. *Dir:* Alfred E. Santell. *Sc:* Blanche Merrill and Paul Schofield. *With* Ben Lyon, Lois Wilson, Dorothy Sebastian, Diane Kane, Sam Hardy, Wilfred Lytell. *Prod:* First National. 8 reels.

THE FAR CRY (1926). Post-war drama of rich American expatriates abroad; as Claire Marsh. *Dir:* Sylvano Balboni (under the editorial supervision of his wife, June Mathis). *Sc:* Katherine Kavanaugh (from the play by Arthur Richman). *With* Jack Mulhall, Myrtle Stedman, Hobart Bosworth, Leo White, Dorothy Revier, Julia Swayne Gordon, John Sainpolis. An Italian festa sequence was shot in Technicolor. *Prod:* First National. 8 reels.

THE LADY FROM HELL (AKA, GB, *The Interrupted Wedding*) (1926). Melodrama of a man falsely convicted of murder; as Lady Margaret Darnely, who discovers proof that frees her Scottish lover. *Dir:* Stuart Paton. *Sc:* J. Grubb Alexander (from a story, "My Lord of the Double B," by Norton S. Parker). *With* Roy Stewart, Ralph Lewis, Frank Elliott, Edgar Norton. *Prod:* Associated Exhibitors. 6 reels.

DIPLOMACY (1926). Comedy drama of international intrigue; as Dora, the wife. *Dir:* Marshall Neilan. *Sc:* Benjamin Glazer (from the play by Victorien Sardou). *With* Neil Hamilton, Arlette Marchal, Matt Moore, Gustav von Seyffertitz, Earle Williams, Arthur Edmund Carewe, Julia Swayne Gordon. (Filmed previously, 1916, as a vehicle for Marie Doro.) *Prod:* Paramount. 7 reels.

SINGED (1927). Romance of the oil fields; as Dolly Wall, a saloon hostess, who stakes a tin-horn gambler. *Dir:* John Griffith Wray. *Sc:* Gertrude Orr (from a story, "Love o' Women," by Adela Rogers St. Johns). *With* Warner Baxter, Claude King, Ida Darling, Mary McAllister, Edgar Norton. *Prod:* Fox. 6 reels.

THE WOMAN IN WHITE (1929). Drama of greed and deception; in a dual role: as sisters, Laura and Ann Fairlie. *Dir:* Herbert Wilcox. *Sc:* Wilcox and Robert J. Cullen (from the novel by Wilkie Collins). *With* Haddon Mason, Louise Prussing, Cecil Humphries, Frank Perfitt, Minna Grey. (Previously made by Thanhouser, 1918, with Florence La Badie; by Mae Murray, Pathé/Stoll, 1920, as *The Curse of Greed;* by Warner Bros., 1948, with Eleanor Parker.) *Prod:* British and Dominion Films. 6702 ft.

ALWAYS FAITHFUL (1929). Romantic comedy; as a wife whose husband assigns his male secretary to taking her to the theatre. A single-reel Vitaphone short, which provided for Miss Sweet's *début* as a talking film actress. *With* George B. Middleton. *Prod:* Warner's Vitaphone. 1 reel.

THE WOMAN RACKET (AKA, GB, *Lights and Shadows*) (1930). Gangster melodrama; as Julia Barnes, a night-club hostess who marries a cop. *Dir:* Robert Ober and Albert Kelley. *Sc:* Albert Shelby Le Vino (from a play, "The Night Hostess," by Philip and Frances Dunning). *With* Tom Moore, Robert Agnew, Sally Starr, John Miljan. *Prod:* M-G-M. 8 reels.

SHOWGIRL IN HOLLYWOOD (1930). Romantic comedy, with a Hollywood setting; as a one-time great movie star forgotten after the advent of sound. *Dir:* Mervyn LeRoy. *Sc:* Harvey Thew and James A. Starr (from a novel, "Hollywood Girl," by J. P. McEvoy). *With* Alice White, Jack Mulhall, Ford Sterling, John Miljan, Virginia Sale, Spec O'Donnell, Lee Shumway, Herman Bing. Song and dance sequences in Technicolor. *Prod:* First National. 80m.

THE SILVER HORDE (1930). Drama of the rivalry among Alaskan fishing companies; as Queenie. *Dir:* George Archainbaud. *Sc:* Wallace Smith (from the novel by Rex Beach). *With* Evelyn Brent, Jean Arthur, Joel McCrea, Raymond Hatton, Louis Wolheim, Gavin

Gordon. (Previously filmed, 1920, with Myrtle Stedman and Betty Blythe.) *Prod:* RKO-Radio. 8 reels.

Addenda

Miss Sweet appeared with her husband, Marshall Neilan, in Goldwyn's 1923 *Souls for Sale;* it was a cameo bit, and they appeared as themselves.

Lew Cody, Blanche Sweet, and Ronald Colman in *His Supreme Moment.*

PART TWO
SOUND ONLY

12
FLORENCE BATES

I think everyone who has had any connection with show business has encountered at least one man or woman who has withstood everything life can dish out with a valour that renewed one's own confidence in the human race.

The actress who did this for me was not a star but a player of character roles. She was Florence Bates, and she did not make her film *début* until she had passed her fiftieth birthday.

She was born Florence Rabe, in San Antonio, Texas, on April 15, 1888. Her father, who ran an antique shop, was a German Jew, and her mother a Portuguese one. There was one other child — an older sister.

In her youth, Florence was considered a musical prodigy, and she once told me she had been "the most obnoxious Quiz Kid you ever saw. I thought I knew everything there was to know about music. Fortunately for me, I injured one hand, and that put an end to any career as a pianist."

She entered the University of Texas, aged fifteen, and graduated three years later. She then taught school, and occupied her spare time with welfare work. In the course of the latter, she met and married a Texan, whose only claim to fame apparently was that he was her first husband; she soon withdrew from teaching to become mother of a daughter.

"My husband was a very handsome man," she once told me, "and he loved me and our baby daughter so much that he just couldn't tear himself away from our sides. What jobs he got he promptly lost because he wanted to stay home all the time and tell us how much he loved us. Well, that was all very well, but I didn't want us to starve, so the baby and I moved in with my parents. I filed suit for divorce, and began wondering what lay around that next turn in the road for me."

An elderly judge who was an old family friend and had always admired Florence's intelligence, was responsible for the surprising turn her destiny took. On his walk past her father's San Antonio home, he paused one day to talk to her as she played on the lawn with her baby daughter, named Ann. He remarked that it was a shame that Florence was letting her receptive and retentive mind go to waste.

"But what can I do?" she asked him.

Much to her surprise, the old gentleman suggested that she turn her attention to the legal profession. He said he possessed one of the best private law libraries in Texas and that she was welcome to borrow books and study at home.

MORE FROM HOLLYWOOD

Six months later, she passed the bar examination, and became the first woman lawyer in the State of Texas. She was only twenty-six years old.

"I don't mind saying I was pretty, and somewhat sexy," she once explained. "That I was also brainy drove most of my rival *confrères* out of their male minds. They had to treat me courteously or forego being thought of as gentlemen — a horrible fate for any Texan. But I knew that behind my back they thought of me in four and five-letter words. I didn't mind as long as I kept winning my cases, which I did.

"The judges, however, weren't much help. They had their legal ways of making things a bit difficult. Most of them scheduled the cases for the clients I represented first on the day's calendar. I never complained, for I always loved the early morning — the earlier the better, for me. I was as bright and shining as a Texas sunflower when court convened at eight a.m., and the juries always decided in my clients' favour."

Florence did well in San Antonio legal circles for four years. Then, within a short time of one another, her father and mother died. What should she and her sister do about the antique business they inherited? Florence decided to give up law and join her sister in carrying on their parents' business in the antique buying and selling world.

She loved every moment of the next ten years. "The purity of antiques was in great contrast to the corruption I'd found in Law practice," she said, and added: "The work was restful." It also enabled her to travel all over Europe and the Orient searching for new treasures to sell in Texas. Sometimes she and her sister, of whom she was very fond, went on their buying trips together, but more often she went alone. Florence had always had an ear for languages, and could speak, besides English, German, Portuguese, French, Spanish, and Hebrew, and she read both Latin and Greek.

The antique business left her with idle time, and she became a commentator on a San Antonio radio show designed to foster the good neighbour policy between the United States and Mexico; it also required her to speak Spanish as well as English, and she became both fluent and colloquial in the language.

The 1929 stock market crash ruined their antique business. There were debts, and before they could all be settled, her sister died. The only compensation was that in the midst of these disasters, on December 9, 1929, she married Will Jacoby, with whom she was in love until the day he died.

She told me that at the time they married he was "a Texas oil man" and that within a few months he lost his Texas holdings. But he retained possession of some sixty thousand acres in Mexico west of Tampico, and they decided to go there and develop oil wells. Throughout the time in Tampico, Florence wore pants, boots, and cotton shirts; kept the drilling-log, typed; ran the river boat that occasionally took them to Tampico; and conducted school for the children of their workers. They were beginning to see daylight when the Mexican Government expropriated their land.

They managed to reach El Paso, where Jacoby took a $25-a-week job, and when they had accumulated a few hundred dollars, they went on to Los Angeles. There, on Washington Boulevard, they opened a bakery with the help of a Russian couple they knew who owned a bakery in Pasadena. Jacoby was at work long before dawn; Forence was behind the counter by eight.

"I loved the bakery smells," she told me, "and making friends with the

266

customers. We learned to make a good product, and were proud of it. Prouder still when we made profits. In time, we could have lived and dressed better, but we talked it over and decided we'd rather put everything back into the business until we were out of debt.''

Florence had another reason for being proud. Her daughter had graduated from an Eastern college with the highest honours, and soon thereafter married a young lawyer named Oppenheimer, and returned to Texas to live. The times Florence loved best were the few trips she made to Texas to visit her.

One of Florence's new friends, Therese Lyon, who acted in little theatre productions, suggested one Sunday that Florence accompany her to the Pasadena Playhouse, where there was to be an open reading for a new stage production. Florence says she herself didn't intend to read, but thought it might be a diversion to watch her friend do so while she, herself, knitted. She was always knitting when her hands weren't otherwise occupied — dresses and sweaters for herself, sweaters and socks for her husband.

But she didn't get much knitting done that Sunday.

The play that was being read for was a dramatisation I had made of Jane Austen's "Emma," which Gilmor Brown, in charge of production at the Playhouse, intended giving at his own Playbox, an intimate theatre-in-the-round adjacent to his home. Philip Van Dyke, who was directing, called me in to hear Florence when he'd asked her to read a second time. Her first reading had brought down the house, which was made up of both professional and amateur actors seeking a showcase for their talents. When Florence finished, I turned to Van Dyke and said, with no hesitation whatever: "Give her the part."

It was obvious she was a born actress. She achieved instant communication with the audience — more than communication, in fact, for admiration and affection were coupled in the audience response. Even when Florence played an unsympathetic role — and she did so later on both stage and screen — you were forced to admire what she created. Florence knew instinctively how to entice "the inward-curving smile" from an audience. That Sunday night she made Miss Bates, the giddy, talkative spinster Jane Austen had created, a human delight.

It didn't matter that she was physically all wrong for the role. Florence was small but plump, and had a head as oversized as Gloria Swanson's or Louella O. Parsons's. Her big eyes missed nothing, and her voice, even in a first sight reading, missed none of the comic subtleties of Miss Austen's characterisations and dialogue. Florence read as if she had been an actress all her life. Nobody could believe it was the first time she had tried out for a role in a play.

I do not drive a car, but Florence did, and she'd pick me up in Hollywood and we'd drive over to Pasadena every day for rehearsals. We clicked almost at once, and remained the best of friends until she died.

The cast adored Florence. She never dried up on anybody, onstage or off, and she was a good listener. When she had a story to tell, everybody listened. And when she threw back her head and laughed, her hearty laughter was infectious.

Florence quickly perceived that most actors are hungry, and that even those blessed with dinner money didn't like to take time out to eat. So she always arrived at rehearsal with a cake, or a large fruit-filled kuchen, or cookies. At rehearsal break, the cast joined her in coffee and refreshment. She was as generous with what she had, and as eager to learn from others, as any teen-aged novice.

"Emma" proved so successful with the subscription audiences at the Playbox that Gilmor Brown moved it to main stage of Pasadena Playhouse, where it became one of the year's most popular attractions. Florence was the acting discovery of the year.

When she contracted with an agent to represent her for film work, she made a surprising stipulation: she didn't want any movie jobs for at least two years. Gilmor Brown had promised to keep her busy constantly, and she wanted to learn everything she could about acting, and go from one part to another, often rehearsing one production by day while acting in another at night.

She told me she had decided to use "Florence Bates" as her professional name because she regarded the "Miss Bates" Jane Austen had created as a good luck charm, and she didn't mean to relinquish it. I think her listing as "Florence Jacoby" on the programme of "Emma" is just about the only time she ever used her real name as an actress.

All this happened late in 1935 and during the first months of 1936, and her husband was as pleased with her success as she. That he adored Florence, and she him, was apparent to everybody who met them. I never knew them to quarrel, or even to have a difference. If Florence didn't agree with him, she never argued, or even said she didn't agree. And he never took issue with anything she did or said. Will Jacoby was an excellent example of an exceptional type that's almost disappeared — the strong but silent male. As a matter of fact, he looked not unlike William S. Hart, who made that masculine image in films his own.

Then, in the midst of their happiness over Florence's new activity, Fate handed her a terrible blow. Her daughter had given birth to a child, a girl, and a telegram came saying there were post-natal complications. Florence fled from rehearsal and flew to Texas. Her daughter died of septic poisoning.

When Florence returned to Los Angeles, she was like somebody who was almost ready to give up. But then she decided to live, and, now aged fifty, "to start life all over again."

For the next four years, she was one of the regular, and most popular members of the Pasadena Playhouse acting group. She acted every kind of part — a German mountain climber in "Autumn Crocus"; silly Mrs. Bennet trying to get her daughters married off in another Jane Austen dramatisation, "Pride and Prejudice"; Juliet's nurse in "Romeo and Juliet" — these were only a few of her many parts.

And, finally, she got a plum. It isn't often that the lead of a play is the character woman's, but Zoë Akins based the star-role of "O Evening Star!" on the character of Marie Dressler, and Jobyna Howland first played it on Broadway. Florence Bates re-created it at Pasadena, where it became her best-remembered role. It was so popular that she returned about ten years later to play it again, in a new production re-staged because of popular demand.

After "O Evening Star!," Florence was constantly being taken by her agent to some Hollywood studio for an interview with a director or producer. At first, she accepted a few walk-ons, timidly, like a beginner paddling near the shore. It was no more than day-work, and film fanatics can catch fleeting glimpses of her as "background" in several features of the late Thirties. But

269

they were unimportant and uncredited appearances, and she soon told her agent she preferred to bide her time and wait for the right role for her real film *début*.

Besides, she still thought of herself as learning, and regarded every role at Pasadena as a challenge. Her credo for acting was: "Never underestimate the intelligence of an opponent, an audience, or a child. Whenever you do, you get your come-uppance, and you jolly well deserve it."

In 1939, her agent took her to David O. Selznick's studio for an appointment with Alfred Hitchcock regarding the role of Mrs. Van Hopper in his forthcoming production of *Rebecca,* his *début* as a director in America.

Mr. Hitchcock appraised her meditatively and asked: "Miss Bates, have you ever been on the London stage?"

"No," replied Florence. "The broad 'a' I'm using is a phoney. I was born and reared in Texas."

Hitchcock frowned. "Then what have you done on the New York stage?"

"Nothing. I don't know anything about the stage, and I know less about the movies. So what do you propose to do about it?"

Hitchcock's eyes twinkled as he said: "I propose to give you a screen test in the morning."

Florence got the role. In her time, she had known many prototypes of Mrs. Van Hopper in various parts of the world — the rich, vulgar, selfish, vain, domineering American dowager who demands attention and is willing to pay for it, and God help anybody who is stuck with her, or, even worse, is beholden to her.

The actors with whom Florence played her scenes in the film's opening sequences — Laurence Olivier and Joan Fontaine — were experienced camera actors. Florence was determined to be as much in the scene as her co-players, to let neither Hitchcock, her fellow actors, nor herself, down. She made mistakes, of course, and was promptly bawled out by Hitchcock, but she came back. He was patient and helpful, and she gave him, finally, exactly what he wanted.

When the picture was press-shown, Florence Bates was acclaimed, and, afterwards, in the lobby of Grauman's Chinese Theatre, where the picture had been previewed, Charles Laughton, whom she had never met, singled her out and planted a congratulatory kiss on her cheek. She couldn't help the happy tears that rose to her eyes.

She was in!

There were immediate disappointments, of course. The most grievous was losing the Marie Dressler role in a re-make of *Tugboat Annie,* for which she tested twice. Then, Mrs. Edward Small, who had liked her performance in *Rebecca,* insisted that her husband give her the role of Joan Bennett's duenna-companion in his production of *The Son of Monte Cristo.*

After that, roles came, and she even had to decline some because she couldn't fit them into her schedule. Then M-G-M put her under contract, and for that studio she played the first of many comically obnoxious mothers-in-law — in *Love Crazy.* Another comedy role, in *The Chocolate Soldier,* with Rise Stevens and Nelson Eddy, followed.

For two of her favourite roles she was borrowed — by RKO for *The Tuttles of Tahiti,* and by Albert Lewin for *The Moon and Sixpence,* which was released by United Artists. She especially loved *The Tuttles* because its star

FLORENCE BATES

was Charles Laughton, who had so impulsively welcomed her into the film-acting world with a kiss.

The Jacobys sold their bakery and invested the money in a new car and a beautiful hillside home off Sunset Plaza Drive in the hills above the Strip. Almost at once, their new home became a centre for dinner parties and fun-evenings. Their next-door neighbours were cameraman Stanley Cortez and his pretty blonde wife, and the Jacobys and Cortezes became a familiar quartet.

Florence never lost her love of the theatre, and was constantly in the audience at Pasadena Playhouse. She started an endowment fund that made scholarships for worthy students possible there, and was always ready to give personal advice and financial help to any aspirant she deemed promising. And she played in several local stage productions in the Southern California area, including one of "Light Up the Sky," sponsored by the Selznick-La Jolla group.

I was often a guest in her friendly, comfortable home, and she frequently prepared the meals herself. She liked to cook, but had a birdlike appetite, and laughed at her own food idiosyncrasies, one of which was using sweet butter on her bread or rolls but salting it from a shaker before eating it. She had two pets: a Mexican hairless dog named "Lupe," and a parrot.

She *enjoyed* playing her screen roles, especially that of Mrs. Bellup, the social dictator in *Saratoga Trunk* who helps Ingrid Bergman crash society.

Florence Bates, Gary Cooper, Ingrid Bergman in *Saratoga Trunk*.

Florence Bates with Irene Dunne in *I Remember Mama*.

She liked working with Gypsy Rose Lee in *The Belle of the Yukon,* for Miss Lee was also a knitter, and between takes the two of them would knit and exchange stories. During the war, Florence worked regularly at the Hollywood Canteen and frequently brought service men home for dinner. Every six months she donated a pint of her blood to the Red Cross.

I'd always hoped she would play in a screenplay I wrote, and was very pleased when Harriet Parsons and George Stevens chose her to play the successful authoress, Florence Dana Moorhead, in *I Remember Mama*. On the day she first came on set for the role, her eyes were gleaming, and I knew she had a tale to tell. She said that as she was driving to the studio, a car driven by a young man had almost collided with her and that the young driver yelled at her furiously: "You old bitch!"

"I just waved my hand," said Florence, "and called: 'Hi, son!'"

Director George Stevens was convulsed with mirth, and forgot the ulcer pains that were then making his life miserable.

The scene in *I Remember Mama* in which Irene Dunne and Florence exchange recipes for literary advice is a perfect example of two pros playing so well they never miss a trick.

Florence was aware that a day would come when she would no longer be in demand. "At fifty, women find the world cut out from under them," she told the late Hedda Hopper. "Their children are usually married and gone. Housekeeping has become a routine, small job. There's nothing left to do. Many of them turn to bridge clubs, or such, to kill time — precious time. What a horrible waste of woman-power! Life has by no means ended for a woman of fifty. When I'm no longer wanted as an actress, I want to teach public relations to younger players. When we are too old to be fruit trees, Hedda, we can always be shade trees for the youngsters."

The time never came when Florence was not wanted as an actress, and she was so grateful to the motion picture industry that she was incensed when she read Lillian Ross's "New Yorker" *exposé* of making of M-G-M's *The Red Badge of Courage*. On her own volition, she wrote a letter to "The Hollywood Reporter," in which she defended Hollywood's film industry, and said: "I have found producers eager, yes, to finish a picture on schedule; but they have been gentle and considerate, and, in the main, efficient. I have found directors tactful and fastidious, anxious and able, to make a solid pattern of accomplishment out of the bits and pieces that go to make up this many-faceted enterprise. So with assistants and crew and helpers. Of course mistakes are made, boners pulled, banalities uttered. The miracle is there are not more in a business as intricate as this."

Without warning, on October 31, 1951, Fate struck her again. That night she was studying her lines in bed for the next day's shooting of *The San Francisco Story* when she heard her husband sigh in the bed next to hers.

"Are you awake, Will?"

He did not respond. She got up and went to him. He had died of a heart attack in his sleep.

Mechanically, with the help of the Cortezes, she did everything she had to

Florence Bates with Dorothy McGuire and Jerome Cowan in *Claudia and David*.

do — called the doctor, the coroner, the undertaker. And the next day she reported for work at the studio.

"Thank God I have something to do," she said when the production manager offered to revise the shooting schedule."

Doggedly, she went on working — the Stanley Cortezes virtually adopted her — but six months later she nearly had a serious nervous breakdown.

"I think I must have been living on sheer nerves," she told me. "I didn't want to give way after Will died, but now I realise I'd been existing in a state of suspended shock. Suddenly, I just had to let go, to give way to grief."

Florence never got over the shock of losing her husband, who had never been ill a day in his life (he was seventy when he died). She forced herself to work whenever a role came up, and she even made televison appearances, but she was losing weight alarmingly, and the laughter was gone from her eyes.

Madge Kennedy and she came to my apartment for dinner one night, and as soon as dinner was finished, she excused herself, and Miss Kennedy drove her home. Some time later, I took Hillary Brooke, who had never met her, to tea at Florence's. For an hour, Florence warmed to Hillary, but then fatigue was visible in her eyes, and we bade her farewell.

It was the last time I saw her.

She suffered several severe heart attacks, and finally agreed to be hospitalised. Mrs. Cortez told me later that when she went next door to drive her to the hospital, Florence was already in her car, impatient to be gone. She died of the heart ailment on January 31, 1954, in St. Joseph's Hospital in Burbank, a few months before her sixty-sixth birthday.

She is the only person I've ever known who actually died of a broken heart, something I had always regarded as a sentimental conceit of Victorian novelists.

FLORENCE BATES FILMOGRAPHY

REBECCA (1940) Romantic suspense drama; as Mrs. Van Hopper. *Dir:* Alfred Hitchcock. *Sc:* Robert Sherwood and Joan Harrison (from the novel by Daphne Du Maurier). *With* Joan Fontaine, Laurence Olivier, George Sanders, Judith Anderson, Nigel Bruce, Reginald Denny, C. Aubrey Smith, Gladys Cooper, Melville Copper, Leo G. Carroll, Leonard Carey, Lumsden Hare, Edward Fielding, Philip Winter, Forrester Harvey. *Prod:* Selznick/United Artists. 131m.

CALLING ALL HUSBANDS (1940). Domestic comedy; as Emmie Tripp. *Dir:* Noel Smith. *Sc:* Robert E. Kent (from the play, "Broken Dishes," by Martin Flavin). *With* Ernest Truex, George Tobias, Lucille Fairbanks, George Reeves, Charles Halton, Virginia Sale, Vera Lewis. (Previously filmed, 1930, as *Too Young to Marry* with Emma Dunn and O. P. Heggie; re-made, 1936, as *Love Begins at 20*, with Dorothy Vaughn and Hugh Herbert in the Bates-Truex roles.) *Prod:* Warner Bros. 7 reels.

THE SON OF MONTE CRISTO (1940). Romantic adventure in the principality of Lichtenburg; as Mathilde, duenna-companion to the principality's grand duchess Zona. *Dir:* Rowland V. Lee. *Sc:* George Bruce. *With* Louis Hayward, Joan Bennett, George Sanders, Lionel Royce, Montagu Love, Ralph Byrd, George Renevant, Michael Visaroff, Rand Brooks, Theodore von Eltz, James Seay, Henry Brandon, Jack Mulhall, *Prod:* Small/United Artists. 102m.

HUDSON'S BAY (1940). Biographical adventure based upon the life of the French trapper, Pierre Esprit Radisson; as a Duchess at the court of Charles II. *Dir:* Irving Pichel. *Sc:* Lamar Trotti. *With* Paul Muni, Gene Tierney, Laird Cregar, John Sutton, Virginia Field, Vincent Price, Nigel Bruce, Morton Lowry, Frederic Worlock, Montagu Love, Ian Wolfe, Jody Gilbert. *Prod:* 20th Century-Fox. 95m.

KITTY FOYLE (1940). Romantic comedy drama; as a querulous customer in a department store. *Dir:* Sam Wood. *Sc:* Dalton Trumbo and Donald Ogden Stewart (from the novel by Christopher Morley). *With* Ginger Rogers, Dennis Morgan, James Craig, Eduardo Ciannelli, Ernest Cossart, Gladys Cooper, Odette Myrtil, Mary Treen, Katharine (K.T.) Stevens, Walter Kingsford, Cecil Cunningham, Nella Walker, Edward Fielding, Kay Linaker, Heather Angel, Tyler Brooke. *Prod:* RKO-Radio. 107m.

ROAD SHOW (1941). Romantic carnival farce; as Mrs. Newton. *Dir:* Hal Roach and Gordon Douglas. *Sc:* Arnold Belgard, Harry Langdon and Mickell Novak (from a novel by Eric Hatch). *With* Adolphe Menjou, Carole Landis, John Hubbard, Charles Butterworth, Patsy Kelly, George E. Stone, Margaret Roach, Polly Ann Young, Edward Norris, Marjorie Woodworth, Willie Best, The Charioteers. *Prod:* Roach-United Artists. 87m.

STRANGE ALIBI (1941). Prison blackmail courtroom melodrama; as Katie, a gambling saloon hostess. *Dir:* D. Ross Lederman. *Sc:* Kenneth Gamet (from a story by Leslie T. White). *With* Arthur Kennedy, Joan Perry, Jonathan Hale, John Ridgely, Charles Trowbridge, Howard Da Silva. *Prod:* Warner Bros. 63m.

LOVE CRAZY (1941). Marital comedy; as Mrs. Cooper, a mother-in-law. *Dir:* Jack Conway. *Sc:* William Ludwig, Charles Lederer, David Hertz (from a story by Ludwig and Hertz). *With* Myrna Loy, William Powell, Gail Patrick, Jack Carson, Sidney Blackmer, Sig Rumann, Vladimir Sokoloff, Donald McBride, Sara Haden, Kathleen Lockhart, Elisha Cook Jr., Clarence Muse. *Prod:* M-G-M. 99m.

THE CHOCOLATE SOLDIER (1941). Romantic comedy; as Madame Helene, voice coach and personal maid to the opera star heroine. *Dir:* Roy Del Ruth. *Sc:* Leonard Lee and Keith Winter (from the play, "The Guardsman," by Ferenc Molnar, with music from Oscar Straus' "The Chocolate Soldier" and with other operatic and classical selections). *With* Nelson Eddy, Rise Stevens, Nigel Bruce, Dorothy Gilmore, Nydia Westman, Max Barwyn, Charles Judels. (The Lunts filmed *The Guardsman* for M-G-M, 1931.) *Prod:* M-G-M. 102m.

WE WERE DANCING (1941). Romantic comedy; as Mrs. Vanderlip. *Dir:* Robert Z. Leonard. *Sc:* Claudine West, Hans Rameau, George Froeschel (from, in part, Noel Coward's "Tonight at 8.30"). *With* Norma Shearer, Melvyn Douglas, Gail Patrick, Lee Bowman, Marjorie Main, Reginald Owen, Alan Mowbray, Heather Thatcher, Nella Walker, Connie Gilchrist. *Prod:* M-G-M. 94m.

THE DEVIL AND MISS JONES (1941). So-cial comedy; as a customer in a department store. *Dir:* Sam Wood. *Sc:* Norman Krasna. *With* Jean Arthur, Robert Cummings, Charles Coburn, Edmund Gwenn, Spring Byington, S. Z. Sakall, William Demarest, Walter Kingsford, Montagu Love, Richard Carle, Charles Waldron, Edwin Maxwell. *Prod:* RKO-Radio. 92m.

MEXICAN SPITFIRE AT SEA (1942). Romantic farce on a cruise; as Mrs. Baldwin. *Dir:* Les Goodwins. *Sc:* Jerry Cady and Charles E. Roberts. *With* Lupe Velez, Leon Errol, Charles (Buddy) Rogers, ZaSu Pitts, Elisabeth Risdon, Marion Martin, Ferris Taylor. *Prod:* RKO-Radio. 73m.

THE TUTTLES OF TAHITI (1942). South Sea island comedy; as Emily, who owns a ferocious fighting cock. *Dir:* Charles Vidor. *Sc:* Lewis Meltzer and Robert Carson (from the adaptation by James Hilton of the novel, "No More Gas," by Charles Nordhoff and James Norman Hall). *With* Charles Laughton, Jon Hall, Peggy Drake, Victor Francen, Gene Reynolds, Curt Bois, Adeline de Walt Reynolds, Mala, Leonard Sues, Jody Gilbert. *Prod:* RKO-Radio. 91m.

THE MOON AND SIXPENCE (1942). Drama based on the life of Paul Gauguin in the South Seas; as Tiare Johnson, an island innkeeper. *Dir/Sc:* Albert Lewin (from the novel by W. Somerset Maugham). *With* George Sanders, Herbert Marshall, Steve Geray, Doris Dudley, Eric Blore, Albert Basserman, Molly Lamont, Elena Verdugo, Heather Thatcher, Irene Tedrow, Devi Dja and her Bali-Java Dancers. *Prod:* United Artists. 89m.

MY HEART BELONGS TO DADDY (1942). Romantic comedy; as Mrs. Saunders, a bossy ex-mother-in-law who continues to live in the home of her widower son-in-law. *Dir:*Robert Siodmak. *Sc:* F. Hugh Herbert. *With* Richard Carlson, Martha O'Driscoll, Cecil Kellaway, Frances Gifford, Mabel Paige, Velma Berg, Francis Pierlot. *Prod:* Paramount. 76m.

THEY GOT ME COVERED (1943). Musical espionage comedy; as a gypsy woman. *Dir:* David Butler. *Sc:* Harry Kurnitz (from a story by Leonard Q. Ross and Leonard Spigelgass. *With* Bob Hope, Dorothy Lamour, Lenore Aubert, Otto Preminger, Eduardo Ciannelli, Marion Martin, Donald Meek, Philip Ahn, Walter Catlett, John Abbott, Mary Treen. *Prod:* RKO-Radio. 94m.

MR. LUCKY (1943). Comedy romance of a gambler who gets roped into war work; as Mrs. Van Every, who teaches Cary Grant how to knit. *Dir:* H. C. Potter. *Sc:* Milton Holmes and Adrian Scott (from a story by Holmes, "Bundles for Freedom"). *With* Cary Grant, Laraine Day, Charles Bickford, Gladys Cooper, Alan Carney, Henry Stephenson, Paul Stewart, Kay Johnson, Walter Kingsford, Erford Gage,

J. M. Kerrigan, Edward Fielding, Vladimir Sokoloff. *Prod:* RKO-Radio. 100m.

SLIGHTLY DANGEROUS (1943). Romantic comedy; as an elegant dowager, Mrs. Roanoke-Brooke. *Dir:* Wesley Ruggles. *Sc:* Charles Lederer and George Oppenheimer (from a story by Ian McLellan and Aileen Hamilton). *With* Lana Turner, Robert Young, Walter Brennan, Dame May Whitty, Eugene Pallette, Alan Mowbray, Howard Freeman, Millard Mitchell, Ward Bond, Pamela Blake, Ray Collins, Paul Stanton, Almira Sessions. Working titles: *Nothing Ventured;* then *Careless. Prod:* M-G-M. 94m.

MISTER BIG (1943). Juvenile comedy; as Mrs. Davis, head of a drama school. *Dir:* Charles Lamont. *Sc:* Jack Polexfen and Dorothy Bennett (from a story by Virginia Rooks). *With* Gloria Jean, Donald O'Connor, Peggy Ryan, Robert Paige, Elyse Knox, Samuel S. Hinds, Bobby Scheerer, Richard Stewart, Ray Eberle. *Prod:* Universal. 74m.

SARATOGA TRUNK (1943) Romantic period drama; as Mrs. Coventry Ballop, society dowager. *Dir:* Sam Wood. *Sc:* Casey Robinson (from the novel by Edna Ferber). *With* Gary Cooper, Ingrid Bergman, Flora Robson, Jerry Austin, John Warburton, John Abbott, Curt Bois, Ethel Griffies, Minor Watson, Louis Payne, Adrienne d'Ambricourt, Helen Freeman, Jacqueline de Wit, Ruby Dandridge, Thurston Hall, Edward Fielding, Lane Chandler, Theodore von Eltz, Monte Blue. *Prod:* Warner Bros. 125m.

HEAVEN CAN WAIT (1943). Comedy drama; as a fashionable candidate for Heaven, who gets to Hell in a hurry on the hot seat. *Dir:* Ernst Lubitsch. *Sc:* Samson Raphaelson (from the play, "Birthday," by Lazlo Bus-Fekete). *With* Don Ameche, Gene Tierney, Charles Coburn, Marjorie Main, Laird Cregar, Spring Byington, Allyn Joslyn, Eugene Pallette, Signe Hasso, Louis Calhern, Helene Reynolds, Michael Ames, Clarence Muse, Dickie Moore, Dickie Jones, Trudy Marshall, Clara Blandkick, Anita Bolster, Claire Du Brey, Maureen Rodin-Ryan. *Prod:* 20th Century-Fox. 112m.

HIS BUTLER'S SISTER (1943). Musical romance, billed as "a fable of the day before yesterday;" as Lady Sloughberry. *Dir:* Frank Borzage. *Sc:* Samuel Hoffenstein and Betty Reinhardt. *With* Deanna Durbin, Pat O'Brien, Franchot Tone, Evelyn Ankers, Else Janssen, Walter Catlett, Akim Tamiroff, Alan Mowbray, Frank Jenks, Sig Arno, Franklin Pangborn, Andrew Tombes, Hans Conried, Iris Adrian. *Prod:* Universal. 94m.

THE MASK OF DIMITRIOS (1944). Suspense espionage drama; as Mme. Chavez. *Dir:* Jean Negulesco. *Sc:* Frank Gruber (from a novel by Eric Ambler). *With* Sydney Greenstreet, Zachary Scott, Faye Emerson, Peter Lorre, George Tobias, Victor Francen, Steve Geray, Eduardo Ciannelli, Kurt Katch, Marjorie Hoshelle, Georges Metaxa, John Abbott, Monte Blue, David Hoffman. *Prod:* Warner Bros. 95m. Working titles: *Mask for Dimitrios* and *A Coffin for Dimitrios.*

SINCE YOU WENT AWAY (1944). Romantic drama of the home front during the Second World War in America; as a hungry passenger on a train. *Dir:* John Cromwell. *Sc:* David O. Selznick (Jeffrey Daniel) from the adaptation by Margaret Buell Wilder of her own novel). *With* Claudette Colbert, Jennifer Jones, Joseph Cotten, Shirley Temple, Monty Woolley, Lionel Barrymore, Robert Walker, Agnes Moorehead, Keenan Wynn, Albert Basserman, Nazimova, Gordon Oliver, Craig Stevens, Guy Madison, Hattie McDaniel, Lloyd Corrigan. *Prod:* Selznick-United Artists. 171m.

KISMET (1944). Romance of Old Bagdad; as Karsha, maidservant to the young heroine. *Dir:* William Dieterle. *Sc:* John Meehan (from the play by Edward Knoblock). *With* Ronald Colman, Marlene Dietrich, James Craig, Edward Arnold, Hugh Herbert, Joy Ann Page, Harry Davenport, Hobart Cavanaugh, Robert Warwick. (Previously filmed by Robertson-Cole in 1920; by First National in 1930; and a musical version by M-G-M, 1955). *Prod:* M-G-M. 100m.

THE BELLE OF THE YUKON (1944). Romantic comedy, with music; as Viola, maid to Gypsy Rose. *Dir:* William A. Seiter. *Sc:* James Edward Grant (from a story by Houston Branch). *With* Randolph Scott, Gypsy Rose Lee, Dinah Shore, Bob Burns, Charles Winninger, William Marshall, Guinn Williams, Robert Armstrong, Victor Kilian, Wanda McKay, Edward Fielding, Joel Friend, Albert Ruiz. *Prod:* RKO-Radio. 84m.

TAHITI NIGHTS (1945). Romance of the South Seas, with music; as Queen Liliha. *Dir:* Will Jason. *Sc:* Lillie Hayward. *With* Jinx Falkenburg, Dave O'Brien, Mary Treen, Cy Kendall, Eddie Bruce, Pedro de Cordoba, Hilo Hattie, Carole Mathews, Isabel Withers. Working title: *Song of Tahiti. Prod:* Columbia. 62m.

TONIGHT AND EVERY NIGHT (1945). Musical romance about London's Windmill Theatre, which never closed in the days of the Big Blitz; as May Tolliver, the Windmill's proprietress. *Dir:* Victor Saville. *Sc:* Lesser Samuels and Aben Finkel (from a play, "Heart of a City," by Lesley Storm). *With* Rita Hayworth, Lee Bowman, Janet Blair, Marc Platt, Leslie Brooks, Professor Lamberti, Dusty Anderson, Jim Bannon, Stephen Crane, Ernest Cossart, Philip Merivale, Shelley Win-

276

FLORENCE BATES

ters, Adele Jergens, Queenie Leonard. *Prod:* Columbia. 92m.

OUT OF THIS WORLD (1945). Musical comedy; as Harriet Pringle, rich dowager. *Dir:* Hal Walker. *Sc:* Walter DeLeon and Arthur Phillips (from stories by Elizabeth Meehan and Sam Coslow). *With* Eddie Bracken, Veronica Lake, Diana Lynn, Cass Daley, Donald McBride, Parkyakarkus, The Four Crosby Boys, Olga San Juan, Mabel Paige, Esther Dale, Carmen Cavallaro, Ted Fiorito, Henry King, Ray Noble, Joe Reichman. *Prod:* Paramount. 96m.

SAN ANTONIO (1945) Western romance; as Henrietta, the duenna companion of an entertainer. *Dir:* David Butler. *Sc:* Alan LeMay and W. R. Burnett. *With* Errol Flynn, Alexis Smith, S. Z. Sakall, Victor Francen, John Litel, Paul Kelly, John Alvin, Monte Blue, Robert Shayne, Robert Barrat, Pedro de Cordoba, Tom Tyler, Chris-Pin Martin, Lane Chandler. *Prod:* Warner Bros. 111m.

WHISTLE STOP (1946). Drama of smalltown life; as Molly Veech, mother of Raft. *Dir:* Leonide Moguy. *Sc:* Philip Yordan (from the novel by Maritta M. Wolff). *With* Ava Gardner, George Raft, Victor McLaglen, Tom Conway, Jorja Curtright, Jane Nigh, Charles Drake, Charles Judels, Carmel Myers. *Prod:* United Artists. 83m.

THE DIARY OF A CHAMBERMAID (1946). Period drama of France in the mid-1880s; as Rose. *Dir:* Jean Renoir. *Sc:* Burgess Meredith (from the novel by Octave Mirabeau and the play dramatised therefrom). *With* Paulette Goddard, Burgess Meredith, Hurd Hatfield, Francis Lederer, Reginald Owen, Judith Anderson, Irene Ryan, Almira Sessions. (Remade in France, 1965, by Luis Buñuel, with Jeanne Moreau.) *Prod:* United Artists. 86m.

CLUNY BROWN (1946). Comedy romance about an uninhibited lady plumber; as a dowager. *Dir:* Ernst Lubitsch. *Sc:* Samuel Hoffenstein and Elizabeth Reinhardt (from the novel by Margery Sharp). *With* Jennifer Jones, Charles Boyer, Peter Lawford, Helen Walker, Reginald Gardiner, C. Aubrey Smith, Reginald Owen, Richard Haydn, Margaret Bannerman, Sara Allgood, Ernest Cossart, Una O'Connor, Queenie Leonard, Billy Bevan, Michael Dyne, Rex Evans. *Prod:* 20th Century-Fox. 101m.

CLAUDIA AND DAVID (1946). Romantic drama, a sequel to *Claudia;* as Nancy Riddle, a gossiping neighbour. *Dir:* Walter Lang. *Sc:* Rose Franken and William Brown Meloney (from the adaptation by Vera Caspary of some of Miss Franken's short stories). *With* Dorothy McGuire, Robert Young, Mary Astor, John Sutton, Gail Patrick, Rose Hobart, Harry Davenport, Jerome Cowan, Else Janssen, Clara Blandick, Pierre Watkins, Betty Comp-

son. *Prod:* 20th Century-Fox. 78m. (Compare listing in Betty Compson filmography.)

THE TIME, THE PLACE AND THE GIRL (1946). Romantic musical; as Mme. Lucia Cassel. *Dir:* David Butler. *Sc:* Francis Swann, Agnes Christine Johnston and Lynn Starling (from a story by Leonard Lee.) *With* Dennis Morgan, Jack Carson, Janis Paige, Martha Vickers, S. Z. Sakall, Alan Hale, Donald Woolf, Monte Blue, Vera Lewis, Carmen Cavallaro and his Orchestra. (No relationship to the play or the previous movie of this title.) *Prod:* Warner Bros. 105m.

NIGHTSONG (1947). As a San Francisco music lover. *Dir:* John Cromwell. *Sc:* Frank Fenton and Richard Irving Hyland (adapted by DeWitt Bodeen from a story by Hyland.) *With:* Merle Oberon, Dana Andrews, Ethel Barrymore, Hoagy Carmichael, Arthur Rubenstein, Eugene Ormandy, New York Philharmonic Orchestra. *Prod:* RKO Radio. 102m.

THE BRASHER DOUBLOON (AKA, GB, *The High Window*) (1947). Detective murder mystery; as Mrs. Murdoch, the murderess. *Dir:* John Brahm. *Sc:* Dorothy Hannah (from the adaptation by Leonard Praskins of the novel by Raymond Chandler). *With* George Montgomery, Nancy Guild, Conrad Janis, Roy Roberts, Fritz Kortner, Marvin Miller, Houseley Stevenson. *Prod:* 20th Century-Fox.

LOVE AND LEARN (1947). Comedy romance, with music; as Mrs. Davis, a landlady. *Dir:* Frederick de Cordova. *Sc:* Eugene Conrad, Francis Swann and I. A. L. Diamond (from a story by Harry Sauber). *With* Jack Carson, Martha Vickers, Robert Hutton, Janis Paige, Otto Kruger, Barbara Brown, Tom D'Andrea, Craig Stevens, Grady Sutton, Creighton Hale, Iris Adrian, Sarah Padden. *Prod:* Warner Bros. 83m.

THE SECRET LIFE OF WALTER MITTY (1947). Comedy fantasy, with songs; as Mrs. Griswold, a prospective mother-in-law. *Dir:* Norman Z. McLeod. *Sc:* Ken Englund and Everett Freeman (from a story by James Thurber). *With* Danny Kaye, Virginia Mayo, Boris Karloff, Ann Rutherford, Thurston Hall, Fay Bainter, Gordon Jones, Konstantin Shayne, Reginald Denny, Doris Lloyd, Fritz Feld, Frank Reicher. *Prod:* Goldwyn / RKO. 110m.

DESIRE ME (1947). Romantic drama; as a village character. No director's credit. *Sc:* Marguerite Roberts and Zoë Akins (from the adaptation by Casey Robinson of the play, "Karl and Anna," by Leonard Frank). *With* Greer Garson, Robert Mitchum, Richard Hart, Morris Ankrum, George Zucco, Cecil Humphreys, David Hoffman. Working title: *Sacred and Profane. Prod:* M-G-M. 91m.

THE INSIDE STORY (1948). Comedy drama

277

about money; as a rich hotel resident. *Dir:* Allan Dwan. *Sc:* Mary Loos and Richard Sale (from a story by Ernest Lehman and Geza Herczeg). *With* Marsha Hunt, William Lundigan, Charles Winninger, Gail Patrick, Gene Lockhart, Allen Jenkins, Roscoe Karns, Robert Shayne, Will Wright, William Haade, Hobart Cavanaugh, James Kirkwood, Frank Ferguson. Re-issued in 1954 as *The Big Gamble.* Working title: *The Storm. Prod:* Republic. 85m.

I REMEMBER MAMA (1948). Comedy drama of a Norwegian family in San Francisco about 1910; as Florence Dana Moorehead, a stylish travelling authoress. *Dir:* George Stevens. *Sc:* DeWitt Bodeen (from the play by John Van Druten and a collection of short-stories, "Mama's Bank Account," by Kathryn Forbes). *With* Irene Dunne, Barbara Bel Geddes, Oscar Homolka, Philip Dorn, Sir Cedric Harwicke, Edgar Bergen, Rudy Vallee, Barbara O'Neil, Ellen Corby, Peggy McIntyre, June Hedin, Steven Brown, Hope Landin, Edith Evanson, Tommy Ivo. *Prod:* RKO-Radio. 116m.

WINTER MEETING (1948). Romantic drama; as Mrs. Castle, housekeeper. *Dir:* Bretaigne Windust. *Sc:* Catherine Turney (from the novel by Ethel Vance). *With* Bette Davis, James Davis, Janis Paige, John Hoyt, Walter Baldwin, Ransom Sherman. *Prod:* Warner Bros. 104m. Working title: *Strange Meeting.*

RIVER LADY (1948). Romantic drama; as Ma Dunnigan, waterfront salookeeper. *Dir:* George Sherman. *Sc:* D. D. Beauchamp and William Bowers (from a story by Houston Branch and Frank Waters). *With* Yvonne De Carlo, Dan Duryea, Rod Cameron, Helena Carter, Lloyd Gough, John McIntire. *Prod:* Universal. Technicolor. 78m.

TEXAS, BROOKLYN AND HEAVEN (AKA, GB, *Girl from Texas*) (1948). Character comedy; as the ex-pickpocket mother adopted by the heroine. *Dir:* William Castle. *Sc:* Lewis Meltzer (from the adaptation by Earl Baldwin of a novel, "Eddie and the Archangel Mike," by Barry Benfield). *With* Guy Madison, Diana Lynn, James Dunn, Michael Chekov, Lionel Stander, William Frawley, Roscoe Karns, Margaret Hamilton, Irene Ryan, Moyna MacGill, Audie Murphy. *Prod:* United Artists. 76m.

MY DEAR SECRETARY (1948). Romantic comedy; as Mrs. Reeves, landlady. *Dir/Sc:* Charles Martin. *With* Kirk Douglas, Laraine Day, Keenan Wynn, Helen Walker, Rudy Vallee, Alan Mowbray, Grady Sutton, Irene Ryan, Gale Robbins, Gertrude Astor. *Prod:* United Artists. 95m.

A LETTER TO THREE WIVES (1948). Romantic comedy; as Mrs. Manleigh, a radio executive's wife. *Dir/Sc:* Joseph Mankiewicz (from the adaptation by Vera Caspary of a story by John Klempner). *With* Jeanne Crain, Linda Darnell, Ann Sothern, Kirk Douglas, Paul Douglas, Barbara Lawrence, Jeffrey Lynn, Connie Gilchrist, Hobart Cavanaugh, Thelma Ritter, Stuart Holmes, Celeste Holm's voice. *Prod:* 20th Century-Fox. 103m. Working title: *A Letter to Five Wives.*

PORTRAIT OF JENNIE (AKA, GB, *Tidal Wave*) (1948). Love story; as Mrs. Jekes, a landlady. *Dir:* William Dieterle. *Sc:* Paul Osborn and Peter Berneis (from the adaptation by Leonardo Bercovici of the novel by Robert Nathan). *With* Jennifer Jones, Joseph Cotten, Ethel Barrymore, Lillian Gish, Cecil Kellaway, David Wayne, Albert Sharpe, Henry Hull, Felix Bressart, Clem Bevans, Maude Simmons. *Prod:* Selznick. 86m.

THE JUDGE STEPS OUT (1949). Character comedy; as a Mexican chorewoman. *Dir:* Boris Ingster. *Sc:* Ingster and Alexander Knox (from a story by Ingster). *With* Alexander Knox, Ann Sothern, George Tobias, Sharyn Moffett, Frieda Inescort, Myrna Dell, Ian Wolfe, H. B. Warner, Martha Hyer, James Warren, Whitford Kane, Harry Hayden, Anita Bolster. Working title: *Indian Summer. Prod:* RKO-Radio. 91m.

THE GIRL FROM JONES BEACH (1949). Romantic farce; as Miss Shoemaker, spinster. *Dir:* Peter Godfrey. *Sc:* I. A. L. Diamond (from a story by Allen Boretz). *With* Ronald Reagan, Virginia Mayo, Eddie Bracken, Dona Drake, Henry Travers, Lois Wilson, Jerome Cowan, Helen Westcott, Paul Harvey, Lloyd Corrigan, Myrna Dell, William Forrest. *Prod:* Warner Bros. 78m.

ON THE TOWN (1949). Ballet-musical about three sailors on the town; as the imbibing Mme. Dilyovska, dance teacher. *Dir* Gene Kelly and Stanley Donen. *Sc:* Adolph Green and Betty Comden (from their Broadway musical). *With* Gene Kelly, Frank Sinatra, Betty Garrett, Ann Miller, Jules Munshin, Vera-Ellen, Alice Pearce, George Meader. *Prod:* M-G-M. 98m.

BELLE OF OLD MEXICO (1950). Romantic comedy, with music; as Nellie Chatfield. *Dir:* R. G. Springsteen. *Sc:* Bradford Ropes and Francis Swann. *With* Estrelita Rodriguez, Robert Rockwell, Dorothy Patrick, Thurston Hall, Fritz Feld, Gordon Jones. *Prod:* Republic. 70m.

COUNTY FAIR (1950). Comedy drama of harness racing; as Ma Ryan. *Dir:* William Beaudine. *Sc:* W. Scott Darling. *With* Rory Calhoun, Jane Nigh, Warren Douglas, Raymond Hatton, Emory Parnell, Joan Vohs, Clarence Muse, Bob Carson, Heine Conklin, Rory Mallinson, Jack Mower. *Prod:* Monogram. 76m.

278

THE SECOND WOMAN (1951). Psychological suspense drama; as Amelia Foster. *Dir:* James W. Kern. *Sc:* Robert Smith. *With* Robert Young, Betsy Drake, John Sutton, Morris Carnovsky, Henry O'Neill, Jean Rodgers, Jason Robards Sr., Steve Geray. Working titles: *Here Lies Love; Ellen; 12 Miles Out.* *Prod:* United Artists. 90m.

THE LULLABY OF BROADWAY (1951). Backstage comedy, with music, as Mrs. Hubbell, nagging wife. *Dir:* David Butler. *Sc:* Earl Baldwin. *With* Doris Day, Gene Nelson, S. Z. Sakall, Billy DeWolfe, Gladys George, Anne Triola, Hanley Stafford, Herschel Daugherty. Working titles: *My Irish Molly O; Just Off Broadway.* *Prod:* Warner Bros. 91m.

FATHER TAKES THE AIR (1951). One of the "Latham Family" comedy series; as Minerva Bobbin. *Dir:* Frank McDonald. *Sc:* D. D. Beauchamp. *With* Raymond Walburn, Walter Catlett, Gary Gray, Barbara Brown, M'liss McClure, Jim Brown, George Nokes. *Prod:* Monogram. 60m.

THE TALL TARGET (AKA, *The Tall Target Man*) (1951). Suspenseful drama about the attempted assassination of President Lincoln in Baltimore on the eve of his first inauguration; as Mrs. Charlotte Alsop. *Dir:* Anthony Mann. *Sc:* George Worthing Yates and Art Cohn (from a story, "The Man on the Train," by Yates and George Homes). *With* Dick Powell, Paula Raymond, Adolphe Menjou, Marshall Thompson, Ruby Dee, Will Geer, Richard Rober, Victor Kilian, Katherine Warren, Leif Erickson, Leslie Kimmell. *Prod:* M-G-M. 78m.

HAVANA ROSE (1951). Romantic comedy, with music; as Mrs. Fillmore, a millionaire's wife who controls the purse-strings. *Dir:* William Beaudine. *Sc:* Charles E. Roberts and Jack Townley. *With* Estrelita Rodriguez, Bill Williams, Hugh Herbert, Fortunio Bonanova, Leon Belasco, Tom Kennedy. *Prod:* Republic. 77m.

THE SAN FRANCISCO STORY (1952). Romantic drama of San Francisco in the 1850s; a waterfront gin-mill harridan. *Dir:* Robert Parrish. *Sc:* D. D. Beauchamp from a novel by Richard Summers). *With* Joel McCrea, Yvonne De Carlo, Sidney Blackmer, Richard Erdman, Onslow Stevens, John Raven, O. Z. Whitehead, Ralph E. Dumke, Robert Foulk, Lane Chandler. *Prod:* Warner Bros. 80m.

LES MISERABLES (1952). The classic novel of Old France; as Mme. Bonnet, a vicious old woman. *Dir:* Lewis Milestone. *Sc:* Richard Murphy (from the novel by Victor Hugo). *With* Michael Rennie, Debra Paget, Robert Newton, Edmund Gwenn, Sylvia Sidney, Cameron Mitchell, Elsa Lanchester, James Robertson Justice, Joseph Wiseman, Rhys Williams, Merry Anders, Norma Varden, Queenie Leonard, Mary Forbes, Moyna MacGill, John Rogers. (Previously filmed, 1918, by Fox, with William Farnum; by France, 1913 (12 reels); 1925 (32 reels); 1934 (10 reels); by France, Italy, East Germany, 1957 (Technicolor), by Italy, 1946; by 20th Century-Fox, 1935, with Fredric March and Charles Laughton.) *Prod:* 20th Century-Fox. 105m.

MAIN STREET TO BROADWAY (1953). Romance of small town vs. Broadway; as a character in a fantasy sequence wherein Tallulah Bankhead plays a sweet housewife. *Dir:* Tay Garnett. *Sc:* Samson Raphaelson (from a story by Robert E. Sherwood). *With* Tom Morton, Mary Murphy, Agnes Moorehead, Herb Shriner, Rosemary de Camp, Clinton Sundberg; and with many cameo appearances of Broadway stars and personalities, ranging alphabetically from Tallulah Bankhead to John Van Druten. *Prod:* M-G-M. 78m.

PARIS MODEL (1953). Four-episode comedy revolving around the history of an exclusive Paris model gown; as Mrs. Norah Sullivan, a wife who holds the purse-strings. *Dir:* Alfred E. Green. *Sc:* Robert Smith. *With* Paulette Goddard, Marilyn Maxwell, Eva Gabor, Barbara Lawrence, Cecil Kellaway, Robert Hutton, Leif Erickson, Tom Conway, "Prince" Michael Romanoff, El Brendel, Robert Bice, Aram Katcher, Bryon Foulger. Original title: *Nude at Midnight. Prod:* Columbia. 81m.

13
CLINT EASTWOOD

"I was a bit of a screw-up, a loner," says Clint Eastwood. "Basically, I'm a drifter, a bum. As it turns out, I'm lucky because I'm going to end up financially well-off for a drifter."

And on another occasion he told Rex Reed: "Whatever success I've had is a lot of instinct and a little luck. I just go by how I feel."

But it's more than luck and instinct, and he is much more than a drifter and a bum. Eastwood is, first and foremost, a survivor. His life and career testify to that. He survived the Depression Era of his youth; he survived two dreary years doing his hitch in the Army; he survived three years being pushed around and ignored by Hollywood; he survived more than seven years as the co-star and then the star of a CBS TV weekly hour-long series. Now he is a superstar in films, and his luck is still holding; he has survived a succession of mediocre vehicles that fortunately for him have done nothing but make money. In 1971 he had three good and varied features in a row to his credit, one marking his *début* as a director; and 1971 also saw him forge ahead to become Number One Worldwide Box-Office Star.

In 1968 he first made the Top Ten in America, placed in fifth position, being surpassed by Sidney Poitier, Paul Newman, Julie Andrews, and John Wayne. He held fifth position the next year, being topped then by Paul Newman, John Wayne, Steve McQueen, and Dustin Hoffman. Great Britain in that year was the first country to give a hint of honours to come, for in 1969 he was named leading money-making star by 1,600 British cinema managers. By 1970 Eastwood had jumped to No. 2 spot in America, preceded only by Paul Newman, and by January of 1971 he had moved securely ahead of every other film star to occupy by a large margin the top spot. In the 1972 list he was topped only by John Wayne, who has appeared twenty-two times among the Top Ten, a record for star endurance. When the 1973 list was published, it revealed that Eastwood had moved again to Number One spot in America, once more ahead of Wayne.

Clint Eastwood is no publicity manager's invention; he came after the decline of the studios, and no studio invented him or helped him edge to the top. He is very modest about his success, and grins engagingly: "Any actor going into pictures has to have something special. That's what makes a star while a lot of damn good actors are passed by. The public recognises their work as good but they don't run out to see them with their $3 for a ticket. The public goes to see the stars. I didn't invent those rules; that's just the way it is."

MORE FROM HOLLYWOOD

Whether one swears by astrology or not, horoscope analysts are not just making idle predictions when they claim that successful actors born under the sign of Gemini never become just stars; they are the superstars of the business. John Wayne, Errol Flynn, Bob Hope, Laurence Olivier, Rosalind Russell, Jeanette MacDonald, Marilyn Monroe, Judy Garland were all born under the sign of Gemini.

So was Clint Eastwood, born in San Francisco, California, on May 31, 1930.

He remembers his childhood as a time of constant travelling. As he told Wayne Warga for a 1969 "Los Angeles Times" piece: "It was during the Depression and for my father jobs were hard to get and hard to maintain. I must have gone to ten different schools in ten years. My father always kept telling me you don't get anything for nothing, and although I rebelled, I never rebelled against that.

"I was never an extrovert, but I longed for independence, even though I got along great with my parents. I went to work right after I graduated from Oakland Technical High School — we had by then settled in Oakland — lumbering in Oregon. I wanted to be by myself and earn my own way. Then I went into the Army and still I didn't know what I really wanted to do. I was never that fortunate to know."

He was stationed at Ford Ord, only a few miles south of his natal city. Army personnel discovered he was a champion swimmer, so he was made Fort Ord's swimming instructor. Today, talking about it, he grins and shrugs. "How could I protest? I love swimming, and I got to live alone down at the pool. It was a long pool, and most of the guys taking the test couldn't make it, and I'd have to dive in and pull them out."

Once, when he had leave, Eastwood went up to Seattle to visit his parents, and hitched a ride back to Monterey on a service plane. The plane crashed at sea off Point Reyes, and Eastwood swam the three miles to shore. "I still haven't met the pilot," he confesses. "He had a Mae West, and I didn't. We both made it, but I had the most work to do. I didn't mind the swim; but that five-mile hike before I found a highway really bothered me."

Universal-International Studios sent a company up to Fort Ord around this time, and an enterprising assistant director called the director's attention to Eastwood. Even then, standing very tall at 6 feet 4 inches, long waisted and lanky, with green eyes shining like a healthy cool cat's, Eastwood had the kind of physical presence that made people turn and look at him a second time. The director asked him to read a scene. Eastwood had never thought about being an actor; in fact, while in Junior High, he'd been forced to take part in a play and was terrified. But he obligingly read for the director, who told him to look him up at Universal when he'd finished his Army training.

Accordingly, when he was discharged, Eastwood went down to Hollywood and reported to Universal, only to be told that the director was no longer with the studio. He thought, "Well, that's that," and was tempted to go to the University of Washington on the G.I. Bill, but instead enrolled at Los Angeles City College. He had a part-time job working as a gas station mechanic, and ten months after landing in Hollywood he married Maggie Johnson, a pretty blonde model whom he had met on a blind date. Twenty years later, they're still man and wife, and very happy.

Clint Eastwood at 'The Eastwood', the charity tennis tournament at Pebble Beach, California on behalf of the Behavioral Services Institute; July 1973.

He still didn't quite know what he wanted to specialise in at City College. "I was taking Business Administration," he says, "what everybody takes when he doesn't know what he wants to do. Acting was the only profession to come along that was sort of specific. A couple of friends of mine from the service were working at Universal — a cameraman and a director. They thought I would photograph well and they made a test. It was one of those silent tests where you walk in front of the camera and look into the lens — scared to death — and if you photographed well, okay. What a kookie way to get going!"

He survived that test for all its kookie crudities, and in 1954 signed a stock acting contract at Universal, guaranteeing him forty weeks out of fifty-two at $75 a week. About that time I was working as a writer on two assignments at Universal (one for Ted Richmond and another for Ross Hunter; neither was filmed), and I well remember seeing Eastwood on the lot. It was hard to miss him. His rangy height, his intense interest in anything to do with film, his wide-smiled friendliness made him stand out, even when he was playing bits in Rock Hudson and George Nader features, and they were then the two white-haired boys at Universal. I didn't see how Eastwood could fail.

Today it must give him some sense of ironic satisfaction. During that first year-and-a-half, when he was a mere contract player, I don't think he ever crossed the threshold of the spacious offices occupied by Milton Rachmil, then head of Universal Studios. Now Eastwood's own company, Malpaso, is housed in those same offices, re-designed and enlarged to accommodate his present needs.

The middle Fifties was a good time for an actor who wanted to learn about picture-making to be at Universal-International. The company annually made a whole series of very successful programme features, and Eastwood managed to appear in six of them where he got billing and footage. He played in others unbilled — voice off camera, the office worker who, back to camera, opens a door to admit a star... But in *Revenge of the Creature* and *Tarantula*, he is in there helping hero John Agar battle giant monsters. In his second release, *Francis in the Navy*, he not only had credit and good camera exposure, but the critics listed him by name and some called him "engaging" or "handsome" or "promising."

But when a year-and-a-half had rolled by, Universal did not pick up its option on his services. Eastwood went over to RKO, and made two films. In the first, a comedy, *The First Travelling Saleslady*, he had excellent billing, and the "Hollywood Reporter" noted that "Clint Eastwood is very attractive as Carol Channing's beau." Unfortunately, *The First Travelling Saleslady* was a real dud. Critics preferred to overlook it, and audiences passed it by as unfunny. Eastwood had just a bit in *Escapade in Japan* at RKO as Dumbo, a screwball pilot who precipitates the whole adventure for the two juvenile leads. But by then RKO had been relinquished by Howard Hughes and was in a decline; the film was eventually — and ironically — taken over by Universal for American release.

During the next two years Eastwood was tempted more than once to throw in the towel. As a free-lance actor, he got two above-average roles — one in a low-budget Western, *Ambush at Cimarron Pass*, released by 20th Century-Fox; and the other a First World War romance, *Lafayette Escadrille* (G. B.: *Hell Bent for Glory*) at Warner Bros., in which at least he had a chance to work under the skilful direction of William Wellman. Actually, in that 1957-58

Clint Eastwood with Carol Channing in *The First Travelling Saleslady*.

period, Eastwood made more money working with a friend digging swimming pools for a contracting company. On one of the jobs, the boss lost his temper with Eastwood's buddy and fired him. Eastwood laid his shovel aside. "You quitting?" the boss asked. "I drove my friend out here," Eastwood explained. "He hasn't any way to get home unless I drive him." And then Eastwood grinned and added, "But yes, you're right. I'm quitting."

It is that kind of loyalty which Eastwood has never lost. Some of his best friends he first met in the days of his early adversity. Today his companies and crews are known for their respect and abiding loyalty to him.

In the last years of the Fifties, the film studios were reluctantly heeding the death knell, and most of them had long abandoned contract lists of any kind. The only hope was television, and even if an actor got a show and it lasted a couple of seasons, he was a dead duck once the show was cancelled. Stars of last year's television hits rarely even had a chance to hold down a running part in the new season's hit, let alone find so much as a bit in a feature film.

Eastwood took television roles whenever one came his way; but it was pure luck and being in the right place at the right time that gained Eastwood his first really big break. One day he was in the neighbourhood of CBS Television City in Hollywood, and went to the upstairs office of Sonia Chernus, CBS Television's story consultant.* She was a friend of him and his wife, and the

*Today Miss Chernus is story editor for Eastwood's Malpaso Productions.

call was purely a social one. But while he was in the outer office talking to Miss Chernus, Robert Sparks, CBS Television's executive producer in charge of all filmed programmes, happened to come out and take a casual look at Eastwood, and then a good second look.

"You an actor?" he asked.

"Yeah — Eastwood's the name."

"Come in, Eastwood," said Sparks. "I want to talk to you and introduce you to somebody. We might do business."

Sparks had been discussing casting problems on a new CBS show, *Rawhide,* with producer-director Charles Marquis Warren. It was a series about a cattle drive that simply went on and on, and an actor named Eric Fleming had been cast as the lead, the trail boss. The role of the younger No. 1 ramrod Rowdy Yates was equally important, and Sparks and Warren hadn't been able to find the right actor for the part, one whose personality would contrast favourably with Fleming's. They were impressed when Eastwood read a scene for them; they were more impressed when they looked at him on film; and they knew he was the actor they were seeking when they saw him together with Fleming. He was signed as co-star, and on January 9, 1959, *Rawhide* was premiered on CBS. Overnight it became one of the real hits of the television season, and its steady popularity lasted for more than seven years.

Eastwood had a good contract, and remembering all the years of struggle, kept quiet during the first three years of the show, even though CBS blithely ignored many of the provisions they had originally agreed to honour. Finally, he lost his temper and complained to Hank Grant, who in the "Hollywood Reporter" for July 13, 1961, noted Eastwood's complaint: "I haven't been allowed to accept a single feature or TV guesting offer since I started the series. Maybe they figure me as the sheepish, nice guy I portray in the series, but even a worm has to turn sometime. Believe me, I'm not bluffing — I'm prepared to go on suspension, which means I can't work here, but I've open features in London and Rome that'll bring me more money in a year than the series has given me in three."

CBS, not wanting to lose Eastwood, called him in, and the pipe of peace was smoked. Thereafter, during the subsequent summer lay-off periods, Eastwood guested, appeared on talk shows, and made it known that he was available to film a feature during those free months. Having got what he wanted, Eastwood used the television medium as a means of learning about acting in front of a camera. If he wanted to try something new in his characterisation of Rowdy Yates, he could afford to try it on TV. If it worked, fine — he'd learned something; if it didn't, oops sorry! — he knew he wouldn't try that again.

In the spring of 1964, he received a hurried and harried call from Italy. An amalgamate company, Jolly-Constantin-Ocean, was going to film a Western in Spain, budgeted at $200,000, and directed by Sergio Leone. The lead had been offered to several American actors working abroad, but they were tied up. One of them, Richard Harrison, suggested they try to get Clint Eastwood. He was available, and agreed to do the film for a flat $15,000. He flew to Spain, and production started on *Per un pugno di dollari,* to be known in English-speaking countries as *A Fistful of Dollars.*

288

CLINT EASTWOOD

The story was patently a Western re-write of a successful Japanese film made by Kurosawa, *Yojimbo*. The samurai hero, originally played by Mifune, became a lone occidental stranger who rides laconically on a mule into a town torn by hates. The stranger wears a soiled serape over a worn fleece-lined leather vest; a flat brimmed hat shades his eyes; he never stops chewing on an unlit cheroot; and he is a real pistolero known as The Man with No Name. He looks over the little town of San Miguel, and comments tersely: "There's money to be made in a place like this."

He cashes in almost at once. Two families are at war with one another and The Man with No Name goes to work for both of them, helping each knock off the other. Dialogue is kept to an admirable sparseness. In one sequence, Eastwood tells the coffin-maker to have three coffins ready. After the shoot-out, in which Eastwood kills four adversaries, he merely turns to the coffin-maker and says, "Sorry — *four* coffins."

The little town of San Miguel suffers a blood bath that is more than just "estupendo," and The Man with No Name survives every kind of horrendous beating to ride off in lonely silence for the final fade-out, the only one to have profited in the venture.

The film was completed on schedule, and Eastwood returned to Hollywood to start filming a new season of hour-long TV scripts for *Rawhide*. He had little to say around the lot about his summer in Spain, saving a few prize anecdotes for appearances on TV talk shows.

By the end of the year, word was leaking out of the Italian boot: *Per un pugno di dollari* was enjoying hysterical popularity; in Italy it had already outgrossed both *My Fair Lady* and *Mary Poppins,* and the picture eventually earned $7,000,000 alone in Europe. Meanwhile, Eastwood was filming the *Rawhide* series for the 1964-65 season, and European friends wrote him jubilantly about his success in the first of the big spaghetti Westerns. Called "El Cigarillo," Eastwood was known as "the fastest draw in the Italian cinema." Vittorio De Sica was proclaiming him to be "absolutely the new Gary Cooper." In South America he was becoming known as "El Pistolero con los ojos verdes" (The Gunman with the Green Eyes). Very quietly, Eastwood noted all this and pigeon-holed the facts, waiting.

In the spring of 1965, Sergio Leone approached him about starring in a sequel Western, in which he would again play The Man with No Name. There would be another American actor in the cast, Lee Van Cleef, while a promising young Italian actor, Gian Maria Volonté (five years later to star brilliantly in *Investigation of a Citizen above Suspicion*) would be the bastardly, drug-addicted killer both Eastwood and Van Cleef, as bounty hunters, would be running down. The picture would again be filmed in Spain, and budgeted at $600,000. Eastwood agreed to do it for $50,000 plus a percentage and fringe benefits.

He flew to Spain in 1965 and filmed the sequel which was to be called in English *For a Few Dollars More*. While abroad, Eastwood also played opposite Silvano Mangano in an Italian-made anthology drama, *The Witches (Le streghe),* each segment of which was made by a different director. De Sica directed the Mangano-Eastwood episode called *A Night Like Any Other*.

When Eastwood returned to Hollywood, he found there had been some shake-ups at CBS. Eric Fleming had been dropped as co-star of *Rawhide*, and without any explanation to viewers why Rowdy Yates was now trail boss, Eastwood was promoted to solo star billing.* The front office at CBS was raging with more than a few minor brouhahas. James Aubrey had cancelled *Rawhide* when he took over the network, but once Aubrey was out at CBS, every show he had cancelled was at first re-scheduled. But *Rawhide* was suddenly dropped irrevocably, and with seventeen segments unfilmed. Eastwood settled his CBS pact on February 8, 1966 for $119,000 cash.

He was a free man.

He had survived a fantastically successful television series, and instead of the oblivion which most stars of a cancelled series inevitably faced, he knew that he had already made it in Europe, Asia, and South America as a big and important new film star. It was a unique position. Steve McQueen, James Garner, and Lee Marvin, onetime TV stars, had survived the demise of their series and subsequently become big stars in feature films, but Eastwood was a top film star even before his television series was cancelled!

Negotiations were already proceeding for a third Western to be made in Spain starring him with Lee Van Cleef and Eli Wallach, this one eventually to be called *The Good, the Bad and the Ugly*. Its violence would be dramatic and excessive to suit the new vogue in the Western film. The picture was to be budgeted at $1,200,000, and Eastwood to be paid $250,000 cash plus ten per cent of the Western hemisphere profits.

He had become a superstar and a rich man in his own right, and as yet not one of the films in the "paella trilogy," as the three features were known in Europe, had been shown in the United States. Leone's company had neglected to buy the American rights to *Yojimbo*, and it took some time before a compromise settlement could be worked out with a Japanese company.

In 1967 both *A Fistful of Dollars* and *For a Few Dollars More* opened in the U.S.A., and by the following year *The Good, the Bad and the Ugly* was also showing everywhere. Vincent Canby, "New York Times" critic, remarked succinctly of its sado-masochistic violence — "Zane Grey meets the Marquis de Sade" — and some time later Canby, after praising Eastwood for not trying to act up a storm on the screen, noted the following: "I'm one of the few people I know who will publicly admit to having liked the Sergio Leone, Italian-Spanish westerns that made Eastwood an international star. In those spare, bloody, nihilistic nightmares, photographed in the powdery colours of the Almeria desert, Eastwood's fathomless cool was framed with style. The movies required absolutely nothing of him except that he exist, the perfect physical specter haunting a world in which the evil was as commonplace as it was unrelenting."

All three foreign-made Westerns are still being shown and whenever an American cinema manager suffers a bad season, he often books all three on a triple replay bill — 387 minutes of Clint Eastwood — and packs the house again. Eastwood made a cinema image for himself in playing The Man with No Name, and has managed to survive even that.

United Artists had released the paella trilogy in the U.S.A., and they negotiated with Eastwood to film in New Mexico a spaghetti Western type of

---

*Fleming went over to MGM to play in a Doris Day comedy, *The Glass Bottom Boat*, and then in '66 flew to Peru on location for the pilot film in MGM-TV's *High Jungle*, he was accidentally drowned there in the headwaters of the Amazon.

290

feature, made after the style of Leone and the other "Via Veneto kids." For *Hang 'Em High,* his first American-made Western, Eastwood received $400,000 plus twenty-five per cent of the net. *Hang 'Em High* is a well-made, fast-moving, violent but honest Western, dramatising an innocent man's revenge on a group of lusty villains who had lynched him and left him for dead. Saved from death by hanging, the man returns to life with a Count of Monte Cristo purpose — to make each of his enemies suffer and die. Well directed by Ted Post, it quickly went into the money-making ranks.

Eastwood has always felt that he is indebted only to the public for his fame, and he is determined to remain true to that public. "Bogart once said he owed it to the movie-going public — and to them alone — to do his best," he commented. "I feel that way, too." Consequently, when Jolly, one of the small companies co-producing *A Fistful of Dollars,* released in 1966 a feature entitled *The Magnificent Stranger* as a new Eastwood film, Eastwood protested legally, proved that the picture was a blend of two segments bought from CBS's *Rawhide,* and *The Magnificent Stranger* was promptly withdrawn. Again, the following year another small Italian company, Lucas, claimed that they had a new Eastwood feature called *El Gringhero,* and again when Eastwood protested, the picture was junked when it was proved to be a compilation of two other segments bought from *Rawhide.*

On May 19, 1968, Clint and Maggie Eastwood became the parents of a son, Kyle Clinton, born in Santa Monica. They had waited fourteen years before having children. Says Eastwood: "By then Maggie and I knew we could get along well enough to last, that we'd stay together. My wife is very beautiful and our son Kyle is — in my opinion, and I am prejudiced — absolutely handsome!"

1968 also saw the birth of Eastwood's own company, Malpaso, in which he owns the controlling stock; he does not hold office, but permits himself to be a commodity hired out by Malpaso in transactions usually arranged by Irving Leonard, Malpaso's president and Eastwood's personal business manager. He thus makes around a million dollars a picture, usually payable at $50,000 annually, plus other percentages, and he makes no picture in which he is not guaranteed a piece off the top of the Italian gross. Every picture he's ever starred in has been a top grosser in Italy, the first country to recognise him as a star.

The first Malpaso-produced feature was released by Universal: *Coogan's Bluff,* a modern thriller about an Arizona deputy extraditing a killer from Manhattan. "Time" magazine's cinema critic noted: "Eastwood, who has hitherto displayed nothing more than a capacity for iron-jawed belligerency in a series of Italian-made westerns, performs with a measure of real feeling in the first role that fits him as comfortably as his tooled leather boots." The role of the Arizona deputy did indeed fit him. When Coogan looks over the Manhattan of today and remarks that he's just "trying to picture the way it was before people fouled it up," he is merely elaborating on one of Eastwood's own oft-quoted remarks explaining why he avoids big cities and prefers to be, in his way, a loner: "Civilisation spoils things."

Actually filmed in Arizona and New York, *Coogan's Bluff* is also the first Eastwood picture to be directed by Don Siegel. The Siegel-Eastwood combo became one of the most harmonious pairings in contemporary picture-making. To date, they have been associated in four pictures, and it is a director-star team in which each brings out the best in the other. *

For his next picture, Eastwood flew to London and then to the Austrian Alps, where he co-starred with Richard Burton in a wildly improbable tongue-in-cheek action melodrama, *Where Eagles Dare*. It was well received everywhere, and is still getting good return bookings. Burton and he became good friends during the shooting, and Elizabeth Taylor was often on the set, frequently reading scripts that had been submitted to her. She passed one on to Eastwood, *Two Mules for Sister Sara,* and when he said he liked it, she said that she'd like to do it with him. Eastwood sent the script to Universal, and they bought it.

Meanwhile, Malpaso arranged a loan-out to Paramount for a big Joshua Logan-directed musical, *Paint Your Wagon,* to be filmed in Oregon with Eastwood co-starring with Lee Marvin and Jean Seberg. None of the three was noted as a singer, but the big song of the piece, "They Call the Wind Maria," was entrusted to a lusty-voiced professional, Harve Presnell. Eastwood had already cut several records which never set the world on fire but revealed him to have a pleasant high baritone. As he said modestly, "It's not exactly Howard Keel, but I think it'll work."

Eastwood came off better than anybody else in *Paint Your Wagon*. Charles Champlin, in the "Los Angeles Times" for October 23, 1969, wrote: "Among the performances, Clint Eastwood's stoic and handsome dignity stands out, and he sings in an unscholarly baritone, which is fine." *Paint Your Wagon,* however, went way over schedule and with the lax box-office reception of it and another musical, *Darling Lili,* Paramount nearly went bankrupt.

Two Mules for Sister Sara was ready to start production in Mexico, with Don Siegel again directing. Unfortunately, by the time the picture was ready to go, Elizabeth Taylor was no longer available, and Shirley MacLaine was cast as the feminine lead, a whore in Maximilian-ruled Mexico forced to masquerade in an escape ruse as a nun. Eastwood, disappointed because Miss Taylor wasn't going to make the film with him, remarked, "The film is really a two-character story, and the woman has the best part — something I'm sure Shirley noticed. It's kind of *African Queen* gone West."

Eastwood was cast as a Texan mercenary named Hogan, but he performed and costumed the character much as if he were playing The Man with No Name in a tamale rather than a spaghetti Western. It worked for him, and if Elizabeth Taylor had been Sister Sara, the whole picture might have come off as an amusing bit of panache camp. Miss MacLaine was not right for the part,

---

*Donald Siegel had been born in Chicago on October 26, 1912. He was educated at Jesus College, Cambridge, in England, and became a professional actor after studying at the Royal Academy of Dramatic Art. He came back to America and went to Hollywood, where in 1933 he joined Warner Bros. as assistant film librarian, but was soon promoted to assistant editor and then head of the Insert Dept. At Warner Bros. he organised an expert Montage Dept., where he wrote and directed all montage sequences. He directed several documentary films, and in 1945 won an Academy Award for distinctive achievement in documentary production with *Hitler Lives*. In 1946 he was assigned his first feature to direct at Warner Bros. — *The Verdict,* and since then the list of Siegel-directed films is not only impressive but has drawn a following that amounts to a cult. In Paris and London, Siegel has been honoured with retrospectives which include such films as *Invasion of the Body Snatchers, Private Hell 36, Riot in Cell Block 11, The Big Steal, Night unto Night, Flaming Star, Madigan,* among others. "Sometimes," Siegel has said, "I feel like a prophet without honour in my own land."

got along with nobody, and when she was bedded with a miserable case of the 'flu and production had to be held up, she let it be known that she wanted "to finish this picture and get the hell back to humanity and civilisation." Nearly everybody else on the set was stricken with either the 'flu or Montezuma's curse. It could hardly be called a happy company. Only Eastwood remained perfectly healthy, and never seemed to get his fill of eating fresh pineapples and papayas.

Eastwood flew to Yugoslavia for his next film, *Kelly's Heroes,* a Second World War comedy about Private Kelly, played by Eastwood, who organises a military mission and how on a three-day leave of absence his group robs a bank in which the Germans have stored away sixteen million dollars in gold bullion. Again, Eastwood was the only actor in a big all-male cast to emerge with any honours. He played Kelly absolutely straight, as if he were The Man with No Name wearing an American private's uniform.

The first of the three Eastwood pictures released in 1971 was *The Beguiled,* filmed in Louisiana by Don Siegel, with Eastwood playing a wounded Union corporal who is taken into a young ladies seminary. Each of the females is beguiled by him, and he plots to use each in getting exactly what he wants. But, as Siegel explained the story, "It's a yarn about a man who zigged when he should have zagged." Eastwood ends trapped, himself the beguiled one, the pawn of the revenge-hungry women, and while they preserve among each other the legend of their beneficence, they gently but firmly murder him.

It is not only a different picture for Eastwood, but in my opinion it is his best film, in which he gives a real performance, one that has nothing to do with his Man with No Name characterisation or any of the strong but silent Gary Cooper derivatives. For the first time he is not a man in complete control, able to handle everything. He is defeated by a group of war-weary women whom he has deceived and dishonoured, and they simply gang up on him.

It is also an intensely beautiful film. From the opening shots of battle presented in a kind of Matthew Brady sepia, the mood of the picture is established and then heightened as Bruce Surtees's camera moves through the forest boughs laden with Spanish moss to pick out the little pinafored girl searching the woods for mushrooms. As the camera moves in on her, colour begins to creep into the forest scene, and suddenly the frame is ablaze with blood red as the girl discovers the wounded, semi-delirious Corporal McBurney. She helps him hobble to the seminary gates, believing as he tells her that he is a Quaker wounded while aiding the injured, although we have already seen and know that he is a deserter wounded while running away from the battle fire.

The entire cast of women, headed by Geraldine Page and Elizabeth Hartman, performs in the best style of the Nineteenth century romance. "Time" magazine called the film "A Southern Gothic horror story that is the most scarifying film since Rosemary birthed her satanic baby." In the "Hollywood Reporter" of March 8, 1971, Larry Cohen wrote: "The performances are uniformly excellent, with Clint Eastwood being the most impressive, particularly in the second half of the film in which he is called upon to break with the more passive dimensions of the role and demonstrate a greater versatility and range than his best past work has indicated."

The tragedy of *The Beguiled* was that Universal did not know how to distribute or exploit it. Announced to open at a first-run house in the Los Angeles area, the Picwood, the picture was cancelled the very week it was due, after all the Sunday publicity had appeared; then several weeks later it opened city-wide on a double bill. Critical response was either wildly enthusiastic or completely negative. Exploitation did not help. One catch-phrase, "Clint Eastwood Has Never Been in a More Frightening Situation" was acceptable, but the art-work was evasive, and Western addicts who attended the film because they thought it was a Western were puzzled and not receptive, while many of those who liked suspense and horror were not aware that the picture was right up their alley. Universal, apparently realising suddenly that they had a picture which might be built carefully through the art house medium into a real cult favourite, withdrew all prints, and scarcely a month later opened it as a solo feature in a small quasi-art house, the Four-Star, on Wilshire Blvd. But the damage had been done, and *The Beguiled* did not make it. Within months, however, it attained through word of mouth the status of a real cult favourite, and everybody who admired the artistic horror film was asking, "Have you seen *The Beguiled?*"

In the autumn, *The Beguiled* opened belatedly and quietly in Paris and then in London. Paris reviews were better than good — "Le plus grand du Grand-Guignol d'Amérique" — and Don Siegel, who was in Paris at the time, must have been gratified at the response. In London also, the picture found its admirers. Tom Milne, reviewing it in "The Times" for December 3, wrote: "...suddenly it blooms orchid-like into a rarefied piece of Southern Gothic. I am not sure that the change entirely works, but it does make for a remarkably beguiling film."

Only once did Eastwood state his feelings publicly about the studio's obvious mismanagement of the film; he was too busy preparing *Play Misty for Me,* in which he would not only star but make his *début* as a director. He must have expressed himself forcefully to the front office, however, because when *Play Misty for Me* opened in Los Angeles, it was given a build-up and opened at a deluxe house, the Cinerama Dome, where it settled in for a good engagement.

Eastwood had long had a hankering to try his talents as a film director. "He is a natural," Don Siegel said of him. "The times I've directed him we would end up shooting scenes we called 'Clint's shots,' scenes which were Clint's ideas that I'd steal. I figured it was time for him to start getting credit for them himself."

Play Misty for Me takes place in the Monterey area — Big Sur and Carmel, where the Eastwoods make their home and where they retreat whenever pre- and post-production does not require Eastwood to be at the studio. Eastwood engaged Siegel to play a small role for him as a kind of good luck charm, and Siegel is very good as Murphy, the bar-tender, in whose bar the meeting between Eastwood and Jessica Walter takes place. But Siegel finished his role quickly and returned to Hollywood, saying to those who thought he might stay on and lend a helping hand to Eastwood, "He doesn't need my help. He's in complete command of the situation."

Eastwood plays a disc jockey stud who has so many women at his beck and call that the girl he really likes loses heart and temporarily leaves town. Every night at the radio station a woman calls in a sultry voice to say, "Play Misty for me,'' which Eastwood does. Then one night he meets her at the bar, and takes her home with him. To him she is little more than a one-night stand; to her he is a man to possess as exclusively hers. What has begun as a rather amusing casual romance, with some breath-takingly beautiful shots of the Monterey coast area, suddenly erupts into the most horrifying of situations. Evelyn, the pretty little pick-up who had liked Errol Garner's ''Misty'' so much, suddenly reveals herself in her true colours — a homicidal maniac who will stop at nothing to gain Eastwood and, when that becomes impossible, to destroy him.

Eastwood as an actor deliberately stepped aside and so directed Jessica Walter that her performance of psychotic evil dominates the picture. She is terrifying, completely winning in her initial sophisticated *naïveté*, all the more shocking when her pathologically possessive madness takes over. Of Eastwood as a director, Miss Walter said: ''He's not insecure like some directors who impose things on you because they are nervous. He made me feel like I could do it whatever it was, and he left the role up to me. He has faith in people.''

For his next, Eastwood moved Malpaso headquarters temporarily over to Warner Bros., when he agreed to take on the lead in a crime thriller, *Dirty Harry*. The property had been bought originally for Frank Sinatra, who, due to hand injury and subsequent surgery, found himself unable to play so action-riddled a part. Don Siegel was engaged to direct, and the entire picture was shot in San Francisco, Eastwood's birthplace.

Dirty Harry opened just before Christmas in Los Angeles, and it is likely to be the most popular and biggest grossing of all Eastwood's American-made films. He plays Police Detective Harry Callahan, assigned to track down a killer sniper known as Scorpio, whose senseless murders hold the city in terror. Callahan runs the slayer down and then walks out when he is reprimanded by the district attorney for his ruthless tactics in apprehending the criminal, who, according to law, has constitutional rights which have been violated. Released, the killer is soon back at his maniacal manoeuvres and kidnaps a busload of seven schoolchildren, holding them as hostages. Callahan moves in again on Scorpio, and this time tricks him into being slain. But disgusted with a law which harbours and protects the criminal, Callahan rips off his badge and hurls it into the murky backwaters of the Bay.

The picture is expertly made, and Eastwood takes over the fast-moving film with an admirable force and virility. He is again the man in complete control, but this time it is the law itself that nearly defeats him. The action requires some death-defying stunt work, and it is obvious that Eastwood is using no double. There is no doubt that it is he who rides up six stories in a fireman's escalator to apprehend a would-be suicide on a cornice, or that it is really he who jumps off a railway bridge to land on top of a moving bus. Critics applauded *Dirty Harry*, and ''Time'' magazine indicated the general tenor of the reviews: ''One of the year's ten best. A superb job of film-making. Eastwood gives his best performance.''

Eastwood spent the last months of 1971 up in the Sierras, in the Arizona and California high country filming *Joe Kidd*. John Sturges directed, and it was a 1972 spring release in the U.S.A. It is full of terse, biting surprise switches in both story-line and characterisation; and it boasts a sequence that will be long remembered where Eastwood drives a train off the end of the tracks directly

Clint Eastwood, directing *Breezy*, with William Holden and Kay Lenz.

through the saloon where the villains are waiting to ambush him and his cohorts.

Later in 1972, Eastwood chose as his second directorial job a Western story by Ernest Tidyman, *High Plains Drifter,* which he shot in the Inyo National Forest country of Eastern California. It is a violent, picaresque tale of bloody revenge, with Eastwood also playing the central role, a return to his Man with No Name character, one regarded with almost supernatural fear as The Stranger. It became a Memorial Day release for 1973.

Eastwood had long wanted to direct a story his company owned written by Jo Heims, a girl whom he had known back in the days when he was a struggling young actor. Miss Heims wrote *Play Misty for Me.* Her romantic comedy, *Breezy,* Eastwood announced several times with himself as director, but he stated that he himself did not want to act in this one; he wished to concert his entire attention and energies on the film's direction. He secured William Holden to play the male lead, and signed an unknown nineteen-year-old, Kay Lenz, to play the title role, a young Laurel Canyon California hippie. Eastwood began shooting his picture in the Los Angeles area on November 13, 1972. Obviously he had done his homework well, because the picture finished shooting on December 19, 1972, requiring only a little more than a month before the cameras. It was marked for a late-summer release.

Early in 1973, he bowed to the inevitable. *Dirty Harry* had been so successful a film in every way that a sequel was more than in order; it was obligatory. Once again he moved Malpaso headquarters to Warner Bros. in Burbank, where *Dirty Harry* had been produced, and started pre-production plans for the production of *Magnum Force,* which continues the adventures of Harry Callahan. This time he wanted to concentrate solely on his acting performance, filled, as he knew it would be, with strenuous action, so he engaged Ted Post, who had directed him in *Hang 'Em High,* to serve as director, and in April of 1973, the company moved up to San Francisco and the Bay area, where the picture was shot.

It is obvious what Eastwood is aiming for: he has no intention of giving up acting roles now when he is top of the heap, but he has become more and more interested in film direction, and is already on the way to establishing himself as a top director. Before acting becomes a secondary consideration to him, I hope he will make a definitive film written by one of the classic Western writers. Owen Wister created a character of the Old West named Lin McLean, who is perfect for Eastwood to play. Lin McLean appears not only in *The Virginian,* but in a number of Wister short-stories that have the true ring of the Old West about them. The title role of *The Virginian* is also a real Eastwood part. Eastwood is older than that hero, was, but they are both ageless. Eastwood was born to deliver that classic line — "When you call me that, *smile.*"

Vincent Canby once noted in the "New York Times" of Eastwood that "by simply reacting well, he has become an important actor of movies." Says Eastwood: "I just believe that everybody ought to know his job and do it well, or find something else to do." To quote him again from his 1971 syndicated interview with Rex Reed: "There are two kinds of actors — one sits in a dressing-room waiting for his call, and the other gets out into the business and polishes his craft by absorbing everything. I don't know enough; I'll never learn everything I need to learn. When a guy thinks he's already learned it, he can only go backwards.''

Although his wife and he maintain a home in San Fernando Valley in Sherman Oaks, not more than fifteen minutes from Universal Studios, they are not often there, for their real home is the unassuming house with spacious acreage which they own in Carmel. Eastwood has also acquired about a thousand acres of land around Carmel, through which the stream, the Malpaso, flows, and it is his intention to build a larger home there. In Carmel Eastwood lives as he pleases, going about like any other beach resident in jeans and a T-shirt. With a friend, he opened and runs a charming restaurant know as The Hog's Breath Inn. He owns a Ferrari and three motor-cycles as well as a Chevy pick-up. But in Carmel he walks by himself most of the time, and every morning jogs three or four miles along the beach. Sometimes he's to be seen walking the Eastwood basset hound, Symphony Syd. When he has to drive, it's in the pick-up or one of the motorcycles. His idea of a relaxing evening is to ride one of his motorcycles up into San Francisco, have a couple of beers, shoot some pool, and ride back home.

Every summer around the Fourth of July, both his wife and he — and she is tops in amateur tennis — host the Clint Eastwood Invitational Tennis Tournament at Pebble Beach on behalf of the Behavioral Services Institute. They have made the tournament an attractive charity enterprise, with such film celebrities as George Peppard, Jim Brown, Dick Smothers, Charlton Heston, Efrem Zimbalist Jr., Lloyd Bridges, Jim Franciscus, Doug McClure, Dinah Shore, Burt Reynolds, and amateur players from other professions competing in the matches. At one of the most recent tournaments, John Wayne stood on a roof on the sidelines, and cheered the players on.

Physically, Eastwood has matured better than his contemporaries. Handsome in his youth, he still, now in his middle years, is so striking a figure that he makes people turn and look at him a second time.

Although his pictures have all been marked with scenes of dramatic and, even, excessive violence, Eastwood is himself a very gentle, civilised and non-violent man. Both his wife and he have devoted time to animal protection causes; he wouldn't even kill a rattlesnake in *Two Mules for Sister Sara,* and became very angry at a native bus driver who liked to run down stray dogs on the highway.

Early in the summer of 1972, the Eastwoods became parents for a second time, when Maggie Eastwood became mother to a daughter — again in a hospital at Santa Monica. They named the little girl Alison.

''Maggie's very happy these days,'' says Eastwood. ''My good luck, or success, if you want to call it that, hasn't really affected her. She would have been content as long as I earned enough money to keep her in tennis rackets.'' He adds: ''To me love for a person is respect for individual feelings — respecting privacy and accepting faults,'' and he has characterised his wife as ''a woman who knows how much room I need.''

CLINT EASTWOOD FILMOGRAPHY

REVENGE OF THE CREATURE (1955). Science-fiction melodrama about the return of the prehistoric Gilled Man first seen in *Creature from the Black Lagoon* (1954); as Jennings. *Dir:* Jack Arnold. *Sc:* Martin Berkeley (from a story by William Alland). *With* John Agar, Lori Nelson, John Bromfield, Nestor Pavia, Grandon Rhodes, Brett Halsey. *Prod:* Universal-International. 82m. Shot in 3-D.

FRANCIS IN THE NAVY (1955). Comedy of mistaken identity revolving around Francis, the talking mule, drafted into the Navy and about to be sold as surplus; as Jonesy, a sailor. *Dir:* Arthur Lubin. *Sc:* Devery Freeman (based on the character "Francis" created by David Stern). *With* Donald O'Connor (in a dual role), Martha Hyer, Richard Erdman, Jim Backus, David Janssen, Martin Milner, Paul Burke, Phil Garris, Chill Wills (as the *Voice of Francis*). *Prod:* Universal-International. 80m.

LADY GODIVA (AKA, GB, *Lady Godiva of Coventry)* (1955). Romantic drama of early England, when the Normans were scheming to get the better of the Saxons and how a virtuous lady saved the day by baring all and taking a now-historic ride; as The First Saxon. *Dir:* Arthur Lubin. *Sc:* Oscar Brodney, Harry Ruskin (from a story by Brodney). *With* Maureen O'Hara, George Nader, Victor McLaglen, Rex Reason, Torin Thatcher, Eduard Franz, Henry Brandon, Arthur Shields, Grant Withers, Robert Warwick, John O'Malley, Rhodes Reason, Arthur Gould-Porter, Leslie Bradley. *Prod:* Universal-International. 89m. Technicolor.

TARANTULA (1955). Science-fiction, about the menace of an atomically unstabilised giant spider, finally burned to death by the Air Force; as the First Pilot. *Dir:* Jack Arnold. *Sc:* Robert M. Fresco, Martin Berkeley (from a story by Fresco and Jack Arnold). *With* John Agar, Mara Corday, Leo G. Carroll, Nestor Paiva, Ross Elliott, Ed Rand, Raymond Bailey. *Prod:* Universal-International. 80m.

NEVER SAY GOODBYE (1956). Romantic drama about a woman suffering from amnesia; as Will. *Dir:* Jerry Hopper. *Sc:* Charles Hoffman (from screenplay of *This Love Of Ours* (1945) by Bruce Manning, John Klorer and Leonard Lee, as adapted from a play, "Come prima meglio di prima" ("As Before, Better than Before") by Luigi Pirandello). *With* Rock Hudson, Cornell Borchers, George Sanders, Ray Collins, David Janssen, Shelley Fabares, Gia Scala. *Prod:* Universal-International. 96m. Technicolor.

THE FIRST TRAVELLING SALESLADY (1956). Romantic comedy about a Woman's Lib corset designer of 1897 who marries an inventor of the horseless carriage; as Jack Rice. *Dir/Prod:* Arthur Lubin. *Sc:* Devery Freeman, Stephen Longstreet. *With* Ginger Rogers, Barry Nelson, Carol Channing, Brian Keith, James Arness, Robert Simon, Frank Wilcox, John Eldredge, Kate Drain Lawson, Lane Chandler, Clarence Muse. *Prod:* RKO. 88m. Technicolor.

STAR IN THE DUST (1956). Western melodrama set between sun-up and sundown of one day, with a killer to be hanged at sundown; as a Ranchhand. *Dir:* Charles Haas. *Sc:* Oscar Brodney (from a novel by Lee Leighton, "Law Man," which had won the 1953 Western Writers of America prize). *With* John Agar, Mamie Van Doren, Richard Boone, Leif Erickson, Coleen Gray, James Gleason, Randy Stuart, Paul Fix, Henry Morgan, Stanley Andrews. *Prod:* Universal-International. 80m. Technicolor.

ESCAPADE IN JAPAN (1957). Suspense action drama, filmed in Japan, about an American and Japanese boy who run away together; as an Air Pilot known as "Dumbo." *Dir:* Arthur Lubin. *Sc:* Winston Miller. *With* Teresa Wright, Cameron Mitchell, Jon Provost, Roger Nakagawa, Philip Ober. *Prod:* RKO (U.S.: U-I release). 92m. Technicolor, Technirama.

AMBUSH AT CIMARRON PASS (1958). Post-Civil War Western about a band of Union soldiers who join a handful of Confederate men in order to get through the Apache line; as Keith Williams. *Dir:* Jodie Copelan. *Sc:* Richard G. Taylor, John K. Butler (from a story by Robert A. Reeds, Robert W. Woods). *With* Scott Brady, Margie Dean, Baynes Barron, William Vaughan, Irving Bacon, Keith Richards, Dirk London, Frank Gerstle. *Prod:* Regal for 20th Century-Fox. 73m. Regalscope.

LAFAYETTE ESCADRILLE (AKA, GB, *Hell Bent for Glory)* (1958). First World War romantic air drama about one of the most famous fighting units in aviation history; as George Moseley, flyer. *Dir/prod/story:* William A. Wellman. *Sc:* A. S. Fleischman. *With* Tab Hunter, Bill Wellman Jr., Etchika Choreau, Jody McCrea, Marcel Dalio, Dennis Devine, David Janssen, Paul Fix, Will Hutchins, Bob Hover, Brett Halsey, Henry Nakamura. *Prod:* Warner Bros. 96m.

For more than seven years (Jan. 9, 1959-Feb. 8, 1966) Clint Eastwood filmed 250 hour-long TV shows for "Rawhide" at CBS. It was about a cattle drive, and for seven years Eastwood appeared on TV screens every week as the No. 1 ramrod Rowdy Yates, co-starring with Eric Fleming, who played Gil Favor, trail boss. For the last twenty-two episodes, Fleming was dropped and Eastwood was moved up into solo starring status as the trail boss.

PER UN PUGNO DI DOLLARI (GB,US: *A Fistful of Dollars*) (1964). An Italian Western (directed by an Italian, filmed in Spain, with an Italian, German, and Spanish cast, and an American star) about a stranger who comes riding into a feuding western town, plays each side against the other and when everybody is dead, rides off alone; as "The Man with No Name," (sometimes called "Joe," synonymous in America with "John Doe," or any unknown man). *Dir:* Sergio Leone. *Sc:* No screenplay credit on the screen, but adapted from the Japanese classic, *Yojimbo* (1961), written by Akira Kurosawa and Ryuzo Kikushima (later screenplay credit was given to Sergio Leone and Duccio Tessari). *With* Marianne Koch, John Welles (Gian Maria Volonté), W. Lukschy, S. Rupp, Antonio Prieto, Jose Calvo, Margherita Lozano, Daniel Martin, Josef Egger, Benny Reeves, Richard Stuyvesant, Carol Brown. *Prod:* Jolly/Constantin/Ocean for United Artists. 96m. Technicolor, Techniscope. Released G.B.-U.S.A., 1967.

PER QUALCHE DOLLARO IN PIU (GB,US: *For a Few Dollars More*). (1965). Sequel to *A Fistful of Dollars* and the second film in the "paella trilogy," about two bounty hunters who, after the Civil War, track down a sadistic, drug-addicted, insane cut-throat named "Il Indio"; as "Il Monco," the name given to "The Man with No Name" by the Italians. *Dir:* Sergio Leone. *Sc:* Luciano Vincenzoni and Sergio Leone (from a story, "Two Magnificent Rogues," by Leone and Fulvio Morzella). *With* Lee Van Cleef, Gian Maria Volonté, Josef Egger, Rosemary Dexter, Maria Krup, Klaus Kinski. *Prod:* P.E.A./Gonzales/Constantin for United Artists. 130m. Technicolor, Techniscope. Released G.B.-U.S.A, 1967.

IL BUONO, IL BRUTTO, IL CATTIVO (GB-US: *The Good, the Bad, and the Ugly*). (1966). Third Western in the "paella trilogy," about a post-Civil War search for a tombstone, where a great fortune is reputedly buried; as "The Good" of the title, known as "Joe" (from the Western colloquial "Good Joe"), referred to derisively by the Eli Wallach character as "Blondie," but still obviously "The Man with No Name." *Dir:* Sergio Leone. *Sc:* Luciano Vincenzoni, Sergio Leone (from a story by Age, Scarpelli, Vincenzoni and Leone, first titled "The Magnificent Rogues"). *With* Lee Van Cleef ("The Ugly"), Eli Wallach ("The Bad"), Aldo Guiffre, Mario Brega, Luigi Pistilli, Rada Rassimov, John Bartha, Antonio Casas, Aldo Sambrell, Enzo Pepito, Al Mulloch, Sergio Mendizibal, Molino Rojo, Lorenzo Robledo, Silvana Bacci, Livio Lorenzon, Paolo Stoppa, Chelo

Alonso. *Prod:* P.E.A. for United Artists. 180m. (Italy), 161, (U.S.A), 148m (G.B). Technicolor, Techniscope. Released G.B. / U.S.A, 1968.

LE STREGHE (US: *The Witches*) (1967). five-part anthology about witchcraft, each directed by a different director and all starring Silvana Mangano; as Giovanna's husband in the last sequence, *A Night Like Any Other*. *Dir:* Vittorio De Sica. *Sc:* Cesare Zavattini, Favio Carpi, Enzio Muzil. *With* Silvana Mangano. (Players in other segments included Annie Girardot, Massimo Girotti, Helmut Berger, Alberto Sordi, Totò). *Prod:* Dino De Laurentiis-United Artists. (U.S.A: Lopert). 100m. Technicolor.

HANG 'EM HIGH (1968). Period Western about an innocent man who survives an aborted lynching and then seeks revenge in the classic style of the Count of Monte Cristo on each of those who had sought to kill him; as Jed Cooper. *Dir:* Ted Post. *Sc:* Leonard Freeman, Mel Goldberg. *With* Inger Stevens, Ed Begley, Pat Hingle, Arlene Golonka, Charles McGraw, James MacArthur, L.Q. Jones, Alan Hale Jr., Dennis Hopper, Bruce Dern, Ben Johnson, Ruth White, James Westerfield, Bob Steele, Bert Freed, Todd Andrews, Michael O'Sullivan. *Prod:* Leonard Freeman for United Artists. 114m. De Luxe Color.

COOGAN'S BLUFF (1968). Modern thriller (called a "psychedelic Eastern-Western) about an Arizona deputy who is sent to Manhattan to extradite a prisoner who is in Bellevue recovering from an acid trip; as Deputy Sheriff Walt Coogan. *Dir/Prod:* Don Siegel. *Sc:* Herman Miller, Dean Riesner, Howard Rodman (from an unpublished story by Miller). *With* Lee J. Cobb, Susan Clark, Betty Field, Don Stroud, Tisha Sterling, Melodie Johnson, Tom Tully, James Edwards, David Doyle, Seymour Cassel. *Prod:* Universal-Malpaso. 94m. Technicolor. (Filmed in Arizona and Manhattan.)

WHERE EAGLES DARE (1969). High action adventure about seven men and a woman who are parachuted into Wartime Germany to rescue a top Allied officer held captive in the inaccessible Castle of the Eagle; as Lt. Morris Schaffer, American Ranger. *Dir:* Brian G. Hutton. *Sc:* Alistair MacLean. *With* Richard Burton, Mary Ure, Michael Hordern, Patrick Wymark, Robert Beatty, Anton Diffring, Donald Houston, Ferdy Mayne, Neil McCarthy. *Prod:* Gershwin-Kastner-M-G-M. 158m. Metrocolor. Super Panavision. 70mm. (Filmed in the Austrian Alps.)

PAINT YOUR WAGON (1969). Musical Western, a *ménage à trois,* about a beautiful blonde who shacks up with two buddies, but stays put with the more romantic one while the other goes off seeking the next gold strike; as

"Pardner" (Sylvester) Newel. *Dir:* Joshua Logan. *Sc/Lyrics:* Alan Jay Lerner (adaptation by Paddy Chayefsky, based on the Lerner-Frederick Loewe musical play). *With* Lee Marvin, Jean Seberg, Harve Presnell, Ray Walston, Tom Ligon, Alan Dexter, William O'Connell, Ben Baker, Alan Baxter, Paula Trueman, Robert Easton, Geoffrey Norman, Roger Herren. *Prod:* Lerner-Malpaso-Paramount. 169m. Technicolor, Panavision. 70mm. Eastwood sings two solos: "I Still See Eliza" and "I Talk to the Trees;" and he sings along with cast members three other songs: "I'm on My Way," "Best Things," "Gold Fever." (Filmed in Wallowa National Park, Oregon.)

KELLY'S HEROES (1970). Second World War comedy-melodrama, about the private heist of sixteen million dollars in gold bullion stored away by the Germans in a town they are occupying; as Private Kelly. *Dir:* Brian G. Hutton. *Sc:* Troy Kennedy Martin (first titled *The Warriors*). *With* Telly Savalas, Don Rickles, Stuart Margolin, Jeff Morris, Richard Davalos. *Prod:* Katzka-Loeb-M-G-M. 144m. Colour. Panavision. (Filmed in Yugoslavia.)

TWO MULES FOR SISTER SARA (1970). Romantic Western of the 1865 era, about a Texas mercenary who comes to the aid of a nun terrorised by bandits, and takes her to a place of safety, where he learns that she's really a prostitute in masquerade; as Hogan. *Dir:* Don Siegel. *Sc:* Albert Maltz (from a story, "Two Guns for Sister Sara", by Budd Boetticher). *With* Shirley MacLaine, Manolo Fabregas, Alberto Morin, Armando Silvestre, John Kelly. *Prod:* Malpaso-Sanen-Universal. 114m. Technicolor, Panavision. (Filmed in Mexico).

THE BEGUILED (1971). Romantic Gothic Civil War drama, about a wounded Union soldier taken in by some women and girls in a Young Ladies' Seminary, and destroyed by them; as Corporal John McBurney, known as "McB." *Dir/Prod:* Don Siegel. *Sc:* John E. Sherry and Grimes Grice (pseudonyms for Albert Maltz and Irene Kamp), (from a novel by Thomas Cullinan). *With* Geraldine Page, Elizabeth Hartman, Jo Ann Harris, Mae Mercer, Pamelyn Ferdin, Darleen Carr, Pattye Mattick, Melody Thomas, Peggy Drier, Patrick Culliton. *Prod:* Malpaso-Universal. 105m. Technicolor. (Filmed in the country near Baton Rouge, Louisiana.)

PLAY MISTY FOR ME (1971). Romantic suspense thriller, about a happy-go-lucky stud whose life is nearly destroyed by a psychopathic girl whom he has rejected; as Dave Garver, disc jockey. *Dir:* Clint Eastwood. *Sc:* Jo Heims, Dean Riesner (from a story by Miss Heims.) *With* Jessica Walter, Donna Mills, John Larch, James McEachin, Jack Ging. Malpaso-Universal. 102m. Technicolor. (Filmed at Big Sur, Carmel and Monterey, California.)

DIRTY HARRY (1971). Crime thriller, about a tough police detective who goes after a mad sniper terrorising a city; as Harry Callahan, of the San Francisco Police Dept. *Dir/Prod:* Don Siegel. *Sc:* Harry Julian Frank, R.M. Frank, Dean Riesner (from a story, "Dead Right," by the Franks). *With* Harry Guardino, Reni Santoni, John Vernon, Andy Robinson, John Larch, John Mitchum, Mae Mercer, Lyn Edgington. *Prod:* Malpaso-Warner Bros. 103m. Technicolor. (Filmed in San Francisco, California.)

JOE KIDD (1972). Western of the high country; as Joe Kidd. *Dir:* John Sturges. *Sc:* Elmore Leonard (from his story, "Sinola"). *With* Stella Garcia, John Saxon, Don Stroud, James Wainwright, Robert Duvall, Gregory Walcott, Lynne Marta, Clint Ritchie. *Prod:* Malpaso-Universal. 100m. Technicolor, Panavision. (Filmed at Lone Pine, California, and in Tucson, Arizona.) (Working title: *Dancer.*)

HIGH PLAINS DRIFTER (1973). Period Western melodrama; as "The Stranger." *Dir:* Clint Eastwood. *Sc:* Ernest Tidyman. *With* Verna Bloom, Mariana Hill, Mitchell Ryan, Jack Ging, Stefan Gierasch, Ted Hartley, Billy Curtis, Geoffrey Lewis, Scott Walker, Walter Barnes, Paul Brinegar, Dan Vadis, Belle Mitchell, John Mitchum. *Prod:* Malpaso-Universal. 105m. Technicolor, Panavision. (Filmed in Inyo National Forest.)

"BREEZY" (1973). Romantic comedy; did not act in the film. *Dir:* Clint Eastwood. *Sc/assoc. prod:* Jo Heims. *With* William Holden, Kay Lenz, Dennis Olivieri, Jamie Smith Jackson, Marj Dusay, Roger C. Carmel, Shelley Morrison, Scott Holden. *Prod:* Malpaso-Universal. Technicolor, Panavision. 100m. (Filmed in Laurel Canyon and other Los Angeles backgrounds.)

MAGNUM FORCE (1973). Crime thriller, sequel to the very successful *Dirty Harry;* as Harry Callahan, who well knows that bullets, as well as champagne, come in magnums. *Dir:* Ted Post. *Sc:* Mike Cimino (from a story by John Milius, and original characters as created by Harry Julian Frank and Rita M. Frank). *With* Hal Holbrook, Felton Perry, Mitchell Ryan, David Saul, Margaret Avery, Richard Devon. *Prod:* Malpaso-Warner Bros. Technicolor, Panavision. (Filmed in San Francisco, California.)

THUNDERBOLT AND LIGHTFOOT (1974). Thriller, as Thunderbolt. *Dir/Sc:* Mike Cimino. *With* Jeff Bridges, George Kennedy, Geoffrey Lewis, Dub Taylor. *Prod:* Malpaso-United Artists. Technicolor, Panavision. (Filmed in Montana.) 114m.

14
VAL LEWTON

Over thirty years ago, in the time of the Second World War, a series of films made at the RKO-Radio Studios in Hollywood attracted the highest of critical praise and proved so profitable that the studio emerged from the "red," where the films of Orson Welles had consigned it.

Each of these pictures is still fondly and vividly remembered, and almost all of them are often revived here and abroad. All are top favourites of today's television viewers.

The series was started as a deliberate experiment: the production of low-budget but high-in-quality films dealing with some phase of psychological horror.

The man most responsible for the success these films still enjoy was the producer for the RKO unit that filmed them. It was his good taste and keen analytical story judgement that raised those programme movies, from the childish banality into which horror-suspense thrillers had fallen, to a level of creative film entertainment.

That man was Val Lewton.

I first met him in 1941 when he was Story Editor for David O. Selznick. He had seen and admired a performance of a play I'd written based upon the lives of the Brontës, "Embers at Haworth," and he remembered me and my play when Mr. Selznick started production plans for a movie to be based on Charlotte Brontë's "Jane Eyre." He arranged to borrow me from RKO, where I was working as a reader, to act as research adviser for that picture. I was to be at the call of Aldous Huxley, who was writing the screenplay, and I was to work closely with William Pereira, who was designing the production, and Robert Stevenson, who would direct it. I spent many days at the Huntington Library in San Marino gathering data for a 100-page reference book Mr. Selznick later referred to as "the Bible." But it was Val who supervised my work, and he whom I saw nearly every day.

One day at lunch he confided that he probably would be leaving the employ of Mr. Selznick before I finished my research job for him. Half in jest, he insinuated he was being kicked upstairs for not having sufficiently appreciated either the novel "Gone With the Wind" or the movie Mr. Selznick made of it. Apparently Val had tried to persuade Mr. Selznick to forget Margaret Mitchell's epic novel of the War between the States and film "War and Peace" or "Vanity Fair," or both, instead. Val delighted in pointing out similarities in the plots of those two classics and of *Gone With the Wind*.

MORE FROM HOLLYWOOD

In spite of the fact that Val had committed the unforgivable and had not only slept but snored through some daily rushes of *Gone With the Wind,* Mr. Selznick had forgiven him and was, in fact, promoting him. Val hastily explained that a meeting had been arranged for him with Charles Koerner, RKO's new production head, and afterwards Koerner negotiated a contract whereby Val was to head a new production unit that would specialise exclusively in low-budget horror programmers.

"They may think I'm going to do the usual chiller stuff which'll make a quick profit, be laughed at and be forgotten," Val said, "but I'm going to fool them. They may fight me all along the way, but I'm going to do the kind of suspense movie *I* like."

This attitude was to be typical of his whole career as a producer. He was given assignments which most contract producers would have filmed on the back lot and shrugged off as evil necessities, but he approached each assignment as a challenge. Forced to submit to exploitation titles, he was determined that the pictures hiding behind the horror titles should be films of good taste and high production quality.

He then suggested that he and I might be able to work in harmony as producer and writer, and said he would like to hire me as screenwriter for whatever assignment Mr. Koerner eventually handed him at RKO. I promised to call him as soon as I saw my research job for *Jane Eyre* coming to an end.

Val departed for RKO two weeks before I'd finished my work at Selznick's, and when I phoned him, as I had promised, he quickly made arrangements for me to be hired at RKO as a contract writer at the Guild minimum, which was then $75 a week. When I reported for work, he ran off for me some American and British horror and suspense movies which were typical of what he did not want to do. We spent several days talking about possible subjects for the first script.

Mr. Koerner, who had personally welcomed me on my first day at the studio, was of the opinion that vampires, werewolves, and man-made monsters had been over-exploited, but that "nobody has done much with cats." He added that he had successfully audience-tested a title he considered highly exploitable — *Cat People*. "Let's see what you two can do with that," he ordered.

When we were back in his office, Val looked at me glumly and said: "There's no helping it — we're stuck with that title. If you want to get out now, I won't hold it against you."

I had no intention of withdrawing, and he and I promptly started upon a careful examination of the cat in literature. There was more to be examined than we had expected. Val was one of the best-read men I've ever known, and the kind of avid reader who retains what he reads.

He had been born in Yalta, on May 7, 1904, and his given names were Vladimir Ivan. In 1906, his mother, a remarkable woman, left her profligate husband, and brought Val and his older sister Lucy to Berlin, and subsequently, in 1909, to America. She had forsaken not only her husband but his name, preferring to revert to her maiden surname. "Leventon," which she shortened, once she got to America, to "Lewton." Nina Lewton was the sister of Alla Nazimova, the great Russian-born actress, who made theatrical and film history in America, and Val's early years were spent in a society

306

VAL LEWTON

Val Lewton, at his desk at RKO.

Left to right: Mark Robson, director; Glenn Vernon, Jean Brooks, Kent Smith, players; and Val Lewton, producer, on set of RKO's *Youth Runs Wild*.

peopled by practitioners of the arts. He was always more than a little afraid of both his mother and his distinguished aunt; he always resisted women who had distinguished themselves in any field, especially writing of any kind.

After two years of studying journalism in Columbia University, Val terminated his formal education, took an apartment on West Tenth Street, and began writing journalism, short stories, and poetry. He always spoke nostalgically of his days as a writer in Greenwich Village and his good friend, Donald Henderson Clarke, a star reporter and novelist who helped Val get newspaper assignments. Val took me to lunch once to meet Mr. Clarke, whom I found not only charming but very quiet, not at all voluble as one would expect a man of his accomplishments to be. Val was very pleased when Clarke later accepted a screenplay assignment from him, and wrote one of the best screenplays Val produced, *The Ghost Ship*.*

His mother, a small, soft-spoken woman of Continental dignity and learning, had gained some distinction as a writer and translator, and was also highly regarded in M-G-M's Eastern literary department, where she had a position of some importance, originally gained for her by Nazimova's power at Metro, but maintained by her through her own superior abilities when Metro amalgamated with Goldwyn and Mayer, and became Loew's, Inc. She was always kind to beginning writers, and many in high places today owe their start to her original interest. I met her once in New York while I was working for Val, and lunched with her at the Algonquin. She regarded the successful pictures Val was then making with marked distaste, but confessed she had not seen any of them. The horrendous publicity had frightened her off.

"I don't understand my son," she said several times, always adding: "He's really very intelligent."

Val told me later that the brilliance of his mother and aunt had made him determined to make a living on his own as a writer. In looking through a popular movie magazine of the early Thirties, I once came across a fictionised version of Garbo's *Inspiration*, based on Daudet's "Sapho," which bore the credit: "Fictionised by Val Lewton." I brought it to his attention, and he laughed sheepishly, and rattled off a series of pseudonyms under which he had published both good and hack stuff. Cosmo Forbes, Sidney Valentine, H. C. Kerkow — these were only some of the names he employed as a writer; his favourite was Carlos Keith, and that was the name he used on his later screenwriting credits.

He was proudest of his novel, "No Bed of Her Own," a depression story, which received good reviews and was widely translated and published in foreign countries; it was purchased by Paramount, but only because, he learned later, they wanted its title for a picture co-starring Carole Lombard and Clark Gable. Censorship prevented Paramount from using the title, however, and the picture, released as *No Man of Her Own*, has absolutely nothing to do with Lewton's novel. Val was delighted when he learned that a German translation of the novel had been sufficiently disliked by the Nazis to be included in one of their book-burnings.

Val always said that it was a now out-of-print history of the Russian

*RKO withdrew *The Ghost Ship* from circulation after a legal battle involving plagiarism, which the studio lost. Even today, *The Ghost Ship* is rarely seen, and is the only Lewton film which is actually difficult to see.

Cossack which brought him to the attention of David O. Selznick, at the time Selznick was preparing a production of *Taras Bulba*.* Selznick brought him to Hollywood to work on a screenplay of Gogol's novella, and although the picture, as planned under Selznick's aegis, never got before the cameras, Val was kept on by Selznick and served as his Story Editor for more than eight years.

When I first knew Val, he was only thirty-seven — a huge, burly, kindly man with a quick sense of humour and pleasant and courteous manners. He was extremely shy, and easily hurt if his superiors failed to go along with him on story and production plans, for he was remarkably honest and well-disciplined, and accepted only the best, get it how he could. He lived quietly in Brentwood with his wife, Ruth, a daughter Nina, and a son named Val after him.

He loathed physical contact on a social basis; he withdrew when people patted or embraced him, and even a handshake could put him off. He said to me once: "One of the things I like about you is that you're not demonstrative; I've noticed you don't even shake hands unless the other party offers his hand." I smiled, and confessed: "I don't like to shake hands, because I'm convinced it's the simplest way of one person's transferring germs to another." He nodded his head approvingly. "I must remember that," he said; "it makes a good excuse."

When one of his pictures was shooting, he practically opened the studios at dawn, but when no picture was going, he loathed working in his office during the morning hours. He preferred to arrive there just before noon, and to have his biggest story or production conference at the lunch-table, and then to work on, often until late at night, sometimes until after midnight. Writers working with him had little social life of their own; he did not demand that they give him all their time; he simply expected them to be available at all hours. During the first picture I wrote for him, I did not accept invitations to dinner, and I gave up going to the theatre, the ballet, and opera, because if I bought tickets in advance, I always had to cancel out and stay at the studio to work.

Val spent weekends on a boat he owned and anchored at the Santa Monica pier. Wartime sailing restrictions only permitted him to sail around the harbour, to circle the entrance buoy, and so he would anchor in the quietest spot — and fish. Many story problems, needless to say, were discussed and settled on these Sunday sailing and fishing excursions.

After we had both read everything we could find pertaining to the cat in literature and the arts, Val had virtually decided to make his first movie from a short story, Algernon Blackwood's "Ancient Sorceries," which admirably lends itself to cinematic interpretation and could easily be re-titled *Cat People*. Negotiations had begun for the purchase of the screen rights when Val suddenly changed his mind.

He arrived at his office unusually early and called me in at once. He had spent a sleepless night, he confessed, and had decided that instead of a picture with a foreign and period setting, he would do an original story laid in contemporary New York City. It was to deal with a triangle — a normal young

*I later learned that the "out-of-print history of the Russian Cossack" was really a novel, "The Cossack Sword," originally published in England, and subsequently in the U.S.A. under the title "Rape of Glory."

man falls in love with a strange foreign girl who is obsessed by abnormal fears, and when her obsession destroys his love and he turns for consolation to a very normal girl, his office co-worker, the discarded one, beset by jealousy, attempts to destroy the young man's new love.

We talked over this story-line for nearly a week. Viewing all those horror pictures had shown us there were basically two kinds of horror pictures: first, the Hollywood kind which had enjoyed great success, especially at Universal, and which begin with a spine-tingling first reel and then slowly taper off to an obvious conclusion and never top the opening sequences; and, second, the more Continental type of story, which opens at a leisurely pace, allowing one to understand and sympathise with the main characters, each sequence growing in suspense until there would be three frightening situations topped by a fast-moving concluding episode.

It was the latter type of story Val was determined I should develop for him.

At the end of a week, I had a two-page story-line incorporating the points on which we had come to definite agreement. The star role was to be, naturally, the girl obsessed. Both Val and I were great admirers of Simone Simon, who had recently played, for RKO, the witch girl in *All That Money Can Buy* (the original release-title for *The Devil and Daniel Webster*). Val had good reason to believe he could get RKO to negotiate for her services as the heroine of *Cat People*. Therefore I was to design the picture around her as its star.

We agreed upon her name — Irena Dubrovnik — and that she was to be a Balkan-born girl working successfully as a dress designer in Manhattan. Val always insisted that all his characters have occupations or professions *and be shown working in their jobs*.

The Central Park Zoo was to be the scene of much of the action, and the first real horror sequence was to be a pursuit late at night on one of the transverses that cut through Central Park from Fifth Avenue to Central Park West.

Irena Dubrovnik was to have a modest studio in a brownstone-front house near the park. Val had decided upon that because a multi-storied staircase built by Orson Welles for his *The Magnificent Ambersons*, which ascended almost to the top of one of the mammoth sound stages, was still standing at RKO-Pathe in Culver City, and, with very few changes in set-dressing, could be used for many of our interior sequences.

The hero was to be named Oliver, and he and his feminine co-worker, Alice, were to be draughtsmen in a ship designer's office.

We had two of the necessary horror sequences — the pursuit on the transverse and an attack in the deserted draughting-office. I would have to devise a middle sequence.

"Go home," said Val, after he had okayed the storyline, "and don't let me see you until you bring back the complete story." But he added that he didn't want the customary screen treatment. I was to write a long short story — as long as I wanted — keeping in mind all the story points we had discussed and feeling free to invent new sequences if they came to me. I was to write as I would for magazine publication, and not for adaptation to the screen.

It was wise counsel, for it permitted me to develop several themes that were later to provide excellent substance for cinematic re-statement. And being on my own, creatively, I was able to come up with the missing middle horror sequence — the attack in the deserted swimming-pool late at night. This was

310

based upon a personal experience of my own, when, swimming alone at night in a pool, I had almost drowned.*

A fortnight later I delivered the story of *Cat People*. Val was elated, as were Jacques Tourneur, who in the interim had been signed to direct the picture, and Mark Robson, then one of RKO's top contract film editors, who had been assigned to edit the movie.

The four of us — producer, writer, director, and film editor — then sat down and discussed, analysed, tore apart, and re-developed what I had written. We agreed on one thing: although the heroine was to be obsessed with the fear of turning into a destructive cat if she were to fulfil her marriage vows, the change of woman to cat and back again was only to be suggested camera-wise and never be actually shown.

We were all also convinced that most talkies were talking too much and that dialogue should be used sparingly, and then only to advance the story when it could not be made wholly comprehensible through the mediums of visual action and natural sound. Later, when D. W. Griffith saw the picture one night in a studio projection room, he commented upon the good use of silent passages, much to Val's pleasure. I remember that when I would turn in a sequence to Val, he would thumb through it quickly and brighten approvingly if there was little dialogue; I learned that if I had a scene to write demanding expository dialogue, I always warned him in advance that unfortunately there would be some pages of dialogue in the upcoming sequence; otherwise, even before he read the scene, he would note the amount of dialogue, and say reprovingly, "DeWitt!"

I suspect someone connected with the production of *The Bad and the Beautiful* must have known Val Lewton at the time Lewton was preparing *Cat People*. In *The Bad and the Beautiful,* Kirk Douglas, as the aspiring movie producer, is faced with a problem of presenting in his picture cat people wearing ridiculous moth-eaten costumes, and he solves the dilemma by never actually showing the people as cats. He goes to a light switch, turns it off, and, in the darkness, with sound effects and voice, suggests more horror than could ever be shown in fact.

This was a favourite stunt of Val's. Time after time, in telling the story of *Cat People,* he would move to the light switch of his office, turn off the lights quietly, and continue recounting the story in the darkened room.

Each of Val's pictures dealt not with realistic horror, but with a cinematic, or camera-suggested, expression of some universal fear or superstition. The stories he produced are dramatisations of the psychology of fear. Man fears the unknown — the dark, that which may lurk in the shadows, death and the dead, mental blackness, being entombed while still alive. What he knows and what he sees with his eyes, man cannot fear. But the unknown, and that which he cannot see, fills him with basic and understandable terror.

I wrote a first-draft of the screenplay of *Cat People* from the revised story-line of my original story evolved in Val's conferences. A copy of this first-draft was immediately dispatched to Simone Simon then in New York and she wired back at once that she would do the picture. That took care of the

*I have read in recent years that director Jacques Tourneur also had such an experience; I never knew about it from him or anybody else when I was writing *Cat People*.

major casting problem, but while I was writing the final shooting script, the casting of the hero and second female lead had to be decided.

It is very hard for a writer to make normal, average, workaday Johns and Janes into interesting screen characters, and it is equally or even more difficult to cast actors who can play such roles with intelligence, sympathy, and charm. Val solved this problem himself.

He had noticed a good-looking young man riding a bicycle from Beverly Hills to the studio every morning and surmised he was an actor. He inquired and learned that he was indeed an actor — that he was Kent Smith, a well-known Broadway leading man who had been put under contract by RKO and was nearing the end of the first year of his contract without having appeared in a single film. He had been borrowed by the Army for a series of training films, and this footage, in which Smith spoke only technical facts, revealed that he was just the matter-of-fact but pleasant hero Val had been seeking.

There was, however, a hitch. Any producer who chose to use Smith would be required to attach all salary that had been paid to him and was unaccounted to any specific picture, to the budget of the film for which Smith was wanted. Val was determined to have him nevertheless, and Kent Smith became the most expensive member of the cast. He proved to be one of its most important members, for he brought a direct honesty and believability to the hero's role that few other leading men available in Hollywood could have demonstrated.

The second feminine role was also filled by an RKO contract player — Jane Randolph.* Most of RKO's contract girls were of the standard type then popular in Hollywood — blonde, bosomy, and vacuously pretty. Jane Randolph was pretty, but brunette, tall, athletic, and intelligent. Val read her in a scene with Kent Smith and promptly handed her the part. Like Smith, she brought believability to her role.

Val was very compatible with Tom Conway, who, like Val, had been born in Russia. Conway was brother to George Sanders, and, if you closed your eyes, his voice sounded like Sanders's own. Val always referred to him as "the nice George Sanders with a giggle." He had been playing the lead in RKO's *Falcon* series and Val signed him to play Dr. Louis Judd, the psychiatrist who beguiles, is himself beguiled, and destroys the heroine even as she destroys him.

Simone Simon arrived and loved her part. She already knew and loved Jacques Tourneur. She loved Val; she loved Mark Robson; she loved me. She wanted to know immediately who her leading man was to be, and, when she met Kent Smith, she loved him. Simone was, and is, one of the most loveable actresses I've ever known. Men never have any difficulty with her.

It's unfortunate that Hollywood nearly ruined her screen career in the beginning by trying to make a stereotyped ingenue of her. A Frenchwoman always, she could be fitted into no Hollywood standard. She was unique; she was Continental; and she was a real movie star. She also distrusted women. Miss Randolph wisely avoided her, as did Elizabeth Russell, who had a brief but memorable role as the cat-faced woman who recognises Simone as "her sister" in the café wedding-party scene.

*Miss Randolph left films to marry Jaime del Amo, and went to live with him in Madrid, where she became one of that city's most prominent society leaders. Since her husband's death in recent years, Miss Randolph spends time both in Los Angeles and Madrid.

VAL LEWTON

There was only one woman connected with the production whom Simone liked and trusted — Babe Egan, the wardrobe woman, who worked in terror of being required to do more than sew on a button, since she actually couldn't sew a stitch. She had been a set-musician in the days of the silents, when emoting stars wanted mood music to background their scenes, and she had also been an Orpheum headliner and had toured Europe with her all-girl band, "Babe Egan and Her Redheads." Now, through pull, she had got herself a job as wardrobe woman, there being nothing open in the music department. One day, when I went to Simone's portable dressing-room between shots to cue her in her lines for the next scene, I found her blithely sewing a torn hem in Babe's skirt. Simone, the practical Frenchwoman, could acquit herself with needle and thread, and sewed on her own buttons — and kept Babe's secret.

Val had decided that since I was still being paid so nominal a salary, the picture's budget could afford me as dialogue director, so I was kept on in that capacity during the entire shooting. The same thing happened later with *Curse of the Cat People*.

Val himself supervised every detail of the picture's production. Scene designers, set dressers, costume and make-up people, all soon learned that the ordinary could not be palmed off on him. He demanded, and got, the best and the truly unique from every department. He had been lucky to get Nick Musuraca as cameraman, and Musuraca brought a haunting, low-key mood in photography that matched the mood of the story. Simone always looked to Nick after a sequence was shot and was never satisfied unless he said, "Good kid." One day she hummed a bewitching little nursery tune at Val's request for Roy Webb of the Music Department, and that simple little rhyme became the *leitmotif* of the film's music score.

Observant moviegoers may have recognised certain feline accoutrements in *Cat People:* the statue of Bubastis in the museum sequence; the tiger lilies in the florist shop window; the cat's claws on the base of the bathtub when Simone tries to cleanse herself of guilt after murdering the lambs; the cats in the Goya reproduction hanging over her mantel when she tells the hero of her past and hints at her abnormal fears. None "just happened." Each had been weighed and approved before it was inserted in the screenplay itself. Val himself dictated the good taste which graced his pictures.

He was apprehensive and nervous at the first preview of *Cat People* — on a week night at the Hillstreet in downtown Los Angeles, a tough audience at best and murder on a week night. The preview was preceded by a Disney cartoon about a little pussy-cat, and Val's spirits sank lower and lower as the audience began to catcall and make loud mewing sounds. "Oh, God!" he kept murmuring, as he wiped the perspiration from his forehead.

The picture's title was greeted with whoops of derision and louder meows, but when the credits were over and the film began to unreel, the audience quieted, and, as the story progressed, re-acted as we had hoped an audience might. There were audible gasps and some screaming as the shock sequences grew. The audience accepted and believed our story, and was enchanted.

After the preview, Val learned from the powers-that-be that the black panther must be shown in the draughting-room sequence moving relentlessly under the tables toward the trapped hero and his new love. This had been *suggested* in the script and in the preview cut by a play of menacing dark shadows. So, to satisfy front-office demands, the black panther and its trainer

313

were re-hired and the revised scene was filmed. Val, refusing to admit defeat, and with the support of his cameraman and editor, had the new footage so spliced in that it was made to seem what the two trapped humans *fancied* they saw rather than what happened in reality.

A weird thing happened on the night these added scenes were shot with the black panther. The assistant director's voice called out: "Close all doors! The panther's loose!" The big soundstage doors were securely closed; the stage itself was flooded with light; and the hunt was on by a few qualified to search, while everybody else stayed exactly where he was in the full light, engaging in quiet small talk, when at any moment a jungle beast might spring down into the scene. In a very few moments the trainer found and controlled the black panther, which had sought refuge, appropriately enough, on one of the cat-walks.

The trade notices of *Cat People* were good, but when the picture opened in New York in a Times Square theatre, it was shuffled off by Manhattan critics as unimportant; after it had been held over week after week, some film critics re-evaluated it. In Hollywood it played thirteen weeks in its first engagement. Both in America and abroad, *Cat People,* along with subsequent Lewton pictures, has a cult of ardent admirers. The big-budget pictures I later wrote at RKO, like *I Remember Mama* and *The Enchanted Cottage,* have their share of admirers, but quite a few moviegoers have surprised me by recounting *Cat People* almost sequence by sequence. A soldier who served in the Pacific told me how he had seen *Cat People* on a Pacific island base projected on an open-air screen under a tropical night sky. Soldiers reclined on beaten-down grass, while all around, in the shadowy periphery of the audience, natives stood and quietly watched the picture. They understood no English, but they too re-acted to this story of a girl obsessed and destroyed by her own fears and superstitions.

Cat People, produced in 1942, had a twenty-four day shooting schedule and was brought in ahead of time at a cost of $134,000. As of thirty years later, it has grossed over $4,000,000 internationally.

Even before *Cat People* had gone before the cameras, Val had been given his second producing assignment. Koerner informed him that his second picture would be based on a Hearst Sunday supplement series entitled "I Walked with a Zombie!" After a day of gloom, his spirits lifted and he told me with a chuckle: "They may never recognise it, but what I'm going to give them in *I Walked with a Zombie* is *Jane Eyre in the West Indies.*"

And that's fundamentally what that picture, with its strangely beautiful photography and first rate performances by Frances Dee, Tom Conway, James Ellison, and Edith Barrett, turned out to be.

Its screenplay was developed by Curt Siodmak and Ardel Wray. Although Val found it difficult to work with female writers, Ardel's easy-going and adaptable nature and her capable work made her an exception. She is the only female writer accredited to any Lewton screenplay.*

My own second assignment for Val was an original called *Seventh Victim,* which I again wrote as a long short story. This time an orphaned heroine is caught in the web of murder, against a background of the Signal Hill oil wells.

*Ardel Wray, like me, had been a reader in RKO's reading department, run by Nan Cochrane. Ardel was the daughter of actress Virginia Brissac and actor-director John Griffith Wray.

Gradually she realises that she will herself be the murderer's seventh victim if she does not discover his identity in time.

Meanwhile, the mounting success of *Cat People* obliged RKO to tear up my old contract and award me a new long-term one at a substantial raise, plus a bonus of two weeks in New York City, with all expenses paid. Before I left, Val told me the studio wanted a sequel to *Cat People* and that I was to stay longer in New York and do some research on Washington Irving and Tarrytown legends. Val said he was stuck with the title, *Curse of the Cat People,* but that the sequel was to be about a little girl who, out of sheer loneliness, conjures up an imaginary friend, little suspecting that this friend, whose likeness she has only seen once in a half-forgotten photograph, is her father's dead first wife.

When I returned from New York, I discovered that the story I had written for *Seventh Victim* had been discarded and that Val now wanted to tell a tale of an orphaned girl who goes to New York to find her elder sister, little suspecting that her sister has disappeared deliberately because she knows that she is the intended seventh victim of a group of devil-worshippers holding forth secretly in Greenwich Village. I had had an inkling that something like this might be in the works, because Val had written me, without going into details, asking me to try and gain admission to a meeting in Manhattan of a modern witches' coven. I was able to attend such a meeting through RKO's very capable New York force. It was a group of very normal-appearing people, who knitted efficiently and talked pleasantly in between hexing and establishing certain curses. I did not see how Hitler could long survive some of the curses placed on his head that night.

Charles O'Neal, a writer I knew, had already been engaged to develop the new story and screenplay of *Seventh Victim,* and I was to work in collaboration with him.*

Val was working on a number of projects, staggering them without, he hoped, staggering himself. The studio had acquired a Cornell Woolrich novel, "Black Alibi," re-titled it *The Leopard Man,* and Ardel Wray was developing it to Val's requirements, putting the scene of action in Santa Fe, New Mexico. Val thus had four properties in various stages of pre-production — *The Leopard Man, Seventh Victim, Curse of the Cat People,* and *The Ghost Ship.* For the last, he had engaged Donald Henderson Clarke to devise an original story that would utilise RKO's handsome standing set of a big ship.

Seventh Victim went before the cameras as the first directorial assignment of Mark Robson, the film editor whom Val now promoted to full directorship. An enterprising agent, Leon O. Lance, had brought a new young actress to Val's attention named Kim Hunter, for whom Lance had secured a contract from Selznick. Val quietly arranged a screen test for Miss Hunter, which she made with a very talented young contract actor, Russell Wade. Jacques Tourneur directed them in the scene between the "halfway lovers" in "Outward Bound," and Nick Musuraca shot it on the ship set which would be used in *The Ghost Ship.* It remains one of the best screen tests I've ever seen, and it's not surprising at all that the front-office raised no objection to introducing Kim Hunter as a screen personality in the *Seventh Victim's* lead. An interest-

*In later years, "Blacky," as Charles O'Neal was called by his friends, gained additional recognition as the father of Ryan O'Neal, contemporary young screen hero.

MORE FROM HOLLYWOOD

ing cast surrounded her, including, among others, Isabel Jewell, Tom Conway, Evelyn Brent, Ben Bard, Mary Newton, and Elizabeth Russell, who was to create a definite impression as the tubercular Mimi who decides to have one last fling before death claims her. There is also a moody, terrifying scene in a small shower, where Kim Hunter is advised by Mary Newton not to try and find her sister; the menace in this scene would grow into real violence years later when Hitchcock did *Psycho*.

Critics were now calling Lewton's pictures outstanding, and the late James Agee declared in both "Time" and "The Nation" that the most imaginative and creative film work in Hollywood was being done by Val Lewton and his unit.

Curse of the Cat People, which received the kind of notices usually reserved for major films, had its share of production crises. Gunther von Fritsch started as its director, but with the film only half completed and shooting far behind schedule, constant battles with the front-office forced him out — and into the army, which must have seemed like a peaceful haven after the battles of RKO. The film's very able film editor, Robert Wise, took over, and completed the

Simone Simon and Ann Carter in Val Lewton's *Curse of the Cat People*.

picture. It was a difficult and thankless task, and from that day I never doubted that Wise would rise to the top ranks as a film director. Like Robson, Wise owes his initial directorial credit to Val Lewton.

After the preview of *Curse of the Cat People,* there was a thirty-minute celebration in Val's office. He had been pleading with the front-office to change the accursed exploitation title to *Aimee and Her Friend,* and the higher echelon had grudgingly agreed to the change. Vodka was being served to the unit when word came that the title, *Curse of the Cat People,* had been reinstated. Val grunted his disgust and poured himself another drink.

"The picture's good enough," he maintained, "for every major critic to complain of its damned title!"

And that's exactly what almost every major critic did, for *Curse of the Cat People* had a believable story and a tender, haunting mood, and is still run off for classes in child psychology. It was about as near as one could get in Hollywood to the kind of film the French were doing before the Nazi invasion curtailed their film-making. There were outstanding performances by Simone Simon, Kent Smith, and Jane Randolph carrying on their original roles (Simone as a friendly ghost, since she had been killed off at the end of *Cat People).*

For some unexplained reason, a brief montage sequence in which the child admires a picture of a Sleeping Beauty storybook heroine wearing a medieval princess's gown was cut from the completed film, so that when Simone appeared wearing the gown the princess had worn, there was no explanation for her attire. This elicited the only adverse comment the picture received. Some critics even accused Simone of suddenly appearing as a Follies showgirl, of all things.

This picture has an exquisite performance by a very sensitive child actress, Ann Carter, and a performance by Julia Dean as a half-crazed, aged actress that made a new career for her in Hollywood, where she had once been a star in silent films. Most critics also remarked upon the intelligent use of Sir Lancelot, a kindly-faced black calypso singer, in a highly sympathetic supporting role. Lewton, incidentally, was one of the first Hollywood producers to use the black race intelligently in his pictures, as an examination of his full product will prove.

I had had a wonderful and mutually profitable working experience with Val on *Cat People;* we had a few differences on *Seventh Victim;* and we had some larger ones on *Curse of the Cat People.* Val, a frustrated writer himself, could not resist tinkering with a writer's screenplay. He had no ear for dialogue, and the dialogue he changed always emerged as bookish. The character of Julia Farren, the old actress, was entirely mine, and although Val fiddled with the other characters, he left Julia Farren alone. He was always saying, with humour in the beginning that began to be edged with contempt: "No, leave the old actress alone. She's DeWitt's. He *likes* old actresses."

I do think I had something to do with his selection of Julia Dean for the part. Half a dozen elderly ladies with stage background had been suggested by Ben Piazza, head of talent at RKO, for the role, among them Miss Dean, and she was the one I felt was exactly right. I suggested to Mr. Piazza that he phone her and ask her to invite Val and Gunther von Fritsch (then sole director on the film) and me to have tea with her. A script had been sent her, so an

317

Julia Dean and Ann Carter in *Curse of the Cat People.*

invitation to tea was quite proper. Also, there is a scene in the story where the old actress officiates at the tea-table, and an actress can really shine when she demonstrates she knows how to pour tea from a silver service. Miss Dean rose to the occasion admirably; her Belasco training did not fail her; and the very next day Val told me, amused, that he thought I'd be glad to know that Miss Dean had been signed for the part.

A film critic and historian, Tom Milne, who is an admirer of *Curse of the Cat People,* has maintained that it, more than any other Lewton production, is an *oeuvre* in the true sense of the word. Everything that was Val is all through this picture. The whole climax and ending is his, definitely. The screenplay, as I wrote it, had an entirely different ending. In my version, after the death of the old actress on the stairway, Amy, in her first experience with death in a human being, is on the very brink of insanity. In her hysteria, she calls for her friend, and Irena materialises to comfort her. Amy keeps crying, ''But she is dead.'' And then Irena comforts her by telling her that death is not so frightening — it is just the end of life — and when Amy does not understand her, Irena says, ''But, Amy, *I* am dead — and I am your friend.'' Amy is reconciled. Her parents and the troopers enter, and she is no longer afraid. There is a hammering then from behind a locked door, and the troopers unlock

318

it to disclose Mrs. Farren's unwanted daughter, Barbara, who is completely mad, demanding to know who locked the door on her. Only Amy knows that her friend Irena locked the door to save her from Barbara.

This version was shot, but after it was cut into the picture, Val didn't like it at all. By this time I was working on a treatment for *The Enchanted Cottage*, and Val asked me to have lunch with him, during which he told me his idea for the revised climax and ending of *Curse of the Cat People*. I didn't like *it* at all, and told him that in my opinion it smacked too much of Saki's "Sredni Vashtar" and several other short story horror classics. Val was indignant and said rather testily that at least, since I was already busy on a new assignment with another producer, I wouldn't be submitted to writing something I didn't approve of, that he himself would write the revised ending. This he did, and it was shot as an added scene, and all the original film was scrapped. I don't think Val ever forgave me, not for disapproving of his revised ending, but for recognising its source. *Curse of the Cat People* was the last screenplay I did for Val and, as with *Cat People*, I had also worked as dialogue director for the production — but I did not work in any capacity on the revised final scenes.

Val did not resent any of his people working on bigger budget pictures at RKO. Before I went over to Harriet Parsons's unit, Charles Koerner, pleased with the work I had done for Val, spoke of me to Herbert Wilcox, who hired me as writer for an Anna Neagle upper-budget starrer, *The Yellow Canary*. I think what Val did resent was that every effort he made to lift himself out of the small-budget production came to nothing. When Jacques Tourneur went on to direct expensive features and I to write them for directors like John Cromwell and George Stevens, Val always wished us the best of luck when we departed his unit, grudgingly admitting he could no longer afford us.*

He chafed at being a lower-budget producer. Production costs were climbing, and even in 1944 it was impossible to get the same quality of picture he had made in 1942 for so small a cost. All his pictures made money for the studio, and although the front-office unwillingly raised his budgets, it kept him making exploitation budget pictures. His plea to be allowed to make a movie of "The African Queen," a novel he greatly admired, was refused. In 1944 he was allowed to make an exploitation picture about juvenile delinquency, *Youth Runs Wild*, but he was not very happy with it, and, resenting the limitations imposed upon him just as strongly as ever, returned to making suspense films.

When Charles Koerner died suddenly, from leukemia, a series of production heads at RKO was unsympathetic toward Val's filmmaking aspirations. Koerner, at least, had given Val almost complete charge of his unit, but the new chiefs constantly interfered.

In spite of this, Val made *Mademoiselle Fifi* from two DeMaupassant tales, "Mademoiselle Fifi" and "Boule de Suif," and he again starred Simone Simon in it. An earlier French movie had also combined those two short stories, but Val's version was far more effective, and more beautifully and authentically dressed.

The success of *Mademoiselle Fifi* opened the way to his filming another

*Val was constantly saying he could not afford something or somebody. Nazimova was often a guest at small dinner parties at the Lewton home, and I asked her once why she didn't star in a movie for Val. "I don't think he can afford me," she replied with a mischievous smile.

319

literary property in the public domain, Robert Louis Stevenson's *The Body Snatchers,* co-starring Boris Karloff and Bela Lugosi, with Henry Daniell. He then produced a very effective original mood-piece, *Isle of the Dead,* which deals with the universal fear of being buried alive. The performance of Katherine Emery as the unfortunate woman who is buried alive is superb and absolutely terrifying. In 1946, Val made *Bedlam,* with Boris Karloff and Anna Lee, his most expensive and probably his least successful picture at RKO, in spite of the real horrors it showed of London's truly infamous Bedlam. The studio was completely unappreciative of the picture's very fine film qualities and almost sloughed it off after its release.

Val, very much overworked and disheartened, had suffered a heart attack, and had been cautioned to go slowly. The war was over, and Val believed that the popularity of his pictures, at least partially, was a wartime phenomenon. Audiences, he thought, had wanted to be frightened by something other than wholesale slaughter, had wanted danger to be particularised. He was telling himself the new movie audiences no longer wanted to escape to personalised horror tales, but to comedy, big-scale Westerns, and spectacular musical extravaganzas in colour. He was discouraged and felt that his work as a producer, although highly successful, was being relegated to the insignificant and forgotten. He cringed when newspaper columnists, searching for a catch-phrase, called him the "Sultan of Shudders."

RKO, often stuck without a final assignment for an actor on his committed contract, was always asking Val to find parts in his productions for such players. In *Cat People* Jack Holt played a very small role in order to use up an unused studio commitment. James Ellison, for his last picture at RKO, got one of his best parts there in *I Walked with a Zombie.* Val used Richard Dix on a final commitment basis as the star of *The Ghost Ship,* and did the same for Dennis O'Keefe in *The Leopard Man.*

He wanted to write as well as produce his next picture, and he wanted it to be a film which wouldn't be restricted by a tight budget or a close shooting schedule. The new heads at RKO were not in sympathy with Val's dreams and terminated his contract. He went over to Paramount with high hopes, but encountered top resistance to all of his schemes there, and produced only one film, *My Own True Love.* His feminine star, Phyllis Calvert, and he disliked one another on sight, and the whole Paramount experience was hardly what the doctor ordered for a man who had already had one heart attack.

Hopefully, he moved over to M-G-M, after a completely humiliating and disheartening experience in trying to set up an independent unit with Mark Robson and Robert Wise. He had long admired a Joseph Hergesheimer novella, "Wild Oranges," and he and I used to talk about it when I was working for him, because I liked it, too, and we both fondly remembered the version King Vidor had made of it in the silents. Val had even tried, without success, to get RKO to buy it for him. Now, at M-G-M, he was at the studio that owned the silent rights to the property; they bought the talking rights, and he happily began writing his own screenplay of it.

That happiness didn't last long. I saw him only once during that time, and he seemed miserable. He was discouraged with his own efforts as a screenwriter, and when I asked, "Did you ever know a writer who was really fully pleased with what he had written?" he admitted that I had a point, but he was over-analytical, too much of a perfectionist ever to be satisfied with his writing attempts. The hero of "Wild Oranges" is a man whose life is nearly wrecked when he sees the bride he loves accidentally killed before his very eyes; his story becomes one of adjustment and the eventual finding of a new love. It was virtually the very story Clark Gable had experienced. Val had himself succeeded in interesting Gable in starring as the hero of "Wild Oranges," but M-G-M had other plans for Mr. Gable. Like almost ruining his career.

Dore Schary, new head of M-G-M, and Val were not compatible, but Val went ahead and made an insignificant little comedy, *Please Believe Me,* with Deborah Kerr and Robert Walker. He left M-G-M just as the full blow of his disappointment at not being able to make a deal with Robson and Wise hit home; he was, in fact, dropped from the unit.

He went over to Universal-International, and there produced a Technicolor Western, *Apache Drums.* It was beneath his talents, but it was a good action film, and the use of colour in it highly commendable. It did serve to restore a bit of his own faith in himself.

He was ready to admit now that he had had too much faith in the inherent goodness of people. The characters in the movies he produced at RKO were all essentially good people, led into self-destruction and crime only by their weaknesses, fears, and sicknesses. Even the devil-worshippers in *Seventh Victim* were pitiful, misled human beings. He had always refused to believe that he had been deliberately thwarted or betrayed by ruthless and jealous men. But now he had begun to admit that it might be so. Nevertheless, he continued doggedly to hope that somewhere there would be a production chief who would believe in him and allow him full film-making powers.

He thought he had found such a man in Stanley Kramer, and was both resigned and delighted when he was engaged as an assistant producer to work under Kramer on *My Six Convicts* and *The Member of the Wedding.*

He had suffered from several gallstone attacks, and then on the very day he started working for Kramer, he had a second heart attack, and when it was followed by a severe one, he was hospitalised, and placed, protesting, in an oxygen tent. He died on March 14, 1951, only forty-six years old.

"There always comes that time," he was fond of saying, "when a real producer must declare, 'This is it! I will stand or fall by the script as it now is! Every story can be rewritten and analysed out of existence. Next week we put this one before the cameras while it's still alive.'"

The psychological thrillers he produced for RKO-Radio were alive, and still are. And they are finding young and new audiences everywhere.

VAL LEWTON FILMOGRAPHY

Val Lewton was producer for the following feature films:

CAT PEOPLE (1942). Psychological horror study of a girl possessed with the fear that she will turn into a cat and destroy any man who loves her. *Dir:* Jacques Tourneur. *Sc:* DeWitt Bodeen. *With* Simone Simon, Kent Smith, Tom Conway, Jane Randolph, Jack Holt, Alan Napier, Elizabeth Russell, Alec Craig, Elizabeth Dunne, Mary Halsey, Dot Farley, Teresa Harris, Charles Jordan, Betty Roadman, Don Kerr. *Prod:* RKO-Radio. 71m.

I WALKED WITH A ZOMBIE (1943). Voodoo and romantic horror and suspense on an island in the West Indies. *Dir:* Jacques Tourneur. *Sc:* Curt Siodmak and Ardel Wray (from a series of articles in "The American Weekly" by Inez Wallace; and the story suggested by Charlotte Brontë's "Jane Eyre"). *With* Frances Dee, James Ellison, Tom Conway, Edith Barrett, Christine Gordon, James Bell, Richard Abrams, Teresa Harris, Sir Lancelot, Martin Wilkins, Darby Jones, Jeni LeGon, Jieno Moxzer, Arthur Walker, Kathleen Hartfield, Norman Mayes, Clinton Rosemond, Alan Edmiston, Melvin Williams, Vivian Dandridge. *Prod:* RKO-Radio. 68m.

THE LEOPARD MAN (1943). Suspense thriller of a series of murders of young girls, clawed to death, in a little town in New Mexico. *Dir:* Jacques Tourneur. *Sc:* Ardel Wray (with additional dialogue by Edward Dein; from the novel, "Black Alibi," by Cornell Woolrich). *With* Dennis O'Keefe, Jean Brooks, Margo, Isabel Jewell, James Bell, Margaret Landry, Abner Biberman, Richard Martin, Tula Parma, Ben Bard, Ariel Heath, Fely Franquelli, Robert Anderson, Jacqueline de Wit, Bobby Spindola, William Halligan, Kate Drain Lawson, Russell Wade, Jacques Lory, Tola Nesmith, Margaret Sylva, Charles Lung, John Dilson, Mary MacLaren, Tom Orosco, Eliso Gamboa, Joe Dominguez, Betty Roadman, Rosa Rita Varella, Brandon Hurst, Rose Higgins, Rene Pedrini, John Piffle, George Sherwood, John Tettemer. *Prod:* RKO-Radio. 66m.

SEVENTH VICTIM (1943). Psychological suspense drama of a modern devil's worship society operating in Manhattan and their attempt to drive a member who has betrayed them into suicide. *Dir:* Mark Robson. *Sc:* Charles O'Neal and DeWitt Bodeen. *With* Kim Hunter, Tom Conway, Jean Brooks, Isabel Jewell, Evelyn Brent, Erford Gage, Hugh Beaumont, Ben Bard, Chef Milani, Marguerita Sylva, Mary Newton, Eve March, Wally Brown, Feodor Chaliapin, Tola Nesmith, Edythe Elliott, Milton Kibbee, Elizabeth Russell, Marianne Mosner, Joan Barclay, William Halligan, Lou Lubin, Kernan Cripps, Dewey Robinson, Lloyd Ingraham, Ann Summers, Betty Roadman, Tiny Jones, Sara Selby, Eileen O'Malley, Lorna Dunn. *Prod:* RKO-Radio. 71m.

THE GHOST SHIP (1943). Psychological suspense drama of a ship's captain, a megalomaniac driven to kill. *Dir:* Mark Robson. *Sc:* Donald Henderson Clarke (from a story by Leo Mittler). *With* Richard Dix, Russell Wade, Edith Barrett, Edmund Glover, Steven Winston, Ben Bard, Skelton Knaggs, Tom Burton, Robert Bice, Lawrence Tierney, Dewey Robinson, Charles Lung, George De Normand, Paul Marion, Sir Lancelot, Boyd Davis, Harry Clay, Russell Owen, John Burford, Eddie Borden, Mike Lally, Charles Regan, Nolan Leary, Herbert Vigran, Shirley O'Hara, Alec Craig, Bob Stevenson, Charles Norton, Norman Mayes. *Prod:* RKO-Radio. 69m.

CURSE OF THE CAT PEOPLE (1944). Psychological study of loneliness in a child driven to the point where fantasy and reality are the same. *Dir:* Gunther von Fritsch and Robert Wise. *Sc:* DeWitt Bodeen. *With* Simone Simon, Kent Smith, Jane Randolph, Julia Dean, Elizabeth Russell, Ann Carter, Eve March, Erford Gage, Sir Lancelot, Joel Davis, Sarah Selby, Charley Bates, Juanita Alvarez, Gloria Donovan, Ginny Wren, Linda Ann Bieber, Mel Sternlight. *Prod:* RKO-Radio. 70m.

YOUTH RUNS WILD (1944). Juvenile delinquency in a small American town during the Second World War. *Dir:* Mark Robson. *Sc:* John Fante (from a story by Fante and Herbert Kline; with additional dialogue by Ardel Wray; from a story, "Are These Our Children?," in "Look" magazine). *With* Bonita Granville, Kent Smith, Jean Brooks, Glenn Vernon, Ben Bard, Lawrence Tierney, Elizabeth Russell, Tessa Brind, Mary Servoss, Arthur Shields, Dickie Moore, Johnny Walsh, Rod Rodgers, Juanita Alvarez, Gloria Donovan, Jack Carrington, Ida Shoemaker, Claire Carleton, Art Smith, Harold Barnitz, Frank O'Connor, Rosemary La Planche, Joan Barclay, Margaret Landry, Harry Clay, George De Normand, Danny Desmond, Fritz Lieber, Robert Strong, Tom Burton, Russell Hopton, Chris Drake, Edmund Glover, Lee Phelps, Gordon Jones, Harry Harvey, Maxwell Hayes, Bud Wiser. *Prod:* RKO-Radio. 67m.

MADEMOISELLE FIFI (1944). Drama of snobbery and hypocrisy among the bourgeoisie in France during the Franco-Prussian War. *Dir:* Robert Wise. *Sc:* Josef Mischel and Peter Ruric (from two stories, "Boule de Suif" and "Mademoiselle Fifi," by

Guy de Maupassant). *With* Simone Simon, John Emery, Kurt Kreuger, Alan Napier, Helen Freeman, Norma Varden, Jason Robards Sr., Romaine Callender, Fay Helm, Edmund Glover, Charles Waldron, Mayo Newhall, Lillian Bronson, Alan Ward, Daun Kennedy, William Von Wymetal, Max Willenz, Marc Cramer, John Good, Allan Lee, Frank Mayo, Margaret Landry, Rosemary La Planche, Marie Lund, Margie Stewart, Violet Wislon, Tom Burton, Steve Winston, Paul Marion, Ed Allen, Richard Drumm, Victor Cutler. *Prod:* RKO-Radio. 69m.

ISLE OF THE DEAD (1945). Psychological obsession with and fear of being buried alive, set on a Greek island during the war of 1912, when a plague rages. *Dir:* Mark Robson. *Sc:* Ardel Wray and Josef Mischel. *With* Boris Karloff, Ellen Drew, Marc Cramer, Katherine Emery, Helene Thimig, Alan Napier, Jason Robards Sr., Ernst Dorian, Skelton Knaggs, Sherry Hall, Erick Hanson. *Prod:* RKO-Radio. 71m.

THE BODY SNATCHER (1945). Suspense drama of grave robbers in Edinburgh, Scotland, early in the Nineteenth century. *Dir:* Robert Wise. *Sc:* Philip MacDonald and Carlos Keith (Val Lewton) (from the story by Robert Louis Stevenson). *With* Boris Karloff, Bela Lugosi, Henry Daniell, Edith Atwater, Russell Wade, Rita Corday, Sharon Moffett, Donna Lee, Robert Clarke, Mary Gordon, Carl Kent, Jack Welch, Larry Wheat, Jim Moran, Ina Constant, Bill Williams. *Prod:* RKO-Radio. 78m.

BEDLAM (1946). Horror story of Bedlam, London's infamous insane asylum, in the Eighteenth century. *Dir:* Mark Robson. *Sc:* Carlos Keith (Val Lewton) and Mark Robson (suggested by William Hogarth's "Bedlam" — Plate 8, "The Rake's Progress.") *With* Boris Karloff, Anna Lee, Billy House, Richard

Fraser, Glenn Vernon, Ian Wolfe, Jason Robards Sr., Elizabeth Russell, Leland Hodgson, Joan Newton, Victor Holbrook, Robert Clarke, John Meredith, Larry Wheat, Bruce Edwards, John Beck, Ellen Corby, John Ince, Skelton Knaggs, John Goldsworthy, Polly Bailey, Foster Phinney, Donna Lee, Nan Leslie, Tom Noonan, George Holmes, Jimmy Jordan, Robert Manning, Frankie Dee, Frank Pharr, Harry Harvey, Betty Gillette, Victor Travers, James Logan. *Prod:* RKO-Radio. 79m.

MY OWN TRUE LOVE (1948). Romantic drama of a father and son in love with a divorcee in London after the Second World War. *Dir:* Compton Bennett. *Sc:* Theodore Strauss and Josef Mischel (from the adaptation by Arthur Kober of a novel, "Make You a Fine Wife," by Yolanda Forbes). *With* Phyllis Calvert, Melvyn Douglas, Wanda Hendrix, Philip Friend, Binnie Barnes, Alan Napier, Arthur Shields, Phyllis Morris, Richard Webb. *Prod:* Paramount. 84m.

PLEASE BELIEVE ME (1950). Romantic comedy of an English girl who inherits a ranch in the American West. *Dir:* Norman Taurog. *Sc:* Nathaniel Curtis. *With* Deborah Kerr, J. Carrol Naish, Spring Byington, Carol Savage, Drue Mallory, George Cleveland, Ian Wolfe, Bridget Carr, Henri Letondal, Gaby André, Leon Belasco. *Prod:* M-G-M. 88m.

APACHE DRUMS (1951) Western drama in Spanish Boot, climaxed by a raid of the Mescalero Apaches and the town saved by the arrival of the Cavalry in the nick of time. *Dir:* Hugo Fregonese. *Sc:* David Chandler (from a novel, "Stand at Spanish Boot," by Harry Brown). *With* Stephen McNally, Coleen Gray, Willard Parker, Arthur Shields, James Griffith, Armando Silvestre, Georgia Backus, Clarence Muse, Ruthelma Stevens, James Best, Chinto Gusman, Ray Bennett. *Prod:* Universal-International. Technicolor. 75m.

15
JEANETTE MacDONALD

The image that Jeanette MacDonald projected from the screen had almost nothing to do with her own personality. In real life she was never arch, coy, spoiled or petulant, but realistic, hard-working and ambitious — a woman of whom it could be said, as it has been of Lillian Gish, "Her head may be in the clouds, but her feet are planted firmly in the box-office."

She was also a warm and friendly woman; she loved to entertain and played the hostess better than any actress I've ever known. "Twin Gables," the attractive English home in Bel-Air that Gene Raymond gave her when they married in 1937, was the scene of many *well*-remembered social occasions.

She always claimed to be "as absent-minded as the professor who kissed the cat goodnight and put his wife out the front door," but at one of her dinner parties I saw her recall with exactitude who had given them the china, silver and crystal. "I love using our wedding gifts," she said, "because then I think of the friends who gave them."

She was a generous woman, but not an extravagant one, and she was always a lady, to the despair of publicists who could find nothing scandalous in her personal life. "I've always made a point of controlling myself," she said once, "because I always thought it was the thing to do."

Her ancestry was Scottish, Irish, and English. "I've been told I have an Irish temper," she once said. "I know I have Scottish thrift, and like the English I love a good show." She was happy when Louella O. Parsons, after a Hollywood Bowl concert, told her she was Hollywood's greatest show-woman. She knew what her public wanted of her, and gave it graciously.

And she had the courage of her convictions. Her Scottish Presbyterian training made her impatient of anything off-colour or vulgar. I once saw her scold a Beverly Hills cinema manager for showing a film she considered pointless and in bad taste. Yet the tolerance and wit of the sophisticate was also hers when she was faced with the truth. When Gene Raymond and she came to Pasadena to see a performance of a play I'd written about Lord Byron, she was astonished and intrigued to learn of Byron's relationship with his half-sister Augusta, and made a point of phoning the next day to tell me she couldn't wait to get home to check the facts in her own library and thought I'd handled a delicate situation that might have been offensive with great taste.

The blatant way in which contemporary theatrical writers and film-makers present sex she found unimaginative and ugly, and didn't mind saying so. "I had my earliest training in films with Lubitsch," she said, "in the days when he was a real boudoir diplomat. He could suggest more with a closed door than all the hay-rolling you see openly on the screen nowadays, and yet he never offended.''

Jeanette MacDonald was also one of the few stars who could "talk story" in terms beyond the limitations of her own role. She invested in a number of story properties and personally engaged writers to develop them into screen-plays and teleplays. I wrote one for her, adapting it from a property she owned, and can testify that at a story conference she was always alert to all the implications of the story itself. She would have made an excellent film producer in her own right, for with her the story came first, and she was willing to fight for the story even if it meant a diminution of her own acting part.

She was born in Philadelphia on Arch Street (an area now considerably run-down, but in the first decade of this century it was representative of the affluent middle class). Long before she ever entered films, she was giving 1907 as her birth year, but her school records at Washington Irving High School and Julia Richman High School in Manhattan state that Jeanette MacDonald, who transferred there from West Philadelphia High School on November 11, 1919, presented as evidence of age a birth or baptismal certificate stating her date of birth as June 18, 1903.* She was the youngest of three daughters born to Daniel and Anne M. (Wright) MacDonald. The father was a contractor and politician, and both he and his wife realised early that all three of their daughters were gifted. They sent them to schools specialising in dramatics, dancing and singing, and before she was nine Jeanette had memorised opera-tic arias from recordings, and had made a professional appearance in a children's revue in Philadelphia.

Some years later, when her next older sister, Blossom, secured a chorus job in New York, Jeanette was allowed to visit her. She was watching the chorus in the Capitol Theatre from the wings one day when producer Ned Wayburn was attracted by her red hair and beauty and put her in the chorus of "The Demi-Tasse Revue," in which she made her New York *début* in January 1920.

Her father's business had so declined at that time that he agreed to move the family home to New York. In April, Jeanette appeared in a bit role in "The Night Boat," which led her to jobs modelling furs and lingerie. She then got a small role in "Irene," and, in October 1921, a bigger one in "Tangerine." A year later she had her first important role, at the Greenwich Village Theatre, in "A Fantastic Fricassee;" and in October 1923 she was such a success in the second female lead in "The Magic Ring," a singing part, that she was placed under exclusive contract by Henry Savage. In 1925 he gave her the *ingénue* prima donna role in George Gershwin's "Tip Toes."

For the next four years Miss MacDonald starred in musicals for Savage and the Shuberts — "Bubbling Over"; "Yes, Yes Yvette"; "Sunny Days"; "Angela"; and "Boom! Boom!" a featured player of which was also Archie Leach, who went to Hollywood and became better known as Cary Grant.

In 1928, when she was playing the Princess Angela, Richard Dix saw her and prevailed upon Paramount to test her for the leading lady's role in his next film, *Nothing But the Truth*. She didn't get that part, although the test was

*I am most grateful to Eleanor Knowles, of Manhattan, for this information. It's credibility is very sensible, because it would indicate that she began her stage career not quite at seventeen, and not at thirteen, which is a little indecent. And that Jeanette MacDonald never was.

329

exceptional, and Dix did everything he could to throw it her way; the Shuberts, however, held her to her contract with them.

The reel of test-film stayed in the vaults for almost a year until Ernst Lubitsch, searching for a leading lady opposite Maurice Chevalier in *The Love Parade,* chanced to see it, and was impressed by her beauty and vivacity. "If she can sing and dance," Lubitsch said, "I'd give her the part." Contracts were drawn and Miss MacDonald entrained for Hollywood.

Her mother accompanied her, for Mr. MacDonald had died. Her sister Blossom was enjoying success as a New York stage actress under the name of Marie Blake; and the oldest sister, Elsie (Mrs. Bernard Scheiter), had opened a dramatic school in Philadelphia.

Lubitsch was delighted to find his new discovery was not only beautiful but talented, eager, and hardworking. And she was just right as Chevalier's foil, the haughty young Queen Louise of mythical Sylvania. In the beginning, Lubitsch called her "Mac." She didn't like it and said: "Don't call me Mac or I'll call you Lu." He then started calling her "Donald," but stopped when she threatened to call him "Itsch." She was always "Jeanette" to her friends, and to acquaintances "Miss MacDonald," and later, "Mrs. Raymond."

In 1929, Jeanette MacDonald also made her recording debut for RCA Victor. She sang her two big numbers from *The Love Parade* — the haunting "Dream Lover" and the rousing "March of the Grenadiers," both by Victor Schertzinger and Clifford Grey.

The Love Parade was a perfect example of a film bearing "The Lubitsch touch," and was instantaneously such a hit that Paramount gave Miss Mac-Donald the singing role of Katherine opposite Dennis King in *The Vagabond King,* a big two-toned Technicolor production.

Curiously, Paramount did not use her in its English language version of *Paramount on Parade,* but she was mistress of ceremonies for the Spanish version, *Galas de la Paramount,* for she was multi-lingual, speaking both Spanish and French as fluently as she did English.

Lubitsch used her again opposite Jack Buchanan this time in his production of *Monte Carlo,* in which she sang "Beyond the Blue Horizon" for the first time, in a sequence that directorially and photographically was highly imaginative, and has since been much imitated. Leo McCarey then gave her a singing role in the wild *mélange* of star-studded comedy and slapstick called *Let's Go Native,* obviously suggested by Barrie's "The Admirable Crichton."

Miss MacDonald's career was then being managed by Robert Ritchie, and for a time they were engaged to marry. She had helped set Ritchie up as a talent manager by becoming his first important client, and she remained with him until he was firmly established in Hollywood and she was a long-term contract star at M-G-M. "Something stops me from going into marriage," she said at the time. "Others have made such a dismal failure of it." She had several managers in the years that followed, but she largely relied for advice on Helen Ferguson, who handled her public relations account. After Ritchie's death in 1972, many "in the know" claimed there to be evidence that Miss MacDonald and he had once been secretly married and just as secretly divorced in Europe.

After *Let's Go Native,* she did a big musical for United Artists called *The Lottery Bride,* which, in spite of its Friml songs, didn't come off as it should

Jeanette MacDonald with Maurice Chevalier in Mamoulian's *Love Me Tonight*.

have. She then went to Fox and filmed three comedies which were not musicals but had incidental songs.

In 1931, a French newspaper had announced that she had been killed in France in an automobile accident, and nothing she could do or say seemed to quash the rumors. She decided that a concert tour of Europe would at least convince Europeans that she was alive and singing. She appeared at the Empire in Paris in September 1931 in a repertory of songs, and then appeared in person in other European capitols. Her London *début* was at the Dominion Theatre.

When she returned to Hollywood, she also returned to Paramount and Lubitsch. He was producing another musical, *One Hour with You* (a musical re-make of his silent comedy success, *The Marriage Circle*), and because he was busy finishing another film, he assigned George Cukor to direct it. Cukor has recently said: "Lubitsch was doing another picture at the time, and I was assigned to direct *One Hour with You*. I don't think they were very pleased with my work — with the best intentions in the world I couldn't have directed it as Lubitsch did. First he supervised it, and then after a few weeks he really took over. It was a very painful time for me because I stood there more or less on the sidelines and watched my Ps and Qs. Certainly it was wholly a Lubitsch picture in style. The script, after all, was his, and I suppose that he directed most of it. I gave what help I could, though. I was there all the time." Miss MacDonald always admired Cukor as a director, and several times expressed regret that she never worked for him later when they were both at M-G-M.

She again appeared opposite Chevalier, this time in a picture with songs by Rodgers and Hart, *Love Me Tonight,* which Rouben Mamoulian produced

331

and directed. In my opinion, it is not only hers and Chevalier's best picture, but one of the very best and brightest movie musicals ever made, thanks largely to Mamoulian. It so impressed Louis B. Mayer that he became convinced Jeanette MacDonald belonged at M-G-M, and in 1933 she signed with that studio. The association was a long and lucrative one.

Her first M-G-M picture was *The Cat and the Fiddle,* in which she co-starred with Ramon Novarro, and in her third one, *Naughty Marietta,* she was co-starred for the first time with Nelson Eddy. The MacDonald-Eddy team was surefire box-office from the beginning, and as a team they remained top grossers through seven more pictures, all of which were the kind of romantic escapism worldwide audiences craved in the depression years before Second World War.

Not long before her death, Miss MacDonald defended these pictures. "Today, anything that has a suggestion of sentiment is quickly dismissed as corn," she said. "Frankly, what's wrong with it? Have we become so suffi-cient that we can live without sentiment? Sentiment, after all, is basic. Without it, there is no love, no life, no family."

Her second M-G-M picture was *The Merry Widow,* and Lubitsch chose her for the part of Sonia despite the fact that Chevalier, who was to play Prince Danilo, had pressured Thalberg to engage Grace Moore for the role. M-G-M had tried Miss Moore in two earlier pictures, and she had failed to register. Mayer, Thalberg, and Lubitsch were agreed on casting Miss MacDonald as Sonia, and then Chevalier learned that if Miss Moore played it, he would have to take billing beneath her. He capitulated, but was delighted when Miss Moore did become a big musical film star at Columbia with *One Night of Love.*

Although Miss MacDonald and Chevalier appear as the most charming and romantic of lovers in *The Merry Widow,* the personal feeling between them was cool, and they never again appeared in a picture together. Actually, Chevalier comes off second best in the picture, and Miss MacDonald's performance is the film's chief distinction. She is exquisitely gowned, sings and dances superbly, and it is obvious that Lubitsch and she were working in perfect harmony.

She also sang charmingly and looked beautiful in *Rose Marie* her second teaming with Nelson Eddy — and the screenplay by Frances Goodrich and Albert Hackett, with Alice Duer Miller, was one of the most cinematic of all the MacDonald-Eddy musicals. *Rose Marie* is a stunning musical romance.

It was a picture made with neither Eddy nor Chevalier which paved the way for solo stardom for Miss MacDonald. This was *San Francisco,* a romantic thriller, in which she was teamed with Clark Gable and Spencer Tracy. It was a box-office bonanza, and is still one of the favourite features on television, and is also frequently revived for theatrical showings. It is said that Gable resisted playing with her at first, but the MacDonald charm and earnest professionalism soon won him over.

Her first solo starring picture, *The Firefly,* released in 1937, proved her name alone could carry a feature. She was supported in it by Allan Jones, whose musicianship she always admired.

Her favourite of all her pictures was *Maytime.* Among her reasons: "There was, too, the satisfaction of working with Robert Z. Leonard, not only one of

332

Jeanette MacDonald with Clark Gable in *San Francisco*.

the ablest all-around directors but one who, being a singer himself, was deft and sympathetic in his handling of the musical phases of the story. He didn't believe in the iron-handed technique, but preferred that the actors follow their own instincts at first, and re-do a scene only when they felt ideas different from their own would improve a performance. Leonard always kept us pliable and spontaneous. Once he relieved a period of tension by arranging for me to find, to my horror, a strange man asleep on my couch when I went to my dressing-room — a man who, on closer inspection, turned out to be a dummy."

Miss MacDonald was always professional and once, when she inadvertently kept a whole crew waiting for her arrival, she arranged the next day to have herself hauled on set in a large doghouse, from which she descended to apologise, before everybody, to director W. S. Van Dyke.

The MacDonald-Eddy musicals continued to be some of the biggest money-makers in the history of M-G-M. Now and then the team was broken up and they would do a solo, but the studio always re-teamed them. The pictures they made still pack them in at revival houses. My own favourite is *Sweethearts*, in which Jeanette was beautifully photographed in Technicolor and wore some of the most dazzling modern clothes ever designed for a star at M-G-M. It also boasted a script that was almost impudently happy, as devised by Dorothy Parker and Alan Campbell. *The Girl of the Golden West*, first shown in becoming sepia tones, was also well-liked; and *New Moon*, *Bitter Sweet*, and *I Married an Angel* have their admirers.

After breaking up with Robert Ritchie, Miss MacDonald usually chose to attend Hollywood parties alone. One night she went to dinner at Rozika Dolly's beach home and a too-busy butler delayed answering the door. A young man who was also waiting to get in, introduced himself as Gene Raymond. They were formally polite, even painfully so, Miss MacDonald later recalled, and when the butler did admit them, Miss Dolly came up to them saying: "How nice that you came together!"

They kept running into each other socially, and Miss MacDonald once told me that when Raymond saw Howard Hughes send her a note at a party, Raymond sought her out afterwards and said he hoped she wasn't going to date Hughes. Finally, he phoned her, saying that since columnists were coupling their names, how about going out to dinner with him? She accepted, and before long they were going everywhere together. She consented to marry him when he proposed one night at the Ambassador's Cocoanut Grove.

Their wedding on June 17, 1937, in the Wilshire Methodist Church, was attended by three hundred invited guests, and was Hollywood's biggest since Vilma Banky's and Rod La Rocque's in 1927. Shortly before she retired, Louella O. Parsons wrote: "So many memories of Jeanette MacDonald come crowding back — none more vivid than her beauty when she walked down the aisle, her strawberry red hair set off with pink veil and gown, when she married Gene Raymond twenty-eight years ago." And Hedda Hopper: "I remember so well the joint wedding reception for the Raymonds and Mary Pickford and Buddy Rogers in the Basil Rathbones' garden. It was a great social event."

Miss MacDonald never ceased studying music, and at one time went to live in Santa Barbara so she could study daily with Lotte Lehmann. Sometimes

Jeanette MacDonald and Nelson Eddy in *Girl of the Golden West*.

1025-219

Louis B. Mayer complained that her tastes were becoming too classical, and Bosley Crowther in his biography of Mayer, "Hollywood Rajah," says Mayer once got down on his knees in front of Miss MacDonald "and sang 'Eli, Eli,' the Jewish lament, in order to show her how he wanted her to get more *schmaltz* into her voice." She, however, went right on with her studies and knew what she was talking about when she told student singers: "Always be natural, never let anyone talk you out of singing naturally."

Her husband and she made only one picture together — *Smilin' Through* (1941). They both had dual roles in it, and it was less an operetta than a romance with music. Raymond then joined the Air Corps.

Miss MacDonald concluded her long-term contract at M-G-M in 1942 in a somewhat ineffectual film, *Cairo,* and thereafter devoted much of her time to tours of our military establishments. In a film about such tours, *Follow the Boys,* made by Charles K. Feldman for Universal, she played herself, and sang two numbers — "Beyond the Blue Horizon" and "I'll See You in My Dreams."

She also did concert singing during those war years. The house was always a sell-out, whether it was New York's Carnegie Hall or Los Angeles' Shrine Auditorium, or the Hollywood Bowl. After the war, she gave a successful concert in London's Albert Hall.

I was working at RKO-Radio when producer Richard Berger was trying to interest RKO's head of production, Charles Koerner, in re-uniting Miss MacDonald with Nelson Eddy in a movie version of the Romberg operetta, *East Wind.* An audition was held in Miss MacDonald's home, and I was impressed anew by her thorough musicianship. She not only played the piano well, but she transposed on sight the key to one that suited Eddy's harmonising with her. Her suggestions for production numbers were always inspirationally right. Unfortunately, Koerner died suddenly of leukemia, and nothing came of the venture.

Miss MacDonald had always recorded for Victor, and her red-seal records, both as a solo artiste and with Eddy, enjoyed the best of sales. But neither that nor her film success entirely satisfied her. Her all-consuming ambition was to sing in grand opera, and she trained diligently, with the best coaches, to achieve it.

She made her operatic *début* in Montreal, Canada, in 1943, singing *Romeo and Juliet* with Ezio Pinza and Armand Tokatjian. Shortly thereafter she made her American *début* in the same opera, with the Chicago Civic Opera Company, and also sang Marguerite in *Faust,* with Pinza as Mephistopheles. These performances were sold-out. So, later, were her appearances in such popular operettas as *Bitter Sweet* and *The King and I.*

In 1948 she returned to M-G-M, at the insistence of Joe Pasternak, for the mother role in *Three Daring Daughters,* in which she had as her daughters Jane Powell, Mary Eleanor Donohue, and Ann E. Todd, and was courted by Jose Iturbi. The following year she made her final screen appearance, as a widowed concert singer in a Technicolor Lassie film, *The Sun Comes Up.* Ironically, there is more of the real-life Jeanette MacDonald in this final screen performance than in any of her biggest box-office successes.

In 1951, Gene Raymond and she co-starred in an Eastern tour revival of Molnar's "The Guardsman." Subsequently, they made many television appearances together; I particularly remember her in a live production with Raymond of "Charley's Aunt," in which she appeared in the final act as the real aunt of Charley.

In 1957, she was the star of a night-club act at the Sahara in Las Vegas, and later appeared in another such act at the Cocoanut Grove in Los Angeles.

Gene Raymond was away on Air Force Reserve duty while she was performing in Las Vegas, and when they both returned to Hollywood, they issued belated invitations for a celebration of their twentieth wedding anniversary. They took over the Rodeo Room in the Beverly Hills Hotel and it was an enchanting evening. After dinner, for over an hour, Jeanette, in a lilac-coloured Empire gown, sang the songs she liked best, and those her guests requested.

I knew she was frequently busy writing the story of her life, often with the assistance of a reputable writer, and she told me once she would have liked to title it *Do-Re-Mi* because "I came to Hollywood frankly for the dough; then when I was a star, I met the 'Re' — Gene — and we were married; and it was then, as Mrs. Raymond, that I really found me." When a book was published with that title, however, she looked at me with a chuckle one day and said, "What do you think of my calling this autobiography 'The Iron Butterfly'? It's one way of letting everybody know I know that's what some people call me. Besides, I think it'd sell copies."

One of her last public appearances was in 1957 at the funeral of Louis B. Mayer, when she sang "Ah, Sweet Mystery of Life."

In the summer of 1959, her husband and she travelled extensively in Europe. I happened to be in Sweden when they visited Stockholm and the reception accorded them was genuinely warm. Stockholm is supposed to have more cinema houses per population than any other city in the world, and the Swedes were as fond of Miss MacDonald as of any of their own sopranos, from Jenny Lind on.

For all her acclaim in every part of the globe she remained an American woman. She loved America, and loved "coming home." On their return to Southern California, they sold their Bel-Air home, because, she confessed, it had become too difficult to get the proper servants for its upkeep. They bought an apartment in a fashionable section of western Los Angeles.

Miss MacDonald had known for some years that she had a heart murmur, but she took good care of herself, and the condition was not serious until 1963, when she went to the Methodist Hospital in Houston, Texas, for an arterial transplant. She was stricken again in December 1964, and on Christmas Eve was operated on for adhesions at the UCLA Medical Center. Early in January 1965 she went again to Houston, to prepare herself for open heart surgery. Her condition worsened, and she had to be fed intravenously.

On the afternoon of January 14, she roused from a drowsy sleep, and saw her husband standing beside her bed.

"I love you," she said.

"I love you, too," he told her.

She smiled, and died.

JEANETTE MacDONALD FILMOGRAPHY

THE LOVE PARADE (1929). Romantic comedy, with music, set in the mythical kingdom of Sylvania; as Queen Louise. *Dir:* Ernst Lubitsch. *Sc:* Ernest Vajda and Guy Bolton (from the play, "The Prince Consort," by Leon Xanrof and Jules Chancel). Music by Victor Schertzinger and Clifford Grey. *With* Maurice Chevalier, Lupino Lane, Lillian Roth, E. H. Calvert, Andre Cheron, Yola d'Avril, Edgar Norton, Lionel Belmore, Albert Roccardi, Carl Stockdale, Eugene Pallette, Russell Powell, Margaret Fealy, Virginia Bruce, Winter Hall, Ben Turpin. *Prod:* Paramount. 12 reels.

THE VAGABOND KING (1930). A romantic fragment, with song, from the court of Louis Xl of France and the poet, François Villon; as Katherine, Villon's lady love. *Dir:* Ludwig Berger. *Sc:* Herman J. Mankiewicz (from the novel, "If I Were King," by Justin Huntly McCarthy; and the operetta, "The Vagabond King," by Rudolf Friml, William H. Post and Brian Hooker). *With* Dennis King, O.P. Heggie, Lillian Roth, Warner Oland, Arthur Stone, Thomas Ricketts, Lawford Davidson. ("If I Were King" was filmed by Fox in 1920 with William Farnum, and again by Paramount in 1938 with Ronald Colman and Frances Dee; Paramount re-made *The Vagabond King,* 1955, with Oreste and Kathryn Grayson.) *Prod:* Paramount. 12 reels. Two-toned Technicolor.

GALAS DE LA PARAMOUNT (1930). The Spanish version of *Paramount on Parade;* as Mistress of Ceremonies, partnered with Ramon Pereda and Barry Norton, speaking and singing in the Spanish language. Besides all the players from the English-speaking version, which included nearly every actor then under contract to Paramount, the Spanish-speaking version also included Ernesto Vilches playing bits from his stage successes; baritone Juan Pulido; dancers La Argentinita and Rosita Moreno; and a skit in Spanish with George Bancroft and Hal Skelly. *Prod:* Paramount. Two-toned Technicolor sequences. 13 reels.

MONTE CARLO (1930). A sophisticated romance between a countess down to her last few francs and a count posing as a hairdresser; as the Countess Vera von Conti. *Dir:* Ernst Lubitsch. *Sc:* Ernest Vajda (with additional dialogue by Vincent Lawrence; from the comedy, "The Blue Coast," by Hans Muller). With songs by Leo Robin, Richard A. Whiting and W. Franke Harling. *With* Jack Buchanan, ZaSu Pitts, Tyler Brooke, Claude Allister, Lionel Belmore, John Roche, Albert Conti, Helen Garden, Donald Novis, David Percy, Erik Bey. *Prod:* Paramount. 10 reels.

LET'S GO NATIVE (1930). A wild burlesque of shipwrecked castaways on a desert isle, full of songs, dances, gags; as Joan Wood. *Dir:* Leo McCarey. *Sc:* George Marion Jr. and Percy Heath. Music by Richard A. Whiting and George Marion Jr. *With* Jack Oakie, James Hall, Skeets Gallagher, William Austin, David Newell, Kay Francis, Charles Sellon, Eugene Pallette. *Prod:* Paramount. 9 reels.

THE LOTTERY BRIDE (1930). Romance in Norway and the Arctic Circle, with songs; as Jenny, a Bride won in a lottery. *Dir:* Paul Stein (Arthur Hammerstein production). *Sc:* Desmond Carter, Howard Dietz, Arthur Schwartz, J. Keirn Brenren and Rudolf Friml (from the operetta, "Bride 66," by Herbert Stothart; with songs by Rudolf Friml *With* John Garrick, Joe E. Brown, ZaSu Pitts, Robert Chisholm, Joseph Macaulay, Harry Gribbon, Carroll Nye. *Prod:* United Artists. Two-toned Technicolor sequences. 10 reels.

OH, FOR A MAN! (1930). Romantic comedy of a prima donna who falls in love with a burglar posing as a singer; as Carlotta Manson. *Dir:* Hamilton Macfadden. *Sc:* Philip Klein and Lynn Starling (from a story, "Stolen Thunder." by Mary F. Watkins). *With* Reginald Denny, Marjorie White, Warren Hymer, Albert Conti, Bela Lugosi, Alison Skipworth, Andre Cheron, Bodil Rosing, William Davidson, Donald Hall, Evelyn Hall. *Prod:* Fox. 9 reels.

DON'T BET ON WOMEN (AKA, GB, *More than a Kiss*) (1931). Romantic comedy; as Jeanne Drake. *Dir:* William K. Howard. *Sc:* Lynn Starling and Leon Gordon (from a play, "All Women Are Bad," by William Anthony McGuire). *With* Edmund Lowe, Roland Young, J. M. Kerrigan, Una Merkel, Henry Kolker, Helene Millard. *Prod:* Fox. 6300 ft.

ANNABELLE'S AFFAIRS (1931). Romantic comedy; as Annabelle Leigh. *Dir:* Alfred Worker. *Sc:* Leon Gordon (from a play, "Good Gracious, Annabelle," by Clare Kummer). *With* Victor McLaglen, Roland Young, Sam Hardy, William Collier Sr., Ruth Warren, Joyce Compton, Sally Blane, Andre Beranger, Walter Walker, Hank Mann, Jed Prouty, Ernest Wood, Louise Beaver. (Filmed as a silent by Paramount in 1919 with Billie Burke.) *Prod:* Fox. 6800 ft.

ONE HOUR WITH YOU (1932). Romantic marital comedy; as Colette Bertier. *Dir:* Ernst Lubitsch and George Cukor. *Sc:* Samson Raphaelson (from a story by Lothar Schmidt which had formed the basis for Lubitsch's silent 1924 Warner Bros. comedy, *The Marriage Circle*). Songs by Oscar Straus, Leo Robin, Richard A. Whiting. *With* Maurice Chevalier, Genevieve Tobin, Charles Ruggles, Roland Young, George Barbier, Josephine Dunn,

338

JEANETTE MacDONALD

Richard Carle, Charles Judels, Barbara Leonard. (Miss MacDonald played the same role in the French version, *Une Heure avec toi*, with Lili Damita in the Tobin role.) *Prod:* Paramount. 9 reels.

LOVE ME TONIGHT (1932). Romantic comedy, with music; as the Princess Jeanette. *Dir:* Rouben Mamoulian. *Sc:* Samuel Hoffenstein, Waldemar Young, George Marion Jr. (from a French play by Leopold Marchand and Paul Armont). Music by Richard Rodgers and Lorenz Hart. *With* Maurice Chevalier, Charles Ruggles, Charles Butterworth, Myrna Loy, C. Aubrey Smith, Elizabeth Patterson, Ethel Griffies, Blanche Friderici, Joseph Cawthorn, Ethel Wales. *Prod:* Paramount. 89m.

THE CAT AND THE FIDDLE (1934). Romantic comedy, with music, of two lovers in Paris; as Shirley. *Dir:* William K. Howard. *Sc:* Bella and Sam Spewack (from the Jerome Kern and Otto Harbach operetta). *With* Ramon Novarro, Frank Morgan, Charles Butterworth, Jean Hersholt, Vivienne Segal, Frank Conroy, Henry Armetta, Adrienne d'Ambricourt, Joseph Cawthorn, Yola d'Avril, Sterling Holloway, Henry Kolker, Irene Franklin. *Prod:* M-G-M. 88m. (Compare listing in Ramon Novarro filmography.)

THE MERRY WIDOW (1934). Romantic comedy, with music, of the mythical kingdom, Marsovia; as Sonia. *Dir:* Ernst Lubitsch. *Sc:* Ernest Vajda and Samson Raphaelson (from the Franz Lehar operetta, with new lyrics by Lorenz Hart and Gus Kahn). *With* Maurice Chevalier, Edward Everett Horton, Una Merkel, George Barbier, Minna Gombell, Ruth Channing, Sterling Holloway, Donald Meek, Herman Bing, Henry Armetta, Barbara Leonard, Akim Tamiroff. A version in the French language, *La veuve joyeuse*, was shot simultaneously, with Miss MacDonald and Chevalier in their original parts. (Previously filmed, 1925, with Mae Murray and John Gilbert; filmed again, 1952, with Lana Turner and Fernando Lamas. *Prod:* M-G-M. 97m.

NAUGHTY MARIETTA (1935). Romantic comedy drama taking place in France in the reign of Louis XV and across the sea to Louisiana; as Marietta (The Princess Marie). *Dir:* W.S. Van Dyke. *Sc:* John Lee Mahin, Frances Goodrich and Albert Hackett (from the Victor Herbert-Rida Johnson Young operetta). *With* Nelson Eddy, Frank Morgan, Elsa Lanchester, Douglas Dumbrille, Joseph Cawthorn, Cecelia Parker, Walter Kingsford, Greta Meyer, Akim Tamiroff, Harold Huber, Edward Brophy. *Prod:* M-G-M. 104m.

ROSE MARIE (1936). Romantic drama, with music, of the city and the Canadian Northwest; as Marie de Flor, an opera singer. *Dir:* W.S. Van Dyke. *Sc:* Frances Goodrich and Albert Hackett, and Alice Duer Miller (from the Otto Harbach and Oscar Hammerstein

operetta, with music by Rudolf Friml and Herbert Stothart). *With* Nelson Eddy, Reginald Owen, Allan Jones, James Stewart, Alan Mowbray, Gilda Gray, George Regas, Robert Grieg, Una O'Connor, Lucien Littlefield, David Niven, Herman Bing, Mary Anita Loos, Dorothy Gray, Aileen Carlyle, Halliwell Hobbes, William Stack. (Previously filmed, 1928, as a silent with Joan Crawford; subsequently filmed, 1954, as a musical with Ann Blyth and Howard Keel.) *Prod:* M-G-M. 110m.

SAN FRANCISCO (1936). Romantic drama of San Francisco, culminating in the earthquake and fire of 1906; as Mary Blake. *Dir:* W.S. Van Dyke. *Sc:* Anita Loos (from a story by Robert Hopkins). Songs by Nacio Herb Brown and Arthur Freed, and with operatic sequences. *With* Clark Gable, Spencer Tracy, Jack Holt, Jessie Ralph, Ted Healy, Shirley Ross, Margaret Irving, Harold Huber, Al Shean, William Ricciardi, Kenneth Harlan, Roger Imhof, Charles Judels, Russell Simpson, Bert Roach, Warren Hymer, Edgar Kennedy. *Prod:* M-G-M. 115m.

MAYTIME (1937). Romantic drama, with music; as Marcia Mornay. *Dir:* Robert Z. Leonard. *Sc:* Noel Langley (from the Rida Johnson Young-Sigmund Romberg operetta; with opera selections and an opera, *Czarita*, arranged by Herbert Stothart and based on Tchaikovsky's Fifth Symphony). *With* Nelson Eddy, John Barrymore, Herman Bing, Tom Brown, Lynne Carver, Raffaela Ottiano, Charles Judels, Paul Porcasi, Sig Rumann, Walter Kingsford, Guy Bates Post, Anna Demetrio and the Don Cossacks Chorus. (Previously filmed as a silent with Ethel Shannon, Harrison Ford and Clara Bow). *Prod:* M-G-M. 130m.

THE FIREFLY (1937). Romantic drama, with music, of Spain at the time of the Napoleonic Wars; as Nina Maria. *Dir:* Robert Z. Leonard. *Sc:* Frances Goodrich and Albert Hackett, and Ogden Nash. Music by Otto Harbach-Rudolf Friml-Gus Kahn. Miss MacDonald's first solo starring vehicle. *With* Allan Jones, Warren William, Billy Gilbert, Henry Daniell, Douglas Dumbrille, Leonard Penn, Tom Rutherford, Belle Mitchell, George Zucco, Lane Chandler, Jason Robards Sr., Theodore von Eltz, Pedro de Cordoba. *Prod:* M-G-M. (Sepia tones). 140m.

THE GIRL OF THE GOLDEN WEST (1938). Romantic drama, with music, of Old California; as Mary (once Minnie) Robbins, owner of the Polka Saloon. *Dir:* Robert Z. Leonard. *Sc:* Isabel Dawn and Boyce DeGaw (from the David Belasco play which had starred Blanche Bates on Broadway). Music by Sigmund Romberg and Gus Kahn. *With* Nelson Eddy, Walter Pidgeon, Leo Carrillo, Buddy Ebsen, Leonard Penn, Priscilla Lawson, Bob Murphy, Olin Howland, Cliff Edwards, Billy

Bevan, Brandon Tynan, H.B. Warner, Monty Woolley, Charles Grapewin, Noah Beery, Bill Cody Jr. (Previously filmed by Jesse Lasky, 1915, with Mabel Van Buren; by First National, 1923, with Sylvia Breamer; and again by First National, 1930, as a talkie with Ann Harding.) *Prod:* M-G-M. (Sepia tones) 121m.

SWEETHEARTS (1938). Romantic comedy drama of two stars of the American theatre; as Gwen Marlowe. *Dir:* W. S. Van Dyke. *Sc:* Dorothy Parker and Alan Campbell (from a modern story by them). Music from the Victor Herbert operetta. *With* Nelson Eddy, Frank Morgan, Ray Bolger, Florence Rice, Mischa Auer, Herman Bing, George Barbier, Reginald Gardiner, Fay Holden, Allyn Joslyn, Olin Howland, Lucile Watson, Gene Lockhart, Kathleen Lockhart, Berton Churchill, Terry Kilburn, Raymond Walburn, Douglas McPhail, Betty Jaynes. *Prod:* M-G-M. Technicolor. 114m.

BROADWAY SERENADE (1939). Romantic drama, with music, of the theatre; as Mary Hale. *Dir:* Robert Z. Leonard. *Sc:* Charles Lederer (from a story by Lew Lipton, John Taintor Foote and Hans Kraly). *With* Lew Ayres, Ian Hunter, Frank Morgan, Wally Vernon, Rita Johnson, Virginia Grey, William Gargan, Katherine Alexander, Al Shean, Esther Dale, Franklin Pangborn, E. Allwyn Warren, Paul Hurst, Frank Orth, Esther Howard, Leon Belasco, Kitty McHugh. *Prod:* M-G-M. 113m.

NEW MOON (1940). Romantic drama, with music, of two *émigrés* from France who find love and a new life in the new world; as Marianne de Beaumanoir. *Dir:* Robert Z. Leonard. *Sc:* Jacques Deval and Robert Arthur. Music from the Hammerstein-Mandel-Schwab-Romberg operetta. *With* Nelson Eddy, Mary Boland, George Zucco, H. B. Warner, Grant Mitchell, Stanley Fields, Richard Purcell, John Miljan, Ivan Simpson, William Tannen, Bunty Cutler, Claude King, Cecil Cunningham, Joe Yule, George Irving, Robert Warwick, Hillary Brooke. (Previously filmed by M-G-M, 1930, with Grace Moore and Lawrence Tibbett.) *Prod:* M-G-M. 105m.

BITTER SWEET (1940). Romantic drama, with music, of Old Vienna; as Sarah Millick. *Dir:* W. S. Van Dyke. *Sc:* Lesser Samuels (from the operetta by Noël Coward). *With* Nelson Eddy, George Sanders, Ian Hunter, Felix Bressart, Edward Ashley, Lynne Carver, Diana Lewis, Curt Bois, Fay Holden, Sig Rumann, Janet Beecher, Charles Judels, Veda Ann Borg, Herman Bing, Greta Meyer, Dalies Frantz. (Previously filmed in England, 1933, with Anna Neagle.) *Prod:* M-G-M. 93m.

SMILIN' THROUGH (1941). Romantic drama of two centuries; in a dual role: as Moonyeen of the Nineteeth century; and as Kathleen of the Twentieth. *Dir:* Frank Bor-

zage. *Sc:* Donald Ogden Stewart and John Balderston (from the play by Jane Cowl and Jane Murfin). Music consisted of the title song and well-known English and Irish ballads. *With* Brian Aherne, Gene Raymond, Ian Hunter, Frances Robinson, Patrick O'Moore, Eric Lonsdale, Jackie Horner, David Clyde, Frances Carson, Ruth Rickaby, Wyndham Standing. (Previously filmed as a silent, 1922, with Norma Talmadge; as a talkie, 1932, with Norma Shearer.) *Prod:* M-G-M. Technicolor. 100m.

I MARRIED AN ANGEL (1942). Romantic comedy fantasy, with music; as Anne (Briggitta). *Dir:* W. S. Van Dyke. *Sc:* Anita Loos (from the Richard Rodgers and Lorenz Hart musical comedy). *With* Nelson Eddy, Edward Everett Horton, Binnie Barnes, Reginald Owen, Douglas Dumbrille, Mona Maris, Janis Carter, Inez Cooper, Leonid Kinskey, Anne Jeffreys, Marion Rosamond, Odette Myrtil, Maude Eburne. *Prod:* M-G-M. 84m.

CAIRO (1942). Romantic drama of counterespionage in Egypt; as Marcia Warren, movie star. *Dir:* W. S. Van Dyke. *Sc:* John McClain (from a story by Ladislas Fodor). *With* Robert Young, Ethel Waters, Reginald Owen, Grant Mitchell, Lionel Atwill, Eduardo Ciannelli, Mitchell Lewis, Dooley Wilson, Larry Nunn, Dennis Hoey, Mona Maris, Rhys Williams, Cecil Cunningham, Harry Worth, Frank Richards, Bert Roach, Pat O'Malley. *Prod:* M-G-M. 101m.

FOLLOW THE BOYS (1944). Charles K. Feldman production glorifying those who entertained in the Armed Services; as herself. *Dir:* Edward Sutherland. *Sc:* Lou Breslow and Gertrude Purcell. Miss MacDonald sang "Beyond the Blue Horizon" and "I'll See You in My Dreams." The main story co-starred George Raft and Zorina; but the picture was filled with guest spots from other stars who had entertained in the Army Camps at home and abroad, including Orson Welles, Marlene Dietrich, Dinah Shore, Sophie Tucker, Arthur Rubinstein, Carmen Amaya, W. C. Fields, and others. *Prod:* Universal. 122m.

THREE DARING DAUGHTERS (AKA, GB, *The Birds and the Bees*) (1948). Modern romance of a divorced mother with three adolescent daughters; as Louise Morgan. *Dir:* Fred M. Wilcox. *Sc:* Albert Mannheimer, Frederick Kohner, Sonya Levien, John Meehan (from a play by Kohner and Mannheimer). *With* Jose Iturbi, Jane Powell, Edward Arnold, Harry Davenport, Moyna MacGill, Mary Eleanor Donahue, Ann E. Todd, Tom Helmore, Kathryn Card, Larry Adler, Amparo Iturbi, Thurston Hall, Richard Simmons. Working title: *Pigtails*. *Prod:* M-G-M. 115m.

THE SUN COMES UP (1949). Romantic drama; as Helen Lorfield Winter, opera and

JEANETTE MacDONALD

concert singer. *Dir:* Richard Thorpe. *Sc:* William Ludwig and Margaret Fitts (from a story by Marjorie Kinnan Rawlings). *With* Lloyd Nolan, "Lassie," Claude Jarman Jr., Lewis Stone, Percy Kilbride, Nicholas Joy, Margaret Hamilton, Hope Landin, Esther Somers. *Prod:* M-G-M. Technicolor. 93m.

Jeanette MacDonald in *The New Moon*.

INDEX

343

344

INDEX

345

INDEX

INDEX

351

354

INDEX